SUPPLEMENT TO THE INDEX OF
MIDDLE ENGLISH VERSE

ROSSELL HOPE ROBBINS
JOHN L. CUTLER

Supplement
TO THE INDEX OF
Middle English Verse

CARLETON BROWN AND ROSSELL HOPE ROBBINS

LEXINGTON
University of Kentucky Press
1965

Copyright © 1966 by the University of Kentucky Press

Library of Congress Catalog Card No.
43-16653

The publication of this book has been made possible through a grant from the Margaret Voorhies Haggin Trust, established in memory of her husband, James Ben Ali Haggin.

PREFACE

The initial stimulus to bring out this *Supplement to the Index of Middle English Verse* came from my friend and colleague, Professor John L. Cutler. By 1961, Professor Cutler had completed a sizable manuscript of addenda and corrigenda to entries in the *Index,* primarily listing those texts printed after 1943 (the date of publication of the *Index*) and some texts printed prior to that date (but inadvertently overlooked), with corrections of the errors that persistently sneak into any bibliographical work.

The University of Kentucky Press, wishing to publish Professor Cutler's manuscript, considerately inquired about my intentions to revise the *Index*. With publication in some form assured by the University of Kentucky Press, I decided this was the time to join forces with Professor Cutler and publish a thoroughgoing revision of the *Index* based not only on the additional printings of texts but above all on a recanvass of the manuscripts, a task I had been systematically pursuing since 1947 on numerous prolonged visits to England. This *Supplement* is thus the result of our joint research.

Acknowledgments are few. But to some dedicated scholars, all good friends of long standing, I owe a real debt of gratitude:

In America, to Curt F. Bühler and Francis Lee Utley, who allowed me to check their annotated copies of the *Index;* to Charlotte D'Evelyn, who gave us valuable help on the homily cycles; to William A. Ringler, Jr., who opened his relevant files for later poems.

In England, my gratitude is especially due to Neil Ker, who for the past twenty years or so has discussed with me his gleanings from out-of-the-way manuscripts; to A. Ian Doyle, who for as long a time has helped me especially in locating obscure manuscripts; to Douglas Gray; and to my Literary Executor, Val M. Bonnell.

On the other hand, were I to list the librarians who have helped me, the names would fill several pages. To avoid the inadvertent omission of any friend, I make here an omnibus and anonymous "Thank You."

Over the years I recall with affection so many pleasant library forays, not only at the major libraries (whose generosity to scholars is constantly chronicled), but in smaller holdings: for example, the cloistered chambers of the librarian at Hereford Cathedral; the unheated and unlit library at the English College in Rome one cold November; the Pepys Library, under the old dispensation in 1934 and under the affluent new in 1963; the Senate House Library in London; the comprehensive English Library at Oxford (of which Mrs. Robbins and I have the proud distinction to be Honorary Members); the Chetham Library in the oldest library building in England; the charming little observatory-turned-manuscript-room at Trinity College, Dublin, where the lunch-enjoying Irish were consternated by my voluntary incarceration from ten to four; King's College, Aberdeen, rich in early printed books as it is in manuscripts; the elegant library at Leeds University; the Newberry Library, where I studied in 1938; Lambeth Palace, where, in 1947, I worked among the remains of charred buildings and charred books; the National Library in Naples with its sole ME manuscript; the Huntington Library one hot summer long ago; Canterbury Cathedral one cold December just after the war; the Bibliothèque nationale; the Rylands Library, whose pseudo-Gothic is transmuted by the graciousness of its staff; and so many more smaller but still essential libraries.

And in this "Thank You" to librarians, I include also those who only serve and fetch. In the long run, it is these ministering assistants on whom a scholar depends so much—in many ways far more than on the senior librarians.

To the University of Kentucky Press, not only are Professor Cutler and myself indebted, but as well the whole community of scholars. The Press encouraged the *Supplement* from its early beginnings under Professor Cutler and persevered with it to final publication—a courageous and monumental undertaking for a relatively small and not wealthy press. We are also indebted to the Kentucky Research Fund for an outright grant to help underwrite some of the costs of publication.

In the final paragraph it is traditional to proclaim fealty to the spouse. For Professor Cutler, I can surely vouch for the loyal encouragement and support of his Ann. For myself, I place on record for the ninth time my indebtedness to my devoted wife, Helen Ann. It is with especial pleasure that I date this Preface on the twenty-fifth anniversary of our marriage, thereby linking the *Supplement,* through the *Index* (1943), to *The Register of Middle English Religious Verse* (1916, 1920). For the *Register's* author, Carleton Brown, not only honored me by collaboration on the *Index,* but in the offices of the Modern Language Association in New York solemnized our marriage.

Katsbaan Onderheugel, Saugerties, New York   R. H. R.
Festival of the Translation of St. Edmund, 1964

Dr. Robbins' generous proposal in 1961 of collaboration on the *Supplement* gave me a rôle in updating and otherwise extending the usefulness of what I had long regarded as a monumental scholarly work. I must acknowledge here my great indebtedness to him, my pleasure in the friendship between the Robbins and the Cutlers to which this joint enterprise led, and my pride in the task accomplished.

To my colleague's list of "Thank You's" I would add three, deeply felt: to Caroline Hammer, Head of the Acquisitions Department, University of Kentucky Libraries; to Norma Cass, former Head of the Reference Department; and to Francis Lee Utley, who trained me in scholarly method and who has ever been a source of encouragement, advice, and direct assistance.

I would also warmly endorse the tribute to our wives, who survived with unfailing good humor the vexations of unavoidable delay and the fractiousness accompanying long periods of unremitting effort in the collaboration now so rewardingly concluded.

Lexington, Kentucky   J. L. C.

CONTENTS

PREFACE — *page* v

INTRODUCTION — xi

FURTHER SELECT LIST OF ABBREVIATED TITLES — xxv

A NOTE: How to Use the *Supplement* — xxix

INDEX OF FIRST LINES: Addenda and Corrigenda — 1

APPENDIX A: Conversion Table of Acephalous Poems in the Brown-Robbins *Index* — 502

APPENDIX B: Further Bodleian Summary Catalogue Numbers Used in the *Supplement* — 503

APPENDIX C: Manuscripts in Private Possession: Present Locations — 505

APPENDIX D: Preservation of Texts — 521

APPENDIX E: Corrigenda for Subject and Title Index in the Brown-Robbins *Index* — 525

SUBJECT AND TITLE INDEX — 526

INTRODUCTION

This *Supplement* expands some 2,300 of the 4,365 entries in the original *Index* and adds some 1,500 new entries.

The basis of this *Supplement* continues to be the MS—the working title of its predecessor had been "A Manuscript Index of Middle English Verse," dropped only because it seemed cumbersome. Some reviewers pointed out certain inadequacies in this approach, such as listing as primary sources MSS which were in fact derived from early prints[1] and, more especially, omitting entirely Middle English poems known only from incunabula.[2] In the *Supplement*, I have now listed these poems, including the 29 items in Ringler's list,[3] as well as those from other early printed books. But Middle English remains essentially MS, and Ringler's 29 incunabular additions to the over 4,000 MS entries merely emphasize this preeminence.

The *Supplement*, in addition to listing entries from MSS not included in 1943, records the present location of those MSS still in private possession and completes the cataloguing of those MSS not available for examination during the war years.

In the relocation of MSS there is, as expected, a further increase in the holdings of the great American libraries, such as the Pierpont Morgan Library and Harvard and Yale (the two universities having benefited by the deposit of private collections, like the Richardson, and the Osborn and Wagstaff). In 1916 Brown's *Register* listed only five American collections; for this *Supplement* I have used thirty-six. More significant is the appearance of MSS at university libraries which hitherto possessed few or no Middle English MSS, such as Princeton, Illinois, and Pennsylvania. The number of private collections has also increased; and several major MSS still in sale catalogues may find homes in America even while this *Supplement* is at press.

A similar change in ownership has occurred in England: the breaking up of the traditional great MS collections—few remain in

---

[1] Actually, a mere half dozen, e.g., Bodl. 3356, Bodl. 4099, Huntington HM 144.

[2] E.g., Skelton's *Bowge of Court* [1470.5] or Earl Rivers' trans. Proverbs of Christine de Pisan [3372.1]. Cf. Curt F. Bühler, *Papers Bibl. Soc. America* XXXVII. 161-5.

[3] William A. Ringler, Jr., "A Bibliography and First-Line Index of English Verse Printed Through 1500," *Papers Bibl. Soc. America* XLIX. 153-80.

[xi]

private hands today, Longleat being a notable exception—has siphoned those MSS not bought for America to small public holdings. Many British provincial universities now boast a few Middle English MSS in their libraries: for example, some of the Wollaton Hall MSS passed over the dividing fence to the adjoining University of Nottingham.

In the detailed recanvass of the MSS used for the *Index* and the inspection of other MSS—some idea of the increase can be gathered by the expansion of the 400 Bodleian MSS in the *Index* to 500 in the *Supplement,* or by the inclusion of another 36 public libraries in Britain beyond the 50 used for the *Index*—many new texts of entries in the *Index* cropped up. Thus the *Pricke of Conscience* extends its lead over the second most popular text in medieval England, the *Canterbury Tales:* 117 to 64. Nine new MSS of Lydgate's *Dietary* [824, 1418], 5 of *Erthe upon erthe* [703-5, 3939-40, 3985], 10 of the poem on *Phlebotomy* [3848], 7 of the "Rules to Find Easter" [1502], and 6 of the "Prayer by the Holy Name" [1703] are but a few of the more notable increases. The most astounding increase lies in MSS with alchemical poems, as a comparison with Singer's *Catalogue of Alchemical Manuscripts* (1928-31) reveals: for example, for Ripley's *Compende of Alkemye* [595], 24 to Singer's 7; for the *Sapientia Patris* [1276], 13 to 2; for Norton's *Ordinal of Alchemy* [3772], 26 to 2; for *Preparing the Philosopher's Stone* [2656], 23 to 9; and for *Verses on the Elixir* [3249], 33 to 4. Many of the standard literary texts show additions: 4 new MSS of *Piers Plowman* [1459], for example, and 2 of the *Confessio Amantis* [2662]. New MSS of the prolific Lydgate have been discovered: 4 of the *Fall of Princes* [1168], 2 of the *Troy Book* [2516], 2 of the *Life of Our Lady* [2574], and 4 of the *Siege of Thebes* [3928]. Even new MSS of Chaucer have been discovered since the *Index:* 3 new MSS of "Truth" [809], 3 of the "ABC Hymn" [239], 3 of "Lak of Stedfastnesse" [3190], 3 of "Purse" [3787], and one each of the "Envoy to Bukton" [2662] and "Gentilesse" [3348]. In a few entries, reexamination of MSS has laid a few ghosts, like the reference (not remarked in twenty-one years) to a fragment of Chaucer's Squire's Tale [4019, MS 81], actually a fragment of Lydgate's *Troy Book* (Bodl. 13679, item 2; I. 460-527, 523-701). The *Supplement* deletes one MS of Lydgate's "Five Joys" [2791], for example, and 2 MSS of Robert of Gloucester's Chronicle [727]. Additions and alterations to some entries have made complete relisting of the MSS essential, such as "The Kings of England" [444], a poem on herbs [2627], the *Libel of English Policy* [3491], the

Chaucer-Merlin Prophecy [3943], the *First Scottish Prophecy* [4029] in 17 MSS, and the *Second Scottish Prophecy* [4008], also established in some 17 MSS. In all, 147 entries occur in 8 or more MSS (123 in the *Index*).

Other MS changes in the *Supplement* include the recataloguing of entries erroneously listed by a burden or verse heading, so that *Index* 3565 now appears as 2079.5 (the original first line being retained for cross reference), and the relisting in regular alphabetical order of the 78 entries formerly grouped separately as "Acephalous," so that *57 (for example) now appears as *3339.5. I have increased cross references, including variant first lines (especially of romances) and burdens which are sometimes used as titles or identifications for the whole poem (e.g., "Blow northern wynd" or "Mynyon go trym"), corrected first lines, completed foliation and pagination wherever omitted in the *Index*, given the new revised foliation of MSS recently repaginated, and extended the identification of related poems (e.g., 2667 is actually 1881; 2797 has now disappeared under a cross reference to 2538, Hoccleve's *Male régle*, of which it forms a part).

Attention is directed to these important features of the *Supplement* by the four Appendices. Appendix A gives a conversion table of the old acephalous numbers of the *Index* and the new asterisked numbers in the *Supplement*. Appendix B gives the Summary Catalogue numbers of the Bodleian MSS not included in the *Index;* Appendix C shows the present locations of over 500 MSS now or recently in private possession; and Appendix D lists the 147 poems occurring in eight or more MSS.

Readers will also observe editions of poems published since 1943: many entries come from recent anthologies and readers, such as my own collections, *Secular Lyrics, Historical Poems,* and *Early English Christmas Carols,* John Stevens' *Mediaeval Carols* and *Music at the Court of Henry VIII* (both in the Musica Britannica series) and *Music and Poetry in the Early Tudor Court,* Greene's *Selection of English Carols;* the editions of individual MSS, like those by Nita S. Baugh, J. A. W. Bennett, G. L. Brook, and Rudolph Brotanek; critical works like Wilson's *Lost Literature;* anthologies like that of Davies and texts like those of Dickins-Wilson and Rolf Kaiser. Many older printings (overlooked for the *Index*) have been added. It is indeed surprising to realize how much material was available to xix century scholars, although the editions were often of limited circulation. For some texts these early editors are now the sole authorities, the original MSS having since disappeared, like Hawkins (*History of Music*, 1776), Fry (*Rare Pieces*, 1818), or Robert Dexter (*Certain Worthye Manuscript Poems*, 1597).

*   *   *   *

The 1,500 new entries in the *Supplement* are the result not only of prolonged MS research, but a broadening of the original criteria by which poems were included.

After two decades of working with the *Index*, it had become apparent that its efficiency as a tool of research would be strengthened if the monolithic rigidity of the previous cut-off date (1500) were relaxed.

Tradition has conjured the beginning and ending of a century into an albatross: the magic in a number with a double zero *ipso facto* entailed a break or change. We tend to regard the series of years 1 to 99, 100 to 199, and so on, as a pattern of colored bricks, neatly piled together—with all the bricks of any one century one color and all the bricks of another some different color. Thus we expect what is produced or what happened in 1498 to be quite different from an event in 1502, without realizing that literature, itself a part of history, is continuous. Some try to avoid the crippling of thinking in centuries by various devices: packaging literary history into segments like The Age of Shakespeare or The Age of Dryden, taking periods of 150 rather than 100 years, so that 1250 to 1400 becomes one unit, and 1400 to 1550 another, or setting a time schedule with different *termini a quo* and *ad quem*. If counting the centuries started from the presumed *death* of Christ, the hurdle of 1500 would disappear very conveniently in 1533. However, the problem of deciding whether any poem were pre or post 1533 would be as debatable as that which plagues the traditional dividing line.[4] Fifteen hundred, liberally interpreted,

---

[4] In his review of Brown's *Register* (*JEGP* XX. 270-5), Patterson noted in BM Addit. 4900 what he thought a medieval poem—"it would be hard to find a song more typically medieval:"

> What harte can thincke or tonge express
> The harme þat groweth of Idleness

"Yet this song," he continued, "does not appear in the *Register*, for our oldest text was apparently written a few years after 1500." A full text, however, occurs in BM Addit. 15223, f. 44a, signed by John Heywood, who lived from 1497 to 1580. The change from the xv to xvi century is really an illustration of a quantitative change becoming qualitative. So we can easily distinguish

must continue to serve. What will ultimately be needed, of course, is an Index of Tudor and Early Elizabethan Verse—and with this aid, the particular problem will evaporate (and another take its place).

Strict adherence to pre and post 1500 standards—although one poem [2343], dated October 4, 1500, crept in[5]—had become a barrier which, in fact, impaired the usefulness of the *Index*.

For example,[6] a series of pageant verses in Cotton Vitellius A. xvi for the festivities to welcome Princess Catharine and Prince Arthur was excluded because composed in 1501. Yet any scholar studying the pageants honoring celebrities in the late xv century, such as the series that in 1496 greeted Henry VII at York, Worcester, Hereford, and Bristol (in Cotton Julius B. xii—1186, 2214, 2215, 2216), or the ceremonial verses at Coventry in 1498 for Prince Arthur [1075, 2834] would certainly need to know about the Vitellius series (otherwise for many students effectively frozen in MS obscurity). Yet while the Vitellius poems of 1501 were excluded, two comparable pageants found only in MSS about the turn of the century were listed, precisely because they could *not* be positively dated: the *Festum Natalis Domini* [3807], a Christmas pageant in Trinity Camb. 599, and a pageant address to a London Lord Mayor [1547.5] in Trinity Camb. 181, written moreover in an early xvi century hand. In the *Supplement*, the medieval pageants inserted by Fabyan in his *New Chronicles*, 1516, have been included, despite possible late contamination.[7]

Many MSS can be dated only as plus or minus 1500. Many other MSS are certainly in early xvi century hands, but just as certainly some of their poems (because they also appear in xv century MSS) are pre 1500. Balliol 354 is an excellent illustration. When dealing

---

between a complete xv century anthology and a xvi century anthology, but the distinction between border-line poems is not so easy.

[5] Other post 1500 entries in the *Index*: 1806 is dated *ca.* 1536; it is now deleted. 4004, Hawes' *Passetyme of Pleasure*, A.D. 1506, is retained.

[6] Another overlapping genre consists of the laments on the deaths of celebrities. Apart from major poets, like Lydgate and Skelton [2192, 1378, 520], there is a series of such poems: 205, 3838, 5, 4066, 4062, 1505. Also 3430, 3206, 2411. In Balliol 354 is 3720, probably written soon after A.D. 1441, followed in MS by a lamentation of Queen Elizabeth, A.D. 1503, ascribed to Thomas More [4263.3]. A medievalist discussing this genre must refer to this poem, and also to 2409.5 (A.D. 1521), 3962.5, and 2552.5, along with 158.9, if he wishes a complete study.

[7] 227.5, 578.5, 728.5, 1924.4, 1929.3, 3785.8, 3866.3.

with a MS like Rawlinson C. 813, in the *Index* I relied on 'hunches' to admit the poems—hunches actually amounting to a quick judgment based on vocabulary, phrases, clichés, imagery, stanza form, subject matter, and presence or absence of revealing clues (like an attack on the pope or mass, or a prevalence of classical references).[8] In the *Supplement* I have now let them all in.

The inviolability of the year 1500 caused further complication in anthologies of poems traditionally considered medieval. In the *Index*, 42 of the carols in Greene's *Early English Carols* had been excluded because of their late date; while strictly justifiable, it worked hardship on a scholar discussing this genre to find that some of Greene's carols had an *Index* number and others not. The *Supplement* now lists all Greene's carols (even including the 2 ascribed to Wyatt). *Early English Lyrics* has been the traditional anthology of Middle English lyrics, but many of its poems were similarly excluded, making for similar difficulties; now all items are listed in the *Supplement,* with the exception of 6 'hard core' xvi century lyrics.[9]

For these reasons—the difficulty of dating with certainty borderline poems, the need to continue a genre beyond 1500, and the practical value of listing the largest number of items in any one modern anthology—I decided to include in the *Supplement* the following categories, into which many of the new entries fall:

(1) The so-called Scottish Chaucerians. All of Dunbar and Skelton, as well as Hawes and Douglas, are now entered. Hitherto, while Henryson had been fully listed in the *Index*, Dunbar was represented only by his 'pre 1500' poems: consequently, his "Praise of London," written in 1501 for a London banquet, was omitted. Our decision was strengthened by the policy of the English II Group of the Modern Language Association of America to include, in its revision of the Wells' *Manual,* the Scottish Chaucerians.

I am aware that by listing the Scottish Chaucerians I am adding to the problems of dating, since many of their poems in the typical MSS parallel poems which I have excluded. However, the *Supplement* is designed for the medievalist, and its aim is to list poems

---

[8] For problems of dating in Rawlinson C. 813 cf. Bolle, *Anglia* XXXIV. 274. From Ashmole 48 I have included *Chevy Chase* [960.1], but omitted the other poems, which are xvi century even when employing medieval forms, e.g., "When I do cawll to mynd" with the refrain: "Ys worcce thene yngnorance," pr. Wright, *Roxburghe Club* LXXVIII. 40-4.

[9] Nos. XXXIX, XL, XLII, XLIV, LXXXVIII, CXXXII.

written in the medieval period (arbitrarily set as ending about 1500) rather than poems written in the medieval manner (which extends far beyond 1500). Who would dare decide whether the following lines are medieval or Elizabethan:[10]

> Excellent princes potent and preclair
> Prudent peirless in bontie and bewtie

or these:[11]

> Dreid god and luif him faythfullie . . .
> Hait pryde invy and lichorie
> All yre sweirnes and glutonie

These latter, incidentally, are by Sir Richard Maitland, excluded for his late date (1496-1586). Other lines from formal Scottish verse immediately evoke the xv century world:[12]

> Welcum oure rubent roiss vpoun þe ryce
> Welcum oure Iem and Ioyfull genetryce

But this couplet—it could be religious or secular—is found in a long poem, "ane new ʒeir gist to the quene mary quhen scho come first hame" in 1562.

These MSS, notably Bannatyne and Maitland Folio, are especially rich in evidences of a cultural time lag.[13] Consequently,

[10] Pepys 2553, p. 30, Poem XIX; pr. STS n.s. VII. 34.
[11] STS n.s. VII. 36.
[12] From Maitland Quarto MS; STS n.s. XXII. 235-42.
[13] Sometimes specific allusions remove ambiguity over the date. An item in Pepys 2553, p. 35 (STS n.s. VII. 40) begins:

> O gratious god almychtie and eterne
> ffor Iesus saik þi sone we ask at þe
> ws to defend consarwe ws and guberne

but later continues:

> Now is protestanis sissin ws amang
> sayand thai will mak Reformatioun

So another poem, Advocates 1. 1. 6, f. 93a (STS n.s. XXII. 245), duplicating the incipits of 1693 and 1694, opens like a traditional Middle English prayer:

> Iesu chryst þat deit on tre
> Send ws thy grace doun frome the hevin
> As thou was borne of a virgin fre
> Keip ws fra deidly synnis sevin

but concludes with a reference to the 'regentis in this realme' for James V of Scotland (an 18-month-old babe on his accession in 1513). Cf. C. S. Lewis, *Oxford Hist. Eng. Lit.*, III. 105-8.

unless poems are ascribed to one of those poets conventionally termed Scottish Chaucerian, or exist in variant texts in earlier or borderline MSS, or can be closely paralleled in medieval poems, they are omitted.

(2) The late xv and early xvi century MSS, including the 'Tudor songbooks,' like Royal Appendix 58, BM Addit. 5465, BM Addit. 5665, and BM Addit. 31922. These have been listed *in toto,* even though some of their items are xvi century. Many of these songs overlap and parallel others which are earlier, and in any case it is inconvenient to refer only to selected items when discussing an entire and complicated MS.

The problems inherent in the poems of the Scottish Chaucerians are repeated here. *The Chaunce of the Dolorous Lover,* printed by de Worde in 1520,[14] includes an address to his mistress, very reminiscent of a lyric in Rawlinson C. 813 [2421]:

> O rubycunde ruby and perle most oryent
> O gyloffer gentyll and swete floure delyce
> O daynty dyamounde and moost resplendent
> O doulset blossome of a full grete pryce

I have included a very few early xvi century poems (ca. 1500-1510) where they exist in minor libraries or are found (uncatalogued) on flyleaves—without registration such poems could easily be lost for a long time. But the masses of Tudor and early Elizabethan poems, uncatalogued or indifferently catalogued, have been left undisturbed in their MSS.[15]

It is certainly not my intention to trespass here into the fields of the Tudor and early Elizabethan experts. But it is easier for a medievalist to disregard a superfluous entry (probably post 1500) than to search for a reference to a poem on the borderline of 1500 which might have been omitted. My aim has been usefulness.[16]

[14] Cf. Dibdin, *Typo. Antiquities,* II. 383.

[15] The interrelations between the xv and xvi century courtly verse demand much further investigation. A notable start has been made (even if her identification by anagrams be rejected) by Ethel Seaton, *Sir Richard Roos.* See also J. Copley, *N&Q* n.s. IX. 174 for Middle English clichés in Wyatt, and P. J. Frankis, *Anglia* LXXIX. 304: "The habits of the lesser anonymous lyric poets of the late fifteenth and early sixteenth centuries may throw some further light on Skelton, and even the verse of Wyatt may be seen to have sprung in part from medieval English sources, and not simply to have been transplanted from the Mediterranean hot-house of Renascence culture."

[16] The *Index* included 4004, Hawes' *Passetyme of Pleasure.* Later, two poems in the *Index* were found to be extracts from 4004: a little poem to his

(3) Verse items of only two lines, including many preachers' tags and proverbs, gnomic sayings, and English lines in Latin stories. These new entries will assist in identifying lines which may have become separated from their originals and have assumed a separate identity.[17] Continued examination of MSS for scraps and scribbles will no doubt produce some further examples.

(4) Tombstone inscriptions or epitaphs recorded only on brasses, on stones, or as wall inscriptions—seldom in MSS. Here Weever's *Ancient Funerall Monuments* has been the primary source, but Stow, Leland, and Dugdale have been consulted, and the secondary compilations of Pettigrew and Ravenshaw. Most of these verses have scant literary merit. Bouquet in his *Church Brasses* comments: "When finally English arrives as the main medium of communication, many inscriptions take the form of long doggerel verses, sometimes not much better than those which figure today in the 'In Memoriam' columns of our country newspapers, but occasionally verging upon the borderline of poetry."[18] Such waifs have their place in historical criticism, since some are variants of well-known poems and show how the more formal verse, like Lydgate's *Dance of Death*, filtered down into everyday use. Others include popular prayer tags, and still others popular proverbs.

*   *   *   *

Despite the increase in new entries and additions to the old, the general picture of Middle English verse has changed very little since 1943.

Nevertheless, some attractive and curious items have landed in the nets. First should be noted the carols with polyphonic music in Egerton 3307, edited (in modernized spelling) with the music by John Stevens in his invaluable *Mediaeval Carols*, and (as Middle English texts) by Richard Leighton Greene in his *Selection of English Carols*. Another of the very few runs of poems occurs in the Felton MS now in the Victoria Public Library at Melbourne: fourteen additional lyrics, not found in any of the other ten MSS, inserted in the prose translation of de Guileville. A series of eleven poems in the mid xvi century Dyce 45 at the Victoria and Albert

---

mistress [2318] added in a Hunterian Mus. MS which 'passed' as medieval, and a long poem praising his mistress [2532.5] as an item in the series of lyrics in Rawlinson C. 813.

[17] Such entries were useful in identifying the wall verses at Launceston [4135.5]; cf. Robbins, *Archiv* CC. 338-43.

[18] A. C. Bouquet, *Church Brasses*, London 1956, p. 167.

Museum continues medieval themes and forms, and introduces some new pseudo-carols. An especially attractive series of late love lyrics is contained in Bodleian 6658; these items deserve a wider public.[19]

Individual poems may perhaps be overlooked in the welter of additional entries, and I would like to introduce here some which seem to be of special interest: a quatrain from a Robin Hood ballad [2830.5]; a couplet fragment in *English* preserved in the Cornish mystery play of the Three Marys [158.3]; two children's tags for Blindman's Buff [28.5] and How Many Miles to Beverley [0.3], anticipating by many years the rhymes collected by the Opies for their *Oxford Dictionary of Nursery Rhymes*. An unusual piece of verse, communicated to me by A. J. Bliss, preserved on a xv century tile from a ruined church in County Louth, Ireland, gives emergency instructions for tending a sick horse until the leech arrive [1426.2]. The writing of verse on tiles is, of course, not unique [cf. 3565.5]. A fragment of a Robin Hood drama was overlooked in the *Index*, though printed in Child and in other editions; it is now in the *Supplement* [3118.4].

Then there are two unpublished dramatic pieces, listed for the first time here, from a MS at Winchester College [3352.5 and 3430.5]; other verses for a pageant or mumming are listed from a xylographic broadside [*338.5]; and new entries in drama include 2741.5 and 3117.2, two prologues for plays. Mandeville's *Travels* is versified in the Coventry City Record Office MS [248.5, now being edited]. There are many new prophecies and charms, mainly xv century, too numerous to be listed here separately. Some items will interest historians of medieval education, like 378.5, an unpublished schoolboy exercise in translation with the original Latin, similar to 430.8, 1632.5, and 4028.6. An advertisement for Hailes Abbey, describing some of the alleged miracles [311.5], forms a pendant to the already known and published set of miracles [3153].

Some two or three dozen new religious and secular lyrics are listed in this *Supplement*, all pleasant but generally not outstanding. There are several new poems with the intriguing 'O and I' refrains [2614.5 and 3098.5], a beautiful religious lullaby [4242.5], an amusing riddle on the names of several lady loves [597.5], and a virelai by Earl Rivers, a form rare in Middle English verse, which occurs in six MSS [3193.5]. Two entries come with polyphonic music

---

[19] Edited by Wagner, *MLN* L. Recently discussed by Seaton, *passim*.

similar to that for the songs in Arch. Selden B. 26 [270 and *317.5]. A scrap which may prove valuable for deciding the use of English on the continent is hinted at in a chansonnier in the Trent Codices [135.3]. Its scribe did not understand English and tried to write by ear (like the men who wrote the English lines in the Mellon and Escorial chansonniers: 138, 2183, 3165; 2782—this last actually an extract from Lydgate's *Temple of Glas*). Attention should be called to the new readings under ultra-violet light of the lyric fragments in Rawlinson D. 913;[20] to the Drexel Fragments in the New York Public Library;[21] and to the late xv century song titles.[22] Other scraps hint at the continuity of the secular lyric through the xiv century, like 1531.5, 3899.6, and 3902.5, and especially the several secular scraps quoted in some xiv century English sermons in Berlin Preussische Staatsbibliothek Lat. theol. fol. 249, now on deposit at the University of Tübingen.[23] One looks forward to full documentation of the Middle English secular lyric in a continuing line of descent from the earliest pencilled courtly poem [3512] about 1200 down to Wyatt and beyond.

* * * *

If the two decades since 1943 have seen addenda-corrigenda needed for more than half the original entries in the *Index*, and their total number increased one third by new entries, it is pertinent to speculate whether a second supplement will be needed about 1984.

So far as new entries go, I doubt whether in the future more than a hundred new poems will be found—not unless a veritable treasure trove of Middle English MSS be miraculously discovered. What new entries might accrue will consist of short proverbial tags and shards, pieces embedded in prose texts, occasional poems on flyleaves, alchemical and medical tracts, early xvi century lyrics, and pre 1500 additions to printed books. Curt F. Bühler in his series of *"Libri impressi cum manuscriptis notis"* has made a start to this end, but to be inclusive this task calls for the examination of *every* early printed book, at least in British libraries. If the help of the keepers of early printed books and of antiquarian booksellers

[20] Dronke, *N&Q* n.s. VIII. 246.
[21] Noted by Stevens, *Music and Poetry*, pp. 426-8.
[22] Hanham, *RES* n.s. VII. 270-4: 2437.5, 2182.3, 2657.5, 925, 2236.5.
[23] These sermons are being examined by Dr. Helmut Gneuss, to whom I am indebted for transcriptions; 3900.5 and 3167.3 are very attractive. Other tags are 1631.3, 2794.6, 3897.5. See Robbins, *Anglia* LXXXII. 1-13.

could be enlisted, this work would be especially valuable for any future index of Tudor (or Early Elizabethan) verse.[24]

It is always possible that important new MSS will be found, but not very likely. After Neil Ker's peregrinations up and down the length and breadth of the British Isles, Ian Doyle's perambulations over the continent, and my own questings in the major libraries, very few Middle English MSS in public collections can now remain unknown. If the pattern of recent discoveries continues, hitherto uncatalogued MSS will for the most part merely duplicate already known texts. The Coventry Lydgate MS (to which vague and inaccurate references have cropped up for many years), for example, contains *De Regimine Principum*, *Titus and Vespasian*, *The Siege of Thebes*, and new texts of six of Chaucer's minor poems. Similarly, other MSS only recently made known (also by Neil Ker) at Peterborough Public Library and at the Hertford County Record Office contain further texts of Lydgate [875, 882; and 3632], and a MS at Chichester has a fourth text of the "Mourning Song" [560]. Probably the sole repository where new poems will continue to be found is the Public Record Office, but such items will appear as the by-products of research in other areas. In the last three decades, for instance, four valuable and charming love lyrics have been inadvertently discovered in documents in this collection [1414.5, 1531.5, 2293.5, and 3706.9].

The possibility of discovering new items is somewhat greater in MSS in private possession. Scholars are still finding MSS not previously recorded. Thus Neil Ker learned that Lady Richmond (of Islip, Oxon.) has a Book of Hours with a text of de Caistre's hymn [1727] and that Miss Littledale (of Oxford) now owns the Pudsey MS (from which Collier in 1857 printed the prayer to Henry VI [333.5]).

Some privately owned MSS have been partially described and located (frequently by the Historical Manuscripts Commission). When such MSS come to be examined in detail, there is always the chance that new poems will be found.

Longleat 29, for example, had been partly listed by Brown and

[24] Cf. F. R. Brown, Histon, Cambridge, England, Catalogue 19 (March-May, 1940), Item 205a: Franciscus Luca, *Sermones*, Cologne 1483. On the verso of the last leaf is an English poem of 44 lines written in an early xvi century hand, beginning:

> Heavens rare pleasure is the earthe
> My treasure is the minde

Allen.[25] Based on these accounts, some thirteen entries had been included in the *Index;* but further examination has now added five entries to the *Supplement* [2017.5, 2250, 2270, 4035, 4056]. Again, a personal inspection of the Talbot Hours (formerly Yates Thompson 83 and now Fitzwilliam Museum 40-1950) has added three new entries [1786.5, 2154, 2388.5] to the two contained in the *Index* [914, 1727].

Not that it is always easy to gain access to a privately owned MS —in the xx century one hesitates to marry the collector's daughter. Some years ago I requested permission to examine a MS belonging to a family in the county of my birth; I was told that the MS reposed on a high shelf in the library, that the owner was invalid, and that he was unable to lift down the MS. In reply I expressed my concern over the owner's health, adding it was a pity that such a valuable MS could not be made available to scholars. A few months later, after a London sale, the Keeper of Western Manuscripts wrote me the Bodleian had acquired the MS, and I was thereafter able to give detailed entries for twenty-three poems. Not all researchers are so fortunate.

There are relatively few MSS still in private hands and not too many MSS which have been inadequately catalogued and whose present whereabouts are not known. The location of MSS which have been competently catalogued, while necessary, is not so pressing. The Cardigan Chaucer, sold at Sotheby's in February, 1959, and described minutely by Manly and Rickert (I. 71-8), is too major a MS to remain hidden for very long. Nor does it hinder literary research to be ignorant of the current ownership of, say, the Berkeley MS, because Carleton Brown in 1916 had listed its three verse prayers; or of the Billyng MS, which was seen, described, and printed as long ago as 1814; or the Clumber MS of the *Voyage to Jerusalem,* which was described in 1937 in a Sotheby Sale Catalogue.

About three dozen MSS were never fully described, and their present locations are unknown. In addition, it is probable that some other MSS are being retained for gradual release by dealers. One hopes to find these MSS and to examine them, for they may *possibly* contain either new entries or provide further texts of entries already listed: for example, the Aldenham *Horae* whose "last eleven leaves contain fifteen prayers in English" (? in verse, perhaps); the Aldenham *Destruction of Jerusalem,* offered in a

---

[25] Brown, *Register*, I. 473-4; Allen, *Writings Ascribed to Rolle*, pp. 34-6.

Goldschmidt Sale Catalogue (No. 55, Item 59) as having on f. 87b "some verses on the vanity of the world"; or the xiv century Phillipps 1805, later Preussische Staatsbibliothek Lat. 194, reputedly now in East Berlin, with three leaves of English verses.

However, examination and reexamination of privately owned MSS, though the most promising field for finding new texts, is (barring some unforeseen discoveries) unlikely to add significantly to the corpus of Middle English verse. Any second supplement in 1984 will be a slim volume.

New texts will of course continue to be published, new editions of previously printed major texts will be needed (like some of the buried poems in the Roxburghe and Maitland Club editions), and complete editions of Middle English MSS (like BM Addit. 37049, or Trinity Camb. 1450—this latter already in preparation), focusing attention on the problems of the whole MS rather than providing editorial *minutiae* on one text known only in photofacsimile—in other words, a trend from the poem in isolation to the poems in society. The first half of the xx century has pretty well completed the culling of Middle English verse.

The second half of the century must inevitably be concerned with prose. Much research has already been conducted on devotional writings, but this is but a small part of all Middle English prose. The same problems that faced the student of poetry before 1920 (and 1943)—namely, the need to spend years of preparatory research examining catalogue after catalogue in the often vain hope of establishing the texts—today face those students desirous of working on Middle English prose. In my opinion, the preparation of the charts for these little sailed seas is the greatest desideratum for Middle English studies—taking precedence even over exhaustive bibliographies, which can never be definitive because they rely on printed editions.

It is perhaps poetic justice that I, who have labored so long with MSS of vernacular verse, should be drawing attention to their complement. Yet I hope that this *Supplement* will in effect write Finis to its own field, and that the appreciation of its usefulness will inspire others to start preparing the groundwork—if only on sections (like Sermons, Devotional Prose, Medical Prose, Letters) or on separate MS collections (like Harley, Royal, Douce, or Trinity Camb.)—for an *Index of Middle English Prose*.

R. H. R.

FURTHER SELECT LIST OF ABBREVIATED TITLES

Adams, *Chief Pre-Sh. Dramas*—Joseph Quincy Adams, *Chief Pre-Shakespearean Dramas*, Boston 1924.
Allen, *Eng. Writings of Rolle*—Hope Emily Allen, *English Writings of Richard Rolle*, Oxford 1931.
Allen, *Rolle*—Hope Emily Allen, *Writings Ascribed to Richard Rolle*, New York 1927.
[Anderson,] *Poets of Great Britain*—[R. Anderson,] *Complete Edition of the Poets of Great Britain*, Vol. I, Edinburgh 1793 and London 1795.
Aspin, *AN Pol. Songs*—Isabel Stewart Tod Aspin, *Anglo-Norman Political Songs*, Oxford 1953.
Bannatyne MS., Hunt. Club—*The Bannatyne Manuscript*, Hunterian Club, Transactions 1873-1881, Vols. XVI, XXXII, XL, XLVI, L, LVI. [Pagination continuous in four parts.]
N. S. Baugh, *Worcestershire Misc.*—Nita Scudder Baugh, *A Worcestershire Miscellany*, Philadelphia 1956.
Beattie, *Edinb. Bibl. Soc.*, 1950—William Beattie, *The Chepman and Miller Prints*, Edinburgh Bibliographical Society, Edinburgh 1950.
Beauties of England—John Britton and Edward Wedlake Brayley, *The Beauties of England and Wales*, 18 vols., London 1801-1815.
Bennett, *England Chaucer-Caxton*—Henry Stanley Bennett, *England from Chaucer to Caxton*, London 1928.
Brandl and Zippel, *ME Sprach- u. Literatur.*—Alois Leonhard Brandl and Otto Zippel, *Mittelenglische Sprach- und Literaturproben*, 2nd ed., Berlin 1927; *Middle English Literature*, New York 1947.
Briggs, *Songs & Madrigals*, PMMS 1891—Henry Bremridge Briggs, *A Collection of Songs and Madrigals of the 15th Century*, Plainsong and Medieval Music Society, 1891.
Brook, *Harley Lyrics*—George Leslie Brook, *The Harley Lyrics*, Manchester 1948, rev. ed. 1956.
Brotanek, *ME Dichtungen*—Rudolph Brotanek, *Mittelenglische Dichtungen aus der Handschrift 432 des Trinity College in Dublin*, Halle 1940.
Brusendorff, *Chaucer Tradition*—Aage Brusendorff, *The Chaucer Tradition*, Copenhagen 1925.
Brydges and Haslewood, *Brit. Bibliographer*—Sir Samuel Egerton Brydges and Joseph Haslewood, *The British Bibliographer*, London, Vol. I, 1810, Vols. II & III, 1812, Vol. IV, 1814.
Bullen, *Carols and Poems*—Arthur H. Bullen, *Carols and Poems*, London 1866; repr. *Songs and Carols*, London 1885.
Cambridge Book Prose & Verse—George Sampson, *Cambridge Book of Prose and Verse*, Cambridge 1924.
Chalmers, *English Poets*—Alexander Chalmers, *The Works of the English Poets*, London 1810.

Chambers, *Eng. Lit. Close MA*—Sir Edmund Kerchever Chambers, *English Literature at the Close of the Middle Ages* (Oxford History of English Literature), Oxford 1945.

Chappell, *OE Pop. Music*—William Chappell, *Popular Music of the Olden Time*, 2 vols., London 1853, 1859; rev. H. Ellis Wooldridge, *Old English Popular Music*, 2 vols., London 1893.

Comper, *Life & Lyrics of Rolle*—Frances M. M. Comper, *The Life of Richard Rolle, Together with an Edition of his English Lyrics*, London 1928, 1933.

Davies, *Med. Eng. Lyrics*—Reginald T. Davies, *Medieval English Lyrics*, London 1963, Evanston 1964.

Dibdin, *Typo. Antiquities*—Thomas Frognall Dibdin, *Typographical Antiquities*, rev. Joseph Ames and William Herbert, 4 vols., London 1810, 1812, 1816, 1818.

Dickins and Wilson, *Early ME Texts*—Bruce Dickins and Richard M. Wilson, *Early Middle English Texts*, Cambridge 1951.

Dodgson, *English Woodcuts*—Campbell Dodgson, *English Woodcuts*, Strasbourg 1936.

Ellis, *Specimens*—George Ellis, *Specimens of the Early English Poets*, London 1790; 3 vols., 1801; rev. ed., 1 vol., 1863.

Förster, *Festschrift zum XII Deutschen Neuphilologentage*—E. Stollreither, *Festschrift zum XII Allgemeinen Deutschen Neuphilologentage*, Erlangen 1906; Max Förster, "Die Mittelenglische Sprichwörtersammlung in Douce 52," pp. 40-64.

Funke, *ME Reader*—Otto Funke, *A Middle English Reader*, Bern 1944.

Greene, *Sel. Eng. Carols*—Richard Leighton Greene, *A Selection of English Carols*, Oxford 1962.

[Hailes,] *Anc. Scot. Poems*—[Sir David Dalrymple, Lord Hailes,] *Ancient Scottish Poems*, Edinburgh 1770; repr. London 1815.

Hall, *Early Middle English*—Joseph Hall, *Selections from Early Middle English*, Oxford 1920, 1951.

Haupt, *Altdeutsche Blätter*—Moriz Haupt and August Heinrich Hoffmann, *Altdeutsche Blätter*, 2 vols., Leipzig 1836, 1840.

Hawkins, *Hist. Music*—Sir John Hawkins, *A General History of Music*, 5 vols., London 1776.

Husk, *Songs*—William Henry Husk, *Songs of the Nativity*, London [1868].

Kaiser, *Anthologie*—Rolf Kaiser, *Alt- und mittelenglische Anthologie*, Berlin 1954; *Medieval English*, Berlin 1958.

Laing, *Dunbar*—David Laing, *The Poems of William Dunbar*, 2 vols., Edinburgh 1834; *Supplement*, 1865.

Laing, *Remains*, 1822; rev. Hazlitt, 1895—David Laing, *Select Remains of the Ancient Popular and Romance Poetry of Scotland*, rev. J. Small, Edinburgh 1885; rev. W. C. Hazlitt, *Early Popular Poetry of Scotland*, London 1895.

Marsh, *Hist. Eng. Language*—George P. Marsh, *Origin and History of the English Language*, New York 1866.

[Masters,] *Rymes of Minstrels*—[James Edwin Masters,] *Rymes of the Minstrels*, Shaftesbury, Dorset, 1927.

Morris, *Specimens*, 1867—Richard Morris, *Specimens of Early English*

A.D. 1250-A.D. 1400, Oxford 1867; rev. (with W. W. Skeat) Part I, A.D. 1150-A.D. 1300, Oxford 1882, 2nd ed., 1885; Part II, A.D. 1298-A.D. 1393, Oxford 1872, 2nd ed., 1894.

Mossé, Handbook—Fernand Mossé, tr. James A. Walker, *A Handbook of Middle English*, Baltimore 1952.

Mustanoja, *How the Good Wife*—Tauno F. Mustanoja, *How the Good Wife Taught her Daughter*, Helsinki 1948.

Neilson and Webster, *Chief British Poets*—William Allan Neilson and Kenneth Grant Tremayne Webster, *Chief British Poets of the 14th and 15th Centuries*, Boston 1916.

Owst, *Preaching in Med. England*—Gerald Robert Owst, *Preaching in Medieval England*, Cambridge 1929, rev. ed., New York 1961.

Padelford, *Early XVI Cent. Lyrics*—Frederick Morgan Padelford, *Early Sixteenth Century Lyrics*, Boston 1907.

Person, *Camb. ME Lyrics*—Henry Axel Person, *Cambridge Middle English Lyrics*, Seattle 1953.

Pettigrew, *Chronicles of Tombs*—Thomas Joseph Pettigrew, *Chronicles of the Tombs*, London 1875.

Pinkerton, *Anc. Scot. Poems*—John Pinkerton, *Ancient Scotish Poems*, 2 vols., London 1876.

Poets of Eng. Lang.—Wystan Hugh Auden and Norman Holmes Pearson, *Poets of the English Language* (Viking Portable Library), Vol. I, New York 1950.

Ramsay, *Evergreen*—Allan Ramsay, *The Evergreen*, 2 vols., Edinburgh 1724; repr. *Ramsay and Early Scottish Poets*, London n.d.

Ravenshaw, *Anc. Epitaphes*—Thomas Fitz-Arthur Torin Ravenshaw, *Ancient Epitaphes from A.D. 1250 to A.D. 1800*, London 1878.

Reed, *Xmas Carols*—Ernest Bliss Reed, *Christmas Carols Printed in the Sixteenth Century* [= Kele, ca. 1550], Cambridge, Mass., 1932.

Rickert, *Anc. Eng. Xmas Carols*—Edith Rickert, *Ancient English Christmas Carols*, London 1910.

Rimbault, *Anc. Vocal Music*—Edward Francis Rimbault, *Ancient Vocal Music*, London 1847.

Rimbault, *Songs & Ballads*—Edward Francis Rimbault, *A Little Book of Songs and Ballads*, London 1851.

Ringler—William A. Ringler, "A Bibliography and First Line Index of English Verse Printed Through 1500," *Papers of the Bibliographical Society of America* XLIX. 153-80.

Robinson, *Chaucer*, 1933, 1957—Fred Norris Robinson, *The Works of Geoffrey Chaucer*, Boston 1933; 2nd ed., 1957.

Robbins, *Early Eng. Xmas Carols*—Rossell Hope Robbins, *Early English Christmas Carols*, New York and London 1961.

Robbins, *Historical Poems*—Rossell Hope Robbins, *Historical Poems of the XIVth and XVth Centuries*, New York 1959.

Robbins, *Sec. Lyrics*—Rossell Hope Robbins, *Secular Lyrics of the XIVth and XVth Centuries*, Oxford 1952; rev. ed., 1955.

Schipper, *DKAW*—Jakob Schipper, *Denkschriften der Kaiserlichen Akademie der Wissenschaften in Wien, philosophisch-historische Class*, Vol. XL (II & IV), XLI (IV), XLII (IV), XLIII (I).

Schipper, *Dunbar*—Jakob Schipper, *The Poems of William Dunbar*, Vienna 1894.
Seaton, *Sir Richard Roos*—Ethel Seaton, *Sir Richard Roos: Lancastrian Poet*, London 1961.
Segar, *Med. Anthology*—Mary G. Segar, *A Mediaeval Anthology*, London 1915.
Sibbald, *Chronicle Scot. Poetry*—John Sibbald, *Chronicle of Scottish Poetry*, 4 vols., Edinburgh 1802.
Singer—Dorothy Waley Singer, *Catalogue of Latin and Vernacular Alchemical Manuscripts*, 3 vols., Brussels 1928-1931.
Stafford Smith, *Eng. Songs*—John Stafford Smith, *A Collection of English Songs in Score for 3 and 4 Voices*, London 1779.
Stevens, *Med. Carols*—John Stevens, *Mediaeval Carols*, Musica Britannica IV, London 1952, 2nd ed., 1958.
Stevens, *Music at Court*—John Stevens, *Music at the Court of Henry VIII*, Musica Britannica XVIII, London 1961.
Stevens, *Music & Poetry*—John Stevens, *Music and Poetry in the Early Tudor Court*, London 1961.
Sylvester, *Xmas Carols*—Joshua Sylvester, *A Garland of Christmas Carols*, London 1861.
Tilley—Morris Palmer Tilley, *Dictionary of the Proverb in England*, Ann Arbor 1950.
Utley—Francis Lee Utley, *The Crooked Rib*, Columbus 1944.
Weever, *Anc. Funerall Monuments*—John Weever, *Ancient Funerall Monuments*, London 1631.
Wehrle, *Mac. Hymn Trad.*—William Otto Wehrle, *The Macaronic Hymn Tradition in Medieval English Literature*, Washington, D.C., 1933.
Wilson, *Early ME Lit.*—Richard M. Wilson, *Early Middle English Literature*, London 1939, 1951.
Wilson, *Lost Lit.*—Richard M. Wilson, *The Lost Literature of Medieval England*, London 1952.
Williams, *New Book Eng. Verse*—Charles Williams, *New Book of English Verse*, New York 1936.
Wordsworth and Littlehales, *Old Service Books*—Charles Wordsworth and Henry Littlehales, *The Old Service Books of the English Church*, London 1904.
Wright, *Camden Soc. XVI*—Thomas Wright, *The Latin Poems of Walter Mapes*, Camden Society XVI.

A NOTE

How to Use the *Supplement*

This *Supplement* is based on *The Index of Middle English Verse,* by Carleton Brown and Rossell Hope Robbins (The Index Society: Columbia University Press, 1943), and to be fully effective should be used side by side with the *Index.*

To locate a poem, first check the *Index,* and then the *Supplement.* Even if the poem is listed in the *Index,* nevertheless examine the *Supplement* under that number for corrections or additions.

New entries

New entries not in the *Index* (or entries in the *Index* which have been renumbered because of transfer from the Acephalous Poems or because of corrected first line) are indicated by a decimal point and figure. All entries with a decimal point are complete in themselves.

All new entries follow the format in the *Index*: (1) First line; (2) Description of contents and poetic form; (3) Manuscripts containing the poem; and (4) Printed editions of the poem.

These new entries are distributed among the *Index* entries according to their appropriate alphabetic order, based on the modern spelling of the Middle English word. Thus under *When* will appear poems beginning *Quhen* [3923.5], *Whanne* [3927.6], *Whane* [3958], *Wan* [cross reference], *Qwen* [3973.5], *Quhone* [4005.5], *Qwhen* [4008], and *Chwen* [4018.5]. By the same principles *Yf, Yff, ȝyf, Gif* are all entered as if spelled *If;* various spellings are subsumed under *Christ,* though *Crist* is most common.

Old entries

The *Supplement* corrects and expands the *Index* with data assembled since 1943. About 2,300 entries in the *Index* are changed; for the others the original entry remains unchanged.

To avoid reprinting the entire entry, corrections are made only for those parts of the entry needing change, and additions are given for further printings, manuscripts, cross references, &c.

Cross references

Where appropriate, cross references are made to Utley *(Crooked Rib),* Ringler (handlist of poems from incunabula), Singer *(Alchemical Manuscripts),* and Tilley *(Dictionary of Proverbs),* as well as to other entries both in the *Index* and in the *Supplement.*

INDEX OF FIRST LINES
Addenda and Corrigenda

0.1 A for Alyn Mallson þat was armyde in a matt
A 'Crosse Rowe' poem ribald in character—46 lines in long couplets.
1. BM Printed Book I A 3420, ff. 270b-271b.
Bühler, *JEGP* LVIII. 249-50.

A (interjection)

0.2 A a my herte I knowe yow well
A song of penitence—one 8-line stanza.   [Cf. 13].
1. BM Addit. 5465, f. 3b.
Fehr, *Archiv* CVI. 52; Stevens, *Music & Poetry*, p. 352.

0.3 Ha ha petipas / ȝuot ich am / þer ich was
Children's rime used in game: How many miles to Beverley.
[Cf. *Oxford Dict. Nursery Rhymes*, no. 26; also Langbaine, *Adversaria*, Bodl. 8617, p. 384].
1. Balliol 320, f. 153b.
Mynors, *Cat.*, p. 242.

1   four 7-line stanzas.
2. New York Pub. Lib. Drexel Fragments 4180.
1. Stevens, *Music & Poetry*, pp. 374-5.

A blysful lord an hy what schal I do   See 540.

2   MacCracken, *JEGP* IX. 63-4 (as Epilogue to 367).

4   'That ons was leffe . . .' [The refrain appears as a proverb in Rylands Lib. Latin 394, f. 3b, pr. Pantin, *BJRL* XIV. 94].
Robbins, *Sec. Lyrics*, pp. 133-5; Kurvinen, *Neuphil. Mitteilungen* LIV. 53-5.

5   1. Conybeare, *Archaeologia* XVIII. 22; Marsh, *Hist. Eng. Lang.*, p. 288; Sisam, *XIV C. Verse & Prose*, pp. 157-60; Robbins, *Hist. Poems*, pp. 102-6; Kaiser, *Med. Eng.*, p. 384.

          A gentill Jhesu
          Burden (in BM Addit. 5465 only) to 3845.

5.5   A for goddis will / What meane ye syrs to stond so styll
          Fulgens & Lucrece, by Henry Medwall (ca. A.D. 1497). *Fulgens & Lucrece*, Rastell, n.d. (STC 17778); *facs.* de Ricci, 1920; Boas and Reed, 1926.

11.5   A lord kyng of myȝt þat levyn woldust þi myȝt
          Irregular riming lines in Rolle's Meditations on the Passion (Text A only)—ten and four lines.
          1. Camb. Univ. Ll. 1. 8, f. 204a.
            Horstmann, *York. Wr.*, I. 87; Ullman, *Eng. Stn.* VII. 458; Allen, *Eng. Writings of Rolle*, pp. 24-5.

          A man I haue yeuyn and made   See 4184.

12   Davies, *Med. Eng. Lyrics*, p. 243.

13   [Cf. 0.2].
          Kirke, *Reliquary* IX. 77; Stevens, *Music & Poetry*, p. 375.

13.3   A most fayre and true / ye cause me rue
          On the absence of his mistress—three 6-line stanzas with a 4-line heading refrain: 'Parting, parting &c.'
          1. Bodl. 6659, f. 100a.
            Wagner, *MLN* L. 454.

          A my dere a my dere son   See 3597.

13.5   Ah my hart / ah this ys my songe
          The lover reproaches his mistress for her hard heart—seven 7-line stanzas with a 4-line refrain: 'Adewe pleasure &c.' [A religious parody in *Gude & Godlie Ballatis*, 1567, *repr.* Mitchell, STS XXXIX. 139].
          1. Bodl. 6659, f. 99a.
            Wagner, *MLN* L. 453-4.

13.8 A Robyn gentyl Robyn / Tel me how thy lemman doth
Women kind and unkind—in MS. 3 eleven lines in three stanzas; in MSS. 1, 2, attributed to Wyatt and expanded to five quatrains and burden. [Utley 202].
1. Egerton 2711, f. 37a; 1a (transcript). BM Addit. 28636, f. 34a; 2. BM Addit. 17492, ff. 22b, 24a; 3. BM Addit. 31922, f. 53b.
1. Foxwell, W*iat*, I. 106; Padelford, *Early XVI Cent. Lyrics*, p. 10; Tillyard, *Wyatt*, p. 90; 1a, 3. Flügel, *Anglia* XII. 272, 241-2; 1a. Flügel, *Neuengl. Lesebuch*, p. 23; 3. Reese, *Music in Renaissance*, p. 770; Stevens, *Music & Poetry*, pp. 111, 405; Stevens, *Music at Court*, pp. 38-9; *facs.* Foxwell, W*iat*, I. 62 facing.

14 A sone tak hede to me whas son þou was
fourteen couplets. [Preceded by riming address on tribulations of B. V. See 427.5].
1. *Rel. Lyr. XIV C.*, p. 228; 2. Owst, *Lit. & Pulpit*, pp. 541-2.

14.5 A the syghes þat cum from my hart
Recollections of love's joys—four quatrains.
1. Royal App. 58, f. 3a; 2. BM Addit. 31922, f. 32b.
1, 2. Flügel, *Anglia* XII. 258, 235; Chappell, *OE Pop. Music*, I. 35-6; Stevens, *Music at Court*, p. 25; 1. Stafford Smith, *Musica Antiqua*, I. 27; Padelford, *Early XVI Cent. Lyrics*, p. 79; Briggs, *Songs & Madrigals*, PMMS 1891, pp. xvii, 10; 2. Flügel, *Neuengl. Lesebuch*, p. 134; Stevens, *Music & Poetry*, p. 395.

16 1. Gregor, *STS* XXI. 100; Wehrle, *Macaronic Hymn Trad.*, p. 119; Davies, *Med. Eng. Lyrics*, pp. 159-60.

18 1, 3. Stevens, *Med. Carols*, pp. 19, 85; Robbins, *Early Eng. Xmas Carols*, pp. 28, 25; 1. Greene, *Sel. Eng. Carols*, p. 65; 2. Rickert, *Anc. Eng. Xmas Carols*, p. 53.

19 1. Gregor, *STS* XXI. 100-1; Wehrle, *Macaronic Hymn Trad.*, p. 119.

A (indefinite article)

20 1, 2. Rickert, *Anc. Eng. Xmas Carols*, pp. 52-3, 49-50.

21   [Cf. Copley, *N&Q* n.s. VI. 387-9].
   1, 3. Stevens, *Med. Carols*, pp. 20, 8; 1. Robbins, *Early Eng. Xmas Carols*, p. 78; 2. Greene, *Sel. Eng. Carols*, p. 83; 3. Rickert, *Anc. Eng. Xmas Carols*, pp. 167-8.

22   3. NLW Deposit: Porkington 10, ff. 201a-202a (st. 1, 3-8, 11, with Latin text interspersed: *Christe qui lux es et dies*). Harvard Coll. Lib. H. C. L. 25258. 27. 5, p. 8; *repr.* Greene, *ELH* VII. 235-6; 2. Husk, *Songs*, p. 52; Dyboski, *EETS* ci. 21-3; Rickert, *Anc. Eng. Xmas Carols*, pp. 72-4; Segar, *Med. Anthology*, pp. 76-7 (7 st. only); Greene, *Sel. Eng. Carols*, pp. 101-3; 3. Sylvester, *Garland of Xmas Carols*, p. 41; Davies, *Med. Eng. Lyrics*, pp. 197-8.

A babe is born to blis vs brynge / I hard a mayd lulley &c. See 22.

23.5   A bastar schall come owt of the west
   'When England shall be Britain,' a political prophecy—one cross-rimed quatrain.
   1. NLW Peniarth 26, p. 117.

25   2. Horstmann, *Archiv* LVII. 290-7.

26   11. Morris, *Specimens*, 1867, pp. 148-51.

28   [Cf. Pace, *Mediaeval St.* XXIII. 363-7].
   2. Robinson, *Chaucer*, 1933, p. 629; 1957, p. 534.

28.5   A bobbid a bobbid a biliried / Smyte not her bot þu smyte a gode
   A tag used in game: Blindman's Buff or Hot Cockles.
   1. Bodl. 649, f. 82a.
   Owst, *Lit. & Pulpit*, p. 510.

A burgeis was in Rome town
   Extract (Telltale Bird) from *Seuyn Sages of Rome* (Advocates 19. 2. 1): See 3187.

28.8   A breffe conclusion declare I shall
   Count Ugolino of Pisa—vv. 254 in quatrains.
   1. New York: Corning Mus. of Glass 6 [*olim* Currer], ff. 119a-123b.

29   Kaiser, *Med. Eng.*, p. 290; Greene, *Sel. Eng. Carols*, p. 59.

30   1. Greene, *Sel. Eng. Carols*, p. 97.

31   Stevens, *Med. Carols*, p. 92.

32   2. Horstmann, *Archiv* LVII. 278-9.

33   [For Prohemium see 731.5; for Envoy see 4258.3. Singer 1059. Ringler 11].
        1. Delete this MS.; 3. Harley 614, f. 4a; 6. Morgan Lib. M. 875 [*olim* Helmingham Hall], f. 7a.
          de Worde, 1495, f. 1a (STC 1536); *repr.* Dibdin, *Typo. Antiquities*, II. 311; Rohde, *OE Herbals*, p. 47; 2. Robbins, *Sec. Lyrics*, pp. 94-5.

33.3   A dragoun with a rede ros þat ys of grete fame
        An English prophecy, with Latin interpolations, including 'Cast of the Dice' (cf. 4018)—vv. 85 in cross-rimed quatrains.
        1. NLW Peniarth 53, pp. 131-6.

33.5   A faythfull frende wold I fayne fynde
        'Gramercy myn own purse'—five 8-line stanzas. [Cf. 1484 and 3959. Ringler 1].
        Boke of Hawkynge and Huntynge, de Worde, 1496 (STC 3309); *repr.* Ellis, *Specimens*, 1805, I. 363-5; Dibdin, *Typo. Antiquities*, II. 60; Ritson, *Anc. Songs*, 1790, p. 89; 1829, II. 6; 1877, p. 151; Bethune, *British Female Poets*, 1848, pp. 14-5; Arber, *Dunbar Anthology*, pp. 182-3.

33.6   A fals beginingge
        Cupiditas est—three lines.
        1. Advocates 18. 7. 21, f. 32b.

33.8   A fals by-hetyng / A lyeres auansyng / A bitynde fonding
        Three monoriming lines in a sermon.
        1. Harley 7322, f. 185a.
          Furnivall, *EETS* 15. orig. ed. 242; rev. ed. 270.

33.9   A fastyng bely / may neuer be mery
A proverbial couplet. [Cf. Tilley B 303].
1. Balliol 354, f. 200a.
Flügel, *Anglia* XXVI. 202; Dyboski, *EETS* ci. 131.

34.5   A floure is sprongen þat shall never faile
Song at the Nativity: poem occurring in only this MS. of Eng. tr. of *Pèlerinage de l'Ame*—five stanzas rime royal.
1. Melbourne: Victoria Pub. Lib., f. 197b.

34.8   A foles blote / ys sone yshote
A proverbial couplet. [Tilley F 515. Cf. 433, v. 421; 1669, st.7; cf. also Meech, *MP* XXXVIII. 130].
1. Bodl. 1851, f. 101b; 2. Bodl. 14526, f. 54b (in 3502); 3. Bodl. 15444, f. 142a; 4. Harley 2321, f. 149a.
1. Schleich, *Anglia* LI. 224; 2. Zupitza, *Archiv* XC. 246; 3. Meech, *MP* XXXVIII. 121; 4. *Rel. Ant.*, I. 208.

A fowle syngyng   See 3743.6.

35   Dickins and Wilson, *Early ME Texts*, pp. 63-70; Mossé, *Handbook*, pp. 178-87 (omits vv. 1-70); Brandl and Zippel, *ME Sprach- u. Literatur.*, pp. 114-8; Kaiser, *Med. Eng.*, pp. 487-8 (vv. 208 only).

35.5   A fryer an heyward a fox and a fulmer sittyng on a rewe
Nonsense verses—one long couplet.
1. Bodl. 10234, f. 52a.
Robbins, *Anglia* LXXXII. 10.

36   [Cf. 4120.6].
4. Leyden Univ. Vossius 9, f. 101b (3 addit. st.).
1 (with 4). MacCracken, *EETS* 192. 445-7.

37   Davies, *Med. Eng. Lyrics*, p. 281.

37.3   A gulden begh in a soghes wrot / A faire wyman and a sot
On erring women—one couplet.
1. BM Addit. 33956, f. 125a.
Register, I. 410.

37.5 A gode begynnyng / makyth a gode endyng
A proverbial couplet. [Cf. 2078; 4049.3; Tilley B 259].
1. Bodl. 15444, f. 140a; 2. Bodl. 21626, f. 28a; 3. Balliol 354, f. 191b; 4. BM Addit. 37075, ff. 70a-71b (beginning a series of irregularly riming proverbs); 5. Rylands Lib. Latin 394, f. 18b.
1. Meech, *MP* XXXVIII. 117; 2. Förster, *Festschrift zum 12 Deutschen Philologentage*, p. 55; 3. Dyboski, *EETS* ci. 129; 5. Pantin, *BJRL* XIV. 105.

38 2, 4. Horstmann, *AE Leg.* 1875, pp. 68-81.

39 [Cf. also 348, 1585.5].

39.5 A good scoler yf þou wilt be / Arise erly & worship þe trinite
A proverbial couplet (followed by 54 other proverbs, some in couplets, many single-lined).
1. Balliol 354, f. 200a.
Flügel, *Anglia* XXVI. 201; Dyboski, *EETS* ci. 129.

40.5 A good wyf and a fayre / Is to her husbonde a pleasure
A proverbial couplet.
Salomon and Marcolphus, Leeu, Antwerp, ca. 1492 (STC 22905); *facs*. Duff, London 1892.

42.3 A greate prynce may have no more vice
Four couplets concluding his translation from the Latin of *The Moste Pitevous Cronicle of th' Orribill Dethe of the Kyng of Scottes*, by John Shirley.
1. BM Addit. 5467.
Stevenson, *Maitland Club* 42. 66-7; Pinkerton, *History of Scotland*, I, Appendix.

42.5 A grehounde shulde be heded like a snake
'The propreteis of a goode grehounde'—ten couplets. [Ringler 2. Tilley S 283].
Boke of Huntyng, St. Albans, 1486 (STC 3308); de Worde, 1496 (STC 3309); *facs.* Blades, 1881; Dibdin, *Typo. Antiquities*, II. 58; *repr.* Tilley, p. 596.

44 Greene, *Sel. Eng. Carols*, p. 122.

45 8. Morris, *Specimens*, 1867, pp. 154-8.

46 5. Rosenthal, *Vitae Patrum in Old & ME Lit.*, p. 161.

48   1. Sloane 3548, f. 118b.

50   4. D'Evelyn and Mill, *EETS* 235. 227.

52   1. Bodl. 9914, f. 252b and f. 253a (var. xvii cent. hand);
      2. Harley 7332, f. 28a (xvii cent. transcript).

54   1. Asloan, f. 257a; 1a (xix cent. transcript). Edinb. Univ. La. IV. 27/8.
      1. Craigie, *STS* n.s. XVI. 175-86.

54.5 A kynges sone and an emperoure
      'Proface,' a Christmas carol—four stanzas and burden: 'This day ys borne a chylde of grace &c.'
      1. BM Addit. 5665, f. 39b.
      Fehr, *Archiv* CVI. 274; Sandys, *Xmas Carols*, p. 10; Wright, *Carols*, Percy Soc. IV. 53; Rickert, *Anc. Eng. Xmas Carols*, p. 217; *Early Eng. Carols*, p. 10; Stevens, *Med. Carols*, p. 96; Robbins, *Early Eng. Xmas Carols*, p. 82.

56   4. D'Evelyn and Mill, *EETS* 235. 229.

57   4. D'Evelyn and Mill, *EETS* 235. 235; 9. Boyd, p. 15.

58   4. D'Evelyn and Mill, *EETS* 235.234.

59   [Cf. 1641, 2446.5].
      4. D'Evelyn and Mill, *EETS* 235. 231; 10. Boyd, p. 11.

60   [Utley 4].

      A leche oþ þe lasours lawfulliche y-leuyd
      Three riming lines preceding 1848.

61   Rickert, *Anc. Eng. Xmas Carols*, pp. 5-6

62   *Gentleman's Magazine*, May 1842, pp. 467-8.

63   [For a variant see 3635].
      Rickert, *Anc. Eng. Xmas Carols*, pp. 42-3.

63.5   A lyoun raumpaund wit his powe
       Two couplets in a collection of friar sermons.
       1. Basle Univ. B. VIII. 4, f. 113a.
           Meyer and Burckhardt, *MA HSS. der Univ. Basel: Beschreibendes Verzeichnis*, Abt. B, p. 853.

63.8   A little in the morninge nothing at noone
       A proverb—one couplet. See 3772.5.
       1. Harley 2321, f. 147a.
           Rel. Ant., I. 208.

       A litell ragge of rethorike / A less lumpe of logyke
       Prefatory verses to Skelton's 'Replycacioun.'   See 3773.5.

64   1. Advocates 19. 3. 1, f. 1a (with concluding scribal rubric, 467.5).

65.5   A losse of hele and likyng / A body dressede to dying
       Four short riming lines in a Latin sermon.
       1. Bodl. 29746, f. 123b.
           Little, *Franciscan Papers*, 1943, p. 248.

66   [Utley 5].
           Segar, *Med. Anthology*, pp. 49-54 (19 st. only); Dickins and Wilson, *Early ME Texts*, pp. 104-9; Kaiser, *Med. Eng.*, pp. 219-21.

66.5   A mayd perles / hathe borne godys Son
       In praise of the Virgin Mother—three stanzas with burden.
       XX· *Songes*, de Worde, 1530, f. 11a (STC 22924); Flügel, *Anglia* XII. 591; Imelmann, *Shakespeare-Jahrbuch* XXXIX. 127-8; *Early Eng. Lyrics*, p. 156; Rickert, *Anc. Eng. Xmas Carols*, pp. 22-3; Segar, *Med. Anthology*, p. 75; *facs.* Reed, *Xmas Carols*, pp. 5-8.

67   *Early Eng. Carols*, p. 44.

67.5   A man is a mirroure of soro and wo
       The ephemeral nature of man—two couplets. [Cf. 1134.5].
       1. Hereford Cath. O. iii. 5, f. 48a.

68   'War before'—one 6-line stanza.

A man of ple and motyng   See 3743.3.

69.5   A mon þat hathe a wart abowne ys schin / he schall neuer nede non of hys kyn
   A proverb—one couplet.
   1. NLW Peniarth 356, p. 297.

70   1. Morgan Lib. M. 876 [*olim* Helmingham Hall], ff. 103b-152b.
   [For early prints see 1515].

71   [Utley 7].
   1. Bodl. 3880, f. 3a; 3. Camb. Un. Ll. 4. 14, f. 173a (lacks the 'Moralyte'); 4. Trinity Camb. 599, ff. 240a-244b (vv. 188 and vv. 82 for 'Moralyte'); 4a (xix cent. transcript by Hartshorne). Bodl. 30161, f. 1a.
   1. Hazlitt, *Remains*, II. 2-15.

72   Arber, *Dunbar Anthology*, p. 191; *Early Eng. Carols*, p. 257; Robbins, *Hist. Poems*, pp. 146-7; Greene, *Sel. Eng. Carols*, p. 139.

76   Rickert, *Anc. Eng. Xmas Carols*, pp. 164-5.

77   A man without mercy mercy shall mysse
   On mercy—one couplet. [Cf. 432 and 832. Tilley M 895].
   1. Bodl. 6926, f. 1a; 2. Balliol 354, f. 113b; 3. Lansdowne 699, f. 95b; 4. Sloane 747, f. 58b; 5. Sloane 3215, f. 38b; 5. Hunterian Mus. 230, f. 248b (in 1628.8); 6. NLW Peniarth 394, p. 90.
   2. Flügel, *Anglia* XXVI. 226; Dyboski, *EETS* ci. 141; 4. *Register*, I. 373.

A man wot whan he goth   See 3199.5 (MSS. Bodl. 21626 and Harley 3362).

78   Rickert, *Anc. Eng. Xmas Carols*, p.159.

*78.5   *. . . . .a myrow and led vs with pryd
   A quatrain in English.
   1. Royal 8. F. vii, f. 54b.

A monk ther was in oon abbay   See 4123.

79.5 A new songe anewe / vnto yow louers blynde
Beware of a false mistress—four cross-rimed quatrains. [Utley 8].
1. Bodl. 12653, f. 14b.
Padelford and Benham, *Anglia* XXXI. 328.

80 Greene, *Sel. Eng. Carols*, p. 124.

81 Stevens, *Med. Carols*, p. 22.

81.5 A nyce wyfe A backe dore / Makyth oftyn tymys a ryche man pore
On erring wives—one couplet. [Tilley W 370].
1. Harley 2252, f. 3a; 2. Royal 12. E. xvi, f. 34b (preceded by 106.5); 3. Royal 18. B. xxii, f. 44b.
3. Nichols, *Boke of Noblesse,* Roxburghe Club LXXVII, lvi; Warner and Gilson, *Cat.*, II. 295.

82 17. Lambeth 223, f. 100a.
3, 4. Morris, *EETS* 46. 36-47; 7. D'Evelyn and Mill, *EETS* 235. 174.

83 2. NLW Peniarth 394, p. 33.
1. Furnivall, *EETS* 15 orig. ed. 83-93; rev. ed. 114-33.

84 *Gentleman's Magazine,* May 1842, p. 467.

86 A philisophre a good clerk seculer
[Utley 9].

86.3 A pyte withowten trewthe
Four types of pity—two couplets in a Latin sermon by Friar Nicolas Philip.
1. Bodl. 29746, f. 175a.

A place as man may see   See 1523.

86.5 A pope in hys solempnyte
Technical terms for rulers' titles—four lines.
1. Harley 2259, f. 144b.

[11]

86.8   A prelat negligent / A discipil inobediente
The Twelve Abuses—twelve lines. [Cf. 1820].
1. Cotton Faustina B. vi, Part II, f. 8b.
Comper, *Life & Lyrics of Rolle*, p. xix.

87.5   A prety wenche may be plesur
Spend your money on a pretty wench—two 3-line stanzas and a 'Joly felowe' burden.
XX Songes, de Worde, 1530, f. 22b (STC 22924); Flügel, *Anglia* XII. 593; Imelmann, *Shakespeare-Jahrbuch* XXXIX. 131; *Early Eng. Carols*, p. 304.

88   four quatrains and burden.
2. Rickert, *Anc. Eng. Xmas Carols*, pp. 203-4; Stevens, *Med. Carols*, p. 4; Robbins, *Early Eng. Xmas Carols*, p. 30.

89.5   A ruler of al remis
A tag in an English prose homily. [Cf. 91.5, 1628.5, 1848, 3101].
1. Worcester Cath. F. 10, f. 47b.
Grisdale, *Leeds Texts & Monographs* V. 50.

91.5   A softenes of a souereyn
A tag in an English prose homily.
1. Worcester Cath. F. 10, f. 45b.
Grisdale, *Leeds Texts & Monographs* V. 42.

91.8   A solitari here / hermite life i lede
Verses surrounding a picture of Rolle, in two MSS. of the *Desert of Religion* (672)—four long monoriming lines with internal rimes. [For alternative text see 1367.3].
1. Cotton Faustina B. vi, Part II, f. 8b; 2. Stowe 39, f. 16b.
1, 2. Hübner, *Archiv* CXXVI. 74, 63 (*facs.*); Comper, *Life & Lyrics of Rolle*, pp. xix, 205 (*facs.*); 1. Horstmann, *York. Wr.*, II. xxxiv; Allen, *Rolle*, p. 310.

93   Stevens, *Med. Carols*, p. 28; Robbins, *Early Eng. Xmas Carols*, p. 42.

94   two monoriming quatrains.

95   The 'Bodley' Burial &c.
1. Bodl. 3692, ff. 140a-156b, 156b-179a.
Furnivall, *EETS* lxx. 171-226.

95.5   A sowre appul whan it is hoote / Shytes out all þat he woote
            A proverbial couplet.
            1. Rylands Lib. Latin 394, f. 19a.
               Pantin, *BJRL* XIV. 106.

95.8   A sufficyent salve for eache disease
            The Virtue of Pacience—one cross-rimed quatrain.
            1. Durham Univ. Cosin V. iii 9, f. 83a.
               Furnivall, *EETS* lxi. 224.

97   2. Horstmann, *Archiv* LVII. 256.

98.5   A thorne hath percyd my hart ryght sore
            No remedy for falling in love—three 5-line stanzas and introductory 2-line burden.
            1. BM Addit. 31922, f. 108b.
               Flügel, *Anglia* XII. 251; Stevens, *Music & Poetry*, pp. 419-20; Stevens, *Music at Court*, p. 80.

99   [Anderson,] *Poets of Great Britain*, I. 575-7.

100   [Utley 12].
            A Text: 4a (xix cent. transcript). Camb. Un. Add. 2793; 8. BM Addit. 9832, ff. 4a-42b (vv. 1-1985; interleaved with William Bonham's ed. of Chaucer, 1542, which continues as ff. 43-47); 9. BM Addit. 28617 (fragments only: begins v. 513), ff. 1-17.
            B Text: 1. Bodl. 2078, ff. 48a-95b.
               A4 and B2. Robinson, *Chaucer*, 1933, pp. 567-611; 1957, pp. 480-518.

101   Furnivall, *EETS* 15 orig. ed. 230; rev. ed. 257.

102   Furnivall, *EETS* 15 orig. ed. 232; rev. ed. 260.

102.3   A . . . . vpon a strawe / Cudlyng of my cowe
            A nonsense carol—six quatrains and 2-line burden: 'Newes newes.'
            1. Cotton Vesp. A. xxv, f. 126b (MS. damaged).
               Rel. Ant., I. 239; Böddeker, *Jahrbuch rom. u. engl. Sprache- u. Literatur.*, N.F. II. 90; Baskervill, *Elizabethan Jig*, p. 61 (2 st. only); *Early Eng. Carols*, pp. 317-8.

102.5   A vertu callid of full grete reuerence
   The Balade to 4042—five stanzas rime royal elaborating the refrain: 'Tong brekith bone of his nature though he hymself haue none.' [Cf. 3792.5].
   1. Bodl. 1475, f. 49a.
   MacCracken, *EETS* 192. 795-6.

103   Rickert, *Anc. Eng. Xmas Carols*, p. 51.

103.5   A war wys lokere / A war wys kepere
   On true love—three riming lines in a Latin-English sermon.
   1. Merton Oxf. 248, f. 131b.
   Pfander, *Pop. Sermon*, p. 50.

105   [Reconstructed as eight 6-line stanzas with 5-line refrain]. Brook, *Harley Lyrics*. pp. 40-1; Degginger, *JEGP* LIII. 84-5 (text), 88-90 (reconstruction); Kaiser, *Med. Eng.*, p. 472 (reconstructed text); Davies, *Med. Eng. Lyrics*, pp. 80-2.

105.5   A qwheel about þe turnyng
   Man's transitory life compared to a wheel, a ship, a shadow, and a flower—two couplets in a Latin sermon. [Cf. 3743.6].
   1. Bodl. 12158, f. 92a.

106   The Poor Widow and the Rich Man—five couplets in a collection of tags.
   Person, *Camb. ME Lyrics*, p. 49.

106.5   A wyld beest a man may tame / A womanes tunge will never be lame
   One couplet satirizing a woman's tongue.
   1. Sidney Sussex Camb. 99 (vv. 4); 2. Royal 12. E. xvi, f. 34b (followed by 81.5); 3. Hunterian Mus. 230, f. 248a (included in 1628.8).

107   *Christmas Carolles*, Copland, ca. 1550 (Douce fragments f. 48); *facs.* Reed, *Xmas Carols*, p. 10.

108.5   A woman oftymes will do / þat she is not bede to do
   A proverbial couplet.
   1. Balliol 354, f. 200b.
   Flügel, *Anglia* XXVI. 203; Dyboski, *EETS* ci. 132.

108.7 A woman thatt ys wylfull ys a plage off the worste
Fortunes according to cards, mainly satirical attacks against women—ten couplets from 'an ancient set of ten fortune cards' in Chetham Lib. [Utley 14. Cf. 2251; and cf. also *Rel. Ant.* I. 249. Utley 308].
Rel. Ant., II. 195-6.

A ȝung man chiftane wittles   See 1820.

A yong wyf and an arvyst gos   See 3533.5.

109   Person, *Camb. ME Lyrics*, p. 25.

110   Frölich, *De Lamentatione S. Marie*, p. 94.

111   1, 2. Stevens, *Med. Carols*, pp. 31, 8.

112   1, 2 (comp. text), 3. Rickert, *Anc. Eng. Xmas Carols*, pp. 97-8; 1. Bullen, *Carols & Poems*, pp. 19-20; Greene, *Sel. Eng. Carols*, p. 71; 2. Segar, *Some Minor Poems*, pp. 9-10; *Oxford Book Carols*, p. 208; 3. Pollard, *XV Cent. Prose & Verse*, p. 272; Duncan, *Story of Carol*, p. 76; Cutts, *Ren. News* X. 5-7.

112.5   Aboffe all thynge / Now lete us synge
A song perhaps celebrating the birth of Prince Henry in A.D. 1511—one 6-line tail-rime stanza. [Cf. 120.4].
1. BM Addit. 31922, f. 24b.
Chappell, *Archaeologia* XLI. 382; Flügel, *Anglia* XII. 232; Stevens, *Music & Poetry*, p. 391; Stevens, *Music at Court*, p. 18.

113   FitzGibbon, *E. E. Poetry*, pp. 233-4; Robbins, *Hist. Poems*, pp. 134-7.

113.5   Absens of ȝou causeth me to sygh and complayne
Ease my heart, mistress—one stanza rime royal. [Cf. 380].
1. BM Addit. 5665, f. 67b.
Fehr, *Archiv* CVI. 279; Stevens, *Music & Poetry*, p. 340.

113.8   *Accipe* that longeth to the
Four lines of moral advice.
1. Wellcome Hist. Med. Lib. 41, f. 5a.
Moorat, *Cat.*, p. 27.

[15]

117 Rickert, *Anc. Eng. Xmas Carols*, pp. 163-4; *Oxford Book Christian Verse*, pp. 18-9; Williams, *New Book Eng. Verse*, p. 23; *Poets of Eng. Lang.*, I. 27; Chambers, *Eng. Lit. Close MA*, p. 91; Kaiser, *Med. Eng.*, p. 290; Davies, *Med. Eng. Lyrics*, pp. 160-1.

118 1. Sloane 2593, f. 4a.
Rickert, *Anc. Eng. Xmas Carols*, pp. 162-3.

119 History of the World from Adam to 1518, in centuries, with numerous digressions and prayers to O.T. heroes, Christian saints, and an introductory prose prologue—generally in interlocking cross-rimed quatrains.
1. Bodl. 3692, ff. 1b-108a.

120 1. Camb. Un. Gg. 4. 27, Ib, f. 35a.
2. Brusendorff, *Chaucer Tradition*, p. 57; Robinson, *Chaucer*, 1933, p. 628; 1957, p. 534.

120.2 Adam that ys ower father be kynde
A version of '*Jesus conditor alme*'—six 7-line stanzas.
1. Bodl. 6616, f. 85b (added in xvi cent. hand).

120.4 Adew adew le company / I trust we shall mete oftener
A song to celebrate the birth of Prince Henry in A.D. 1511 —four macaronic lines. [Cf. 112.5].
1. BM Addit. 31922, f. 74b.
Chappell, *Archaeologia* LXI. 382; Flügel, *Anglia* XII. 247; Stevens, *Music & Poetry*, pp. 249, 413; Stevens, *Music at Court*, p. 54.

120.5 Adewe adewe my hartes lust
A complaint, perhaps of one exiled, by Cornish—one cross-rimed quatrain (following 158.8).
1. Bodl. 6659, f. 100a; 2. BM Addit. 31922, f. 23b.
1. Seaton, *Sir Richard Roos*, p. 405; 2. Flügel, *Anglia* XII. 232; Stevens, *Music & Poetry*, pp. 14, 390; Stevens, *Music at Court*, p. 17.

120.6 Adew corage adew / Hope & trust
A love song—four lines.
1. BM Addit. 31922, f. 42b.
Flügel, *Anglia* XII. 239; Stevens, *Music & Poetry*, p. 401; Stevens, *Music at Court*, p. 32.

120.7   Adew der hart / be man depart
           The comfortless lover—twelve lines in 7-line stanzas with burden: 'My luf mornes for me.'
           1. Camb. Un. Kk. 1. 5, Part VII, f. 179b (ends imperfectly).
           Stevenson, *Lancelot of Laik*, Maitland Club 1839, p. xix.

Adewe pleasure welcome mornynge
    Refrain of 13.5.

Auise the wele let reson be thy guyde   See 3955.5.

Avyse youe wemen wom ye trust
    Burden to 1630.

Isope myn auctor makis mencioune   See 3703 (Asloan).

Affraid alas and whi so sodenli
    Burden to 3131.

Eftir asking we will speik of taking   See 121.5.

Eftir everie asking followis nocht   See 2621.5.

121.5   Eftir geving I speik of taking
           'Of discretioun in taking' by William Dunbar—ten 5-line stanzas with refrain: 'In taking sowld discretioun be.' [Cf. 2621.5 and 3768.3].
           1. Camb. Un. Ll. 5. 10, f. 22b; 2. Pepys 2553, p. 261 (lacks st. 4 & 8); 3. Advocates 1. 1. 6, f. 62b.
             2. Craigie, *STS* n.s. VII. 292-4; 3. Ramsay, *Evergreen*, II. 87-9; repr. *Ramsay & Earlier Scot. Poets*, pp. 275-6; [Hailes,] *Anc. Scot. Poems*, pp. 63-5; *Select Poems of Dunbar*, Perth 1788, pp. 57-8; Sibbald, *Chronicle*, II. 8-10; Laing, *Dunbar*, I. 170-1; Paterson, *Dunbar*, pp. 242.5; *Bannatyne MS.*, Hunt Club, I. 170-1; Small, *STS* IV. 90-1; Schipper, *Dunbar*, pp. 253-4; and *DKAW* XLI (IV). 54-7; Baildon, *Dunbar*, pp. 125-6; Ritchie, *STS* n.s. XXII. 154-5; 3 (with 2 addit. st. from 2). MacKenzie, *Dunbar*, pp. 35-6.

122   —in couplets. [Singer 865].

124   6. Coventry Corp. Record Office, ff. 40-43a.
           4. Furnivall, *EETS* lxi. 95-110.

126	9. Trinity Oxf. 57, f. 21b.
127	3. Winchester Coll. 33, f. 53b. 2. D'Evelyn and Mill, *EETS* 235. 33.
130.5	After þe sayyngus off men þat ben holde On Discretion—five lines. 1. Camb. Un. Nn. 4. 12, f. 57b.
134	fourteen lines.
134.5	Ageynst þe frenchemen in the feld to fyght A modified carol probably for the invasion of France in 1513—one monoriming quatrain and refrain: 'Helpe now þi king,' and 2-line introductory burden. 1. BM Addit. 31922, f. 100b. Chappell, *Archaeologia* XLI. 383; Flügel, *Anglia* XII. 250; Flügel, *Neuengl. Lesebuch*, p. 161; Stevens, *Music & Poetry*, pp. 417-8; Stevens, *Music at Court*, p. 74.

Agaynst the prowde Scottes clatteryng   See 1931.3.

135.3	Agwillare habeth stan diff yn lantern chis tale me [t]old Fragment of a chanson (or ballade) apparently in English, misunderstood by a foreign scribe. [Cf. Ficker, *Musical Qr.* XXII. 131-7]. 1. Trienter Codices 88, ff. 209b-210a. Adler and Koller, *Denkmäler der Tonkunst in Osterreich* XI (1). 120.
135.5	Alac alac what shall I do Three lines of a love song (preceding 3635.5). 1. BM Addit. 31922, f. 35b. Flügel, *Anglia* XII. 236; Trefusis, *Songs Henry VIII*, Roxburghe Club CLXI. 72; Stevens, *Music & Poetry*, p. 396; Stevens, *Music at Court*, p. 26.
137	seven 8-line stanzas. 1. Bodl. Lat. misc. c. 66 [*olim* Capesthorne], f. 94b. Robbins, *PMLA* LXV. 272-4.
138	[Cf. 146]. 1. Yale Univ. 91, ff. 77b-79a. Bukofzer, *Musical Qr.* XXVIII. 42-5; Menner, *MLQ* VI. 386; Robbins, *Sec. Lyrics*, pp. 150-1.

139	Robbins, *Sec. Lyrics*, pp. 156-7; Person, *Camb. ME Lyrics*, p. 31.
141.5	Alas alas that ever I was born / ffor body and soule The Sinner's Lament (≡142), occurring separately. 1. Lincoln Cath. 234, f. 163a. Owst, *Preaching in Med. England*, p. 273.
142	[Cf. 141.5].
143	[Delete entire entry]. Allas allas vel yuel y sped See 3825. Alas ales þe wyle / þout y on no gyle Burden to 1849.
143.5	Alas dere hart what ayleth the A lover protests his devotion—four quatrains, each including refrain: 'Yt were my death to se you dye.' 1. Bodl. 1502, f. 135a (flyleaf).
143.8	Alasse Dethe alasse a blessful thyng ye were An epitaph, including a warning to 'galaunts,' in Hungerford Chapel, Salisbury—two stanzas rime royal. Pettigrew, *Chronicles of Tombs*, pp. 170-1.
145	On Deceit—one 8-line stanza. [Cf. 674]. Robbins, *Sec. Lyrics*, p. 100; Davies, *Med. Eng. Lyrics*, p. 161. Allace depairting grund of wo See 767 (MS. Advocates 1. 1. 6).
146	[Cf. 138]. Robbins, *Sec. Lyrics*, p. 150; Menner, *MLQ* VI. 386; *Oxford Hist. Music*, 1932, II. 4-5.
146.5	Alas for lak of her presens On the absence of his mistress—one stanza rime royal. [Cf. 1334].

147   1. BM Addit. 5465, f. 30b.
Stafford Smith, *Eng. Songs*, p. 12; Fehr, *Archiv* CVI. 57; Stevens, *Music & Poetry*, p. 360.

147   1. Camb. Un. Gg. 4. 27, Ia, ff. 509b-516b (vv. 1-254, 331-562); 2. Sloane 1212, ff. 4a-4b (vv. 439-505 only); 3. BM Addit. 16165, ff. 231a-241b (lacks vv. 157-176).

148   2. Delete this MS.

149   Ross, *Speculum* XXXII. 281-2.

150   *Bagford Ballads*, I. 519; Robbins, *Sec. Lyrics*, pp. 28-30.

152   1. NLW Peniarth 26, p. 108.
Robbins, *Sec. Lyrics*, pp. 152-3.

153   [Delete entire entry].

155   Furnivall, *EETS* 15 orig. ed. 234; rev. ed. 264.

155.5   Alas it is I that wote nott what to say
The rejected lover—one stanza rime royal. [Followed by 1273.3].
1. BM Addit. 5465, f. 17b.
Burney, *Hist. Music*, 1782, II. 548-50; Fehr, *Archiv* CVI. 55; Stevens, *Music & Poetry*, p. 357.

157   three 7-line stanzas.

Hallas men planys of litel trwthe   See 2145.

158.2   Alas myne eye whye doest þou bringe
'Why art thow thus my mortall foe'—one quatrain.
1. Bodl. 6659, f. 99a.
Wagner, *MLN* L. 453; Seaton, *Sir Richard Roos*, p. 179.

158.3   Ellas mornyngh y syngh mornyng y cal / our lord ys deyd that bogthe ovs al
Fragment of an English song ['*cantant*'] in the Cornish mystery play of the Three Marys in the *Ordinale de Resurrexione Domini Nostri Jhesu Christi*.
1. Bodl. 2639, f. 64b; 1a (1695 English translation). Bodl.

28556, p. 278; 1b (1695 Cornish transcript). Bodl. 28557, p. 427.
1. Norris, *Anc. Cornish Drama*, 1859, II. 58, 60; Peter, *Old Cornish Drama*, 1906, p. 31; Halliday, *Legend of Rood*, p. 13; Robbins, *Anglia* LXXXII.5.

158.4   Alas my childe how haue ye dighte
'A lamentacioun of our lady for sweryng,' with examples of typical oaths, swearers' lamentations, and concluding moralization—vv. 83 in quatrains, couplets, and rime royal.
1. Trinity Dublin 432, f. 65a.
Brotanek, *ME Dichtungen*, pp. 99-102.

158.6   Alas poor man what chans hav y
Secret love—two quatrains.
1. Balliol 316 B, f. 114a.
Mynors, *Cat.*, p. 334.

158.7   Allace so sobir is the micht
A warning to woman against false men by 'Mersar'—four 8-line stanzas. [Utley 19].
1. Advocates 1. 1. 6, f. 269a.
[Hailes,] *Anc. Scot. Poetry*, pp. 196-7; Sibbald, *Chronicle*, I. 195-6; Ellis, *Specimens*, 1811, I. 374-6: *Bannatyne MS.*, Hunt. Club, p. 782; Ritchie, *STS* n.s. XXVI. 48.

Alas the woo þat we are wroght
Scriveners' Play: see 1273.

158.8   Alas to whom should I complayne
A lover's complaint—one cross-rimed quatrain (followed by 120.5), actually st. 1 of 158.9.
1. Bodl. 6659, f. 100a.
Wagner, *MLN* L. 455; Seaton, *Sir Richard Roos*, p. 405.

158.9   Alas to whom shuld I complayne
A Farewell by Edward Stafford, Third Duke of Buckingham, executed in A.D. 1521—twenty-two quatrains, each ending with 'remedyles.' [First st. occurring separately, as lover's complaint, 158.8. Cf. 2409.5].
1. Harley 2252, ff. 2b-3a.

159   Robbins, *PMLA* LXIX. 635-6; Person, *Camb. ME Lyrics*, p. 32.

159.5   Alas what shall I do for love
         A late love lyric, ascribed to Henry VIII—six lines.
         1. BM Addit. 31922, f. 20b.
            Chappell, *Archaeologia* XLI. 374; Flügel, *Anglia* XII. 231; Flügel, *Neuengl. Lesebuch,* p. 133; Trefusis, *Songs Henry VIII,* Roxburghe Club CLXI. 7-8; Padelford, *Early XVI Cent. Lyrics,* p. 78; Stevens, *Music & Poetry,* p. 390; Stevens, *Music at Court,* p. 16.

         Alas what shulde yt be to yow
         See 1086 (MS. 7, vv. 229-36).

159.8   Alas what thing can be more grevous payne
         The pangs of absence—six stanzas rime royal.
         1. Bodl. 12653, f. 13b.
            Padelford and Benham, *Anglia* XXXI. 327-8.

160   in quatrains with 'Wo worth' anaphora.
         1. Nottingham Univ. Mi Dc 7 [*olim* Wollaton Hall], outside cover.
            Hist. MSS. Comm. Report, 1911, pp. 267-8.

161   Utley, *Harvard Theol. Rev.* XXXVIII. 145; Person, *Camb. ME Lyrics,* pp. 42-3; Robbins, *Hist. Poems,* pp. 166-8; Kaiser, *Med. Eng.,* p. 323; Davies, *Med. Eng. Lyrics,* pp. 265-6.

161.5   Alas wharto shall y now take
         The sinner forsaken by heaven and earth—three monoriming lines.
         1. Balliol 149, f. 79b.
            Mynors, *Cat.,* p. 133.

163   [Masters,] *Rymes of Minstrels,* p. 22; Greene, *Sel. Eng. Carols,* p. 155; Speirs, *Med. Eng. Poetry,* pp. 88-9.

168   2. Harley 2251, ff. 287b—293b (ends imperfectly).

172   1, 2. Bolle, *Anglia* XXXIV. 292; 2. Padelford and Benham, *Anglia* XXXI. 317.

173.5   Al clerkyn lou clercyn lou / Ys y-wyrt at Oxinfort
         Three couplets translating '*Omnis amor clerici amor clerici.*'
         1. Leicester City. Lib., Old Town 4, p. 38.
            Retrospective Rev. 1853, I. 419.

174	James and Jenkins, *Cat.*, p. 133 (vv. 6 only).
176	Zupitza, *Archiv* XC. 247.
177	Person, *Camb. ME Lyrics*, p. 28.
179	five monoriming lines. Wilson, *Lost Lit.*, p. 180; Dronke, *N&Q* n.s. VIII. 246.

All hayle and be gladde most noble & moder dere / Of Ihesu
See 3955.5.

180	Kaiser, *Anthologie,* pp. 211-3; Kaiser, *Med. Eng.,* pp. 249-51 (vv. 120 only).
182	1. Hunterian Mus. 83, f. 12a. Robbins, *MLN* LVIII. 41-2; Stevens, *Med. Carols,* p. 111.
183	2. MacCracken, *Archiv* CXXXI. 45-6.
184	12. D'Evelyn and Mill, *EETS* 236. 460.
187	Furnivall, *EETS* 15 orig. ed. 224; rev. ed. 253.
187.5	Al holy chyrch was bot a thrall Carol to St. Thomas of Canterbury—seven 5-line stanzas with 2-line burden. 1. Egerton 3307, f. 62b. Greene, *Journal American Musicological Soc.* VII. 7; Stevens, *Med. Carols,* p. 48; Greene, *Sel. Eng. Carols,* p. 80.
189.5	All ys gode but best ys thys A couplet at the end of a prose 'most souereyn medycyn for the pestilence.' 1. Pepys 1047, f. 18a.
190.3	Alle it is for woo / þat þe hen synges in þe snowe A proverbial couplet. 1. Bodl. 21626, f. 18b; 2. Rylands Lib. Latin 394, f. 8b. 1. Förster, *Festschrift zum 12 Deutschen Philologentage,* p. 47; 2. Pantin, *BJRL* XIV. 97.

190.5 All lust and lykyng I begyn to leue
A lover's plea—one quatrain and three 8-line stanzas.
1. Trinity Camb. 599, f. 3b.
Wilson, *Anglia* LXXII. 405-6.

192 Furnivall, *EETS* 32 rev. ed. 381-4.

193.5 Al maters wel pondred and wel to be regarded
'Against venemous tongues' by John Skelton—vv. 82 in couplets and monorimed sequences.
Workes, Marshe, 1568 (STC 22608); *repr.* [? J. Bowle,] 1736; Chalmers, *English Poets*, II. 235-6; Dyce, *Skelton*, I. 132-6; Dyce and Child, *Skelton & Donne*, I. 154-9; Henderson, *Skelton*, 1931, pp. 138-42; 1948, 1959, pp. 245-9.

193.8 All mi blod for þe is sched / Reu on me þat am for bled
Christ's appeal—one couplet.
1. Advocates 18. 7. 21, f. 119a.

194 Robbins, *Sec. Lyrics*, p. 12; Kaiser, *Anthologie*, p. 310; Kaiser, *Med. Eng.*, p. 476; Dronke, *N&Q* n.s. VIII. 246.

194.5 All noble men of this take hede
'The Relucent Mirror' by John Skelton—thirty lines. [Also used as prefatory lines to 813.3].
Certayne Bokes, Kynge and Marche, ca. 1560 (STC 22599); and other early prints; Kele, n. d. (STC 22615); *repr.* Dyce, *Skelton*, II. 26-7; Dyce and Child, *Skelton & Donne*, II. 276-7; Flügel, *Neuengl. Lesebuch*, p. 62; Henderson, *Skelton*, 1931, pp. 338-9; 1948, 1959, pp. 308-9; *Workes*, Marshe, 1568 (STC 22608); *repr.* [? J. Bowle,] 1736; Chalmers, *English Poets*, II. 266 and 271.

Alle of the herbys o Ierlonde   See 3754.

*196.5 *All owr mischeuis haue in þy syht
A prayer to the Virgin—vv. 45 in couplets.
1. Egerton 3245 [*olim* Gurney], f. 198a.
Robbins, *PMLA* LIV. 385-6.

197.5 Al oure wonder & al oure wo / is torned to wele & blisse al so
A couplet in a Latin sermon.
1. Camb. Un. Ii. 3. 8, f. 144a.

197.8 Alle perisches and passes þat we with eghe see
First lyric inserted in Rolle's *Ego Dormio*—8 or 10 irregular alliterative lines.
1. Bodl. 3938, f. 338a; 2. Bodl. 11272, f. 96a; 3. Camb. Un. Dd. 5. 64, Part III, f. 24b; 4. Pepys 2125; 5. BM Addit. 22283, f. 150b; 6. Trinity Dublin 155; 7. Westminster School; 8. *olim* Gurney; 9. Longleat 29; 10. Paris: Bibl. Mazarine 514; 11. Paris: Bibl. St. Geneviève 339.
2, 3. Horstmann, *York. Wr.*, I. 53; 3. Allen, *Eng. Writings of Rolle*, p. 64.

199   12. BM Addit. 12195, f. 121b (st. 6 only).
10. Sibbald, *Chronicle*, III. 221-2; FitzGibbon, *E. E. Poetry*, pp. 78-9.

199.5 Al schul we hen / whedir ne when / may no man ken / But god aboue
An epitaph on a brass at Pakefield, Suffolk.
S.E., *East Anglian* II. 321.

200   2. Longleat 29, ff. 54b-55a.

201   12. D'Evelyn and Mill, *EETS* 236.463.

202   [Cf. 3910.5].
1. Cotton Vesp. B. xii, f. 3a.

203   1. Advocates 19. 2. 1, ff. 16b-21a.

205   1. Camb. Un. Add. 4407, Art. 19: Fragments a (vv. 6-12), b (vv. 20-29), c (vv. 83-8 with 4 new lines); 2. Harley 2253, ff. 73a-73b (vv. 91).
2. Percy, *Reliques*, 1765, II. 7; Warton, *Hist. Eng. Poetry*, 1824, I. 106; Zupitza, *Uebungsbuch*, pp. 158-60; Aspin, *AN Pol. Poems*, pp. 90-2; Kaiser, *Anthologie*, p. 367; Kaiser, *Med. Eng.*, p 357; Robbins, *Hist. Poems*, p. 21; Davies, *Med. Eng. Lyrics*, pp. 91-4.

209   4. Kendal Grammar School: A. de Clavasio, *Summa de casibus conscientiae*, Nuremberg 1498, fragment in binding (vv. 127-90, 572-653 of MS. 1).

210   [For a similar burden cf. 1280. Utley 20].
1. Bodl. 29734, f. 23a.

FitzGibbon, *E. E. Poetry*, p. 239; [Masters,] *Rymes of Minstrels*, p. 9; Williams, *New Book Eng. Verse*, p. 109; *Oxford Book Light Verse*, p. 63; Robbins, *Sec. Lyrics*, pp. 39-40.

210.5 Alle þat leuen in god lystneþ to my lore
A blessing—one couplet (in the *Speculum Sacerdotale*).
1. Bodl. 11247, f. 25a; 2. BM Addit. 36791, f. 68a.
2. Weatherly, *EETS* 200. 121.

211 seventy-one 6-line stanzas.

213 B. 4. *Register*, I. 371.

215 Bowers, *MLN* LXX. 250-2.

220 14. Ipswich County Hall Deposit: Hillwood [*olim* Brome], f. 5a.

221 [For similar lines see 141, 3311, 3397, 3398].
1. Furnivall, *EETS* 15 orig. ed. 232; rev. ed. 261; 2. Patterson, *JEGP* XX. 275.

222.5 Alle þe wordis þat drawen to senne / þenk þat wenym is þerinne
A couplet translating '*Omne seminarium voluptatis venenum puta.*'
1. Advocates 18. 7. 21, f. 12a.

223 2. Pepys 2553, p. 171 (8 st.).
Chepman and Myllar, 1508 (8 st., following 1567) (STC 11984); *facs.* Beattie, Edinb. Bibl. Soc. 1950, pp. 49-51.

223.5 Al thyngys contryued by mannys reason
'Magnyfycence' by John Skelton—in varied stanzas.
Magnyfycence A Goodly Interlude, ? Rastell, 1533 (STC 22607); *repr.* Roxburghe Club 1821; Dyce, *Skelton*, I. 226-310; Dyce and Child, *Skelton & Donne*, II. 3-124; Ramsay, *EETS* xcviii; Farmer, *Tudor Facsimile Texts*, 1910; Henderson, *Skelton*, 1931, pp. 173-256; 1948, 1959, pp. 165-244.

All this before Ihesu tham sayde   See 1189.

224 twenty-six lines.
Horstmann, *Leben Iesu*, 1873, pp. 5-6.

225 [Cf. 474.5].
Robbins, *Sec. Lyrics*, pp. 24-5; Greene, *Sel. Eng. Carols*, p. 162.

226 1. BM Addit. 40166 (C), f. 12b.

227.5 All tho that been enemyes to the kynge
Pageant verses for the return of Henry VI to London, A.D. 1432—one stanza rime royal. [Adapted from 3799].
Fabyan, *New Chronicles*, Pynson, 1516 (STC 10659); *repr.* Ellis, 1811, p. 603; Gattinger, *Wiener Beiträge* IV. 24-5.

228 All tho þat list of wemen evill to speik
[Utley 21].
Chaucer, Thynne, 1532 (STC 5068); *Chaucer*, Speght, 1598 (STC 5077); *Chaucer*, Stow, 1561 (STC 5075); Urry, *Chaucer*, 1721, p. 456; Bell, *Poets of Great Britain*, X. 127; [Anderson,] *Poets of Great Britain*, I. 444; *British Poets*, Chiswick 1822, IV. 295; Chalmers, *Eng. Poets*, I. 344-5; 1. *Bannatyne MS.*, Hunt. Club, IV. 799.

228.5 Alle to late all to late / when þe weyne is at þe 3ate
A proverbial couplet. [Cf. Hendyng].
1. Bodl. 21626, f. 26a; 2. Rylands Lib. Latin 394, f. 15b.
1. Förster, *Festschrift zum 12 Deutschen Neuphilologentage*, p. 52; 2. Pantin, *BJRL* XIV. 102.

228.8 All vnder sunne is wyt swynk her yvonne
Worldly wealth makes trouble—three long lines with medial rime.
1. Corpus Christi Camb. 405, p. 22.
Person, *Camb. ME Lyrics*, p. 71.

229 [Preceded immediately by 3730].
3. Longleat 29, ff. 53b-54b.
1. Allen, *Eng. Writings of Rolle*, p. 49; 2 (coll. 1). Comper, *Life & Lyrics of Rolle*, pp. 264-8.

230 [Cf. 3428, *Pricke of Conscience*, vv. 1273].

230.5 Alle we liuien hapfulliche
Two couplets translating 'Viuimus hic sorte &c.'
1. Advocates 18. 7. 21, f. 87b.

231 Skeat, *Athenaeum* 1894, CIV. 98; Skeat, *Minor Poems* 1896, p. 461.

All wylde beasts a man maye tame   See 106.5.

231.5 All wyth a throwe and a lowe and lully / I haue Ioly a pryn for þe mastry
Two English lines (followed by *probationes pennae*).
1. Sloane 3160, f. 24b.
Robbins, *Anglia* LXXXII. 12.

All womein Ar guid noblle and excellent   See 232.

232 one stanza rime royal. [For two similar poems see 3174.5 and 3909.6. Cf. also 1593; Hughey, II. 211].
1. BM Addit. 17492, f. 18b; 3. Pepys 2553, p. 356; 4. Arundel, Harington, f. 107b; 4a (transcript). BM Addit. 28635, f. 57b.
1, 4. Hughey, II. 209, I. 185; 1. Padelford, *Early XVI Cent. Lyrics*, p. 94; Muir, *Proc. Leeds Philos. & Lit. Soc. (Lit. & Hist. Section)*, VI. 260; 3. Pinkerton, *Anc. Scot. Poems*, p. 244; Craigie, *STS* VII. 433.

233 [Ringler 3].
8. Camb. Un. Kk. 1. 7, f. 35a; 9. BM Addit. 34193, f. 32a; 10. Hatfield; 11. Melbourne: Victoria Pub. Lib., f. 126a.
Pylgremage of the Sowle, Caxton, 1483 (STC 6473); *repr.* Cust, 1859, pp. 46-7.

All ye men þat by me wendene   See 2596.

236 1. Rickert, *Anc. Eng. Xmas Carols*, pp. 22-3.

All ye that have soughte many a daye
A second part (usually a few couplets) in some MSS. of 3249.

237 [See Gray, *N&Q* n.s. VIII. 135].
Robbins, *Sec. Lyrics*, p. 119; Davies, *Med. Eng. Lyrics*, p. 188.

All you that fayne woulde be speade
Introduction (vv. 5) in some MSS. to 1276.

239 [Inserted in the prose translation. . .in MSS. 1, 4, 8, 12, 13, and 16].
14. Coventry Corp. Record Office, f. 75a; 15. Durham Univ. Cosin V. I. 9, f. 203a (st. 1-2 only); 16. Melbourne: Victoria Pub. Lib., f. 74b.
4. Wright, *Roxburghe Club* XCI. 165-70; Furnivall and Locock, *Roxburghe Club* CXLV. 528-33; Robinson, *Chaucer*, 1939, pp. 617-9; 1957, pp. 524-6; 15. Doyle, *Durham Philobiblon* I. 54-5.

241 [Incorporated into 2451].
4. Harley 2406, f. 8b (followed by 1790.5); 5. Longleat 29, f. 57b (4 st.).
2, 3. Person, *Camb. ME Lyrics*, pp. 1-3; 4. Davies, *Med. Eng. Lyrics*, p. 194.

242.5 Almyghty god in trenite / fadir and sone and holy gost /as wis as y beleve in the
Verses against thieves—vv. 27 in couplets. [For a variant text cf. 1952.5].
1. Yale Univ. 163, f. 15b.
Vann, *Speculum* XXXIV. 637.

245 1. Bodl. 1885, f. 47a; 35. Liverpool Univ. [*olim* Gower, *olim* Quaritch Sale Cat. 328, Item 577], f. 1a; 36. Bodl. Lyell 28, ff. 79 (imperfect at beginning and end); 37. Nottingham Univ. Mi LM 9 [*olim* Wollaton Hall], f. 1a; 38. Harley 5977, f. 90 (a single leaf); 39. Robert Taylor (Princeton) [*olim* Petre, *olim* Sotheby Sale 10 March 1952, Lot 143, *olim* Quaritch Sale Cat. 704, Item 350, *olim* Laurence Witten].
31. Fischer, *Eng. Stn.* LX 258-61; Wordsworth, *Surtees Soc.* CXXXII. 165-7; 37. *Hist. MSS. Comm. Report*, 1911 (Col. Middleton MSS.) (extract).

246 four couplets (followed by 1950.5).
1. Lincoln Cath. 91, f. 191b; 2. Egerton 3245 [*olim* Gurney], f. 191a; 3. Princeton Univ. 21 [*olim* Huth], f. 112b.
1. Comper. *Life & Lyrics of Rolle*, pp. 293-4; 3. Bühler, *MLN* LXVI. 314.

247 1. Goldberg, *Die Catonischen Distichen*, Leipzig 1833, pp. 13-5.

248   6. Folger Lib. 420312 [*olim* Clopton], f. 84b.

248.5   Almyghti god in trenite / oo god and persones thre
             A versification of Mandeville's *Travels*—vv. 2947 in couplets. (Cf. 3117.6].
             1. Coventry Corp. Record Office, ff. 77b-97b.

250.5   Almytty god Iesu crist þat deydest upon de rode tre
             A prayer for grace by the wounds of Christ—four quatrains.
             1. Plimpton Addenda 2, f. 5b.

253   3. Bodl. Lat. Lit. e. 17, ff. 51a-53a (9 st.).

             Allemysty god that all has wroght   See 694.

258   a prose tract, *Antidotarium Nicholai.*

259   1a (transcript). Bodl. 21639, ff. 1a-92b.
             Friedman and Harrington, *EETS* 254.

260   vv. 363 in 6-line stanzas.

261   fifty-nine couplets.
             1. Egerton 3143 [*olim* Clumber], ff. 60b-63a.
             Haslewood, *Roxburghe Club* 1824, pp. 49-56; Bazire, *EETS* 228. 72-6.

263   [Ringler 4].
             8. Camb. Un. Kk. 1. 7, ff. 34b-35a; 9. BM Addit. 34193, f. 31b; 10. Hatfield; 11. Melbourne: Victoria Pub. Lib., f. 125b.
             Pylgremage of the Sowle, Caxton, 1483 (STC 6473); *repr.* Cust, 1859, pp. 45-6.

263.3   Alone alone alone alone alone alone / alone in wyldernes
             A refrain, probably of a love song.
             1. Royal App. 58, f. 8a.
             Flügel, *Anglia* XII. 262.

             Alone alone alone alone / Here I sytt alone
             Burden to 364.

             Alone alone alone alone / Sore I sygh
             Burden to 377.5.

263.5   Alone alone / here y am myself alone
Doleful cheer — two quatrains including refrain.
1. BM Addit. 5665, f. 140b.
    Fehr, *Archiv* CVI. 283; Stevens, *Music & Poetry*, p. 346.

263.8   Alone alone / murning alone
A warning to lovers — six 8-line tail-rime stanzas.
1. BM Addit. 5665, f. 133b.
    Fehr, *Archiv* CVI. 282; Stevens, *Music & Poetry*, p. 342.

264   2. Camb. Un. Add. 2585 (1), f. 1a.
Robbins, *MLN* LXVI. 504.

265   2. Advocates 1. 1. 6, p. 30 and f. 46b.
1. FitzGibbon, *E. E. Poetry*, pp. 88-9; 2a. Ritchie, *STS* 3 s. V. 50-2; 2b. Eyre-Todd, *Med. Scot. Poetry*, pp. 98-100; Laing, *Henryson*, 1865, p. 15; Wood, *Henryson*, pp. 195-6.

265.5   Allon he drawys fro company
Christ's love for his 'drury' — six lines.
1. Trinity Dublin 277, p. 188.

266   [Delete entire entry].

Alone I lyue alone and sore I syghe for one
Burden to 2293.5.

266.3   Alone y lyue alone
Fragment heading 3971 apparently to indicate title of a popular air. [Cf. 266.5].
1. Caius 383, p. 41.
    James, *Cat.*, II. 436; *Early Eng. Carols*, p. 280.

266.5   Alone I leffe alone / And sore I sygh for one
A round — one couplet. [For these lines used as burden, cf. 377.5 and 2293.5; cf. also 266.3].
1. BM Addit. 31922, f. 22a.
    Flügel, *Anglia* XII. 231; Briggs, *Songs & Madrigals*, PMMS, 1891, pp. 3-4; Stevens, *Music & Poetry*, p. 390; Stevens, *Music at Court*, p. 17.

267   *Chaucer*, Speght, 1598 (STC 5077); Urry, *Chaucer*, 1721, p. 555; Bell, *Poets of Great Britain*, 1782, XII. 123; [Ander-

son] *Poets of Great Britain,* I. 584; Godwin, *Life of Chaucer,* 1803, II. 356; *British Poets,* Chiswick 1822, V. 178; Moxon, *Chaucer,* 1843, p. 439; [Pickering's] *Aldine Brit. Poets,* 1845, VI. 286; 1866, VI, 305; Bell, *Chaucer,* III. 426; Robbins, *Sec. Lyrics,* pp. 162-3; Kaiser, *Anthologie,* p. 297; Kaiser, *Med. Eng.,* p. 470; Davies, *Med. Eng. Lyrics,* pp. 255-6.

268   Person, *Camb. ME Lyrics,* p. 29.

269   'The Falcon,' the wounds of Christ against the sins—fifteen couplets.
Ross, *Speculum* XXXII. 278-9; Kaiser, *Med. Eng.,* p. 296; Bowers, *Univ. of Florida Monographs, Humanities* XII. 32.

269.5   Also þe lanterne in þe wynd þat sone is aqueynt
The transitoriness of life (? perhaps by William Herebert)— two couplets.
1. BM Addit. 46919 [*olim* Phillipps 8336], f. 204b.
Rel. Ant., II. 229.

*269.8   *Also þe stonden þer so. . .
The sixth line of a much-effaced 10-line poem on the Annunciation, written in pencil in a xiii cent. hand.
1. Camb. Un. Hh. 4. 18, f. 111b.

Also use not to pley at the dice
An extract (*Rel. Ant.,* II. 27) from 1540 (Bodl. 1479).

270   A lover's complaint, fragmentary English love song with music. [Cf. *317.5].
1. BM Loan 29/333: Portland, verso.

271   1. Egerton 3245 [*olim* Gurney], f. 183b.

Allways six is the best caste of the dyse   See 734.8.

271.5   Allway to say sothe thu shalt neuer com fore the
On speaking the truth—two long couplets.
1. Bodl. 15444, f. 168b.

*272.5   *. . .am I lent by diuyne prouidence / . . .we mankynde
On the Seven Virtues—seven 8-line stanzas. [Ringler 97].
BM single sheet, printed on one side, ca. 1500 (STC 17037).

[32]

273   6. B. D. Brown, *EETS* 169. 76.

274   *Early Eng. Carols*, p. 329; Wilson, *Lost Lit.*, p. 183.

275   Don't meddle—a single couplet.
         Skeat, *EETS* 38. viii.

276.5   Amang thir freiris within ane cloister
         'Of the passioun of Christ' by William Dunbar—twelve 8-line stanzas with refrain: 'O mankynd for the lufe of the.' [Followed without break by 2161.5].
         1. Pepys 2553, p. 203; 2. Arundel 285, f. 168a; 3. Asloan, f. 290b; 3a (xix cent. transcript by Chalmers). Edinburgh Univ. La. III. 450/1; 3b (xix cent. transcript). Edinburgh Univ. La. IV. 27/8.
         1. Small, *STS* IV. 239-43; Schipper, *Dunbar*, pp. 375-7; and *DKAW* XLII (IV). 72-5; Baildon, *Dunbar*, pp. 199-201; Craigie, *STS* n.s. VII. 229-32; MacKenzie, *Dunbar*, pp. 155-7; Kinsley, *Dunbar*, pp. 2-6; 2. Bennett, *STS* 3 s. XXIII. 266-7; 3. Craigie, *STS* n.s. XVI. 242-5; 3a. Paterson, *Dunbar*, pp. 81-3; Laing, *Dunbar*, I. 243-6.

277   seven 8-line stanzas. [Utley 26].
         2. Laing, *Dunbar*, II. 91-2; Sibbald, *Chronicle*, I. 363.

*282.5   *[An an] gel sche sent to him anon
         The clerk blinded by the glory of the B. V.
         1. Advocates 19. 2. 1, f. 37b.
         Horstmann, *AE Leg. 1881*, pp. 499-502; Boyd, p. 24.

284   8 (with vv. 1-144 from 3). Small, *Met. Hom.*, pp. 78-92.

285   eighty-six stanzas rime royal, with Complaint in seven 9-line stanzas. [Utley 1].
         1. St. John's Camb. 235, Part II, f. 1a (xvi cent.); 3. Bodl. 29640, pp. 476-509 (Eng. from Thynne, with Latin tr. by Kinaston, ca. 1639).
         Charteris, 1593 (STC 13165); *repr.* Chalmers, *Bannatyne Club*, 1824, I. 294-9; Sibbald, *Chronicle*, I. 157-76 (extracts); Eyre-Todd, *Med. Scot. Poetry*, pp. 103-25; Arber, *Dunbar, Anthology*, pp. 156-78; Neilson and Webster, *Chief Brit. Poets*, pp. 367-74; Wood, *Henryson*, pp. 105-26; Dickins, Edinb. 1925; Elliott, pp. 90-107; Anderson, [Glasgow,] 1663; 3. Smith, *STS* LXIV. cv-cxlvi.

285.5   An Egyll shall ryse with a bore bold
A political prophecy—forty-five irregular riming lines.
1. Lansdowne 762, ff. 53b-54a.

286.5   An evyll favouryd and a fowle blacke wyf
A description of Marcolphus' wife Polycena, tr. from the Latin—two couplets. [Ringler 5].
Salomon and Marcolphus, Leeu, Antwerp, ca. 1492 (STC 22905); *facs.* Duff, London, 1892.

287   2. Rosenthal, *Vitae Patrum in Old & ME Lit.*, p. 153.

288   5. Rosenthal, *Vitae Patrum in Old & ME Lit.*, p. 161.

289   13. Bodl. Lat. misc. b. 17 [*olim* Robartes], one leaf (corresponds to Bodl. 6923, f. 132b).

293.5   Ane murlandis man of uplandis mak
'Tydingis fra the sessioun' by William Dunbar—eight 7-line stanzas.
1. Camb. Un. Ll. 5. 10, f. 37a; 2. Pepys 2553, pp. 314-5; 3. Advocates 1. 1. 6, f. 59a.
2. Craigie, *STS* n.s. VII. 374-5; 3. Ramsay, *Evergreen*, I. 98-100; *repr. Ramsay and Earlier Scot. Poets*, pp. 234-5; [Hailes,] *Anc. Scot. Poems*, pp. 48-50; *Select Poems of Dunbar*, Perth 1788, pp. 46-9; Sibbald, *Chronicle*, I. 247-9; Laing, *Dunbar*, I. 102-4; Paterson, *Dunbar*, pp. 140-2; *Bannatyne MS.*, Hunt. Club, I. 160-2; Small, *STS* IV. 78-80; Schipper, *Dunbar*, pp. 79-80; and *DKAW* XL (II). 78-80; Ritchie, *STS* n.s. XXII. 145-7; Baildon, *Dunbar*, pp. 29-30; MacKenzie, *Dunbar*, pp. 79-80; Kinsley, *Dunbar*, pp. 73-4.

295   1. Cotton Calig. A. ix, ff. 3a-194b.
Hall, Oxford 1924 (selections); Brook and Leslie, *EETS* 250.

Ane soung man chiftane witles   See 1820.

*295.5   *And a woman of hauntynge moode
'*Disputacio inter Clericum et Philomenam*'—vv. 85 in alternate stanzas of 8 and 10 lines. [Cf. 1452].
1. Bodl. 14528, f. 5a (first leaf missing).
Robbins, *Sec. Lyrics*, pp. 176-9.

*295.8 *And alle þe to þer þat were þer pers
One leaf of a poem on King Arthur, possibly a version of the *Morte d'Arthur,* containing the victory of the Britons over the Romans.
1. Bodl. 13679, Item 3.

*296.3 *And as I passid in my preiere þer prestis were at messe
Mum and the Sothsegger—in alliterative lines.
1. Camb. Un. Ll. 4. 14, ff. 107b-119b ('Richard the Redeles,' vv. 857; ends imperfectly); 2. BM Addit. 41666, ff. 1a-19b (1751 different vv.; begins and ends imperfectly).
1, 2. Day and Steele, *EETS* 199; 1. Wright, *Camden Soc.* III. 1-30; Wright, *Pol. Poems,* I. 368-417; Skeat, *EETS* 54. 469-503; Skeat, *Piers Plowman,* I. 603.

*296.6 *And as þy worde came on þys wyse / To þe thefe
A prayer on the Words of Christ from the Cross—ten 6-line stanzas.
1. Camb. Un. Dd. 5. 76, f. 1a.
Person, *Camb. ME Lyrics,* pp. 6-8.

297 [Delete entire entry].

And at Warwike that Erle so fre   See 979.

298   Chambers, *Eng. Lit. Close MA,* p. 111; Jacob, *XV Cent.,* p. 662; Greene, *Sel. Eng. Carols,* p. 130.

*298.5 *Ande Dyomedes byrdes þai ware / Callit thare-eftre
The Scottish Troy Fragments, inserted in two MSS. of Lydgate's *Troy Book* (2516)—in couplets.
Fragment A.
1. Camb. Un. Kk. 5. 30, ff. 11a-19a (vv. 596; beginning corresponds to *Troy Book* I. 876); Part II, ff. 28a-71a (extracts copied in A. D. 1612).
Fragment B ('Barbour').
1. Bodl. 21722, ff. 290a-300b (vv. 1-918), 307a-336b (vv. 1181-1562 continuing to v. 3118); 2. Camb. Un. Kk. 5. 30, ff. 304b-308a (vv. 1-1562).
A1, B1, B2. Horstmann, *Barbours Leg. Samml.* 1881, pp. 218-27, 229-304.

299 [Utley 28].
5. Coventry Corp. Record Office, ff. 43-49.

2. Hammond, *Eng. Verse Chaucer-Surrey*, p. 69 (extracts).

299.5 And ever þe hyer þat þowe art
One couplet introducing a series of proverbs (317) in one MS., with a concluding couplet.
1. Bodl. 6943, f. 73a.

*And euill thryfte on thy hede saide lytell John   See 1915 (STC 13688).

299.8 And for swet smell at thi nose stink sall thou find
Against Gallants—three couplets in Fordun's *Scotichronicon* (Book XIV, Cap. xxx).
Hearne, *Joannis de Fordun Scotichronicon*, Edinb. 1759, II. 374-5.

*And he seyȝe me wiþ his eyȝe   See 1873.5.

301 [Following 1163].

*301.3 *And his fadire of wyf wat nocht
The Life of St. Agnes in the *Scottish Legendary*.
1. Camb. Un. Gg. 2. 6, f. 348a.
Horstmann, *Barbours Leg. Samml.*, II. 151-6; Metcalfe, STS XXV. 346-57.

301.5 And I am soked in my synne / Lang liggand þare in
An irregular couplet in Rolle's English Psalter (Ps. III). [For further MSS. see Allen, *Rolle*, pp. 170-7].
1. Bodl. 4127, f. 8a; 2. Univ. Coll. Oxf. 64.
1. Allen, *Eng. Writings of Rolle*, p. 9; 2. Bramley, Oxford 1884, p. 14.

302 [See 3614].
1. Harley 1251, f. 184a; 3. Cotton Titus C. xix, f. 144a; 4. Egerton 1151, f. 159a.
1. Littlehales, *EETS* 109. xlviii; Wordsworth and Littlehales, *Old Service Books*, p. 61; Coulton, *Life in the MA*, II. 118; Bennett, *England Chaucer-Caxton*, p. 161.

And I mankynd have not in mynd   See 4094.3.

*And I waited on that wold how wondirly bilt   See 653.

302.5　　　　And I war a maydyn / As many one ys
　　　　　　　A girl's progress in love—three quatrains. [The first line occurs in Harley 1517, f. 94b, pr. *Early Eng. Carols*, p. 326; as title in Bodl. 29634, f. 54b, pr. *Early Eng. Carols*, p. 60; *Thersites*, pr. Dodsley, ed. Hazlitt, *Old Plays*, I. 405. Utley 29].
　　　　　　　1. BM Addit. 31922, f. 106b.
　　　　　　　　　Flügel, *Anglia* XII. 250; Stevens, *Music & Poetry*, pp. 42, 418-9; Stevens, *Music at Court*, pp. 78-9.

303　　　　　one 6-line stanza, with preceding couplet.
　　　　　　　1. BM Addit. 43490, f. 23a.
　　　　　　　　　Coulton, *Life in the MA*, III. 135; Bennett, *England Chaucer-Caxton*, p. 21; Stevens, *Music & Poetry*, p. 205; Davis, Oxford 1958, p. 106; Matthews, *Later Med. Eng. Prose*, pp. 90-91.

　　　　　　　And yf ye will to the medcyn applie　　See 3721.

*303.3　　　*And in þis fair way persaif I wele a thing
　　　　　　　The Talis of the Fyve Bestes—vv. 422 in couplets.
　　　　　　　1. Asloan ff. 229a-235b; 1a (xix cent. transcript). Edinburgh Univ. La. IV. 27/8.
　　　　　　　　　Craigie, *STS* n.s. XVI. 127-40.

*303.6　　　*And liued in dedeli sinne / Seyn Patrike hadde rewthe
　　　　　　　Owayne Miles—in 6-line stanzas. [Cf. 982 and 1767].
　　　　　　　1. Advocates 19. 2. 1, f. 25a.
　　　　　　　　　Turnbull and Laing, *Owain Miles*, 1837; Kölbing, *Eng. Stn*. I. 98-112.

*304.5　　　*And Martha kepid swiþe wel / Hir londes
　　　　　　　Life of St. Mary Magdalene—in couplets.
　　　　　　　1. Advocates 19. 2. 1, f. 62a.
　　　　　　　　　Turnbull, *Leg. Cath.*, pp. 213-57; Horstmann, *AE Leg. 1878*, pp. 163-70.

305　　　　　[Delete entire entry].

　　　　　　　And more they shulde vndertake　　See 979.

305.5   And now and ȝe uollen dwelle / The uirtues of the lylye
One couplet introducing a prose herbal (with other couplets throughout, sometimes used as rubrics).
1. Sloane 2457, f. 2a.

And now my pen alas wyth wyche I wryte
Couplet from *Troilus and Criseyde* (IV. 13-14) introducing 2577.5.

*And of whete grete plente   See 1979 (MS. 7A).

*306.3   *And our lord wente out of þe temple in hudels al one
A fragment from the *South English Legendary*—ten lines.
1. Camb. Un. Add. 4544: fragment.

*306.5   *And sayde I dreede no threte / I haue founde youe here
The Jeaste of Syr Gawayne—vv. 541 in 6-line stanzas.
1 (transcript, ca. 1564, of an early print by E.B.). Bodl. 21835, f. 15a; 2. Harley 5927, Art. 32 (a single leaf from an early print).
1. Madden, *Syr Gawayne*, Bannatyne Club 1839, pp. 207-23; 2. Furnivall, *Captain Cox*, Ballad Soc. VII. xxxv-vi.

306.8   And save thys flowre wyche ys oure kyng
A song for victory in France, A.D. 1492—five quatrains and burden.
1. Cotton Domitianus XVIII, f. 248b.
Rimbault, *Songs & Ballads*, no. 33; Flügel, *Neuengl. Lesebuch*, pp. 160-1; Robbins, *Neuphil. Mitteilungen* LV. 293; Robbins, *Hist. Poems*, p. 96.

And she yt lose and you yt fynde   See 302.

*308.5   *And lx yen barons fulle bolde shall be brittend to dethe
A political prophecy—forty-five alliterative lines.
1. Camb. Un. Ll. 1. 18, ff. 128a-b (a single leaf).
Day, *RES* XV. 63-4.

*309.5   *And so betyd a tyme þat he / of Alexandir to þe cite
The Life of St. Katherine in the *Scottish Legendary*.
1. Camb. Un. Gg. 2. 6, f. 380a.
Horstmann, *Barbours Leg. Samml.*, II. 197-213; Metcalfe, *STS* XXV. 445.

310   3. Cotton Julius A. v, f. 150a; 8. Delete this MS.; 10. Harley 114, ff. 138b-139a.
        2, 11. Wright, *Camden Soc.* VI. 307, 396; 10. Wilson, *Lost Lit.*, p. 211.

        *And spatte a luyte on is fingur   See 3452 (MS. Bodl. 1486).

*310.5 *And suffred for sow wondes smert
        Exhortation to worship by the Passion—ten couplets.
        1. BM Addit. 37787, f. 170a.
        N. S. Baugh, *Worcestershire Misc.*, p. 153.

        And there withall I alraide   See 316.6 (Caxton).

311   forty short couplets.
        Bowers, *PMLA* LXX. 214-6.

*311.5 *And their did. . .mekely for his loue
        An advertisement for Hailes Abbey, including four miracles associated with the Holy Blood of Hailes—thirty-six stanzas rime royal. [For another version see 3153].
        Gloucester Pub. Lib. Deposit: *Divers Miracles of Christ's Blood in Hayles,* Pynson, ca. 1515, f. 7a. [See Oates, *Library* 5 s. XIII. 275].

312   An admonition to officers of justice at Lovedays. . .(including a variant of 3621).
        Bowers, *MLR* XLVII. 374 (vv. 1-24 only).

312.5   And thow wyst what thyng yt were
        An ABC poem on morals and manners—vv. 82 in doggerel couplets in hand of Richard Kaye (xvi cent.). [Cf. 1270.1].
        1. Corpus Christi Oxf.: Glanville, *De Proprietatibus Rerum,* 1488.
        Milne and Sweeting, *MLR* XL. 237.

313   3. Cotton Julius A. v, f. 168b; 8. Delete this MS.; 10. Harley 114, f. 158a.
        2, 10. Wright, *Camden Soc.* VI. 323, 399; 10. Wilson, *Lost Lit.*, p. 211.

        And wyll ye serue me so
        Burden to 1485.5.

*316.3 *And whan they had resceyved her charge
'Why I Can't be a Nun'—in 8-line stanzas. [Utley 30].
1. Cotton Vesp. D. ix, ff. 177a-182b, 190a-b (begins and ends imperfectly: vv. 392).
 Furnivall, *E. E. Poems*, pp. 138-50.

316.6 And wyth the noyse of them two
Conclusion added to Chaucer's incomplete *House of Fame* (991)—six couplets. [Ringler 6].
 The Book of Fame, Caxton, ca. 1486 (STC 5087); repr. Furnivall, *Parallel Texts MP*, Chaucer Soc., p. 241.

317 2. Bodl. 6943, f. 73a (vv. 14).
  3. Person, *Camb. ME Lyrics*, p. 25.

*317.5 *And southe that seldes newe ioyes
A love poem—six 8-line stanzas (first st. erased). [Cf. 270].
1. BM Loan 29/333: Portland, verso.

Angeles of pees shall haue dominacioun See 2200.

320 Robbins, *Hist. Poems*, pp. 62-3; Greene, *Sel. Eng. Carols*, p. 85.

Ane See A, An, or One.

320.5 *Ante ffinem termini / Baculus portamus*
The song of the schoolboy at Christmas—seven Latin and English couplets.
1. Sloane 1584, f. 33a.
 Rel. Ant., I. 116; Furnivall, *EETS* 32. rev. ed. 387.

Anthiocus þat heythyn kyng See 944.

Aperte thefte does he that man See 245 (MS. 24).

Apon See Upon.

322 Ekwall, *Studien i Modern Sprakvetenskap* XVII. 42-3; Aspin, *AN Pol. Songs*, pp. 6-9; Kaiser, *Med. Eng.*, p. 216.

324 [See also 317, 596, &c. Ringler 7].

9. Trinity Dublin 516, f. 27a; 11. BM Printed Book I B 49408; Alliaco, *Meditationes,* Caxton, n. d., f. 34b (vv. 16); 12. Plimpton Add. 2, f. 4b (vv. 9).

Boke of Huntyng, St. Albans, 1486 (STC 3308); de Worde, 1496 (STC 3309); Dibdin, *Typo. Antiquities,* II. 59; *facs.* Blades, *Life & Typography of Caxton,* II. 50 (vv. 11); Lydgate, *Stans puer,* Caxton, ca. 1477 (STC 17030); *repr.* Dibdin, *Typo Antiquities,* II. 224; 3. Furnivall, *EETS* 32 orig. ed. 359; rev. ed. 247; *Now and Then,* No. 83 (Spring, 1951), p. 22; 10. Kurvinen, *Neuphil. Mitteilungen* LIV. 60; 11. Bühler, *Eng. Lang. Notes* I. 82.

325   [Delete entire entry].

Arise ȝe gudely folkes and see
Second line of couplet heading to 3627.5.

326.5   As a man may sle himself with his owne knyif / So he may synne wyth his owne wyif
One couplet.
1. Salisbury Cath. 103, f. 52b.
Brandeis, *EETS* 115. 161.

326.8   As a man rode faste by þe way
'The wordes of a good horse to his mayster'—seven couplets, with rubric: '*In illis diebus* when horse coude speake.'
1. Plimpton 259, f. 15a (added in xvi cent. hand).
Plimpton, priv. pr.

As bricht Phebus schene soverane hevinnis E   See 1842.5.

333   Envoy of two stanzas rime royal. [For a text without introductory Prologue see 4244].

333.5   As far as hope will yn lengthe / on the kyng Henry
Prayer to Henry VI—two stanzas rime royal. [Cf. 2393].
1. Littledale (Oxford) [*olim*Pudsey].
Collier, *Camden Soc.* LXVII. 59-60.

334.5   As flowers in feeld thus passeth lif
Epitaph, A.D. 1469, for Robert Dalusse at St. Martin's Church, London—four lines.
Weever, *Anc. Funerall Monuments,* p. 406 (STC 25223); Pettigrew, *Chronicles of Tombs,* p. 431; Ravenshaw, *Antiente Epitaphes,* p. 13.

335   *Gentleman's Magazine*, May 1842, p. 472.

337   As for yowre prayes yn fame þat is vpbore

337.5   Als free make I thee / As heart can wish or egh can see
A single couplet inscribed in Beverley Church, Yorks. (attributed to Athelstan); and also in St. Austin's Church, Hedon, Yorks.
Weever, *Anc. Funerall Monuments*, 1631, p. 181 (STC 25223); *Beauties of England*, pp. 436, 445.

*338.5   *[As] her am I sent by diuyne prouidence
Moralizing verses for a pageant or mumming, spoken by Faith, Charity, Temperance, Justice, Force, Hope, and Prudence—seven 8-line stanzas. [For emendations see Mabbott, *MLN* LXV. 545].
BM Blockbook broadside, ca. 1480; *repr.* Schreiber, *Handbuch der Holz-und Metallschnitte des XV Jahrhunderts*, VI. 52-3 (No. 2984).

339   1. Rylands Lib. Latin 395, f. 119a.

340   1a (transcript ca. 1818). BM Addit. 39864, f. 160a; 3. Egerton 3307, f. 65b (6 st.).
1, 3. Greene, *Journal American Musicological Soc.* VII. 81, 80; 2. Davies, *Med. Eng. Lyrics*, pp. 218-9; 3. Stevens, *Med. Carols*, p. 52; Greene, *Sel. Eng. Carols*, pp. 62-3.

340.5   As I came by a bowre soo fayre
The prisoner of love—eight cross-rimed quatrains.
1. Bodl. 12653, f. 1b.
Padelford and Benham, *Anglia* XXXI. 312-3.

As I came by a grene forest syde
Burden to 418.

342   Brydges and Haslewood, *Brit. Bibliographer*, IV. 193-200 (extracts); Brandl and Zippel, *ME Sprach- u Literatur.*, pp. 118-23; Kaiser, *Med. Eng.*, pp. 482-5 (vv. 396 only).

342.5   As I cam fro deuys dall / With brede and cheche
On the good use of provisions—two couplets.
1. NLW Peniarth 356, p. 299.

343	Rickert, *Anc. Eng. Xmas Carols*, pp. 102-3.
344	[For a poem with the same refrain see 1338. Utley 31]. Robbins, *Sec. Lyrics*, pp. 180-1.
347	Clive, *Roxburghe Club* L. 238-57.
348	[Cf. 1585.5]. 4. Rosenthal, *Vitae Patrum in Old & ME Lit.*, p. 155.
351	6. N. S. Baugh, *Worcestershire Misc.*, pp. 107-21.

As y lay on ʒoleis nyʒt   See 352 (Camb. Un. Add. 5943).

352	1. L. S. M[ayer,] *Music, Cantelenas, Songs*, 1906, pp. 40-1; Robbins, *MLR* LIV. 221; Stevens, *Med. Carols*, p. 110; Robbins, *Early Eng. Xmas Carols*, p. 73; 2. James and Macaulay, *MLR* VIII. 72-3; 4. Davies, *Med. Eng. Lyrics*, pp. 112-4.
353	sixteen quatrains (a virelai). 1. Copley, *Seven Eng. Songs*, 1940; Stevens, *Med. Carols*, p. 112.
354	1, 3. Stevens, *Med. Carols*, pp. 16, 3; 3. Robbins, *Early Eng. Xmas Carols*, p. 54.
355	124 8-line stanzas. 1. Camb. Un. Ff. 2. 38, f. 28a (begins at v. 451); 2. Pepys 1584, ff. 28a-36b. 1 with 2. Kreuzer, *Traditio* VII. 370-85.
356	[Cf. 2376]. Robbins, *Hist. Poems*, pp. 147-8.
359	Cook, *Reader*, pp. 462-4; Brook, *Harley Lyrics*, pp. 65-6; Funke, *ME Reader*, pp. 49-51; Davies, *Med. Eng. Lyrics*, pp. 78-80.
360	*Early Eng. Carols*, p. 305; *Poets of Eng. Lang.*, I. 21-2; Kaiser, *Anthologie*, p. 291; Kaiser, *Med. Eng.*, p. 463; Greene, *Sel. Eng. Carols*, p. 161; Davies, *Med. Eng. Lyrics*, pp. 77-8.
361	1. Rickert, *Anc. Eng. Xmas Carols*, pp. 68-9.

364   five quatrains and burden: 'Alone alone alone alone / Here
            I sytt alone alas alone.'
            Kirke, *Reliquary* IX. 76-7; *Oxford Book Christian Verse*,
            p. 44; Stevens, *Music & Poetry*, p. 365.

365   [See 3889.5].
            1. Bodl. 13814, ff. 92a-93*a (vv. 1-132, 181-201); 3. Cotton
            Vitell. E. x, ff. 255b-258a (imperfect: vv. 564); 4. Lansdowne
            762, ff. 24a-31 (vv. 491, including 4029, vv. 81); 5. Sloane
            2578, ff. 6a-11b (imperfect: lacks Fytte I; vv. 321. Followed
            by 4029); 6. Lincoln Cath. 91, ff. 149b-153b (imperfect: vv.
            636 and Prologue of vv. 24).
            Fragments: a. Bodl. 4062; b. Bodl. 6683; c. Bodl. 8258; d.
            Harley 559; e. BM Addit. 6702.
            Whole Prophesie of Scotland, Waldegrave, Edinb. 1603;
            repr. Laing, *Bannatyne Club* XLIV. 18; 3. Scott, *Minstrelsy
            of Scottish Border*, rev. Henderson, Edinb. 1932, IV. 92;
            5. Brandl, *Sammlung englischer Denkmäler* II. 75; 6. Child,
            Pop. Ballads, no. 37, App., I. 326-94 prologue and prophe-
            cies omitted); *crit. ed.* Flasdieck, *Wort und Brauch* XXII.

366   Robbins, *Sec. Lyrics*, pp. 204-6.

366.5   As I mused in my dys mekyll towart
            A political prophecy—vv. 152 generally in couplets.
            1. NLW Peniarth 26, pp. 112-6.

366.8   As I musyng myself alone
            The Lamentacion of the Kyng of Scottes (on the misfortunes
            of Flodden)—fifteen 8-line stanzas. [Cf. 2547.3, 2549.5].
            1. Harley 2252, ff. 43b-45b.
            Halliwell, *Palatine Anthology*, p. 208; Dolman, *Gentle-
            man's Magazine* 1886, CCXXI. 13.

367   [Cf. 2, considered as Epilogue].

            As I out rode this enderes night
            See 112 (Sharp), inserted in 3477.

368   in rime royal stanzas.
            1. Cotton Julius A. v, f. 131b (8 st.); 2. Bodl. 12653, f. 30a
            (10 st.).
            Copland, n. d.; *repr.* [Haslewood,] 1824; 2. Padelford and
            Benham, *Anglia* XXXI. 350-2.

370	fifteen 8-line stanzas. 1-3. Wilson, Ann Arbor 1957.
	As I walked by a fforest side Burden to 418.
372	the wicked counsel of Queen Margaret. . .fifty-three lines in quatrains (ends imperfectly). Robbins, *Neuphil. Mitteilungen* LVI. 97-9; Robbins, *Hist. Poems*, pp. 196-8.
	As I walked the wod so wild See 1333.
374.5	As I was so be ye Moral verses for an epitaph at St. Olaf's Church, London, including gnomic lines on giving (cf. 3272.5)—three couplets. Weever, *Anc. Funerall Monuments*, 1631, p. 423 (STC 25223); Bühler, *Renaissance News* VIII. 11.
375	[Cf. 376]. 1. Greene, *Sel. Eng. Carols*, p. 137; 2. Segar, *Med. Anthology*, p. 100; Segar, *Some Minor Poems*, p. 41; Kaiser, *Med. Eng.*, p. 290; Blench, *Preaching in England*, pp. 322-3.
376	[Cf. 375]. *Early Eng. Carols*, p. 249.
377	As I went on Yol day in owre prosession *Oxford Book Light Verse*, p. 53; Kaiser, *Anthologie*, p. 312; Kaiser, *Med. Eng.*, p. 477; Robbins, *Sec. Lyrics*, pp. 21-2; Speirs, *Med. Eng. Poetry*, pp. 82-3; Greene, *Sel. Eng. Carols*, p. 166; Davies, *Med. Eng. Lyrics*, p. 162.
377.5	As I went this enders day / alone walkyng A *Planctus Marie* carol—five quatrains and burden: 'Alone alone &c.' [For burden cf. 266 and 2293.5]. *Christmas Carolles*, Kele, ca. 1550 (STC 5205); *facs.* Reed, *Xmas Carols*, pp. 35-6; *repr. Early Eng. Carols*, pp. 123-4.
378	1. Rickert, *Anc. Eng. Xmas Carols*, pp. 174-6.
378.5	As I went to þo kyrk wepand An exercise in translation, with the original Latin—vv. 16.

[Cf. 430.8].
1. Durham Univ. Cosin V. iii. 10, f. 72b.

379   *Retrospective Rev.* I. 307-12; Child, *Ballads*, 1864, 1878, I. 273-6; and *Pop. Ballads*, no. 38, App., I. 333-4 (prophecies omitted).

380   [Cf. 113.5].
1. Camb. Un. Ff. 1. 6, f. 154b.
Robbins, *Sec. Lyrics*, pp. 157-8.

383   [Following 3361].
Vollmer, *Berliner Beiträge zur germ. u. rom. Phil.* XVII. 44-5; Robbins, *Sec. Lyrics*, p. 155; Person, *Camb. ME Lyrics*, pp. 32-3.

384   [Delete entire entry].

As it befell and happinnit into deid   See 442.5.

397   Two couplets in a series of proverbs, followed by other scattered single lines and couplets. [Cf. 2785.5, 2818.3, 4049.5, &c].

As Mary was grette with Gabryell   See 3992 (de Worde).

399   [For extracts see 1377, 2697, and 3923.5].
1. Cotton Nero D. xi, f. 3a; 2. Lansdowne 197, ff. 3a-259b (abridged version); 9a (transcript). Harley 6909, ff. 1a-270a. 1, 9 (with vv. 1-64 from MS. 5 and vv. 65-686 from MS. 4). Amours, *STS* 50, 53, 54, 56, 57; 1. Pinkerton, *Anc. Scot. Poems*, II. 500-19 (extracts only); *Rel. Ant.*, II. 162 (extracts only); 3. Eyre-Todd, *Early Scot. Poetry*, 1891, pp. 144-76 (extracts only).

399.5   As moche as gnawes / Bestes long inneþ dawes
A translation of lines in Virgil in Trevisa's translation of Higden's *Polychronicon* (Book II, Cap. 44)—one quatrain.
1. St. John's Camb. 204; 2. Cotton Tiberius D. vii; 3. Harley 1900; 4. Stowe 65; 5. BM Addit. 24194; 6. Aberdeen Univ. 21; 7. Chetham Lib. 11379; 8. Hunterian Mus. 83; 9. Penrose 12; 10. Morgan Lib. 875.
    Trevisa, *Discripcion of Britayne*, Caxton, 1480 (STC 13440a); de Worde, 1498 (STC 13440b); Trevisa, *Prolicronycon*,

Caxton, 1482 (STC 13438); de Worde, 1495 (STC 13439); Treveris, 1527 (STC 13440); 1. Babington and Lumby, *Rolls Series* XLI, ii. 39.

401   5. Trinity Camb. 601, f. 298a.

As ofte as I consydre these olde noble clerkes
Prologue (3 st. rime royal) to 2183.5.

Als oft as men says þis orisoun
Four monoriming lines serving as rubric to 1734.

402   1. MacCracken, *Archiv* CXXVII. 323.

403.5   As other men hathe in londe
Four gnomic lines.
1. Bodl. 655, f. 114b.

As poverte causithe sobernes   See 2820 (BM Addit.).

404.5   As righte to rule is reason / So tyme doeth trye out treason
One couplet. [Cf. 952].
1. Bodl. 4130, f. 168b.
Bergen, *EETS* cxxi. 75.

406   A. 11. Halliwell, *Yorkshire Anthology*, 1851, p. 287 (begins v. 84).

As that I me stode in studeying loo Aloone   See 370.

407.5   As the cause requyrithe to stody is goode
A warning to scholars: 'But allway to be in stody dryethe vp a mannes blode' — one couplet.
1. Royal 18. D. ii, f. 202b.

407.6   As the Child Merlin sat on hys fathers knee
The Argument of Morien and Merlin: alchemical verses — vv. 370 in couplets. [Cf. 3616].
1. Bodl. 7630, Part VI, f. 27a.
Ashmole, *Theatrum Chemicum*, pp. 427-8 (vv. 77-94, 100-14 only); Taylor, *Chymia* I. 26-35.

407.8 As þe cocke croweth / so þe chekyn lernyth
A proverbial couplet. [Heywood's *Proverbs*, 1562].
1. Bodl. 21626, f. 18b.
Förster, *Festschrift zum 12 Deutschen Neuphilologentage*, p. 48.

409.5 As the holy growth grene
A Holly and Ivy carol turned into a love lyric, ascribed to Henry VIII—four cross-rimed quatrains with a 4-line burden: 'Grene growth the holy.'
1. BM Addit. 31922, f. 37b.
Chappell, *Archaeologia* XLI. 374-5; Flügel, *Anglia* XII. 237-8; Flügel, *Neuengl. Lesebuch*, p. 135; Trefusis, *Songs Henry VIII*, Roxburghe Club CLXI. 13; *Early Eng. Lyrics*, p. 54; *Oxford Book Carols*, p. 130; Padelford, *Early XVI Cent. Lyrics*, p. 77; *Oxford Book XVI C. Verse*, pp. 34-5; *Early Eng. Carols*, p. 304; Stevens, *Music & Poetry*, pp. 398-9; Stevens, *Music at Court*, p. 28; Davies, *Med. Eng. Lyrics*, pp. 290-1; *facs*. Briggs, *Musical Notations*, PMMS, plate xx.

410 Attributed to George Ripley, with Epistle (in Ashmole, *Theatrum Chemicum*, pp. 109-11) dedicating 595 to Edward IV. [Singer 810A].
1. Bodl. 6954, ff. 103a-105b (vv. 168); 5. Sloane 3667, ff. 157b-160b (vv. 168).
Ashmole, *Theatrum Chemicum*, 1648, pp. 111-6.

411.5 As þe smyte wyth an axe in an hard tre / Beware that the chippes falle not in youre ye
A proverbial couplet. [Cf. 1149.5].
Salomon and Marcolphus, Leeu, Antwerp, ca. 1492 (STC 22905); *facs*. Duff, London 1892.

412 Hearne, *Roberti de Avesbury Historia*, 1720, pp. 264-5; Brydges and Haslewood, *British Bibliographer*, II. 80-1.

412.5 As þou Lord dyddest stope and staye
'A charm agaynst thy enemyes'—eleven couplets.
1. Bodl. 7798, pp. 61-2.
Cat. Ashmole MSS., p. 1063.

*As walnot barke his hare is salowe   See *1426.8.

As ye haue herde accomplysshed the gladnes   See 447.

417.5   As sung Awrora with cristall haile
'The fenseit freir of Tungland' by William Dunbar—two 24-line stanzas sandwiching five 16-line stanzas, all in tail-rime.
1. Advocates 1. 1. 6, f. 117a; 2. Asloan, f. 211b (vv. 1-69 only); 2a (transcript by Chalmers). Edinburgh Univ. 521.
    1. Ramsay, *Evergreen*, I. 91-7; repr. *Ramsay and Earlier Scot. Poets*, pp. 233-4; [Hailes,] *Anc. Scot. Poets*, pp. 20-5; Sibbald, *Chronicle*, I. 305-9; Laing, *Dunbar*, I. 39-44; Paterson, *Dunbar*, pp. 190-7; *Select Poems of Dunbar*, Perth 1788, pp. 23-8; *Bannatyne MS.*, Hunt. Club, III. 333-7; Small, *STS* IV. 139-43; repr. Browne, *Early Scot. Poets*, 1896, pp. 123-7; Eyre-Todd, *Med. Scot. Poetry*, pp. 199-203; Schipper, *Dunbar*, pp. 221-6; and *DKAW* XLI (IV). 21-8; Baildon, *Dunbar*, pp. 105-8; Ritchie, *STS* n.s. XXII. 311-5; MacKenzie, *Dunbar*, pp. 67-70; Kinsley, *Dunbar*, pp. 44-8; 2. Craigie, *STS* n.s. XVI. 92-4.

417.8   Astrologye ther been of hem too / The long & the round also
Materia medica: the virtues of herbs (Asfodyll, Betayne, Centorye, &c.)—in couplets. [Cf. 2627].
1. Trinity Camb. 905, ff. 134b-139b, 144b-148a.

418   1. Balliol 354, f. 178a.
Padelford, *Early XVI Cent. Lyrics*, p. 138 (de Worde, p. 75); Rickert, *Anc. Eng. Xmas Carols*, p. 139.

420   Mason, *Humanism & Poetry*, p. 149; Davies, *Med. Eng. Lyrics*, p. 212.

423   Horstmann, *EETS* 98. 157-61; Boyd, p. 44.

427   four cross-rimed quatrains and concluding couplet.

427.5   At his burth thow hurdist angell syng
The tribulations of the Virgin—in couplets (followed by 14).
1. Balliol 149, f. 11a (vv. 4); 2. Worcester Cath. F. 10, f. 25a (vv. 12).
    1. Coxe, *Cat.*, p. 46; 2. Floyer and Hamilton, *Cat.*, p. 6; Owst, *Lit. & Pulpit*, p. 541.

429   five 8-line stanzas with refrain: 'Honour with age to everie vertew drawis.'
2. Advocates 1. 1. 6, p. 38 and f. 52b.
    2a. Ritchie, *STS* 3 s. V. 63-4; Sibbald, *Chronicle*, I. 365-6.

430.5 At my begynnyng Crist me spede / In vertv and lernyng for to spede
A couplet, the opening of 430 and 432, used as a tag to be learned by a child.
1. Camb. Un. Ii. 6. 36, flyleaf; 2. Harley 3362, f. 89a; 3. Royal 12. E. xvi, f. 106b; 4. Durham Univ. Cosin V. iii. 9, f. 17b; 5. Lincoln Cath. 189, f. 5b; 6. Trinity Dublin 340, f. 166a; 7. Bühler 5, marginal note.
4. Furnivall, *EETS* lxi. 126.

At my commyng the ladys euerychone   See 1086.

430.8 At my howse I have a Jaye
Animal noises: a schoolboy's exercise in translation, with Latin original—six couplets. [Cf. 378.5; 1632.5].
1. Harley 1002, f. 72a.
Herrtage, *EETS* 75.82; Wright, *RES* n.s. II. 117.

432 [See Mustanoja, *Neuphil. Mitteilungen* IL. 127-8].
1. Harley 2252. . . .see 77; with another couplet in 832. . .
2. St. George's Chapel, Windsor, E. I. I, f. 95b (fragment, variant).
2. James, *MSS. of St. George's Chapel, Windsor*, p. 74.

At our begynyng god vs spede   See 432 (St. George's Chapel).

433 2, 3. Morris, *EETS* 49. 103-38; 3. Segar, *Med. Anthology*, pp. 127-32; 3 comp. Brandl and Zippel, *ME Sprach- u. Literatur.*, pp. 145-55; *crit. text*. Arngart, Lund 1955.

436 Rickert, *Anc. Eng. Xmas Carols*, p. 257; Robbins, *Sec. Lyrics*, p. 48.

437 1a (xix cent. transcript by Hartshorne). Bodl. 30161.
Förster, *Anglia* XX. 139-52.

438

439 6. Chetham Lib. 6709, ff. 180a-189b.

440 At the short game of tablis forto play
Gentleman's Magazine, May 1842, p. 463 (extracts).

441	Davies, *Med. Eng. Lyrics*, pp. 130-2.
	At þis court þis lawe is set See 442.
442	2. Basle Univ. B. VIII. 4, f. 93b. 2. Meyer and Burckhardt, *MA HSS. der Univ. Basel: Beschreibendes Verzeichnis*, Abt. B, 1960, p. 852.
442.5	At Tweidis mowth thair standis a nobill toun 'The Freiris of Berwick,' sometimes ascribed to William Dunbar—vv. 589 in couplets (with introductory couplet: 'As it befell and happinit into deid &c.'). 1. Pepys 2553, p. 113; 2. Advocates 1. 1. 6, f. 348b. Aberdeen 1662; 1. Pinkerton, *Anc. Scot. Poems*, 1786, I. 65-85; Baildon, *Dunbar*, pp. 211-24; Craigie, *STS* n.s. VII. 133-48; 2. Sibbald, *Chronicle*, II. 372-90; Laing, *Dunbar*, II. 3-32; *Bannatyne MS.*, Hunt. Club, IV. 1004-20; Small *STS* IV. 285-304; Ritchie, *STS* n.s. XXVI. 261-77; Mackenzie, *Dunbar*, pp. 182-95; *crit. text.* Schipper, *Dunbar*, pp. 394-432; and *DKAW* XLIII (I). 1-44.
	Atte Warwyk the Erle so fre See 979 (Harmsworth).
444	—in couplets. [See also 882, 3632]. [Revise listing of MSS. as follows:] 1. Bodl. 1787, f. 49b (various English verses up to Edward I scattered throughout); 2. Bodl. 1999, ff. 140b-144a (vv. 194); 3. Bodl. 7081 (roll); 4. Bodl. 11951, ff. 187a-189a; 5. Bodl. 29284 (roll: vv. 192); 6. Cotton Julius D. viii, f. 27a; 7. Cotton Julius E. iv, f. 2a (vv. 224); 8. Harley 78, ff. 69b-72a; 9. Harley 4205, ff. 1a-8a (vv. 217, with elaborate paintings of kings); 10. Sloane 1986, ff. 103a-111b; 11. Coll. of Arms LVIII, ff. 335-343 (concluding interpolation in 727). 5. MacCracken, *EETS* 192. 717-22.
445	1, 2. Robbins, *Sec. Lyrics*, p. xxxix; 2. *Early Eng. Carols*, p. xxxv; Brook, *Harley Lyrics*, p. 5; Wilson, *Lost Lit.*, p. 174; Mustanoja, *How the Good Wife*, p. 226; Davies, *Med. Eng. Lyrics*, pp. 24, 31.
447	3. Trinity Camb. 601, f. 157a; 5. Cotton App. XXVII, f. 1a (st. 8-23); 7. Delete this MS.
454	Rickert, *Anc. Eng. Xmas Carols*, p. 8.

454.5   *Ave* quene of heven ladi of erthe welle of all bownte
Prayers to the Virgin (with account of Joys and Sorrows) and Jesus—vv. 181 in couplets.
1. Harvard Univ. Deposit: Richardson 22, ff. 78a-82b.

455   Brotanek, *ME Dichtungen*, pp. 128-9; Robbins, *Hist. Poems*, pp. 206-7.

455.5   Awake synner out of thi slepe
Fragment of a Tudor song. [Cf. Stevens, *Music & Poetry*, p. 106].
1. Pembroke Camb., folder of music fragments.

455.8   Awake ye ghostly persons awake
ABC poem against pride of clergy, attributed to William Thorpe (ca. A. D. 1407)—three stanzas rime royal.
Foxe, *Acts and Monuments*, ed. Townshend, IV. 259 (from an old Register; MS. not identified).

456.5   Ay besherewe yow be my fay
'Manerly Margery Mylk and ale,' an amorous flyting, perhaps by John Skelton—four stanzas of five monoriming lines each stanza with a 2-line refrain (which appears also in 729.5, v. 1198).
1. BM Addit. 5465, f. 96b.
Hawkins, *Hist. Music*, 1776, III. 3-8; 2. Ritson, *Anc. Songs*, 1790, p. 100; Dyce, *Skelton*, I. 28-9; Dyce and Child, *Skelton & Donne*, I. 35-6; Flügel, *Neuengl. Lesebuch*, p. 148; Henderson, *Skelton*, 1931, p. 38; 1948, 1959, p. 24; Stevens, *Music & Poetry*, pp. 378-9.

Backe & syde goo bare goo bare   See 554.5.

458   2. BM Addit. 29729, f. 135b.

459   An amulet for a baker against the fever—two couplets.
Mynors, *Cat.*, p. 235.

461.5   Beith all glad and mery that sitteth at this messe
A sotelty for a bridal feast—one couplet. [See also 1270.8, 1331.5, 1386.5].
1. Bodl. Lat. misc. c. 66 [*olim* Capesthorne], f. 68b.
Furnivall, *EETS* 32 rev. ed. 359.

461.8	Be clenly clad
Moral counsels: don't be at strife with your betters, your fellows, or your subjects—eight lines.
1. Bodl. 14526, f. 1b.
462	5. Cotton Claudius A. ii, f. 102a.
463	2. Rickert, *Anc. Eng. Xmas Carols*, p. 22.
	Be gladde O London be glad and make grete Ioy See 3799.
465	and concluding quatrain (see 1833.5), a prayer.
*465.3	*Be her of wel stille / & sey mid gode wille
On the efficacy of the *Ave Maria*: the B. V. appears to a monk.
1. Bodl. 1485, first flyleaf.
Napier, *MLN* IV. 275-6.
465.5	Be hit beter be hit werse / folo hym þat berit þe pursse
A proverbial couplet. [Cf. 686.5 and Heywood. Tilley P 646].
1. Bodl. 15444, f. 141b; 2. Bodl. 21626, f. 22b; 3. Balliol 354, f. 200a; 4. BM Addit. 37075, f. 70b.
1. Meech, *MP* XXXVIII. 120; 2. Förster, *Festschrift zum 12 Deutschen Neuphilologentage*, p. 49; 3. Flügel, *Anglia* XXVI. 202; Dyboski, *EETS* ci. 130.
	Be hit knowyn to all that byn here See 4184.
466	Harris, *EHR* IX. 647; Wilson, *Lost Lit.*, p. 198.
467	[For a moralization see Hazlitt, *Remains*, III. 2-22. Utley 36].
2. BM Addit. 27879, p. 420 (twenty 12-line st.; incomplete).
Arnold, *Customs of London*, 1502, p. 75 (STC 782); 1521; repr. London 1811, pp. 198-203; Child, *Ballads*, 1864, 1878, IV. 144-57; FitzGibbon, *E. E. Poetry*, pp. 212-25; Arber, *Dunbar Anthology*, pp. 184-90.
467.5	Be hyt trew or be hitt fals / hitt is as þe copy was
Concluding rubric by the scribe concerning the poems copied—one couplet.
1. Advocates 19. 3. 1, f. 7a (to 64); f. 157b (to 1724); f. 216a (to 3184).

469 1. Person, *Camb. ME Lyrics*, p. 21; 2. Kaiser, *Med. Eng.*, p. 296.

470 Segar, *Med. Anthology*, p. 111 (4 st.); Greene, *Sel. Eng. Carols*, p. 133.

   Be merye be merye / I pray you euerychon
   Burden to 88.

470.5 Be mirry man and tak nocht far in mynd
   'Without glaidnes awailis no tressour' by William Dunbar—five 8-line stanzas with this refrain.
   1. Pepys 2553, p. 221; 2. Aberdeen: Town Clerk's Office, Register of Sasines III; 3. Advocates 1. 1. 6, f. 98a.
    1. Craigie, *STS* n.s. VII. 249-50; 2. MacKenzie, *Dunbar*, pp. 148-9; 3. [Hailes,] *Anc. Scot. Poems*, pp. 68-9; *Select Poems of Dunbar*. Perth 1788, pp. 60-1; Laing, *Dunbar*, I. 193-4; Paterson, *Dunbar*, pp. 51-3; *Bannatyne MS.*, Hunt. Club, II. 279-80; *Blackwood's Magazine*, Feb. 1835; Small, *STS* IV. 108-9; Schipper, *Dunbar*, pp. 340-2; and *DKAW* XLII (IV). 38-40; Baildon, *Dunbar*, pp. 176-7; Ritchie, *STS* n.s. XXII. 259-60.

473 [Cf. 471].

474 1. NLW Mostyn Welsh 129, p. 19.

474.5 Be pes ye make me spille my ale
   An amorous flyting, a dialogue between a wooer and a lady—three 8-line stanzas. [Cf. 225].
   1. BM Addit. 5665, f. 66b.
   Ritson, *Anc. Songs*, 1792, p. 102; Stevens, *Music & Poetry*, p. 339.

475.5 Be the chorel nevyr so hard , He shall qwake be þe berde / ar he passe zyzarde
   A tag in Wey's Latin *Itinerary to Compostella*—three lines.
   1. Bodl. 2351, f. 100a.
   Williams, *Roxburghe Club* LXXVI. 155.

475.8 Be the fader what may be / well is þe childe þat may thee
   A proverbial couplet.
   1. Bodl. 21626, f. 28a; 2. Harley 665, f. 295b; 3. Rylands Lib. Latin 394, f. 18b.

1, 3. Pantin, *BJRL* XIV. 106, 105; 1. Förster, *Festschrift zum 12 Deutschen Neuphilologentage*, p. 55.

477   three couplets (followed by 513).

478   four 18-line stanzas with wheel rime, with additional couplet.
Bühler, *Anglia* LXXVIII. 418-20.

479   Kurvinen, *Neuphil. Mitteilungen* LIV. 52-3.

479.5   Be ȝe ane luvar think ye nocht ȝe suld
'Gude counsale' by William Dunbar—three 8-line stanzas. [Cf. 1440.5].
1. Advocates 1. 1. 6, f. 212b.
Laing, *Dunbar*, I. 177; Paterson, *Dunbar*, pp. 88-9; *Bannatyne MS.*, Hunt. Club, IV. 602-3; Small, *STS* IV. 162-3; Eyre-Todd, *Med. Scot. Poetry*, p. 185; Schipper, *Dunbar*, pp. 324-5; and *DKAW* XLII (IV). 21-3; Baildon, *Dunbar*, pp. 165-6; Ritchie, *STS* n.s. XXIII. 244-5; MacKenzie, *Dunbar*, pp. 142-3.

480   [For a short ME prose tract, 'according to Seynt Gregore,' see Bodl. 2103, f. 101a.]

481   1. Bodl. Lat. misc. c. 66 [*olim* Capesthorne], f. 93b.
Robbins, *PMLA* LXV. 267.

482   The Lay of Sorrow...
Wilson, *Speculum* XXIX. 716-9.

483   [Cf. 3766, 3767].

484   2. Trinity Dublin 155, pp. 149-238 (ends imperfectly).

484.5   Before thou pretend any evill in thy harte
Remember the end—one couplet, 'quod Carter.'
1. Durham Univ. Cosin V. iii. 9, f. 54b.
Furnivall, *EETS* lxi. 181.

488   Greene, *Sel. Eng. Carols*, p. 67.

488.5   Beholde & see how byrds dothe fly
Nonsense verses—riming irregularly.

XX *Songes*, de Worde, 1530 (STC 22924); Flügel, *Anglia* XII. 596-7; Imelmann, *Shakespeare-Jahrbuch* XXXIX. 136.

489   Behold and see o lady free / *Quem meruisti portare*

490.5   Beholde he saide my creature
         Christ's Complaint to Man—one stanza rime royal with 4-line burden: 'In a slumbir late as I was.'
         1. BM Addit. 5465, f. 122b (perhaps incomplete).
         Fehr, *Archiv* CVI. 70; *Early Eng. Carols*, p. 189; Stevens, *Music & Poetry.* p. 385.

493.5   Beholde man lere and se / What prayer god made for þe
         One couplet.
         1. Harley 2406, f. 1a.

496   Attributes of the Virgin and Christ—two couplets.
         Robbins, *Sec. Lyrics.* p. 241.

497   2. BM Addit. 5465, f. 63b and f. 73b (3 st.); 3. Bodl. Lyell 24 [*olim* Quaritch *Cat. Illuminated MSS.* 1931, no. 66], f. 100a (vv. 16, added later); 4. Rosenbach 678. . .Deventer 1496.
         1. Hearne, *Johannis de Fordun Scotichronicon*, 1722, V. 1397-9; Davies, *Med. Eng. Lyrics*, pp. 202-3; 2 (with 2 addit. st. from MS. 4). Dyce, *Skelton*, I. 141-3; Dyce and Child, *Skelton & Donne*, I. 165-7; Henderson, *Skelton*, 1931, pp. 12-13; 1948, 1959, pp. 11-12; Hughes, *Poems by Skelton*, London 1924, pp. 7-9; Pinto, *Selection*, 1950, pp. 22-4; Stevens, *Music & Poetry*, pp. 369-70.

498   4. Woolf, *RES* n.s. XIII. 7.

         Behold o man lefte up thy eye & see
         Clopton Chapel extracts of 2759.

500   2. Harley 2251, f. 228a.
         1. Robbins, *Hist. Poems*, pp. 174-5.

501   two couplets.

502   Furnivall, *EETS* 15 orig. ed. 226; rev. ed. 254; Comper, *Spiritual Songs*, p. 130.

502.5　　　Behold we wrecches in this world present
　　　　　　Moralizing verses—twenty-four quatrains, and Latin headings.
　　　　　　1. Coventry Corp. Record Office, f. 167b.

503　　　　　　Greene, *Sel. Eng. Carols*, p. 95.

506.5　　　*Benedicite* whate dremyd I this nyȝt
　　　　　　'Thi lady hath forgoten to be kynd'—one stanza rime royal. [Translated into Latin by Thomas More: cf. Sabol, *MLN* LXIII. 542].
　　　　　　1. BM Addit. 5465, f. 13b.
　　　　　　　Hawkins, *Hist. Music*, 1776, III. 30; Stafford Smith, *Musica Antiqua*, I. 21; Fehr, *Archiv* CVI. 55; *Early Eng. Lyrics*, p. 74; *Oxford Book XVI C. Verse*, p. 44; Ault, *Elizabethan Lyrics*, p. 22; *Poets of Eng. Lang.*, I. 426-7; Stevens, *Music & Poetry*, p. 357.

507　　　　　three 5-line stanzas and burden.
　　　　　　　Stafford Smith, *Musica Antiqua*, I. 23, 21; Rickert, *Anc. Eng. Xmas Carols*, p. 19; *Early Eng. Carols*, p. 138; Stevens, *Med. Carols*, p. 62; Robbins, *Early Eng. Xmas Carols*, p. 56.

　　　　　*Bens be þe nek Petron hent　　See *295.8.

508　　　　　A grace before meat to SS. Katherine, Mary, and Margaret—four quatrains.
　　　　　　Brotanek, *ME. Dichtungen*, pp. 135-6.

510　　　　　*Gentleman's Magazine*, May 1842, p. 446 (extracts).

　　　　　Betonye sethyn þese lechys bedene　　See 2627.

512.5　　　Better ytt ys smalle howsolde too holde / Then to lye in pryson wyth fetters of golde
　　　　　　The Golden Mean—one couplet.
　　　　　　1. Harley 172, f. 90b; 2. Harley 2247, f. 79b; 3. Lansdowne 699, f. 95b; 4. Durham Univ. Cosin V. iii. 9, f. 79a.
　　　　　　4. Furnivall, *EETS* lxi. 218.

512.8　　　Better it is to suffer fortoun and abyd
　　　　　　The Golden Mean—a couplet (513) followed by other riming proverbial lines on the same subject (including 1151). [Cf. 3256.6].

        1. Advocates 1. 1. 6, f. 75b.
Bannatyne MS., Hunt. Club, p. 205; Ritchie, *STS* n.s. XXII. 187.

513 [Also = vv. 9-10 of 4137; and concluding couplet of 3256.6. Cf. also 512.8].
2. Bodl. 1486, f. 238b (follows 477); 3. Harley 665, f. 281a (vv. 4); 4. Royal 17. D. vi, f. 150b; 5. Durham Univ. Cosin V. iii. 9, f. 85b; 6. NLW Peniarth 356, p. 196 (preceded by 1940.8).
5. Furnivall, *EETS* lxi. 228.

514 [Utley 37a].
1. Camb. Un. Ii. 3. 8, f. 68b.

515 Manly, *Eng. Poetry*, pp. 12-13; Warren, *Treasury of Eng. Lit.* 1908, II. 62-3; *Oxford Book Eng. Verse*, pp. 2-3; *Poets of Eng. Lang.*, I. 24-5; Segar, *Med. Anthology*, pp. 98-9; Brook, *Harley Lyrics*, p. 33; Kaiser, *Anthologie*, p. 293; Kaiser, *Med. Eng.*, p. 466; Speirs, *Med. Eng. Poetry*, pp. 56-7; Davies, *Med. Eng. Lyrics*, pp. 67-8.

515.5 Betuix twell houris and ellevin
'þe amendis to þe telyouris and sowtaris for the turnament maid on thame' by William Dunbar—ten quatrains with refrain: 'Telȝouris and sowtaris blist be ȝe.' [Cf. 2289.8].
1. Pepys 2553, p. 317; 2. Advocates 1. 1. 6, f. 112b.
1. Craigie, *STS* n.s. VII. 378-9; 2. Ramsay, *Evergreen*, I. 253-5 (lacks st. 7); Laing, *Dunbar*, I. 59-60; Paterson, *Dunbar*, pp. 220-1; *Bannatyne MS.*, Hunt. Club, III. 319-21; Small, *STS* IV. 127-8; Eyre-Todd, *Med. Scot. Poetry*, pp. 197-8; Schipper, *Dunbar*, pp. 139-40; and *DKAW* XL (IV). 49-50; Baildon, *Dunbar*, pp. 70-1; Ritchie, *STS* n.s. XXII. 298-300; MacKenzie, *Dunbar*, pp. 126-7; Kinsley, *Dunbar*, pp. 57-8.

517.5 Bewar man I come as thef
A tag in Grimestone's sermon notes. [Cf. Owst, *Lit. & Pulpit*, p. 532].
1. Advocates 18. 7. 21, f. 86b.

Bewar my lytyl fynger
Burden to 4265.5.

518 'Cusse hym not to ofte'—three short couplets.

  Beware the or thou arte not wyse   See 1920 (printed fragment).

  Bides a while and holdes soure pais   See 110.

520   [Delete entire entry].

  Bydynge al alone with sorowe sore encombred   See 2818.6.

521   Bryd one brere brid brid one brere / kynd is come of luue
     Robbins, *Sec. Lyrics*, pp. 146-7; Wilson, *Lost Lit.*, p. 184; *New Oxford Hist. Music*, III. 113; Stemmler, *Die englischen Liebesgedichte des MS. Harley 2253*, Bonn 1962, p. 89.

521.5   Bryd on brere y telle yt / to non o þer y ne dare
     Fragment of a love song, preserved as indication of tune of carol 1330.
     1. Caius Camb. 383, p. 210.
     James, *Cat.*, II. 437; *Early Eng. Carols*, p. 308; Robbins, *Sec. Lyrics*, p. 17; Wilson, *Lost Lit.*, p. 181.

522   *Eng. Lyr. XIII C.*, p. 176.

524   'Greenacres a lenvoye upon John Bochas'—four stanzas rime royal at end of one MS. of *Fall of Princes* (1168). [Ringler 8].
     1. Bodl. 3354, f. 118b (one st. only at end of *Troilus and Criseyde*, 3327); 2. Rylands Lib. English 2, f. 184b.
     Falle of Princis, Pynson, 1494 (STC 3175); Tottel, 1554; 2. Bergen, *EETS* cxxiii. 1023.

527   Rickert, *Anc. Eng. Xmas Carols*, pp. 45-6.

527.5   Blessid be the swettest name of our lord / Jhesu crist
     'Balade'—one stanza rime royal translated from Latin by Caxton. [Cf. 927.5 and 3830.5. Ringler 9].
     1. Chetham Lib. 6709, f. 156a (copied from Caxton).
     Lydgate, *Lyf of Our Lady*, Caxton, 1484 (STC 17023); *facs.* Blades, *Life & Typography of Caxton*, II. 172; *repr.* Dibdin, *Typo. Antiquities*, I. 341; Duff, *XV C. English Books*, p. 75; Crotch, *EETS* 176. 85; Aurner, *Caxton*, p. 294; Lauritis, Klinefelter, and Gallagher, *Life of Our Lady*, p. 52.

528.5   Blisside be þou holy trinite
　　　　　Song at Trinity: poem occurring in only this MS. of Eng.
　　　　　tr. of *Pèlerinage de l'Ame*—five stanzas rime royal.
　　　　　1. Melbourne: Victoria Pub. Lib., f. 212b.

　　　　　Blissyd John Baptist for thy name so precious　　See 3563.5.

534　　　 2. Thompson (Portland, Oregon) [Amherst 20], f. 12b.
　　　　　　1. Davies, *Med. Eng. Lyrics*, p. 204.

　　　　　Blessyd marie virgin of nazareth　　See 914.

535　　　 [Utley 38].

539.5　　Blind and dyaf and alsue dumb
　　　　　Personal lines preceding *Ayenbite of Inwyt*.
　　　　　1. Arundel 57, f. 2a.
　　　　　　Morris, *EETS* 23. 1.

540　　　 6. Camb. Un. Kk. 1. 7, ff. 10a-15b; 7. BM Addit. 34193, ff.
　　　　　11b-14b; 8. Hatfield; 9. Melbourne: Victoria Pub. Lib., f.
　　　　　102a.
　　　　　　Pylgremage of the Sowle, Caxton, 1483 (STC 6473); *repr.*
　　　　　Cust, 1859, pp. 11-17; Dibdin, *Typo. Antiquities*, I. 154-5
　　　　　(5 st. only).

541.5　　Blyth Aberdeane thow beriall of all tounis
　　　　　'The Queinis Reception at Aberdein,' A.D. 1511, by William
　　　　　Dunbar—nine 8-line stanzas with refrain.
　　　　　1. Camb. Un. Ll. 5. 10, f. 7a.
　　　　　　Laing, *Dunbar*, I. 153-5; Paterson, *Dunbar*, pp. 288-91;
　　　　　Small, *STS* IV. 251-3; Schipper, *Dunbar*, pp. 298-301; and
　　　　　DKAW XLI (IV). 99-103; Baildon, *Dunbar*, pp. 154-6;
　　　　　Craigie, *STS* n.s. XX. 55-8; MacKenzie, *Dunbar*, pp. 137-9;
　　　　　Kinsley, *Dunbar*, pp. 16-18.

541.8　　Blood swetyng / Herd byndyng
　　　　　The seven torments of Christ—seven short monoriming lines.
　　　　　1. Balliol 149, f. 33a; 2. Magdalen Oxf. 93, f. 137b; 3. Trinity
　　　　　Dublin 277, p. 188.

542　　　 On the Host—four monoriming lines.
　　　　　1. Hereford Cath. O. iv. 14, f. 225a.

Blow northerne wynd   See 515.

Blow the winde styl & blow nat so shyl   See 3112.

Blow þy horne hunter   See 3199.8.

543   [For burden appearing separately see 1137.5].
           [Masters,] *Rymes of Minstrels*, p. 8.

544   Collier, *Camden Soc.* LVII. 68.

545   [Singer 860].

548   [Cf. 1318].
           Segar, *Some Minor Poems*, pp. 48-9; Segar, *Med. Anthology*, pp. 80-1 (4 st.).

548.3   Breke owte & not blynne
           A couplet tr. '*Erumpe et clama*' in an English sermon. [Cf. 664.5].
           1. Royal 18. B. xxiii, f. 127b.
           Ross, *EETS* 209. 218.

*548.5   *Bricht as ane angell schyning in his weid
           The Romance of Clariodus—in couplets: Book I (vv. 1576), II (vv. 1938), III (vv. 2442), IV (vv. 2860), V (vv. 3029).
           1. Advocates 19. 2. 5 [*olim* Hailes], f. 8a (begins and ends imperfectly).
           Irving, *Maitland Club*, 1830.

Bryght as the stern of day begouth to schyne   See 2820.5.

548.8   Brynge þe oxe to þe halle / and he wolle to þe stalle
           A proverbial couplet.
           1. Rylands Lib. Latin 394, f. 2a.
           Pantin, *BJRL* XIV. 92.

549   1. Rickert, *Anc. Eng. Xmas Carols*, p. 245; [Masters,] *Rymes of Minstrels*, p. 21; Bullen, *Carols & Poems*, p. 187; Kaiser, *Anthologie*, p. 311; Kaiser, *Med. Eng.*, p. 478; Robbins, *Sec. Lyrics.*, pp. 9-10; Greene, *Sel. Eng. Carols*, p. 154; Speirs, *Med. Eng. Poetry*, pp. 87-8; Davies, *Med. Eng. Lyrics*, p. 217; 2. Coulton, *Life in the MA*, III. 140-1.

550.5   Bird us neure bliþe be / Wen we þenke on pinges þre
Recollections of mortality—six 6-line tail-rime stanzas.
1. Camb. Un. Add. 2585 (2).

551   Warning against lechery.
1. Harley 7578, f. 16a.
Robbins, *PQ* XXXV. 93-5; Bowers, *MLN* LXX. 397-8; Davies, *Med. Eng. Lyrics,* p. 260 (st. 1-3 only).

552.3   Burnys ne battelles brytten at schall be
Political prophecy using emblems or devices—fourteen cross-rimed quatrains.
1. NLW Peniarth 26, pp. 60-1.

552.5   Busy in stody be þou child
Advice on good behaviour—two short couplets.
1. Balliol 354, f. 200a.
Flügel, *Anglia* XXVI. 202; Dyboski, *EETS* ci. 130.

But and the wyf oons happe to go astraye
Extract (pr. *Rel. Ant.,* II. 27) from 1540 (MS. Bodl. 1479).

*552.8   *Bot fals men make her finges feld / & doþ hem wepe wel
Praise of women (? by Lynne)—in 11-line stanzas with bob. [French original in Harley 2253: cf. *Archiv* CX. 102. Utley 42].
1. Advocates 19. 2. 1, ff. 324a-325b (vv. 330; begins and ends imperfectly).
Leyden, *Complaynt of Scotland,* 1801, p. 161; Laing, *A Penni Worth of Witte,* Abbotsford Club, 1857, pp. 107-18; Kölbing, *Eng. Stn.* VII. 103-7; Holthausen, *Archiv* CVIII. 290-9.

553   *Gentleman's Magazine,* May 1842, p. 467 (2 st. only); Sauerstein, *Charles d'Orleans,* 1899, pp. 42-3.

553.5   Bot god that good may geue
A simple prayer—three couplets.
1. Trinity Dublin 423, f. 203a (added in xvi cent. hand).

*554.3   *But y the goste of guydo him. . .
Gast of Gy—fragment of fifteen lines in couplets. [Cf. 3028. Ringler 98].

Pynson, ca. 1492, two-strip fragment (STC 12477); *repr.* Duff, *Athenaeum*, Aug. 24, 1901, p. 254; Duff, *XV C. English Books*, no. 169.

554.5　　But yf that I maye have trwly
A drinking song—eight stanzas mostly 11-lined, with 4-line pseudo-burden. [A shorter version, four 8-line stanzas and burden in *Gammer Gurton's Needle*, Act II. Cf. also Hawkins, *Hist. Music*, 1776, III. 21-2].
1. Victoria and Albert Mus., Dyce 45, f. 23b.
Dyce, *Skelton*, I. vii; Bullen, *Lyrics from Eliz. Dramatists*, 1893, pp. 288-90; Gayley, *Rep. Eng. Comedies*, I. 259; *Early Eng. Lyrics*, pp. 229-31; *Oxford Book XVI C. Verse*, pp. 94-6.

556　　1. Bodl. Lat. misc. c. 66 [*olim* Capesthorne], f. 94a.
Robbins, *PMLA* LXV. 271-2.

But spend yt on a prety wenche　　See 87.5.

556.5　　But Suthfolke Salesbury and Say
Against the Earl of Suffolk, A.D. 1448—three lines.
Piggot's Chronicle, repr. Kingsford, *Eng. Hist. Lit.*, p. 370; Wilson, *Lost Lit.*, p. 199; Robbins, *Hist. Poems*, p. xxxviii.

*But þis ston vp shal turned be　　See 1425.

But þou gloryouse lord þou quykenyst þe dede　　See 11.5.

*557.3　　*Bot yhene of þam oft with þam to mete / For all seme þai
A treatise on shrift. [For variant text see 694].
1. Sion Coll. Arc. L. 40. 2 / E. 25, ff. 1a-12b.

557.5　　But why am I so abusyd
A lover's complaint—one stanza rime royal.
1. BM Addit. 5465, f. 20b.
Fehr, *Archiv* CVI. 55; Stevens, *Music & Poetry*, p. 358.

558.3　　By a banke as I ley / musyng In my mynd
A song in praise of Henry VIII. [For a political variant see 558.5. Cf. also Ravenscroft, *Deuteromelia*, 1609, p. 19; *repr.* Chappell, *OE Pop. Music*, I. 49; Rimbault, *Songs & Ballads*, p. 55].

XX *Songes,* de Worde, 1530 (STC 22924); Flügel, *Anglia* XII. 597; Flügel, *Neuengl. Lesebuch,* pp. 161-2; Imelmann, *Shakespeare-Jahrbuch* XXXIX. 136-7.

558.5 By a bancke as I lay / musyng my sylfe alone
A May song of love—three 7-line stanzas. [Cf. 558.3].
1. Royal App. 58, f. 10b.
Phillipps, *Archaeologia* XXVIII. 13; Furnivall, *Captain Cox,* Ballad Soc., 1871, p. xii; Flügel, *Anglia* XII. 204-5; Flügel, *Neuengl. Lesebuch,* p. 139; Rimbault, *Songs & Ballads,* p. 53; Chappell, *OE Pop. Music,* I. 46-7; Collier, *Extracts from Registers of Stationers' Company,* I. 193; *Oxford Book XVI C. Verse,* pp. 40-1.

559 1. Camb. Un. Ff. 5. 48, ff. 112b-113b (15 st.).
2. Arber, *Dunbar Anthology,* pp. 142-4; Robbins, *Sec. Lyrics,* pp. 107-9; Kaiser, *Med. Eng.,* p. 450 (8 st. only).

560 3. NLW Deposit: Porkington 10, ff. 203a-207b (26 st.); 4. Chichester: West Sussex Rec. Office, Cowfold Churchwardens Accounts, at end.

561 [Cf. also 2736.6].
8. Bodl. Lat. misc. e. 85, ff. 79a-81a (9 st.).

By by lullaby   See 1448.5.

564 'The Lufaris Complaynt,' a letter with a Prologue of nine stanzas rime royal and text of twelve stanzas, generally 9-lined.
1. Wilson, *Speculum* XXIX. 719-23.

566 thirteen couplets.
1. Camb. Un. Ll. 5. 10, f. 10a; 2. Pepys 2553, pp. 8, 316.
2. Schipper, *Dunbar,* pp. 44-5; and *DKAW* XL (II). 44-5; Baildon, *Dunbar,* pp. 9-10; MacKenzie, *Dunbar,* pp. 55-6.

567 [For xvi cent. versions see Wells, *Manual,* pp. 133-4].
A. J. Bliss, London 1960.

568 2. Bradfer-Lawrence [*olim* Lyell], f. 118a.

569 seven lines.
1. Bodl. 3041, f. 2a.

572	1. Bodl. Lat. misc. c. 66 [*olim* Capesthorne], f. 93a. Robbins, *PMLA* LXV. 264-6.
574	2. Horstmann, *AE Leg. 1875*, pp. 81-2 (vv. 277-322).
575	[Delete entire entry].

By hym that all dothe embrase　　See 1547.5.

*By name þat theobaldus hyȝt　　See 1645 (Harvard).

By one foreste als I gan walke　　See 560.

By saynt Mary my lady　　See 729.5.

576　　6. Ipswich County Hall Deposit: Hillwood [*olim* Brome], f. 80b; 7. Wellcome Hist. Med. Lib. 673, f. 7b (3 st.); 8. Rome: English Coll. 1306, f. 74b.
7. Kane, *London Med. St.* II (Part I), pp. 60-1.

576.5　　By the grace of our lord omnipotent / with suffrage of Mary
An English metrical version of the *Biblia Pauperum* (perhaps xvi cent.)—forty-three stanzas rime royal.
1. Caius 793, pp. 161-71.

By þe ath þat I swere to þe　　See 565.

577　　[Delete entire entry].

By þe see of Galilee oure lord in a tyme he wende
See 3452.

578.5　　By these two trees whiche here growe vpryght
Pageant verses recited by a Tree of Jesse at the return of Henry VI to London, A.D.1432—two stanzas rime royal. [Adapted from 3799].
　　Fabyan, *New Chronicles*, Pynson, 1516 (STC 10659); *repr.* Ellis, 1811, p. 606; Gattinger, *Wiener Beiträge* IV. 28-9.

579　　1. Bodl. 1689, f. 97b.
Robbins, *Sec. Lyrics*, p. 246.

580　　Person, *Camb. ME Lyrics*, p. 28.

581	Rickert, *Anc. Eng. Xmas Carols*, p. 181; Stevens, *Med. Carols*, p. 109; Robbins, *Early Eng. Xmas Carols*, p. 36.
583	1. Varnhagen, *Anglia* VII. 282-7.
584	*comp. text.* MacCracken, *EETS* 192. 772-5 (13 st.).
585	Marsh, *Hist. Eng. Language*, 1866, p. 281; Hall, Oxford 1914, pp. 27-30; Robbins, *Hist. Poems*, pp. 34-7.

585.5   Calliope / As ye may se / Regent is she
       On his service to Calliope by John Skelton—three 8-line tail-rime stanzas.
       Workes, Marshe, 1568 (STC 22608); *repr.* [? J. Bowle,] 1736; Chalmers, *English Poets*, II. 236; Dyce, *Skelton*, I. 197-8; Dyce and Child, *Skelton & Donne*, I. 219-20; Henderson, *Skelton*, 1931, p. 257; 1948, 1959, p. 346.

586   Candelmasse ys a feste heye & holy þor ʒe alle þyng

       Card lye down and whele stond styll   See 1163.5.

*586.5   *Cassamus roos aftre this talkynge
       The courtly game of '*Le roi qui ne ment*,' an extract from the *Voeux du Paon* (vv. 1604-1977). [Cf. 803, 2251].
       1. Camb. Un. Ff. 1. 6, ff. 166a-177b (vv. 566).
       Rosskopf, *Editio princeps des Me. Cassamus*, Erlangen 1911.

       Catesby the cat and Lovel the dogge / Rule all England under the hog   See 3318.7.

587	Horstmann, *AE Leg. 1881*, pp. lxliii-lxlv (vv. 171).
588	An acrostic on St. Katirin. 1. Trinity Camb. 257, f. 9b. Robbins, *Sec. Lyrics*, p. 273; Wilson, *MLN* LXIX. 21.
588.5	Celestial Princess thow blessyd vergyn Marie Epitaph, A. D. 1486, for Margaret Cantelowe of Streatham, Surrey—one 8-line stanza. Ravenshaw, *Antiente Epitaphes*, pp. 14-5.
589	Clive, *Roxburghe Club* L. 212-38.

590   *Chaucer,* Speght, 1598 (STC 5077); Urry, *Chaucer,* 1721, p. 554; Bell, *Poets of Great Britain,* 1782, XIII. 117; [Anderson,] *Poets of Great Britain,* I. 582; 1. Robbins, *Sec. Lyrics,* pp. 165-8.

591.5   Change þi lawe if þou wolt wel spede
    English lines in a friar sermon—one quatrain.
    1. Basle Univ. B. VIII. 4, f. 93b.
    Meyer and Burckhardt, *MA HSS. der Univ. Basel: Beschreibendes Verzeichnis,* Abt. B, pp. 852-3.

592   Furnivall, *EETS* 15 orig. ed. 236; rev. ed. 264.

593.5   Charite is chasyd al abowte
    The absence of charity—two couplets in a Latin sermon.
    1. Bodl. 29746, f. 175a.

*593.8 *. . .Charlis doghti knyȝtes. .ta. .le as þat a waywarde spedde
    Sir Firumbras—in couplets (vv. 1-3410) and 6-line stanzas (vv. 3411-7130).
    1. Bodl. 25166, ff. 1a-77b (a corrected draft by the author of the opening lines appears on the cover).
    1. Herrtage, *EETS* xxxiv.

594   10. Lincoln Cath. 234, f. 164a (in sermon).
    9. *Register,* I. 451; 9, 10. Owst, *Preaching in Med. England,* p. 272.

595   [Cf. 410, 3372.8. Singer 810].
    1. Bodl. 3652, ff. 41a-65a; 6. Bodl. 7010 [Ashmole 1490], ff. 114a-136b; 7. Bodl. 14614, ff. 35b-68b; 8. Bodl. 14674, f. 2a; 10. Camb. Un. Ff. 2. 23, f. 1b; 12. Caius Camb. 399, Part II, ff. 31a-87; 13. Trinity Camb. 1120, Part II, ff. 82a-131b; 15. Harley 367, ff. 55a-76a (variant); 17. Delete this MS.; 24. John Scott [present location not known]; 25. Univ. of Pennsylvania, Smith 4, ff. 10b-30.

597.5   Chyldern profyt & lycor faylyng
    Riddles concealing names of ladies—in couplets.

    1. Bodl. 2059, f. 417b (vv. 8); 2. Bodl. 21831, f. 77a (vv. 4, variant); 3. Balliol 354, f. 219a (vv. 6).
    1-3. Robbins, *Eng. Lang. Notes* I. 2-3; 2. *Rel. Ant.,* II. 112; 3. Flügel, *Anglia* XXVI. 228; *Early Eng. Lyrics,* p. 1 (vv. 3).

598	1. Wilson, *Lost Lit.*, p. 172; 3. Hall, *Early Middle English* I. 5; Reese, *Music in MA*, p. 241.
600	1. BM Addit. 46919 [*olim* Phillipps 8336], f. 208a.
601	Greene, *Sel. Eng. Carols*, p. 79.
603.5	Cryste crosse me spede ABC / The grace of the graye distaffe 'How þe gosyps made a royal feest'—in couplets. *Cryste Crosse me Spede*, de Worde, n.d. [Cf. Dibdin, *Typo. Antiquities*, II. 368].
604	Person, *Camb. ME Lyrics*, pp. 5-6.
605	Robbins, *Hist. Poems*, pp. 227-32.
605.5	Crist for clenesse of thin incarnacion / þe merit of thi woundes A charm. [Cf. 624]. 1. Boston Pub. Lib. 1546 [*olim* Sowter, *olim* Le Neve *Horae*], f. 110b.
607	twenty-two stanzas rime royal.
607.3	Crist hathe made hys complainte A prophecy—vv. 96 in quatrains. 1. Victoria and Albert Mus., Dyce 45, f. 18a.
607.5	Crist is offred for mannes sake / Of senne fre man to make One couplet in Grimestone's sermon notes. 1. Advocates 18. 7. 21, f. 121b.
607.8	Crist ys woundid for oure wikkednesse 'We buþ ful heled of oure siknesse'—a couplet in a Latin sermon. 1. Camb. Un. Ii. 3. 8, f. 121b.
608	Rickert, *Anc. Eng. Xmas Carols*, p. 187.
611	[St. 4 = st. 4 of 3691]. Davies, *Med. Eng. Lyrics*, pp. 139-41.

611.5	Cryste on crosse his blode þat bled / And lyfe for lyfe he layd to wed

Treatise on the Birth and Prophecy of Merlin—vv. 2786. [See 1162, 1675].
   de Worde, 1510 (STC 17841).

612
   1. Advocates 1. 1. 6, p. 13 and f. 21a.
      1a, 1b. Ritchie, *STS* 3 s. V. 21-3; *STS* n.s. XXII. 50-1;
      1b. *Bannatyne MS.*, Hunt. Club, pp. 52-4.

615   Cryst þat art [boþe d]ay & lyht / thow vnhilist þe mirknasse
   1. Egerton 3425 [*olim* Gurney], f. 201a.

616   Robbins, *Harvard Theol. Rev.* XLVII. 59-60.

620   3. Hereford Cath. O. iv. 14, f. 199a.
   3. *Register*, I. 446.

620.5   Cryst that day ert and lyght
   A version of '*Criste qui lux es et dies*'—five quatrains.
   1. Harley 1260, f. 196a.
   Robbins, *Harvard Theol. Rev.* XLVII. 58-9.

621.5   Crist þat deyde vp on þe crosse for sauacion of mankynde
   A prayer for grace at death, in Lavynham's *Tretis*—three long monoriming lines.
   1. Bodl. 655, f. 23a; 2. Bodl. 12146, f. 1a; 3. Bodl. 21634, f. 193a; 4. Camb. Un. Ff. 6. 31, f. 11a; 5. Trinity Camb. 305, f. 243a; 6. Harley 211, f. 35a; 7. Harley 1197, f. 9a; 8. Harley 1288, f. 64a; 9. Harley 2383, f. 65a; 10. Royal 8. C. 1, f. 144a; 11. Leeds Univ., Brotherton 501, f. 68a; 12. London: Dr. Williams' Lib. Anc. 3, f. 133b; 13. Norwich: St. Peter Hungate Mus. 48. 158. 926, f. 31a; 14. Soc. of Antiquaries [*olim* Bright], p. 383.
   6. Zutphen, *A Litil Tretys by Lavynham*, p. 1.

624   Crist that was in Bedelem born / & bapteisyde was in flum iordan
   A charm to staunch blood—in irregular lines. [Cf. 627.5 and 1946.5].
   [Revise listing of MSS. as follows:]
   1. Bodl. 3548, f. 1b (and var. ff. 2a, 3a); 2. Bodl. 31379, f. 10b (vv. 9); 3. Egerton 833, f. 20b (vv. 8); 4. Royal 12. B. xxv, f. 60b (vv. 4); 5. Royal 17. A. viii, f. 49b (vv. 4); 6. Sloane 56, f. 100b (vv. 14); 7. Sloane 2584, f. 103b (vv. 6);

8. BM Addit. 33381, f. 151b (vv. 7, var.); 9. BM Addit. 33996, f. 147a (vv. 7); 10 Wellcome Hist. Med. Lib. 404, f. 20a; 11. Wellcome Hist. Med. Lib. 406, f. 4b; 12. Wellcome Hist. Med. Lib. 542, f. 9a; 13. Boston Pub. Lib. 1546 [olim Sowter, olim Le Neve Horae], ff. 109b-110b.

1. Briggs, Folklore LXIV. 454; 9. Heinrich, ME Medizinbuch, Halle 1896, p. 122; [MS. not identified: not Sloane 88] Rel. Ant. I. 315.

Crist that was of infynyt myght   See 1731.

627.3   Crist was done on a tre

A charm against 'heuyll' by the wounds of Christ—six lines.

1. BM Addit. 33381, f. 151b.

Crist was i-bore in bedlehem   See 624.

627.5   Crist was of þe wirgine Marie born

A charm for staunching blood—one quatrain. [Cf. 624].

1. Stockholm Royal Lib. X. 90, p. 110.

Stephens, Archaeologia XXX. 401; Holthausen, Anglia XIX. 81.

627.8   Cristys blood clensyth and kepyth mannys sowls fro dedely synne

Three long monoriming lines added to a Disputacio de sanguine Christi. [Cf. 628].

1. H. P. Kraus, Sale Cat. 93 (1960), Item 91: Michael de Hungaria, Sermones, J. Paderborn, Louvain, ca. 1480.

A. Apponyi, Hungarica LII. 37.

Crystys crosse be my spede   See 0.1.

631.5   Christene man þu lerne of love

Appeal of Christ to sinner, comparing Christ on the Cross to a 'bok of loue'—nine 6-line stanzas.

1. olim George Smith [olim Harmsworth Sale, Lot 2018, Oct. 1945] (Sotheby Sale, Lot 317, Feb. 2, 1960), f. 105a.

Mead, MLR LV. 234-5.

631.8   Cronykillis and annuall bookis of kinges

House of Percy: Metrical Chronicle by William Peeris. [Cf. prose chronicle in Bodl. 2986, roll].

    1. Bodl. 4192, ff. 119a-140b (lacks 19 st. at f. 123a); 2. Royal 18. D. ii, f. 186a.
      1. J. B[esly], *Rare Tracts*, Newcastle, 1845, I. 9.

633.5   Cir-cum-staunt-ly thre Kings came by nynght
  Mnemonic verses on the saints' days in each month, adapted from the French—twelve quatrains.
    Sarum Prymer, Paris 1529 (Morgan Lib. Acc. No. 28432); *Horae*, Rouen 1557 (Morgan Lib. Acc. No. 1036); &c. Bühler, *St. in Renaissance* VI. 230-2.

Clamabant in a day go we to þe tyre wyth hay hay   See 1445.6.

635.5   Clym clam the cat lepe over the damme
  A tag in Nicolas Bozon's *Contes moralisés*.
    1. Harley 1288, f. 99a; 2. BM Addit. 46919 [*olim* Phillipps 8336], f. 125a; 3. Gray's Inn 12, f. 42a.
    1-3. Ross, *Neuphil. Mitteilungen* L. 209; 1, 3. Smith, *SATF*, pp. 212, 145; Förster, *Festschrift zum 12 Deutschen Neuphilologentage*, p. 59; 3. Wilson, *LSE* VI. 46; Owst, *Lit. & Pulpit*, p. 44.

Clime not to hie / lest chipis fall in thin eye   See 1149.5.

636   1. Asloan, ff. 301b-303a.

636.5 Close þi herte from enwye
  Counsels of sage conduct—two couplets in a Latin sermon by Friar Nicholas Philip.
    1. Bodl. 29746, f. 173b.

637   Ross, *Speculum* XXXII. 279-81; Kaiser, *Med. Eng.*, p. 261.

638   Hales and Furnivall, *Percy Folio MS.*, I. 61.

Come home dere hert your tarieng   See 3878.

Come over the burne Besse   See 3318.4.

642.5 Come ouer the woodes fair & grene
  An amorous dialogue with gathering flowers imagery—twenty cross-rimed quatrains.

	1. Bodl. 12653, f. 58b.
	Padelford and Benham, *Anglia* XXXI. 377-80; Zupitza, *Archiv* LXXXVII. 433; *Early Eng. Lyrics*, p. 64.
643	1. BM Addit. 46919 [*olim* Phillipps 8336], f. 207b.
644.5	Come wynde come reyne / come he neuer agayne
	Proverbial couplet translating '*Ventus cum pluuia* &c.'
	1. Bodl. 15444, f. 143b.
	Meech, *MP* XXXVIII. 124.
648	1. *Rel. Lyr. XV C.*, pp. 131-3; Stevenson, *STS* LXV. 293-5; Bennett, *STS* 3 s. XXIII. 255-7; Davies, *Med. Eng. Lyrics*, pp. 274-6.
648.5	Complayn I may / And right well say
	'Dame Pitiles:' a lover's complaint—seven 8-line tail-rime stanzas (st. 7 may be later: cf. Seaton, *Sir Richard Roos*, p. 187).
	MS. not established.
	Hawkins, *Hist. Music*, 1776, III. 27-8.
649	[Cf. 649.5].
649.5	Complayne I may whereuyr I go
	'I-wiss yet will I not me complayne'—one stanza rime royal. [Cf. 649].
	1. BM Addit. 5465, f. 46b.
	Stafford Smith, *Eng. Songs*, no. 13; Fehr, *Archiv* CVI. 59; Stevens, *Music & Poetry*, p. 365.
649.8	Complane I wald wist I quhome till
	A complaint to the King by William Dunbar—vv. 76 in couplets.
	1. Camb. Un. Ll. 5. 10, f. 13b; 2. Pepys 2553, p. 16.
	2. Pinkerton, *Anc. Scot. Poems*, I. 109-11; Sibbald, *Chronicle*, I. 340-1; Laing, *Dunbar*, I. 142-4; Paterson, *Dunbar*, pp. 224-7; Small, *STS* IV. 212-4; Schipper, *Dunbar*, pp. 267-70; and *DKAW* XLI (IV). 68-72; Baildon, *Dunbar*, pp. 134-6; Craigie, *STS* n.s. VII. 17-19; MacKenzie, *Dunbar*, pp. 39-41.
650	Skeat, *Minor Poems*, p. 222; Robinson, *Chaucer*, 1933, pp. 638-9; 1957, p. 542.

651   1a. *Early Eng. Carols,* pp. 185-6.

651.5   Concordans musycall Iugyd by the ere
        Praise God for music—one stanza rime royal. [Cf. 1931.8].
        XX *Songes,* de Worde, 1530 (STC 22924); Flügel, *Anglia*
        XII. 596; Imelmann, *Shakespeare-Jahrbuch* XXXIX. 135.

652   1. *Tractatus Sancti Bonaventure doctoris...de Quatuor
        Exerciciis,* added on flyleaves [present location not known].
        [John Fry,] *Pieces of Ancient Poetry,* Bristol 1814, pp. 41-4.

653   8. Rome: English Coll. 1306, f. 76a.
        1. Chalmers, *English Poets,* I. 555-6; 7. MacCracken, *EETS*
        192. 839-44.

654   [Singer 997].
        4. Hunterian Mus. 104, ff. 1a-58b (begins and ends imperfectly; several lacunae).

655   1. Person, *Camb. ME Lyrics,* pp. 44-8.

657   Robbins, *PMLA* LXIX. 636; Davies, *Med. Eng. Lyrics,*
        pp. 240-1.

658   [Ringler 10].
        11. Leyden Univ. Vossius 9, f. 80b; 12. Huntington HM
        144 &c. (copied from first ed. Caxton).
        Caxton, ca. 1477 (STC 17018) (vv. 1-462); de Worde, ca.
        1499 (STC 17020); *repr.* Sykes, *Roxburghe Club* 1822; *facs.*
        Jenkinson, 1906; 12. Bühler, *MLN* LV. 566-7 (addit. var. st.).

661.5   Curtaise catoun / þus endis his resoun
        On Cato, pagan yet Christian—five tail-rime stanzas of 6
        short lines.
        1. Bodl. 3894, f. 123b.
        Furnivall, *N&Q* 4 s. II. 176.

662.5   Credo Peter began to saye
        The Apostles and the Creed—five 12-line stanzas. [Cf. 311, 1374, 2700].
        1. Shrewsbury School 3, ff. 45b-46b.

Calvert, *Trans. Shropshire Hist. Arch. & Nat. Hist. Soc.* 1894, p. 11.

663   3. Harley 78, f. 3a (vv. 172-207).
Wolfe, London, 1553 (STC 19904); *repr.* T. D. Whitaker, London 1814; Rogers, London, 1561 (STC 19908); 1. Wright, *Vision & Creed*, 1842, 1856; Skeat, *EETS* 30. 1-32; 3. Doyle, *Speculum* XXXIV. 435-6.

664   Davies, *Med. Eng. Lyrics*, p. 209.

Crosse was made all of red   See 33.

*664.3   *. . .crowne of thorne so scharpe & kene / throw my heyd
Fragment of a poem on Christ's passion and pleading.
1. New York Pub. Lib. Drexel Fragments 4180.
Stevens, *Music & Poetry*, p. 426.

664.5   Crye to Crist and not blynne / and haske
A couplet in a prose sermon. [Cf. 548.3].
1. Royal 18. B. xxiii, ff. 105b, 107a.
Ross, *EETS* 209. 153, 157.

Colle to me the rysshys grene   See 835.5.

665   1. Longleat 254, verso of last leaf.
Bergen, *EETS* cxxiv. 19.

666   [Utley 49].
9. Durham Univ. Cosin V. ii. 13, f. 100a; 11. BM Addit. 17492, f. 89b (vv. 344-50, 64-77), f. 91a (vv. 302-8) [see 1069.5 and 4217.6].
5. Arber, *English Garner*, 1882, IV. 54-71; Pollard, *XV C; Prose & Verse*, pp. 14-31.

667   [Utley 50].
[Masters,] *Rymes of Minstrels*, pp. 14-16.

668   Dickins and Wilson, *Early ME Texts*, pp. 132-5; Brandl and Zippel, *ME Sprach- u. Literatur.*, 1947, p. 203; Kaiser, *Anthologie*, p. 304; Kaiser, *Med. Eng.*, p. 486.

670   [Utley 51].
Copley, *Seven Eng. Songs*, 1940.

Dangler *cum* jasper
False transcription of first line of 1655.5.

671 [All texts show &c...For complete ed. and chart see Mustanoja, *How the Good Wife Taught her Daughter*, Helsinki 1948, pp. 18-9].
1. Emmanuel Camb. 106, f. 48b (with introduction; 28 st.); 2. Trinity Camb. 599, f. 211a (with introduction; 31 st.); 4. Delete this MS.; 5. Delete this MS.; 6. Huntington HM 128 [*olim* Ashburnham 130], f. 216b (with introduction).
Certaine Worthye Manuscript Poems, Dexter, 1597 (STC 21499); *repr.* Edinb. 1812; Gibbs, *Roxburghe Club* 1873, pp. 163-71; *repr.* with 1-3, 6. Mustanoja, *How the Good Wife*, pp. 158-72, 197-216; 3. Coulton, *Social Life in Britain*, pp. 446-51; 6. Hindley, *Old Book Collector's Misc.*, London 1876, II. 1.

671.5 Doughter Kateryn I alphons remember
The speech of Alphouns at the pageant celebrating the marriage between Prince Arthur and Princess Catharine—seven stanzas.
1. Cotton Vitell. A. xvi, ff. 189a-190a.

Dowsteryn if ye wol be vertuous   See 3196 and 3784.

672 [For a tag with a picture see 1367.3].

Dere doghterne and yhe wyll be vertuus   See 3196.

672.3 Dere is þe hony bouȝt / þat on thornes is souȝt
A proverbial couplet. [Cf. Hendyng, st. 29; 2078; Tilley H 554].
1. Bodl. 21626, f. 23b; 2. Rylands Lib. Latin 394, f. 13a.
1. Förster, *Festschrift zum 12 Deutschen Neuphilologentage*, p. 51; 2. Pantin, *BJRL* XIV. 100.

Dere sonnes let not ydelnes yowe enslombre   See 3196.

672.4 Dethe began by cause of syn
We all must die—seven 8-line stanzas and 4-line burden. *Christmas Carolles*, Kele, ca. 1550 (STC 5205); *facs.* Reed, *Xmas Carols*, pp. 25-8; *repr. Early Eng. Carols*, pp. 251-2.

672.5   Deth bringith down lowe þat ben bolde
        The inevitability of death—three couplets in a Latin sermon.
        1. Bodl. 29746, f. 174b.

673   2. Bodl. 12158, ff. 92b-93a.

673.5   Deth of frendes maketh fon
        Dread of dying—two couplets.
        1. Hereford Cath. O. iii. 5, f. 49b.

674   [Cf. 145].
        12. Bodl. Auct. 7 Q. 21, end papers.
            2. Robbins, *Sec. Lyrics,* p. 100; 10. Kurvinen, *Neuphil. Mitteilungen* LIV. 62.

675   1. Fitzwilliam Mus. McClean 182, f. 138b (twice, and again on f. 139a).

        Deme no thyng þat is in dowt   See 675.5.

675.5   Deme þe best of euery dowt / Tyll the trowth be tryed owt
        A moralizing couplet. [Also appears on a late xiv cent. bronze jug; *repr.* Evans, *English Art,* 1949, p. 90].
        1. Balliol 354, f. 200b; 2. BM Addit. 31922, f. 79b.
            1. Flügel, *Anglia* XII. 247; Dyboski, *EETS* ci. 131; 2. Stevens, *Music & Poetry,* p. 413; Stevens, *Music at Court,* p. 57.

675.8   Demyd wrongfully / In absent
        No remedy: a lover's complaint—four stanzas of 7 short lines, the first and last lines of each stanza: 'Demyd wrongfully.'
        1. BM Addit. 5465, f. 9b.
            Fehr, *Archiv* CVI. 53; Stevens, *Music & Poetry,* p. 353.

676.5   Departure is my chef payne / I trust ryght wel of retorn agane
        A late love song, ascribed to Henry VIII—a round: one couplet.
        1. BM Addit. 31922, f. 60b.
            Flügel, *Anglia* XII. 243; Flügel, *Neuengl. Lesebuch,* p. 136; Trefusis, *Songs Henry VIII,* Roxburghe Club CLXI. 23-4; Stevens, *Music & Poetry,* p. 408; Stevens, *Music at Court,* p. 44.

679 [Utley 54].
Chepman and Myllar, 1508; *facs.* Beattie, *Edinb. Bibl. Soc.* 1950, pp. 145-6; *repr.* Stevenson, *STS* LXV. 217-8; Sibbald, *Chronicle*, I. 197; 2. Pinkerton, *Poems from Scarce Editions*, III. 130.

679.5 Devout soules that pass this way / For Stephen Foster
An epitaph, allegedly on a copper plate in the chapel at Ludgate — three couplets.
Ogilvy, *Relics of London City*, 1910, p. 57.

679.8 Deuorit with dreme devysing in my slummer
'A general satyre' ascribed to William Dunbar (and also to James Inglis) — sixteen 5-line stanzas with internal rime and refrain.
1. Pepys 2553, p. 187: 2. Advocates 1. 1. 6, p. 47 and f. 60a.
1. Schipper, *Dunbar*, pp. 314-21; and *DKAW* XLII (IV). 9-19; Baildon, *Dunbar*, pp. 162-4; Craigie, *STS* n.s. VII. 211-3; 2a, 2b. Ritchie, *STS* 3 s. V. 79; n.s. XXII. 147-50; 2b. Ramsay, *Evergreen*, I. 102-6; *repr. Ramsay and Earlier Scot. Poets*, pp. 235-6; [Hailes,] *Anc. Scot. Poems*, pp. 51-5; *Select Poems of Dunbar*, Perth 1788, pp. 49-52; Sibbald, *Chronicle*, I. 373-7; Laing, *Dunbar*, II. 24-7; Paterson, *Dunbar*, pp. 291-5; *Bannatyne MS.*, Hunt. Club, I. 162-5; Small, *STS* IV. 81-3; MacKenzie, *Dunbar*, pp. 151-3; Kinsley, *Dunbar*, pp. 70-2.

680 *Early Eng. Carols*, p. 70; Stevens, *Med. Carols*, p. 65.

681 Bullen, *Carols & Poems, frontis.*; Rickert, *Anc. Eng. Xmas Carols*, p. 218; Stevens, *Med. Carols*, p. 67; Robbins, *Early Eng. Xmas Carols*, p. 9.

681.5 Dysdayne me not wythout desert
'Refuse me not' — five quatrains with added bob. [Cf. variant ascribed to Wyatt in *Tottel's Miscellany*].
1. BM Addit. 18652, f. 163b.
Reed, *Anglia* XXXIII. 369.

683 2. Advocates 19. 2. 1, ff. 278a-279b (fragment: vv. 7760-8021 of MS. 1); 3. Lincoln's Inn 150, ff. 28a-90a (vv. 1-4713, 5180-8021 of MS. 1); 4. St. Andrew's Univ.: two fragments (formerly part of MS. 2; vv. 150 between v. 6856 and v. 7194 of MS. 1).
BM *Bagford Ballads*, Vol. I, no. 27; *repr.* with 1-4. Smithers, *EETS* 227; 1-3. Brandl and Zippel, *ME Sprach- u. Litera-*

    tur., pp. 66-71 (extracts); 3 (with gaps filled by vv. 1217 of MS. 1). Weber, *Metr. Rom.*, I. 3-327; 2. Nicholson, *Rouland and Vernagu*, Abbotsford Club, 1836, pp. xx-xxvii.

684   Wilson, *Lost Lit.*, p. 187.

686   [Cf. 687.5 and 2060].
    2. Balliol 354, f. 147b (following 2060).
    Flügel, *Anglia* XXVI. 167; Dyboski, *EETS* ci. 138.

   Do thow better do thow worse / Do after hym that beryth the purse   See 465.5.

687   Girvan, *STS* 3 s. XI. 174-5.

687.3   Dou way Robin the child wile wepe
    Fragment of the tenor words to a motet. [Music, without words, also appears in Cotton Fragments XXIX, f. 36a].
    1. Princeton Univ. Garrett 119.
    Levy, *Journal American Musicological Soc.* IV. 225; *New Oxford Hist. Music*, III. 112.

687.5   Do well whill þou art here / & þou shalt haue well els wher
    A proverbial couplet. [Cf. 686].
    1. Balliol 354, f. 200a.
    Flügel, *Anglia* XXVI. 202; Dyboski, *EETS* ci. 130.

688   3. Bodl. 3478, f. 21b; 4. Bodl. 6668, f. 210a; 5. Cotton Vitell. A. i, f. 18b.

688.3   Done is a battell on the dragon blak
    On the Resurrection, by William Dunbar—five 8-line stanzas with refrain: '*Surrexit Dominus de sepulchro.*' [Cf. 3225.5].
    1. Advocates 1. 1. 6, f. 35a.
     [Hailes,] *Anc. Scot. Poems*, pp. 107-8; *Select Poems of Dunbar*, Perth 1788, pp. 89-91; Laing, *Dunbar*, I. 247-8; Paterson, *Dunbar*, pp. 85-6; *Bannatyne MS.*, Hunt. Club, I. 94-6; Small, *STS* IV. 156-7; Schipper, *Dunbar*, pp. 379-81; and *DKAW* XLII (IV). 77-9; Baildon, *Dunbar*, pp. 203-4; Ritchie, *STS* n.s. XXII. 88-9; MacKenzie, *Dunbar*, pp. 159-60; Kinsley, *Dunbar*, pp. 7-8; Davies, *Med. Eng. Lyrics*, pp. 253-4.

688.5   Doun by ane rever as I red
'Do for thy self quhill thov art heir,' attributed to William Dunbar—ten 8-line stanzas with this refrain.
1. Advocates 1. 1. 6, p. 32 and f. 48b.
   1a, 1b. Ritchie, STS 3 s. V. 53-6; n.s. XXII. 122-4; 1b. Laing, *Dunbar*, II. 51-4; *Bannatyne MS.*, Hunt. Club, II. 133-5; Small, STS IV. 305-7; Schipper, *Dunbar*, pp. 406-8; and DKAW XLIII (I). 57-60; Baildon, *Dunbar*, pp. 231-3.

Doune from heaven from heaven so hie   See 112 (Sharp).

688.8   Downbery doun / Now am I exild my lady fro
To his mistress—a round: seven lines.
1. Royal App. 58, f. 4a; 2. BM Addit. 31922, f. 25a.
   1, 2. Flügel, *Anglia* XII. 260, 232; Stevens, *Music at Court*, p. 18; 2. Stevens, *Music & Poetry*, p. 391.

Drawe me nere
Burden to 1194.5.

693   Davies, *Med. Eng. Lyrics*, pp. 170-1.

Dremand me thocht that I did heir   See 3634.6.

694   [Cf. *557.3].

Dryngker fylle another ale   See 3259.

Dros of hors & gyl of fisch   See 597.5 (Bodl. 21831).

*dronken dronken dronken y-dronken   See 4256.6.

694.5   *Dum ludis floribus velud lacinia*
A macaronic Latin, French, and English (vv. 2) lyric to his Parisian mistress—five quatrains.
1. Harley 2253, f. 76a.
   Wright, *Spec. Lyric Poetry*, Percy Soc. IV. 64; Brook, *Harley Lyrics*, p. 55; *Early Eng. Lyrics*, pp. 276-7.

695   4. Pembroke Camb. 258, f. 134b.

696   [Entry transferred to 1320.5.]

698 [Utley 57].

700 1, 2. Brotanek, *ME Dichtungen,* pp. 152-9; 1. Furnivall, *EETS* 15 orig. ed. 1-3; 2. Robbins, *Hist. Poems,* pp. 218-21.

701 4. BM Addit. 37787, f. 12b (with 6-line verse rubric, 3448.5).
4. N. S. Baugh, *Worcestershire Misc.,* p. 98.

Airlie on as woddinsday   See 2821.3.

702.5 Erth goyth vpon erth as mold vpon
A variant of 'Erthe upon erthe' (704) used as an epitaph in Edmonton Church, London—four lines.
Weever, *Anc. Funerall Monuments,* 1631, p. 534 (STC 25223).

703.3 Erth my bodye I giue to the / On my sowle Iesu haue pite
A brief epitaph, A.D. 1400, at Great Ormsby, Norfolk—one couplet.
Ravenshaw, *Antiente Epitaphes,* p. 10.

703.5 Earthe oute of earthe clensen pure
Alchemical verses—six couplets.
1. Bodl. 7654, f. 72a.

704 [For 8-line tombstone inscription in Melrose Abbey see Wass, *Melrose Abbey,* p. 24, and Flügel, *Anglia* XXVI. 218]. 12a (xix cent. transcript). Egerton 2257, f. 100a; 14. Univ. of Pennsylvania, Lat. 33, f. 91b [*olim* Harmsworth; *olim* Dewick; Sotheby Sale, Oct. 15, 1943, Lot 2053; Raphael King Ltd., Sale Cat. 53, No. 215, Dec. 1951]; 17. *olim* Tenison [present location not known: see *Repressor,* RS, I. lxxii, n.]; 18. Davis and Orioli Sale Cat. 135, 1949, No. 2A.
2-4, 6-16. Murray, *EETS* 141; 16. J. G. Nichols, *Anc. Allegorical Hist. & Leg. Painting,* 1836; 4. Flügel, *Anglia* XXVI. 217-9; 6. Laing, *Dunbar,* I (Supplement). 317 (vv. 1-5 only); 12. Davies, *Med. Eng. Lyrics,* p. 180.

705 3. Wellcome Hist. Med. Lib. 1493, f. 9a.
3. Kane, *London Med. St.* II (Part I), p. 66.

Erþe toc of erþe erþe wyþ woh   See 3939 (Harley 2253).

706   Five lines of precepts: 'Be man noʒt hors noþer asse.'
1. Coxe, *Cat.*, p. 1; Skeat, *EETS* 54. xxvii; Kölbing and Day. *EETS* 188. vii.

707.5   *Ecclesiae tres sunt / qui servitium malle fallunt*
Two macaronic lines on Tutivillus. [Cf. 1214.9, 1655.5 and 3812].
1. *olim* Phillipps 58, f. 35b.
Rel. Ant., I. 90; Wright, *Piers Plowman*, 2d ed. 1856, p. 543.

708   Davies, *Med. Eng. Lyrics*, pp. 64-7.

709   Warton, ed. Hazlitt, *Hist. Eng. Poetry*, 1871, III. 10-12; Ritson, *Poems by Minot*, p. 13; Mätzner, *AE Sprachproben*, I. 326; Morris, *Specimens*, II. 131; FitzGibbon, *E. E. Poetry*, pp. 9-12; *Cambridge Book Prose & Verse*, p. 363; Mossé, *Handbook*, pp. 234-7.

710   John Hardyng's *Metrical Chronicle*, generally with a Dedication to Henry VI; some MSS. with concluding Envoy to Edward IV, and other end-matter. . . .For later continuations see 4174.5 and Bodl. 21916, ff. 1a-20b, rime royal, fragmentary. [Cf. also Kingsford, *EHR* XXVII. 462-82].
12. Bühler 5, p. 1 (begins p. 117 of Ellis' ed.); 13. Harley 3730, ff. 1a-1b (verses from Epilogue only); 14. Harvard Coll. Eng. 1054, ff. 1a-149b; 15. Univ. of Illinois 83 [Robinson Sale Cat. 72, No. 182], ff. 1a-224b.
8. Kingsford, *EHR* XXVII. 740-53 (extracts only).

711   On the Duke of Gloucester—seven stanzas rime royal from *The Fall of Princes* (1168), vv. 372-420, appearing separately.
Furnivall, *Russell's Boke of Norture*, Roxburghe Club 1867, LXXXVII. xv-xvi.

*Eke in iiij maners who so can take hede   See *3844.8.

*711.5   *eke to þe sowlys þy mercy
A prayer to Christ by Dominus Iohannes arcuarius Canonicus Bodmine—first legible line of six irregular couplets.
1. Harley 2399, f. 47a.

Ek ye wymmen whiche been enclyned   See 2602.

714	1553 and 1565 versions: Waterhouse, *EETS* civ. 8-18; 1565 version only: Fitch, *Norfolk Archaeology*, 1856; Manly, *Spec. Pre-Sh. Drama*, 1897, I. 1; Adams, *Chief Pre-Sh. Dramas*, pp. 88-93.
715	Cawley, *Wakefield Pageants in Townley Cycle*, 1958 (Plays 2, 3, 12, 13, 16, 21).
716	5. Harley 2124, f. 1a (A.D. 1607; lacks Banns); 11. NLW Peniarth 399 (Antichrist only).
	4 (Banns, Noah, Herod only). Markland, *Roxburghe Club* 1818, XXI; 10. F. M. Salter, 1935; 11, 12. Greg, *Play of Antichrist*, Oxford 1935.
717	Riddle on the word IHC—three or four irregular lines. [Cf. 1528.5].
	1. *Cat. Douce MSS.*, p. 41; 1, 2. Robbins, *Eng. Lang. Notes* I. 3; 2, 3. Robbins, *Sec. Lyrics*, pp. 253, 80.
*717.5	*Either oþur þus to cloþun and fede
	Life of St. Paula.
	1. Bodl. 3938, f. 89a col i.
	Horstmann, *AE Leg. 1878*, pp. 3-8.
718.5	Elendoune Elendoune þi lond is fulle rede
	A couplet on the Battle of Ellendune in de Brunne's tr. of Langtoft.
	1. Inner Temple, Petyt 511, Part VII.
	Hearne, Oxford 1725, I. 14; Wright, *Rolls Ser.* XLVII, i. 298; Wilson, *Lost Lit.*, p. 34.
720	A promise of pardon to all who honor the 11,000 Virgins with *Pater Nosters* and *Aves*—one 8-line stanza.
	1. Huntington HM 140 [*olim* Phillipps 8299], f. 155b.
721	1-5, 7-13. F. Schubel, *Die südengl. Legende von den 11,000 Jungfrauen*, Greifswalder, Beiträge zur Literatur und Stilforschung XXI. 151; 10, 12, 13. Liljegren, *Eng. Stn.* LVII. 98, 103, 108; 7. D'Evelyn and Mill, *EETS* 236. 443.
722	Adams, *Chief Pre-Sh. Dramas*, pp. 207-11.
724	To his mistress—nine quatrains.
	Strutt, *Horda Angel-Cynnan*, III. 153; Robbins, *Sec. Lyrics*, pp. 160-2.

726   'Acquaynt the wyth connyng' — one quatrain (= st. 131) taken from Burgh's *Cato Major* (854).

    1. Person, *Camb. ME Lyrics*, p. 49.

Enforce yourselfe as goddis knyght   See 3206.5.

England and walles as to thair soffrayne

Verses in Harley 3730 from Epilogue to Hardyng's *Chronicle* (710).

England be glad pluk up thy lusty hart   See 134.5.

Engelond glad þou beo vor þou miȝt wel eþe

Quatrain introducing the Life of St. Thomas of Canterbury in 4171 (Stow 949) and in 907 (Bodl. 6924 and Cotton Jul. D. ix).

727   A Text.

    1. Cotton Calig. A. xi, f. 3a (vv. 12049; and vv. 34 copied later from now lost Allen MS.); 4. BM Addit. 18631, f. 4a; 17. BM Addit. 50848, ff. 1-6 (= missing six leaves of MS. 5, vv. 561-630, 1467-1676, 1817-1955). [Cf. Hill, *N&Q* CCX. 47-9].

    B Text.

    11. Sloane 2027, ff. 98a-169b (begins imperfectly); 12. London Univ. 278 [*olim* Mostyn Hall 259], f. 1a.

    C Text.

    14. Delete this MS.; 15. Delete this MS.; 16. Coll. of Arms LVIII, f. 6a (a garbled version, with many prose insertions; also includes 444, 1979, 3539, 3632).

    1. Hearne, Oxford 1724, *repr.* 1810 (pp. 1-464 from MS. 3; pp. 465-571 from MS. 1; pp. 610-11 from Allen MS.); Stevenson, *Church Historians of England*, V, i. 351-81 (extracts: vv. 1500 only).

728   The Life of St. Thomas of Canterbury, without the introductory section (vv. 202), dealing with Gilbert, St. Thomas' father.

[For complete 'Laud' text see 4171; for 'Harley' text see 907].

[Revise listing of MSS. as follows:]

1. Bodl. 1596, f. 141a; 2. ? Bodl. 29430, ff. 8b-18b (ends imperfectly); 3 ? Camb. Un. Add. 3039, f. 79b.

728.5   Ennok first with a benygne chere
    Pageant verses by Enok and Eli at the return of Henry VI to London, A.D. 1432—two stanzas rime royal. [Adapted from 3799].
    Fabyan, *New Chronicles*, Pynson, 1516 (STC 10659); *repr.* Ellis, 1811, pp. 605-6; Gattinger, *Wiener Beiträge* IV. 28.

729   An affirmation of devotion to his mistress, a love epistle— vv. 32.

729.3   Eoves her wonede ant was swon
    Seal of Evesham Abbey—one couplet.
    Victoria County Hist. Worcestershire, II. 127.

729.5   Arectyng my syght towarde the zodyake
    'The Garlande of Laurell' by John Skelton—vv. 1604, chiefly in rime royal.
    1. Cotton Vitell. E. x, ff. 223a-240b (fragmentary).
        R. Fawkes, 1523 (STC 22610); *repr.* Dyce, *Skelton*, I. 361-427; Dyce and Child, *Skelton & Donne*, II. 170-241; Flügel, *Neuengl. Lesebuch*, pp. 45-59 (extracts); Henderson, *Skelton*, 1931, pp. 395-451; 1948, 1959, pp. 347-96; Hughes, *Poems by Skelton*, 1924, pp. 149-206; *Workes*, Marshe, 1568 (STC 22608); *repr.* [? J. Bowle,] 1736; Chalmers, *English Poets*, II. 236-50; 1. Hammond, *Eng. Verse Chaucer-Surrey*, pp. 342-60.

    Isope myn auctor makis mencioune
        The Twa Mys (only):   see 3703 (Asloan).

731.5   Eternall lawde to god grettest of myght / Be hertely
    Trevisa's translation of *Prohemium* to Bartholomeus *De Proprietatibus Rerum*—twelve stanzas rime royal. [Ringler 12. For Envoy see 4258.3].
    de Worde, 1495 (STC 1536); *repr.* Hawkins, *Hist. Music*, 1776, II. 277-8; Dibdin, *Typo. Antiquities*, II. 315-7; Aurner, *Caxton*, p. 67 (st. 1 only).

733.1   Evyn as mery as I make myght
    A letter by a lady to her real love—four quatrains.
    1. Bodl. 12653, f. 58b.
    Padelford and Benham, *Anglia* XXXI. 377.

    Even as you lyst   See 813.6.

733.3   Eueir asse mon liuit lengore / so is dom iwrt strengore
A couplet translating Latin 'Quanto longiorem pacienciam &c.'
1. Trinity Camb. 323, f. 46a.
James, *Cat.*, I. 444.

733.5   Evere beginnit ure tale / of drunkenesse and of alle
A couplet tag in a Latin sermon on confession.
1. Balliol 220, f. 219b.
Mynors, *Cat.*, p. 216.

733.8   Euer cursyd be that man / that callyth me thorpe for womyndham
A tag by William Womyndham, Canon of Kirkeby.
1. Trinity Camb. 1144, f. 107a.

734   [Followed by 4272.5].
Robbins, *Sec. Lyrics*, p. 156.

734.5   Euer is the eie to the wude leie / þerinne is þet ich luuie
A proverbial saying, followed by miscellaneous lines and snatches, possibly verse, found in the *Ancren Riwle*. [Cf. 3513].
1. Cotton Cleo. C. vi, f. 38a; 2. Cotton Nero A. xiv, f. 23b (one line only); 3. Trinity Dublin 97, f. 273b.
1, 2. Wilson, *LSE* V. 36; Wilson, *Lost Lit.*, p. 174; 1. Morton, *Ancren Riwle*, Camden Soc., p. 96; *Eng. Lyr. XIII C.*, p. xi; Whiting, *Speculum* IX. 219; Dobson, *Ancren Riwle*; 2. Day, *EETS* 225. 42.

734.8   Euer is six the best chance of þe dyce
A political prophecy according to the throw of the dice—in couplets. [In MSS. 2, 3, 4, and 6 followed by 3308.5. For texts which add a 4-line introduction see 4018].
1. Bodl. 13814, f. 93b (vv. 14); 2. Trinity Camb. 1157, f. 41a (vv. 2); 3. Cotton Cleo. C. iv, f. 123b (vv. 12); 4. Harley 559, f. 39a (vv. 10); 5. Harley 7332, f. 28b (vv. 10); 6. Lansdowne 762, f. 96a (vv. 10); 7. Sloane 2578, f. 45b repeated at f. 67a, and variants at f. 45b, 52b, 64b; 8. Trinity Dublin 516, f. 118a (vv. 10).
5. Furnivall, *Ballads from MSS.*, Ballad Soc. I. 319; 8. Furnivall, *Thynne's Animadversions*, Chaucer Soc. 2s. XIII. xlv; Furnivall, *EETS* 9. xlv; Robbins, *Hist. Poems*, p. 120.

Euermore schalle the 6 be the best cast of the dyce   See 734.8.

735   [An acrostic to Elin. Cf. 737].
             1. Bodl. Lat. misc. c. 66 [*olim* Capesthorne], f. 92b col. ii,
             and repeated at f. 94b col. i.
             Robbins, *PMLA* LXV. 262.

735.3   Euer lenger þe wors / Lokys þe blynde hors
             A proverbial couplet.
             1. Bodl. 21626, f. 15b; 2. Rylands Lib. Latin 394, f. 7b.
             1. Förster, *Festschrift zum 12 Deutschen Neuphilologentage*,
             p. 45; 2. Pantin, *BJRL* XIV. 96.

735.5   Everlasting welthe with owte disconfeture
             Acrostic on Elisabetha Timwaw, Queen to Henry VII — vv. 16.
             1. Quaritch Cat. Illuminated MSS. 1931, No. 73.
             Quaritch Sale Cat. 532, Item 403.

736   repr. Science, *EETS* 170. xliii-iv.

737   [Cf. 735].
             1. Bodl. Lat. misc. c. 66 [*olim* Capesthorne), f. 93b.
             Robbins, *PMLA* LXV. 267.

738.5   Eueri day me comes tiþinge þre
             Three sorrowful things — three couplets. [Cf. 695, 1615, 3711-
             3, 3969].
             1. Pembroke Camb. 258, f. 134b.

739   Davies, *Med. Eng. Lyrics*, p. 156.

746   [Followed in one MS. by 3256].
             1. Furnivall, *EETS* 9. 122-6.

746.5   Euerich nyȝt þere a cok / Wakeþ som man or it dawe
             Verses on a table of brass, in Trevisa's translation of Higden's
             Polychronicon (Book I, Cap. 24) — five cross-rimed quatrains.
             1. St. John's Camb. 204; 2. Cotton Tiberius D. vii; 3.
             Harley 1900; 4. Stowe 65; 5. BM Addit. 24194; 6. Aberdeen
             Univ. 21; 7. Hunterian Mus. 83; 8. Penrose 12; 9. Morgan
             Lib. 275.

Trevisa, *Discripcion of Britayne,* Caxton, 1480 (STC 13440a); de Worde, 1498 (STC 13440b); Trevisa, *Prolicronycon,* Caxton, 1482 (STC 13438); de Worde, 1495 (STC 13439); Treveris, 1527 (STC 13440); 1. Babington and Lumby, *Rolls Series* XLI, i. 237, 239; Matzner, *AE Sprachproben,* II. 367.

747 Vuele men goid þe siechen / so deit þe seke þene leche

748 [Delete entire entry].

Yul mowth he spede / where þat he go   See 1442.5.

749 Rosenthal, *Vitae Patrum in Old & ME Lit.*, pp. 151-3.

750 2. Harley 2388, f. 57b.

751 four stanzas rime royal (defective), followed by 2308.5.
1. Cotton Vesp. D. ix, f. 188a.
Robbins, *Sec. Lyrics,* pp. 200-1.

752 thirty-four quatrains. [Cf. 2421].
Strutt, *Horda Angel-Cynnan,* III. 152; Robbins, *Sec. Lyrics,* pp. 209-14.

752.5 *Exilium* is contrari to his Ioyeng
On the casting of the dice according to the signs of the Zodiac—eleven irregular riming lines with some extra tags.
1. Harley 671, f. 1a.

753 Rickert, *Anc. Eng. Xmas Carols,* pp. 166-7; Copley, *Seven Eng. Songs,* 1940; Stevens, *Med. Carols,* p. 11; Robbins, *Early Eng. Xmas Carols,* p. 32.

Fayn I wolde blissed lorde yf it like þe   See 3563.5.

753.3 Fane wald I luve but quhair about
'Counsale in Luve,' attributed to William Dunbar—seven 5-line stanzas with refrain. [Utley 60].
1. Advocates 1. 1. 6, f. 255a.
Sibbald, *Chronicle,* I. 368-9; Laing, *Dunbar,* II. 31-2; *Bannatyne MS.,* Hunt. Club, IV. 744; Small, *STS* IV. 308-9; Schipper, *Dunbar,* pp. 433-4; and *DKAW* XLIII (I). 44-6; Baildon, *Dunbar,* pp. 224-5; Ritchie, *STS* n.s. XXVI. 13-14.

753.5   Faine wald I with all diligence
'The Danger of Wryting,' attributed to William Dunbar—seven 5-line stanzas with refrain: 'This watt I nocht quhairof to wryte.'
1. Pepys 2553, p. 210.
Pinkerton, *Anc. Scot. Poems*, II. 195-6; Laing, *Dunbar*, II. 49-50; Small, *STS* IV. 310-11; Schipper, *Dunbar*, pp. 437-8; and *DKAW* XLIII (I). 49-50; Baildon, *Dunbar*, pp. 227-8; Craigie, *STS* n.s. VII. 237-8.

753.8   Fayre and discrete fresche wommanly figure
A lover's offer of service—nine lines. [Cf. 754, 2318].
1. BM Addit. 5665, f. 72b.
Fehr, *Archiv* CVI. 280; Stevens, *Music & Poetry*, p. 342.

754   A letter from a lover to his mistress—six stanzas (vv. 59).
Robbins, *Sec. Lyrics*, pp. 202-4.

754.5   Faire laydis I pray yow tell me / Whos this ij fayre children be
A riddle—seven lines.
1. Westminster School: 3, f. 231b.
Wilson, *N&Q* CCX. 327.

Fayre lordings if you list to heere   See 1688 (Jhones print).

Fayrest of fayer and goodleste on lyve
The introductory stanza (vv. 6) to the Envoy (923) to *The Ile of Ladies* (3947): the power of his mistress for the poet's happiness (in Speght, 1598, f. 365b).

757   twenty lines, most of them illegible because of stains.

758   seven 8-line stanzas with refrain.
2. Laing, *Henryson*, 1865, p. 18; Wood, *Henryson*, pp. 215-6.

761   [Ringler 13].
2. BM Printed Book I B 49408: Alliaco, *Meditationes*, Caxton, n.d., f. 34b.
Boke of Huntyng, St. Albans, 1486 (STC 3308); *facs.* Blades, 1881; de Worde, 1496 (STC 3309); *repr.* Dibdin, *Typo. Antiquities*, II. 59; 2. Bühler, *Eng. Lang. Notes* I. 83.

762   Haupt and Hoffman, *Altdeutsche Blätter*, I. 396; Kuriyagawa, *Eigo Seinen* CI. nos. 5-8 (with Japanese tr.); Robbins, *Hist. Poems*, pp. 121-7.

763   Robbins, *Sec. Lyrics*, p. 207.

         Farewell aduent & haue good daye   See 905.5.

763.5   Fare well fare well / All fresh all chere
         'My true harte hathe slayne me,' a love letter in irregular stanzas with refrain: 'Alas for pure pite / From cruell dethe I cannot stert / My paynes be so mortal.'
         1. Coughton Court (roll) (probably xvi cent. hand).
         Rickert, *MP* XXXI. 198-9.

765   [This epitaph was frequently inscribed on monuments or brasses: a. St. Michael's, Crooked Lane, London, A.D. 1487; b. Romford, Essex; c. Northleach, Gloucestershire; d. Baldock, Hertfordshire; e. St. Martin's, Ludgate Hill, London (var.); f. Royston, Hertfordshire (var.); g. Maldon, Essex (var. in 6-line st., incl. st. 1 of 769). It forms the last stanza of 769.
         a-g. Gray, *N&Q* n.s. VIII. 133-4; b, d, e, g. Weever, *Anc. Funerall Monuments*, 1631, pp. 649, 545, 387, 610 (STC 25223); a. Stow, *Survey of London*, 1598, p. 175; g. Ravenshaw, *Antiente Epitaphes*, p. 10].

765.3   Fairweill my Hairt fairweill boyth freind and fa
         A love letter with anaphoric lines—four stanzas rime royal.
         1. Advocates 1. 1. 6, f. 225a.
         Bannatyne MS., Hunt. Club, III. 645; Ritchie, *STS* n.s. XXIII. 283.

765.5   Farewell my joy and my swete hart
         To his mistress: a lover on departing—two cross-rimed quatrains.
         1. BM Addit. 31922, f. 66b.
         Flügel, *Anglia* XII. 244; Flügel, *Neuengl. Lesebuch*, p. 136; Stevens, *Music & Poetry*, p. 409; Stevens, *Music at Court*, pp. 48-9.

766   Robbins, *Sec. Lyrics*, p. 207.

767   2. Advocates 1. 1. 6, f. 225a (var. st. 2, 3, 4).
         1, 2. Bolle, *Anglia* XXXIV. 297; 1. Robbins, *Sec. Lyrics*, pp. 208-9; 2. *Bannatyne MS.*, Hunt. Club, III. 646; Ritchie, *STS* n.s. XXIII. 284-5.

768   1. Bodl. Lat. misc. c. 66 [*olim* Capesthorne], f. 93b.
         Robbins, *PMLA* LXV. 268.

769   [For st. 5 occurring separately see 765].
         3. Delete this MS., and delete pr. *Rel. Ant.*, I. 268.
         2. Davies, *Med. Eng. Lyrics*, pp. 206-7.

769.5   Fart on hyll / and fart ther þu nylle
         A proverbial couplet.
         1. Rylands Lib. Latin 394, f. 16b.
         Pantin, *BJRL* XIV. 103.

770   1. Hereford Cath. O. iv. 14, f. 213b.

771   3. Sion Coll. Arc. L. 40. 2/E. 25, ff. 39a-47b (vv. 1-413 of MS. 2).

772   *Sydrac and Boctus* (longer version), translated from the French by Hugh of Campeden—about 22,250 lines in couplets. [For the abridged version see 2147; see also *Boccus and Sydrake*, ca. 1532; and cf. Bülbring, *Sidrac in England*, Halle 1902].
         2. Lansdowne 793, ff. 1a-181a; 3. *olim* Meyerstein [*olim* Wrest Park; Sotheby Sale, Dec. 17, 1952, Lot 466; Quaritch Sale Cat. 713, 1953, Lot 467] (begins and ends imperfectly).

772.5   ffader & son and holy gost / Gret god in trinite
         A carol to the Trinity—three quatrains and burden (st. 1 = st. 1 of 774).
         1. Egerton 3307, f. 55a.
         Stevens, *Med. Carols*, p. 40; Greene, *Sel. Eng. Carols*, p. 120.

774   (st. 1 = st. 1 of 772.5).

775   2. N. S. Baugh, *Worcestershire Misc.*, pp. 104-5, 125-8.

778   [For extracts occurring separately see 516 and 937].
         2. Camb. Un. Ii. 4. 9, f. 97a (lacks Prologue); 5. Osborn 5 [*olim* Bowes Midland], Yale Univ. Deposit; 6. Folger Lib. 420312 [*olim* Clopton], ff. 1a-84a.

779   1. *Rel. Lyr. XIV C.*, pp. 219-22.

780	4. BM Addit. 37787, f. 142a. 4. N. S. Baugh, *Worcestershire Misc.*, pp. 122-4.
782	[Cf. 782.5]. Greene, *Sel. Eng. Carols*, p. 118.
782.5	Father I am thine onlye soone '*Nolo mortem peccatoris*'—twenty-three 6-line stanzas with this refrain. [Cf. 782]. 1. BM Addit. 15233, f. 37a.
782.8	Fadir y may no la[n]gir duhel Nine English couplets following a Latin tale about a householder who loved a boy '*carnaliter.*' 1. Leicester City Lib., Old Town 4, p. 41.
783	Robbins, *Sec. Lyrics*, p. 100.
786	1. Ipswich County Hall Deposit: Hillwood [*olim* Brome], f. 15a.
787	Camden, *Remains*, 1633, p. 24; 1870, p. 29; Haupt and Hoffman, *Altdeutsche Blätter*, II. 141-2.
790	1. Egerton 3245 [*olim* Gurney], f. 1b.
790.5	Fader sone and holy goost / Lord to the I make my moone *Oracio devota in anglicis verbis:* to the Trinity—thirty quatrains. 1. Bodl. Lyell 30, ff. 62b-65b.
	Fader þat hart in heuene See 2074 (Pavia).
790.8	Fader to þe bowe / þe sune to þe lowe A proverbial couplet. Maitland, *Bracton's Note Book*, London 1887, III. 501.
791	19. Winchester Coll. 33, f. 33a. 8. D' Evelyn and Mill, *EETS* 235. 128.
	Feld haþ eye wode haþ ere See 3502.5

793.5 ffelow yff þou haste þe kyde
Proverbial lines in a Latin and English collection—two couplets.
1. NLW Peniarth 356, p. 298.

795 *Early Eng. Lyrics,* p. 201; Robbins, *MLN* LXXIV. 199; Robbins, *Sec. Lyrics,* p. 8; Stevens, *Med. Carols,* p. 113.

798 10. Furnivall, *EETS* 15 orig. ed. 233-4; rev. ed. 262.

799 [Cf. inscription in Oxford tavern, pr. Hole, *Eng. Custom & Usage,* p. 106].
1. Ipswich County Hall Deposit: Hillwood [*olim* Brome], f. 1b.

800 1. Bowers, *MLN* LI. 429-31.

Fyrst blak and wyte and also rede
Continuation of 2656 (Trinity Camb. 916, p. 152). [Singer 850].

801 [Sometimes used as conclusion to 2666. Singer 8].
2. Bodl. 7654, f. 74b.
Ashmole, *Theatrum Chemicum,* p. 33 (vv. 19).

ffurst yn thi mesure looke ther be no lak
See 576 (st. on *Justitia*).

802 1. Bodl. 4127, f. 212a.
Bloomfield, *Seven Deadly Sins,* p. 169.

802.5 First loke and aftirward lepe / Avyse the well or thow speke
A proverbial couplet against hasty tongue.
1. Bodl. 21626, f. 31b.
Förster, *Festschrift zum 12 Deutschen Neuphilologentage,* p. 57.

803 1. Bodl. 2078, ff. 195a-203b (f. 195 torn; ff. 197, 201 mutilated); 2. Bodl. 3896, ff. 148b-154a.

First of thy Rising   See 799 (Oxford inscription).

[92]

805   First IJ and then J than IIJ and than V / than IJ and than
        IJ and IIIJ go belyve
           'Seynt Thomas Lottis,' a puzzle—one couplet.

806   Person, *Camb. ME Lyrics,* pp. 22-3.

           Five hundreth thowsande for to say   See 3443.

807.5   Flaterie flourith / Treuth plourith
           Couplet in a sermon by Thomas Brinton.
           1. Harley 3760, f. 62b.
              Devlin, *Speculum* XIV. 334; Devlin, *Camden Soc.* 3 s.
              LXXXV. 113.

808   2. Harley 3362, f. 24a (vv. 33).

809   [Ringler 14].
           2. Bodl. 3356, f. 210b (3 st.); 18. Leyden Univ. Vossius 9,
           f. 96a; 21. BM Cat. 643. m. 4: transcripts by William Thomas
           in 1721 of burned Cotton Otho A. 18, pasted into copy of
           Urry's *Chaucer,* II. 548; 22. Coventry Corp. Rec. off., f. 77a;
           23. Nottingham Univ. Me LM 1 [*olim* Mellish], flyleaves.
           Temple of Bras, Caxton, ca. 1478 (STC 5091); de Worde;
           and later prints; Clarke, *Riches of Chaucer,* 1835, II. 314
           (mod.); 8. 15, Pace, *MLN* LXIII. 458-60; 7. Girvan, *STS*
           3 s. XI. 175; 13. Brusendorff, *Chaucer Tradition,* pp. 246-8;
           Robinson, *Chaucer,* 1933, p. 631; 1957, p. 536; Davies,
           Med. Eng. Lyrics, pp. 135-6; 21. Pace, *Speculum* XXVI.
           366-7.

811   [Cf. 2010. Utley 65].
           2. Armagh, Bishop John Swayne's Register (two 6-line st.).
           1. Wright, *Pol. Poems,* II. 252.

811.5   Folke discomforted bere heuy countenaunce
           The letter of Dydo—Prologue in nine stanzas rime royal,
           Letter to Aeneas in 242 lines of heroic couplets, and an Envoy
           in two stanzas rime royal.
              The Boke of Fame, Pynson, 1526 (STC 5088).

813   Jones, *Inst. Hist. Medicine Bull.* V. 575; [Masters,] *Rymes
           of Minstrels,* p. 13; Robbins, *Sec. Lyrics,* p. 102; Kaiser,
           Anthologie, p. 312; Kaiser, *Med. Eng.,* p. 523; Davies,
           Med. Eng. Lyrics, p. 235.

813.3   For age is a page / For the courte full vnmete
'Why come ye nat to Courte?' by John Skelton—vv. 1248 in 'skeltonics.' [For prefatory lines see 194.5].
1. Bodl. 12653, f. 36a (incomplete).
Kele, ca. 1545 (STC 22594); *repr.* Dyce, *Skelton*, II. 27-67; Dyce and Child, *Skelton & Donne*, II. 276-320; Skeat, *Specimens*, 1887, pp. 138-47 (extracts); Flügel, *Neuengl. Lesebuch*, pp. 62-7; Henderson, *Skelton*, 1931, pp. 338-75; 1948, 1959, pp. 308-45; Williams, *Selection*, 1902, pp. 142-80; Wyght, n.d. (STC 22595); Kytson, n.d. (STC 22596); *Workes*, Marshe, 1568 (STC 22608); *repr.* [? J. Bowle,] 1736; Chalmers, *English Poets*, II. 271-81; 1. Zupitza, *Archiv* LXXXV. 429-36.

813.5   ffor all þe blod I sched for þe / bot hertely luffe I aske to me
A couplet in a scroll attached to a drawing of the wound in Christ's heart.
1. Bodl. Lat. misc. c. 66 [*olim* Capesthorne], f. 129b.

813.6   For as ye lyst my wyll ys bent
'Even as ye lyst,' ascribed to Thomas Wyatt—seven 5-line stanzas with this refrain, and (MS. 1 only) 2-line burden. [Cf. Greene, *RES* n.s. XV. 178-9].
1. BM Addit. 17492, f. 20a; 2. BM Addit. 18752, f. 89b.
1, 2. *Early Eng. Carols*, pp. 315-6; 1. Foxwell, I. 276; Muir, p. 106; 2. Reed, *Anglia* XXXIII. 362.

813.8   ffore better hit were stil to be
Against the sin of 'rabylding' divine service by 'ianglers, haukers, and hunters'—three lines in a prose treatise.
1. Bodl. 21876, f. 32b.

814   one 6-line stanza (preceded by eight French stanzas).
3. Camb. Un. Gg. 1. 1 (with one extra st.); 4. Cotton Julius A. v, f. 149a; 9. Delete this MS.; 13. Harley 114, f. 138a (A Text).
11. Wilson, *Lost Lit.*, p. 210.

815   Seventeen quatrains...with an introductory and a concluding stanza in rime royal.

816   2. Camb. Un. Add. 2585 (I), f. 1b.
1. Davies, *Med. Eng. Lyrics*, pp. 181-2; 2. Robbins, *MLN* LXVI. 504-5.

817   Robbins, *Hist. Poems*, pp. 39-44.

817.5   For feyre wyfes / mony losyn her lyfes
           A proverbial couplet.
           1. Rylands Lib. Latin 394, f. 3b.
           Pantin, *BJRL* XIV. 93.

818   Hearne, *Hemingi Chartularium Ecclesiae Wigorniensis*, 1723, II. 663; Robbins, *Hist. Poems*, p. 203.

*819.5   *For full fayne I wold do that myght you please
           The Romans of Partenay or of Lusigen (The Tale of Melusine) —vv. 6615 in rime royal stanzas.
           1. Trinity Camb. 597, f. 1a (imperfect).
           Skeat, *EETS* 22.

820   Goldberg, *Die Catonischen Distichen*, Leipzig 1883, pp. 15-24.

822   Robbins, *Hist. Poems*, pp. 108-10.

823   [Following 2386].
           Robbins, *Sec. Lyrics*, p. 288; Seaton, *Sir Richard Roos*, p. 114; Bennett, *RES* n.s. XIII. 176.

*823.3   *For he it seiȝe wiþ siȝt / Now bigin ichil of him
           Roland and Vernagu—vv. 880 in 12-line stanzas.
           1. Advocates 19. 2. 1, ff. 263a-267b (imperfect at beginning and end).
           Maidment, *Abbotsford Club* 1836; Herrtage, *EETS* xxxix. 37-61.

823.5   ffor he mai leefe & he mai fynde
           Christ's love for man—two couplets in a Latin sermon.
           1. Bodl. 29746, f. 177b.

824   [Sometimes preceded by three stanzas: see 4112. For a disarranged and defective version see 1418. Ringler 15].
           14. Trinity Camb. 263, f. 112b; 18. Harley 541, ff. 209b, 207a, 207b (leaf misplaced); 25. Royal 17. B. xlvii, f. 2a (11 st.); 30. BM Addit. 10099, f. 211b (disarranged: 13 st.); 39. Trinity Dublin 516, f. 27b; 42. Leyden Univ. Vossius 9, f. 99a; 43. Nat. Lib. of Medicine 4, ff. 64-7; 45. Fitzwilliam Mus. 261, ff. 30a-32; 46. Bodl. Lat. th. d. 15, f. 132a; 47. Trinity Camb.

1117, ff. 132b, 132a; 48. Cotton Titus D. xx, ff. 93a-94a (begins v. 35); 49. Nottingham Univ. Me LM 1 [*olim* Mellish], endleaves; 50. Wellcome Hist. Med. Lib. 406 [*olim* Loscombe, *olim* Ashburnham 122], f. 39b (var., ca. 1575); 51. Wellcome Hist. Med. Lib. 411, f. 2b; 52. Rome: English Coll. 1306, f. 87b; 53. *olim* Schwerdt [Sotheby Sale, Mar. 12, 1942; present location not known].

7. Neilson and Webster, *Chief Brit. Poets*, pp. 221-2; Robbins, *Sec. Lyrics*, pp. 73-6; 25. cf. *The Gouernayle of Helthe*, Caxton, 1489 (STC 12138); de Worde, ca. 1510 (STC 12139); 34. *Bannatyne MS.*, Hunt. Club., pp. 196-9; Ritchie, *STS* n.s. XXII. 178-80; 35. Stevenson, *STS* LXV. 30-2; 36. [Delete this reference]; 43. [Delete this reference].

825   Rickert, *Anc. Eng. Xmas Carols*, p. 188.

825.3   for honger gred y the to feden
           The practical works of mercy—seven lines.
           1. Bodl. 8714, f. i verso.

825.5   ffor I am dughti of dede wo so will me knowe / be þe kyte he may se þe pocok and þe crowe
           An English couplet in a Latin sermon.
           1. Camb. Un. Ii. 3. 8, f. 42a.

825.8   For I ham pore withouten frendes
           Two couplets translating '*Si fas esset loqui &c.*'
           1. Advocates 18. 7. 21, f. 87b.

826   On the value of prayer—twenty-nine riming lines in the prose treatise, *Pupilla Oculi*.
           Person, *Camb. ME Lyrics*, p. 30.

           For ȝif þe louerd bidd fle   See 1426.5.

827.5   for it is mery to ben a wyfe / deye I wylle and lese my lyfe
           A couplet translating '*Nupcie moriar quia nubere dulce est.*' [Occurs in some MSS. of *Fasciculus Morum*].
           1. Caius 71, f. 88a; 2. Caius 364, f. 145a; 3. Harley 7322, f. 45b.
               1. Robbins, *Sec. Lyrics*, p. xxxix; 3. Furnivall, *EETS* 15 rev. ed. 250.

*827.8   *ffor it es pryuelaged als we se
           A tract on the *Pater Noster*—about 2800 lines in couplets.
           1. Harley 6718, ff. 16a-33a.

828   [Originally a triple ballade].
           1. MacCracken, *Archiv* CXXVII. 236; 2 (with st. 5 from 1). Cohen, *Ballade*, pp. 287-9.

832   Two moral couplets advocating mercy (vv. 3-4 = 77).

834   For loue of Iesu my swete herte / y morne & seke wyþ teres smert
           A couplet in a Latin homily (and repeated *passim*).

           ffor man without mercy of mercy shall misse   See 77.

*834.5   *For myne owne ware / I tell the syr
           Fragment of a Robin Hood ballad—vv. 124 in 12-line tail-rime stanzas.
           Two leaves, n.d. [Lambeth Palace]; *repr*. Maitland, *Early Printed Books at Lambeth*, 1845; Gutch, *Robin Hood*, 1847, II. 46-50.

835.5   ffor my pastyme vpon a day
           A lover's plaint—four quatrains and burden: 'Colle to me the rysshys grene.'
           1. Royal App. 58, f. 4a (burden only again at f. 14b). Ritson, *Anc. Songs*, 1829, I. lxxv; Furnivall, *Captain Cox*, Ballad Soc., 1871, p. cliii; Flügel, *Anglia* XII. 259-60; Chappell, *OE Pop. Music*, I. 38-9; Padelford, *Early XVI Cent. Lyrics*, p. 83.

836   Counsels of prudence—one quatrain. [Followed by 2356]. Macray, *Cat.*, V. 79.

837.5   For nowe vpon þis first day I wil my choys renuwe
           A lover's New Year gift, 'Amerous balade by Lydegate'—twenty-three 3-line stanzas with introductory couplet: 'In honnour of þis hegh fest of custome &c.'
           1. BM Addit. 16165, f. 253b.
           Hammond, *Anglia* XXXII. 194-6; MacCracken, *EETS* 192. 424-7; *Poets of Eng. Lang.*, I. 225-8.

839   1. Edinburgh Univ. 27, f. 288a.

For Scotes at Dunbar See 848.

841 [See 3558.5 for *Brut* version. Ringler 73a].
1. Bodl. 3904, f. 8a; 4. Cotton Julius A. v, f. 148a; 9. Delete this MS.; 13. Harley 114, f. 137a (A Text).
1, 3, 7. Wright, *Camden Soc.* VI. 298, 395; 4. Wilson, *Lost Lit.*, p. 210.

*842.5 *For that power haven not we / Him hol to Maken in non degre
The Holy Grail, by Henry Lovelich—in couplets.
1. Corpus Christi Camb. 80, f. 197a (leaves misplaced; vv. 23932).
Furnivall, *Seynt Graal or The Sank Ryal*, Roxburghe Club, 1861, 1863, LXXX; Furnivall, *EETS* xx, xxiv, xxviii, and xxx.

843.5 For þe loue of God & in the way of charitie
Epitaph on John Maners, A.D. 1492—one stanza rime royal.
Dugdale, *Warwickshire*, 1656, facing p. 349.

847 1. Balliol 149, f. 35b; 2. Magdalen Oxf. 93, f. 140a; 3. Trinity Dublin 277, p. 193.

848 Meyer, *Romania* XV. 314 (vv. 4-9 only); Wilson, *Lost Lit.*, p. 211.

For ther wottys no creature what peyn that I endure See 303.

848.5 for thylke grounde þat beareth the wedes wycke
One stanza (I. 946-52) from *Troilus and Criseyde* (3327) occurring separately.
1. BM Addit. 17492, f. 59b.
Southall, *RES* n.s. XV. 144.

849 Robbins, *Hist. Poems*, p. 62.

849.5 For thou haste pleyde enough I saye
Couplet tag in *Gesta Romanorum*. [Cf. 3818.5].
1. BM Addit. 9066, f. 65a.
Herbert, *Cat. Rom.*, III. 258.

850 Furnivall, *EETS* 15 orig. ed. 241; rev. ed. 269.

For though I had yow to-morow
Extract (BM Addit. 17492, f. 91a) from 3670.

851 [For further extracts occurring separately cf. 2782. Ringler 16].
6. Sloane 1212, f. 1a (vv. 736-54), f. 2a (vv. 98-162).
Temple of Glas, Caxton, ca. 1478 (STC 17032); *facs.* Jenkinson, 1905; de Worde, ca. 1498 (STC 17032a); de Worde, ca. 1500 (STC 17033); Pynson, ca. 1505 (STC 12954); Berthelet, n.d. (STC 12955); Berthelet, ca. 1530 (Selden D. 45) (STC 17034).

*851.3 *. . .for þi sake man to whom yf þou call at a
Fragment of a poem on Christ's pleading, with a fragment of a burden.
1. New York Pub. Lib. Drexel Fragments 4180.
Stevens, *Music & Poetry*, p. 426.

*851.6 *For þi self man þou may see
'How *iudicare* come in crede'—in 8-line stanzas. [Cf. 3819. Cf. Tilley, J 98].
1. Lambeth 491, Part II, f. 295a.
Bülbring, *Archiv* LXXXVI. 387-8; Utley, *Medieval St.* VIII. 304-5.

For to kenne þe veynes to late blood
See 3848 (Trinity Camb. 921, var.).

853 ten 6-line stanzas.
1. Camb. Un. Ff. 1. 6, f. 143b.
Robbins, *PMLA* LXIX. 636-8; Person, *Camb. ME Lyrics*, pp. 56-8.

853.2 for to saye havyng non atorryte
One stanza rime royal signed by John Mereley on unusual behaviour by 'ane ydell parson.'
1. Bodl. 2285, f. 5a.

853.3 forto stoppe þe strem of loue þat draws to synne
A couplet in a Latin sermon.
1. Balliol 149, f. 72b.

853.4 ffor was hyt neuer myn kynd / Chese in welle to fynd
A couplet in Nicolas Bozon's *Contes moralisés*.
1. Harley 1288, f. 100b; 2. BM Addit. 46919 [*olim* Phillipps 8336], f. 126a; 3. Gray's Inn 12, f. 43a.
    1, 3. Ross, *Neuphil. Mitteilungen* L. 210; 1. Herbert, *Cat. Rom.*, III. 104; 3. Smith, *SATF*, p. 151.

853.6 For when þe hounde knawithe þe bone / þan of felishippe kepeþ he none
One proverbial couplet in a sermon.
1. Royal 18. B. xxiii, f. 81b.
    Ross, *EETS* 209. 89.

853.8 For whan the roof of thyn hous lyth upon thy nese
'Al thys werldly blisse to the ne is worith a pese'—a proverbial couplet in a sermon by Brinton. [Cf. 3998].
1. Harley 3760, ff. 201a, 244b.
    Devlin, *Speculum* XIV. 334-5; Devlin, *Camden Soc.* 3 s. LXXXVI. 337, 402.

For why goode lord thou haste me saved & kepte
Additional stanza (Bodl. 6943, f. 134b) to 951.

854 [See also 726. Ringler 17].
14. Harley 172, f. 52b; 32 Göttingen Univ. Cod. philol. 163 n, ff. 45b-72a; 33. Rome: English Coll. 1306, f. 90b.
    Paruus Catho, Caxton, ca. 1477 (STC 4850); *facs.* Jenkinson, 1906; Caxton, ca. 1478; ca. 1480; 1 (with 8, st. 1-7). Förster, *Archiv* CXV. 304-23, CXVI. 25-34.

*854.3 *For wynde or Rayne ffor water or colde or hete
The Three Kings of Cologne, attributed to Lydgate—vv. 859 in rime royal stanzas.
1. BM Addit. 31042, ff. 100a-119b (about vv. 100 missing at beginning).
    MacCracken, *Archiv* CXXIX. 50-68.

854.5 For Winefrede virgine pure / That ouercomminge
Hymn to St. Winifred, in a Litany of St. Winifred in English—seven stanzas with concluding couplet.
1. Rylands Lib. Latin 165, quire c.

854.8 ffor wodecoke snyte curlew also
Recipe for preparing woodcock—eleven couplets. [Cf. 2361].
1. Pepys 1047, f. 15b.

855 1. Bodl. Lat. misc. c. 66 [*olim* Capesthorne], f. 94b.
Robbins, *PMLA* LXV. 274-5.

856 Wood, *Henryson,* pp. 199-201; Elliott, pp. 112-4.

856.5 fformynge in me the maner off my lyffe
'A blisful thynge were comyn gouernaunce'—one 8-line stanza, actually st. 77 of Walton's *Boethius* (1597) occurring separately. [Cf. 2820].
1. Bühler 17, flyleaf 4b.
Bühler, *English Lang. Notes* II. 4.

858.5 fforsake youre synne þat doon amys / And sue þe weye þat ledeth to blis
A couplet (based on Eph. III) used as heading to Latin sermon.
1. Caius 230, f. 91b.

858.8 fore-swore fore-lore / ffore evyr more / Tak þis fore lore
A tag written in a margin.
1. Royal 8. C. vii, f. 161a.

*Forht com ay knyth of that land   See *4194.5.

Forth went we thoo vnto dame hopes place
'*Tractatus de Spe*' at end of 3406.

859.5 Fortunate is he who hathe the happe
Felix quem faciunt aliena pericula cautum'—one couplet.
1. Durham Univ. Cosin V. iii. 9, f. 82b.
Furnivall, *EETS* lxi. 224.

860 3. BM Addit. 34360, f. 19a (20 st.).

860.3 Fortune ys varyant ay tornyng her whele / He ys wyse þat ys ware or he harm fele
A proverbial couplet included in a series of six (4137).
1. Balliol 354, f. 160a.
Flügel, *Anglia* XXVI. 174; Dyboski, *EETS* ci. 139.

860.5 Foule fende away thou flee
St. Katherine's charm for banishing despair (in *Gesta Romanorum*)—four lines.
1. BM Addit. 9066, f. 77a.
Herrtage, *EETS* xxxiii. 404.

861 Four victims of tyranny—two couplets.

861.5 Four maner of folkis ar evill to pleis
'Of folkis evill to pleis' by William Dunbar—seven quatrains with refrain: 'And wald have part fra utheris by.'
1. Camb. Un. Ll. 5. 10, f. 3a; 2. Advocates 1. 1. 6, p. 47 (vv. 9-24) and f. 66b (lacks st. 7).
1. Laing, *Dunbar*, I. 173-4; Paterson, *Dunbar*, pp. 89-90; Schipper, *Dunbar*, pp. 278-9; and *DKAW* XLI (IV). 80-1; Baildon, *Dunbar*, pp. 141-2; Craigie, *STS* n.s. XX. 45-6; MacKenzie, *Dunbar*, pp. 48-9; 2a, 2b. Ritchie, *STS* 3 s. V. 78; n.s. XXII. 163; 2b. [Hailes,] *Anc. Scot. Poems*, pp. 210-11; Sibbald, *Chronicle*, III. 224; *Bannatyne MS.*, Hunt. Club, II. 180.

861.8 Vour þynges ȝe ofte ysoeth
Four sorrowful things—two short couplets in AN poem on Morality.
1. BM Addit. 46919 [*olim* Phillipps 8336], f. 85a.

864 Patterson, *Shakespearean Studies*, 1916, pp. 436-7; Trend, *Music & Letters* IX. 112; Dickins and Wilson, *Early ME Texts*, p. 119; Kaiser, *Anthologie*, p. 291; Kaiser, *Med. Eng.*, p. 463; Mason, *Humanism & Poetry*, p. 158; Stemmler, *Die englischen Liebesgedichte des MS. Harley 2253*, Bonn 1962, p. 89; Davies, *Med. Eng. Lyrics*, p. 52.

864.5 ffrance and fflaunders than shall ryse
A political prophecy—one cross-rimed quatrain.
1. Lansdowne 762, f. 53b.

865.5 ffree lusti fresch most goodly
Opening words only of a love song, preserved with one staff of music.
1. Camb. Un. Kk. 6. 30, f. 130a.
Stevens, *Music & Poetry*, p. 438.

865.8   Fredome honour and nobilness
'Of covetyce' by William Dunbar—eleven quatrains with refrain: 'All all for causs of cuvetice.'
1. Camb. Un. Ll. 5. 10, f. 9a; 2. Pepys 2553, p. 6; 3. Advocates 1. 1. 6, f. 64b.
2. Craigie, STS n.s. VII. 5-6; 3. Ramsay, *Evergreen*, II. 95-7; *repr. Ramsay and Earlier Scot. Poets*, p. 277; *Poems in Scot. Dialect*, 1748, pp. 28-9; [Hailes,] *Anc. Scot. Poems*, pp. 212-4; Sibbald, *Chronicle*, II. 17-8; Laing, *Dunbar*, I. 175-6; *Bannatyne MS.*, Hunt. Club, I. 175-6; Small, STS IV. 158-9; Schipper, *Dunbar*, pp. 309-11; and *DKAW* XLII (IV). 7-9; Baildon, *Dunbar*, pp. 160-2; Ritchie, STS n.s. XXII. 159-60; MacKenzie, *Dunbar*, pp. 141-2.

866   1. BM Addit. 43491, f. 22a.
Fenn, *Paston Letters*, II. 234.

867   Bullrich, *Über Charles d'Orleans*, 1893, p. 22 (2 st. only); Arber, *Dunbar Anthology*, pp. 120-2.

868   Furnivall, *EETS* 15 orig. ed. 41-2; rev. ed. 69-70.

869   [Cf. 3291].
1. Robbins, *Sec. Lyrics*, pp. 129-30.

870   A plea to his mistress—a roundel. [Cf. 3751.3].
Robbins, *Sec. Lyrics*, p. 159.

870.5   ffrere gastkyn wo ye be
Against over-wandering friars, "quod Raff Drake"—thirteen macaronic couplets.
1. Royal App. 58, f. 24b.
Rimbault, *Songs & Ballads*, p. 35; Flügel, *Anglia* XII. 268.

870.8   ffrere tamas stanfeld / god almegtheie hem it ȝelde
John Crophill's Loving Cups, an ale-wives' poem—eight 8-line stanzas with a concluding 6-line stanza.
1. Harley 1735, f. 48a.

871   Robbins, *Hist. Poems*, pp. 164-5.

    ffrend an we ar ffer In det   See 1608 (Harley).

871.5   Frende of that ere I knew / & I lowe and schal
        To his mistress—six quatrains.
        1. Trinity Dublin 641, f. 1a.

873.5   ffrendschupe þat chawnachit nowth / Enles lordschupe þat deyth nowth
        A couplet in a Latin sermon.
        1. Camb. Un. Ii. 3. 8, f. 167a.

873.8   ffro al maner thevys and vntrew men
        A charm against thieves—twelve couplets and two Latin quatrains.
        1. Bodl. 817, f. 2b.

874   'Delicta iuuentutis mee'—three couplets.
        1. Robbins, *Neophilologus* XXXVIII. 39.

        *Fra chamber went Gy   See *4194.5.

875   5. Leyden Univ. Vossius 9, f. 17a; 6. Harvard Coll. Eng. 530, f. 4b; 7. Peterborough Pub. Lib., ff. 54a-63b.

        Fram heven into the clerkes bour   See 282-5.

878   Rickert, *Anc. Eng. Xmas Carols*, pp. 32-3; Segar, *Med. Anthology*, pp. 83-4; Segar, *Some Minor Poems*, pp. 11-12.

        From her childhoode as I fynde that she fled
        Printed as fragment of otherwise unknown ballad by Dibdin, *Typo. Antiquities*, I. 60; actually a leaf of *Canterbury Tales:* VII. 2255-65, IX. 9-20. [Ringler 17a].

        From stormy wyndis & grevous wethir
        Burden to 2394.5.

879.5   Fro þe seed of sorwe þat is synne
        A prayer for heaven's bliss—one long couplet in Lavynham's *Tretys*.
        1. Bodl. 655; 2. Bodl. 12146; 3. Bodl. 21634; 4. Camb. Un. Ff. 6. 31; 5. Trinity Camb. 305; 6. Harley 211, f. 46b; 7. Harley 1197; 8. Harley 1288; 9. Harley 2383; 10. Royal 8. C. i; 11. Leeds Univ., Brotherton 501; 12. London: Dr. Williams' Lib. Anc. 3; 13. Norwich: St. Peter Hungate Mus. 48. 158. 926; 14. Soc. of Antiquaries [*olim* Bright].
        6. Zutphen, *A Litil Tretys by Lavynham*, pp. xiii, 25.

882   2. Delete this MS.; 3. Peterborough Pub. Lib., ff. 49a-52b.

883   William Wey's *Itineraries to Jerusalem:* Part I only (Parts II & III in Latin)—vv. 352 in couplets. [For a text with many similar lines see 986].
           Bandinel, *Roxburghe Club* LXXVI. 8-19.

884   Robbins, *Hist. Poems*, pp. 127-30.

886   [Utley 72].

886.5   Full oft I muse and hes in thocht
           'Best to be blyth' by William Dunbar—eight 5-line stanzas with refrain.
           1. Camb. Un. Ll. 5. 10, f. 43a (7 st.); 2. Pepys 2553, p. 337 (7 st.); 3. Advocates 1. 1. 6, f. 98b and f. 115b (vv. 1-9 only).
           2. Small, *STS* IV. 110-11: Craigie, *STS* n.s. VII. 410-11; 3. [Hailes,] *Anc. Scot. Poems*, pp. 73-5; Pinkerton, *Sel. Scot. Ballads*, 1783, II. 60-2; *Sel. Poems of Dunbar*, Perth 1788, pp. 64-5; Laing, *Dunbar*, I. 187-8; *repr. Blackwood's Magazine*, Feb. 1835; *Bannatyne MS.*, Hunt. Club, II. 281-2, 329; Paterson, *Dunbar*, pp. 48-9; Eyre-Todd, *Med. Scot. Poetry*, pp. 211-2; Schipper, *Dunbar*, pp. 335-7; and *DKAW* XLII (IV). 33-5; Baildon, *Dunbar*, pp. 173-4; Ritchie, *STS* n.s. XXII. 260-1; MacKenzie, *Dunbar*, pp. 143-4; Kinsley, *Dunbar*, pp. 66-7.

887   Stevens, *Med. Carols*, p. 70.

888   [Cf. 3305].
           Trend, *Music & Letters* IX. 114; *New Oxford Hist. Music*, III. 116; Davies, *Med. Eng. Lyrics*, pp. 100-1.

889   3. Robbins, *MLN* LVIII. 40-1; Stevens, *Med. Carols*, p. 111; Robbins, *Early Eng. Xmas Carols*, p. 64.

890   2. Balliol 354, f. 221b (4 st.).
           2. Rickert, *Anc. Eng. Xmas Carols*, p. 29; Segar, *Med. Anthology*, p. 85.

891   Robbins, *Sec. Lyrics*, p. xxxvi; Wilson, *Lost Lit.*, p. 188.

892   Furnivall, *Academy* 1896, No. 1269, p. 146; Robbins, *Hist. Poems*, pp. 138-9.

892.5   Galauntis purse penyles *per vicos ecce vagrantur*
                One macaronic couplet on 'Galaunt.'
                1. Lansdowne 762, f. 92a.
                Rel. Ant., I. 288.

                Gardein ways cumfort of flowres   See 597.5.

896   1. Longleat 30, f. 22b.

897   2. Furnivall, *EETS* 15 orig. ed. 145-6; rev. ed. 174-5.

                Gaudeamus synge we *in hoc sacro tempore*   See 2111.

899   The Battle of Barnet—four 8-line stanzas.
                Robbins, *Hist. Poems*, pp. 226-7.

903   Robbins, *Sec. Lyrics*, pp. 10-11; Greene, *Sel. Eng. Carols*, p. 153; Speirs, *Med. Eng. Poetry*, pp. 86-7; Davies, *Med. Eng. Lyrics*, pp. 276-7.

904   By 'Richardoune.'

905.5   Get the hence what doest thou here
                Farewell to Advent—two quatrains and burdens. [Cf. 4197].
                Christmas Carolles, ? Copland, ca. 1550 (Douce fragments *f. 48*); *facs.* Reed, *Xmas Carols*, p. 14; *repr.* Flügel, *Anglia* XII. 588; Flügel, *Neuengl. Lesebuch*, p. 124; Rickert, *Anc. Eng. Xmas Carols*, pp. 54-5; *Early Eng. Carols*, p. 5.

906   [See ed. Herrtage, p. 360. Cf. 2078.5, 2167, and 2818.2].
                12. Delete this MS.; 13. Trinity Dublin 517, f. 132b; 16. Bodl. 1654, f. 10a (var. vv. 3); 17. Bodl. 2649, f. viii recto (var. vv. 7); 18. Bodl. 21681, f. 55a; 19. Trinity Camb. 1157, f. 72a (vv. 1-4 lacking); 20. Rylands Lib. Latin 394, f. 15b (var. vv. 4); 21. Cox [*olim* Harmsworth; Sotheby Sale, Oct. 1945, Lot 1956].
                5, 10. Robbins, *Hist. Poems*, pp. 143-4, 326-7; 2, 15. Brown, *Archiv* CXXVIII. 76; 3, 10. Herrtage, *EETS* xxxiii.

500, 360; 9. Madden, *Roxburghe Club* 1838, LV. 398; 14. Peter, *Complaint & Satire*, p. 68; 16. Förster, *Eng. Stn.* XXXI. 15; 20. Pantin, *BJRL* XIV. 102; 21. J. S. Cox, *Lit. Repository* 1957, IV. 1.

907 13. Bodl. 6924, f. 228b; 14. Cotton Jul. D. IX, f. 232b.
   4. D'Evelyn and Mill, *EETS* 236. 610; 10. Mätzner, *AE Sprachproben*, p. 177 (vv. 1787-2398); 13. Thiemke, *Palaestra* CXXXI. 14.

908.2 ʒeue me and I the / and so shull we frendes be
   A proverbial couplet.
   1. Bodl. 21626, f. 13b; 2. Rylands Lib. Latin 394, f. 5a.
   1. Förster, *Festschrift zum 12 Deutschen Neuphilologentage*, p. 44; 2. Pantin, *BJRL* XIV. 95.

908.4 Gyff hem heuen forto see
   A blessing on good hosts—three lines.
   1. Camb. Un. Ff. 1. 6, f. 109b.
   Robbins, *PMLA* LXIX. 626.

908:6 ʒif þis lomb to heouen kyng / ffor our synnes in offeryng
   A sacrifice—a couplet in a Latin sermon by Nicolas Philip.
   1. Bodl. 29746, f. 167a.

908.8 Gyff where gyftes may aweyle / ffor luff ys feynte where gyftes do feyle
   A moral couplet.
   1. Bodl. 11272, f. 105b.

909 Davies, *Med. Eng. Lyrics*, pp. 215-6.

910 'God kepe oure kyng and saue the croun' &c. [= Henry V].
   Robbins, *Hist. Poems*, pp. 45-9.

912.5 Gladythe thoue queyne of Scottis regioun
   A compliment to Queen Margaret, ca. 1506, by William Dunbar—five 8-line stanzas with refrain: 'Gladethe thoue Queyne ot Scotish regioun.'
   1. Aberdeen Town Clerk's Office, Register of Sasines, III.
   Laing, *Dunbar*, I (Supplement), 281-2; Small, *STS* IV.

274-5; Schipper, *Dunbar*, pp. 121-2; and *DKAW* XL (IV). 31-2; Baildon, *Dunbar*, pp. 59-60; MacKenzie, *Dunbar*, pp. 179-80.

913 [For *Complaint of Venus* see 3542. Ringler 18].
Mars and Venus, Notary, ca. 1500 (STC 5089); Chaucer, Stow, 1561 (STC 5075); *repr.* Chalmers, *English Poets*, I. 360; 2. Robinson, *Chaucer*, 1933, pp. 623-7; 1957, pp. 529-37.

914 1. Balliol 354, f. 209a (st. 1 lacking); 4. Blairs Coll. 22, f. 96a; 6. York Minster XVI. G. 5, f. 170a; 7. *olim* Ashburnham 49; 8. Longleat 30, f. 17a; 9. Fitzwilliam Mus. 40-1951 [*olim* Thompson 84, Beauchamp Hours], f. 54a (st. 16 lacking); 10. Fitzwilliam Mus. 40-1950 [*olim* Thompson 83, Talbot Hours], f. 81a (6 st.).
Matyns of Our Lady, de Worde, 1513 (STC 15914); 5 (with st. 1-5 from MS. 6). Wordsworth, *Surtees Soc.* CXXXII. 161-4; 6 (one st. to B.V. only). Simmons, *EETS* 71. 200.

916 Rickert, *Anc. Eng. Xmas Carols*, pp. 190-1.

917 1. Folger Lib. 5031 [*olim* Macro 5, *olim* Gurney 170], ff. 38a-75.
Adams, *Chief Pre-Sh. Dramas*, pp. 265-87 (abridged).

918 three 5-line stanzas and burden.
Rickert, *Anc. Eng. Xmas Carols*, p. 183; Stevens, *Med. Carols*, p. 90.

918.5 Gloryouse lord so doolfully dyȝte
A variant of st. 5 of 2273, occurring separately in Rolle's *Meditations on the Passion* (Text A only).
1. Camb. Un. Ll. 1. 8, f. 204a.
Ullmann, *Eng. Stn.* VII. 458; Horstmann, *York. Wr.*, I. 86; Allen, *Eng. Writings of Rolle*, p. 24.

Glory & preyse laude & hye honour   See 2574 (MS. 30).

919 [Utley 75]
2. Camb. Un. Ff. 1. 6, f. 156a (9 st. only); 4. Rome: English Coll. 1306, f. 81b (17 st.).
de Worde, 1509 (STC 19119); *repr.* Collier, *Percy Soc.* I; 1 (with 7 addit. st. from de Worde). Wright, *Camden Soc.* XVI. 295-9.

Go bet peny go bet go
Burden to 2747.

920   [Ringler 19].
Temple of Glas, de Worde, ca. 1498 (STC 17032a); *repr.* Duff, *XV C. Eng. Books,* p. 76; de Worde, ca. 1500 (STC 17033); *repr.* Dibdin, *Typo. Antiquities,* II. 304; Duff, *XV C. Eng. Books,* p. 77; [Anderson,] *Poets of Great Britain,* I. 579; Clarke, *Riches of Chaucer,* II. 305 (mod.); Robbins, *Hist. Poems,* pp. 232-3.

921   1. Lansdowne 796, f. 1b.
Robbins, *Hist. Poems,* pp. 168-73.

Go forthe lytelle boke and lowly þow me commende
Envoy to 1514.

922   1, 2. Sauerstein, *Charles d'Orleans,* 1899, p. 64; 3. Robbins, *Sec. Lyrics,* pp. 182-3.

923   An Envoy to his mistress—three stanzas rime royal with refrain (following 3947).
1. BM Addit. 10303, f. 9a; 2. Longleat 256, f. 24b.
Chaucer, Speght, 1598 (STC 5077); *repr.* Urry, *Chaucer,* 1721, p. 587; Bell, *Poets of Great Britain,* XI. 84; [Anderson,] *Poets of Great Britain,* I. 479; Chalmers, *English Poets,* I. 394; *British Poets,* Chiswick 1822, V. 138; Moxon, *Works of Chaucer,* p. 405; [Pickering's] *Aldine Brit. Poets,* 1845, VI. 242; 1866, V. 153; Bell, *Works of Chaucer,* III. 508; Sherzer, Berlin 1903; Cohen, *Ballade,* p. 279.

*[Go fro my] vindow go go fro my window
Burden to 4284.3.

925   The wounds of love—one 5-line stanza. [The first line, as a title, in Public Rec. Office C. 47/37/11, f. 3b; pr. Hanham, *RES* n.s. VIII. 272].
1. Bodl. 6668, f. 192b.
Copley, *Seven Eng. Songs,* 1940; Harvey, *Gothic England,* p. 85; Robbins, *Sec. Lyrics,* p. 150; Davies, *Med. Eng. Lyrics,* p. 245.

926 1. Bodl. Lat. misc. c. 66 [olim Capesthorne], f. 94a.
Robbins, *PMLA* LXV. 271; Robbins, *Sec. Lyrics*, p. 195; Davies, *Med. Eng. Lyrics*, p. 258.

927 Davies, *Med. Eng. Lyrics*, pp. 201-2.

Goo litill boke and mekely me excuse
Lines used as Envoy to 935, actually from 447.

927.5 Goo lityl book and submytte the / Vnto al them
Epilogue to *Lyf of Our Lady* (2574) by William Caxton—one stanza rime royal. [Followed by 3830.5 and 527.5. Ringler 20].
1. Chetham Lib. 6709, f. 156a (copied from Caxton).
Caxton, 1484 (STC 17023); *facs.* Blades, *Life & Typography of Caxton*, II. 171; *repr.* Dibdin, *Typo. Antiquities*, I. 340; Duff, *XV C. Eng. Books*, p. 75; Aurner, *Caxton*, p. 294; Crotch, *EETS* 176. 85; Lauritis, Klinefelter, and Gallagher, *Life of Our Lady*, p. 52.

928.5 Go lytyl boke for dredefull ys thy message
A lover's Envoy to his sovereign lady—in rime royal stanzas. [Following 2478.5].
1. Trinity Camb. 599, ff. 7a-8b, continued at f. 154a.

929 Robbins, *Sec. Lyrics*, p. 97.

930 Neilson and Webster, *Chief Brit. Poets*, pp. 204-5.

931 3. Bodl. Lat. misc. c. 66 [olim Capesthorne], f. 107b (lacks vv. 1-21; vv. 50-56 follow v. 112; vv. 396-7 reversed).
2 (with st. 1 & 2 from MS. 1). Glauning, *EETS* lxxx. 2-15.

Go little quaire apace
Envoy to Skelton's *Replycacioun* (3772.5).

932 Robbins, *Sec. Lyrics*, p. 87.

932.5 Go piteous hart rasyd with dedly wo
Disconsolate love by John Skelton 'at the instance of a nobyll lady'—two stanzas rime royal with refrain.
Dyuers Balettys, ? Pynson, n. d. (STC 22604); *repr.* Dyce, *Skelton*, I. 27; Dyce and Child, *Skelton & Donne*, I. 33-4; Henderson, *Skelton*, 1931, p. 34; 1948, 1959, p. 32; Davies, *Med. Eng. Lyrics*, p. 266.

Go thou little quayer and recommaund me   See 2663.5.

Go ye before be twayne and twayne / Wysly that ye be not
See 2358.5 (Cotton Titus).

933   seven 9-line stanzas and burden.

935   [Further English prose texts include: Ashmole 59, ff. 1a-12b;
Rawl. C. 83, ff. 1-8; Rawl. B. 490, ff. 28b-72; Royal 18. A.
vii, ff. 1a-26b. Singer 29].
4. Balliol 329, f. 80a; 20. Caius 336, ff. 104a-124a (fragment:
st. 328-31, 353-90, 170-91, 193-4, 195-213, 234-7, 228-33, 238-71,
273-89, 64, 43, 65, 68).
Governaunce of Kynges and Princes, Pynson, 1511 (STC
12140, 17017); *repr.* Starnes, Gainesville, Florida, 1957;
Pynson, 1527.

936   1. Bodl. 6943, f. 134a.
Robbins, *Hist. Poems*, p. 196.

938   [See 942, 2796.5].

939   A prayer against robbers—four couplets (followed by 1293.5).
2. Bodl. 817, f. 2b.
1. Robbins, *Sec. Lyrics*, p. 245.

God and the holy trenete   See 939.

940   [Also in printed *Horae*, e.g., Pynson, 1514 (STC 15917);
Fawkes, 1521. See Dibdin, *Typo. Antiquities*, II. 111; Butterworth, *Eng. Primers*, p. 6; Bühler, *St. in Renaissance* VI.
224-6].
1. Bühler, *St. in Renaissance* VI. 224.

941   2. Harley 545, ff. 136b-138b; 3. Lambeth 306, f. 49a.
1. Wilson, *Lost. Lit.*, p. 204; Robbins, *Hist. Poems*, p. 63;
2. Madden, *Archaeologia* XXIX. 138; Gairdner, *Camden
Soc.* n.s. XXVIII. 94.

944   2. Longleat 257, f. 119a (begins imperfectly: *De matre cum
vij pueribus*).
1. Kalen, *Götesborgs Högskolas Arsskrift* XXVIII. 5 (vv.
1-6000); Ohlander, *Gothenburg St. in English* V (vv. 6001-
6924); XI (6925 to end).

*944.5 *God for hys grace schylde vs from schame / Her basnettys
Firumbras, a translation of the *chanson de geste* of *Fierabras*
—vv. 1842 in couplets.
1. BM Addit. 37942 [*olim* Fillingham], f. 1a (imperfect).
O'Sullivan, *EETS* 198.

945.5 God grant me gras to gehte agayn / þe luffe þat I haue loste
A two-line fragment.
1. Trinity Camb. 1434, f. 1a (written twice).
James, *Cat.*, III. 461; Wilson, *Lost Lit.*, p. 182.

945.8 God graunt vs al therin to be frended
A couplet at the end of Usk's *Testament of Love*.
Chaucer, Thynne, 1532, f. ccclxi (STC 5068); Skeat, *Oxf. Ch.*, VII. 145.

God honoured women in his life
Extract from 1596.

950 1a (late xviii cent. transcript). Bodl. 21749, f. 1.
French and Hale, *ME Met. Rom.*, pp. 239-84 (vv. 1491-2118, 2175-3038, 3151-3225).

952 2. Advocates 1. 1. 6, p. 24 and p. 60; 3. NLW Mostyn Welsh 129, p. 19.
2a, 2b. Ritchie, *STS* 3 s. V. 40; n.s. XXIII. 2.

956 Robbins, *Sec. Lyrics*, pp. 248-9.

956.5 God maker of alle thyng / Be at oure begynnynge
A prologue to Mirk's *Festial*—two couplets.
1. Cotton Claudius A. ii, f. 1b.
Blades, *Life & Typography of Caxton*, II. 135.

958 2. Patterson, *JEGP* XV. 406-18.

960.1 God prosper long our noble king
Chevy Chase, a broadside version of the *Hunting of the Cheviot* (3445.5), composed in the 16th century—64 quatrains. [Found in many late collections of ballads].
1. BM Addit. 27879, pp. 188-91.
Coll. Old Ballads, Glasgow, 1747, I. 108; Percy, *Reliques*, 1765, I. 235; Hales and Furnivall, *Percy Folio MS.*, II. 7;

Child, *Ballads,* 1864, 1878, VII. 43-54; and *Pop. Ballads,* no. 162, III. 311-14; Sargent and Kittredge, *Pop Ballads,* pp. 397-400; Arber, *Dunbar Anthology,* pp. 68-78; Leach, *Ballad Book,* pp. 454-60.

960.3 God safe kyng hare wherehever he go or ryde
'Sent george be hys forman hovre blyssyd lady be hys gyde' —one long couplet. [Probably for Henry VIII].
1. Trinity Camb. 1157, f. 24b.
James, *Cat.,* III. 170.

960.5 God save king henry wheresoer he be
Anthem for marriage of Henry VII and Elizabeth, A.D. 1486—five lines with music by Thomas Ashwell. [Cf. similar opening lines in song against Cardinal Wolsey in Harley 2252, f. 156a, pr. Flügel, *Neuengl. Lesebuch,* pp. 102-4].
1. Camb. Un. Dd. 13. 27, f. 31a; 2. St. John's Camb. 234, f. 28b.
2. *Lives of Queens of England,* 1853, IV. 40.

962 Stevens, *Med. Carols,* p. 107.

*God shild þat day my soul fro care   See 1759 (Edinb. Univ.).

964.5 God spede þe plouȝ / and sende us korne I-now
A caption for a picture of a man ploughing (in one MS. of *Piers Plowman*)—one couplet. [Cf. Tilley G 223].
1. Trinity Camb. 594, f. iii verso.
James, *Cat.,* II. 64.

965 2. N. S. Baugh, *Worcestershire Misc.,* p. 96.

968 2. Plimpton Addenda 3 [*olim* Pratt], f. 241b; 3. Delete this MS.
1. Brook, *Harley Lyrics,* pp. 68-9.

God that all this worlde dyde make / And dyed for us vpon a tree
See 979 (Skot's print).

969 The Expedition of Henry V into France, in three passus: The Siege of Harfleur, The Battle of Agincourt, The Triumph in London—in 8-line stanzas with additonal refrain lines: 'Wot ye right well that thus it was / Gloria tibi Trinitas.'
1. Bodl. 11951, ff. 178a-186a (69 st.); 2. Cotton Vitell. D. xii,

II, f. 214 (var., Passus I, vv. 221; Passus II, vv. 251; lacks refrain); 3. Harley 565, ff. 102a-114a.

Batayll of Egyngscourte, Skot, ca. 1530 (STC 198); 2. 3. Nicolas, *History of Battle of Agincourt*, 1833, pp. 303-25, 301-29; Arber, *Eng. Garner*, VIII. 13; Pollard, *XV C. Prose & Verse*, pp. 2-12; 3. Evans, *Old Ballads*, 1810, II. 334.

970   9. Nat. Lib. of Medicine 49, ff. 96b-107b (copied from early print).

973   2. Advocates 19. 3. 1, f. 11a (vv. 757).

975   3. BM Addit. 22283, f. 157b.
2. N. S. Baugh, *Worcestershire Misc.*, p. 145.

977   de Worde, ca. 1510 (STC 14522); *facs.* Jenkinson; 1. Zupitza, *Archiv* CX. 66-82.

978   Copland, n.d. (STC 17036).

979   [Revise entire entry as follows:]
The Siege of Rouen, ascribed to John Page, sometimes inserted into the prose *Brut*—in couplets. [Prose chronicles ending at 1419 give only a prose paraphrase; those continuing to 1430 give fuller prose paraphrase with last part in verse; only complete text is MS. 6. Each MS. shows considerable variants].

1. Bodl. 3652, ff. 28a-42b (vv. 1-946; ends imperfectly); 2. Balliol 354, ff. 128a-138b; 3. Camb. Un. Hj. 6. 9, ff. 258b-261a; 4. Trinity Camb. 1413, ff. 195b-197a; 5. Cotton Galba E. viii, ff. 140a-143b (vv. 669); 6. Egerton 1995, ff. 87a-109b; 7. Harley 226, ff. 136b-142b; 8. Harley 753, ff. 177a-182b; 8a (xix cent. transcript). Egerton 2257, ff. 17a-19a (vv. 82 only); 9. Harley 2256, ff. 189a-193b (vv. 1-1312); 10. BM Addit. 27879, pp. 523-5 (badly damaged: vv. 1-119, 176-202, 226-85, 349-76 of MS. 6); 11. Lambeth 331, ff. 107b-112a; 12. *olim* Buccleugh (Quaritch Sale Cats. 303, 304); 13. *olim* Charlemont, ff. 23 (present location not known); 14. Holkham Hall 670, ff. 125a-b (vv. 637-773 only); 15. *olim* Harmsworth (Sotheby Sale Oct. 15, 1945, Lot 1951).

Batayll of Egyngscourte, Skot, ca. 1530 (STC 198); 6. Brie, *EETS* 135. 404; *crit. ed.* Huscher, *Kölner Anglistische Arbeiten* I. 138.

981	[Cf. 3760.5].
	4. Egerton 3245 [*olim* Gurney], f. 189b (vv. 6; part of 1729).
	1-4. Robbins, *MP* XXXVI. 338, 342-3.

981.3 God that is most of myghte
The House of Stanley: *The Most Pleasant Song of Lady Bessy*, perhaps by Humphrey Brereton—vv. 1082 in quatrains. [For a later variant cf. 986.5].
1. Harley 367, f. 89a; 2. BM Addit. 27879, p. 463; 3. Bateman (present location not known).
1, 3. Halliwell, *Percy Soc.* XX; 2. Hales and Furnivall, *Percy Folio MS.*, III. 321-63; 3. Heywood, 1829; Jewett, *Ballads of Derbyshire*, 1867, p. 12.

981.5 God þat is so foul of meght / Saue hare solys bothe day & neght
A prayer tag by John Crophill—one couplet.
1. Harley 1735, f. 42b.

983 Douce fragments E. 20 (cf. STC 24133; 13075).

985.5 God that made boythe daye & neight
To the new moon—six lines [Followed by 1513.5].
1. Lansdowne 96, f. 104a.
Sparrow-Simpson, *Journal Brit. Archaeol. Assoc.* XLVIII. 45.

986 in couplets with occasional quatrains.

986.5 God that shope both sea and land / & ffor all creatures dyed
The House of Stanley: *Bosworth Field*—vv. 656 in quatrains. [A late variant of 981.3; for a later variant, ca. A.D. 1605, cf. Harley 542, ff. 31a-33b].
1. BM Addit. 27879, p. 434.
Hales and Furnivall, *Percy Folio MS.*, III. 235-59.

987 Evans, *Old Ballads*, 1810, II. 296; Marsh, *Hist. Eng. Language*, p. 278; Mätzner, *AE Sprachproben*, I. 324; Morris, *Specimens*, II. 126.

987.5 God þat set ope boþe se & sande
A tale of Henry II— in 6-line tail-rime stanzas.
1. Harley 5396, f. 311b (fragment: vv. 24).

God þat was borne in þe borough of bethelem   See 624.

988 [Delete: Compare 1663].

God the endewe with a crowne of glorye   See 3866.3.

989 910 lines in 6-line stanzas. [Cf. 1764].
Hales and Furnivall, *Percy Folio MS.*, II. 557-94; Laing, *Remains*, rev. Hazlitt, I. 252-83.

991 2. Bodl. 3896, f. 154b.
Caxton, ca. 1486 (STC 5087); Pynson, 1526; 2. Robinson, *Chaucer*, 1933, pp. 332-53; 1957, pp. 282-303.

993 A charm against wolves and thieves (perhaps originally addressed to Woden)—in rough couplets.
1. Paris: Bibl. nat. n.a. latines 693 [*olim* Ashburnham 120], f. 191a.
Priebsch, *Academy* IL, May 23, 1896, p. 428 (vv. 14); Robbins, *Sec. Lyrics*, p. 245 (vv. 4).

994.5 God wot grete cause these wyffys haue amonge
'In besenysse'—five triplets with this refrain. [Utley 77].
1. BM Addit. 22718, f. 86b.
Bühler, *Library* 4 s. XV. 318.

God wold that euery wife that wonnyth in this land   See 671.

*995.2 *Godes boure as tu gane bilde / us fra sinne and syame sylde
A prayer to the B.V.—vv. 76 in 9-line stanzas.
1. Camb. Un. Add. 2585 (2).

995.3 Goddys chosyn who so wil be
A glorious garland of eight roses, at end of Latin text of Rolle's *De modo vivendi*—four couplets.
1. Harley 5398, f. 20b.

995.4 Goddis grace is redy bothe erly & late
On nurture and kind—in 8-line stanzas.
1. Harley 541, f. 212a (vv. 68).

995.6 Godes grete godnysse and hys longe abydynge
Monoriming quatrain in a Latin sermon.
1. Caius 334, f. 179b.
Owst, *Preaching in Med. England*, p. 273 n.

995.8 Godes hore / Cristes lore
Inducements to repentance—four short lines translating a Latin text.
1. Harley 7322, f. 167a.
Furnivall, *EETS* 15 rev. ed. 267.

997 Rickert, *Anc. Eng. Xmas Carols*, pp. 173-4.

998 Kirke, *Reliquary* IX. 74; Rickert, *Anc. Eng. Xmas Carols*, pp. 41-2; Davies, *Med. Eng. Lyrics*, pp. 222-3.

1001.5 Godis wreche late arecheit / An wonne he smit / ful sor he hit
A three-line tag translating Latin '*Lento pede procedet divinitas* &c.'
1. Trinity Camb. 323, f. 46a.
James, *Cat.*, I. 444.

1002 Davies, *Med. Eng. Lyrics*, p. 130.

1004 Rickert, *Anc. Eng. Xmas Carols*, p. 219; Stevens, *Med. Carols*, p. 12; Robbins, *Early Eng. Xmas Carols*, p. 16; Davies, *Med. Eng. Lyrics*, p. 214.

1007 Robbins, *Sec. Lyrics*, p. 85.

1008 1. Bodl. 13679, Item 1 (g).
Robbins, *MLN* LXXIV. 200; *Poets of Eng. Lang.*, I. 25-6; Robbins, *Sec. Lyrics*, p. 11; Speirs, *Med. Eng. Poetry*, p. 60; Davies, *Med. Eng. Lyrics*, p. 99.

Grayce and good manners maketh man   See 1009.3.

1009.3 Grace and manears maketh a man / But woe be vnto him þat no good cane
A proverbial couplet (the first line used as motto of Winchester College).
1. Christchurch Oxf. 152, f. 1a; 2. Egerton 2862, f. 50a.
1. Manly and Rickert, *Canterbury Tales*, I. 90, 690.

Grace in thys lyf and aftirwarde glorie   See 2200.

1009.5 Grace of oure offendynge / Space to oure amendynge / And his face to see at oure endynge
A pious aspiration—three lines at end of Vegetius.
1. Morgan Lib. M. 775, f. 121b.

Grasles galante in all thy luste and pryde   See 143.8 (st. 2).

1010   Wilson, *Lost Lit.*, p. 183; Robbins, *Sec. Lyrics*, pp. 144-5.

1011   2. Thompson (Portland. Oregon) [*olim* Amherst 20], ff. 10a-12a. *Gloryous Medytacyon of Jhesus Crystes Passyon*, R. Faques, ca. 1521 (STC 14550); 1. Gray, *N&Q* n.s. X. 50-1.

1011.5 Grant gracious God grant me this time
The House of Stanley: *Scottish Feilde*—422 alliterative lines. [For a later version, post 1544, cf. *Flodden Field*, vv. 513 in quatrains, in Harley 293, ff. 55a-61b; Harley 367, ff. 120a-125a; BM Addit. 27879, p. 117; pr. Weber, *Flodden Field*; Evans, *Old Ballads*; Hales and Furnivall, *Percy Folio MS.*, 1. 318-40].
1. BM Addit. 27879, pp. 79-90; 2. Lyme; 2a. Bodl. Dep. c 130 (*facs*.).
1. Hales and Furnivall, *Percy Folio MS.*, I. 212-34; Oakden, *Chetham Soc.* n.s. XCIV; 2. Robson, *Chetham Soc.* XXXVII.

1011.8 Grant me þe will of wepynge / With teris
Devotions to the crucified Christ—fifteen 8-line stanzas.
1. *olim* Huth (Sotheby Sale Cat., 1911, I. 154, Lot 538) (roll).

1013.5 Grette aporte in hynes
'*Ista tria sunt dyshonowret quia sunt confusores cuiuscunque regni et ciuitatis*'—three lines.
1. Bodl. 2508, f. 31b.

1014   vv. 218 in couplets. [Cf. *Pricke of Conscience* (3428), vv. 1090].

1014.5 Gret huntyng by ryuers and wode / Makythe a manys here to growe thorowe hys hoode
The dangers of excessive sports—a couplet.
1. Egerton 1995, f. 64b.

1016   [Also called 'Chaucer's Chronicle.' Utley 80].
Gaertner, *John Shirley*, Halle 1904, p. 66.

1017.5   Grene flowryng age of your manly countenance
Let never the love of true lovers be lost: a young lady to her lover—fifteen lines.
1. Bodl. 12653, f. 53b.
Padelford and Benham, *Anglia* XXXI. 370.

Grene growith þe holy so doth þ ᵊ Iue   See 409.5.

1018   [For a religious parody cf. 1018.5].
Robbins, *Sec. Lyrics*, pp. 214-7; Davies, *Med. Eng. Lyrics*, pp. 185-7.

1018.5   Grevouse ys my sorowe / bothe Even & morow
Appeal of Christ to man, a religious parody of 1018—seven 8-line stanzas including refrain: 'Ye wil not frome synne refrayne.' [Cf. *Gude and Godlie Ballates*, p. 132; *repr.* Laing, 1868, pp. 132-7; Mitchell, STS XXXIX. 151-7].
1. Victoria and Albert Mus., Dyce 45, f. 17a.

1021   *Bannatyne MS.*, Hunt. Club, III. 401-4; Laing, *Henryson*, 1865, p. 43; Wood, *Henryson*, pp. 152-60.

Gup Cristian Clowte gup Iak of the Vale
Refrain of 456.5.

1021.5   Gup Scot / Ye blot / *Laudate*
'Against Dundas' by John Skelton—vv. 63 in English and Latin 'skeltonics.'
Workes, Marshe, 1568 (STC 22608); *repr.* [? J. Bowle,] 1736; Chalmers, *English Poets*, II. 305; Dyce, *Skelton*, I. 192-4; Dyce and Child, *Skelton & Donne*, I. 213-6; Henderson, *Skelton*, 1931, pp. 463-5; 1948, 1959, pp. 147-9.

1024   a type of acrostic, each stanza beginning with a word of 'Heil Marie' (1062).

1026   with a word-type acrostic (*Aue Maria*). [Cf. 1024].

1028   Watts, *Love Songs of Sion*, 1924, p. 136 (mod.).

Heyl boe þov Marie ful of godes grace   See 1062.

1030.5   Hayle be thou Mary most of honowr
          To the Virgin—four stanzas and burden.
          1. Egerton 3307, f. 67a.
             Stevens, *Med. Carols*, p. 54; Robbins, *Early Eng. Xmas Carols*, p. 52; Greene, *Sel. Eng. Carols*, p. 109.

1032   5. Trinity Dublin 516, f. 25b.
          2. *Register*, I. 252; 5. *Rel. Lyr. XV C.*, pp. 41-2.

1034.5   Ayl be þow ster of se / godis moder blessed þow be
          Ave maris stella—seventeen couplets.
          1. Merton Oxf. 248, f. 167a.
             Rel. Lyr. XIV C., pp. 55-6.

1035   [A verse rendering of the prose *Hundred Meditations* in Bodl. 1873, ff. 79b-86, as a supplement to Suso's *Horologium Sapientiae*].

1036   *Ave Maria*—one stanza and burden.
             Robbins, *MLN* LXXIV. 200; Stevens, *Med. Carols*, p. 25; Robbins, *Early Eng. Xmas Carols*, p. 49.

1037.3   Hayl blyssyd laḍe qwych hays born / God Son
          'Qwen the angel sayd *Aue*'—one irregular quatrain.
          1. Bodl. 3340, f. 23a (added after 3385).
             Early Eng. Carols, p. 168.

*1037.5   *Heyll blessid Marie
          Fragment of a hymn to the B.V. (? on the Five Joys) in twelve 8-line stanzas. The first two st. are nearly completely lost, and of the other lines only the ends remain. Nearly all the st. begin with the phrase: 'Heyll blessid Marie.' In the school of Lydgate.
          1. St. John's Oxf. 56, ff. 84b-85b.

1038.5   Hayle cheftane Cristes aghen confessour
          A prayer to St. Robert to help the monastery—eighteen couplets (following 3677).
          1. Egerton 3143, f. 63a.
             Haslewood, *Roxburghe Club*, 1824, pp. 55-6; Bazire, *EETS* 228. 76-7.

Hail comely and clean
Song of the Shepherds in the *Secunda Pastorum*, Towneley Plays (715).

1039   eight quatrains, followed by concluding rubric couplet.

1040   vv. 1715 in rime royal stanzas.
Bennett, *STS* 3 s. XXIII. 7-63.

1041   2. Pepys 1584, f. 102a.
1. Person, *Camb. ME Lyrics*, pp. 11-13.

1041.3   Haile festivale day with al honoure
Song at the Annunciation: poem occurring in only this MS. of Eng. tr. of the *Pèlerinage de l'Ame*—five stanzas rime royal.
1. Melbourne: Victoria Pub. Lib., f. 199a.

1041.5   Hayle flower of virgynyte
Hymn to the Virgin, 'more in dygnyte þan all seyntes'—one 6-line tail-rime stanza.
1. Bodl. 3493, p. 162 (end flyleaf).

1044   Bennett, *STS* 3 s. XXIII. 294-8.

1045   2. Longleat 30, f. 25a.

1046   A hymn on the Five Joys, ascribed to an anchoress of Maunsfeld by Shirley (MS. 1) and to Lydgate by Stow (MS. 4)—five 8-line stanzas.
3. Delete this MS.

1047   six long lines with medial rime.
Person, *Camb. ME Lyrics*, pp. 14, 71.

1048.5   Haill goddis sone of mychtis maist
A praising of Christ and the Virgin—thirteen 8-line stanzas with alternating refrains: '*Beatus venter qui te portauit*' and '*Beata vbera que suxisti.*'
1. Advocates 1. 1. 6, f. 28a.
Bannatyne MS., Hunt. Club, II. 72; Ritchie, *STS* n.s. XXII. 68-71.

1048.8   Hayle heremete mast þat ys of myght
'*Oracio ad beatum Robertum*'—twenty-nine couplets (following 3677).
1. Egerton 3143, f. 37b.
Haslewood, *Roxburghe Club*, 1824, pp. v-vii; Bazire, *EETS* 228. 80-1.

1053   1. *facs*. B. D. Brown, *Bodl. Qr. Record* VII, facing p. 1;
2. Comper, *Life & Lyrics of Rolle*, pp. 269-71.

Hail King I thee call
Song in the *Prima Pastorum*, Towneley Plays (715).

1054   1. BM Addit. 46919 [*olim* Phillipps 8336], f. 207a.

1058   Cumming, *EETS* 178. xxxi-xxxvii.

1062   2. Person, *Camb. ME Lyrics*, p. 27.

1064   Person, *Camb. ME Lyrics*, p. 14.

1070.3   Haill Mary quhais concepcioun / Wes caus of our mirthe
'Ane devoit orisoun till our Lady callit *Ave cuius concepcio*'—twenty-two irregular lines.
1. Arundel 285, ff. 188b, 189a.
Bennett, *STS* 3 s. XXIII. 287.

1070.5   Hayl most myghty in þi werkyng
Aue Rex anglorum: an Epiphany carol—one quatrain and burden.
1. Egerton 3307, f. 55b.
Stevens, *Med. Carols*, p. 40; Robbins, *MLN* LXXIV. 203; Robbins, *Early Eng. Xmas Carols*, p. 45; Greene, *Sel. Eng. Carols*, p. 90.

1077   Bennett, *STS* 3 s. XXIII. 298; Davies, *Med. Eng. Lyrics*, p. 290.

1078   1a. BM Addit. 20091, ff. 65a-73a (xix cent. transcript).

1078.5   Hayle Saint Robert a confessour
'*Oracio Presidentis*' in ruling the house, invoking St. Robert—forty-seven couplets (following 3677).

1. Egerton 3143, ff. 35b-37b.
Haslewood, *Roxburghe Club*, 1824, pp. i-iv; Bazire, *EETS* 228. 77-80.

1082.5 Hale sterne superne hale in eterne
'Ane ballat of Our Lady' by William Dunbar—seven aureate 12-line stanzas with Latin bob: *'Ave Maria gratia plena.'*
1. Asloan, f. 303a; 1a (xix cent. transcript by Chalmers). Edinburgh Univ. La. III. 450/1.
1. Small, *STS* IV. 269-71; Laing, *Dunbar*, I. 239-42; Schipper, *Dunbar*, pp. 369-71; and *DKAW* XLII (IV). 67-9; Smith, *Spec. Middle Scots*, pp. 14-7; Baildon, *Dunbar*, pp. 195-7; Craigie, *STS* n.s. XVI. 275-8; MacKenzie, *Dunbar*, pp. 160-2; Kinsley, *Dunbar*, pp. 8-9 (3 st. only); Davies, *Med. Eng. Lyrics*, pp. 247-8 (3 st. only).

1083.5 Heil þou festful day
A verse insert in a prose text on Adam and Melchisedech.
1. Bodl. 2322, Part E.
Capgrave, *Solace of Pilgrimes*, p. 160; *repr*. C. A. Mills, 1912.

1086 [Utley 82].
1. Bodl. 3896, f. 50b; 5. Sloane 1710, ff. 164a-176b (vv. 93-140, 191-764); 7. BM Addit. 17492, f. 90a (vv. 717-24, 229-36).
The Boke of Fame, Pynson, 1526 (STC 5088) (with *Lenvoy de limprimeur,* 6 added st. rime royal, pr. Hammond, *Eng. Verse Chaucer-Surrey,* p. 432); *Chaucer.* Thynne, 1532 (STC 5068); Reynes, 1542 (STC 5070); Stow, 1561 (STC 5075); Speght, 1598 (STC 5077); Urry, *Chaucer*, 1721, p. 422; Bell, *Poets of Great Britain,* X. 133; [Anderson,] *Poets of Great Britain,* 1793, I. 446; Todd, *Illustrations of Gower & Chaucer,* p. 296; Chalmers, *English Poets,* I. 518; 1 (coll. Thynne, 4). Skeat, *Oxf. Ch.* VII. 299; 2. Furnivall, *EETS* 15 rev. ed. 80; 4. Furnivall, *EETS* 15 orig. ed. 52-80.

1087 Halfe in a dede sclepe not fully revyved
poem of fifteen stanzas rime royal, one concluding 8-line stanza and Envoy in one stanza rime royal.
Todd, *Illustrations of Gower & Chaucer,* pp. 302-9.

Hange I wyl my nobyl bow   See 1303.5.

1088.5	happe is harde grace hath no pere / Rych is nygarde worshippe is dere
	A couplet on the evils of the age.
	1. Balliol 354, f. 205b; 2. Royal 17. D. vi, f. 1b.
	1. Flügel, *Anglia* XXVI. 174; Dyboski, *EETS* ci. 140.
	Herde hevy hote and dry See 3721.
1090	1. Horstmann, *Archiv* LXXXI. 97.
1091	1. Kaiser, *Med. Eng.*, p. 284.
1097	[Singer 858].
	Alchemical verses on making the hot bath—thirteen couplets.
1101	10. Rylands Lib. Eng. 50, f. 103a (vv. 1-659 only).
1105	3. Cotton Caligula A. ix, f. 14a (a single leaf, vv. 48).
	Herkenythe lordynges curteys and hende See 3187.
	Herknies me a luytel þrowe See 3310 (Bodl. 1486).
1109.5	Herkenes of me I lytyll spekyn / for vrenes I woll you tellyn
	On the colors of urines—twenty-four couplets followed by a prose tract on the same subject, ff. 76b-78a (in turn followed by 1201.3).
	1. Sloane 120, ff. 75a-76a.
1112	'*Prophecia de Merlyn.*' [Cf. French texts in Camb. Un. Gg. 1. 1, f. 120a; Cotton Julius A. v, f. 177b; Harley 746; Latin texts in Cotton Vesp. E. vii, f. 89, abridged, and Harley 6148].
	2. Bodl. 4062, ff. 43a-45a (var., vv. 136); 3. Harley 559, ff. 45a-47b (var., vv. 141).
	Whole Prophesie of Scotland, Waldegrave, Edinburgh 1603 (cf. STC W 2060); Andro Hart, Edinburgh 1617 (STC 17842); *repr.* Edinburgh 1714, 1718, 1745; Falkirk, 1782; Laing, *Collection of Anc. Scot. Prophecies,* Bannatyne Club XLIV; 1. Hall, *Poems of Minot,* 1914, pp. 103-11.
	Herkyn to me both olde & yonge See 1914.
1113	1. Longleat 55, f. 42b.

1114 2. Camb. Un. Add. 4407, Art. 19 (three fragments, d, e, f: vv. 174-83; 341-64, 537-49).

1. K. Botzenmayer, *Heroic Deeds & Knightly Adventures*, Westermann Texte, Englische Reihe nr. 129.

1116 1. Advocates 19. 3. 1, f. 60a; 1a (xix cent. transcript). Egerton 2257, ff. 169a-170a.

Herkneth true y ou telle

'Whose wole of loue be trewe do lystne me'—eight 6-line stanzas with 5-line refrain: 'Ich wolde ich were a threselcock.' Reconstructed first line and text of 105.

1119 *Christmas Carolles*, Kele, ca. 1550 (STC 5205); *facs*. Reed, *Xmas Carols*, pp. 20-3; *repr*. Dyce and Child, *Skelton & Donne*, I. 168-71; Henderson, *Skelton*, 1931, pp. 21-4; 1948, 1959, pp. 16-8; 1. Bennett, *STS* 3 s. XXIII. 261-5.

1119.3 Harry harry hobillschowe

'The manere of the crying of ane playe' by William Dunbar —vv. 173 in eleven 16-line tail-rime stanzas.

1. Advocates 1. 1. 6, f. 118b; 2. Asloan, f. 240a (ends v. 165); 2a (xix cent. transcript). Edinburgh Univ. 521.

1. Ramsay, *Evergreen*, I. 258-64; *Poems in Scot. Dialect*, 1748, pp. 38-42; *Ramsay and Earlier Scot. Poets*, pp. 257-8; [Hailes,] *Anc. Scot. Poems*, pp. 219-24; Pinkerton, *Select Scot. Ballads*, 1783, II. 75-80; Sibbald, *Chronicle*, II. 350-4; *Bannatyne MS.*, Hunt. Club, III. 337-41; Small, *STS* IV. 314-20; Ritchie, *STS* n. s. XXII. 315-20; 2. Craigie, *STS* n.s. XVI. 149-54; MacKenzie, *Dunbar*, pp. 170-4; Kinsley, *Dunbar*, pp. 102-7; 2a. Laing, *Select Remains*, 1822; Laing, *Dunbar*, II. 37-43; Schipper, *Dunbar*, pp. 191-7; and *DKAW* XL (IV). 100-7; Baildon, *Dunbar*, pp. 89-93.

1119.5 Herry Notingham & his wyffe lyne here / þat maden this chirche stepull

Epitaph on monumental brass at Holme-by-the sea, Norfolk, A.D. 1405—three couplets.

Pettigrew, *Chronicles of Tombs*, p. 44; Morison, *Blackletter Text*, 1942, title page; Bouquet, *Church Brasses*, p. 200.

1119.8 Hatest thou Urse / have thou Gods curse

A prophetic curse ascribed to Aldred, last Saxon Bishop of York, by William of Malmesbury (*Gesta Pontificum*, Cap. 115).

Hamilton, *Rolls Ser.* LII. 253; Morley, *Sh. Eng. Poems*,

III. 241; *Grundriss*, 2nd. ed., II, i. 1096; Förster, *Archiv* CXIX. 433; Zupıtza, *AE Uebungsbuch*, 1928, p. 86; Wells, *Manual*, p. 221.

1120 [The first four lines occur as vv. 9-12 of 2245.1].
2. Canterbury Cath. fragment (st. 1).
   1. Robbins, *Sec. Lyrics*, pp. 135-6; Kurvinen, *Neuphil. Mitteilungen* LIV. 57-8.

1120.3 Have as ofte as þi will sorow and sikynge / As þou haddiste in þi synne lust and likyng
A malediction—one long couplet.
1. Bodl. Lat. lit. e. 17, f. 53a.

1120.5 Haue god day my leman
A fragment of a popular song in The Red Book of Ossory.
1. Kilkenny: Red Book of Ossory, f. 72a.
Hist. MSS. Comm. Report X, App. V. 245; Graves, *N&Q* 1 s. II. 385; Seymour, *Anglo-Irish Lit.* 1200-1582, p. 97; *Early Eng. Carols*, p. cxviii; Wilson, *LSE* V. 40; Wilson, *Lost Lit.*, p. 188.

1121 Robbins, *Sec. Lyrics*, p. 148; Wilson, *Lost Lit.*, p. 185.

1123 Wilson, *Lost Lit.*, p. 187.

1123.5 Haath mercy on me mercy on me / ȝe þat my freendes be
A couplet in a Latin sermon.
1. Bodl. 12158, f. 92a.

1123.8 Haue mercy vppon me oo god
The psalm '*Miserere*' arranged as a translation of the *Asperges*—in couplets with a 4-line pseudo-burden.
1. BM Addit. 32427, f. 141a; 2. Salisbury Cath. 152, f. 159b.
   1. Frere, *Antiphonale Sarisburiense*, I. 78; 2. Kingdon, *Wiltshire Arch. & Nat. Hist. Mag.*, XVIII. 65-6, *facs.* facing p. 66; Wordsworth and Littlehales, *Old Service Books*, p. 51.

1126 2. Pepys 1584, f. 107b; 5. St. Cuthbert's Coll., Ushaw, 28.
1. Person, *Camb. ME Lyrics*, p. 24.

1128 [For a variant text see 2250].

1129   6. Royal 8. F. vii, f. 45b (5 couplets &c.); 8. Bodl. 8714, f. i verso (vv. 12).
        4. Horstmann, *York. Wr.*, I. 111.

1130   1 (with st. 20-21 from MS. 3). MacCracken, *EETS* cvii. 77-84.

        Hay   See   Hey

        *He ete brede bot a quantite   See 1645 (Harvard).

1132   *Early Eng. Carols*, p. 221; Rickert, *Anc. Eng. Xmas Carols*, p. 193; Williams, *New Book Eng. Verse*, p. 112; Niles, *Carol Study Book*, p. 35; Gilchrist, *JFSS* IV. 35; Segar, *Med. Anthology*, pp. 35-6; Greene, *Med. Aevum* XXIX. 10-11 (with 3 trad. versions); Chambers, *Eng. Lit. Close MA*, p. 111; Mason, *Humanism & Poetry*, p. 146; Greene, *Sel. Eng. Carols*, p. 128; Speirs, *Med. Eng. Poetry*, pp. 76-7; Davies, *Med. Eng. Lyrics*, p. 272.

*1132.5   *He beheld ladys with laughinge cher
        The Song of Roland—vv. 1049 in alliterative couplets.
        1. Lansdowne 388, ff. 381a-395b (incomplete).
           Herrtage, *EETS* xxxv. 107-36; Michel, *Chanson de Roland*, Paris 1837, App. VIII, pp. 279-84 (extracts only; vv. 100).

1134.5   He is a bird þat synges of soro
        The ephemeral nature of man—two couplets. [Cf. 67.5].
        1. Hereford Cath. O. iii. 5, f. 48a.

1135   [Delete entire entry].

        He is a fole eke as seneke seythe
        On careful speaking: an extract of Lydgate's *Order of Fools* (st. 6, 10, 12-14) occurring separately: see 3444.

1136.3   He ys in sowle ful sekely / lyggande on his couche
        '*Contra obstinatos*'—two short quatrains.
        1. Harley 2388, f. 58b.

1136.5   He is no good swayn / þat lettith his Iorney for þe rayn
        A proverbial couplet. [Tilley S 1022].
        1. Balliol 354, f. 200b.
           Flügel, *Anglia* XXVI. 203; Dyboski, *EETS* ci. 131.

1137　　　　Furnivall, *EETS* 15 orig. ed. 234.

1137.3　　　He is wyse & happy þat can be ware / be an oder mannys harme
　　　　　　　A proverbial tag translating Latin. [Cf. 1139].
　　　　　　　1. BM Addit. 12195, f. 114a.

1137.5　　　He ys wyse and wel y-taȝth / þat beryth a horne & blow hym noȝth
　　　　　　　On the cuckold—a single couplet. [For these lines used as burden see 543].
　　　　　　　1. Bodl. 15444, f. 142a; 2. Rylands Lib. Latin 394, f. 3a.
　　　　　　　Meech, *MP* XXXVIII. 121; 2. Pantin, *BJRL* XIV. 93.

1138　　　　2. Bodl. 1947, f. ii recto (vv. 4).
　　　　　　　1. Madden, *Archaeologia* XXIX. 325; Wright, *Pol. Poems*, II. 225.

1139　　　　[Cf. 1137.3].
　　　　　　　4. Hereford Cath. O. iv. 14, Part II, pastedown; 5. Trinity Dublin 158, f. 48b.
　　　　　　　2. Patterson, *Shakespearean Studies*, p. 450.

1140.5　　　He makt himself in gret richesse / þat nith & day flet wrechednesse
　　　　　　　A couplet translating '*Hic bene se ditat qui semper inania vitat.*'
　　　　　　　1. Advocates 19. 2. 1, f. 32b.

1142　　　　Wilson, *Lost Lit.*, p. 177; Robbins, *Sec. Lyrics.* p. 238.

1142.5　　　He may lightli swim / that is hold wp by þe chin
　　　　　　　A proverbial couplet. [Cf. Heywood; Tilley C 349].
　　　　　　　1. Bodl. 15444, f. 141a; 2. Balliol 354, f. 191b.
　　　　　　　1. Meech, *MP* XXXVIII. 119; 2. Dyboski, *EETS* ci. 129.

1145　　　　seven lines in a Latin homily.
　　　　　　　Brown, *MLN* LXIX. 394.

1145.5　　　He sthey open þe rode þat barst helle clos
　　　　　　　Christ's Resurrection, a couplet by William Herebert.
　　　　　　　1. BM Addit. 46919 [*olim* Phillipps 8336], f. 210b.
　　　　　　　Gneuss, *Anglia* LXXVIII. 183.

1147 [For a similar rubric in prose see Lambeth 559, f. 140a].

1147.2 He that doth as can / blame him no man
A proverbial couplet.
1. Bodl. 21626, f. 13a; 2. Rylands Lib. Latin 394, f. 5a.
1. *Bodl. Sum. Cat.*, IV, Part 2, p. 505; Förster, *Festschrift zum 12 Deutschen Neuphilologentage*, p. 44; 2. Pantin, *BJRL* XIV. 95.

1147.4 He that fast spendyth must nede borowe / But whan he schal paye aȝen then ys al the sorowe
On borrowing—one long couplet.
1. Harley 116, f. 125a.

1147.6 He that fool sendyth / fool abydeth
A proverbial couplet.
1. Salisbury Cath. 103, f. 124b.
Owst, *Lit. & Pulpit*, p. 44.

1147.8 He þat hadd inou to help him self wital / Sithen he ne wold I ne wile ne I ne schal
A couplet in Nicolas Bozon's *Contes moralisés*.
1. BM Addit. 46919 [*olim* Phillipps 8336], f. 132b; 2. Gray's Inn 12, f. 24b.
2. Smith, *SATF*, p. 44; Wilson, *LSE* VI. 45; Ross, *Neuphil. Mitteilungen* L. 207.

1147.9 He that had Londyn for-sake / Wolde no more to hem take
A couplet in Gregory's *Chronicle* on the approach of the Earl of March ('thys fayre whyte ros and herbe') to London, A.D. 1461.
1. Egerton 1995, f. 206b.
Gairdner, *Camden Soc.* n.s. XVII. 215; Wilson, *Lost Lit.*, p. 204.

1148 Bowers, *Eng. Lang. Notes* I. 164.

1148.5 He that hes gold and grit riches
'Ane his awin ennemy' by William Dunbar—five 5-line stanzas with refrain.
1. Pepys 2553, p. 212; 2. Advocates 1. 1. 6, f. 115b.
1. Craigie, *STS* n.s. VII. 239-40; 2. Ramsay, *Evergreen*, I. 204; repr. *Ramsay & Earlier Scot. Poets*, p. 252; [Hailes,]

Anc. Scot. Poems, p. 66; Pinkerton, Select Scot. Ballads, 1783, II. 55-6; Sibbald, Chronicle, I. 345; Laing, Dunbar, I. 107; Paterson, Dunbar, pp. 91-2; Select Poems of Dunbar, Perth 1788, pp. 59-60; Bannatune MS., Hunt. Club, II. 329-30; Small, STS IV. 134-5; Schipper, Dunbar, pp. 236-7; and DKAW XLI (IV). 38-9; Baildon, Dunbar, p. 115; Ritchie, STS n.s. XXII. 308-9; MacKenzie, Dunbar, p. 2; Kinsley, Dunbar, p. 59.

1149 1. Harley 116, f. 170b.

He that hath thoughte / ful inwardly and ofte See 4129.

1149.5 He that heweth to hye / þe chippis will fall in his ye
A proverbial couplet. [Cf. 411.5 and 3382, st. 3. Tilley C 354, C 357].
1. Bodl. 21626, f. 29b; 2. Balliol 354, f. 191b and f. 200b; 3. Rylands Lib. Latin 394, f. 21b.
1. Förster, *Festschrift zum 12 Deutschen Neuphilologentage*, p. 55; 2. Flügel, *Anglia* XXVI. 203; Dyboski, *EETS* ci. 129, 132; 3. Pantin, *BJRL* XIV. 107.

1149.8 He þat hyȝt hym wyþ hys kyn
Examples of foolish behaviour—three couplets.
1. BM Addit. 30338, f. 191b.

1150.3 He that in this booke beginneth to read
Patris Sapientiae, an alchemical poem—in quatrains. [For a similar but shorter poem cf. 1276].
1. Bodl. 7010, ff. 336a-342b (120 st.); 2. Bodl. 7630, Part V, ff. 8b-14a (120 st.); 3. Sloane 2352, ff. 86a-91b; 4. Massachusetts Hist. Soc., Winthrop 20 c, ff. 14b-19b (114 st.).
Ashmole, *Theatrum Chemicum*, pp. 194-209.

1150.5 He that in youthe no care will take
A proverb—two couplets. [Cf. 1151].
1. Morgan Lib. M. 898, f. 17b.
Bühler, *PMLA* LXXVI. 22.

1151 [See 512.8, 1150.5, 1817, 3502 (vv. 9-10), 3847, and 4151. Tilley Y 37].
3. Balliol 354, f. 213b; 4. Trinity Oxf. 49, f. 139b (var.); 9. Bodl. 1851, f. 99a; 10. Royal 17. D. vi, f. 150b; 11. Durham Univ. Cosin V. iii. 9, f. 46a (imperfect) and f. 79a (followed by 512.5); 12. Hunterian Mus. 400, flyleaf e verso.

4, 6, 8. Robbins, *Sec. Lyrics,* pp. 81-254, xxxii; 3. Flügel, *Anglia* XXVI. 225; 4. Manly and Rickert, *Canterbury Tales*, I. 540, 690; 9. Schleich, *Anglia* LI. 221; 11. Furnivall, *EETS* lxi. 169, 218.

1151.5 He that in youthe to sensualite / Applythe his mynde
On living in ease—one stanza rime royal.
1. Hunterian Mus. 239, f. 102b (in xvi cent. hand).

1152.5 He þat is befor tyme warned / Litill or nowgth is hurte or harmyd
A proverbial couplet.
1. Egerton 1995, f. 112b.

*1153.5 *He that is der and buried in syght
Prophecia Bridelyngton, Banistor, Merlyn and Thomas Assheldon. [Cf. 3889.5].
1. NLW Peniarth 50, p. 3 (first 16 lines illegible because of reagent).

1156 'Quod More.' [Cf. 4135.5].
2. Bodl. 2712, f. 268a.
1, 2. Robbins, *Archiv* CC. 342; 1. *Oxford Dict. Eng. Proverbs*, 1935, p. 188; Manly and Rickert, *Canterbury Tales*, I. 378.

1157 Wright, *Retrospective Rev.* n.s. II. 198.

He that made both heven and erthe
An extract (*Rel. Ant.*, II. 84) from 1184.

1159 Horstmann, *AE Leg. 1881*, pp. 242-58.

1161 1. Bibl. Bodmeriana, Coligny, Genève [*olim* Ireland Blackburn], ff. 35a-59a.

1162 [See 611.5 for longer version].
4. Lincoln's Inn 150, ff. 2, 3, 13a-27b (vv. 2490).

162.5 He that may not suffre wele / with unskyle he pleynith hym þei he wo þole
Proverbium—one couplet.
1. Camb. Un. Ff. 5. 47, f. 1b (added in xvi cent. hand).

1162.6   He that may thrive and will not
             A gnomic warning—four monoriming lines.
             1. Royal 17. A. xxxii, f. 122a.

1162.7   He þat mokyt / schall noȝt be owyn mokyt
             A couplet translating '*Qui me deridet non inde risus abibit.*'
             1. Bodl. 15444, f. 144a.
                Meech, *MP* XXXVIII. 125.

1162.8   He that no good can nor non will lern
             'Who shall him warne?'—one long couplet.
             1. Balliol 354, f. 191b.
                Dyboski, *EETS* ci. 129.

1162.9   He that of wast takys no hede / he shall wante wen he hasse nede
             A proverbial couplet included in 1628.8. [Cf. 1163].
             1. Hunterian Mus. 230, f. 248b.

1163   [Cf. 1162.9, 1328.5, 3546. Tilley M 1275].
             4. Bodl. Lyell 34, back cover (vv. 6).
                Rhodes; *repr.* Furnivall, *Roxburghe Club* LXXXVII. 49;
                2. Robbins, *Sec. Lyrics*, p. 81; 3. Patterson, *Shakespearean Studies*, p. 450; Tilley, p. 483.

1163.5   He þat smythth with a stafe off oke
             Fragment of a refrain-song, 'Card lye down.'
             1. New York Pub. Lib., Drexel Fragments 4185.

1165   [Cf. 1410].
             3. Royal 18. B. xxii, f. 44b; 5. Jesus Oxf. 29, f. 143b; 6. A. G. Thomas: Sarum *Horae*, (Sotheby Sale, Dec. 10, 1962, Lot 145), flyleaf.
                2, 3, 4b. Robbins, *Sec. Lyrics*, pp. 85, 254; 1. James. *Cat.*, III. 36; 2. Bishop, *EETS* 109. xlix; Coulton, *Life in the MA.*, II. 118 (mod.); Bennett, *England Chaucer-Caxton*, p. 161; Kaiser, *Med. Eng.*, reverse of title page; 3. Nicolas, *Boke of Noblesse*, Roxburghe Club LXXVII. lvi; 5. Hill, *Med. Aevum* XXXII. 209; 6. *Sotheby Sale Cat.*, Dec. 10, 1962.

1166.5   He that to women hys credens gyffe
             Beware the snares of woman—two couplets.
             1. Bodl. 11224, f. 111b (added in xvi cent. hand).

1168 [Ringler 22].
19. Rylands Lib., English 2 [*olim* Osterley Park], f. 1a; 21 = 29. *olim* Rosenbach 475 [*olim* Harmsworth, *olim* Leighton], f. 1a; 22. Longleat 254; 23. *olim* Wollaton Hall, f. 1a (Quaritch Sale Cat. 1931, Item 100; Cat. 775, Item 5); 30. Rosenbach Foundation 439/16 [*olim* Phillipps 4254], f. 1a; 31. Houghton 9, Queenstown, Maryland [*olim* Mostyn Hall 272, *olim* Rosenbach 477], f. 1a; 32. Balliol 329, ff. 127a-171b (begins I. 967); 33. *olim* Lyell (Quaritch Sale Cat. 699, 1952, Item 28); 34. Illinois Univ. 84, ff. 1-386; 35. Newberry Lib., Louis H. Silver 4.

Extracts: [For further extracts see 1592, 3744. Cf. also 3535].
7. Trinity Camb. 599, ff. 2a-3a (=1592); 8. Trinity Camb. 600, p. 368 (= 674; and III. 1569-75); 9. Fitzwilliam Mus., McClean 182, f. 11 a (VI, ii) and f. 49b (II, ii; IV, xv; III, xx; I, xiii; III, ix; III, xiv); 15. Harley 4011, f. 1b; 17. Sloane 2452 (fragment, 8 leaves, begins I. 1023); 18. Sloane 2577, Part A; 20. Leyden Univ. Vossius 9, ff. 65b (VIII. 2661), 75a (VIII. 1023), 104a (VII. 1153); 25. Morgan Lib. M. 4, ff. 74b-75b (Envoy); 26. *olim* Phillipps 23554 (one leaf, III, vi end to beg. viii) (Maggs Sale Cat. 849, Item 30 A).

Pynson, 1494 (STC 3175).

1170 Three essentials for love — one stanza rime royal.
Wilson, *MLN* LXIX. 22; Davies, *Med. Eng. Lyrics*, p. 219.

1170.5 He þat wyle furþer streche
On over-ambition — three proverbial monoriming lines. [A variant of 4113 occurring separately. Cf. Tilley A 316].
1. Harley 3362, f. 4a.

1171 1, 2. Förster, *Anglia* LXVII. 134, 136 (brief extracts only).

1172 [For prose versions cf. Canterbury Cath. Z. 8. 33, *olim* Ingilby, f. 1a; NLW Deposit: Porkington 10, f. 132a].
5 = 6. Newberry Lib. Gen. Add. 12 [*olim* Condover Hall, Robinson Sale Cat. No. 63, Item 71] (roll).
1, 4 (vv. 554-914). Furnivall, *EETS* 15 orig. ed. 113-44; rev. ed. 143-73; 3. N. S. Baugh, *Worcestershire Misc.*, p. 106.

1172.5 He that wyll in Eschepe ete a goose so fat
Advice against extravagant living, '*secundum Aristotilem*' — one quatrain.
1. Trinity Camb. 599, f. 208b.
James, *Cat.*, II. 73.

1172.8   He that will not spare
            A moralizing couplet on a late xiv cent. bronze jug.
            Evans, *English Art*, 1949, p. 90.

1173   [For similar lines in *Fasciculus Morum* see 4151; cf. also 1151; 1669, st. 39, MS. 2 only; Heywood, *EETS* 32.107, vv. 4; *Roxburghe Club* LXXXVII. 45. Further refs. in Meech, *MP* XXXVIII. 126].
            [Revise listing of MSS. as follows:]
            1. Bodl. 15444, f. 140a; 2. Bodl. 21626, f. 31a; 3. Camb. Un. Ee. 4. 37, f. ii verso; 4. Harley 2247, f. 79b; 5. Durham Univ. Cosin V. iii. 9, f. 85b; 6. Rylands Lib. Latin 394, f. 24b; 7. Morgan Lib. M. 124, f. 157b.
            1. Meech, *MP* XXXVIII. 117; 2. Förster, *Festschrift zum 12 Deutschen Neuphilologentage*, p. 57; 5. Furnivall *EETS* lxi. 228; 6. Pantin, *BJRL* XIV. 108; 7. Bergen, *EETS* cxxiv. 85.

            He that will sadly behold me with his ie / Maye see his own Merowr and lerne to die
            One couplet, introducing 4238.5.

1174.5   He that wyll with the devyll ete / A long spone must he gete
            A proverbial couplet. [Tilley S 771].
            1. Harley 2321, f. 149a; 2. Sloane 747, f. 66a.
            1. *Rel. Ant.*, I. 208; 2. Förster, *Anglia* LXII. 203.

            *Heo tok forþ a wel fair þing / Of hire finger a riche ryng
            Floris and Blauncheflur (Camb. Un. MS.):   see 2288.8.

1174.8   He was neuer wyse / þat went on þe yse
            A proverbial couplet.
            1. Bodl. 21626, f. 19b.
            Förster, *Festschrift zum 12 Deutschen Neuphilologentage*, p. 48.

            *He wil my corse all beclip & clap [me] to his breist
            See 3845.5 (v. 104, early print).

1176   [For prose versions see...Huntington HU 1051...and *Boke of Huntyng*, St. Albans, 1486 (STC 3308)].

[134]

Heded like a snake   See 42.5.

Her and se and hold the styll   See 3081.

1176.5   Harte be tru & don not amys
Remember me—three lines. [Probably secular; cf. 1176.8].
1. Trinity Camb. 1157, f. 59a.
Robbins, *Anglia* LXXXII. 12.

1176.8   hartte be trwe and true loue kepe
Remember your lover—two couplets. [Cf. 1176.5].
1. Sloane 3501, f. 53a.
Fehr, *Archiv* CVII. 53.

1179   Euen it es a rich ȝ ture

1179.5   Heueli mote he hit brouke
A colophon—six irregular riming lines.
1. Vatican Lib. Borghese 298, f. 201b.
Pelzer, *Revue néo-scolastique*, Aug.-Nov. 1913, pp. 54-5.

1180   An Envoy to his mistress: a love epistle. [Cf. Seaton, p. 152].

1181   2. Brechin Castle.
1. Hazlitt, *Remains*, I. 301-3.

1181.5   Ector þat was off alle knyghtes flowr
The Nine Nobles—nine quatrains.
1. Harley 2259, f. 39b.
Furnivall, *N&Q* 7 s. VIII. 22; Loomis, *MP* XV. 216.

1182   1. Stockholm Royal Lib. X. 90, p. 146.
Robbins, *Sec. Lyrics*, p. 58.

1184   1. Bodl. 6922*, f. 9a (vv. 822); 6. Cotton Calig. A. ii, f. 130a; 7. Advocates 19. 3. 1, f. 48a; 10. Naples Nat. Lib. XIII. B. 29, p. 114 (fragment: vv. 122).
10. *Rel. Ant.*, II. 67 (vv. 19 only).

1185   Four lines on Henry (Hotspur) Percy.
1. Egerton 3309 [*olim* Castle Howard], p. 204.
Wilson, *Lost Lit.*, p. 203.

Henry Notingham & his wyffe   See 1119.5.

1186   1. York City House Book VI, f. 17b; 2. Cotton Julius B. xii, f. 11b.

 1, 2. Smith, *London Med. St.*, 1939, pp. 394-5; 1. Raine, *Yorks. Arch. Soc. Record Ser.* XCVIII. 158-9.

1186.5   Hurre fayre speche ys turnyd into grutchyng / Here swete smelle and sawowurys turnyd into stynggyng

A couplet in Bozon's *Contes moralisés*.

1. Harley 1288, f. 97a.

Herbert, *Cat. Rom.*, III. 104; Smith, *SATF*, p. 209; Förster, *Festschrift zum 12 Deutschen Neuphilologentage*, p. 60; Ross, *Neuphil. Mitteilungen* L. p. 213.

1187   one stanza rime royal (with acrostic Hvmfrey).

1. Bodl. Lat. misc. c. 66 [*olim* Capesthorne], f. 92b and f. 95a.

Robbins, *PMLA* LXV. 262-3.

1187.5   Here are beryd vnder this stoon in the clay

Epitaph for Thomas and Margery Amys, A.D. 1445, on a brass in Barton Church, Norfolk. [Cf. 1285.5].

Blomefield, *Norfolk*, XI. 5; L'Estrange, *East Anglian* III. 319.

1188   [For prose versions see Bodl. 3938; Bodl. 12143, f. 52, with rimes; Harley 1704, f. 48b; Harley 1706; pr. Horstmann, *York. Wr.*, I. 110-11; &c.].

1188.5   Heer biginneþ a good tretis / þat seint Edmound

Verse introduction to a prose *Mirror of St. Edmund*—one monoriming quatrain.

1. Bodl. 3938, f. 355a.

Horstmann, *York. Wr.*, I. 240.

Here begynneth a lytell propre jeste   See 603.5.

1189   vv. 501 in couplets.

Bowers, *Univ. of Florida Monographs, Humanities* XII. 19-32.

1190   vv. 117 in couplets.

Bowers, *Southern Folklore Qr.* XX. 120-3.

Here bygynneþ a tretys / þat is yclept
Introductory heading to 3270.

1192   [Delete this entry].

Here begynneth of Saynt Margarete / The blessed lyfe   See 2673.

Here begynithe the Compende of Alkamie   See 595.

1192.5   Here begynneth þe medicyns both goode & true / To hele all sores
   The properties and medicines of a horse—twelve couplets.
   de Worde, ca. 1502 (STC 13827.1).

1194.5   Here beside dwellithe a riche barons dowghter
   The Juggler and the Baron's Daughter—fourteen long couplets and bob with 2-line burden: 'Drawe me ner.' [Cf. Sidgwick, *Pop. Ballads*, III. 211-16].
   1. Balliol 354, f. 251a.
      Flügel, *Anglia* XXVI. 278; Dyboski, *EETS* ci. 115; *Early Eng. Lyrics*, p. 251; Davies, *Med. Eng. Lyrics*, pp. 284-6.

1195   [Utley 85].
   Sylvester, *Xmas Carols & Ballads*, p. 159; Sylvester, *Garland of Xmas Carols*, p. 143; Husk, *Songs of Nativity*, p. 129; Bullen, *Carols & Poems*, pp. 255-6; Rickert, *Anc. Eng. Xmas Carols*, p. 262; Patterson, *Shakespearean Studies*, 1916, p. 444; Robbins, *Sec. Lyrics*, p. 46.

1197   [Cf. 1197.8].
   G. C. V. Harcourt, *Legends of SS. Augustine, Antony, and Cuthbert*, 1868.

1197.1   Here endiþ as ȝe may see / *Stimulus Consciencie*
   A colophon ascribing the *Pricke of Conscience* to 'Richard þe holy ermyte'—two couplets.
   1. Egerton 3245 [*olim* Gurney], f. 156a.
      Allen, *Rolle*, p. 375.

1197.2   Here endys haukyng with medysyns and castyng / And all that longys to goode hauke kepyng
   A couplet following a collection of prose notes on hawking derived from Juliana Berners.
   1. Pepys 1047, f. 23b.

1197.3   Here endiþ þe Bible / Jesu helpe us for we ben feble
Concluding rubric at end of Wycliffite Bible.
1. Trinity Dublin 67, endleaf.

Here endith the boke of Sapience / How man hadde first Redemcioun
Epilogue to 3406.

1197.4   Here endiþ þe book / of vertu and of synne
A recommendation for the *Speculum Vite* (245), which immediately precedes—two cross-rimed quatrains joined with riming tails.
1. Trinity Dublin 423, f. 203a.

1197.5   Here endeth þe medicynes sothe & trwe
Six lines concluding a collection of veterinary directions in prose.
1. Sloane 686, f. 65b.

1197.6   Here endeþ þe rule of seint Benet
Ten lines in irregular couplets forming a colophon for a prose commentary.
1. Lib. of Congress, Washington, 4, f. 36a.

1197.8   Here fader and moder of sanct Austine
On St. Augustine—twenty-two couplets on the back of Carlisle Cathedral choir stalls. [Cf. 1197].
Harcourt, *Legends of SS. Augustine, Antony, and Cuthbert*, 1868.

1198   Rickert, *Anc. Eng. Xmas Carols*, p. 225; Greene, *Sel. Eng. Carols*, p. 96.

1199   Robbins, *Sec. Lyrics*, p. 60.

1201   Robbins, *Sec. Lyrics*, p. 9.

1201.3   Here I woll tel yow a medecyn / for euery maner of vryn
On the colors of urines—fifteen couplets, followed by a prose tract. [Cf. 1109.5].
1. Sloane 120, ff. 78a-79a.

1201.5   Here I will you wyse make / when ye will a Iurney take
Astrological prognostications for traveling—sixteen couplets.
[Cf. 1436.2].
1. Sloane 636, f. 103a.

1202   2. N. S. Baugh, *Worcestershire Misc.*, p. 87; Mahoney, *Speculum* XXXIV. 98.

1203   [Singer 853].
3. Sloane 1098, f. 9a (vv. 40).

1204   14. Canterbury Cath. D. 14.

1204.5   Here is ybyried under this grave / Harry Hawles
Epitaph on a brass, ca. 1430, for Harry Hawles, in Arreton Church, Isle of Wight—two couplets.
Pettigrew, *Chronicles of Tombs*, p. 46; Ravenshaw, *Antiente Epitaphes*, p. 9.

1205   to a Latin text, ff. 58a-64b, *De lapide philosophorum*. [Singer 855].

1205.5   Here lieth byrryd under thys stone off marbyll / Margaret
Epitaph at Raveningham, Norfolk, A.D. 1483—four couplets.
East Anglian III. 327.

1206   Robbins, *Sec. Lyrics*, p. 119.

1206.1   Here lyth grauyn vndyr this ston / Thomas Knowles
Epitaph (xv cent.) at St. Anthony's [Antlins] Church, London —ten lines.
Weever, *Anc. Funerall Monuments*, 1631, p. 402 (STC 25223); Ravenshaw, *Antiente Epitaphes*, p. 6.

1206.2   Here lyeth graven [vnder] thyis stoon / Christine Savage
Epitaph, A.D. 1450, for Robert and Christine Savage of Busshead, Sussex—eight lines.
Pettigrew, *Chronicles of Tombs*, p. 243; Ravenshaw, *Antiente Epitaphes*, p. 11.

1206.4   Here lieth i-dolven vnder this stone / Roger hunt & Johone
Epitaph, A.D. 1473, at Great Linford, Bucks.—four couplets.
Records of Bucks., III. 113.

1206.6 Here lyth John Brigge under this marbil ston
Epitaph on a brass, A.D. 1454, in Salle Church, Norfolk—three couplets.
Pettigrew, *Chronicles of Tombs*, p. 46; Cotman, *Sepulchral Brasses in Norfolk*, 1839.

1206.7 Here lythe Rychard þe sone and þe Eyer
Epitaph, A.D. 1445, for Richard Mansfield of Taplow, Bucks.—one 8-line stanza followed by a 3-line prayer tag.
Ravenshaw, *Antiente Epitaphes*, pp. 10-11.

1206.8 Here lyth þe bones of Rychard Adare
Epitaph, A.D. 1435, for Richard and Maryon Adare of Kelshall, Herts.—vv. 14 (including Abuses of the Age: cf. 906, 2818.2).
Ravenshaw, *Antiente Epitaphes*, p. 9.

1206.9 Here lith the fresshe flour of Plantagenet
Epitaph on Queen Elizabeth, wife of Henry VII—nine couplets (following 4263.3 and a Latin version).
1. Balliol 354, f. 176a.
Flügel, *Anglia* XXVI. 188; Dyboski, *EETS* ci. 99; Campbell, *Eng. Works of Sir Thomas More*, p. 312.

1207 1. Harley 665, f. 295a.
Chambers, *Eng. Lit. Close MA*, p. 139; Robbins, *Sec. Lyrics*, p. 118; Davies, *Med. Eng. Lyrics*, p. 188.

1207.5 Here lies William Banknot and Anne his wyff / Swete Iesew grant to them and us euerlastyng lyff
Epitaph, A.D. 1400—four lines.
Weever, *Anc. Funerall Monuments*, 1631, p. 334 (STC 25223).

1209 Horstmann, *AE Leg. 1881*, p. 3.

Here now endeth as ye maye see
Couplet colophon concluding de Worde, *Siege of Thebes*, 1495, f. 87a: see 3928.

1210.5 Her sal I duellen loken vnder stone
Two couplets translating '*Hic habitabo clausus in tumulo.*'
1. Advocates 18. 7. 21, f. 87b.

[140]

1211.5   Here the redman and his whyte wiffe
'The wordes of þe first sphere'—four couplets.
1. Bodl. 7630, Part I, f. 38b.

1211.7   Here vnder lyth a man of Fame / William Walworth
Epitaph, (allegedly) A.D. 1383, for William Wentworth, Mayor of London, at St. Michael's, Crooked Lane, London—six couplets.
Weever, *Anc. Funerall Monuments*, 1631, p. 410 (STC 25223).

1211.8   Here vndyr rests this marble ston / Jone Spenser
Epitaph, A.D. 1407—six couplets.
Pettigrew, *Chronicles of Tombs*, p. 430.

1211.9   Here vndyr this ston lyes Piers Ion / And Elizabeth his wyeff
Epitaph, A.D. 1473—seven lines.
Weever, *Anc. Funerall Monuments*, 1631, p. 650 (STC 25223).

Here ye may lerne wisdom ful goode   See 3848.

Herfor and þerfor and þerfor I came   See 3552.

1212   Sandys, *Carols*, p. 18; Rickert, *Anc. Eng. Xmas Carols*, p. 128; Stevens, *Med. Carols*, p. 82.

1213   1. BM Addit. 46919 [*olim* Phillipps 8336], f. 205a.
Kaiser, *Anthologie*, p. 240; Kaiser, *Med. Eng.*, p. 283.

1214   [Singer 183].
2. Trinity Camb. 1137, f. 37a (at end of Latin version); 3. Harley 3542, f. 14a; 4. Harley 3542, f. 41b (at end of Latin version).
1, 3, 4. Singer, *Alchemical MSS.*, I. 160, III. 1134.

Heryed be thou blysfull heuen quene   See 1243.

Heryed be thou blysful lord aboue   See 1244.

Herry Notingham & his wyffe lyne here   See 1119.5.

Hey doune doune / These women all   See 3559.8.

1214.2   Hay hay the wythe swan / By Godes soule I am thy man
A motto of Edward III.
Palliser, *Historic Devices*, p. 361.

1214.4   Hay how the cheualdoures / woke al nyght
The entertainers at a wake: a fragment in the Red Book of Ossory.
1. Kilkenny: Red Book of Ossory.
Hist. MSS. Comm. Report X, App. V. 245; Graves, *N&Q* 1 s. II. 385; Seymour, *Anglo-Irish Lit. 1200-1582*, p. 97; Wilson *LSE* V. 40; Robbins, *Sec. Lyrics*, p. xxxvi; Wilson, *Lost Lit.*, p. 188.

1214.5   Hay how the mavys on a brere
A *chanson d'aventure* dialogue between a mavis and a disconsolate lover—three 10-line tail-rime stanzas.
1. BM Addit. 5665, f. 146b.
Fehr, *Archiv* CVI. 284; Stevens, *Music & Poetry*, p. 349.

Hey nony nony nony nony no
Burden to 3635.5.

1214.6   Hey now now
Three words used as a round.
1. BM Addit. 31922, f. 21b and again (with different music) at f. 25b.
Stevens, *Music & Poetry*, pp. 390, 391; Stevens, *Music at Court*, pp. 16, 19.

Hey troly loly lo / Mayde whether go you   See 2034.5.

1214.7   Hey troly loly loly / my loue is lusty plesant and demure
A round—ten lines.
1. BM Addit. 31922, f. 80a.
Chappell, *Archaeologia* LXI. 375; Flügel, *Anglia* XII. 248; Stevens, *Music & Poetry*, p. 414; Stevens, *Music at Court*, p. 57.

1214.9   *Hi sunt qui psalmos corrumpunt nequitur almos*
Macaronic lines on Tutivillus—four lines. [Cf. 707.5, 1655.5, and 3812].
1. Balliol 354, f. 201b; 2. Camb. Un. Ff. 1. 14; 3. Lansdowne 762, f. 101b; 4. Sloane 1584, f. 13b.

1. Flügel, *Anglia* XXVI. 204; Dyboski, *EETS* ci. 137; 2. Horstmann, *York. Wr.*, II. xxxiii; 3. *Rel. Ant.*, I. 291; Wright, *Percy Soc.* VIII. 225; Wright, *Piers Plowman*, 1856, p. 543; 4. Wright, *Camden Soc.* XVI. 148.

1215 Sibbald, *Chronicle*, I. 14-54 (160 st. only); Eyre-Todd, *Med. Scot. Poetry*, pp. 1-74; Lawson, 1910, pp. 3-101; Neilson and Webster, *Chief British Poets*, pp. 347-66; W. A. MacKenzie, 1939.

1216 Brook, *Harley Lyrics*, pp. 46-8.

1217 Furnivall, *EETS* 15 orig. ed. 229; rev. ed. 256.

1218 Hingeston, *Capgrave's Chronicle*, RS I. xxvi; Person, *Camb. ME Lyrics*, p. 53.

1218.5 Hym were bettre that he ne were ne neuer born / for liif and soule be his forloren

Illustrative couplet to conclude a specimen *exemplum* in a '*Liber Exemplorum ad usum praedicantium*' —one couplet. [Cf. 3901].
1. Durham Cath. B. iv. 19, f. 50a.
Little, *Brit. Soc. Franciscan St.*, I. 45; Pfander, *Pop. Sermon*, p. 47.

1218.8 Himselfe by geving receyvethe a benefithe

Give to those worthy—one couplet.
1. Durham Univ. Cosin V. iii. 9, f. 58b.
Furnivall, *EETS* lxi. 188.

Hiry hary hubbilschow See 1119.3.

1219 [For an earlier version in couplets see 2036 &c. For Kele's version see 2111].

Early Eng. Carols, p. 118; Greene, *Sel. Eng. Carols*, p. 104.

*1219.5 *His Brothere Ruffin of hym greate marvell hade

Legend of SS. Wulfhade and Ruffyn—only fragments of the first leaf are preserved (the first complete line is v. 70).
1. Cotton Nero C. xii, f. 182a.
Horstmann, *AE Leg. 1881*, pp. 308-14.

1220 2. Hereford Cath. O. iii. 5, f. 48a.

His myrth is slaket   See 1220 (Hereford Cath. MS).

1220.5   Hys signe ys a ster bryth
An Epiphany carol—three quatrains and burden.
1. Egerton 3307, f. 58b.
Stevens, *Med. Carols*, p. 43; Greene, *Sel. Eng. Carols*, p. 90.

1222   Robbins, *Sec. Lyrics*, pp. 33-4.

1223.5   Holde þy thombe in thy fyst / And kepe þe welle fro Had I wyst
A proverbial couplet.
1. Bodl. 21626, f. 26a; 2. Rylands Lib. Latin 394, f. 16b.
1. Förster, *Festschrift zum 12 Deutschen Neuphilologentage*, p. 53; 2. Pantin, *BJRL* XIV. 103.

1224   2. Arthur, *Archaeologia* LVII. 55-7.

1225   [Utley 86].
Husk, *Songs*, p. 128; Bullen, *Carols & Poems*, p. 256; Sylvester, *Garland of Xmas Carols*, p. 141; Rickert, *Anc. Eng. Xmas Carols*, p. 262; Robbins, *Sec. Lyrics*, pp. 45-6.

1226   [Utley 87 and 88].
Copland, 1561; 1, 2. Rickert, *Anc. Eng. Xmas Carols*, pp. 264-6; Greene, *Sel. Eng. Carols*, pp. 93, 92; Davies, *Med. Eng. Lyrics*, pp. 280, 175; 1. Mason, *Humanism & Poetry*, p. 154; Speirs, *Med. Eng. Poetry*, pp. 85-6; 2. Husk, *Songs*, p. 131; Sylvester, *Garland of Xmas Carols*, p. 144; Ritson, *Anc. Songs*, 1877, p. 113.

Holy angell to whom pusance deuine   See 914 (st. 8).

1227   Holy archan[g]le Michael / saynt Gabriel and Raphael
two couplets (followed by 1961.3).
1. Arundel 57, f. 2a.

Holy Chyrch of hym makyth mynd   See 340.

1230   1. Stevens, *Med. Carols*, p. 14; 2. Rickert, *Anc. Eng. Xmas Carols*, p. 18.

1232   1. BM Addit. 46919 [*olim* Phillipps 8336], f. 207b.
Brown, *Sources and Analogues of Chaucer's CT*, p. 469.

1234   4. Egerton 3307, f. 66b.
          3, 4. Stevens, *Med. Carols,* pp. 88, 53; 4. Greene, *Sel. Eng. Carols,* p. 131.

1235   1. BM Addit. 46919 [*olim* Phillipps 8336], f. 208a.

1236   James, *Cat.,* II. 90; MacCracken, *Archiv* CXXX. 309.

1237   Kirke, *Reliquary* IX. 76-7.

1238   A letter to his heart's sovereign—five stanzas rime royal.
          1. Robbins, *Sec. Lyrics,* pp. 192-3.

1239   *Gentleman's Magazine,* May 1842, p. 461 (2 st. only).

1240   Robbins, *Sec. Lyrics,* pp. 184-5.

1240.5   Honowre of kyngys in every mannys syght / Of comyn costome louythe equyte and ryghte
          A 'scripture' or descriptive title in a London pageant—one couplet (in Gregory's *Chronicle*).
          1. Egerton 1995, f. 180a.
          Gairdner, *Camden Soc.* n. s. XVII. 174.

1241   Robbins, *Sec. Lyrics,* p. 196; Kurvinen, *Neuphil. Mitteilungen* LIV. 56-7.

1241.5   Onowryd and blyssed motte he be
          Epilogue, praising God, to an alchemical tract in prose—one quatrain.
          1. Copenhagen Old Coll. 248, f. 1b.
          Retrospective Rev. 1854, II. 409.

1242   [Ringler 96].
          8. Camb. Un. Kk. 1. 7, f. 119a; 9. BM Addit. 34193, f. 93a; 10. Hatfield; 11. Melbourne: Victoria Pub. Lib., f. 204b (with addit. st.).
          Pylgremage of the Sowle, Caxton, 1483 (STC 6473).

1243   [Ringler 24]
          7. Camb. Un. Kk. 1. 7, f. 117a; 8. BM Addit. 34193, f. 91a;

9. Hatfield; 10. Melbourne: Victoria Pub. Lib., f. 199b (3 addit. st.).

Pylgremage of the Sowle, Caxton, 1483 (STC 6473).

1244 [Ringler 25].
8. Camb. Un. Kk. 1. 7, f. 121b; 9. BM Addit. 34193, f. 94a; 10. Hatfield; 11. Melbourne: Victoria Pub. Lib., f. 206b.

Pylgremage of the Sowle, Caxton, 1483 (STC 6473).

1245 [Ringler 26].
7. Camb. Un. Kk. 1. 7, f. 114b; 8. BM Addit. 34193, f. 90b; 9. Hatfield; 10. Melbourne: Victoria Pub. Lib., f. 196a.

Pylgremage of the Sowle, Caxton, 1483 (STC 6473).

1246 [Ringler 27].
8. Camb. Un. Kk. 1. 7, f. 36a (last 2 lines only); 9. BM Addit. 34193, f. 32b; 10. Hatfield; 11. Melbourne: Victoria Pub. Lib., f. 127a.

Pylgremage of the Sowle, Caxton, 1483 (STC 6473); *repr.* Cust, 1859, pp. 48-9.

1247 [Ringler 28].
8. Camb. Un. Kk. 1. 7, f. 34a; 9. BM Addit. 34193, f. 31a; 10. Hatfield; 11. Melbourne: Victoria Pub. Lib., f. 125a.

Pylgremage of the Sowle, Caxton, 1483 (STC 6473); *repr.* Cust, 1859, p. 44 (2 st. only).

1248 [Ringler 29].
8. BM Addit. 34193, f. 95b; 9. Hatfield; 10. Melbourne: Victoria Pub. Lib., f. 209a (2 addit. st.).

Pylgremage of the Sowle, Caxton, 1483 (STC 6473); *repr.* Cust, 1859, pp. 80-1.

1249 [Ringler 30].
8. Camb. Un. Kk. 1. 7, f. 120a; 9. BM Addit. 34193, f. 93b; 10. Hatfield; 11. Melbourne: Victoria Pub. Lib., f. 205b.

Pylgremage of the Sowle, Caxton, 1483 (STC 6473); *repr.* Cust, 1859, pp. 78-9.

1249.5 Honoured be þou lorde of myghte
Song at the Assumption: poem occurring in only this MS. of Eng. tr. of the *Pèlerinage de l'Ame*—five stanzas rime royal.

1. Melbourne: Victoria Pub. Lib., f. 201a.

1251.5　　Hope ne were / hert brostun were
　　　　　A proverbial couplet, also appearing in *Gesta Romanorum* (pr. *Roxburghe Club*, 1838, p. 374; Herrtage, *EETS* xxxiii. 228; cf. Owst, *Lit. & Pulpit*, p. 43) and *Pricke of Conscience* (3428), vv. 7263-6. [Tilley H 605].
　　　　　1. Bodl. 21626, f. 29b; 2. Balliol 354, f. 191b; 3. Harley 3362, f. 4a; 4. Rylands Lib. Latin 394, f. 21b.
　　　　　　1. Förster, *Festschrift zum 12 Deutschen Neuphilologentage*, p. 55; 2. Dyboski, *EETS* ci. 129; 4. Pantin, *BJRL* XIV. 107.

1252　　　Lambarde, *Dictionarium Angliae*, 1730, p. 36; Wright, *Pop. Superstitions*, II. 260; Wilson, *Early ME Lit.*, p. 270; Wilson, *Lost Lit.*, p. 207.

1253　　　Hote and moyste ys Aquarius as ys the eþe[r] men tellyth vs byfore
　　　　　　twelve quatrains.

1253.5　　How a lyon shal be banished and to Berwyke gone
　　　　　A late Merlin prophecy.
　　　　　1. Bodl. 12653, Art. 53.

1254　　　The Port of Peace: Not Death but God—one 8-line stanza from Walton's translation of Boethius (1597), Book III, Metre 10. [Cf. 'The lyf ys longe that lothesumlye dothe last,' Bodl. 6933, st. 6: 'Dethe ys a port wherby we passe to joy,' pr. Wright, *Roxburghe Club* LXXXVIII. 36-7].
　　　　　Greg, *RES* XVI. 198; Greene, *MLN* LXIX. 307.

1255　　　Brie, *Eng. Stn.* XXXVII. 32; Lloyd, *RES* V. 303; Henderson, *Skelton*, 1931, p. 143; Person, *Camb. ME Lyrics*, p. 26.

　　　　　How frendly was Medea to Jason
　　　　　Extract (BM Addit. 17492, f. 91a) from 666.

1256.5　　Howe hurtfull is the thing
　　　　　Two moralizing couplets on Evil Tongue (following 1586).
　　　　　1. Royal 17. A. xxxii, f. 122b.

1258　　　[Delete entire entry].

　　　　　Hou ihesu crist herowede helle　　See 1850.5.

1259　　　3. Pepys 1584, f. 14a; 4. Pepys 2125, f. 60b.

1260   Two couplets in a Latin homily on 'Audi filia et vide' (Ps. XLIV. 11). [For a translation of the 'text' see 2231.8].
Pfander, *Pop. Sermon*, p. 46.

1261   2. Huntington HM 183 [*olim* Hawkins, *olim* Phillipps 8923], f. 4a (written twice).
2. Bowers, *MLN* LXVII. 332-3.

How shall Y plece a creature uncerteyne   Burden to 4283.5.

How shall I report   See 2756.5.

1264.5   How sould I rewill me or in quhat wys
'How sall I governe me' by William Dunbar-ten 5-line stanzas with refrain.
1. Camb. Un. Ll. 5. 10, f. 38a; 2. Pepys 2553, p. 323; 3. Advocates 1. 1. 6, f. 66a.
1. MacKenzie, *Dunbar*, pp. 24-6; 2. Craigie, *STS* n. s. VII. 388-9; 3. [Hailes,] *Anc. Scot. Poems*, pp. 76-8; *Sel. Poems of Dunbar*, Perth 1788, pp. 65-7; Sibbald, *Chronicle*, II. 4-6; Laing, *Dunbar*, I. 184-6; Paterson, *Dunbar*, pp. 222-4; *Bannatyne MS.*, Hunt. Club, I. 178-80; Small, *STS* IV. 95-7; Schipper, *Dunbar*, pp. 304-6; and *DKAW* XLII (IV). 1-4; Baildon, *Dunbar*, pp. 156-8; Ritchie, *STS* n. s. XXII. 162.

1265   [Perhaps one 5-line stanza aabba: cf. Greene, *Speculum* XXVII. 506]. [Utley 18].
Wells, *Manual*, p. 1176; Robbins, *Sec. Lyrics*, p. xxxvi; Wilson, *Lost Lit.*, p. 187; Davies, *Med. Eng. Lyrics*, p. 31.

1265.5   How slely þe deth schal robben ham
Three monoriming lines in a Latin sermon.
1. Camb. Un. Ii. 3. 8, f. 167b.

How þe book takeþ in honde   See 2361.5.

1267   Furnivall, *EETS* 15 orig. ed. 240; rev. ed. 268.

Hoyda hoyda joly rutterkin   Burden to 2832.3.

Hudo make an ende of thy playe   See 3818.5.

1267.5	Ynguar and Vbbe Beorn was þe þridde / Loþebrokes sunes The three sons of Lothbrog—two alliterative lines. 1. Pembroke Camb. 32, f. 141b. Förster, *Anglia* XLII. 147; Wilson, *Lost Lit.*, p. 43; James, *Cat.*, p. 71; Wells, *Manual*, p. 1052.
1269	[Utley 90]. Furnivall, *EETS* 15 orig. ed. 238; rev. ed. 266.
	I am a joly foster See 4068.6.
1269.5	I am a woman I may be bold A wanton's desires—five couplets and a 10-line heading, abbreviated in repetition as pseudo-burden. [Cf. 1286.5. Utley 120]. 1. Harley 7578, f. 105b. Fehr, *Archiv* CVII. 58.
1269.8	I am a worme & no man / Out castynge of alle men A couplet in a Latin sermon. 1. Balliol 149, f. 56b.
	I am a-knowe / and wot ryght well See 4186.
1270	[Cf. 1381]. 1. Arundel 83, f. 127a; 2. *olim* Yates Thompson 57 [*olim* Ashburnham 230], ff. 179b, 180a. 1. Gray, *N&Q* n.s. X. 167; 2. *Cat. MSS. Ashburnham Place*, London, n.d.
	Ich am agast me þinket i se / þat зonder stonde deuelen þre See 1270 (Thompson MS.).
1270.1	I am Alexander that conquert to paradise yate The Nine Worthies—eight long quatrains in hand of Richard Kaye (xvi cent.). [Cf. 312.5]. 1. Corpus Christi Oxf.: Glanville, *De Proprietatibus Rerum*, 1488. Milne and Sweeting, *MLR* XL. 87-9.
1270.2	I ham as I ham and so will I be The rebellious lover, attributed to Sir Thomas Wyatt—in quatrains. [Utley 92; cf. Utley, *MLN* LX. 106-10].

1. BM Addit. 17492, f. 85a (vv. 40); 2. Advocates 1. 1. 6, f. 250a (vv. 40); 3. Trinity Dublin 160, f. 107a (omits vv. 1-8); 4. Univ. of Pennsylvania Lat. 35 [*olim* Lyell, Quaritch Sale Cat. 699, Item 61], f. 3a flyleaf (vv. 16, with burden).

3, 4. Greene, *RES* n.s. XV. 176-7; 1. Foxwell, *Wiat*, I. 354; Muir, *Collected Poems*, pp. 54-5; 2. *Bannatyne MS.*, Hunt. Club, III. 731; Tillyard, *Wyatt*, p. 126; Ritchie, *STS* n.s. XXVI. 2-3; 3. Muir, *Unpublished Poems*, pp. 81-2; 4. Morford, *Lib. Chronicle Univ. Pennsylvania* XXV. 80-3.

I am as lyght as any roe
Burden to 3782.

1270.4   I am begynnyng & ende that made eche creature
Speech of the Father of Heaven at the Pageant celebrating the marriage of Prince Arthur to Princess Catharine—four stanzas rime royal.
1. Cotton Vitellius A. xvi, f. 192b.

1270.6   I am called Chyldhod in play is all my mynde
Tapestry verses by Thomas More, ca. 1503—eight stanzas rime royal and vv. 12 in Latin.
Workes, Rastell, 1557 (STC 18076); *facs. & repr.* Campbell, *Eng. Works of Sir Thomas More*, pp. 332-5; *repr.* Flügel, *Neuengl. Lesebuch*, pp. 40-2.

1270.8   I am comyng toward your bryde
A 'sotelty' for a bridal feast—three irregular lines. [Cf. 461.5, 1331.5, 1386.5].
1. Bodl. Lat. misc. c. 66 [*olim* Capesthorne], f. 68b.

1273   2. York: Yorkshire Philol. Soc. [*olim* Sykes], ff. 4 (Play 42, Scriveners, only).
1. J. S. Purvis, 1957 (mod.); 2. *History & Antiquities of City of York*, York 1785, II. 128-32; Halliwell, *Yorkshire Anthol.*, London 1851, pp. 198-204; Collier, *Camden Soc.* LXXIII. 3-18; J. H. Turner, *Yorkshire Anthol.*, Bingley 1901, pp. 39-43; Cawley, *LSE* VII *cum* VIII. 74-80.

1273.3   I am he that hath you dayly servyd
Fragment of a love song—four lines (following 155.5).
1. BM Addit. 5465, f. 19b.
Fehr, *Archiv* CVI. 55; Stevens, *Music & Poetry*, p. 358.

1273.5	I am he that wyl not fle / Gyfe me a stafe for charity English couplet translating 'Ego sum illy quy non youlte fugere da mychi bacoulum.' 1. Camb. Un. Add. 3402, f. 2b.
	I am here syre cristesmasse See 681.
1273.8	I am honour whome folk of euery degre 'The speche of Honour' at the Pageant celebrating the marriage between Prince Arthur and Princess Catharine—four stanzas rime royal. 1. Cotton Vitellius A. xvi, f. 194b.
1274	Davies, *Med. Eng. Lyrics*, p. 132.
1275	English couplets on illustrations of the months of the year. 1. Harley 5401, f. 81a.
1276	[For a longer poem cf. 1150.3. Singer 813]. [Revise listing of MSS as follows:] 1. Bodl. 3652, ff. 70-71; 2. Bodl. 7010, f. 46a (vv. 78) and again at f. 143a; 3. Bodl. 7624, Part II, pp. 89-91 (vv. 62) and again at pp. 107-8 (vv. 59); 4. Bodl. 7630, Part V, ff. 21a-21b (vv. 46); 5. Bodl. 7630, Part VIII, ff. 21a-22b (vv. 102), and again at f. 50a (vv. 18); 6. Bodl. 7644, ff. 61b-62a (vv. 61); 7. Bodl. 8343, ff. 62b-64b (vv. 64); 8. Trinity Camb. 1119, f. 90b (vv. 42); 9. Sloane 1092, f. 13b (vv. 13); 10. Sloane 1098, ff. 7b-8b; 11. Sloane 1098, ff. 38a-b; 12. Sloane 3667, f. 117b; 13. Massachusetts Hist. Soc., Winthrop 20 c, ff. 25b-26a.
1276.3	hic am michel of airas / Wl sone ic am virþeten alas A couplet tag. 1. Trinity Camb. 323, f. 28a. James, *Cat.*, I. 441.
1276.5	ic am nout for þisse þinge þo English words in a xii century homily. 1. Bodl. 5136, p. 398 (two lines of music, without words, on p. 396).

1276.8	I am not unkynd to love as I ffynd One line of a love lyric added to flyleaf of a Psalter. 1. Harley 2888, last leaf. Wordsworth and Littlehales, *Old Service Books*, p. 60; Wilson, *Lost Lit.*, p. 190.
1278	Robbins, *Sec. Lyrics*, p. 164.
1279	Robbins, *Sec. Lyrics*, p. 233.
1280	[For a similar burden cf. 210. Utley 93]. Robbins, *Sec. Lyrics*, pp. 34-5; Greene, *Sel. Eng. Carols*, p. 167.
1281.5	I am walked in a veye / Butt wheþur I shall I can not sey Daily reminder of death—one couplet. 1. Royal 18. B. xxiii, f. 107a. Ross, *EETS* 209. 157.
*1285	*I by-leve that crist was borne of mari the virgen
1285.5	I beseche all peple fer and ner / To prey for me Thomas Amys An epitaph, A.D. 1445, on a brass in Barton Church, Norfolk—eight lines. [Cf. 1187.5]. Blomefield, *Norfolk*, XI. 5; L'Estrange, *East Anglian* III. 319.
1286	8. Trinity Dublin 351, f. 25a.
1286.5	I can be wanton and yf I wyll I can be wanton—six cross-riming quatrains. [Cf. 1269.5]. 1. Bodl. 6659, f. 98b. Wagner, *MLN* L. 452-3.
1287	[From Peter Idley's *Instructions* (1540), II. A. 2197-2210].
1288	1a (xix cent. transcript). Egerton 2257, ff. 15a-16b.
	I Kateryn of the court celestyall See 1322.8.
1289	How Christ shall come—four long lines with 'I come' anaphora (immediately following 1353). *Rel. Lyrics XIV C.*, p. 53.

1291   Furnivall, *EETS* lxx. 225-42; Adams, *Chief Pre-Sh. Dramas,* pp. 225-42 (vv. 1-924).

1292   seven couplets (followed by 3709).
1a (xix cent. transcript). Egerton 2257, f. 98a.
Halliwell, *Dict. Archaic & Provincial Words,* p. xxxiii; M. J. Hughes, *Women Healers in Med. Life,* 1943, p. 32.

1293   6. BM Addit. 33996, f. 109b; 7. Wellcome Hist. Med. Lib. 542, f. 14b.

1293.5   I coniour hem in the name of the ffader
A charm against thieves—in couplets (following 939).
1. Bodl. 817, f. 2b (vv. 14, inc. Latin); 2. Camb. Un. Add. 5943, f. 170a (vv. 18).
2. L. S. M[ayer], *Music, Cantalinas, Songs &c.,* p. 42; Robbins, *Sec. Lyrics,* pp. 58-9.

1294.3   I count his conquest greate
Let Reason defeat Will—one cross-rimed quatrain.
1. Durham Univ. Cosin V. iii. 9, f. 83a.
Furnivall, *EETS* lxi. 224.

1294.5   Ic del his bin teche / laht me hauith made ische
An English couplet in a Latin story about a boy with an ulcerated hand.
1. Caius 414, f. 166b.
James, *Cat.,* I. 487.

1295   1. Cotton Julius F. x, f. 141a.

1295.5   I eschew to climbe too high aloft / least for presumption I should not fall soft
The Golden Mean—one couplet.
1. Bodl. 11946, f. 1b.

I ffynde wretyn a noble story   See 1653.

1295.8   I fly / constraynyd am I / with wepynge eyes / to morne & pleyne
No comfort without his mistress—in short lines.
1. Nat. Lib. Scotland 6128, last leaf (fragmentary).
Robbins, *Anglia* LXXXII. 12.

I go to the medowe to mylke my cow   See 2034.5.

1296   [Ringler 31].
        7. Camb. Un. Kk. 1. 7, ff. 21a-24b; 8. BM Addit. 34193, ff. 19b-21a; 9. Hatfield; 10. Melbourne: Victoria Pub. Lib., f. 112a.
        Pylgremage of the Sowle, Caxton, 1483 (STC 6473); *repr.* Cust, 1859, pp. 24-9.

1297   [For a later version expanded into long lines cf. Rawl. poet. 172, f. 12b; Bodl. Gough Norfolk 43, f. 31b; Arundel, Harington, f. 16a, pr. Hughey, I. 79. For a longer and later text cf. Rimbault, *Songs & Ballads,* p. 42; Hawkins, *Hist. Music,* 1776, III. 38; Hughey, II. 3-4; cf. also 1400 and 3960.5].
        1. Bodl. 655, f. 114b; 3. Harley 116, f. 170b (followed by vv. 5-6 of 1400); 6. Delete this MS.; 8. Bodl. 15444, f. 168a (var.); 9. Cotton Titus A. xxvi, f. 73b; 10. Harley 4800, f. 54a.
        3, 9. Robbins, *Sec. Lyrics,* pp. 81, 255; 3. Kaiser, *Med. Eng.,* p. 550; 10. Cummings, *EETS* 178. xviii.

I hange on Cros for loue of þe   See 1321.

1299   Sisam, *Nun's Priest's Tale,* p. 32; Williams, *New Book Eng. Verse,* p. 65; Robbins, *Sec. Lyrics,* pp. 41-2; Davies, *Med. Eng. Lyrics,* pp. 153-4.

1300   'The Discryuyng of a fayre lady:' a mock courtly panegyric of traditional charms—seven stanzas rime royal. [Utley 95].
        2. Leyden Univ. Vossius 9, f. 110b.
        Chaucer, Stow, 1561 (STC 5075); *Chaucer,* Speght, 1598 (STC 5077); Urry, *Chaucer,* 1721, p. 557; Bell, *Poets of Great Britain,* 1782, XIII. 131; [Anderson,] *Poets of Great Britain,* I. 586; Chalmers, *English Poets,* I. 563-4; 1. Patterson, *Shakespearean Studies,* 1916, p. 440 (st. 1-2 only); Person, *Camb. ME Lyrics,* pp. 38-40; 2. van Dorsten, *Scriptorium* XIV. 324.

1301   Woolf, *RES* n.s. XIII. 4-5.

1301.5 Ich aue a mantel i-maket of cloth
        A single line fragment of an English song.
        1. Bodl. 13679, Item 1 (c).
        Heuser, *Anglia* XXX. 174; Wilson, *Lost Lit.,* p. 179.

1302   Robbins, *Sec. Lyrics,* pp. 15-6; Davies, *Med. Eng. Lyrics,* p. 158.

1303   [Cf. *Oxford Dict. Nursery Rhymes,* p. 386].
Child, *Ballads,* 1864, 1878, VIII. 271; and *Pop. Ballads,* I. 415; Sargent and Kittredge, *Ballads,* p. 646; Williams, *New Book Eng. Verse,* pp. 67-8; *Poets of Eng. Language,* I. 27-8; Robbins, *Sec. Lyrics,* pp. 40-1; *Oxford Dict. Nursery Rhymes,* p. 387; Davies, *Med. Eng. Lyrics,* pp. 164-5.

1303.3 Y haue ben a foster long and meney day
A 'jolly forester' song—two quatrains. [Utley 97. Cf. 1303.5; also 'I have benne a lover,' Trinity Dublin 160, f. 113a; pr. Muir, *Unpublished Poems,* Liverpool 1961, p. 32].
1. BM Addit. 5665, f. 53b.
Stafford Smith, *Musica Antiqua,* II. 28-9; Rimbault, *Songs & Ballads,* p. 59; *Rel. Ant.,* II. 199; Flügel, *Neuengl. Lesebuch,* p. 151; *Early Eng. Lyrics,* p. 247; *Early Eng. Carols,* p. 451; Stevens, *Music & Poetry,* p.338.

1303.5 I haue bene a foster / long & many a day
A 'jolly forester' song: the old lover—six 5-line stanzas. [Utley 83. Cf. 1303.3; and for a companion song see 4068.6].
1. BM Addit. 31922, f. 65b.
Chappell, *OE Pop. Music,* 1893, I. 50; Flügel, *Anglia* XII. 244; *Early Eng. Carols,* pp. 313-4; Stevens, *Music & Poetry,* pp. 408-9; Stevens, *Music at Court,* p. 48.

1305   Wilson, *Lost Lit.,* pp. 177-8; Robbins, *Sec. Lyrics,* p. 147.

1306   2. Robinson, *Chaucer,* 1933, pp. 316-29; 1957, pp. 266-79.

I haue loued so many a day   See 3595.

1309   sixteen stanzas rime royal (with twelve lines in French).
Chaucer, Thynne, 1532 (STC 5068) (printed as part of 99); *Chaucer,* Stow, 1561 (STC 5075); *Chaucer,* Speght, 1598 (STC 5077); Urry, *Chaucer,* 1721, p. 539; Bell, *Poets of Great Britain,* 1782, XIII. 91; [Anderson,] *Poets of Great Britain,* I. 576; Chalmers, *English Poets,* I. 547; Skeat, *Oxf. Ch.,* VII. 281-4.

1312   a song with music, eleven lines.
1. Bodl. 21956, f. 20b.
Robbins, *Sec. Lyrics,* p. xxxviii.

1313　　　　*Gentleman's Magazine,* May 1842, p. 464.

1314　　　　[Considered as an English *englyn*, cf. *JEFDSS* IV. 130].
　　　　　　Robbins, *Sec. Lyrics,* p. 42; Chambers, *Eng. Lit. Close MA,* p. 113.

1315　　　　I haue y-soȝfte in many a syde
　　　　　　Early Eng. Carols, pp. 210-1; Stevens, *Med. Carols,* p. 104.

　　　　　　I haue þe soghte many a day　　See 2463.

1316　　　　*Gentleman's Magazine,* June 1842, p. 465.

1317　　　　Ritson, *Anc. Songs,* 1790, pp. 49-51; Gutch, *Robin Hood,* London 1847, II. 36-9; Child, *Ballads,* 1864, 1878, V. 39-42; and *Pop. Ballads,* no. 115, III. 13-14; Sargent and Kittredge, *Pop. Ballads,* pp. 244-5; Leach, *Ballad Book,* pp. 332-4.

1318　　　　[Cf. 548].

1319　　　　Delete: [Sandison, *Chanson d'Aventure,* p. 142].

1320　　　　A *chanson d'aventure* song of the Passion with symbolic letters.
　　　　　　facs. Report of Friends of Bodleian 1930-1931, facing p. 16.

1320.5　　　Ich herde men vpo mold make muche mon
　　　　　　The Song of the Husbandman—seventy-two lines in 8- and 4-line stanzas alternately.
　　　　　　1. Harley 2253, f. 64a.
　　　　　　　　Wright, *Pol. Songs,* pp. 149-52; Wülcker, *Lesebuch,* I. 71; Böddeker, *AE Dicht.,* pp. 102-5; Brandl and Zippel, *ME Sprach- u. Literaturproben,* pp. 134-5; *Cambridge Book Prose & Verse,* pp. 396-8; Kaiser, *Anthologie,* p. 171; Kaiser, *Med. Eng.,* p. 358; Robbins, *Hist. Poems,* pp. 7-9.

1321.3　　　I in study standing
　　　　　　Two-line fragment.
　　　　　　1. BM Addit. 35286, f. 93a (added in xvi cent. hand).

1321.5　　　I John of Gaunt / Do give and do grant
　　　　　　A [? spurious] grant—three doggerel couplets.
　　　　　　Beauties of England, I. 76; *Bedfordshire Magazine* I. 317.

1322	four 5-line stanzas and burden. Sandys, *Carols*, p. 13; Rickert, *Anc. Eng. Xmas Carols*, p. 24; Stevens, *Med. Carols*, p. 68; Greene, *Sel. Eng. Carols*, p. 115.

1322.5   I Julius cesar your high emperour
        On the three worthies: Julius Caesar, Alexander, and Hector—three quatrains. [Cf. 1270.1].
        1. Wellcome Hist. Med. Lib. 225, f. 2a.

1322.8   I Kateryn of the court celestyall
        'The speche of Saynt Kateryn' at the Pageant celebrating the marriage of Prince Arthur to Princess Catharine—four stanzas rime royal.
        1. Cotton Vitellius A. xvi, ff. 184b-185a.

        Ich king Athelstane   See 4183.

1326   Haupt and Hoffman, *Altdeutsche Blätter*, II. 141.

1326.5   I leue on owre holy dryʒt
        On the Creed.
        1. Trinity Dublin 211, at end (b).

        I lente my godes to my frende   See 1297.

1327   Rimbault, *Anc. Vocal Music*, No. 11; Briggs, *Songs & Madrigals*, PMMS 1881, pp. [M] 27-30; Padelford, *Early XVI Cent. Lyrics*, pp. 91-3; Robbins, *Hist. Poems*, pp. 94-5; Stevens, *Music & Poetry*, p. 364; Davies, *Med. Eng. Lyrics*, pp. 263-4.

1328.2   I loue and ffynde cause
        An amatory scribble—five irregular lines.
        1. Bodl. 10173, f. 131a.

1328.3   I loue and y dare nouʒt
        Contrasts: eight monoriming lines in two sets of semi-proverbial aphorisms, one leading to frustration and the other to achievement. [Cf. 1163, 3081. Cf. Utley 100].
        1. Bühler 21, f. iii recto.
        Bühler, *Studies in Med. Lit. to Baugh*, p. 286.

        I loue I loue and whom loue ye   See 1327.

1328.5　　　I loue loued & loued wolde I be
　　　　　　　The faithful lover—one stanza rime royal.　　[Cf. *Wyatt*, ed. Muir, No. 106].
　　　　　　　　1. BM Addit. 5465, f. 28b.
　　　　　　　　　　1. Stafford Smith, *Eng. Songs*, p. 12; Briggs, *Songs & Madrigals*, PMMS 1881, pp. [M] 23-6; Fehr, *Archiv* CVI. 56-7; Stevens, *Music & Poetry*, p. 360.

1328.7　　　I loue so sore I wolde fayne descerne
　　　　　　　The three leaves of true love, according to a woman—nine stanzas rime royal.
　　　　　　　　1. Bodl. 12653, f. 61a.
　　　　　　　　Padelford and Benham, *Anglia* XXXI. 381-2.

1328.8　　　I love trewly without feynyng
　　　　　　　A love song—one quatrain.
　　　　　　　　1. BM Addit. 31922, f. 44b.
　　　　　　　　Flügel, *Anglia* XII. 239; Stevens, *Music & Poetry*, p. 402; Stevens, *Music at Court*, p. 33.

1329.5　　　I loue vnloued suche is myn aventure
　　　　　　　Unrequited love—one stanza rime royal.　[Cf. 1329].
　　　　　　　　1. BM Addit. 31922, f. 122b.
　　　　　　　　Flügel, *Anglia* XII. 255; Stevens, *Music & Poetry*, p. 424.

1330　　　　Robbins, *Sec. Lyrics*, pp. 17-8; Greene, *Sel. Eng. Carols*, p. 166.

1330.3　　　I Luriche for the love of thee / Doe make Coventre tol free
　　　　　　　Couplet in stained glass window in Trinity Church, Coventry, commemorating ride of Lady Godiva.
　　　　　　　　Dugdale, *Warwickshire*, 1656, p. 86.

　　　　　　　*I made of my frend my foo　　See 1400.

1330.5　　　I maister Andro Kennedy / *Curro quando sum vocatus*
　　　　　　　'The testament of Mr. Andro Kennedy' by William Dunbar—thirteen 8-line macaronic stanzas and a concluding 12-line stanza.
　　　　　　　　1. Camb. Un. Ll. 5. 10, f. 24b; 2. Pepys 2553, p. 135; 3. Advocates 1. 1. 6, f. 154a.
　　　　　　　　Chepman and Myllar, ca. 1508 (STC 7348); *repr.* Laing, *Knightly Tale of Golagros*, 1827; Sibbald, *Chronicle*, I. 296; Stevenson, *STS* LXV. 263-6; Small, *STS* IV. 54-8; Mac-

Kenzie, *Dunbar*, pp. 71-4; Kinsley, *Dunbar*, pp. 96-8; *facs.*
Beattie, *Edinb. Bibl. Soc.* 1950, pp. 193-6; 2. Craigie, *STS*
n.s. VII. 155-9; 3. Ramsay, *Evergreen*, II. 76-81; *repr.*
Ramsay & *Earlier Scot. Poets*, p. 273; [Hailes,] *Anc. Scot.
Poems*, pp. 42-7; *Poems in Scot. Dialect*, 1748, pp. 18-22;
Sel. Poems of Dunbar, Perth 1788, pp. 41-6; Laing, *Dunbar*,
I. 137-41; Paterson, *Dunbar*, pp. 143-8; *Bannatyne MS.*,
Hunt. Club, IV. 488-91; Small, *STS* II. 54-8; Schipper,
Dunbar, pp. 211-5; and *DKAW* XLI (IV). 11-17; Baildon,
Dunbar, pp. 100-3; Ritchie, *STS* n.s. XXIII. 62-6.

I may say and so may mo / I wyte myself myne owene wo
Rimed Heading to 1511 (Cotton MS.).

1331   three stanzas rime royal.
         Robbins, *Sec. Lyrics*, p. 158; Person, *Camb. ME Lyrics*,
         p. 33.

1331.5   I mekely unto you sovrayne am sent
         A 'sotelty' for a bridal feast—one couplet. [Cf. also 461.5,
         1270.8, 1386.5].
         1. Bodl. Lat. misc. c. 66 [*olim* Capesthorne], f. 68b.
         Furnivall, *EETS* 32 rev. ed. 358.

1333   fifteen 5-line stanzas including refrain. [The first line occurs
         as a title in Sloane 3501, f. 2b].
         1. Huntington EL 1160, f. 11b (4 st.); 2. BM Addit. 22718,
         f. 14b (first two lines scribbled, and again at f. 54a); 3.
         Trinity Dublin 160, ff. 108a-b.
         1. Robbins, *Sec. Lyrics*, pp. 14-15; Davies, *Med. Eng.
         Lyrics*, p. 261; 3. Muir, *Unpublished Poems*, Liverpool 1961,
         pp. 26-8.

*I ne can telle ʒou nowt / Hou richeliche the fadel was wrout
Floris and Blauncheflur (Advocates MS.): see 2288.8.

1334   Robbins, *Sec. Lyrics*, p. 151.

1335   Royster, *MLR* IV. 509; Wilson, *Early ME Lit.*, p. 269;
         Wilson, *Lost Lit.*, p. 206.

1337   [Utley 103].
         Utley, *Crooked Rib*, p. 31.

1338   [Utley 104].

1338.5　　I patrik larrons of spittale feyld
　　　　　　A lover's plea—in couplets.
　　　　　　　1. Aberdeen Univ. 223, f. 172a (vv. 11; ends imperfectly).

*1339.5　　*I pray daily ther paynys to asswage
　　　　　　Concluding three lines of a love song.
　　　　　　　1. BM Addit. 5465, f. 20a.
　　　　　　　Fehr, *Archiv* CVI. 55; Stevens, *Music & Poetry*, p. 358.

1341.5　　I pray yow all for charite
　　　　　　Epitaph, A.D. 1437, for John Spyeer of Burford, Oxford—eight couplets (including prayer tags, cf. 1965.5).
　　　　　　　Ravenshaw, *Antiente Epitaphes*, p. 10.

1341.8　　I pray you all gyue your audyence
　　　　　　Everyman, a morality play.
　　　　　　　Pynson, 1510 (STC 10603, &c.); *facs.* Farmer, 1892; *repr.* Hawkins, *Origin of Eng. Drama*, 1773, I; Goedeke, Hanover 1865; Hazlitt, 1874; Greg, *Materialien zur Kunde des älteren englischen Dramas*, IV, XXIV, XXVIII; Logeman, *Elckerlijk and Everyman*, Ghent, 1892. And in numerous recent editions.

1342　　　[Ringler 60].
　　　　　　23. Lansdowne 344, f. 34b; 29. Rylands Lib. Latin 341, f. 74b; 30. Ushaw: St. Cuthbert's Coll. 28; 31. Trinity Dublin 159, f. 171a; 32. Trinity Dublin 351, f. 44a; 34. Laurence Witten, New Haven, Cat. 5, Item 51 [*olim* Helmingham Hall LJ. V. 14], f. 82b; 36. Camb. Un. Dd. 4. 51, f. 25a; 37. Camb. Un. Add. 6150, f. 18b; 38. Foyle [*olim* Harmsworth; Sotheby Sale, Oct. 16, 1945, Lot 2131]; 39. Univ. of Illinois 71 [*olim* Harmsworth; Sotheby Sale, Oct. 16, 1945, Lot 2132].
　　　　　　Speculum Christiani, de Machlinia, ca. 1486 (STC 26012); 22, 23. Holmstedt, *EETS* 182. 132-59; 340-2 (vv. 121-72 only).

1343　　　1. Bennett, *STS* 3 s. XXIII. 290-3.

1344　　　one quatrain and eleven couplets.
　　　　　　　1. Bodl. Lat. misc. c. 66 [*olim* Capesthorne], f. 93b.
　　　　　　　Robbins, *PMLA* LXV. 268-9; Robbins, *Sec. Lyrics*, pp. 194-5.

1344.5　　I pray yow maydens euerychone / Tell me
　　　　　　An erotic carol with *double entendre*—six quatrains and burden, 'Podynges at nyght &c.'
　　　　　　　1. Camb. Un. Add. 7350, f. ii verso.
　　　　　　　Robbins, *PMLA* LXXXI.

I praye youe maydys that here be   See 1595.

1346   1. Corpus Christi Oxf. 255, f. 105a; 2. BM Addit. 27879, p. 184.
    1. Cornelius, *PMLA* XLVI. 1025; 2. Child, *Pop. Ballads*, no. 45, I. 410-13; Hales and Furnivall, *Percy Folio MS.*, I. 508-14; Sargent and Kittredge, *Pop. Ballads*, pp. 78-81; Leach, *Ballad Book*, pp. 154-8.

I rede þat þou do right so
Extract (Camb. Un. Ff. 1. 6, f. 81a) from 2662.

1349.5   I recommende me to yow with harte and mynde
A love letter to his mistress—thirteen cross-rimed quatrains. [St. 3 = st. 2 of 3165].
1. Bodl. 12653, f. 2a.
Padelford and Benham, *Anglia* XXXI. 313-5.

1350   Williams, *New Book Eng. Verse*, pp. 66-7.

1351   Rickert, *Anc. Eng. Xmas Carols*, p. 66; Segar, *Med. Anthology*, pp. 66-7; *Oxford Book Carols*, p. 220; Greene, *Sel. Eng. Carols*, p. 98; Davis, *Med. Eng. Lyrics*, p. 166.

1352   Ritson, *Anc. Songs*, 1877, p. xlvii; Rickert, *Anc. Eng. Xmas Carols*, p. 59; Stevens, *Med. Carols*, p. 1; Bukofzer, *Journal American Musicological Soc.* VII. 74; Robbins, *Early Eng. Xmas Carols*, p. 70.

1353   four long lines with 'I sayh' anaphora (followed immediately by 1289).

1354   I saw iij hedles playen at a ball
1. Bodl. 29734, f. 26b; 2. Bodl. 15444, f. 144a (vv. 2 with 4 Latin lines).
    1. Wright, *Percy Soc.* XXIII. 35 (as part of 2049); Robbins, *Sec. Lyrics*, p. 241; 2. Meech, *MP* XXXVIII. 125.

1354.5   I say withowte boste / that the smoke stereth the roste
A proverbial couplet.
1. Balliol 354, f. 200b.
    Flügel, *Anglia* XXVI. 203; Dyboski, *EETS* ci. 131.

1355.5 I sei a sicte þat was vnseire
A song of impossibilities against faithlessness in women: 'Lemmąn whan þe song is soþ / Of loue þou ssalt be trewe' —vv. 24.
1. Westminster Cath. 34. 3, f. 36b.

1356 [Utley 105].

1356.3 I seche a þouthe þat eldyth noȝt
On a religious life—three couplets.
1. Bodl. 1292, f. 1b.

1356.5 I seik about this warld unstabille
'Of the changes of life' by William Dunbar—four 5-line stanzas.
1. Camb. Un. Ll. 5. 10, f. 8b; 2. Pepys 2553, p. 5 and p. 315 (two texts).
2a, 2b. Craigie, STS n.s. VII. 4, 376; 2a. Pinkerton, Anc. Scot. Poems, I. 124; Sibbald, Chronicle, II. 13; Laing, Dunbar, I. 203; Paterson, Dunbar, pp. 63-4; MacKenzie, Dunbar, pp. 140-1; 2b. Small, STS IV. 232; Schipper, Dunbar, pp. 283-4; and DKAW XLI (IV) 85-6; Baildon, Dunbar, pp. 145-6; Kinsley, Dunbar, p. 60.

1356.8 I serue where I no truyst can ffynde
The lover despairs of his mistress—three 5-line stanzas. [Utley 106].
1. BM Addit. 18752, f. 138b.
Reed, Anglia XXXIII. 366.

I saruyd oure lady bothe nythte and day   See 2719.

1359 [Utley 106a].
1. Copenhagen Royal Lib. 29264, f. 163a.
Davies, Med. Eng. Lyrics, p. 195.

1360 I shall telle you a tale / Pampyng & I have piked your male
Riming conclusion to a letter from John Paston I to Margaret Paston, September 20, 1465—ten couplets. [Paston letters No. 528].
1. BM Addit. 34889, f. 33a.
Fenn, IV. 90; Gairdner, II. 237; Coulton, Life in the MA, III. 129-30; Davis, Oxford 1958, p. 52.

1361 [Delete entire entry].

I sale þe teche sone tak hede   See 3195.

1362 [Utley 107. For a version in quatrains cf. 2358.5].
1. FitzGibbon, *E. E. Poetry*, p. 226; Coulton, *Life in MA*, III. 141; Kaiser, *Med. Eng.*, p. 479; Pollet, *Skelton*, pp. 251-4; Greene, *Sel. Eng. Carols*, p. 148.

1363 Rickert, *Anc. Eng. Xmas Carols*, pp. 34-5.

1363.5 I schal you tell þis ilk nyght
A carol to St. Stephen—six quatrains and burden. [Cf. var. 2652.5].
1. Egerton 3307, f. 54b.
Stevens, *Med. Carols*, p. 39; Greene, *Sel. Eng. Carols*, p. 78.

1364 [Singer 854].
2. Sloane 1098, f. 9a.

I shall you tell with plaine declaracion   See 1364.5.

1364.5 I shall you tell without leyssinge
The Emblematical Scroll, attributed to George Ripley, on preparing the Philosopher's Stone—in groups of couplets describing illustrations. [All these MSS. are rolls. Texts vary, and sometimes incorporate sections of 2656].
1. Bodl. 2974 (vv. 137); 2. Bodl. 7662 (vv. 137); 3. Bodl. 8447 (vv. 71); 4. Fitzwilliam Mus. 276* (vv. 127); 5. Wellcome Hist. Med. Lib. 692 (vv. 96); 6. Wellcome Hist. Med. Lib. 693 (ca. A.D. 1600); 7. *olim* Dyson Perrins (Sotheby Sale, Dec. 1958, Lot 42); 8. *olim* Dyson Perrins (Sotheby Sale, Nov. 29, 1960, Lot 147; Kraus Cat. 100, Item 32).
Ashmole, *Theatrum Chemicum*, pp. 375-9 (vv. 114) [Bodl. 8465ee is an interleaved copy].

I sigh and sob both day and nyght for on so fair of hewe
Part of 2007, last seven stanzas, possibly for a separate poem. [Cf. 1715; and Wilson, *RES* n.s. X. 345-6].

1365 2. Cook, *Reader*, pp. 455-7; Brook, *Harley Lyrics*, pp. 59-60; Kaiser, *Anthologie*, pp. 294-5; Kaiser, *Med. Eng.*, p. 293; Davies, *Med. Eng. Lyrics*, pp. 82-4.

1367 [Cf. Copley, *N&Q* n.s. IX. 134-7].
Bullen, *Carols & Poems*, pp. 4-5; Rickert, *Anc. Eng. Xmas Carols*, p. 6; Segar, *Some Minor Poems*, p. 13; *Oxford Book Christian Verse*, p. 30; *Poets of Eng. Language*, I. 29; Chambers, *Eng. Lit. Close MA*, p. 91; *Oxford Book Eng. Verse*, pp. 34-5; Niles, *Carol Study Book*, 1948, p. 27; Mason, *Humanism & Poetry*, p. 175; Speirs, *Med. Eng. Poetry*, pp. 67-8; Manning, *PMLA* LXXV. 8; Davies, *Med. Eng. Lyrics*, p. 155.

*1367.1 *[I sing of kin] ges by the dayes of Arthur
Sir Lamwell—fragments in short couplets.
1. Camb. Un. Kk. 5. 30, a single leaf (vv. 90).
Two fragments of early prints (STC 15187): A (Malone 941) eight leaves; B (Douce fragments e. 40) one leaf only (vv. 61); A, B. Hales and Furnivall, *Percy Folio MS.*, I. 522, 533;
1. Furnivall, *Captain Cox*, Ballad Soc. 1871, VII. xxxi; repr. *New Shakespeare Soc.* 1890.

1367.3 I syt and synge / of luf longynge
Love longing for Jesus, in one MS. of the *Desert of Religion* (672) beneath a picture of several saints—one 6-line stanza (=st. 8 of 1715). [For alternative text see 91.8].
1. BM Addit. 37049, f. 52b.
Hübner, *Archiv* CXXVI. 74; Allen, *Rolle*, p. 310; Allen, *Eng. Writings of Rolle*, p. lxiv.

1367.5 I slepe and my hert wakes / Wha sall tyll my lemman say
Three riming lines in Rolle's *Ego Dormio*.
1. Bodl. 3938, f. 338b; 2. Bodl. 11272, f. 95a (var.); 3. Camb. Un. Dd. 5. 64, III, ff. 27b-28a; 4. Pepys 2125; 5. BM Addit. 22283, f. 151a; 6. BM Addit. 37790, f. 135a; 7. Trinity Dublin 155; 8. Westminster School; 9. Longleat 29, f. 47a; 10. *olim* Gurney; 11. Paris: Bibl. Mazarine 514; 12. Paris: Bibl. St. Geneviève 3390, f. 107a;.
1, 3. Horstmann, *York. Wr.*, I. 59; 3. Allen, *Eng. Writings of Rolle*, p. 70; Kaiser, *Med. Eng.*, p. 203.

1367.8 I slepe & my hert wakes to þe
Couplet attached to scroll for picture of man lying on ground.
1. BM Addit. 37049, f. 30b.
Comper, *Life & Lyrics of Rolle*, p. 315; Allen, *Rolle*, p. 307.

1367.9	I stond as styll as ony stone God amends all—one quatrain. 1. Ipswich County Hall Deposit: Hillwood [*olim* Brome], f. 81a. Smith, *Commonplace Book*, p. 20; *Early Eng. Lyrics*, p. 161.
1368	1. Egerton 3245 [*olim* Gurney], f. 185a.
1370	[For indulgence see 3305.8] 5. Longleat 30, f. 10b; 7. Blairs Coll. 13.
1370.5	I that in heill wes and gladnes 'Lament for the Makars' by William Dunbar—twenty-five quatrains with refrain: '*Timor mortis conturbat me.*' 1. Pepys 2553, p. 189; 2. Advocates 1. 1. 6, f. 109a. Early print: ? Violette, ca. 1508 (STC 7350); *facs.* Beattie, *Edinb. Bibl. Soc.* 1950, pp. 189-92; *repr.* Laing, *Knightly Tale of Golagros*, &c., 1827; Small, STS IV. 48-51; Stevenson, STS LXV. 259-62; MacKenzie, *Dunbar*, pp. 20-3; Kinsley, *Dunbar*, pp. 61-4; 1. Craigie, STS n.s. VII. 214-7; 2. Ramsay, *Evergreen*, I. 129-35; *repr. Ramsay & Earlier Scot. Poets*, pp. 239-40; [Hailes,] *Anc. Scot. Poems*, pp. 94-9; *Select Poems of Dunbar*, Perth 1788, pp. 78-82; Sibbald, *Chronicle*, I. 325-32; Laing, *Dunbar*, I. 211-15; Paterson, *Dunbar*, pp. 248-52; *Bannatyne MS.*, Hunt. Club, III. 308-11; Eyre-Todd, *Med. Scot. Poetry*, pp. 187-91; Schipper, *Dunbar*, pp. 285-90; and *DKAW* XLI (IV). 86-92; Kaufmann, *Traité de la langue. . .Dunbar*, 1873, pp. 23-46; Baildon, *Dunbar*, pp. 146-9; Arber, *Dunbar Anthology*, pp. 23-7; Ritchie, STS n.s. XXII, 287-91; Davies, *Med. Eng. Lyrics*, pp. 250-2 (18 st. only).
1371	[Delete entire entry]. *I that to youre service wolde were able See 2766.
1372	2. Balliol 316 A, f. 110b. 4. N. S. Baugh, *Worcestershire Misc.*, pp. 97-100.
1373.5	I thocht lang quhill sum lord come hame A welcome to the Lord Treasurer by William Dunbar—eight quatrains with refrain: 'Welcome my awin Lord Treasaurair.' 1. Camb. Un. Ll. 5. 10, f. 5b. Laing, *Dunbar*, I. 105-6; Paterson, *Dunbar*, pp. 179-80;

Small, *STS* IV. 264-5; Schipper, *Dunbar*, pp. 229-30; and *DKAW* XLI (IV). 30-2; Craigie, *STS* n.s. XX. 51-2; Baildon, *Dunbar*, pp. 110-11; MacKenzie, *Dunbar*, pp. 49-50.

1374   ten couplets (twelve Apostles named).
Bowers, *PMLA* LXX. 213-4.

1377   1, 9. Amours, *STS* LVII. 90-1; 1. Wilson, *Lost Lit.*, p. 213; Wilson, *LSE* V. 44; 3. Macpherson, *Orygnale Cronykill*; Laing, *Original Chronicle*, II. 436.

1378   *Workes*, Marshe, 1568 (STC 22608); *repr.* [? J. Bowle,] 1736; Chalmers, *English Poets*, II. 306-8; Percy, *Reliques*, 1767, I. 93; 1794, I. 95; Dyce and Child, *Skelton & Donne*, I. 8-18; Henderson, *Skelton*, 1931, 1948, 1959, pp. 4-10.

1378.5   Y wandryng ful wery and walkynge þe ways
An ABC alliterative poem on flowers, one stanza to each letter of the alphabet.
1. Lincoln Coll. Oxf.

1379   2. Pepys 1584, f. 104b; 4. BM Addit. 22283, f. 130a col i.
1. *Rel. Lyr. XIV C.*, pp. 148-51.

1380   [Cf. Ransome, *EHR* IV. 460].
Brotanek, *ME Dichtungen*, pp. 138-41; Robbins, *Hist. Poems*, pp. 215-8.

1381   [Cf. 1270, 3220.5, and 3220.7].

1381.5   I was as yee be now in dust and clay
Epitaph, A.D. 1458, for John Septuaus and his wife in Sittingborne Church, Kent—four lines. [Cf. 1381, 3220.5, &c.].
Weever, *Anc. Funerall Monuments*, 1631, p. 279 (STC 25223).

1382   Scott, Edinburgh 1804, 1811; Eyre-Todd, *Early Scot. Poetry*, 1891, pp. 21-57 (extracts).

1383   Rickert, *Anc. Eng. Xmas Carols*, pp. 78-81.

1384   [Utley 112].
1, 2. Hall, *Early Middle English*, I. 149-75 (lengthy extracts); 2. E. G. Stanley, London 1960; *facs.* Ker, *EETS* 251.

Y was wel fair scuch ssaltou be / for godes loue be war be me
See 1270 (Thompson MS.).

1386.5   I welcombe you brethern godely in this hall
A 'sotelty' for a bridal feast—five lines. [Cf. 461.5, 1270.8, 1331.5].
1. Bodl. Lat. misc. c. 66 [*olim* Capesthorne), f. 68b.
Furnivall, *EETS* 32 rev. ed. 358.

1388   An Amorous Complaint (*Compleint Damours*) attributed to Chaucer &c.
2. Bodl. 3896, f. 197a; 3. Harley 7333, f. 135b.
3. Skeat, *Minor Poems*, p. 218; Robinson, *Chaucer*, 1933, pp. 636-7; 1957, pp. 540-1.

1389.5   Ic chule bere to wasscen doun in þe toun / þat was blac ant þat was broun
A couplet among miscellaneous Latin and English notes.
1. Trinity Camb. 323, f. 27b.
James, *Cat.*, I. 441; Wilson, *Lost Lit.*, p. 181.

1390   [Delete entire entry].

I wyll leue but I no dar   See 1400.

Ich wolle leose my life   See 827.5 (Harley 7322).

1390.3   I will not man þat þou die / But with my bodye I will þe bye
Reply of Mercy to Adam—one couplet in a prose sermon. [Cf. 1509.5 and 3729.5].
1. Royal 18. B. xxii, f. 64b.
Ross, *EETS* 209. 49.

I will nocht reherss all the maner / For quha sa likis
Ballad of the victory of Sir Andrew Hercla in Barbour's *Bruce* (xvi. 519), pr. Skeat, *STS* XXXII. 69.   See 3217.

I wyll please what so betyde / if thou wylt please lay truthe asyde
A proverbial couplet (= vv. 19-20 of 3502), pr. *Oxford Dict. Eng. Proverbs*, 1948, p. 506.   See 3502.

1391.8   I wille that the cokke have the quede / And for his songe he shall be dede

A couplet in the *Gesta Romanorum*. [Cf. 3322.3].
1. BM Addit. 9066, f. 15b.
Madden, *Roxburghe Club* 1838, LV. 308.

I wyll yow tell a full good sport   See 1362.

I wil ȝou tellyn bi & bi   See 2627.

1392   On the need for caution in marriage—a three-line tag. [Cf. 3919. Utley 113a].
1. Lansdowne 762, f. 92a.
Robbins, *Sec. Lyrics*, p. 239.

1392.5   I wondyr mych in þe wrytyng above
Two couplets, the second answering the first, at end of a Latin sermon.
1. Antwerp: Plantin-Moretus Mus. 305.

1393.5   [I] wote a boure so bricht / es kidde with kaiser and knicht
A fragment of a song, perhaps a religious love poem—one quatrain.
1. Camb. Un. Add. 2585 (2).

1394   Warton, *Hist. Eng. Poetry*, 1824, I. 34 (vv. 1-18, 27-30 only); Guest, *Hist. Eng. Rhythms*, 1838, II. 298 (st. 1-3 only); Brook, *Harley Lyrics*, pp. 31-2; Kaiser, *Med. Eng.*, p. 465.

1395   Dickins and Wilson, *Early ME Texts*, pp. 119-21; Brook, *Harley Lyrics*, pp. 48-50; Kaiser, *Anthologie*, pp. 294-5; Kaiser, *Med. Eng.*, p. 467; Mossé, *Handbook*, pp. 208-10; Greene, *Sel. Eng. Carols*, p. 158; Brandl and Zippel, *ME Sprach- u. Literatur.*, pp. 127-8; Davies, *Med. Eng. Lyrics*, pp. 88-91.

1396   '*Anigmata:*' a riddle on the days, weeks, and months of the year, translating '*Est arbor quadam ramos retinens duodenos &c.*'—five lines.
1. Robbins, *Sec. Lyrics*, p. 62.

1397.5   I wate na better wele
One 6-line tail-rime stanza in Rolle's English Psalter (Ps. LXI). [For further MSS. see Allen, *Rolle*, pp. 170-7].

1. Bodl. 4127, f. 90a; 2. Univ. Coll. Oxf. 64, f. 65b.
1. Allen, *Eng. Writings of Rolle*, p. 16; 2. Bramley, Oxford 1884, p. 215.

1398   Against extravagance in dress, an extract from Hoccleve's *De Regimine Principum*, st. 58-73.   See 2229.

1399   2. Furnivall, *EETS* 32. 385; Kaiser, *Med. Eng.*, p. 559; Greene, *Sel. Eng. Carols*, p. 145; Davies, *Med. Eng. Lyrics*, pp. 289-90.

1400   2. Harley 116, f. 170b (vv. 5-6, preceded by 1297); 4. Harley 2321, f. 147a (vv. 3-4).
1. Zupitza, *Archiv* XC. 247-8; 3. Segar, *Some Minor Poems*, p. 39.

1401   I wald noght spare for to speke wist I to spede
Hall, Oxford 1914, pp. 33-4; Williams, *New Book Eng. Verse*, pp. 28-9.

1402   1. Kaiser, *Med. Eng.*, p. 331 (8 st. only); Davies, *Med. Eng. Lyrics*, pp. 127-30.

*I you honoure blesse lawde and glorifie
Last two stanzas rime royal of Proheme (Plimpton MS.) to 3406.

1405.5   I-blessyd be Cristes sonde
'God spede the plowe alle way'—nine 3-line stanzas with 3-line burden: 'The merthe of alle þis londe / maketh þe gode husbonde / wiþ eringe of his plowe.'
1. Bodl. 3340, f. 19a.
Early Bodl. Music, II. 132-3; *Early Eng. Lyrics*, pp. 241-2; Padelford, *Anglia* XXXVI. 104; Chambers, *Eng. Lit. Close MA*, pp. 95-6; Stevens, *Med. Carols*, pp. 112-3; Robbins, *Hist. Poems*, pp. 97-8; Greene, *Sel. Eng. Carols*, p. 147.

1407   Brook, *Harley Lyrics*, pp. 64-5.

1408   3. Stockholm Royal Lib. X. 90, pp. 35-47 (with eight introductory lines); 4. Bühler 21 [*olim* Phillipps 7008], ff. 45b-49b (vv. 202).
3. Müller, *Aus me Medizintexter*, Kölner Anglistische Arbeiten, 1929.

1409   James, *Cat.*, III. 75.

1409.1   Yff a ʒong woman had a c. men take
'A good medesyn yff a mayd have lost her madened to make her a mayd ageyn' — vv. 34 in irregular stanzas. [Utley 117].
1. BM C. 21. d. 7: *Mirrour of the World,* Caxton 1481, flyleaf, *Rel. Ant.,* I. 250-1.

If al that the wolf unto a preest worthe   See 3513.

1409.3   Yf all the erthe were parchment scrybable
An extract (vv. 239-45) of *The Remedy of Love* (3084), here adapted to the praise of women. [Also forms last st. of 1944; for a companion piece cf. 3701.5. Cf. *Oxford Dict. Nursery Rhymes,* p. 436; Linn, *PMLA* LIII. 951-67. Utley 118].
1. BM Addit. 17492, f. 90a; 2. Advocates 1. 1. 6, f. 258b. *Chaucer,* Thynne, 1532 (STC 5068); Chalmers, *English Poets,* I. 540; 1. Muir, *Proc. Leeds Philos. & Lit. Soc.* (Lit. & Hist. Section), VI. 278; 2. *Bannatyne MS.,* Hunt. Club, p. 755; Ritchie, *STS* n. s. XXVI. 23; Mason, *Humanism & Poetry,* p. 52.

1409.5   Yff anye man aske a question of the / In thine answer
One quatrain against hasty tongue.
1. Morgan Lib. Acc. No. 53095, *Greate Herbal,* Kynge, 1561 (STC 13179), added on lower cover.

1409.8   Yf any man askyth ho made this crye / say Robyn Rydesdale Jac Nag and I
A couplet on the rebellion of 1469.
1. Trinity Dublin 516, f. 113b.

1410   [Cf. 1165].
Robbins, *Sec. Lyrics,* p. 256.

1411.5   ʒif euer thys booke don take his flight
A book plate of Stephan Batman — two couplets.
1. Pepys 2498, p. 370.
Påhlsson, *Recluse,* p. x.

ʒyf hope nere hert wolde to berste   See 1251.5.

If I be wanton I wotte well why   See 1269.5.

1413 Gentleman's Magazine, May 1842, p. 462.

1414 Bokenham's 'Life of St. Anne.'
Clive, Roxburghe Club L. 41-61.

1414.5 Yf I had space now for to write / my mortal paynes
The lover's pains—one 8-line tail-rime stanza. [Cf. Seaton, Sir Richard Roos, p. 324. Cf. also 1414.8].
1. Public Rec. Office, S. P. 1/246, f. 28a.

1414.8 Iff I had wytt for to endyght / of my lady
'My hart she hath and euer shall'—six cross-rimed quatrains. [Cf. 1414.5].
1. BM Addit. 18752, f. 58b (5 st.); 2. BM Addit. 31922, f. 34b; 3. Royal App. 58, f. 5b.
2, 3. Flügel, Anglia XII. 235, 260; Flügel, Neuengl. Lesebuch, pp. 134, 138; 1. Reed, Anglia XXXII. 350-1; 2. Padelford, Early XVI Cent. Lyrics, p. 78; Oxford Book XVI C. Verse, pp. 41-2; Stevens, Music & Poetry, p. 396; Stevens, Music at Court, p. 26; comp. text. Early Eng. Lyrics, p. 57.

1415 Greene, Sel. Eng. Carols, p. 134.

1415.5 þyf yc loue in þe / þat y ne hawe in me
De dilectione cadus—four short lines trans. Latin 'Sic in te diligo.'
1. BM Addit. 11579, f. 26b.

1416 1. Bodl. 14526, f. 55a (vv. 18 included in 3502).
1. Zupitza, Archiv XC. 247.

1417 Wright, Carols, 1836, no. xviii; Robbins, Sec. Lyrics, pp. 4-5; Kaiser, Anthologie, p. 393; Kaiser, Med. Eng., p. 416; Greene, N&Q, n.s. XI. 88.

1417.3 If I were in my castell of Bungeie
Hugh Bigot's defiance of Henry III—a popular quatrain (two variants).
Camden, Britannia, art. Suffolk, 1607; Percy, Reliques, Essay on Anc. Minstrels, note u 3; OED s.v. Cockney 2 c (Harrison, England, II. xiv).

1417.5 If it be loste & you it finde
A book plate—two couplets.

          1. Harley 5036, f. 44a; 2. BM Addit. 39659, f. i verso (late xvi cent.).

          2. *BM Cat. Addit. MSS. 1916-1920*, p. 137; Bergen, *EETS* cxxiv. 21.

1418   2. Furnivall, *EETS* 32 orig. ed. 54-8; Stevenson, *STS* LXV. 296-7.

1418.5   Yf it be so that ye so creuel be

          A love complaint—five stanzas rime royal adapted from Chaucer's *Troilus* and *Criseyde* (3327): Book II. 337-51, 778-84, 785-91, 855-61. [Cf. also 2577.5].

          1. BM Addit. 17492, f. 91a.

          Muir, *Proc. Leeds Philos. & Lit. Soc.*, (Lit. & Hist. Section), VI. 279-80.

1419   Brusendorff, *Chaucer Tradition*, p. 251.

1420.5   If Loue now reynyd as it hath bene

          A love song ascribed to Henry VIII—seven couplets.

          1. BM Addit. 31922, f. 48b.

          Chappell, *Archaeologia* XLI. 377; Flügel, *Anglia* XII. 240-1; Trefusis, *Songs Henry VIII*, Roxburghe Club CLXI. 17; Stevens, *Music & Poetry*, p. 403; Stevens, *Music at Court*, p. 35.

1421   Robbins, *Sec. Lyrics*, p. xxxii.

1422   1. Haupt and Hoffman, *Altdeutsche Blätter*, II. 142.

1422.1   Gif no luve is o God quaht feill I so

          'Song of Troyelus'—five stanzas rime royal (extracted from 3327, Book I. 400-34. For further MSS. see 3327 Extracts B, F, J).

          1. Advocates 1. 1. 6, f. 230a.

          Chaucer, Stow, 1561 (STC 5075); Urry, *Chaucer*, 1721, p. 272; 1. *Bannatyne MS.*, Hunt. Club, p. 668; Ritchie, *STS* n.s. XXIII. 304.

1422.3   Yf on the rockes of Scilla and caribdis I doe chaunce

          To his mistress—three long couplets.

          1. St. John's Camb. 34, second cover (added in xvi cent. hand).

          James, *Cat.*, p. 47.

1422.5   Yf onely sight suffyse / my hart to lose or bynde
The lover struggles against jealousy and envy—eight quatrains.
1. Bodl. 7391, f. 129a.

1423   [A xvi cent. trans. of 'Clara dies Pauli' in one quatrain is in NLW Welsh 129, p. 266. Cf. 1426.1. Tilley S 55].
Robbins, *Sec. Lyrics*, p. 63.

If so be þat lechis doon þee faile   See 1418.

*If that he be a crysten man   See 1725 (de Worde, 1500).

1425   2. Bodl. 6922, ff. 1a-7b, 97a, 97b (vv. 216).
2. Furnivall, *Ballads from MSS.*, Ballad Soc. 1863, I. 63; Allen, *Rolle*, pp. 391-2 (extracts).

1426   vv. 104 in couplets.
Gaertner, *John Shirley*, p. 63. Delete: Hammond, *Eng. Stn.* XLIII. 12.

1426.1   If the day of Saint Paule be cleere
'The Saying of *Erra Pater* to the Husbandman:' prognostics for the fortunes of the coming year from St. Paul's Day—four couplets. [Cf. 1423].
1. Bodl. 21702, f. 278b.
Hearne, *Roberti de Avesbury Historia*, Oxford 1720, p. 266; Brydges and Haslewood, *British Bibliographer*, II. 81.

1426.2   If þe leche be noht in þe towne
What to do until the horse doctor comes—in couplets inscribed on slate (about 8 lines legible), discovered at Smarmore, Co. Louth. National Mus., Dublin, No. 1961.8.
Bliss, *Proc. Royal Irish Academy*.

1426.4   Yf the lord byddyth fle / The stewward byddyth sle
A couplet in Bozon's *Contes moralisés*.
1. Harley 1288, f. 92b; 2. BM Addit. 46919 [*olim* Phillipps 8336], f. 120b; 3. Gray's Inn 12, f. 17b.
1-3. Smith, *SATF*, pp. 198, 12; Förster, *Festschrift zum 12 Deutschen Neuphilologentage*, p. 58; Ross, *Neuphil. Mitteilungen* L. 202; 2, 3. Wilson, *LSE* VI. 45; 1. Herbert, *Cat. Rom.*, III. 102.

1426.6   ȝif þe stone is oon / telle what craft brouȝt hym vppon
A riddling couplet inscribed on a pillar, in Trevisa's translation of Higden's *Polychronicon* (Book I, Cap. 24).

1. St. John's Camb. 204; 2. Cotton Tiberius D. vii; 3. Harley 1900; 4. Stowe 95; 5. BM Addit. 24194; 6. Aberdeen Univ. 21; 7. Hunterian Mus. 83; 8. Penrose 12; 9. Morgan Lib. M. 875.

Trevisa, *Discripcion of Britayne,* Caxton, 1480 (STC13440a); de Worde, 1498 (STC 13440b); Trevisa, *Prolicronycon,* Caxton, 1482 (STC 13438); de Worde, 1495 (STC 13439); Treveris, 1527 (STC 13440); 1. Babington and Lumby, *Rolls Series* XLI, i. 227; Mätzner, *AE Sprachproben,* II. 364.

*1426.8   *If þai do so he wil þaim safe / as walnot barke his hare
Last forty-five lines of a description of the appearance of Christ—in quatrains.
1. BM Addit. 37049, f. 25a.
Bowers, *Anglia* LXX. 431-3; Ross, *Speculum* XXXII. 277-8.

1427   An extract from *The Proverbs of Hendyng* (1669) [= st. 41 of MS. 1, and st. 10 of MS. 2. Utley 123a].
Littlehales, *EETS* 109. lxix; Patterson, *Shakespearean Studies,* 1916, p. 450.

1427.5   If þow be stalworth fare þou. . .
Practical counsel—four lines (much faded).
1. Harley 485, f. 99b.

1429   An extract from *The Proverbs of Hendyng* (2078), corresponding to vv. 166-71.
Laing, *Remains,* rev. Hazlitt, 1895, I. 308.

1429.5   If þou fest hym deliciously þan he will sclepe
The nature of Man—two couplets.
1. Hereford Cath. O. iii. 5, f. 48b.

1430   Robbins, *SP* LVI. 560.

1431.5   If þou my trewe lufer wil be
A couplet on a scroll attached to a picture of Christ Child in lap of Virgin.
1. BM Addit. 37049, f. 30b.

1433   Greene, *Sel. Eng. Carols,* p. 138; Davies, *Med. Eng. Lyrics,* pp. 154-5.

1435   Moral precepts preceding a mystical prose devotion in style of Rolle.

1436.2   Yf thow wilt eschew Bytter adventure
How to avoid heartbreak—one cross-rimed quatrain.
1. Durham Univ. Cosin V. iii. 9, f. 65a.
Furnivall, *EETS* lxi. 198.

1436.3   [If þou wylt goo in] to the partes of the este
Prognostics by the moon for a journey—four couplets. [Cf. 1201.5].
1. Bodl. 6795, Part II, f. 21*a.

If thou wylte lyve purelye   See 3087 (Magdalene 13).

1436.5   If þou wyse be wil / six kep þou whilke I þe kenne
Six rules against sins of the tongue—one quatrain inserted in two MSS. of The Book of Vices and Vertues. [For French text cf. Morgan Lib. M. 771, f. 43a].
1. BM Addit. 17013, f. 5a; 2. Huntington Lib. HM 147, f. 21a.
1, 2. Francis, *EETS* 217. lxii, 54.

1438   [Singer 792].

þyf þy bonde ys ylle / Held þy tonge stille
Concluding couplet to 3078.

1439.5   If þi horse have iiij white feet give him to þi foo
The properties of a horse judged by white hooves—two long couplets.
1. Bodl. 8606, f. 59b.

1439.8   If worde and ded agre / Your fyrnd [assured] wyll I be
A single couplet.
1. Morgan Lib. M. 722, title page.

Yf ye wolle to þys medycyn applye   See 3249.

1440.5   Gif ȝe wald lufe and luvit be
'Advyce to luvaris' attributed to William Dunbar—six quatrains with refrain: 'Be secreit trew and pacient.' [Cf. 479.5].
1. Advocates 1. 1. 6, f. 230a.
Laing, *Dunbar,* II. 33-4; *Bannatyne MS.,* Hunt. Club, III. 667-8; Small, *STS* IV. 312-3; Schipper, *Dunbar,* pp. 434-5; and *DKAW* XLIII (I). 46-7; Baildon, *Dunbar,* pp. 225-6; Ritchie, *STS* n.s. XXIII. 303.

1441.5   Ilke a fyngir has a name als men thaire fyngers calle
          The names of the fingers—four couplets: an extract from
          Legend of St. Michael in *South English Legendary* (3029).
          1. Camb. Un. Ff. 5. 48, f. 82a.
             Herrtage, *EETS* 75. 131.

1442   Paraphrase of Rolle's *Form of Living* (chapters 1-6) &c.

1442.5   Yll mowth he spede where þat he go / that lenyth this boke to
          frende or to foo
          A book motto of 'Will. Womyndham Canonicus de Kyrkeby'
          —one long couplet.
          1. Trinity Camb. 1144, ff. 51b-52a.
             James, *Cat.*, III. 142.

1443   *Rel. Lyr. XIV C.*, pp. 194-6.

1444   Davies, *Med. Eng. Lyrics*, p. 279.

1444.5   Illuster Lodovick of France most Cristin King
          Elegy on the death of Bernard Stewart, Lord of Aubigny, by
          William Dunbar—four 8-line stanzas with refrain: 'For he
          is gone the flour of chevalrie.' [Cf. 2811.5].
          1. Camb. Un. Ll. 5. 10, f. 6b.
             Laing, *Dunbar*, I. 133; Paterson, *Dunbar*, p. 271; Small,
             STS IV. 63; Schipper, *Dunbar*, pp. 296-7; and *DKAW* XLI
             (IV). 97-9; Baildon, *Dunbar*, pp. 153-4; Craigie, *STS* n.s.
             XX. 54-5; MacKenzie, *Dunbar*, pp. 133-4.

1445.5   In a busshell of wynnynge / ys not a hondfull of cunnyng
          A proverbial couplet, with Latin version.
          1. Balliol 354, f. 200b.
             Flügel, *Anglia* XXVI. 203; Dyboski, *EETS* ci. 131.

1445.6   In a day go we to the tyre wyth hay hay
          One line fragment of popular song preserved in a Latin poem
          on Neville's Cross.
          1. Bodl. 3041, f. 116a; 2. Bodl. 11566, f. 124b; 3. Cotton
          Titus A. xx, f. 82b.
             2. Wright, *Polit. Poems*, I. 48; Wilson, *Lost. Lit.*, p. 190.

1448.5   In a drem late as I lay / me þought I hard / a maydyn say
          On the Virgin Mother—two stanzas with a Lullaby burden.
          XX Songes, de Worde, 1530 (STC 22924); *repr.* Imelmann,

Shakespeare-Jahrbuch XXXIX. 125-6; Flügel, Anglia XII. 590; Flügel, Neuengl. Lesebuch, p. 145; Rickert, Anc. Eng. Xmas Carols, pp. 67-8.

1449   Brook, Harley Lyrics, pp. 39-40.

1449.5 In a garden vnderneth a tree
        A *chanson d'aventure* of the unhappy lover—six 6-line tail-rime stanzas and a 2-line refrain: 'This nyghtes rest.'
        1. Bodl. 6659, f. 100a.
        Sandison, *Chanson d'Aventure*, pp. 100-1; Wagner, *MLN* L. 455.

1450   and a 4-line burden: 'This day day dawes.'
        Stafford Smith, *Eng. Songs*, p. 10; Briggs, *Songs & Madrigals*, PMMS 1881, pp. [M] 15-8; Robbins, *Hist. Poems*, pp. 93-4; Stevens, *Music & Poetry*, pp. 381-2; Davies, *Med. Eng. Lyrics*, pp. 262-3.

1450.5 In a goodly nyght as yn my bede I laye
        An erotic dream vision—six 8-line stanzas. [Cf. 1841.5].
        1. Bodl. 12653, f. 47a.
        Padelford and Benham, *Anglia* XXXI. 360-1; Davies, *Med. Eng. Lyrics*, pp. 282-3.

        In a lande as I was lente   See 365 (Cotton Vitell.).

1451   1. Penrose 6 [*olim* Delamere], ff. 14a-19b.

1452   thirteen cross-rimed quatrains.   [Utley 129. Cf. *295.5. Delete: Compare *5].
        Robbins, *Sec. Lyrics*, pp. 172-6.

1455.5 In a plesante arboure very queynte & quadrante
        'Vice through violence puttyth vertue vnto flyte'—twelve 8-line stanzas with this refrain.
        1. Victoria and Albert Mus., Dyce 45, f. 19b.

1457   [Delete entire entry].

        In a slumbir late as I was / I harde a voice
        Burden to 490.5.

1459   A Texts [See also 1458]:
9. Morgan Lib. M. 818 [olim Harmsworth, olim Ingilby], f. 16a; 10. Westminster, f. 1a (A Text to XI; C Text XIV-XXIII); 11. Pembroke Camb. fragment; 12. Liverpool Univ. F. 4. 8 [olim Horton Hold Hall, olim Chaderton], f. 1a (A Text I-XI; C Text XIII-XXIII); 13. Nat. Lib. Wales 733B, f. 1a (begins and ends imperfectly; A Text to VIII; C Text XI-XXII); 14. Soc. of Antiquaries 687, pp. 470-549.
C Texts:
16. London Univ. [olim Sterling, olim Clopton], ff. 1a-97b (ends XXIII. 87); 17. London Univ. V. 88 [olim Ilchester], f. 1a.
A5. Kane, London 1960; comp. text. Knott and Fowler, Baltimore 1952; A2, B1, C18. Skeat, 1954.

1460   8. Rylands Lib. Latin 395, f. 138a (st. 11 only).
4. Davies, *Med. Eng. Lyrics*, pp. 148-51; 7. Philip Warner, *Medici Soc. Memorabilia* III. 9-32; 9. Segowa, *Paris Version of Quia Amore Langueo*, Kanezuwa 1934.

1461   twenty-seven quatrains.
Wright, *Camden Soc.* XVI. 346-9.

In a tyme of a somers day   See 1454.

1463   1, 2. Furnivall, *EETS* 15 orig. ed. 150-9; rev. ed. 180-9; 1. *Oxford Book Mystical Verse*, pp. 6-10; *Oxford Book Christian Verse*, pp. 25-9; *Poets of Eng. Language*, I. 30-4; 2. Segar, *Med. Anthology*, pp. 23-6 (12 st. only); Kaiser, *Med. Eng.*, pp. 291-3 (10 st. only).

1464   2. Horstmann, *Archiv* LVII. 288.

1464.5 In age as he growith *sua crescat gracia fructu*
'fful litel he knowith *quanto dolet Anglia luctu*' — one long macaronic couplet.
1. Harley 218, f. 79a; 2. Harley 536, f. 35b.

1465   Life of St. Euphrosine in the Vernon *Golden Legend* — in short couplets.
Horstmann, *Eng. Stn.* I. 304-11.

1466   Bloomfield, *Seven Deadly Sins*, p. 166.

1466.5   In all oure gardyn growis thare no flouris
'Balade [of Unstedfastness]' following *Sir Eglamour* (1725) attributed to William Dunbar—19 lines in 8-line stanzas (ends incomplete).

Chepman and Myllar, ca. 1508 (STC 7542); *facs.* Beattie, *Edinb. Bibl. Soc.* 1950, p. 88; *repr.* Pinkerton, *Poems from Scarce Editions*, 1792, III. 127; Laing, *Knightly Tale of Golagros*, 1827; Laing, *Dunbar*, II. 44; Small, STS IV. 321; Schipper, *Dunbar*, p. 436; and *DKAW* XLIII (I). 47-8; Baildon, *Dunbar*, pp. 226-7; Stevenson, STS LXV. 156.

*In all the londes of crystyente   See 1993 (Douce fragment).

1467   In all this worlde ys none so true / As she that bare our Lorde Jhesu
A single couplet on the Virgin.

1468   [Utley 130].
[Masters,] *Rymes of Minstrels*, p. 7; Robbins, *Sec. Lyrics*, pp. 6-7.

In Almys dar thow do no thyng   See 2714 (Harvard MS.).

In anoþer mannys hous / ne be þou neuer coueytous   See 4135.5 (st. 3).

1469   1. Horstmann, *Archiv* LVII. 300-5.

1470   *Carmina:* a *Bele Aeliz* poem—eleven lines, probably incomplete.
Frankis, *Neuphil. Mitteilungen* LX. 70; Davies, *Med. Eng. Lyrics*, p. 212.

1470.5   In autumpne whanne the sonne in Virgine / By radyante hete
'The Bowge of Courte' by John Skelton—seventy-seven stanzas rime royal. [Ringler 32].

de Worde, ca. 1498 (STC 22597); *repr.* Dyce, *Skelton*, I. 30-50; Dyce and Child, *Skelton & Donne*, I. 37-60; Williams, *Selection*, pp. 37-56; Hughes, *Skelton*, pp. 65-86; Henderson, *Skelton*, 1931, pp. 39-58; 1948, 1959, pp. 37-54; Pinto, *Selection*, pp. 25-43 (omits vv. 365-71, 400-13); *Workes*, Marshe, 1568 (STC 22608); *repr.* [? J. Bowle,] 1736; Chalmers, *English Poets*, II. 250-4.

1470.8   In baill be blyth for þat is best
             'In baill be blyth for it is best'—five 8-line stanzas with this refrain.
             1. Pepys 2553, p. 224.
                Pinkerton, *Anc. Scot. Poems*, p. 202; Craigie, *STS* n.s. VII. 252-3.

1471   1, 2. Rickert, *Anc. Eng. Xmas Carols*, pp. 50, 183-4; 2. Greene, *Sel. Eng. Carols*, p. 61; 3 (bur. only) and 4. Stevens, *Med. Carols*, pp. iii, 5; 4. Nettel, *Carols*, no. 7.

             In Betheleem that noble place   See 2332.

1473   1, 2. Stevens, *Med. Carols*, pp. 27, 2.

1474   [See 276 and 539].
             2. Camb. Un. Add. 6860 [*olim* Macro 18, *olim* Gurney 75], f. 99a.

1477.5   In clench qu becche under ane þorne
             A xii century scrap. [See also 1267.5].
             1. Pembroke Camb. 281, f. 1a.
                Förster, *Anglia* XLII. 147; James, *Cat.*, p. 71; Wells, *Manual*, p. 1052.

1480   [Cf. 2747, 2821.5, and 3209].
             1. Coulton, *Social Life in Britain*, pp. 367-70; 2. FitzGibbon, *E. E. Poetry*, pp. 13-4; Robbins, *Sec. Lyrics*, pp. 51-5.

1481   3. Harley 2251, ff. 55a-70a; 7. Leyden Univ. Vossius 9, f. 49a.

1482   1. Horstmann, *Archiv* LVII. 289-90.

             In ingland whilom wund a knight   See 1641 (Harley 4196).

1484   [Cf. 33.5 and 3959].
             James and Macaulay, *MLR* VIII. 72.

1485   [Utley 136].
             1. [Masters,] *Rymes of Minstrels*, pp. 28-9; 2. Robbins, *Sec. Lyrics*, pp. 35-6; Kaiser, *Anthologie*, p. 311; Kaiser, *Med. Eng.*, p. 478; Greene, *Sel. Eng. Carols*, p. 143; Davies, *Med. Eng. Lyrics*, pp. 221-2.

1485.5   In fayth ye be to blame / for my good wyll me to dyffame
Love scorned—three quatrains with burden: 'And wyll ye serve me so &c.' [Cf. *Wyatt*, Muir, no. 113].
XX Songes, de Worde, 1530 (STC 22924); *repr*. Imelmann, *Shakespeare-Jahrbuch* XXXIX. 131-2; Flügel, *Anglia* XII. 593-4.

In Fevrier when that it was cold   See 1562.

1488   3. Davies, *Med. Eng. Lyrics*, pp. 287-8.

1489   *Rel. Lyr. XV C.*, pp. 266-8.

1489.5   In hond and [herte] true loue kepe
True love—six lines.
1. Morgan Lib. *Royal Book*, Caxton, ca. 1486 (added in xvi cent. hand).

1490.5   In hevene and erth aungell and man
Song at Corpus Christi: poem occurring in only this MS. of Eng. tr. of *Pèlerinage de l'Ame*—twelve stanzas rime royal.
1. Melbourne: Victoria Pub. Lib., f. 214b.

1491   [Ringler 33].
14. Lansdowne 344, f. 7a; 19. Trinity Dublin 159, f. 152a (st. 3 omitted); 20. Trinity Dublin 351, f. 7a; 22. Laurence Witten, New Haven, Cat. 5, Item 51; 24. Camb. Un. Dd. 4. 51, ff. 7a, 8a, 8b, 9a (scraps only); 25. Camb. Un. Add. 6150, f. 5a.
Speculum Christiani, de Machlinia, ca. 1486 (STC 26012).

1492   [Utley 137].
Early Eng. Carols, p. 322.

*1492.5   *In hel ne purgatore non oþer plase
A treatise on the Deadly Sins and their remedies, by John Audelay—vv. 263 in 13-line stanzas.
1. Bodl. 21876, f. 1a.
Halliwell, *Percy Soc.* XIV. 1-10; Whiting, *EETS* 184. 1-10.

1493.5   In hys beyng he [is] god in persons tre
Three lines on Christ in a Latin sermon.
1. Camb. Un. Ii. 3. 8, f. 168b.

1494.5　　　In holy Churche of cristys fovndacion
　　　　　　　Clergy's place in the three estates—sixteen 5-line stanzas (including a 2-line refrain) and burden: 'In towne a &c.'
　　　　　　　1. Victoria and Albert Mus., Dyce 45, f. 22a.

　　　　　　In honour of the ordouris nyne　　See 399.

　　　　　　In honnour of þis heghe fest of custome yere by yere　　See 837.5.

*1496.3　　*In hoote somere þese erbes þou take
　　　　　　　A Book of Medical Recipes in English verse and prose, beginning imperfectly. [Followed by 3848 and 2627, inserted among miscellaneous prose receipts].
　　　　　　　1. Trinity Camb. 921, ff. 1a-33a.

1496.5　　　In hour of our deeþ helpe us lord / In þe day
　　　　　　　A prayer tag in an English primer—one couplet.
　　　　　　　1. BM Addit. 17011, f. 64a.
　　　　　　　　Wordsworth and Littlehales, *Old Service Books*, p. 53.

　　　　　　In illis diebus when horse coulde speake　　See 326.8.

1497　　　　In Iuyli whan the sonne shone shene
　　　　　　　1. Cotton Galba E. ix, f. 113b (7 vv. repeated on f. 3a); 1a (xix cent. transcript). Egerton 2257, ff. 2a-4b; 2. Rome: English Coll. 1306, f. 85b.
　　　　　　　　2. Klinefelter, *PMLA* LXVII. 890-4; Robbins, *Hist. Poems*, pp. 78-83.

1498　　　　2. Glauning, *EETS* lxxx. 16-28.

1498.5　　　In Kent alle care bygan / *Ibi pauci sunt sapientes*
　　　　　　　A macaronic couplet presumably on the Great Rebellion of 1381.
　　　　　　　1. Trinity Dublin 214, flyleaf.

1498.8　　　*In libro* men schul rede
　　　　　　　Verbum domini comparatur—four monoriming lines.
　　　　　　　1. Bodl. 2293, f. 164a.

　　　　　　In lovys daunce / Syth that oure chaunce　　See 2261.4.

*1500.5   *In lyde ioye and blisce bringet me to bide
          End of a song.
          1. Corpus Christi Camb. 8, p. 457.
          New Oxford Hist. Music, III. 111.

1502   How to find Easter Day according to the new moon (C)—
          three couplets.
          9. Bodl. 1689, f. 82b; 10. Trinity Camb. 1450, f. 58b; 11.
          Harley 3810, Part I, f. 52b; 12. Royal 8. F. xii, f. 43a; 13.
          Sloane 747, f. 46a; 14. Leeds: Brooke Horae; 15. Paris: Bibl.
          nat. f. lat. 3638, f. 75a (vv. 1-2 only).
          3. Robbins, *Sec. Lyrics*, p. 63; 6. Littlehales, *EETS* 109.
          xlix; Wordsworth and Littlehales, *Old Service Books*, p.
          60; 14. *Cat. MSS. Thomas Brooke*, London 1891, I. 266.

1502.5   In Marche þou shalt lern / For to angul
          De arte piscandi—four lines.
          1. Sloane 1698, ff. 12a-13.

1503.5   In May as that Aurora did upspring
          'The Merle and the Nichtingaill' by William Dunbar—fifteen
          8-line stanzas with alternating refrains. [Utley 139].
          1. Pepys 2553, p. 165 (vv. 17-32 wanting); 2. Advocates 1. 1.
          6, f. 283a.
             1. Craigie, *STS* n.s. VII. 188-91; 2. [Hailes,] *Anc. Scot.
          Poems*, pp. 112-7; *Select Poems of Dunbar*, Perth 1788, pp.
          93-8; Laing, *Dunbar*, I. 216-20; repr. *Blackwood's Magazine*,
          Feb. 1835; *Bannatyne MS.*, Hunt. Club, IV. 822-6; Paterson,
          Dunbar, pp. 43-7; Small, *STS* IV. 174-8; Baildon, *Dunbar*,
          pp. 178-82; Ritchie, *STS* n.s. XXVI. 87-91; Arber, *Dunbar
          Anthology*, pp. 1-6; MacKenzie, *Dunbar*, pp. 134-7.

1504   [Utley 140].
          Brook, *Harley Lyrics*, pp. 44-5; Kaiser, *Anthologie*, p. 293;
          Kaiser, *Med. Eng.*, p. 466.

1504.5   In may that lusty sesoun
          A courtly maying song—one 9-line tail-rime stanza.
          1. BM Addit. 31922, f. 26a.
             Flügel, *Anglia* XII. 232; Briggs, *Songs & Madrigals*, PMMS
          1891, pp. 6-7; Stevens, *Music & Poetry*, p. 391; Stevens,
          Music at Court, p. 19.

1506   Ellis, *Ch. Soc.*, 2 s. IV. 463 (2 st. only). Delete: Skeat,
          Oxf. Ch., I. 55.

1507	[For another Envoy cf. 2579.5; for extract occurring separately cf. 3911.5].
8 (transcript of Chepman & Myllar). Asloan, ff. 243a-246b and ff. 293a-300b.
Chepman and Myllar, 1508 (STC 5099); *facs*. Beattie, *Edinb. Bibl. Soc.* 1950, pp. 109-33; *repr.* Stevenson, *STS* LXV. 181-203; *Chaucer,* Thynne, 1532 (STC 5068); *repr.* Chalmers, *English Poets,* I. 338-44.
1507.5	In may when myrth moves vpon lofte
A political prophecy—six irregular lines.
1. Cotton Titus A. xxv, f. 105b.

In my begynnyng god be my speade   See 430.5.

1509	2. A. Rosenthal, *Sale Cat.* 1944, V. 11 (added to Guido, *Historia Troiana,* Strassburg, 1494).
1509.5	In my grace þou hope nowsth / For þou shalte haue as þou haste wrought
Reply of Righteousness to Adam—one couplet in a prose sermon (followed by 3729.5 and 1390.3).
1. Royal 18. B. xxiii, f. 64b.
Ross, *EETS* 209. 44.
1510	Robbins, *Sec. Lyrics,* pp. 193-4.
1511.5	In name of God almyghti þe blyssed Trinitee
The Miroure of Mans Saluacioune, a translation of the *Speculum Humane Salvacionis.*
1. Foyle, Beeleigh Abbey [*olim* Huth, *olim* Harmsworth, Sotheby Sale, 1945, Lot 2100; *olim* Maggs, *olim* Breslauer Cat.].
Huth, *Roxburghe Club,* 1888.
1513.5	*In nomine patris* at my Crowne
A night prayer—six lines. [Follows 985.5].
1. Lansdowne 96, f. 104a.
Sparrow-Simpson, *Journal Brit. Arch. Assoc.* XLVIII. 45.
1514	[Cf. 2242].
Rhodes, *Boke of Nurture,* 1577 (STC 20958) (vv. 796); *repr.* Furnivall, *Roxburghe Club* LXXXVII. 1-83; 1. Furnivall, *EETS* 32 orig. ed. 117-99; rev. ed. 1-83.

1515 Fragments of early prints: Sir John Fenn's Letters (parallels vv. 3508-3587); ? de Worde, in bindings of *Michaelis Menoti Sermones Quadragesimales*, Paris 1525, in Trinity Camb. (parallels vv. 8371-8423, 8791-8981); both fragments *repr.* Furnivall, *Roxburghe Club* LXXXV. xxxiii*-xxxv*; xxv-xxx..

In olde tyme straung thynges cam to pass   See 3549.5.

1522 Greene, *Sel. Eng. Carols*, p. 125.

1523 1. *Rel. Ant.*, I. 63-4 (extract); Furnivall, *EETS* 15 orig. ed. 244-50; rev. ed. 271-8.

1524.5 In ryɜtfulnesse doyng
Rules for a man — three monoriming lines in a Latin sermon.
1. Bodl. 29746, f. 45b.

In Rome another miracle wes   See 4123.

1527 nine 7-line stanzas.
1. Camb. Un. Ll. 5. 10, f. 34b; 2. Pepys 2553, pp. 308, 311; 3. Advocates 1. 1. 6, f. 103b.
1. Schipper, *Dunbar*, pp. 37-40; and *DKAW* XL (II). 37-40; Baildon, *Dunbar*, pp. 4-6; 2. MacKenzie, *Dunbar*, pp. 53-5; Craigie, *STS* n. s. VII. 368-70; Kinsley, *Dunbar*, pp. 40-2; Davies, *Med. Eng. Lyrics*, pp. 248-50 (7 st. only); 3. *Ramsay and Earlier Scot. Poets*, p. 262; *Bannatyne MS.*, Hunt. Club II. 296-8.

1528 755 lines in rime royal stanzas, including eleven introductory stanzas and three concluding stanzas.
Chaucer, Thynne, 1532 (STC 5068); *repr.* Skeat, *Oxf. Ch.*, VII. 380-84; *Chaucer*, Stow, 1561 (STC 5075); *repr.* Urry, *Chaucer*, 1721, p. 433; Bell, *Poets of Great Britain*, X. 167; [Anderson,] *Poets of Great Britain*, I. 455; Chalmers, *English Poets*, I. 526-32; *Chaucer*, Speght, 1598 (STC 5077); 2. Pearsall, *Floure and Leafe*, 1962, pp. 105-26.

In Septembre in fallynge of the lefe / Whan phebus   See 3955.3.

1528.5 In seyven foretene & foure / Is all my trust & store
A riddling number couplet. [Cf. 717).
1. BM Addit. 20059, f. 2a.

In soro and car he led hys lyfe   See 4278.

1531.5	In sory tyme my lyf is y-spent The woebegone lover—six lines (possibly incomplete). 1. Public Record Office S. C. 2/175/41, f. 1a. Stanley Neuphil. *Mitteilungen* LX. 287; Robbins, *Anglia* LXXXII. 13.
1533	Gutch, *Robin Hood*, 1847, II. 23-35; Child, *Ballads*, 1864, 1878, V. 18-32; and *Pop. Ballads*, no. 121, III. 109-14; Sargent, and Kittredge, *Pop. Ballads*, pp. 289-93; Leach, *Ballad Book*, pp. 352-60.
1534	1, 2. Child, *Pop. Ballads*, no. 119, III. 97-101; 1. Hartshorne, *Anc. Met. Tales*, p. 179; Ritson, *Robin Hood*, 1832, II. 231; Gutch, *Robin Hood*, 1847, II. 7-20; Jamieson, *Pop. Ballads*, II. 54; Child, *Ballads*, 1864, 1878, V. 1-16; Sargent and Kittredge, *Pop. Ballads*, pp. 282-6; Gummere, *OE Ballads*, pp. 77-90; Leach, *Ballad Book*, pp. 340-9.
1538	[Occurs as vv. 123-346 of MS. 1 of 3560].
*1538.5	*In þat ȝere [s]nowe schal bee / Wete heruest ȝe schal see Prognostics according to the day of the week on which New Year falls—vv. 58 in couplets. [See 3265]. 1. St. John's Camb. 237, p. 39.
1539	2. Bodl. Eng. misc. c. 291 [*olim* Halliday Cat.], ff. 3, 4 (32 st.). *Flower of the Commandments*, de Worde, ca. 1510 (STC 23876).
1540	[Utley 22a, 41a, 93a]. 1. Bodl. 1479, f. 1a (begins imperfectly in Book I; Book II begins f. 35a); 7. Trinity Dublin 160, f. 14a (begins imperfectly at st. 8; ends imperfectly; some leaves missing); 8. Bodl. Eng. poet. d. 45 [*olim* Frampton Court], ff. 1a-37b (slightly imperfect).
1540.5	In þe begynnyng off thys yere A New Year carol—one quatrain and burden. 1. Royal App. 58, f. 9a (burden only) and f. 13a. Flügel, *Anglia* XII. 263, 265.
1541	vv. 975 in 13-line stanzas.
1542	by James Ryman.

1543   1. Stowe 393, f. 99b; 2. Public Record Office, Coram Rege Rolls, Anc. Indictments, K. B. 9, No. 144, m. 31.
1. Robbins, *Hist. Poems*, pp. 60-1; 2. Chambers and Daunt, *Book of London English*, p. 276.

1544   1. Bodl. Lyell 34 [*olim* John Speed Davies], f. 203a.
Brotanek, *ME Dichtungen*, pp. 199-202; Robbins, *Hist. Poems*, pp. 207-210.

1546   8. Brown, *EETS* 169. 63.

1547.5   In the ende of yemps whan phebus had sorchid
A pageant address to a London Lord Mayor—four 6-line stanzas with a couplet heading: 'By hym that all dothe embrase / And nothing his pleasure may compase.'
1. Trinity Camb. 181, f. 172a.

1548   [For French original cf. *Le Debat du cueur et de l'oeil*, in Royal 19. A. iii, ff. 29a-41b; and *Le Jardin de Plaisance*, ca. 1501; *facs. SATF*; and cf. Wright, *Camden Soc.* XVI. 310].
de Worde, n.d. [post 1500] (STC 6915).

In the honour of Christes byrth / Syng we al with ioye and myrthe
Couplet heading to 1575.5.

1552   In the londe of more bretaynge
Robbins, *English St.* XXXVIII, 261-2; Robbins, *Hist. Poems*, pp. 113-5.

1554   2. Asloan, f. 213a.
Chepman and Myllar, ca. 1508 (one leaf fragment) (STC 13594); *facs.* Beattie, *Edinb. Bibl. Soc. Trans.* II. 394; *repr.* Laing, *Adversaria*, 1867; 1. Pinkerton, *Poems from Scarce Editions*, III. 145; *Bannatyne MS.*, Hunt. Club, IV. 867-97; Sibbald, *Chronicle*, I. 62-81 (44 st. only); 2. Craigie, *STS* n.s. XVI. 95-126.

1555   3. Trinity Dublin 516, ff. 116a-b (vv. 65).
1. Turner, *History of England*, 1815, III. 169-70; Collier, *Camden Soc.* LXVII. 72-4; Robbins, *Hist. Poems*, pp. 187-9; 2. Gairdner, *Camden Soc.* n.s. XXVIII. 99.

1555.5   In the monthes of June and July
Alchemical verses—thirteen lines (following 3721; two lines occur in 2656). [Singer 864].
1. Bodl. 6954, f. 55a.

1556   1, 2. Gollancz, *Roxburghe Club* CXXXII; Offord, *EETS*
246; 1. Gollancz, *Select E. E. Poems*, II; Ford, *Age of
Chaucer*, pp. 302-14 (omits vv. 299-630).

   In þe name of oure souereyn sauyour
      Prologue (in MS. Camb. Un. Dd. 1. 1) to 4250.

1557.5 In the name of the fader that settes in trone
   On the different places of a pilgrimage to Compostella,
   Rome, and Jerusalem—vv. 1694 in couplets.
      Purchas, *Pilgrimes*, 1625, ii. 1230-45 (Chap. v of 'the eight
      Book of the First Part') (STC 20509); repr. Glasgow, 1905-7,
      VII. 507-70; King, *Way of St. James*, Hispanic Soc. of
      America, 1920 (first part only).

1558   [Singer 856].
   Alchemical verses: the order of God's universe a justification
   for the Philosopher's Stone—eleven couplets.
      Ashmole, *Theatrum Chemicum*, 1652, p. 211.

1559   Behre, *Götesborgs Högskolas* [Universitets]*Arsskrift* XLVI,
   Götesborg 1940 (vv. 19715-27466); Kaiser, *Festschrift für
   Ernst Otto*, Berlin 1957 (extracts); Kaiser, *Anthologie*, pp.
   363-73 (extracts).

1560   in 8-line stanzas.

1561   8. Coventry Corp. Record Office, ff. 49-56.

1561.5 In the sacrament I am contenyd bothe god and man
   On the Sacrament—one 8-line stanza. [Cf. 3318.2].
   1. Durham Univ. Cosin V. v. 19, f. 72a.

1562   *Chaucer*, Stow, 1561 (STC 5068); repr. Urry, *Chaucer*, 1721,
      p. 556; Bell, *Poets of Great Britain*, XIII. 125; [Anderson,]
      Poets of Great Britain, I. 584; Chalmers, *English Poets*,
      I. 562; *Chaucer*, Speght, 1598 (STC 5077); Clarke, *Riches of
      Chaucer*, II. 311 (mod.).

   In the See wythe outen lese   See 1364.5.

1563   [Preceded by 3252.5 and 4049.6].

1564   A prophecy on the states of Europe—twelve quatrains.
   1. NLW Peniarth 50, pp. 251-2.

1565   [Cf. 4185].
          1. Camb. Un. Mm. 4. 41, f. 147b.
          Person, *Camb. ME Lyrics*, p. 9 (lacks introduction).

1566   4. Bibl. Bodmeriana, Coligny, Genève [*olim* Ireland Blackburn], f. 5a.
          1. Sibbald, *Chronicle*, I. xvii-xxvii (vv. 1-332 only).

1567   Chepman and Myllar, 1508 (STC 11984); *facs.* Beattie, *Edinb. Bibl. Soc.* 1950, pp. 7-48.

1569.5   In the yere of Crist on thowsand four hundryd ful trow wyth four and sixteen / I Rychard Skipwith
          Epitaph, A.D. 1416, at St. Peter's Church, St. Albans — five long and three short lines, irregularly riming.
          Pettigrew, *Chronicle of Tombs*, p. 45; Ravenshaw, *Antiente Epitaphes*, p. 6.

1570.5   In thise wordes *plus pi* ben conteyned
          Acrostic (*Plus pi*) on those not obligated to fast — one stanza rime royal commenting on ten lines of Latin preceding.
          1. Lansdowne 762, f. 91a.
          Rel. Ant., I. 287; Brotanek, *ME Dichtungen*, p. 161.

1570.8   In thyn adversyte thanke thi gode
          A set of pious verses.
          1. Sarum *Officium Mortuorum*, Sotheby Sale, Oct. 10, 1962, Lot 146.

1575   1, 3. Rickert, *Anc. Eng. Xmas Carols*, pp. 52, 47-8.

1575.5   In this tyme of Chrystmas
          Mary plays with the Christ Child, a carol — six quatrains and burden.
          Christmas Carolles, ? Copland, ca. 1550 (Douce fragments f. 48); *facs.* Reed, *Xmas Carols*, p. 15; *repr.* Flügel, *Anglia* XII. 588-9; Flügel, *Neuengl. Lesebuch*, p. 125; Rickert, *Anc. Eng. Xmas Carols*, p. 71; *Early Eng. Carols*, p. 37.

1576   Furnivall, *EETS* 32 orig. ed. 1-9; rev. ed. 250-8.

1578   Rickert, *Anc. Eng. Xmas Carols*, pp. 122-3; Stevens, *Med. Carols*, p. 80.

1580   [Delete entire entry].

In þis werd þat hys so wicke   See *2685.5.

1580.5   In thought dispered not knowyng remedy
A moralizing poem on Fortune—seven stanzas rime royal.
1. Plimpton 256, ff. 131a-b (added in xvi cent. hand).

1581   Kirke, *Reliquary* IX. 75.

1582   1. Leyden Univ. Vossius 9, f. 109b.

1583   8. Robert Taylor (Princeton) [*olim* Petre, *olim* Sotheby Sale, 10 Mar. 1952, Lot 143; *olim* Quaritch Sale Cat. 704, Item 350; *olim* Laurence Witten].

1585.5   In token þat dethe shuld þe lust of man refrayne
A story of Kyng Palaan—one introductory stanza rime royal and nine quatrains. [Cf. 39, 348, 3176].
1. Trinity Dublin 432, f. 62a.
Brotanek, *ME Dichtungen*, p. 52.

*1585.8   *. . .in torne clothis
The third line of 8-line fragment (beginning of lines damaged) apparently attacking extreme fashions in dress by appeal to Christ 'vpon the rode.'
1. Trinity Camb. 1157, f. 74b.

1586   [Followed by 1256.5. Cf. a prose scribble in Hunterian Mus. 232, f. 104a].

1587   [Followed by 2511].

In villa in villa   Burden to 2090.

1587.3   In vice most vicius he excellis
'Aganis treason: Epitaphe for Donald Owre' by William Dunbar—eight 6-line stanzas.
1. Camb. Un. Ll. 5. 10, f. 11a; 2. Pepys 2553, pp. 11-12; 3. Advocates 1. 1. 6, pp. 53-4.
2. Craigie, *STS* n.s. VII. 11-12; 3. Ramsay, *Evergreen*, II. 209; Laing, *Dunbar*, I. 135-6; Paterson, *Dunbar*, pp. 150-1; *Bannatyne MS.*, Hunt. Club, IV. 1094-5; Small, *STS* IV. 190-1; Schipper, *Dunbar*, pp. 208-9; and *DKAW* XLI (IV). 9-11; Baildon, *Dunbar*, pp. 98-100; Ritchie, *STS* 3 s. V. 87; MacKenzie, *Dunbar*, pp. 65-6.

1587.5   In wele be wyis and war or þou be wo / Thouȝ thou mow sle yit do nothyng so
   A couplet motto in a scroll in one MS. of Hoccleve's *De Regimine Principum* (2229).
   1. Camb. Un. Hh. 4. 11, f. 21a.

1587.8   In welth be ware of woo what so þe happes / & bere þe evyn for drede of after clappes
   A proverbial couplet in a series of six (see 4137).
   1. Balliol 354, f. 160a.
   Flügel, *Anglia* XXVI. 174; Dyboski, *EETS* ci. 139.

   In what estate so euer I be   See 2066.5.

1588   Kaiser, *Anthologie*, p. 442; Kaiser, *Med. Eng.*, p. 295; Davies, *Med. Eng. Lyrics*, pp. 171-3.

1589   Segar, *Some Minor Poems*, p. 40.

1589.5   In wyldirnes / ther founde I Besse
   A betrayed maiden, with a *chanson d'aventure* opening—eight 6-line tail-rime stanzas.
   1. Egerton 3002, f. 2b (7 st.); 2. BM Addit. 5665, f. 141a.
   2. Fehr, *Archiv* CVI. 283; Stevens, *Music & Poetry*, p. 346.

1591   3. Kreuzer, *Traditio* VII. 359-403.

1592   An extract in Stow from *The Fall of Princes* (1168) made up of Book IV. 2374-87 and Book III. 1373-1421. [Utley 142].
   1. Trinity Camb. 599, f. 2a (with one added st.).
   [Anderson,] *Poets of Great Britain*, I. 587.

1593   [Cf. 232. Utley 143].
   2. Royal RM 24. d. 2, f. 99b.
   1. Robbins, *Sec. Lyrics*, p. 102; Stevens, *Music & Poetry*, p. 162.

1594   an acrostic of John Wilson.
   1. BM C. 10. b. 23: *Game of Chesse*, Caxton, n. d. (written on margin).
   Blades, *Life & Typography of Caxton*, II. 11.

1595   [Utley 144].

1596   [Utley 145].
            Segar, *Med. Anthology*, p. 109 (extracts).

            In youth in age both in wealth and woe / *Auxilium meum a Domino*
            Burden to 3706.4.

1596.5   Infynite laude wyth thankynges many folde
            Colophon or 'Lenuoye' of de Worde's edition of Hilton—two 8-line stanzas. [Ringler 34].
            Hylton, *Scala Perfeccionis*, de Worde, 1494 (STC 14042); repr. Dibdin, *Typo. Antiquities*, II. 36-7; Plomer, *Wynkyn de Worde*, p. 52.

            Ynguar and Vbbe Beorn was þe þridde   See 1267.5.

1596.8   Instruckt well thy familie / Sucor the pore
            Moral counsel: an acrostic on Isaace Frise—eleven lines.
            1. Newberry Lib. Gen. Lib. Addit. 8, f. 242b (added in xvi cent. hand).

1597   [For extracts occurring separately see 1254, 2820].
            10. Camb. Un. Add. 3573 [*olim* Phillipps 9472], f. 1a; 14. Harley 44, ff. 5a-102 (with a Proheme of 31 st. on f. 2a); 22. Newberry Lib. Gen. Lib. Addit. 8, f. 78a; 23. Rosenbach Foundation 1083/30 [*olim* Phillipps 1099], f. 78a.

1598   1. Advocates 1. 1. 6, p. 44 and f. 57a.
            Chepman and Myllar, 1508; *facs.* Beattie, *Edinb. Bibl. Soc.* 1950, pp. 144-5; *repr.* Laing, *Knightly Tale of Golagros*, 1827; Smith, *STS* LVIII. 107-8; Stevenson, *STS* LXV. 216-7; 1a. Ritchie, *STS* 3 s. V. 73-4; 1b. Pinkerton, *Poems from Scarce Editions*, III. 128; Laing, *Henryson*, 1865, p. 21; Eyre-Todd, *Med. Scot. Poetry*, pp. 101-2; Wood, *Henryson*, pp. 185-6; 2. Elliott, p. 121.

1598.3   Into my Hairtt emprentit is so sore
            On his mistress—three stanzas rime royal. [vv. 1-12 are contained in 2161].
            1. Advocates 1. 1. 6, f. 220b.
            Bannatyne MS., Hunt. Club, p. 629; Ritchie, *STS* n.s. XXIII. 270.

            Into sorwe & care turned is oure pley   See 221.

| 1599 | Person, *Camb. ME Lyrics*, p. 28. |

| 1599.5 | Into thir dirk and drublie dayis |

'Meditatioun in wynter' by William Dunbar – ten 5-line stanzas.
1. Camb. Un. Ll. 5. 10, f. 1a (vv. 1-22 only); 2. Pepys 2553, p. 3 (vv. 23-50) and p. 318

1. Craigie, *STS* n.s. XX. 34-5; 2a, 2b. Craigie, *STS* n.s. VII. 1-2, 380-2; 2a. Pinkerton, *Anc. Scot. Poems*, I. 125-7; Sibbald, *Chronicle*, II. 11-12; Laing, *Dunbar*, I. 253-5; repr. *Blackwood's Magazine*, Feb. 1835; Eyre-Todd, *Med. Scot. Poetry*, pp. 213-4; Paterson, *Dunbar*, pp. 245-7; 2b. Small, *STS* IV. 233-4; Schipper, *Dunbar*, pp. 329-31; and *DKAW* XLI (IV). 26-9; Baildon, *Dunbar*, pp. 168-9; Browne, *Early Scot. Poets*, pp. 131-3; MacKenzie, *Dunbar*, pp. 26-71; Kinsley, *Dunbar*, pp. 64-6.

| 1601 | Rickert, *Anc. Eng. Xmas Carols*, p. 189. |

| 1602 | 2. N. S. Baugh, *Worcestershire Misc.*, p. 148. |

| 1602.5 | Ypocras great wysedomm hadd |

True learning now disregarded – six couplets.
1. Morgan Lib. Acc. No. 673, *Dictes or Sayengis*, Caxton, 1447 (added in xvi cent. hand).

Bühler, *EETS* 211. 333.

| 1603 | Verses at the beginning of a Book of Medicines. [Cf. 1605 and 4182]. |

1. Bodl. 817, f. 72b (vv. 8); 2. Sloane 3160, f. 153a (vv. 6).

| 1604 | [Delete entire entry (prose)]. |

| 1605 | [Cf. 1603 and 4182]. |

1. Sloane 2584, f. 9a; 2. Bodl. 29003, f. 139a; 3. Harley 3383, f. 85b.

| 1605.5 | *Ipse mocat me* / An aple is no pere tree |

A nonsense carol – four 3-line macaronic stanzas and 2-line burden.

Christmas Carolles, Kele, ca. 1550 (STC 5205); *facs.* Reed, *Xmas Carols*, p. 40; *Early Eng. Carols*, p. 319.

| 1606.8 | Is an endynge of sorowe and gynnyngge of blisse |

The water of life – one couplet in a Latin sermon.
1. Bodl. 1871, f. 201a.

[I]ʂ in my remembrauns non but ye alone   See 380.

1607   Arber, *Dunbar Anthology*, p. 123.

1608   Is tell yw my mynd anes tayliar dame
A plea to Annis Taylor for another drink, a Welsh-English 'englyn.'
1, 2. Robbins, *Sec. Lyrics*, pp. 229,5.

1608.5   Is ðeos burch breome geond Breotenrice
Description of Durham—vv. 21 in alliterative lines, at end of Simeon of Durham's *Chronicle*.
1. Cotton Vitell. D. xx (MS. burned in 1731); 2. Camb. Un. Ff. 1. 27, p. 202; 2a (transcript). Harley 533.
1. Hickes, *Thesaurus*; 2. Somner, Twisden's *Historiae Anglicanae Scriptores*, 1652; Oelrich, *Angelsächsische Chrestomathie*, Hamburg, 1798; *Rel. Ant.*, I. 159; Arnold, *Symeonis Monachi Opera*, Rolls Series LXXV, i. 221; Wülcker, *Kleinere AS Dichtungen*; Wülcker, *Bibl. AS Poesie*, I. 389; Craigie, *Spec. AS Poetry*, III. 42; Krapp and Dobbie, *AS Poetic Records*, VI. 27; Kaiser, *Med. Eng.*, p. 144

1609   Robbins, *Sec. Lyrics*, p. 1.

1609.5   Ys thys a fayre avaunte ys thys honor
An extract from Hoccleve's *Lespistre de Cupide* (666), comprising vv. 64-77.
1. BM Addit. 17492, f. 89a.

Isope myn auctor makis mencioune   See 3703 (Asloan).

y-turned into ioye is al my wo / þou hast wrapped me wyst blisse for euere mo
See 3397 (MS. Camb. Un.).

1613   in the Vernon *Golden Legend*—in short couplets.
Horstmann, *AE Leg.* 1878, pp. 22-5.

1615   1. Furnivall, *EETS* 15 orig. ed. 221; rev. ed. 250.

1618   [Ringler 35].
Chaucer, *Compleynt of Anelida*, ca. 1477 (STC 5090); *facs.*

Blades, *Life & Typography of Caxton*, II. 65; Jenkinson, 1905.

1619 [Cf. 4135.5. Ringler 36].
1. Bodl. 2712, f. 268a; 2. Bodl. 11948, f. 31a.
Chaucer, *Compleynt of Anelida*, ca. 1477 (STC 5090); *facs.*
Blades, *Life & Typography of Caxton*, II. 65; 1, 2. Robbins, *Archiv* CC. 342, 343; 2. Furnivall, *EETS* 32 rev. ed. 220.

1620 [For later variants see 3445.5 and 960.1].
1. Cotton Cleo. C. iv, ff. 64a-68b; 2. Harley 293, ff. 52a-54b (57 st. only).
1. Percy, *Reliques*, 1775, I. 22; 1794, I. 18; Child, *Ballads*, 1864, 1878, VII. 5-18; and *Pop. Ballads*, no. 161, III. 295-8; Sargent and Kittredge, *Pop. Ballads*, pp. 387-90; Arber, *Dunbar Anthology*, pp. 50-62; Gummere, *OE Ballads*, pp. 94-104; *Northumberland Garland*, p. 3; Sidgwick, *Ballads*, p. 192; Robbins, *Hist. Poems*, pp. 64-74; Leach, *Ballad Book*, pp. 436-43; 2. Percy, *Reliques*, 1765, I. 21.

1620.5 Is it not sure a deadly pain
The anguish of separated lovers—one stanza rime royal.
1. Public Record Office S. P. 1/246, f. 27a.
Hawkins, *Hist. of Music*, 1776, III. 25; *Early Eng. Lyrics*, p. 85; Saltmarsh, *Antiquaries Journal* XV. 18.

1621 1. BM Addit. 27879, p. 490; 2. York Minster.
1, 2. Child, *Pop. Ballads*, no. 167, III. 338-42; IV. 503-7; 1. Hales and Furnivall, *Percy Folio MS.*, III. 399; Child, *Ballads*, 1864, 1878, VII. 55-71; Sargent and Kittredge, *Pop. Ballads*, pp. 407-12; Gummere, *OE Ballads*, pp. 130-41; Leach, *Ballad Book*, pp. 467-75; 2. Raine, *Surtees Soc.* LXXXV. 64-75 [Delete: from a xvi cent. print &c.]

1622 Robbins, *Sec. Lyrics*, p. 43; Bowers, *JEGP* LI. 393-4; Perkins, *Journal American Folklore* LXXIV. 235-6.

1624 [Cf. *2639.5].
1. Hales and Furnivall, *Eger and Grine*, London 1867.

1626 A poser attacking duplicity.

1627.5 It is but a sympill oke / That [is] cut down
Proverbial couplet in a letter from Elizabeth Brews to John

Paston, February 1477. [Paston Letters No. 782, and repeated in No. 785].
1. BM Addit. 43490, f. 22a.
Fenn, II. 208; Gairdner, III. 169, 172; Coulton, *Life in the MA*, III. 134; Bennett, *England Chaucer-Caxton*, p. 20.

1628.5 It is first þe floritif of fairnes
Three rıming alliterative lines in an English prose homily. [Cf. 1848].
1. Worcester Cath. F. 10, f. 43a.
Register, I. 450.

1628.8 Yt is folly to byene a begare yff it be wyell boyghtt
A series of ten disconnected proverbial couplets signed 'Wyllughby' (including 77, 106.5, 1162.9, 2056, 2072.3).
1. Hunterian Mus. 230, ff. 247a-248b.

1629 in rime royal stanzas. [Immediately preceded by Lydgate's *Horse Sheep & Goose* (658) in this MS. only, and followed by 3504. St. 6 = st. 23 of 3651; st. 7 = st. 1 of 3436 and = 3437. Ringler 37].
1. Huntington HM 144 [*olim* Huth 7], f. 144a (5 st. copied from Caxton).
The Horse the Ghoos & the Sheep, Caxton, ca. 1477 (STC 17018) (7 st.): ca. 1478 (STC 17019); de Worde. ca. 1499 (STC 17020); *repr*. Jenkinson, 1906; de Worde, ca. 1500 (STC 17021).

1630 [Utley 147].

1631.3 Het is i-cume to þis tune / Godith and Godrun
A quatrain in a Latin sermon.
1. Tübingen Univ. Deposit: Berlin Preuss. Staatsbibliothek Lat. theol. fol. 249, f. 134a.

1632.5 Hit ys in heruyst cartes to clater
Aphoristic lines: a schoolboy's exercises, with a Latin translation — five lines. [Cf. 430.8].
1. Harley 1002, f. 72b.
Wright, *RES* n.s. II. 118.

1633 [Masters,] *Rymes of Minstrels*, p. 12.

1634 Furnivall, *EETS* orig. ed. 231; rev. ed. 260.

1634.5   Hyt is mery in hall / when berdys waggyth all
           Proverbial couplet translating *'Aula gaudescit &c.'* [Cf. Heywood; Tilley H 55; and Meech, *MP* XXXVIII. 129].
           1. Bodl. 15444, f. 141b.
              Meech, *MP* XXXVIII. 120.

1635   'Balade by Chaucer' on swiving. [Utley 148. Cf. 2611].
           1. Harley 7578, f. 15a.
           1, 2. Brusendorff, *Chaucer Tradition*, pp. 280-1; 2. Hammond, *MLN* XIX. 38.

1635.5   It is no wyse mannys lore / to tak þe las and leue þe more
           A proverbial couplet.
           1. Rylands Lib. Latin 394, f. 3b.
              Pantin, *BJRL* XIV. 93.

1636.3   Yt is prayse to know hey thyng / but it is scame to forgo
           A proverbial tag translating Latin.
           1. BM Addit. 12195, f. 116b.

1636.5   hit is so praty In euery degre
           The deluded lover—four quatrains and 2-line refrain (possibly an embryonic carol).
           1. BM Addit. 5465, f. 93b; 2. New York Pub. Lib. Drexel Fragments 4180 (st. 1-2 only).
           1. Hawkins, *Hist. of Music*, 1776, III. 24; Rimbault, *Songs & Ballads*, no. 40; Fehr, *Archiv* CVI. 67; Flügel, *Neuengl. Lesebuch*, p. 143; 2. Stevens, *Music & Poetry*, pp. 377-8.

1636.8   It is þe properte of a gentelman/To say the beste þat he can
           A proverbial couplet.
           1. Bodl. 11948, f. 31a.
              Furnivall, *EETS* 32. 220.

1637   [Delete entire entry].

           It is to be titelled now proved withoute obstacle
             'Of the Crafte of Philonomye' (MS. Caius 336): see 935.

1637.2   It is to me a ryght gret joy
           One line only, serving as a round
           1. BM Addit. 31922, f. 61a.

Trefusis, *Songs Henry VIII*, Roxburghe Club CLXI. 25; Stevens, *Music & Poetry*, p. 408; Stevens, *Music at Court*, p. 45.

1637.4 It is to vertu full good & necessary
The speech of Job in the pageant celebrating the marriage of Prince Arthur and Princess Catharine—four stanzas rime royal.
1. Cotton Vitellius A. xvi, ff. 190b-191a.

1637.6 hit is vnknowe / what man bulde þis cete nowe
A verse insert on Chester Castle in Trevisa's translation of Higden's *Polychronicon* (Book I, Cap. 48)—thirteen doggerel couplets. [Cf. 2361.5].
1. St. John's Camb. 204; 2. Cotton Tiberius D. vii; 3. Harley 1900; 4. Stowe 65; 5. BM Addit. 24194; 6. Aberdeen Univ. 21; 7. Chetham Lib. 11379, f. 52b; 8. Hunterian Mus. 83; 9. Penrose 12; 10. Morgan Lib. M. 875.
Trevisa, *Discripcion of Britayne*, Caxton, 1480 (STC 13440a); de Worde, 1498 (STC 13440b); Trevisa, *Prolocronycon*, Caxton, 1483 (STC 13438); de Worde, 1495 (STC 13439); Treveris, 1527 (STC 13440); Babington and Lumby, *Rolls Series* XLI, ii. 81-3.

1637.8 It is well fownde a passyng grete damage
Against 'double intendement'—three stanzas rime royal with refrain.
1. Arundel 26, f. 32a.

1638 Heuser, *Die Kildare-Gedichte*, p. 139.

1639 Furnivall, *EETS* 15. 260 (rev. ed. only); *Register*, I. 353.

1640 [Cf. 3583].
3. Copenhagen Royal Lib. 29264, f. 163a; 4. Durham Univ. Cosin V. v. 19, f. 72b (var.).
1. Davies, *Med. Eng. Lyrics*, p. 196.

1640.3 It standeth wryten in a boke / He that hath no horse muste go on fote
One gnomic couplet.
Salomon and Marcolphus, Leeu, Antwerp, ca. 1492 (STC 22905); *facs.* Duff, London 1892.

1640.5   It þat I gif I haif / It þat I len I craiff
Twelve moralizing lines on lending money. [Cf. 3273, 3088, 4137, 1297, and 4095].
1. Camb. Un. Ll. 5. 10, f. 57b; 2. Pepys 2553, p. 294; 3. Advocates 1. 1. 6, f. 147a.
2. Craigie, STS n.s. VII. 344; 3. Ramsay, Evergreen, I. 107; Ritchie, STS n.s. XXIII. 43.

Y-turnd into ioye is al my wo   See 3397.

1641   [Cf. 59, 2446.5].
12. Harley 4196, f. 147b.

1641.5   It was a mayde of brenten ars
'My ladyes water-myll:' an erotic carol—four 3-line stanzas and burden.
Christmas Carolles, Kele, ca. 1550 (STC 5205); facs. Reed, Xmas Carols, p. 36; repr. Early Eng. Carols, p. 311.

1642   Boyd, ME Miracles, pp. 18-23.

1645   11. Harvard Coll. Eng. 1032, two fragments (var.).

1649   Child, Pop. Ballads, no. 23, I. 243-4, V. 288; Cook, Reader, p. 470; Mossé, Handbook, pp. 205-6; Niles, Carol Study Book, p. 5; Davies, Med. Eng. Lyrics, pp. 75-7; Leach, Ballad Book, pp. 108-9.

1650   1. Greene, Sel. Eng. Carols, p. 109; Davies, Med. Eng. Lyrics, pp. 163-4; 2. Rickert, Anc. Eng. Xmas Carols, p. 7.

Item I shall telle yow a tale   See 1360.

1651.5   Iuy is both fair & gren
A carol in praise of ivy—five 7-line stanzas including bob and burden.
1. Egerton 3307, f. 59b.
Stevens, Med. Carols, p. 44; Greene, Sel. Eng. Carols, p. 94.

1652   Robbins, Sec. Lyrics, p. 164.

1653.5   Jack dawe þou habest blasfemed & reson hast
Jack Upland's Rejoinder (to 4098.3)—in irregular non-riming lines, partly alliterative, partly prose. [Cf. 3782.5].

        1. Bodl. 1642, ff. 2a-16b (added on margins).
        Wright, *Polit. Songs*, II. 39.

1654   [Text preserved in early chronicles, such as Walsingham and Knighton, and followed in most later chronicles. Cf. 1796].
        Annales, Stow, 1615, p. 294; Mackay, *Percy Soc.* I. 3; Wright, *Pop. Superstitions*, II. 260; Lumby, *Chronicon Henrici Knighton*, Rolls Ser. XCII, ii. 139; Eberhard, *Der Bauernaufstand vom Jahr 1381*, AF LI. 21; Lindsay and Groves, *Peasants' Revolt 1381*, p. 87; Hilton and Fagan, *English Rising of 1381*, p. 103.

1654.5   Jack of Norffolke be not to bolde / For Dykon thy maister is bought and solde
        A traditional couplet in early chronicles, a warning, A.D. 1485, to John Howard, Duke of Norfolk.
        Holinshed, *Chronicles*, 1808, III. 444: Weever, *Anc. Funerall Monuments*, 1631, p. 830 (STC 25223); Hall's *Chronicle*, 1809, p. 413.

1655   Lumby, *Chronicon Henrici Knighton*. Rolls Ser. XCII, ii. 139; Eberhard, *Der Bauernaufstand vom Jahr 1381*, AF LI. 20; Lindsay and Groves, *Peasants' Revolt 1381*, p. 87; Hilton and Fagan, *English Rising of 1381*, p. 102.

1655.5   Iangler *cum* jasper lepar galper *quoque* draggar
        Three macaronic lines on Tutivillus. [Cf. 707.5, 1214.9, and 3812].
        1. Lansdowne 762, f. 93b.
        Rel. Ant., I. 291; Wright, *Percy Soc.* VIII. 225-6.

1656   Bowers, *Gast of Gy*, Leipzig 1938, p. 41.

1657.5   Jerusalem reioss for joy
        On the Nativity, attributed to William Dunbar—five 8-line stanzas with refrain: '*Illuminare Jerusalem.*'
        1. Advocates 1. 1. 6, f. 27b.
        Laing, *Dunbar*, II. 57-8; *Bannatyne MS.*, Hunt Club, II. 71-2; Small, *STS* IV. 322-3; Schipper, *Dunbar*, pp. 450-1; and *DKAW* XLIII (I). 62-3; Baildon, *Dunbar*, pp. 235-6; Ritchie, *STS* n.s. XXII. 66-8.

1662   Rickert, *Anc. Eng. Xmas Carols*, pp. 176-7.

1663	three quatrains. Comper, *Life & Lyrics of Rolle*, p. 278.
1664.5	Jhesu be þou my ioy al melody and swetnes Three irregular riming lines in Rolle's English Psalter (Ps. LVI). [For further MSS. see Allen, *Rolle*, pp. 170-7]. 1. Bodl. 4127, f. 85b; 2. Univ. Coll. Oxf. 64, f. 62b. 1. Allen, *Eng. Writings of Rolle*, p. 15; 2. Bramley, Oxford 1884, p. 204.
1666	Entry transferred to 1719.5. Boyd, *ME Miracles*, pp. 38-43.
1669	[For extracts from the *Proverbs of Hendyng* occurring separately see 594, 1427, 1429, 2817, 4143; and cf. *Rel. Ant.*, I. 193 (vv. 1-32, MS. 2), I. 256 (vv. 1-22, MS. 1)].
1674	Perry, *EETS* 26 orig. ed. 91; Comper, *Life & Lyrics of Rolle*, p. 295.
1675	[Cf. 611.5].
1678	Brook, *Harley Lyrics*, pp. 52-3. Iesu chryste hevynnis kyng / Grant vs all his blissyng See 1725.
1683.3	Iesu cryst most mercyful A simple prayer to Christ—three monoriming lines. 1. Camb. Un. Kk. 1. 6, f. 2a.
1683.5	Jesu Christ most of myght / Have mercy on John le Wenlock Epitaph, ca. A.D. 1480, at Luton. 1. Harley 1531, f. 15a. *Beauties of England*, I. 31.
1684	1. Bodl. 3938, f. 114b col. ii and f. 300a col. ii (appended to 3760). 1a. Comper, *Life & Lyrics of Rolle*, p. 280; 1b. Davies, *Med. Eng. Lyrics*, p. 117; 1 (mod.). Segar, *Med. Anthology*, p. 39.
1687	2. Wells Cath. *Statuta Angliae*, at end. 1. Gray, *N&Q* n.s. X. 128.

1688	Ihones, n.d. (STC 79); [de Worde,] n.d. (STC 78); *repr.* Hazlitt, *Remains*, III. 100-18.
1690	6. *Rel. Ant.*, II. 65-7 (selections).
1691	1. Egerton 3245 [*olim* Gurney], f. 193a.
1692	Perry, *EETS* 26 orig. ed. 79-82; rev. ed. 73-5; Comper, *Life & Lyrics of Rolle*, pp. 236-9; Segar, *Med. Anthology*, pp. 21-2 (7 st. only).
1695	1. Furnivall, *EETS* 117. 462-4.
1697	[Cf. *3216.5]. Reese, *Music in MA*, p. 389.
1699	Ihesus doþ him by mene / and spekeþ to synful mon Davies, *Med. Eng. Lyrics*, pp. 152-3.
1700	1. Trinity Dublin 155, pp. 16-7.
1700.5	Jhesu for thi blysfull blod / bryng thoo soulus in to thi blis A simple prayer to Jesus—four lines. 1. Bodl. Lyell 30, f. 285b. Robbins, *Anglia* LXXXII. 4.
1701	1. Balliol 316 A, f. 110a.
1702	[Delete entire entry]. Ihesu for þi blodi heued / þat al wit thornes &c. See 1708.
1703	[For a prose variant see BM Addit. 33381, f. 181b]. 12. Wellcome Hist. Med. Lib. 632 [*olim* Pullen] (roll); 13. Bodl. 15802, f. 63b; 14. Trinity Camb. 1450, f. 89b; 15. Harley 63, f. 44b; 16. Harley 494, f. 105a; 17. Worcester Cath. F. 172, f. 116b. 18. Pepys Lib., *Example of Virtue*, 1510, flyleaf (var., vv. 3, added in xvi cent. hand). *XV Oos*, Caxton, ca. 1490 (STC 20195); *XV Oos*, Copland, 1529 (STC 20196); 6. Bennett, *STS* 3 s. XXIII. 278; 9. Robbins, *SP* LVI. 571; 12. Sparrow-Simpson, *Journal Brit. Archaeol. Assoc.* XLVIII. 39.

1704.5	Ihesu for thi meche myht / Saue alle people that loue trouthe / and hate all vnryht
	A motto on a scroll in one MS. of Hoccleve's *De Regimine Principum* (2229).
	1. Camb. Un. Hh. 14. 11, f. 83b.
1705	Marsh, *Hist. Eng. Language*, p. 255; Brook, *Harley Lyrics*, pp. 57-9.
1706	Gray, *N&Q* n.s. X. 128.
1707	1. Bodl. 2643, f. 147b (rubric), 148a (text).
1708	1. Bodl. 15834, f. 19a and again at f. 62a (st. disarranged: 4, 7, 5, 6, 3, 1, 2).
	1a. *Rel. Lyr. XIV C.*, pp. 218-9.
1709.5	Jesu for þi woundes fiue / þou kepe hem weil in al þaire lyue
	A prayer by the Passion—four lines. [Preceded by 2602.4].
	1. Sloane 2275, endleaf, f. 245a.
	Robbins, *Anglia* LXXXII. 4.
1710	Stevens, *Med. Carols*, p. 102; Robbins, *Hist. Poems*, p. 242; Davies, *Med. Eng. Lyrics*, p. 262.
1711	Gray, *N&Q* n.s. X. 128.
1715	[This poem is inserted into a Southern version of *Incendium Amoris*, 2007, v. 68; 4088, one quatrain, is incorporated into this piece. See also 1367.3].
	Comper, *Life & Lyrics of Rolle*, pp. 240-4.
1717	1. Trinity Dublin 155, pp. 11-14.
1717.3	Ihesus haue mercy vppon vs and this Inglishe nacyon
	Prayer for England as part of Christendom—one couplet in long lines.
	1. Durham Univ. Cosin V. iii. 9, f. 94b.
	Furnivall, *EETS* lxi. 241.

Ihesu kyng in trone / Lord in mageste   See 412.

1719   [Ringler 39].
        7. Camb. Un. Kk. 1. 6, ff. 30b-32a; 8. BM Addit. 34193, f. 28a; 9. Hatfield; 10. Melbourne: Victoria Pub. Lib., f. 121b.
        Pylgremage of the Sowle, Caxton, 1483 (STC 6473); repr. Cust, 1859, pp. 38-40.

1719.5 Jesu lythe my sowle with þi grace
        'A prayer aȝeen dispeyre or mysbeleue: *Illumina*' — two couplets followed by a prose prayer.
        1. Lambeth 541, f. 1a.
        Robbins, *Neophilologus* XXXVIII. 40.

1721   fifty-one stanzas rime royal and concluding 8-line stanza.
        9. St. John's Oxf. Arch. A. 50 (first 2 st. missing).
        Matyns of Our Lady, de Worde, 1513 (STC 15914).

1722   1a (xix cent. transcript). Egerton 2257, f. 95a.

1724   [Cf. 467.5].
        5. Penrose 6, f. 166a (first vv. 10 illegible).

1725   [Ringler 38].
        Syr Eglamoure of Artayes, de Worde, ca. 1500 (STC 7541), one leaf fragment (vv. 59 only = vv. 242-94 in Schleich); R. Bankes, n.d. (fragment); Copland, n.d. (fragment: Selden D. 45); Chepman and Myllar, 1508 (STC 7542); *facs.* Beattie, *Edinb. Bibl. Soc.* 1950, pp. 53-87.

1726   1. NLW Peniarth 53, pp. 103-11.
        Baugh, *Philologica: Malone Anniversary Studies*, pp. 202-7; Robbins, *SP* XLVII. 36-41.

1727   [For early printed primers &c. see Hoskins; Brydges and Haslewood, *Brit. Bibliographer,* 1814, IV. 139-40 ('Psalter of Jesus'); and Bühler, *St. in Renaissance* VI. 235].
        13. Bodl. Lat. misc. c. 66 [*olim* Capesthorne], f. 106a (begins imperfectly at v. 15); 14. Longleat 30, f. 19b; 15. Fitzwilliam Mus. McClean 40-1950 [*olim* Yates Thompson 83, 'Talbot Hours'], f. 134a; 18. Yale Univ. 163 [*olim* Wagstaffe 9], f. 186b; 19. NLW Peniarth 53, p. 103; 20. Paris: Bibl. Mazarine 514, ff. 145b-146b (vv. 42); 21. Islip (Lady Richmond), Horae.

Jesus Psalter, Copland, 1529 (STC 14563); *Our Ladyes Chamber or Parloure,* Robert Wyer, n.d.; Jerome of Ferrara, *Exposit. on Ps. LI.,* tr. 1538 (vv. 20 at end); 8. Bennett, *STS* 3 s. XXIII. 277-8; 10. Davies, *Med. Eng. Lyrics,* pp. 146-8; 12. Warner, *Medici Soc. Memorabilia,* III. 33-9; 13. Robbins, *PMLA* LXV. 275-6; 17. Drake, *N&Q* 4 s. II. 576 (vv. 60).

1728   Ihesu lorde þi blesside life / helpe and counfort our wrecchede life
[Many other copies occur at end of Love's prose *Mirror,* e.g. Camb. Un. Add. 6578, f. 124a; Camb. Un. Add. 6686, p. 233. In Camb. Un. Ii. 4. 9 it follows the Northern Passion].
3. Harley 4011, f. 2b; 4. BM Addit. 19901, f. 8b.
Love, *Mirror,* Caxton, 1488; *repr.* Blades, *Life & Typography of Caxton,* II. 195-6.

1729   3. Egerton 3245 [*olim* Gurney], f. 192b (vv. 12); 4. Bodl. Lyell 30, f. 300b; 5. Paris: Bibl. nat. f. fr. 1830, f. 137a (vv. 8).
2. Davies, *Med. Eng. Lyrics,* p. 115; 3. Robbins, *PMLA* LIV. 378.

1730   Person, *Camb. ME Lyrics,* p. 8.

1730.5 Ihus marcy Lady helpe / for my dogge ys a parillus welp
For my dog (name illegible) — one couplet.
1. Bodl. 12417, f. 1b (added in xvi cent. hand).
Smalley, *Med. & Renaissance St.* III. 226.

1731   Stevens, *Music & Poetry,* p. 367.

1732   1. Furnivall, *EETS* 15 orig. ed. 103-8; rev. ed. 133-8.

1732.5 Jesu most swettest of any þynge / To love sow I haue grete longyng
'A song of loue to owre lorde Iesu Criste' — seventy mono-riming quatrains. [Cf. 3238].
1. Harvard Univ. Deposit: Richardson 22, ff. 72a – 78a.

1733   *facs.* Brown, facing p. 1.

1734   1. York Minster, Chapter House [*olim* Challoner], ff. 206a-207a.
McGarry, *Holy Eucharist in ME Verse,* p. 235 (rubric only).

1735	Comper, *Life & Lyrics of Rolle*, p. 318.
1736	2. Paris: Bib. Mazarine 514, f. 7b (vv. 16). 1. Robbins, *Neophilologus* XXXVIII. 40-1.
1738	Sandys, *Carols*, p. 15; Rickert, *Anc. Eng. Xmas Carols*, pp. 181-2; Stevens, *Med. Carols*, pp. 86, 101.
1739.5	Iesu of Nazareth / þat þoledest for mannes soule deth A prayer for mercy by the Five Wounds — six lines. 1. Wells Cath. *Statuta Angliae*, end flyleaf. Robbins, *Anglia* LXXXII. 4.
1740	1. Camb. Un. Add. 6686 [*olim* Ashburnham 140], p. 270.
1741	Perry, *EETS* 26 orig. ed. 78; Horstmann, *York. Wr.*, I. 364; Comper, *Life & Lyrics of Rolle*, pp. 281-2.
1742	1. BM Addit. 46919 [*olim* Phillipps 8336], f. 209b.
1743	1. Trinity Dublin 155, pp. 14-15.
1745	1. Horstmann, *Archiv* LXXXI. 314.
1747	3. Newberry Lib. D. 26986, f. 135a (20 st.).
1747.5	Jhesu sweet ihesu lorde myne On the Passion — forty monoriming lines in quatrains. [Cf. 3236]. 1. *olim* Llanarth Priory, Raglan, Horae (ends imperfectly) (Quaritch Sale Cat. 742, Item 13). *Life of the Spirit*, Oxford 1946, I. 134-5.
	Jesu swete now wyll I syng See 3238.
1749	(possibly a roundel).
1750	[Followed by 1770]. Bowers, *N&Q* CXCVI. 134.
1751	[Utley 149a]. (imperfect at end).

1752	3. Victoria and Albert Mus., Reid 7, endleaf. *Speculum Spiritualium*, Paris 1510, f. ccii verso.
1753	1. Glazier G. 9, Art 1 [*olim* Berkeley].
1755	2a. Bodl. facs. e. 23 (photo facsimile).
1757	2. Perry, *EETS* 26 orig. ed. 78; Comper, *Life & Lyrics of Rolle*, p. 281.
1758.5	Jhesu that deyed up on a tre / owr sowlys for to wynne A simple prayer against 'þe Fendis myзt'—one quatrain. 1. Harley 211, f. 147b. Robbins, *Anglia* LXXXII. 4.
1761	8. Egerton 3245 [*olim* Gurney], f. 185b; 10. Longleat 30, ff. 49a-51b. 9. Davies, *Med. Eng. Lyrics*, pp. 120-5.
1767	1. Ipswich County Hall Deposit: Hillwood [*olim* Brome], f. 28a.
1768	Iesue that ys most of myght / & made man aboffe all thyng Robbins, *Sec. Lyrics*, pp. 124-6.
1770	[Following 1750]. Bowers, *N&Q* CXCVI. 134.
1770.5	Iesu that sufferyd bitter passion and peyn / Haue mercy &c. Epitaph, A.D. 1487, for John Chamberleyn and his wives at Allhallows the Less Church, London—eight lines. Weever, *Anc. Funerall Monuments*, 1631, p. 409 (STC 25223).
1772	Robbins, *Hist. Poems*, pp. 239-42. Iesu þat was in bedlem born / baptysud was in flum iordan See 624.
1777	two quatrains in a sermon. 1. Bodl. 28746, f. 173a and again at f. 175a (vv. 6).
1778	Pynson, 1520 (STC 14806).

*1779.5   *Iesu thow do me loue the so
          A prayer to Christ—vv. 34. [Cf. 3236, st. 20 of MS. 2].
          1. Quaritch Sale Cat. Illuminated MSS. 1931, Lot 82, and Cat. 609, 1943, Lot 500.

1781   9. Harley 2339, f. 78a; 16. Egerton 3245 [olim Gurney], f. 188b; 17. Camb. Un. Add. 6693 [olim Ashburnham 236], f. 179a (first two lines, added on flyleaf); 18. Maidstone Mus. A. 6, f. ii recto (5 st.).
          Omelia Origensis, W. Faques, London, ca. 1504, f. 10a (STC 18846); repr. Dibdin, Typo. Antiquities, III. 11 (vv. 16); 1. Segar, Med. Anthology, pp. 18-20 (7 st. only); 9. Comper, Life & Lyrics of Rolle, pp. 288-92.

1786.5   Iesu whom ye serue dayly / Vppon 3our enemys
          A prayer for John Talbot—six couplets.
          1. Fitzwilliam Mus. 40-1950 [olim Yates Thompson 83, 'Talbot Hours'], f. 107b.
          de Ricci, Thompson Cat., II. 224-5.

1787   Gray, N&Q n.s. X. 134; Davies, Med. Eng. Lyrics, p. 216.

1788   4. D'Evelyn and Mill, EETS 235. 237.

1789   Furnivall, EETS 15 orig. ed. 38-9; rev. ed. 66-7.

1790.5   John Baker of Briggeswater / Criste helpe the
          A blessing on John Baker and Dame Katherine Moleyns, Prioress of Kingston St. Michael—two couplets (following 241).
          1. Harley 2406, f. 8b.

1790.8   John Ball greeteth you wele all
          Letter of John Ball to the rebels—one quatrain. [Cf. 1791].
          Annales, Stow, 1615, p. 294; Lumby, Rolls Series XCII, ii. 139; Hilton and Fagan, English Rising of 1381, p. 100.

1791   [Cf. 1790.8, 1796 and 2356, variant. Text preserved in early chronicles such as Walsingham and Knighton, and followed in most later chronicles].
          Annales, Stow, 1615, p. 293; Holinshed's Chronicles, 1807, II. 749; Mackay, Percy Soc. I. 1; Riley, Thomae Walsingham Historia Anglicana, Rolls Series XXVIII, ii. 33;

	Thompson, *Chronicon Angliae*, Rolls Series LXIV. 322; Lumby, *Chronicon Henrici Knighton*, Rolls Series XCII, ii. 140; Eberhard, *Der Bauernaufstand vom Jahr 1381*, AF LI. 22, 23; Hilton and Fagan, *English Rising of 1381*, p. 102; Wilson, *Lost Lit.*, p. 202; Robbins, *Hist. Poems*, pp. xliii, 54.
1793	Robbins, *Sec. Lyrics*, pp. 259-60.
1793.5	John Barton lyeth under here / Sometimes of London Epitaph, A.D. 1460, of John Barton and his wife at St. Michael Basinghall—four couplets. Stow, *Survey of London*, 1598, p. 229; Weever, *Anc. Funerall Monuments*, 1631, p. 398 (STC 25223); Pettigrew, *Chronicles of Tombs*, p. 46; Ravenshaw, *Antiente Epitaphes*, p. 12; Gray, *N&Q* n.s. VIII. 135.
1793.6	Ion Clerke of toryton I dar a̴ ow Flyleaf verses—vv. 30. 1. Stanbrook Abbey 3, f. iii. Ker, *Medium Aevum*.
1793.7	John Coppyn of Whitstabell in great devotion Rimed inscription, A.D. 1446. Somner, *Antiq. Canterbury*, 1703, p. 79.
	Jhoone is sike & ill at ease Introductory burden to 1636.5.
1793.9	Ion Ion pyke a bone / tomorrow þu schall pyke none A proverbial couplet tr. Latin. 1. Bodl. 15444, f. 141a. Meech, *MP* XXXVIII. 119.
	John ofte reuolue in thyn rememberance See 3563.5.
1796	[Text preserved in early chronicles, such as Walsingham and Knighton, and followed in most later chronicles. Cf. 1791]. *Annales*, Stow, 1615, p. 294; Holinshed's *Chronicles*, 1807, II. 749; Mackay, *Percy Soc.* I. 2; Wright, *Pop. Superstitions*, II. 260; Riley, *Thomae Walsingham Historia Anglicana*, Rolls Series XXVIII, ii. 34; Thompson, *Chronicon Angliae*, Rolls Series LXIV. 322; Skeat, *Piers Plowman*, 1886, II. lv; Trevelyan, *England Age of Wycliffe*, p. 203; Sisam, *XIV C.*

Verse & Prose, p. 161; Eberhard, *Der Bauernaufstand vom Jahr 1381*, AF LI. 23; Owst, *Lit. & Pulpit*, p. 221; *Early Eng. Carols*, p. cxliv; Lindsay and Groves, *Peasants' Revolt 1381*, p. 86; Hilton and Fagan, *Eng. Rising of 1381*, pp. 101, 103; Kaiser, *Anthologie*, p. 373; Kaiser, *Med. Eng.*, p. 387; Robbins, *Hist. Poems*, p. 55; Rickert, *Chaucer's World*, p. 362.

1796.5 Jon Wellis of London grocer & meyr / To Bristow gave this swerd feir
    Inscription on a sword, the property of Bristol Corporation.

1798 originally perhaps about two 7-line stanzas.
    Wilson, *Lost Lit.*, p. 180; Robbins, *Sec. Lyrics*, p. xl.

Joly felowe joly   See 87.5.

1799 Wilson, *Lost Lit.*, p. 185.

1805 Proheme and Envoy (2 st.) pr. Horstmann, *EETS* 100. xliv-xlv.

Ioie helthe ande euery delle
    An extract (vv. 439-505), occurring separately (Sloane 1212), from *Supplicacio Amantis*.   See 147.

1806 [Delete entire entry].

1807 Joy thu Mary with virgyn flower
    '*Gaude flore virginali*' — vv. 28 mainly in quatrains.
    1. Canterbury Cath. Add. 68 [*olim* Ingilby], ff. 99b-100a. Woodruff, *XV Cent. Guide Book*, pp. 80-81.

1808 five quatrains.
    1. Canterbury Cath. Add. 68 [*olim* Ingilby], f. 98a. Woodruff, *XV Cent. Guide Book*, p. 80.

1808.5 Joy winefred virgine that ouercomminge youthful lures
    A 'himme' to St. Winifred, preceded and followed by prose prayers — seven quatrains.
    1. Rylands Lib. Latin 165, end flyleaves (added in xvi cent. hand).

1809	12. Winchester Coll. 33, f. 15b.
	6. D'Evelyn and Mill, *EETS* 236. 692.
1810	[Delete entire entry].
	Juce of lekes with gotes galle See 2026.5.
1810.5	Justyce now is dede / Trowth with a drowsy hede
	'*En Parlament à Paris*' by John Skelton—vv. 15 in 'skeltonics.' *Garlande of Laurell*, Faukes, 1523 (STC 22610); *repr.* Dyce, *Skelton*, I. 426-7; Dyce and Child, *Skelton & Donne*, II. 243; Flügel, *Neuengl. Lesebuch*, p. 60; Henderson, *Skelton*, 1931, p. 468; 1948, 1959, p. 397; *Workes*, Marshe, 1568 (STC 22608); *repr.* [? J. Bowle,] 1736; Chalmers, *English Poets*, II. 303.
1811	On the chair of a judge—seven lines.
	*Kandidus wroth went oway / And no com ogain See 683 (MS. 2).
1812	Clive, *Roxburghe Club* L. 182-212.
	Kype and save and thou schall have See 3088.
1814.5	Kepe þe fro care / & blesse þe fro þe mare
	A proverbial couplet.
	1. Bodl. 21626, f. 16b.
	Förster, *Festschrift zum 12 Deutschen Neuphilologentage*, p. 46.
1815	2. Pepys 1584, f. 107a; 6. Ushaw: St. Cuthbert's Coll. 28.
1817	1, 4, 6. Robbins, *Sec. Lyrics*, pp. 80-1, 253; 1. Zupitza, *Archiv* XC. 247; 2. Bloomfield, *Seven Deadly Sins*, p. 208.
1817.5	Kepe well thy cowncell as tresor in cheste
	Keep silence: friends may become foes—six lines.
	1. Trinity Dublin 661, p. 44.
1820	[Cf. Tilley W 700].
	7. Advocates 1. 1. 6, f. 122a (vv. 6) and again at f. 147a; 10.

Camb. Un. Add. 6860 [olim Gurney 75, olim Macro 18], f. 42b (var.); 11. Bodl. 2670, f. 88b (var.); 12. Bodl. 12506, f. 1a (vv. 4); 13. Camb. Un. Ll. 5. 10, f. 58a; 14. Sloane 1210, f. 124a (vv. 4).

    1, 5, 6. Heuser, *Bonn. Beit.* XIV. 184; 4, 6. Robbins, *Hist. Poems*, pp. 328, 144; 4. *Register*, I. 235; 5. Förster, *Archiv* CIV. 304; *Early Eng. Carols*, p. 419; 6. Robbins, *Anglia* LXXVII. 193; Peter, *Complaint & Satire*, p. 11; 7a. Ramsay, *Evergreen*, I. 107; *Bannatyne MS.*, Hunt. Club, p. 346; Ritchie, *STS* n.s. XXII. 324; Craigie, *STS* n.s. XXIII. 43; 12. O'Connor, *Art of Dying*, New York 1942, p. 108.

    King Edward wanne þu hauest Berwic   See 3918.5 (Rishanger, *RS* XXVIII).

1820.5   King hart in to his cumlie castell strang
    King Hart, attributed to Gawin Douglas — vv. 960 in 8-line stanzas.
    1. Pepys 2553, p. 226.
        Pinkerton, *Anc. Scot. Poems*, p. 1; Small, *STS* II. 85-120; Craigie, *STS* n.s. VII. 254-84.

1820.8   Kynge Henry is dede bewtye of the worlde for whom great dole
    On the death of Henry III — four couplets (allegedly contemporary) quoted in Fabyan's *Chronicle*. [Cf. 3955.5].
    Fabyan, *New Chronicles*, Pynson, 1516 (STC 10659); *repr.* Ellis, 1811, p. 260.

1821   vv. 23.
    1. BM Addit. 46919 [*olim* Phillipps 8336], f. 209b.
    Gneuss, *Anglia* LXXVIII. 180-2.

1822   12. Furnivall, *EETS* 15 orig. ed. 222; rev. ed. 251.

1822.5   Kynge Jamy Jomy your Ioye is all go
    'A ballade of the scottysshe kynge' attributed to John Skelton — vv. 72 in couplets. [Cf. 1931.3].
    BM C. 39. e. 1 [R. Fawkes, 1513] (STC 22593); *repr.* Dyce, *Skelton*, I. 82; Brie, *Eng. Stn.* XXXVII. 51-3; Flügel, *Neuengl. Lesebuch*, p. 150; Pollet, *Skelton*, pp. 247-9; *facs.* Ashton, *Century of Ballads*, 1882, p. xiii.

1823	[Also cf. 3080.5]. 2. Trinity Camb. 263, f. 113b; 4. Ipswich County Hall Deposit: Hillwood [*olim* Brome], f. 23a (ends v. 236); 5. Bodl. 10239, ff. 45b-47b (Day XI only).
1824.2	Kingdomes are but cares / state ys devoyd of staie The troubles of high estate, (spuriously) attributed to Henry VI—three quatrains. [Cf. *Mirror for Magistrates*]. 1. MS. written by Sir James Haryngton. Harington, *Nugae Antiquae*, 1804, I. 386.
1824.4	Kyngis state giff ȝou will lede Against young men's counsel—four lines in Fordun's *Scotichronicon* (Book XIV, Cap. iv). 1. Harley 712; 2. Edinburgh Univ. 186. Hearne, *Joannis de Fordun, Scotichronicon*, Edinburgh 1759, II. 344.
1824.6	Kysse or thow sclepe Take care—three riming lines. 1. Caius 249, f. vi. James, *Cat.*, I. 300.
1824.8	Kytt hathe lost hur key An erotic carol—five quatrains and burden. [For a later sequel, cf. Collier, *Register of Stationers' Company*, 1848, I. 55. Tilley K 109]. 1. Royal App. 58, f. 6b. Briggs, *Songs & Madrigals*, PMMS 1891, pp. xvii, 1-2; Flügel, *Anglia* XII. 261-2; Flügel, *Neuengl. Lesebuch*, p. 138; *Early Eng. Carols*, p. 310.
	Kytt she wept I axyde why soo See 1824.8.
1825	James, *Cat.*, III. 77.
1826	A Compleynt by the Duke of Suffolk, a testament bequeathing the lover's heart and will.
1827	The glamour of a knight errant—six couplets. Person, *Camb. ME Lyrics*, p. 38.
1829	[Cf. vv. 11-12 of 4137. Utley 151]. 2. Durham Univ. Cosin V. iii. 9, ff. 16b, 37b, 85b.

1. Robbins, *Sec. Lyrics*, p. 37; 2. Furnivall, *EETS* lxi. 124, 156, 228.

1829.2 Know or þou knyte & then þou mayst slake
A proverbial couplet included in a series of six (4137).
1. Balliol 354, f. 160a.
Lidgate, *Stans puer*, Caxton, ca. 1477 (STC 17030); *repr.* Duff, *XV Cent. English Books*, p. 76; 1. Flügel, *Anglia* XXVI. 174; Dyboski, *EETS* ci. 139.

1829.3 Knouwyth that beth and schul be
Inscription over the entrance to Cowling Castle, near Rochester, Kent (late xiv cent.) — four lines.
Beauties of England, VII. 591; Bouquet, *Church Brasses*, p. 167.

1829.5 Know well ore þou knyt to fast / Fore often rape rewyþe at last
A monitory couplet. [Cf. 1829.2 and vv. 39-40 of 3502].
1. Bodl. 14526, f. 54a.
Zupitza, *Archiv* XC. 244; *Oxford Dict. Eng. Proverbs*, p. 253.

1829.8 Knolege acquayntance resort favour with grace
In praise of his beloved, by John Skelton — seven stanzas rime royal with acrostic on Kateryn.
Dyuers Balettys, Pynson, n. d. (STC 22604); *repr.* Dyce, *Skelton*, I. 25-6; Dyce and Child, *Skelton & Donne*, I. 31-3; Henderson, *Skelton*, 1931, pp. 31-2; 1948, 1959, pp. 30-1.

1833.5 Lady for þese ioyes seuene
A simple prayer to the Virgin — a quatrain concluding 465.
1. Huntington HM 127 [*olim* Powis], f. 53a.
Rel. Lyr. XV C., p. 60.

Lady ffor they Ioyes ffyue   See 2099 (Lincoln).

1836   Davies, *Med. Eng. Lyrics*, p. 64.

1838   [Actually st. 3, 4, 5, 10 = st. 3, 7, 11, 15 of 3761].
Robbins, *MLR* XLIX. 290-2; Person, *Camb. ME Lyrics*, pp. 14-16; Wilson, *Anglia* LXXII. 415-8.

1838.5 Ladi quene y pray the to governe me in gode lore
A prayer by Christ's shedding blood — five monoriming quatrains.
1. Bodl. Lat. lit. e. 17, ff. 13b-14a.

1841   Douce Fragment D. 48: [? Copland, ca. 1550] (vv. 10-24, 33-40); *facs.* Reed, *Xmas Carols*, p. 11.

1841.5   Late on a nyght as I lay slepyng
                An erotic dream vision—five quatrains. [Cf. 1450.5].
                1. Bodl. 12653, f. 48a.
                Padelford and Benham, *Anglia* XXXI. 361-2.

1842   1. Bodl. 6943, f. 35a (and a variant of first vv. 12 on f. 34b).

1842.5   Laude honor prasingis thankis infynite
                The XIII Bukes of Eneados, translated by Gawin Douglas—in couplets.
                1. Trinity Camb. 1184, f. 1a; 2. Edinburgh Univ. Elphinston; 3. Edinburgh Univ. Ruthven; 4. Lambeth; 5. Longleat.
                Copland, 1553 (STC 24797); *repr.* (with 3). Ruddiman, Edinburgh, 1710; *Select Works*, Perth 1787, pp. 89-138 (selected prologues only); Smith, Edinburgh 1959, pp. 25-94 (extracts only); 1. Dundas, *Bannatyne Club*, 1839; 2. Sibbald, *Chronicle*, I. 428 (extracts); Small, *Works*, II, III, IV.

1843.8   Laughyng schal be mynged with wo
                A couplet in a Latin sermon.
                1. Balliol 149, f. 25a.

                Lauch liis down our all   See 2787 (Fordun).

1844.5   *Le roy cuuayte nos deneres*
                Macaronic quatrain, apparently from a popular song ca. A.D. 1279, on dislike of Statute of *Quo warranto* in Walter of Guisborough's *Chronicle* (four out of ten MSS. only).
                1. Bodl. 1771; 2. Bodl. 1787; 3. Camb. Un. Dd. 2. 5; 4. Lansdowne 239.
                Hamilton, *Chronicon de Hemingburgh*, II. 7; Wilson, *Early ME Lit.*, p. 269; Wilson, *Lost Lit.*, p. 196; Rothwell, *Camden Soc.* 3 s. LXXXIX. 216 n.

1846   *Rel. Lyr. XV C.*, p. 290.

1848   in an English prose homily (containing other riming tags, e.g., 89.5, 81.5, 1628.5, 3101).
                Grisdale, *Leeds Texts & Monographs* V. 28.

1849	Robbins, *Sec. Lyrics*, pp. 22-4; Kaiser, *Anthologie*, p. 310; Kaiser, *Med. Eng.*, p. 476; Greene, *Sel. Eng. Carols*, p. 164; Davies, *Med. Eng. Lyrics*, pp. 204-6.
1850	Leve in þi rokke ne is no thef / Take oþer maneȝ wulle is hire to lef

A couplet in Nicolas Bozon's *Contes moralisés*.
   1. Gray's Inn 12, f. 38a.
      1. Smith, *SATF*, p. 117; Förster, *Festschrift zum 12 Deutschen Neuphilologentage*, p. 59; Wilson, *LSE* VI. 45; Ross, *Neuphil. Mitteilungen* L. 208.

Lef (adj.)

1850.5	Leve frend nou beth stille

The harrowing of Hell, with versified title: 'Hou ihesu crist herowede helle / Of harde gates ich will telle.' [For a somewhat later text see 185].
   1. Bodl. 1687, f. 119a.
      Rel. Ant., I. 253 (vv. 1-26 only); Halliwell, *Dict. Archaic & Provincial Words*, p. 958 (prologue only); Varnhagen, Erlangen 1898; Hulme, *EETS* c. 2-22.

1852	[Utley 172].
	1. NLW Deposit: Porkington 10, ff. 56b-59b.
1854	3. Pepys 1584, f. 48a.
	5. Horstmann, *York. Wr.*, II. 381-9.
1855	[Utley 154].
1856.5	Leue men þis beoþ þe ten heste

A note on the Ten Commandments—eight couplets.
   1. Bodl. 4061, f. 211a.

1857	1, 2. Robbins, *Hist. Poems*, pp. 325-6, 140-3; 1. Aspin, *AN Pol. Songs*, pp; 62-3; 2. Marsh, *Hist. Eng. Language*, pp. 244-7.
1858	Kirke, *Reliquary* IX. 75 (extract); *Gentleman's Magazine*, May 1842, p. 471.
1859	20. Winchester Coll. 33, f. 33a.
	8. D'Evelyn and Mill, *EETS* 235. 128.

1860   Funke, *ME Reader*, pp. 48-9.

1861   Marsh, *Hist. Eng. Language*, p. 254; Manly, *Eng. Poetry*, p. 13; *Oxford Book Eng. Verse*, pp. 3-5; Brook, *Harley Lyrics*, pp. 43-4; *Poets of Eng. Language*, I. 22-3; Kaiser, *Anthologie*, p. 292; Kaiser, *Med. Eng.*, p. 464; Wright, *Eng. Vernacular Hands*, p. 9 (*with facs.*); Speirs, *Med. Eng. Poetry*, pp. 53-5; Davies, *Med. Eng. Lyrics*, pp. 84-6.

1863.3 Let be wanton your busynes
    An erotic song—one quatrain.
    1. Bodl. 6659, f. 98b.
    Wagner, *MLN* L. 453.

1863.5 Let fal downe thyn e & lift up thy hart
    Behold thy maker: wall inscription at Campsall Church—one 8-line stanza.
    Leland, *De Rebus Brit.*, I. xxxvi.

1863.8 Let for þy senne / And wepe þy senne
    On sin and repentance—five lines with Latin key words, '*Desine* &c.'
    1. BM Addit. 11579, f. 29a.

1864.5 Lett lowe to lowe go kyndly and sowfte
    On the nature of love—eight quatrains.
    1. Bodl. 13679, f. 6a; 2. BM Addit. 18752, f. 85a (st. 1-2, 4-5, 7-8) and f. 84b (st. 3, as separate poem).
    1. Frankis, *Anglia* LXXIII. 300; 2. Reed, *Anglia* XXXIII. 356.

1865   6. Davies, *Med. Eng. Lyrics*, pp. 191-3.

1866   Rickert, *Anc. Eng. Xmas Carols*, pp. 220-1; *Oxford Book Carols*, p. 211; Robbins, *Sec. Lyrics*, p. 3; Greene, *Sel. Eng. Carols*, p. 58; Davies, *Med. Eng. Lyrics*, pp. 277-8; Greene, *N&Q* n.s. XI. 88-9.

1866.5 Let not vs that yong men be
    A love song, perhaps by Henry VIII—two 6-line stanzas.
    1. BM Addit. 31922, f. 87b.
    Chappell, *Archaeologia* LXI. 375; Flügel, *Anglia* XII. 248; *Early Eng. Lyr.*, p. 68; *Oxford Book XVI C. Verse*, pp. 42-3; Stevens, *Music & Poetry*, p. 415; Stevens, *Music at Court*, p. 63.

1866.7   Let reason Rule the þat this booke shall reede
           A book plate—two couplets.
           1. Pepys 2498, p. 44.
              Påhlsson, *Recluse*, p. x.

1866.8   Lett serch your myndis ye of hie consideracion
           A political song on the birth of Prince Arthur, 'the soveren sede'—one stanza rime royal.
           1. BM Addit. 5465, f. 11b.
              Fehr, *Archiv* CVI. 54; Stevens, *Music* & *Poetry*, p. 355.

1867.5   Let þy worke þy worde passe / for bost makyth þy fame lesse
           A proverbial couplet.
           1. Harley 2321, f. 174b.

           Leue (adj.)—see under Lef.

1870   1. Bodl. 1045, f. 215a, repeated at f. 216a; 3. Ipswich County Hall Deposit: Hillwood [*olim* Brome], f. 81a.

1871   [See 2364 and lines in 2787].
           1a (xix cent. transcript). Egerton 2257, f. 183a.

1871.3   *Libro* seryng *In libro* men schul rede
           Four monoriming lines with internal rime on *Verbum Domini*.
           1. Bodl. 2293, f. 164a.

1871.5   Ly þow me ner lemmon in þy narms
           A lyric scrap.
           1. Bodl. 1883, f. 75b.
              Hist. MSS. Comm. Report, Lord De L'Isle and Dudley, I. 194; Furuskog, *Studia Neophilologia* XIX. 163; Wilson, *Lost Lit.*, p. 190; Ker, *EETS* 247. xiii (and *facs.*).

1871.8   lif lestynge loue habbynge
           Bliss evermore—one couplet in a Latin sermon.
           1. Bodl. 1871, f. 201a.

1873   Rickert, *Anc. Eng. Xmas Carols*, pp. 219-220; Greene, *Sel. Eng. Carols*, p. 84; Davies, *Med. Eng. Lyrics*, p. 288.

*1873.5   *Liȝtbern þat angel briȝt / Answerd anon riȝt
           '*Vite Ade et Eve*'—a fragment in couplets.

1a. Advocates 19. 2. 1, ff. 14a-16a; 2. Edinburgh Univ. 218 (1), two leaves (formerly between ff. 13 and 14 of MS. 1). Laing, *A Penni Worth of Witte*, Abbotsford Club 1857, pp. 49-75; Horstmann, *AE Leg*. 1878, pp. 138-47.

1874   in rime royal stanzas. [Cf. 4255].

1. Trinity Camb. 601, f. 247a (22 st.); 2. Rome: English Coll. 1306, f. 78a (32 st.).

A Treatyse of a Galaunt, de Worde, ca. 1510-1520 (STC 24241); *repr*. Brydges, *Censura Lit.*, n.s. V. 37-40; 2d ed. 1815, I. 62-6; Halliwell, *Roxburghe Club* LXXVII; Furnivall, *Ballads from MSS.*, I. 445; Hazlitt, *Remains*, III. 151-60.

1875   6. Leyden Univ. Vossius 9, f. 8b.

2. Halliwell, *Percy Soc*. II. 135-49.

Lustneþ alle a lutel þrowe   See 3310 (MS. Harley).

1879   Brunner, *Eng. Stn*. LXVIII. 189-94.

1881   10. *olim* Aldenham [Goldschmidt Sale Cat. 55, Item 59], ff. 77-99; 11. Coventry Corp. Record Office, f. 98a; 12. Morgan Lib. M. 898 [*olim* Edwardes], f. 2a (begins incomplete at v. 846 of MS. 8); 13. Yale Univ. Deposit: Osborn 32 [*olim* Knowsley Hall], ff. 39.

1882   Mustanoja, *How the Good Wife*, Helsinki 1948, pp. 216-21.

1883   Boyd, *MLN* LXXI. 557 (short extracts); Boyd, *ME Miracles*, pp. 68-87.

1884   [Cf. Child, *Eng. Scot. Pop. Ballads*, V. 104-5. Utley 157]. Jackson, ca. 1580 (STC 14521).

1885   2. Sir Henry Ellis, Introduction, *Doomsday Book*, II. 99; *repr.* Mancel and Trebutien, *L'Établissement de la Fête de la Conception Notre-Dame*, Caen 1842, p. 91.

1887   2. BM Addit. 22283, f. 90b col. ii (vv. 1-104 only).

1888   1, 2. Kurvinen, Helsinki 1957; 2. Ackerman, *Univ. of Michigan Contrib. in Mod. Phil.* VIII.

1889	Pinkerton, *Anc. Scot. Poems,* II. 488-93; Child, *Ballads,* 1864, 1878, VI. 274-83; Böddeker, *AE Dicht.,* pp. 126-34; Brandl and Zippel, *ME Sprach-u. Literatur.,* pp. 129-33; Kaiser, *Med. Eng.,* p. 355; Robbins, *Hist. Poems,* pp. 14-21.
1892	1. Segar, *Some Minor Poems,* pp. 19-20; 3. Rickert, *Anc. Eng. Xmas Carols,* p. 129; Greene, *Sel. Eng. Carols,* p. 82.
1893	*Oxford Book Christian Verse,* pp. 30-1; *Oxford Book Eng. Verse,* pp. 9-10; Speirs, *Med. Eng. Poetry,* pp. 70-1.
1894	Child, *Ballads,* 1864, 1878, VI. 269-74; Böddeker, *AE Dicht.,* pp. 116-21; *Cambridge Book Prose & Verse,* pp. 399-400; Robbins, *Hist. Poems,* pp. 9-13.
1895	2 (transcript, ca. 1564, of an early print). Bodl. 21835, f. 8a (four fragments: vv. 350); 4. Egerton 2862. . . .(vv. 275-436 of MS. 5); 6. Advocates 19. 2. 1, f. 78b (vv. 1065, incomplete). de Worde, n.d. (STC 6470); 5. Hales and Furnivall, *Percy Folio MS.,* III. 16-48.
1897	*How a merchande dyd hys wyfe betray* or *A penniworth of witte*—in couplets. [See *2602.3]. 2. Harley 5396, f. 286a (vv. 175; fragmentary). 1. Ritson, *Anc. Pop. Poetry,* 1791, pp. 69-83; J. E. Masters, Shaftesbury 1933; 2. Sibbald, *Chronicle,* I. 144-52.
	Lystenyt lordyngs more and lees / I bryng yow See 463.
1898.5	Lysten lordinges that of marueyles lyke to heare *Robert the Deuyll*—vv. 1145 in couplets. [Cf. 2780]. de Worde, ca. 1502 (STC 21070); repr. Herbert, 1788; Hazlitt, *Remains,* I. 218-63.
1903	1. BM Addit. 46919 [*olim* Phillipps 8336], f. 210b. Gneuss, *Anglia* LXXVIII. 184.
1904	vv. 128 in couplets.
1905	2. Bodl. 6777 (begins in the Thursday section, v. 85); 3. Trinity Camb. 600, pp. 257-61 (vv. 126); 6. Harley 1735, f. 13b (Prologue, vv. 32), ff. 14b-16b (vv. 120); 7. Wellcome Hist. Med. Lib. 411, f. 1a (begins incomplete; vv. 85). 1. Robbins, *Sec. Lyrics,* pp. 63-7.

1907	12. Harvard Univ. Eng. 1031, two leaves (vv. 888-1018, 1143-1272).
9, 10. Foster, *EETS* 147. 172-6.
1907.5	Listneþ now lordynges and I wil ȝou telle / How þe world ymade was
On the stars and planets—forty lines, imperfect at end. [Cf. 2753].
1. Harley 874, f. 31b.
1909	Halliwell, *Nugae Poeticae*, 1844, pp. 21-36.
1911	19. Winchester Coll. 33, f. 36b.
10. D'Evelyn and Mill, *EETS* 235. 160.
1913	[Revise listing of MSS. as follows:]
1. Bodl. 1234; 2. Bodl. 1476; 3. Bodl. 4138; 4. Bodl. 6420, f. 65a; 5. Bodl. 6928, ff. 1a-18a (xvii cent.); 6. Bodl. 14641, f. 53a (begins v. 267); 7. Christ Church Oxf. 152, ff. 62a-71a; 8. Corpus Christi Oxf. 198; 9. Trinity Oxf. 49; 10. Camb. Un. Ii. 3. 26; 11. Camb. Un. Mm. 2. 5; 12. Fitzwilliam Mus., McClean 181; 13. Egerton 2726, ff. 56a-63; 14. Egerton 2863; 15. Harley 1758, ff. 46a-55a (beg. imperfect); 16. Harley 7334, ff. 59a-70b; 17. Lansdowne 851, ff. 54b-65a; 18. Royal 17. D. xv, ff. 66b-79b; 19. Royal 18. C. ii, ff. 56b-67b; 20. Sloane 1685, ff. 51b-62b; 21. Sloane 1686, ff. 71a-86b; 22. Hunterian Mus. 197; 23. Lichfield Cath. 2; 24. Petworth 7; 25. Morgan Lib. M. 249 [*olim* Ashburnham 124]; 26. Penrose 6 [*olim* Delamere]; 27. Rosenbach: Fdn. 1084/1 [*olim* Phillipps 8137].
Chaucer, Stow, 1561 (STC 5075); *repr.* Urry, *Chaucer*, 1721; Bell, *Poets of Great Britain*; [Anderson,] *Poets of Great Britain*; Chalmers, *Eng. Poets*, I. 607-23; 8, 15, 17, 18, 20, 24. *Chaucer Soc.*, First Series, 8, 9, 10, 13; 16. Wright, *Percy Soc.*, 1847; Bell, *Eng. Poets*, 1854; Furnivall, *Chaucer Soc.* LXXIII; French and Hale, *ME Met. Rom.*, pp. 209.
1914	1. Greene, *Sel. Eng. Carols*, p. 108; 2. Rickert, *Anc. Eng. Xmas Carols*, p. 9.
1915	*The Little Gest of Robin Hood*—456 quatrains. [Ringler 42].
A Lytell Gest of Robyn Hode, de Worde, ca. 1500 (STC 13687), two leaves only (vv. 34); Pynson, ca. 1500 (STC 13688), one leaf (vv. 877-938), two leaves (vv. 908-92, 1248-61, 970-1000, 1307-1337); [? Doesbech, Antwerp, 1510-1515] (imperfect); *facs.* Beattie, *Edinb. Bibl. Soc.* 1950; de Worde, ca. 1519 (STC 13689); *repr.* Laing, *Knightly Tale of Golagros*,

1827; Flügel, *Neuengl. Lesebuch,* pp. 171-86; Stevenson, *STS* LXV. 267-90; Gutch, *Robin Hood,* 1847, I. 145-219; Child, *Ballads,* 1864, 1878, V. 44-123; and *Pop. Ballads,* no. 117, III. 56-78; Sargent and Kittredge, *Pop. Ballads,* pp. 256-78; Gummere, *OE Ballads,* pp. 1-68; Pollard, *XV C. Prose and Verse,* pp. 35-80; Copland, 1548; *repr. Tudor Facs. Texts,* 1914.

1916   1. Bodl. 11951, f. 128b (vv. 853; one leaf wanting).

1917   2. Peter, *Complaint* & *Satire,* p. 101.

1919   [Ringler 44].
1. Balliol 354, f. 160a (Delete: transcript of Caxton, ca. 1477); 2. Oriel Oxf. 79, ff. 88, 89, 78 (Delete: transcript of a lost Caxton *ante* 1477).
The Book of Curtesye, Caxton, ca. 1477-8 (STC 3303); *repr.* Jenkinson, 1907; de Worde, ca. 1492 (STC 3304), two leaves (vv. 337-57); *repr.* with 1, 2. Furnivall, *EETS* iii; *Stans puer ad mensam,* de Worde, post 1501 (at end).

1920   [Ringler 43].
4. Harley 541, ff. 210, 211.
A Lytell Treatyse for to Lerne Englysshe and Frensshe, de Worde, ca. 1500 (STC 24866) (vv. 103); Pynson, ca. 1500 (STC 24867) (vv. 93); ca. 1505, fragment (STC 24868); 4. Furnivall, *EETS* 32 orig. ed. 16-24; rev. ed. 265-73; 6. Gessler, *Deux Manuels de Conversation imprimés en Angleterre,* Bruxelles 1941.

1921   Brook, *Harley Lyrics,* pp. 71-2.

1922   five 8-line stanzas.
1, 2. Brook, *Harley Lyrics,* pp. 88, 70-1 *(with facs., frontispiece);* 1. Wilson, *Lost Lit.,* p. 182.

Lvtel wot hit any mon / hou loue hym haueþ y-bounde
See 1922 (MS. Harley).

1923   Brook, *Harley Lyrics,* p. 88.

1923.5   Lyue not as a glutton styll for to eate
On moderate diet — one couplet.
1. Durham Univ. Cosin V. iii. 9, f. 64a.
Furnivall, *EETS* lxi. 196.

1924	Person, *Camb. ME Lyrics*, p. 26.
1924.3	Lo al þat euer I spent þat sum time had I
	On giving, spending, and lending: common tombstone verses—four gnomic monoriming lines with a Latin version (earliest citation A.D. 1410). [Cf. 1297, 3274].
	Camden, *Remaines*, 1614, p. 375 (STC 4522); Weever, *Anc. Funerall Monuments*, 1631, p. 581 (STC 25223); *repr.* Bühler, *Renaissance News* VIII. 11; *Beauties of England*, VII. 100; Pettigrew, *Chronicles of Tombs*, p. 73; Ravenshaw, *Antiente Epitaphes*, pp. 5, 7.
1924.4	Loo by the sentence of prudent Salamon
	Pageant verses by Cleanness at the return of Henry VI to London, A.D. 1432—two stanzas rime royal. [Adapted from 3799].
	Fabyan, *New Chronicles*, Pynson, 1516 (STC 10659); *repr.* Ellis, 1811, p. 605; Gattinger, *Wiener Beiträge* IV. 27.
1924.5	Lo karmentis þis lady that ye se
	Carmentis, Tubal Cain, and Saturnus—three quatrains. [Cf. 1931.8].
	1. Trinity Dublin 432, f. 65a.
	Brotanek, *ME Dichtungen*, p. 95.
1925	Wilson, *Lost Lit.*, p. 185.
1926	Robbins, *Hist. Poems*, pp. 152-7.
1926.5	Loo he that ys all holly yours soo free
	A love letter: a plea to his mistress—nine stanzas rime royal adapted from Chaucer's *Troilus and Criseyde* (3327) as follows: Book II, vv. 1121-7, 841-7, 869-82; Book IV, vv. 561-7; Book V, vv. 1072-8; Book II, vv. 778-84; Book I, vv. 708-12; Book IV, vv. 260-6, 267-73.
	1. Bodl. 12653, f. 48b.
	Padelford and Benham, *Anglia* XXXI. 362-3; Bolle, *Anglia* XXXIV. 284-7.
1927	Poem on Delight, from a pageant—ten 6-line stanzas.
	Calderhead, *MP* XIV. 6-7.
1929	[A variant text in Fabyan, *New Chronicles*, 1516, STC 10659; *repr.* Ellis, 1811, pp. 600-1. Cf. 3955.5].

1. St. John's Oxf. 57 (MS. not paginated; 3 st.); 2. Cotton Julius B. i, f. 79b; 3. Lansdowne 285, f. 6b; 5. Egerton 1995, f. 177a; 6. Morgan Lib. M. 775, f. 15a.
   2. Harvey, *Gothic England*, pp. 179-80; 4. Robbins, *Sec. Lyrics*, p. 98; 5. Gairdner, *Camden Soc.* n.s. XVII. 169-70; 6. Arthur, *Archaeologia* LVII. 57-8.

1929.3   Lo I chief pryncesse dame sapience
    Pageant verses by Sapience at the return of Henry VI to London, A.D. 1432 — one stanza rime royal. [Adapted from 3799].
    Fabyan, *New Chronicles*, Pynson, 1516 (STC 10659); *repr.* Ellis, 1811, pp. 604-5; Gattinger, *Wiener Beiträge* IV. 26.

1929.5   Lo Kyng Artour ful manly and ful wyse
    King Arthur, Charlemagne, and David — three quatrains.
    1. Bodl. 10234, f. 32a.

1930   Comper, *Life & Lyrics of Rolle*, p. 279; Woolf, *RES* n.s. XIII. 6.

1931   Stevens, *Med. Carols*, p. 24.

1931.3   Lo these fonde sottes / And tratlynge Scottes
    'Agaynst the prowde Scottes" by John Skelton — vv. 218 in couplets and 'skeltonics.' [Cf. 1822.5].
    Certain Bokes, Kynge and Marche, n.d. (STC 22599); *repr.* Dyce, *Skelton*, I. 182-91: Dyce and Child, *Skelton & Donne*, I. 202-10; Flügel, *Neuengl. Lesebuch*, pp. 60-1 (extract); Henderson, *Skelton*, 1931, pp. 164-72; 1948, 1959, pp. 140-7; Pinto, *Selection*, 1950, pp. 78-9 (extract); Day, n.d.; Lant. n.d.; *Workes*, Marshe, 1568 (STC 22608); *repr.* [? J. Bowle,] 1736; *repr.* Chalmers, *English Poets*, II. 261-3.

    Loo this noble and victorious conqueror
    See 3632 (MS. Bodl. 1797 var.).

1931.5   Loe thus saieth Arnolde of the new towne
    Alchemical verses ascribed to 'Chavcer' — in couplets. [Cf. 2330].
    1. Sloane 1092, ff. 8b-9a; 2. Sloane 1098, ff. 17b-18a (vv. 44); 3. Univ. of Pennsylvania, Smith 4, f. 78a.

1931.8 Lo Tubal cayme þat furste fonde arte of songe
The Invention of Music—two couplets. [Cf. 651.5, 1924.5].
1. Trinity Dublin 432, f. 65a.

1933.5 London thou art of townes a per se
To the City of London, attributed to William Dunbar—seven 8-line stanzas with refrain.
1. Balliol 354, f. 199b; 2. Cotton Vitell. A. xvi, f. 200a; 3. Lansdowne 762, f. 7b; 4. London Guildhall, Great Chronicle, ff. 292a-294a; 5. Morgan Lib. MA 717.
1. *Rel. Ant.*, I. 205-7; Flügel, *Anglia* XXVI. 199-201; Dyboski, *EETS* ci. 100-2; 2. Laing, *Dunbar*, I. 277-9; Small, *STS* IV. 276-8; Eyre-Todd, *Med. Scot. Poetry*, pp. 182-4; Schipper, *Dunbar*, pp. 88-90; and *DKAW* XL (II). 87-90; Baildon, *Dunbar*, pp. 36-8; Arber, *Dunbar Anthology*, pp. 31-3; Kingsford, *Chronicles of London*, pp. 253-5; MacKenzie, *Dunbar*, pp. 177-8; 4. Mackie, *King James IV of Scotland*; Bühler, *RES* XIII. 8-9.

1934 [This tag occurs in many MSS. of the Brut Chronicle, some of which are listed below, and in many early printed chronicles. Ringler 45].
[Revise listing of MSS. as follows:]
1. Bodl. 11539; 2. Bodl. 21897; 3. Pepys 2163 (unpaginated); 4. Harley 372; 5. Harley 2279; 6. Trinity Dublin 490; 7. Trinity Dublin 516, f. 118a; 8. Worcester Cath. F. 10, f. 238a.
Chronicles of England, Caxton, 1480 (STC 9991) and later eds.; Brie, *EETS* 131. 249; Strutt, *Horda Angel-Cynnan*, II. 83; Thompson, *Chronicon Galfridi le Baker de Swynebroke*, p. 212; Camden, *Remains*, 1636, p. 194; Fabyan, *New Chronicles*, Pynson, 1516 (STC 10659); *repr.* Ellis, 1811, p. 440 [cf. 3955.5]; Wright, *Pol. Poems*, II. 251; Wright, *Pop. Superstitions*, II. 261; Furnivall, *EETS* 9. xlvi; Henderson, *Scottish Vernac. Lit.*, p. 18; Baskervill, *Elizabethan Jig*, p. 41; Wilson, *LSE* V. 46; Wilson, *Lost Lit.*, p. 197; Owst, *Lit. & Pulpit*, p. 407; Robbins, *Neophilologus* XXXIX. 141; Jones, *MA* XXV. 68; Robbins, *Hist. Poems*, p. xxxviii.

1934.5 Lang heff I maed of ladyes quhytt
'On ane blakmoir' by William Dunbar—five 5-line stanzas with refrain: 'My ladye with the mekle lippis.' [Utley 161].
1. Camb. Un. Ll. 5. 10, f. 45b; 2. Pepys 2553, pp. 341-2.
2. Pinkerton, *Anc. Scot. Poems*, I. 97-8; Laing, *Dunbar*, I. 123-4; Paterson, *Dunbar*, pp. 273-4; Small, *STS* IV. 201-4;

Schipper, *Dunbar,* pp. 206-7; and *DKAW* XLI (IV). 7-9; Baildon, *Dunbar,* pp. 97-8; Craigie, *STS* n.s. VII. 416-7; MacKenzie, *Dunbar,* pp. 66-7; Kinsley, *Dunbar,* p. 20.

1935   15. Canterbury Cath. D. 14.
           5. Foster, *Essays & Studies in Honor of Carleton Brown,* p. 153.

1936.5   Loke and leftes up ȝoure heued on hay / For ȝoure rampson nereȝ ney
           A couplet in a Latin sermon.
           1. Public Record Office C. 47/39/15.

1937   [Cf. an inscription in St. Paul's Cathedral, pr. Camden, *Remains,* London 1636, p. 386; 1876, p. 413].
           2. Harley 1706, f. 204b.
           2. Horstmann, *York. Wr.,* II. 377.

1938   [Utley 165].
           Robbins, *Sec. Lyrics,* pp. 37-8.

1938.5   Loke his wonnyng be clere a dyȝte
           On receiving a guest—two couplets in a Latin sermon by Friar Nicholas Philip.
           1. Bodl. 29746, f. 173a and f. 177b.

1939   Robbins, *Hist. Poems,* pp. 50-3.

1939.5   Lok man above the ys Ioy þat euery schall last
           Heaven and Hell: 'Lok man beneyth the ys paine with owtyn rest'—one couplet.
           1. Bodl. 6621, f. 183b.

1940.5   Loke nu frere / Hu strong ordre is here
           A monkish pledge and response in Giraldus Cambrensis, *Speculum Ecclesie*—two couplets.
           1. Cotton Tiberius B. xiii (Dist. I, cap. xiii).
           Brewer, *Rolls Series* XXI, iv. 209; Wilson, *LSE* V. 39; Wilson, *Lost Lit.,* p. 174.

1941   1. Balliol 354, f. 205a col i.

1941.5 loke or þu speke / and thynke or þu speke
A moralizing tag preceding the proverbial tag (513), in one MS. only.
1. Nat. Lib. Wales, Peniarth 356, p. 196.

1941.8 Loke out here Maier with thy pilled pate
Student abuse of the Mayor of Cambridge in A.D. 1418—forty irregular lines.
1. Harley 247, f. 129a (vv. 30); 2. Cole [present location not known].
2. Hartshorne, *Anc. Met. Tales,* p. 225; Wright, *Pop. Superstitions,* II. 266; G. H. Cooper, *Annals of Cambridge,* V. 1; Coulton, *Soc. Life in Britain,* p. 66; Wilson, *Lost Lit.,* p. 200.

1942 Patterson, *JEGP* XX. 275.

1943 2. Harley 913, f. 28a (vv. 22, with 2047).

1944 [For refrain cf. 2661; also cf. Tilley B 541. Utley 166].
1. Delete this MS.; 5. Rome: English Coll. 1306, f. 75b. *Chaucer,* Stow, 1561 (STC 5075); *repr.* [Anderson,] *Poets of Great Britain,* I. 586; Hammond, *Eng. Verse Chaucer-Surrey,* p. 413; 2, 3. Robbins, *Sec. Lyrics,* pp. 224, 290; 2. Davies, *Med. Eng. Lyrics,* pp. 238-40.

*1944.5 *. . .[lo]kyng for her trew love / long or that yt was day
Fragment of a love song, possibly with this refrain.
1. New York Pub. Lib. Drexel Fragments 4185.
Stevens, *Music & Poetry,* p. 427 (refrain only).

Lord and god alwey / lovere of all mankynde   See 2725.

1946.5 Lord as thou hange upon þe rode
A prayer to staunch blood—seven lines. [Cf. 624].
1. Rylands Lib. Latin 228, f. 74a.

1947 two couplets.
Robbins, *Neophilologus* XXXVIII. 39-40.

Lord blyssyd be þi name   See 1975.

1950 Coxe, *Cat.,* p. 42.

1950.5　　　Lorde god alweldande / I beteche todaye into þi hande
A general morning prayer—in couplets (following 246).
1. Egerton 3245 [*olim* Gurney], f. 191a (vv. 18); 2. Lincoln Cath. 91, f . 191b (vv. 20); 3. Princeton Univ. 21 [*olim* Huth], f. 112b (vv. 20).
　　1. Robbins, *PMLA* LIV. 376; 2. Horstmann, *York. Wr.*, I. 364 (and cf. I. 222); Perry, *EETS* 26.77; Comper, *Life & Lyrics of Rolle*, p. 294; 3. Bühler, *MLN* LXVI. 314.

1951　　　1. Egerton 3245 [*olim* Gurney], f. 185a.

1952　　　Haupt and Hoffman, *Altdeutsche Blätter*, II. 142.

1952.5　　Lord God in Trinite / Fader and Sone and Holy Gost
'For metyng of theues saie thou this charm'—twelve couplets. [Cf. 4154.8 and a variant, 242.5].
1. Sloane 2457, f. 8a.
Bühler, *Speculum* XXXIII. 372.

1953　　　1, 2. Casson, *EETS* 221.

　　　　　Lord god in trinite / þou boutyst man　　　See 250.

1954　　　A Thanksgiving to Christ attributed to Rolle.
Perry, *EETS* 26 orig. ed. 75-6.

1955.5　　Lord god preserve under þy mighty hande/ þe kynge þe qwene þe people and þis land
A prayer tag for England—one couplet [= vv. 6-7 of 2218, occurring separately].
1. Corpus Camb. 61, flyleaf; 2. Trinity Camb. 600, p. 359; 3. BM Addit. 5467, f. 221a; 4. Huntington Lib. EL. 26. A. 13, flyleaf.

1957　　　[Utley 168].

1959　　　3. BM Addit. 37787, f. 158a.
3. N. S. Baugh, *Worcestershire Misc.*, p. 146.

1961　　　[For st. 21 occurring separately see 3824].
10. Longleat 30, f. 26a; 13. Morgan Lib. M. 99, ff. 92a-132a.
　2. Adler and Kaluza, *Eng. Stn.* X. 232; 13. Ellis, Kelmscott Press, 1894; *coll.* Bühler, *MLN* LX. 19-22.

1961.3   Lord iesu almiʒti king / þat madest and lokest alle þyng
           Introductory invocation (following 1227) to *Ayenbite of Inwyt*
           —two couplets.
           1. Arundel 57, f. 2b.
              Morris, *EETS* 23. 1.

1961.5   Lord Iesu Cryst goddes sone on lyve / haue mercy on vs
           A simple prayer by the Five Wounds—one couplet.
           1. Bodl. 10234, f. 17b.
              Gray, *N&Q* n.s. X. 128.

1963   1. York Minster XVI. G. 5, f. 1b.

1963.5   Lord Jhesu Crist ʒat sitit abow hous / of ʒos foul glotunis
           Two couplets translating '*Jhesu Christe Domine qui supra nos sedes* &c.'
           1. Leicester City Lib., Old Town 4, p. 38.
              Retrospective Rev. I. 419.

1965.5   Lord Ihesu thy blesside lyfe / Help and comforte our wrecchid lif
           A simple prayer tag at end of *Speculum Vite Christi* in English.
           1. Advocates [MS. not established].
              Dibdin, *Northern Tour*, II. 600.

           Lorde kynge of glorye / Suche grace   See 1979.

1966   Boyd, *ME Miracles*, pp. 38-43.

1967   A prayer to God the Father attributed to St. Thomas Aquinas. [For the ME prose translations, cf. Doyle, *Dominican St.* I. 229-38].

1967.3   Lorde of us thou haue menynge
           Memento nostri Domine—four quatrains.
           1. Harley 1260, f. 107a.
              Robbins, *Harvard Theol. Rev.* XLVII. 57-8.

1967.5   Lord on alle synful heere knelynge on ther kne
           Oracio—one 8-line stanza (following 3845).
           1. Bodl. 798, f. 95b.
              MacCracken, *EETS* cvii. 254.

[229]

1967.8	Lord sey me for the mayden love that thou thi modir calles 'þe vision of sire William Banestre, knyght' — vv. 118. 1. Bodl. 4062, ff. 37b-38a (fragmentary).
1968	vv. 14. 1. BM Addit. 46919 [*olim* Phillipps 8336], f. 206b. Gneuss, *Anglia* LXXVIII. 180.
1969	3. BM Addit. 22283, f. 159a. 2. N. S. Baugh, *Worcestershire Misc.*, p. 147.
	Lord þat art of mihtes most / þe seuen ʒiftes See 975.
1973	Trounce, *EETS* 224.
1974	[Utley 169]. Dickins and Wilson, *Early ME Texts*, pp. 124-5; Kaiser, *Med. Eng.*, p. 480.
1975	A series of eight prayers to Christ, each beginning 'Lorde' (except 4) scattered throughout a Latin homily &c. 3. Pfander, *Pop. Sermon*, pp. 47, 48 (st. 2 and 4 only).
1979	4. Harley 4690, ff. 109a-111a (fragment: vv. 1608); 5. BM Addit. 31042, f. 125a (var. &c.); 7A. Advocates 19. 2. 1, ff. 326, 327 (vv. 1-34, 1286-7, 1311-1436, 1667-1757, 2783-2957); 7B. Edinburgh Univ. 218 (II), two fragments (originally from MS. 7A: vv. 1753-1928, 2593-2782); 7C. St. Andrew's Univ., two fragments (originally from MS. 7A: vv. 2081-2426); 8. Merton 23. b. 6 (Ker: Pastedowns 919; vv. 2040-2239). de Worde, 1509 (STC 21007); 2. Brunner, *Wiener Beiträge* XLII; 7B. Turnbull and Laing, *Owain Miles*, Edinb. 1837; Kölbing, *Eng. Stn.* VIII. 115-19; 7C. Smithers, *Med. Aevum* XVIII. 3-11.
1981	1. York Minster XVI. G. 5, f. 98b.
1982	1. Bodl. 14530, f. 2b (without refrain); 4. Delete this MS. *Certaine Worthye Manuscript Poems*, Robert Dexter, London 1597 (STC 21499); *repr.* Gibbs; 3. Furnivall, *N&Q* 4 s. II. 125.
1984	Horstmann, *Archiv* LVI. 223; Boyd, *ME Miracles*, pp. 30-32.

1984.5	Lordes & ladyes all bydene / For your goodnes & honour
'A new caroll of our lady' — eight quatrains and 2-line 'Nowell' burden.
Christmas Carolles, Kele, ca. 1550 (STC 5205); *facs.* Reed, *Xmas Carols*, pp. 44-6; *repr.* Bliss, *Bibl. Misc.*, p. 57; Sandys, *Xmas Carols*, p. 21; Bullen, *Songs & Carols*, p. 12; Rickert, *Anc. Eng. Xmas Carols*, pp. 36-8; *Early Eng. Carols*, p. 183.
	Lordynges and ye wyll holde you styll See 1895.
1987	Boyd, *ME Miracles*, pp. 92-104.
1988	Bennett, *England Chaucer-Caxton*, pp. 185-8 (*repr.* from *Rel. Ant.*, I. 61-3).
	Lordinges herkneth to me tale / Is merier than the nightingale See 1993.
1989	2. Wright, *Carols*, Percy Soc. IV. 20-3.
1992	'Symonye and Covetise,' on the evil times of Edward II — vv. 414 in tail-rime stanzas, a redaction of 4165, with vv. 114 not found there.
1. Bodl. 1885, f. 325b (lacks two leaves).
Ross, *Anglia* LXXV. 177-93.
	Lordinges lysten and holde you styl See 1993.
1992.5	Lordinges listen & hold you stil / hearken to me a litle
Durham Field, a ballad on the Battle of Neville's Cross — sixty-five quatrains. [Cf. 3117].
1. BM Addit. 27879, p. 245.
Hales and Furnivall, *Percy Folio MS.*, II. 191-200; Sidgwick, *Ballads Illustrating Eng. Hist.*, p. 22; Child, *Pop. Ballads*, No. 159, III. 284-7.
1993	[Cf. *3405.3. Ringler 41].
A Text:
3. Egerton 2862, ff. 45a-94b, 96a-b.
de Worde, ca. 1500 (STC 1987) (two leaves only: vv. 29-98, 227-92 of B Text, MS. 1); Pynson, ca. 1503 (STC 1988); and other early prints; Thomas East, ca. 1588 (STC 1990); A Text. 4, 5. *Rel. Ant.*, II. 60-4 (extracts); II. 64-5 (vv. 12).
1994	1. Harley 2252, ff. 86a-133b (vv. 3834, slightly imperfect).

1995	1. Bodl. MS not identified (fragment: vv. 13018-13193) [not Bodl. 14099]; 2. Delete this MS.; 3. Inner Temple, Petyt 511, Part VII, ff. 4-14, 180-190.
1996	1. BM Addit. 31042, f. 82a.
1997	1. BM Addit. Roll 63481 B [*olim* Redgrave Hall], a scrap of vellum. Brandl, *Archiv* CXLIV. 255.
1998	Time lost is never recovered—four lines. 2. Trinity Dublin 159, ff. 151a, 156a; 3. Balliol 316 B, f. 82a; 4. Cotton Titus A. xxvi, f. 173b; 5. Sloane 513, f. 136a. 3. Mynors, *Cat.*, p. 334.
	Lost ys my love farewell adewe Refrain to 3707.3.
1998.5	Loth to bedde / and loth fro bed On sloth—two short couplets. 1. Bodl. 21626, f. 21a; 2. Rylands Lib. Latin 394, f. 10b. 1. Förster, *Festschrift zum 12 Deutschen Neuphilologentage*, p. 49; 2. Pantin, *BJRL* XIV. 99.
1999	Lothe to offende / wyllyng to plese On suffrance—two couplets. [Cf. 3170]. 1. Boston Medical Lib. 23, f. 138b (vv. 2); 2. Bodl. 21658, f. iii recto; 3. Bodl. Lyell 34, back cover (repeated in looking glass letters).
1999.5	Loue fayne wolde I / yff I coude spye A love song—one stanza of eight short lines (perhaps incomplete). 1. BM Addit. 5465, f. 11b. Stevens, *Music* & *Poetry*, p. 355.
2000.3	Lowe god and drede shame A book plate of John Kyng of Dammowe—two couplets. 1. Leyden Univ. Vossius 9, f. 125b. Robinson, *Harvard Studies* & *Notes in Philol.* V. 188.
2000.5	Love god and flee synne How to win Heaven—two couplets.

              1. Bodl. 14526, f. 55a (vv. 2 included in 3502); 2. Harley 4486, f. 148a.
                  1. Zupitza, *Archiv* XC. 241.

2003.5   Loue hym wrouste / and loue hym brouste
              Love Him wrought—three stanzas with 'O and I' refrain (vv. 34 in all).
                1. BM Addit. 45896 (roll), Art. 3.
                Smith, *London Med. St.* II. 47-8.

              Loue ys a lady of the ffeminyne kynd
              Stanza 3 of 1864.5 occurring separately (BM Addit. 18752).

2005   [Utley 170].
              Onions, *Bodl. Quarterly Rev.* IV. 114; Stemmler, *Die Englische Liebesgedichte des MS Harley 2253*, Bonn 1962, pp. 90, 201.

2007   A Text: Comper, *Life & Lyrics of Rolle*, pp. 248-51; *Oxford Book Mystical Verse*, pp. 1-6; *Poets of Eng. Language*, I. 35-40.
              B Text: 2. Longleat 29, ff. 51a-53a.
                B. 2. Wilson, *RES* n.s. X. 342-6.

2007.5   Loue is naturall to euery wyght
              One mistress is best—three 5-line stanzas with 4-line burden: 'Smale pathis to the grenewode.'
              1. BM Addit. 5465, f. 112b.
                Fehr, *Archiv* CVI. 68; *Early Eng. Carols*, p. 313; Stevens, *Music & Poetry*, pp. 382-3.

2008   seven lines preceded by Latin version.
              Furnivall, *EETS* 15 orig. ed. 228; rev. ed. 257.

2009   [Utley 171].

2010   [Cf. 811].

2012   Kaiser, *Anthologie*, p. 241; Kaiser, *Med. Eng.*, p. 286.

*2012.3   *. . .love shuld com / On euery syde þe way she pryde
              Fragment of a love song.

    1. New York Pub. Lib. Drexel Fragments 4184.
    Stevens, *Music & Poetry*, p. 427.

   Luve þat is het can no skill See 2013.

2013 [Utley 173].
    2. Advocates 1. 1. 6, f. 265a (var.).
    2. *Bannatyne MS.*, Hunt. Club, IV. 733; Ritchie, *STS* n.s. XXVI. 40.

2014 Furnivall, *EETS* 15 orig. ed. 232; rev. ed. 262.

2015 Love wyll I and leve so may befalle
    A love song—one stanza rime royal.
    1. Bodl. 3509, f. 93b (vv. 4).
    XX Songes, de Worde, 1530 (STC 22924) (complete text); repr. Imelmann, *Shakespeare-Jahrbuch* XXXIX. 132-3; 1. Robbins, *MLN* LXIX. 158.

2016 Robbins, *Sec. Lyrics*, p. 149.

2017 [1. Delete this MS.]
    2. *Early Bodl. Music*, II. 61-2; Robbins, *Sec. Lyrics*, p. 148.

2017.5 Loued be þou king & thanked be þou kyng
    The first song in Rolle's *Form of Living* (Cap. vii)—nine (or eleven) irregular lines. [Cf. a Levacion prayer in *Lay Folks Mass Book* (3507), vv. 427-35, pr. Horstmann, *York. Wr.*, II. 6. For second song see 4056].
    1. Bodl. 1049, f. 53a; 2. Bodl. 1292, f. 11b; 3. Bodl. 1619, f. 83a; 4. Bodl. 1963, f. 146b; 5. Bodl. 3938; 6. Bodl. 11272, f. 90b; 7. Bodl. 12143, f. 50a; 8. Univ. Coll. Oxf. 97, f. 144b; 9. Camb. Un. Dd. 5. 64, Part III, f. 13a; 10. Camb. Un. Ff. 5. 45; 11. Camb. Un. Hh. 1. 12; 12. Camb. Un. Ii. 4. 9; 13. Camb. Un. Ii. 6. 55; 14. Caius 669, f. 183a; 15. Trinity Camb. 322, f. 138b; 16. Trinity Camb. 1053, f. 109b; 17. Harley 1022, f. 55a; 18. Lansdowne 455, f. 37b col ii; 19. Royal 17. B. xvii, f. 10a (in 3507); 20. BM Addit. 22283, f. 149a; 21. Chetham 6690; 22. Hereford Cath. P. i. 9; 23. Trinity Dublin 155; 24. Westminster School; 25. *olim* Gurney; 26. *olim* Harmsworth [*olim* Amherst]; 27. Longleat 29, f. 38a; 28. Huntington HM 127 [*olim* Powis 327]; 29. Paris: Bibl. Mazarine 514, f. 7a; 30. Paris: Bibl. St. Geneviève; 31. Morgan Lib. M. 818, f. 11a.
    8, 9. Horstmann, *York. Wr.*, I. 30; 17, 19. Comper, *Life & Lyrics of Rolle*, p. 221; 9. Allen, *Eng. Writings of Rolle*, p. 107.

2018   1. NLW Deposit: Porkington 10, ff. 53a-56a.

2018.5 Lucina schynnyng in silence of the nicht
'The birth of Antichrist' (or A Dream of Fortune) by William Dunbar—ten 5-line stanzas.
1. Camb. Un. Ll. 5. 10, f. 42b; 2. Pepys 2553, p. 334; 3. Advocates 1. 1. 6, f. 133a.
2. Craigie, *STS* n.s. VII. 405-7; 3. [Hailes,] *Anc. Scot. Poems*, pp. 26-8; *Select Poems of Dunbar*, Perth 1788, pp. 28-30; Sibbald, *Chronicle*, I. 313; Laing, *Dunbar*, I. 36-8; Paterson, *Dunbar*, pp. 187-9; *Bannatyne MS.*, Hunt. Club, III. 375-7; Small, *STS* II. 149-51; Schipper, *Dunbar*, pp. 217-9; and *DKAW* XLI (IV). 18-21; Ritchie, *STS* n.s. XXIII. 4; Baildon, *Dunbar*, pp. 104-5; MacKenzie, *Dunbar*, pp. 70-1; Kinsley, *Dunbar*, pp. 48-50.

2019   Clive, *Roxburghe Club* L. 257-71.

Luce In hys lessoun lerede me to synge   See 2021.

2021   2. BM Addit. 45896 (roll), Art 2 (8 st.).
2. Smith, *London Med. St.* II. 45-7.

2022   Delete 1. Heuser, *Anglia* XXVII. 283.

Lolay lolay   See 352.

2024   Christ weeps in the cradle for man's sin—seven quatrains and burden: 'Lullay lullay litel child / qwi wepest þou so sore.'
2. *Rel. Lyr. XIV C.*, pp. 80-1; *Oxford Book Christian Verse*, pp. 17-8; Greene, *Sel. Eng. Carols*, p. 103.

2025   1. Harley 913, f. 31b; 1a (transcript). BM Addit. 20091, ff. 58b-60a.
Kaiser, *Med. Eng.*, p. 242 (4 st. only); Davies, *Med. Eng. Lyrics*, pp. 106-7.

Lully lulley lully lulley / þe fawcon hath born my mak away
Burden to 1132.

Lullay myn lyking my dere sone my swytyng
Burden to 1351.

Lully lulla þow littell tine child
Burden to 2551.8.

Lullay my child and wepe no more / Slepe and be now styll
Burden to 3596.

2025.5 Lusti yough shuld vs ensue
The best use of youth, ascribed to Henry VIII—seven quatrains.
1. BM Addit. 31922, f. 94b.
Chappell, *Archaeologia* XLI. 376; Flügel, *Anglia* XII. 249-50; Trefusis, *Songs Henry VIII*, Roxburghe Club CLXI. 34-5; Stevens, *Music & Poetry*, pp. 416-7; Stevens, *Music at Court*, pp. 70-1.

2026 Lyarde, a satire on friars and husbands.

2026.5 Macer of erbe who so he sekes / Seth Ypocras as on sett lekes
Macer on the Virtues of Herbs—eighteen couplets.
1. Sloane 140, ff. 52a-53a; 2. Huntington Lib. HU 1051, f. 85a (vv. 21-32).
2. *Hist. MSS. Comm. Report 1928*, p. 422; Robbins, *Sec. Lyrics*, p. 77.

2028 Arber, *Dunbar Anthology*, p. 124.

2028.3 Madame as the noble Alphons kyng
'The speche of Boecius' at the pageant celebrating the marriage of Prince Arthur to Princess Catharine—three stanzas rime royal.
1. Cotton Vitellius A. xvi, f. 191a.

2028.5 Madame d'amours / All tymes ar ours
Loyalty to his mistress—two stanzas in eight short lines.
1. BM Addit. 31922, f. 73b.
Flügel, *Anglia* XII. 247; Padelford, *Early XVI Cent. Lyrics*, p. xxxiii; Stevens, *Music & Poetry*, p. 412; Stevens, *Music at Court*, p. 53.

2028.8 Madame defrayne / Ye me retayne
The faithful lover—three stanzas in eight short lines.
1. BM Addit. 5465, f. 35b.
Fehr, *Archiv* CVI. 57; Stevens, *Music & Poetry*, p. 362.

2029   a balade, three stanzas rime royal. [Utley 175].
   1. Bodl. 3896, f. 194b; 2. Cotton Cleo. D. vii, f. 190a; 3. Harley 7578, f. 17b.
   Chaucer, Stow, 1561 (STC 5075); [Anderson,] *Poets of Great Britain*, I. 579-80; Clarke, *Riches of Chaucer*, II. 312-3; 2. Robinson, *Chaucer*, 1933, pp. 627-8; 1957, p. 540.

2030.2   Madame kateryn because that I & ye / Be comin of noble blood
   'The speche of saynt Vrsula' at the pageant celebrating the marriage of Prince Arthur and Princess Catharine—four stanzas rime royal.
   1. Cotton Vitellius A. xvi, f. 185a.

2030.4   Madame sith ye haue entred the gates of pollycy
   'The speche of Noblesse' at the pageant celebrating the marriage of Prince Arthur and Princess Catharine—four stanzas rime royal.
   1. Cotton Vitellius A. xvi, f. 186b.

2030.6   Madame wan you ar dysposed to pray / remember your assured sarvant alway
   One couplet signed 'T. Roos.' [Cf. 2030.8].
   1. BM Addit. 17012, f. 180a.
   Wordsworth and Littlehales, *Old Service Books*, p. 62.

2030.8   Madame when ye most devoutyst be / have yn remembrance f and p
   One couplet. [Cf. 2030.6].
   1. BM Addit. 17102, f. 180a.
   Wordsworth and Littlehales, *Old Service Books*, p. 62.

2031   [Utley 176].
   Robinson, *Chaucer*, 1933, pp. 627-8; 1957, p. 533; Kökeritz, *MLN* LXIII. 311-2; Davies, *Med. Eng. Lyrics*, pp. 133-4; *facs*. Skeat, *Twelve Facsimiles*.

2032.5   Madame ȝour men said þai wald ryd
   'To the Quene' by William Dunbar: a warning against catching the pox—seven 5-line stanzas with refrain. [Utley 177].
   1. Camb. Un. Ll. 5. 10, f. 46a; 2. Pepys 2553, p. 342.
       2. Pinkerton, *Anc. Scot. Poems*, I. 99-100; Laing, *Dunbar*, I. 115-6; Small, *STS* IV. 203-4; Schipper, *Dunbar*, pp. 125-6; and *DKAW* XL (IV). 35-6; Baildon, *Dunbar*, pp. 62-3; Craigie, *STS* n.s. VII. 417-8; MacKenzie, *Dunbar*, pp. 59-60.

2033   [Utley 178].

*2033.3   *Magi...
            A poem apparently on the visit of the Magi to Bethlehem—
            probably in stanzas of four or five monoriming lines. [Cf.
            3810.3].
            1. Cotton Tib. E. vii, f. 281b. [The MS. is so charred that
            only occasional words can be made out on various lines].

2033.5   Mayde and moder eke thou be
            A prayer to the Virgin with French stanzas alternating with
            English.
            1. Laurence Witten, New Haven, Cat. 5, Item 47 (flyleaf of
            a Latin Psalter).

2034   Brook, *Harley Lyrics,* p. 87.

2034.5   Mayde whether go you / I go to the medewe &c.
            A sophisticated story of love—four quatrains in dialogue
            (with inserted couplets) and introductory heading; 'Hey troly
            loly lo.'
            1. BM Addit. 31922, f. 124b.
                Chappell, *Archaeologia* XLI. 384-5; Flügel, *Anglia* XII. 255;
                Early Eng. Lyr., pp. 62-3; Padelford, *Early XVI Cent.
                Lyrics,* pp. 84-6; *Oxford Book XVI C. Verse,* pp. 43-4;
                Stevens, *Music & Poetry,* pp. 424-5; Stevens, *Music at
                Court,* pp. 95-8.

2035   1. Egerton 3245 [*olim* Gurney], f. 198b (2 st. only; ends im-
            perfectly).

2036   [For later versions, in stanzas, see 1219, 2111, 3575].
            Reed, *Xmas Carols,* p. 82.

2037.5   Maiden in the mor lay
            The Maid of the Moor—four rondel-type 9-line stanzas (prob-
            ably ends imperfectly).
            1. Kilkenny, Red Book of Ossory, f. 71a (first line only); 2.
            Bodl. 13679, Item I (b).
                1. Greene, *Speculum* XXVII. 504; 2. *Cat. Col. MSS. Rawl.
                (Bodl. Cat.* V. iv), p. 137; Heuser, *Anglia* XXX. 175; Sisam,
                XIV Cent. V. & P., p. 167; Robbins, *Sec. Lyrics,* pp. 12-13;
                Poets of Eng. Lang., I. 26; Kaiser, *Med. Eng.,* p. 471; *New
                Oxford Hist. Music,* III. 119; Speirs, *Med. Eng. Poetry,* p.
                62; Davies, *Med. Eng. Lyrics,* p. 102.

2039   Brook, *Harley Lyrics*, pp. 66-8.

2039.3   Maydenes of Engelande sare may ye morne
Song said to have been sung by the Scots after the defeat of the English at Bannockburn—five lines. [This tag occurs in many MSS. of the *Brut Chronicle*, examples listed below, and in many early printed chronicles. Ringler 45a].
1. Bodl. 11539; 2. Cotton Galba E. viii, f. 88a; 3. Cox [*olim* Harmsworth].
Cronicles of England, Caxton, 1480 (STC 9991), and later eds.; Fabyan, *New Chronicles*, Pynson, 1516 (STC 10659); repr. Ellis, 1811, p. 420 (cf. 3955.5); Rastell, *Pastime of People or Chronicles*, 1811, p. 204; Pinkerton, *Anc. Scot. Poems*, II. 494; Aytoun, *Ballads of Scotland;* Eyre-Todd, *Scot. Ballad Poetry*, p. 17; Furnivall, *Captain Cox*, Ballad Soc. VII. clvi; Woods, *TRSL* n.s. VI. 28; Brie, *EETS* 131. 208; Wilson, *Lost Lit.*, p. 213; Wilson, *LSE* V. 44; *Early Eng. Lyrics*, p. liii; Robbins, *Hist. Poems*, p. 262; J. S. Cox, *Literary Repository*, 1957, IV. 1; Baskervill, *Elizabethan Jig*, p. 41.

2039.5   Make we mery in hall and boure
A carol on the Circumcision—six quatrains and burden.
Christmas Carolles, Kele, ca. 1550 (STC 5205); *facs.* Reed, *Xmas Carols*, pp. 41-3; *repr.* Bliss, *Bibl. Miscellanies*, 1813, p. 54; *Early Eng. Carols*, p. 76.

2039.8   Make we oure plentevous feste of gystnyng / In clere clennesse and trewe lyuyng
A couplet translating the text of a Latin sermon (I. Cor. v. 8).
1. Royal 8. D. x, f. 1b.
Warner and Gilson, *Cat.*, I. 248.

Man and Woman God hath wrought
Prefatory verses in some printed texts of 2666 (abstracted from 407.6).

2044   Rickert, *Anc. Eng. Xmas Carols*, pp. 209-10; Stevens, *Med. Carols*, p. 69.

2047   [Cf. 1943].

Man be war and be no fool   See 3306.

Man be ware & wise in dede
Burden to 3820.

2049 [Utley 179].
[Masters,] *Rymes of Minstrels*, p. 17.

Man byholde byfore þee howe þi lyffe wasteþ   See 1937.

2050.5 Man com & se yow schal alle dede be
Epitaph, A.D. 1370, on John the Smith—eight lines on a brass at Brightwell-Baldwin, Oxfordshire.
Ravenshaw, *Antiente Epitaphes*, 1878, p. 4; Skeat, *Proc. Monumental Brass Soc.* V; Bouquet, *Church Brasses*, p. 165; Mustanoja, *Neuphil. Mitteilungen* LIII. 492.

2052 8. Penrose 6 [*olim* Delamere], f. 162b.
4. *Retrospective Rev.* II. 101-4; 5. Leonhard, *Zwei Gesch.* &c.; 7. Furnivall, *EETS* 15 orig. ed. 96-102; rev. ed. 126-32.

2053 1, 4. Stevens, *Med. Carols*, pp. 12, 100.

2056 [Utley 179].
1. Bodl. 29734, f. 26b; 2. Harley 2316, f. 56b; 3. Hunterian Mus. 230, f. 248b (included in 1628.8).
2. Wright, *Percy Soc.* VIII. 83.

2057 Davies, *Med. Eng. Lyrics*, pp. 226-7.

Man hem pleynit of mikil untrewthe   See 2145.

2058 9. *Register*, I. 451.

2059 454 lines in couplets.

2060 1. Balliol 354, f. 147b (one 6-line st. followed by 686).

2061 *Early Eng. Carols*, pp. 126-7.

Man yff thow wylt me mercy gete   See 2714.

2063 [Cf. 2079].
Bowers, *MLN* LXIV. 455-9.

2064   2. Ipswich County Hall Deposit: Hillwood [*olim* Brome], f. 1a.

2066   Manly, *Eng. Poetry*, pp. 13-4; Dickins and Wilson, *Early ME Texts*, pp. 123-4; Brook, *Harley Lyrics*, pp. 69-70; Kaiser, *Anthologie*, p. 307; Kaiser, *Med. Eng.*, p. 473; Speirs, *Med. Eng. Poetry*, pp. 92-3; Davies, *Med. Eng. Lyrics*, pp. 71-3.

2066.5   Man in what state that ever thou be
            '*Timor mortis*' macaronic epitaph of late xv and early xvi century, appearing on tombstones at Northleach, Witney, Luton, and Great Tew.
            Bouquet, *Church Brasses*, p. 195 (Northleach); Brabant, *Oxfordshire*, 1919, p. 27 (Witney); *Early Eng. Carols*, p. 424 (Witney); Greene, *Sel. Eng. Carols*, p. 237 (Witney); Ravenshaw, *Antiente Epitaphes*, p. 17 (Luton); Gray, *N&Q* n.s. VII. 403-4 (Luton, Northleach).

2066.8   Man is but a frele þing
            Two couplets translating '*Est homo res fragilis* &c.'
            1. Advocates 18. 7. 21, f. 87b.

2068.5   Mon yt behoves the oft to have i mynd
            Epitaph on R. Stokes, Hampton-in-Arden, Warwickshire — four lines.
            Bouquet, *Church Brasses*, p. 167.

2070   2. Hall, *Early Middle English*, I. 29; 3. Stevenson, *Ayenbite of Inwyt*, Roxburghe Club 1855, p. 101; 5. Reese, *Music in MA*, p. 243.

2071   [Delete entire entry].

            Man of the self thu haf god mynde   See 2056.

2072   Morris, *Specimens*, 1867, pp. 1-18 (extracts); Hall, *Early Middle English*, I. 197-214 (extracts).

2072.2   Man remember & have yn mynde
            On the need of foresight — five couplets.
            1. Sloane 140, f. 100a.

2072.4　　　Man remember thy end / and thou shalt never be shend
　　　　　　Memento mori—one couplet.
　　　　　　1. Harley 4294, f. 82a.
　　　　　　　Rel. Ant., I. 316; Patterson, *JEGP* XX. 273.

2072.6　　　Man Remembre whens þou com & wheþer þou shalt
　　　　　　On just dealing: '& to thyn evyn Cristyn do no wronge'—
　　　　　　one couplet (following 3969).
　　　　　　1. Balliol 354, f. 213b.
　　　　　　　Flügel, *Anglia* XXVI. 226; Dyboski, *EETS* ci. 141.

2072.8　　　Man sen thy lyf is ay in weir
　　　　　　'Advice to spend anis awin gude' by William Dunbar—ten quatrains with refrain: 'Thyne awin gude spend quhill thow hes space.'
　　　　　　1. Pepys 2553, p. 225; 2. Advocates 1. 1. 6, f. 136a.
　　　　　　　1. Craigie, *STS* n.s. VII. 253-4; 2. Ramsay, *Evergreen*, I. 64-5; *repr. Ramsay & Earlier Scot. Poets*, p. 229; [Hailes,] *Anc. Scot. Poems*, pp. 70-2; *repr.* Pinkerton, *Sel. Scot. Ballads*, 1783, II. 57-9; *Sel. Poems of Dunbar*, Perth 1788, pp. 62-3; Sibbald, *Chronicle*, I. 342-4; Laing, *Dunbar*, I. 191-2; Paterson, *Dunbar*, pp. 54-6; *Bannatyne MS.*, Hunt. Club, III. 383-4; Small, *STS* IV. 152-3; Schipper, *Dunbar*, pp. 338-40; and *DKAW* XLII (IV). 35-8; Baildon, *Dunbar*, pp. 174-5; Ritchie, *STS* n.s. XXIII. 11-13; MacKenzie, *Dunbar*, pp. 147-8.

2074　　　　2. Furnivall, *EETS* 15 orig. ed. 235; rev. ed. 264.

2077　　　　4. Foster, *Essays & Studies in Honor of Carleton Brown*, p. 157.

2077.5　　　Man þat was in wurchipe tok no hede / And þerfore last his worchup for is mysde[de]
　　　　　　A couplet in a Latin sermon.
　　　　　　1. Camb. Un. Ii. 3. 8, f. 101a.

　　　　　　Man that wole of lechecrafte here　　See 3422.

2078　　　　2. Camb. Un. Add 4407, Art. 19 (h) (vv. 2-36 only).
　　　　　　1. Morris, *Specimens*, pp. 96-102.

Man the behovyth oft to haue þis in mind
Four monoriming lines on Abuses of Age (cf. 906) included in an Epitaph: See 2818.2.

2078.5 Man then wel bewar / for warldly good makyth man blinde
Inscription on a pew at Crawley Church, Sussex.
Bouquet, *Church Brasses*, p. 168.

2079 [Cf. 2063].
Bowers, *MLN* LXIV. 459-60.

2079.5 Man þu haue þine þout one me
Appeal of Christ to Man—three 5-line stanzas, with 2-line heading: 'þenc man of mi harde stundes &c.' [Preceded by 3964, without break, but possibly originally separate].
1. Royal 12. E. i, f. 194b.
Rel. Lyr. XIV C., p. 2.

2082 [Masters,] *Rymes of Minstrels*, pp. 10-11; Robbins, *Sec. Lyrics*, pp. 55-6; Davies, *Med. Eng. Lyrics*, pp. 224-5.

2085 1. Camb. Un. Ii. 3. 8, f. 63a; 2. Advocates b. 44. 2.

2086 [var. burden in Royal App. 58, f. 8b. Cf. 3228.3].
Ritson, *Anc. Songs*, p. lxviii; Greene, *Sel. Eng. Carols*, p. 118; Davies, *Med. Eng. Lyrics*, pp. 256-7.

2090 [Utley 180].
3. BM Addit. 22718, f. 86b (st. 10-14).
2. [Masters,] *Rymes of Minstrels*, p. 24-26.

2092 [Utley 181. Singer 806].
[B, vv. 1706-5810 = vv. 1679-5169; &c].
1. Hunterian Mus. 409, f. 2a (vv. 7696 of Fragment A; lacks vv. 1-44, 333-380, 1387-1482, 2395-2442, 3595-3690, 7385-7576).
Robinson, *Chaucer*, 1933, pp. 664-731; 1957, pp. 564-637.

Margaret meke / whom I now seke
Introductory heading to 3270.5.

Marke this songe for it is trewe   See 3549.5.

2096	1. Egerton 3245 [*olim* Gurney], f. 201b.
2097	Rickert, *Anc. Eng. Xmas Carols*, pp. 170-1.
2098	1. Greene, *Sel. Eng. Carols*, p. 111.
2099	[Also on wall paintings of Life of B.V.M. on chancel wall, Broughton Church, Oxon.]. 2. Horstmann, *York. Wr.*, I. 377.
2100	Haupt and Hoffman, *Altdeutsche Blätter*, II. 142.
2101	*Rel. Lyr. XIV C.*, p. 72.
	Marie I praye þe as þu art fre See 3238.
2104	twenty-two couplets.
2105	4. Brown, *EETS* 169. 65.
2106	6. Brown, *EETS* 169. 68.
2107	Davies, *Med. Eng. Lyrics*, pp. 103-5.
2111	*Christmas Carolles*, Kele, ca. 1550 (STC 5205); *facs*. Reed, *Xmas Carols*, p. 49; *repr. Early Eng. Carols*, p. 117; 1. Reed, *Xmas Carols*, pp. 83-4.
2113	Rickert, *Anc. Eng. Xmas Carols*, p. 13; Greene, *Sel. Eng. Carols*, p. 114.
2118	4. Longleat 30, f. 23b (lacks st. 1, 2, 8); 6. ? Brussels: Bibl. royale 2054, ff. 106-108.
2119	[Ringler 46]. 17. Delete this MS.; 20. Lansdowne 344, f. 38b; 26. Ushaw: St. Cuthbert's Coll. 28; 27. Trinity Dublin 159, f. 175a; 28. Trinity Dublin 351, f. 48b; 29. Laurence Witten, New Haven, Cat. 5, Item 51 [*olim* Helmingham Hall LJ. V. 14], f. 85a; 34. Bodl. 6922*, f. 22b; 45. Goldschmidt Sale Cat. 71, 1943, no. 1 [*olim* Greg; *olim* Huth 153], f. 15a; 46. Longleat 29, f. 57b; 49. Yale Univ. 163 [*olim* Wagstaff; *olim* Petworth 8], f. 186b; 50. Bodl. Lyell 30, ff. 142a-143a (two fragments, vv. 44

only); 51. Camb. Un. Add. 6150, f. 20b; 52. Blairs Coll., Book of Hours, f. 15a; 53. Foyle [*olim* Harmsworth; Sotheby Sale, Dec. 16, 1945, Lot 2131]; 54. Univ. of Illinois 71 [*olim* Harmsworth; Sotheby Sale, Dec. 16, 1945, Lot 2132]; 55. *olim* Borneman [Parke-Bennet Sale, Nov. 1955, Lot 796].

Speculum Christiani, de Machlinia, ca. 1486 (STC 26012); repr. Dibdin, *Typo. Antiquities*, II. 13-14; Pollard, *XV C. Prose & Verse*, p. xiii; 36. Marsh, *Hist. Eng. Language*, p. 465; 41. N. S. Baugh, *Worcestershire Misc.*, pp. 143-4.

2120   7. Brown, *EETS* 169. 68.

2121   eight quatrains (followed directly by 2119).
            1. Longleat 29, f. 57b.

2121.5   Marie so fre have minde and pite
            A prayer tag to the Virgin—one couplet.
            1. *olim* Fellowes, f. 171b (Sotheby Sale Cat., June 7, 1964, Lot 231).

2124.5   Mary thou were greet with lovely cheere
            To the Virgin—four monoriming quatrains.
            Speculum Spiritualium, Paris 1510, f. ccvi verso.

2127   5. D'Evelyn and Mill, *EETS* 235. 348.

2128   2. Harley 7333, f. 132b.
            Chaucer, Stow, 1561 (STC 5075); *Chaucer*, Speght, 1598 (STC 5077); Urry, *Chaucer*, 1721, p. 551; Chalmers, *English Poets*, I. 556; 1. Skeat, *Oxf. Ch.*, VII. 450; 2. Furnivall, *Parallel Texts MP*, Chaucer Soc. 1 s., XXI. 98.

2128.5   Mayster Johan eu greteþ of Guldeuorde þo
            Two couplets copied in xvii cent. by Thomas Wilkens from a 'broaken leafe' of the same MS.
            1. Jesus Oxf. 29, f. 228a.
            Warton, *History*, rev. Hazlitt, 1871, II. 38; Heuser, *Bonn. Beit.* XVII. 105; Atkins, *Owl and Nightingale*, p. xxiii; Dickins and Wilson, *Early ME Texts*, p. 50; C. Sisam, *RES* n.s. V. 22.

2131   Maysters that war of craftes sere
            vv. 90 in couplets.
            Robbins, *Sec. Lyrics*, pp. 67-70.

2132	[Delete this entry].
	Mastres your maners are hard to know See 2195.3.
	May y sugge na more so wel me is See 694.5.
2135	1. Camb. Un. Add. 5943, f. 170b. Robbins, *Sec. Lyrics,* pp. 27-8.
2136	an acrostic. [Utley 182]. Cutler, *MLN* LXX. 88.
2138	two quatrains.
2139	Chepman and Myllar, 1508 (7 st.); *repr.* Sibbald, *Chronicle,* I. 199; Stevenson, *STS* LXV. 236-8; *facs.* Beattie, *Edinb. Bibl. Soc.* 1950, pp. 166-8; 1. Pinkerton, *Poems from Scarce Editions,* III. 133; Laing, *Henryson,* 1865, p. 36; *Bannatyne MS.,* Hunt. Club, p. 213; Wood, *Henryson,* pp. 189-91.
2140	[Delete entire entry].
	Me rewis one mary my modyr Stanza 5 of 1119 occurring separately.
2140.5	Me sayth þat game goth on wombe An irregular couplet in a Latin sermon by Friar William Herebert. 1. BM Addit. 46919 [*olim* Phillipps 8336], f. 171b.
2141	Robbins, *Sec. Lyrics,* p. 144.
	Meede in thy lande is domys man See 906 (Cox MS.).
2142	de Worde, ca. 1528 (STC 14128); de Worde, ca. 1530 (STC 5733).
2143	Horstmann, *Archiv* LXXXII. 405-7.
2143.5	*Memento homo quod cinis me* / Think man &c. 'Of manis mortalitie' by William Dunbar—six 8-line stanzas with refrain: *'Quod tu in cinerem reverteris.'* 1. Pepys 2553, p. 193; 2. Advocates 1. 1. 6, f. 47a.

1. Craigie, *STS* n.s. VII. 218-9; 2. [Hailes,] *Anc. Scot. Poems*, pp. 118-20; *Sel. Poems of Dunbar*, Perth 1788, pp. 98-100; Laing, *Dunbar*, I. 249-50; Paterson, *Dunbar*, pp. 65-7; *Bannatyne MS.*, Hunt. Club, II. 127-9; Small, *STS* IV. 74-5; Schipper, *Dunbar*, pp. 384-5; and *DKAW* XLII (IV). 81-3; Baildon, *Dunbar*, pp. 206-7; Ritchie, *STS* n.s. XXII. 117-9; MacKenzie, *Dunbar*, pp. 149-50.

2145   3. Balliol 227, f. 258a; 4. Egerton 2788, f. 53b.

1, 2. *Rel. Lyr. XIV C.*, pp. 54, 259; 3. Mynors, *Cat.*, p. 229.

2146   Me[n hem com]pleynes of vntrewyth / la[we es] dede and þat es rewth
    in couplets.
    1. Bodl. 4031, f. 1b (vv. 7; ends imperfectly).
    Rel. Lyr. XIV C., p. 259; Wells, *Manual*, p. 975.

2147   *Sydrac and Boctus*, the didactic dialogue on morals and doctrines, with 1084 questions—abridged version. Translated by Hugh Campedene from the French (cf. Bodl. 2451; pr. Paris 1486). [For the longer version cf. 772].
    4. Brudenell, Lamport Hall, Northants, ff. 2 (fragment = Questions 282-303 of MS. 1).
    Thomas Godfraye, London [? 1530] (STC 3186).

2148   nine 8-line stanzas.
    FitzGibbon, *E. E. Poetry*, pp. 235-7; Bennett, *England Chaucer-Caxton*, pp. 224-6; Kaiser, *Med. Eng.*, p. 496. [Delete: James, *Cat.*].

2149   Wright, *Pol. Poems*, I. 75-80; Morris, *Specimens*, II. 134; Brandl and Zippel, *ME Sprach- u. Literatur.*, pp. 135-7; Kaiser, *Med. Eng.*, p. 381.

2150   Davies, *Med. Eng. Lyrics*, p. 116.

2151   in short couplets.

2153   10. McGill Univ. 142 (fragment of four leaves: vv. 20129-20314) [identification and location not established].

2153.5   Menskful and myȝty in mynde modyr of maries iij
    '*Stirps beate Anne*'—eight 9-line stanzas.
    1. Aberdeen Univ. 123, f. 131b.

2154   2. Fitzwilliam Mus. 40-1950 [*olim* Yates Thompson 83, 'Talbot Hours'], f. 132b.

2157   twenty 8-line stanzas.
         2. Kreuzer, *MLN* LXVI. 226-31.

2159   Comper, *Life* & *Lyrics of Rolle*, pp. 297-8.

2161   His pitiless mistress—sixteen lines based on phrases from *The Temple of Glas* (851), followed by vv. 736-54, 762-3 from the same poem, adapted to form a personal petition. [Cf. 1598.3 which incorporates vv. 12].
         Robbins, *Sec. Lyrics*, pp. 141-2.

         Merlyn sonn my worldis blys   See 3616.

2161.5   Methocht compassioun wod of feris
         'Of the Passioun of Christ' by William Dunbar—six 8-line stanzas with refrain: 'Thys blissit saluatour chryst Iesu.' [Follows without break 276.5].
         1. Pepys 2553, p. 206; 2. Arundel 285, f. 169b.
         1. Laing, *Dunbar*, I (Suppl.). 285; Small, *STS* IV. 241; Schipper, *Dunbar*, pp. 378-9; and *DKAW* XLII (IV). 75-7; Baildon, *Dunbar*, pp. 201-3; Craigie, *STS* n.s. VII. 232-4; MacKenzie, *Dunbar*, pp. 158-9; Kinsley, *Dunbar*, pp. 6-7; 2. Bennett, *STS* 3 s. XXIII. 268-9.

2162   Robbins, *Sec. Lyrics*, p. 144; Wilson, *Lost Lit.*, p. 178.

2163   one 7-line stanza.
         Trend, *Music* & *Letters*, IX. 111; Dickins and Wilson, *Early ME Texts*, p. 118; Segar, *Med. Anthology*, p. 92; Kaiser, *Anthologie*, p. 291; Kaiser, *Med. Eng.*, p. 463; Davies, *Med. Eng. Lyrics*, p. 51.

         Mirry Margaret / As mydsomer flowre   See 729.5.

2164   2. Bodl. 1595, f. 45b.
         Liber Eliensis (STC 1595); Stewart, 1848, p. 202; *CHEL* II. 397; Williams, *New Book Eng. Verse*, p. 23; Wilson, *Early ME Lit.*, p. 253; Brook, *Harley Lyrics*, p. 4; Wilson, *Lost Lit.*, p. 171; Kaiser, *Anthologie*, p. 363; Kaiser, *Med. Eng.*, p. 160; Davies, *Med. Eng. Lyrics*, p. 30.

2165   6. Chetham Lib. 8009, f. 4a.
           3 (with 4), 5. McKnight, *EETS* 14. 111-36.

2166   Brook, *Harley Lyrics*, pp. 29-31.

2167   [Ringler 47].
           25. Lansdowne 344, f. 32b; 33. Rylands Lib. Latin 341, f. 77b; 34. Ushaw: St. Cuthbert's Coll. 28; 36. Trinity Dublin 159, f. 169b; 37. Trinity Dublin 351, f. 41b; 38. *olim* Gurney 38 &c.; 40. Laurence Witten, New Haven, Cat. 5, Item 51 [*olim* Helmingham Hall LJ. V. 14], f. 81a; 42. Bodl. 29764, ff. 41b, 42a; 43. Camb. Un. Dd. 4. 51, f. 23a; 44. Camb. Un. Add. 6150, f. 17b; 45. Foyle [*olim* Harmsworth; Sotheby Sale, Dec. 16, 1945, Lot 2131]; 46. Univ. of Illinois 71 [*olim* Harmsworth; Sotheby Sale, Dec. 16, 1945, Lot 2132].
            Speculum Christiani, de Machlinia, ca. 1486 (STC 26012); 24, 26. Herrtage, *EETS* xxxiii. 499, 497; 38. *Hist. MSS. Comm. Report* XII, App., Part IX, p. 164.

2168   [St. 1 = st. 1 of 3328.5].

2169   Myghtfull Mari y-crownyd quene / emperesse off heuene and helle
           An orison to the Virgin—nine 8-line stanzas.

2172   five couplets.
           1. Royal 12. C. xiv, f. 1*b col i & ii.
           Bowers, *JEGP* LVI. 441-2.

        Myn auctour Bochas rejoysed in hys lyve
           An extract from *Fall of Princes*, I. 6511-6734. [Utley 185].
           See Extracts, MS. 13, 1168.

2176   1. Sauerstein, *Charles d'Orléans*, 1899, pp. 65-6.

2178   'How þe louer is sett to serue þe floure,' including a reproof to Lydgate. [Utley 186].
           Robbins, *Sec. Lyrics*, pp. 186-9.

2179   a love poem with involved sestina-like stanza-linking.
           Cords, *Archiv* CXXXV. 302.

2182 [For another text in 8-line stanzas see 2247].
1. Bodl. 3896, f. 323b.
Robbins, *Sec. Lyrics*, pp. 189-90.

2182.3 Myne hartys luste
Title of a courtly love lyric mentioned in a bill of a music teacher ca. A.D. 1473-4.
1. Public Record Office C 47 / 37 / 11, f. 3b.
Hanham, *RES* n.s. VIII. 271.

2182.6 Min hartys lust & alle my plesure
A love duet—three 8-line stanzas.
XX Songes, de Worde, 1530 (STC 22924); Hawkins, *Hist. Music*, 1776, III. 35-6; Flügel, *Anglia* XII. 596-7; Imelmann, *Shakespeare-Jahrbuch* XXXIX. 135.

2183 1. Yale Univ. 91, ff. 65b-67a.
Menner, *MLQ* VI. 384.

2183.5 Myne high estate power & auctoryte
The Preface to the *Book of Fortune*, on the cast of the dice, by Thomas More—thirty-seven stanzas rime royal.
1. Balliol 354, f. 104a.
Lady Fortune, Wyer, ca. 1538; *repr.* Huth, *Fugitive Tracts*, 1 s; Furnivall, *Captain Cox*, Ballad Soc. VII. xcv-vi (Pro.); More, *Workes*, Rastell, 1557; *facs. & repr.* Campbell, *Eng. Works*, pp. 338-44; *Book of Fortune*, 1618; 1. Flügel, *Anglia* XXVI. 142; Flügel, *Neuengl. Lesebuch*, pp. 140-41 (Pro., 3 st. & 2 st. tailpiece only); Dyboski, *EETS* ci. 72-80.

2185 Robbins, *Sec. Lyrics*, pp. 13-14; Stevens, *Med. Carols*, p. 111 (burden only).

2186 vv. 956 in couplets.
Mustanoja, *Neuphil. Mitteilungen* XLIX. 149-79.

2187 Person, *Camb. ME Lyrics*, p. 28.

2188 Robbins, *Sec. Lyrics*, pp. 142-3.

Mynyon go trym go trym   See 3632.3.

2189 vv. 88 in couplets.

2191.5   Mis like it noght to þe þo i be of litel body
English translation of Latin elegiacs preceding a *Speculum Medicorum*—eleven lines.
1. BM Addit. 34111, f. 31a.

2192   [Four lines apparently adapted from st. 1, vv. 1-3, 5, appear beneath the Latin epitaph of Thomas Dalby, Archdeacon of Richmond, d. Jan. 26, 1526, in north aisle of choir in York Minster, pr. Leach, *Surtees Soc.* CVIII. xcv].
3. Corning Mus. of Glass 6 [*olim* Currer], ff. 131a-132b.
Richard Lant, ca. 1542; Kynge and Marche, n.d. (STC 22599); *repr.* Dyce, *Skelton*, I. 1-5; Dyce and Child, *Skelton & Donne*, I. 3-7; Henderson, *Skelton*, 1931, 1948, 1959, pp. 1-3; Pinto, *Selection*, 1950, pp. 15-7 (omits st. 4, 7-8); J. Day, n. d.; *Workes*, Marshe, 1568 (STC 22608); *repr.* [? J. Bowle,] 1736; Chalmers, *English Poets*, II. 260-1.

2195   sometimes ascribed to Skelton. [Utley 187].
Brie, *Eng. Stn.* XXXVII. 29-30; Lloyd, *RES* V. 304; Henderson, *Skelton*, 1931, p. 36; 1948, 1959, p. 27.

2195.3   Mastres your maners are hard to know
An attack on women's inconstancy, signed Nycholas Wikes—two stanzas rime royal with refrain: 'Slyppur it is to grype on whome is no holde.' [Utley 188].
1. Royal 17. D. xviii, f. 1b.

2195.5   Moaning my hart doth sore oppresse
'Therfore swet hart loue me agayne'—seven quatrains.
1. BM Addit. 18752, f. 89a.
Reed, *Anglia* XXXIII. 361.

Money money how hay goode day
Burden to 113.

2199.5   Most Cristen prince and frande vnto the feith
Pageant verses, spoken by St. George, St. Ethelbert, and the B.V. to welcome Henry VII in 1486 at Hereford—three stanzas rime royal.
1. Cotton Julius B. xii, f. 17b.

2200   (seven items in all).

2200.3	Most clere of colour and rote of stedfastness The goodness of his mistress—one stanza rime royal. 1. BM Addit. 5465, f. 26b. Stafford Smith, *Eng. Songs*, p. 12; Fehr, *Archiv* CVI. 56; Stevens, *Music & Poetry*, pp. 359-60.
2200.5	Moost dere Cosine of england & fraunce Pageant verses to Henry VII in A.D. 1486 at Bristol—five stanzas rime royal. 1. Cotton Julius B. xii, f. 18b.
	Most excellent most high & nobil prince Letter to Cupid in 4024.
2201	1. Leyden Univ. Vossius 9, f. 112b.
2207	Brook, *Harley Lyrics*, pp. 37-9.
2208	MacCracken, *Archiv* CXXVI. 366-70; Garmonsway and Raymo, *E. E. & Norse Studies Presented to Hugh Smith*, 1963, pp. 89-96.
2209	[Delete entire entry].
	Moost myghtfull myrrore of hy magnyfycens See 451.5.
2212.5	Moost noble prynce our souueraigne hege lorde Pageant verses for Henry VII in A.D. 1486 at Bristol—three stanzas rime royal. 1. Cotton Julius B. xii, f. 19b.
2213	A mumming at Hertford, ca. A.D. 1428, by Lydgate. [Utley 190]. 1. Neilson and Webster, *Chief British Poets*, pp. 223-7.
	Moste pleasaunt princes recorded þat may be See 2781.
2214	1. York City, House Book VI, f. 17b; 2. Cotton Julius B. xii, f. 12a. 1, 2. Smith, *London Med. St.*, I. 393-4, 396; 1. Raine, *Yorks. Arch. Soc. Record Ser.* XCVIII. 158; Robbins, *Sec. Lyrics*, pp. 117-8.

2215   in rime royal stanzas.
1. York City, House Book VI, f. 16b (3 st.); 2. Cotton Julius B. xii, f. 11a (4 st.).
     1, 2. Smith, *London Med. St.*, I. 391-2; 1. Raine, *Yorks. Arch. Soc. Record Ser.* XCVIII. 157.

2216   1. York City, House Book VI, f. 16a; 2. Cotton Julius B. xii, f. 10b.
     1, 2. Smith, *London Med. St.* I. 388-90; 1. Raine, *Yorks. Arch. Soc. Record Ser.* XCVIII. 156-7.

2217   1. Bodl. Lat. misc. c. 66 [*olim* Capesthorne], f. 93b.
     Robbins, *PMLA* LXV. 266-7; Davies, *Med. Eng. Lyrics*, p. 256.

2217.5   Moost souereyn Lorde Chryste [Jesu] / Born of a mayd
'*Miserere nobis:*' a carol to Christ—five 5-line stanzas and burden.
     Christmas Carolles, Kele, ca. 1550 (STC 5205); *facs.* Reed, *Xmas Carols*, p. 65; *repr. Early Eng. Carols*, p. 196.

2218   [Cf. 1955.5].
2. Trinity Camb. 601, f. 245a (with 2 st. from 3190) and again at f. 318a (followed by Envoy from 3190).
     1. Robbins, *Hist. Poems*, pp. 235-9; 2. MacCracken, *MLN* XXIII. 214 (inserts only).

2221   3. Furnivall, *EETS* lxi. 52-6.

2222.5   Moder of Merci shyld hym from thorribul fynd
Probable epitaph of William Caxton: 'Bring hym to lyff eternall that neuyr hath ynd'—one couplet.
     Dibdin, *Typo. Antiquities*, I. cxi; Blades, *Life & Typography of Caxton*, I. 75.

2223   *Chaucer*, Thynne, 1532 (STC 5068); *Chaucer*, Stow, 1561 (STC 5075); *Chaucer*, Speght, 1598 (STC 5077); Urry, *Chaucer*, 1721, p. 358; Bell, *Poets of Great Britain*, XIII. 84; [Anderson,] *Poets of Great Britain*, I. 575; Chalmers, *English Poets*, I. 319; *British Poets*, Chiswick 1822, IV. 197; *Aldine Brit. Poets*, 1845, VI. 255; 1866, VI. 275; Bell, *Chaucer*, III. 413; Skeat, *Oxf. Ch.*, VII. 405.

2224   [Utley 191].

2224.5 Morning my hart doth sore oppresse
'Alas I cannot be lovyd agayne'—seven quatrains with this refrain.
1. BM Addit. 18752, f. 89a; 2. Huddersfield Corp., Ramsden Rental.
1. Reed, *Anglia* XXXIII. 361.

2226 Brandl and Zippel, *ME Sprach- u. Literatur.*, pp. 110-3.

Musike in his melody requirith true soundes   See 3405.8.

2226.5 Musing allone this hinder nicht
'Of deming,' possibly by William Dunbar—eleven 5-line stanzas with refrain: 'May na man now undemit be.'
1. Pepys 2553, pp. 168 and 313; 2. Advocates 1. 1. 6, f. 63b.
1a, 1b. Craigie, *STS* n.s. VII. 191-3, 372-4; 2. Ramsay, *Evergreen*, II. 90-2 (omits vv. 41-5); *repr. Ramsay and Earlier Scot. Poets*, p. 276; [Hailes,] *Anc. Scot. Poems*, pp. 79-81; *Sel. Poems of Dunbar*, Perth 1788, pp. 67-9; Sibbald, *Chronicle*, II. 2-3; Laing, *Dunbar*, I. 181-3; Paterson, *Dunbar*, pp. 160-3; *Bannatyne MS.*, Hunt. Club, II. 171-3; Small, *STS* IV. 92-4; Schipper, *Dunbar*, pp. 306-9; and *DKAW* XLII (IV). 4-7; Ritchie, *STS* n.s. XXII. 156; Baildon, *Dunbar*, pp. 158-60; MacKenzie, *Dunbar*, pp. 23-4.

2227 1. Rylands Lib. Eng. 113 [*olim* Hodson 39], f. iv.
Furnivall, *EETS* 15 rev. ed. 289.

2228 Kingsford, *Eng. Hist. Lit.*, pp. 395-7; Robbins, *Hist. Poems*, pp. 184-6.

2229 Hoccleve's *De Regimine Principum*.
4. Bodl. 6533, ff. 1-99 (766 st. only); 39. *olim* Merton 28 [Breslauer Cat. 90, Item 24], f. 1a; 44. Rosenbach Foundation 1083/30 [*olim* Phillipps 1099], f. 1a; 45. Coventry Corp. Record Office, ff. 1-40.
30. Furnivall, *EETS* lxxii. 196-7 (Envoy only); 41. Furnivall, *EETS* lxi. 61 (Envoy only).

2231 Robbins, *Sec. Lyrics*, p. 148.

2231.3 Mi coloures byn both briʒt & shene
'ffor I am a brid of paradise'—one quatrain (with sketch of a bird).
1. Bodl. Lat. misc. c. 66 [*olim* Capesthorne], f. 95b.

2231.5   My darlyng dere my daysy floure
  The lover deceived, by John Skelton—four stanzas rime royal with couplet heading: 'With lullay lullay like a childe / Thou slepest too long thou art begiled.' [Utley 192].
  Dyuers Balettys, [? Pynson,] n.d. (STC 22604); Dyce, *Skelton,* I. 22-3; Dyce and Child, *Skelton & Donne,* I. 27-8; Henderson, *Skelton,* 1931, pp. 27-8; 1948, 1959, pp. 22-3; *Early Eng. Carols,* pp. 310-11; Pinto, *Selection,* p. 21 (extract); *Poets of Eng. Lang.,* I. 370-1; Davies, *Med. Eng. Lyrics,* pp. 267-8.

2231.8   My doȝter my derlyngge / Herkne my lore y-se my thechyng
  A recurring couplet in a Latin homily translating the text: *'Audi filia et vide'* (Ps. XLIV. 11). [Cf. 1260].
  1. Bodl. 1871, f. 193a *et passim.*
  Robbins, *MLN* LIII. 243; Pfander, *Pop. Sermon,* p. 46.

2232   Robbins, *Sec. Lyrics,* p. 145.

2233   [Cf. Brentano, *Bull. Univ. Kansas, Humanistic St.* V, 2. 48-9. Ascribed to Lydgate. Ringler 48].
  19. Stowe 982, f. 10a; 22. Leyden Univ. Vossius 9, f. 96b; 23. Nat. Lib. of Medicine 4, ff. 65a-66b.
  Lidgate, *Stans puer,* Caxton, ca. 1477 (STC 17030); *repr.* Dibdin, *Typo. Antiquities,* II. 222-4; 21. Coulton, *Social Life in Britain,* pp. 90-3.

2233.5   My dere frendes I you pray / four thingis in your hertis bere away
  Introductory couplet to *Quinta Tabula* in *Speculum Christiani.* [Ringler 49].
  For MSS. cf. 2167.
  Speculum Christiani, de Machlinia, ca. 1486 (STC 26012); *comp. text* Holmstedt, *EETS* 182. 75.

2235   [Delete: For Book II see 3154.]
  Girvan, *STS* 3 s. XI. 1-51.

  My dere sone where so ȝe fare by frith or by fele   See 4064.

2236   Kirke, *Reliquary* IX. 74 (extracts); Dickins and Wilson, *Early ME Texts,* pp. 121-2; Brook, *Harley Lyrics,* pp. 62-3; Kaiser, *Anthologie,* pp. 298-9; Kaiser, *Med. Eng.,* pp. 468-9; Davies, *Med. Eng. Lyrics,* pp. 59-62.

2236.5 My dely wo
        Title of a courtly love lyric mentioned in a bill of a music teacher ca. A.D. 1473-5.
        1. Public Record Office C 47 / 37 / 11, f. 4a.
        Hanham, *RES* n.s. VIII. 272.

2237   [Utley 194].

        My feerful dreme neuyr forgete can I
        Burden to 3750.

2238.5 My felowe for his sothe sawe / hathe loste hys lyfe and lythe ful lawe
        Riming comment of the second cock in the Story of the Three Cocks in the *Gesta Romanorum* —one couplet. [Cf. 3081 and 3322.3].
        1. Harley 5259, f. 60b; 2. Harley 7333, f. 180b; 3. BM Addit. 9066, f. 19b.
        2, 3. Herrtage, *EETS* xxxiii. 175; 1. Herbert, *Cat. Rom.*, III. 206.

2239   Coxe, *Cat.*, I. 97 (vv. 4 only).

2240   2. Davies, *Med. Eng. Lyrics*, pp. 125-6.

2241   thirteen stanzas of varying length, perhaps a proto-carol. [Cf. Robbins, *Anglia* LXXV. 196-7].
        1. BM Addit. 46919 [*olim* Phillipps 8336], f. 206a.

2242   [Cf. 1514].

2243   Arber, *Dunbar Anthology*, p. 122; Saltmarsh, *Antiquaries Journal* XV. 9; Robbins, *Sec. Lyrics*, pp. 183-4; Davies, *Med. Eng. Lyrics*, p. 183.

2244   [Utley 195].
        Early print, n.p., n.d.; *facs.* Beattie, *Edinb. Bibl. Soc.* 1950, p. 192; *repr.* Small, *STS* IV. 52; H. Browne, *Early Scot. Poets*, 1896, pp. 133-5; Pinkerton, *Poems from Scarce Editions*, 1792, III. 141-2; Sibbald, *Chronicle*, I. 358-9; Laing, *Knightly Tale of Golagros*, 1827; Stevenson, *STS* LXV. 262; Zupitza, *AE Uebungsbuch*, pp. 202-3; Neilson and Webster, *Chief British Poets*, pp. 397-8; MacKenzie, *Dunbar*, pp. 169-70; Kinsley, *Dunbar*, pp. 101-2; 1. Laing,

Dunbar, II. 35-6; *Bannatyne MS.*, Hunt. Club, III. 382-3; Schipper, *Dunbar*, pp. 70-2; and *DKAW* XL (II). 69-72; Ritchie, *STS* n.s. XXIII. 10-11.

2244.3   My heid did 3ak yester nicht
'On his heid-ake' by William Dunbar—three 5-line stanzas.
1. Camb. Un. Ll. 5. 10, f. 6a.
Laing, *Dunbar*, I. 128; *repr. Blackwood's Magazine*, Feb. 1835; Paterson, *Dunbar*, p. 163; Small, *STS* IV. 254; Schipper, *Dunbar*, p. 234; and *DKAW* XLI (IV). 35-6; Baildon, *Dunbar*, p. 113; Craigie, *STS* n.s. XX. 53; MacKenzie, *Dunbar*, p. 3; Kinsley, *Dunbar*, pp. 60-1.

2244.6   My herte ys yn grete mournyng
Dame Pitiless—four quatrains including refrain: 'My lady hath forsaken me.' [Cf. 2250.3].
1. BM Addit. 5665, f. 135b.
Fehr, *Archiv* CVI. 282; Stevens, *Music & Poetry*, p. 343.

My hert is set to syng   See 2784.5.

2245   Robbins, *Sec. Lyrics*, p. 151; Stevens, *Music & Poetry*, p. 124.

2245.1   My harte ys sore but yett noo forse
On the absence of his only mistress—nine quatrains. [vv. 9-12 = vv. 1-4 of 1120].
1. Bodl. 12653, f. 57b.
Padelford and Benham, *Anglia* XXXI. 376-7.

2245.3   My hart ys yowrs now kyp het fast
True love—five quatrains.
1. BM Addit. 18752, f. 59a.
Reed, *Anglia* XXXIII. 351.

2245.4   My harte ys yours ye may be sure / And so shall be
Faithful love—one couplet signed 'Bourscher Richard Daniel.'
1. Bodl. 6919, end cover.
Lauritis, Klinefelter, and Gallagher, *Life of Our Lady*, p. 40.

2245.6   My hart my mynde & my hole poure
A pledge of devotion to his lady—four stanzas rime royal.
1. BM Addit. 18752, f. 72a.

XX Songes, de Worde, 1530 (STC 22924); repr. Flügel, Anglia XII. 589; Flügel, Neuengl. Lesebuch, p. 146; Imelmann, Shakespeare-Jahrbuch XXXIX. 132; 1. Reed, Anglia XXXIII. 351.

My harte of golde as true as stele
Burden to 2250.8.

My harte was sett with true entente   See 79.5.

2246   Sauerstein, Charles d'Orléans, 1899, p. 65.

2247   [For a version in rime royal see 2182].
Furnivall, EETS 15 orig. ed. 40; rev. ed. 68.

Mi hartys lust & all my plesure   See 2182.6.

2247.5   My hartis treasure and swete assured fo
'To a Ladye quhone he list to feyne,' by William Dunbar—seven stanzas rime royal. [Utley 199].
1. Pepys 2553, p. 322.
Laing, Dunbar, I. 121; Paterson, Dunbar, pp. 182-4; Small, STS IV. 245-6; Schipper, Dunbar, pp. 118-9; and DKAW XL (IV). 27-8; Baildon, Dunbar, pp. 57-8; Craigie, STS n.s. VII. 386-7; MacKenzie, Dunbar, pp. 99-100.

2249   five cross-rimed quatrains.
1. Harley 3362, f. 90a; 2. BM Addit. 18752, f. 139a.
1. Ritson, Anc. Songs, 1829, II. 22; rev. Hazlitt, 1877, p. 166; 1, 2. Reed, Anglia XXXIII. 366-7.

2250   2. Bodl. 11272, f. 79b and again at f. 97b; 5. Pepys 2125, f. 99b; 6. BM Addit. 37790, f. 134b; 7. BM Addit. 22283, f. 151a; 8. Westminster School; 9. Longleat 29, f. 46a; 10. olim Gurney.
3. Allen, Eng. Writings of Rolle, p. 67; Comper, Life & Lyrics of Rolle, pp. 228-30.

2250.3   My Ladye hath forsaken me / that longe hathe ben her man
The forsaken lover—six cross-rimed quatrains followed by two couplets. [Cf. 2244.6 burden].
1. Bodl. 6659, f. 98a.
Wagner, MLN L. 452 (st. 1 only).

2250.5 My lady hath me in that grace
A devoted mistress—two cross-rimed quatrains and additional refrain: 'Why shall not I,' and a 4-line introductory burden.
1. BM Addit. 31922, f. 107b.
Flügel, *Anglia* XXII. 250-1; Flügel, *Neuengl. Lesebuch*, p. 137; Stevens, *Music & Poetry*, p. 419; Stevens, *Music at Court*, p. 79.

My lady is a prety on   See 3097.6.

My lady is unkynde I wis   See 13.8.

2250.8 My lady went to Caunterbury
A nonsense carol—eight quatrains and 4-line burden. [Cf. Ravenscroft, *Pammelia*, 1609. Utley 203].
Christmas Carolles, Kele, ca. 1550 (STC 5205); *facs.* Reed, *Xmas Carols*, pp. 38-40; *repr.* Husk, *Songs of Nativity*, p. 134; Bliss, *Bibl. Misc.*, p. 53; *Early Eng. Lyrics*, p. 254; Rickert, *Anc. Eng. Xmas Carols*, p. 143; *Oxford Book Light Verse*, p. 87; *Early Eng. Carols*, pp. 318-9.

2251 [Utley 201. For one st. occurring separately see 4091. Cf. Dodsley, *Old Plays*, 1827, XII. 308].
2. Bodl. 3896, f. 47a.
1, 2. Freudenberger, *Ragman Roll: Ein spätmittelenglisches Gedicht*, Erlangen 1909, pp. 2-16; 2. Wright, *Anec. Lit.*, 1844, pp. 83; Hazlitt, *Remains*, I. 69-78.

2253 1. Advocates 19. 2. 1, f. 317a (vv. 1136; slightly imperfect).

2254 Hinckley, *Notes on Chaucer*, Northampton, Mass., 1907, p. 130; Robinson, *Chaucer*, 1933, p. 859; 1957, p. 752; Robbins, *Sec. Lyrics*, p. 152; Davies, *Med. Eng. Lyrics*, p. 246.

My leue leuedi ne be þi wimpil neuere so þelu   See 2285.

2255.3 My lytell fole / Ys gon to play
His coy mistress—one short stanza with a 'How frisca Ioly' refrain.
1. Royal App. 58, f. 55b.
Flügel, *Anglia* XII. 272.

2255.6 My lytell prety one my prety bony one
A jolly wanton—four 5-line stanzas with refrain: 'nou doute she ys a loue of all that euer I see.' [Cf. 3097.6. Utley 204].
1. BM Addit. 4900, f. 62b; 2. BM Addit. 18752, f. 76b.
1. Chappell, *OE Pop. Music*, I. 71; 2. Hazlitt, *Remains*, IV. 234; Reed, *Anglia* XXXIII. 352.

*My lorde the it sente syr mordure   See 1993 (Douce fragment).

2257 Robbins, *Sec. Lyrics*, p. 93.

2258.5 My lordis of Chalker pleis ȝow to heir
'To the lordis of the kingis chalker,' by William Dunbar—four 5-line stanzas.
1. Camb. Un. Ll. 5. 10, f. 6a.
Laing, *Dunbar*, I. 109; Paterson, *Dunbar*, p. 181; Small, *STS* IV. 255; Schipper, *Dunbar*, p. 231; and *DKAW* XLI (IV). 32-2; Baildon, *Dunbar*, p. 111; Craigie, *STS* n.s. XX. 53-4; MacKenzie, *Dunbar*, pp. 50-1.

My loue is lusty plesant and demure   See 1214.7.

My luf mornes for me
Burden to 120.7.

My lufe murnis for me for me
Refrain-heading of 4094.3.

2261.2 My loue she morns ffor me
A fragment of a love song—one couplet. [Cf. 2261.4].
1. Trinity Camb. 1157, f. 24b.
Wilson, *Lost. Lit.*, p. 182.

2261.4 My love sche morneth / For me for me
Defend all true lovers—eleven 6-line tail-rime stanzas. [Cf. 2261.2 and 3706.8; for a religious adaptation cf. 4094.3].
1. BM Addit. 31922, f. 30b.
Flügel, *Anglia* XII. 233-5; Flügel, *Neuengl. Lesebuch*, pp. 133-4; Padelford, *Early XVI Cent. Lyrics*, pp. 80-3; Stevens, *Music & Poetry*, pp. 393-4; Stevens, *Music at Court*, p. 23.

2261.6   My loue so swyte / Iesu kype
            A true love banished—five 6-line tail-rime stanzas.
            1. Sloane 3501, f. 52b.
               Fehr, *Archiv* CVII. 52-3.

            My lovid to me is a sope of myrre
            Concluding erotic prayer to 1035.

2261.8   My loving frende amorous Bune
            A humorous letter from one young woman to another—twenty-three couplets. [Utley 206].
            1. Bodl. 12653, f. 6b.
               Padelford and Benham, *Anglia* XXXI. 320-1.

2262   [Utley 208. Ringler 50].
            1. Bodl. 3896, f. 193b; 2. Coventry Corp. Record Office, f. 75b.
               Mars and Venus, Notary, ca. 1500 (STC 5089); *repr. with* 1. Furnivall, *Parallel Texts MP,* Chaucer Soc., pp. 424-5; 1. Robinson, *Chaucer,* 1933, p. 635; 1957, p. 539.

2262.3   My mayster ys cruell and can no curtesye
            The Five Dogs of London—five quatrains (each with a proverbial heading: cf. 3987) and concluding couplet.
            1. Trinity Dublin 516, f. 22b.
               Robbins, *PMLA* LXXI. 266-8; Robbins, *Hist. Poems,* pp. 189-90.

2262.5   Mi mind is mukel on on þat wil me nost amende
            Lament of a lover—one couplet with medial rime, with illustration showing Gawain and wife of Green Knight.
            1. Cotton Nero A. ix, f. 125a.
               Madden, *Syr Gawayne,* p. 1; *and facs.,* p. 45; *facs.* Gollancz, *EETS* 162.

2263   1. Bodl. Lat. misc. c. 66 [*olim* Capesthorne], f. 94b.
               Robbins, *PMLA* LXV. 274.

2263.5   My name is Parott a byrde of paradyse
            'Speke, Parrot,' by John Skelton—vv. 511 chiefly in rime royal stanzas, and with repeated Envoys [cf. 3318.4].
            1. Harley 2252, ff. 134a-140a.
               Certayne Bokes, Lant, n. d.; *repr. with* 1. Dyce, *Skelton,*

II. 1-25; Dyce and Child, *Skelton & Donne*, II. 245-75; Henderson, *Skelton*, 1931, pp. 259-81; 1949, 1959, pp. 288-307; Hughes, *Skelton*, pp. 1-6. 140-3; Pinto, *Selection*, pp. 98-103 (extracts); Kynge and Marche, n.d.; Day, n.d.; *Workes*, Marshe, 1568 (STC 22608); *repr.* [? J. Bowle,] 1736; Chalmers, *English Poets*, II. 258-60.

2264 [Cf. 3348. Ringler 51].
4. Harley 367, f. 86b (st. 1 only).
Temple of Bras, Caxton, ca. 1478 (STC 5091); *Chaucer*, Thynne, 1532 (STC 5068); *repr.* Skeat, *Oxf. Ch.*, VII. 237-44; *Chaucer*, Stow, 1561 (STC 5075); *Chaucer*, Speght, 1598 (STC 5077); Urry, *Chaucer*, 1721, p. 546; Bell, *Poets of Great Britain*, XIII. 159; Chalmers, *English Poets*, I.552.

2267 1. Camb. Un. Ll. 5. 10, f. 2b.
Schipper, *Dunbar*, pp. 33-4; and *DKAW* XL (II). 33-4; Laing, *Dunbar*, I. 91; Paterson, *Dunbar*, pp. 134-5; Baildon, *Dunbar*, p. 1; Craigie, *STS* n.s. XX. 44-5; MacKenzie, *Dunbar*, p. 51; Robbins, *Sec. Lyrics*, p. 91.

My propir Besse / My praty Besse   See 2263.5.

2267.5 My ryght good lord most knyghtly gentyll knyght
A letter to her absent lord from his devoted mistress—eight stanzas rime royal in the Paston Letters, No. 870.
1. BM Addit. 43491, ff. 27a-b.
Fenn, II. 304; Gairdner, III. 302-3.

2268 Four half-erased lines of verse on the absence of his mistress.

2270 2. Bodl. 11272, f. 98b; 5. Pepys 2125, f. 99b; 6. BM Addit. 22283, f. 151a; 7. BM Addit. 37790, f. 135a; 8. Westminster School; 9. *olim* Gurney; 10. Longleat 29, f. 47a; 11. Paris; Bibl. Mazarine 514.
3. Allen, *Eng. Writings of Rolle*, p. 70; Comper, *Life & Lyrics of Rolle*, pp. 231-4; Kaiser, *Anthologie*, p. 171; Kaiser, *Med. Eng.*, p. 203; Davies, *Med. Eng. Lyrics*, pp. 108-10.

2271 thirteen 8-line stanzas.

2271.2 My soverayne lorde for my poure sake
A lady rejoices at her lover in a chivalric tournament,

perhaps with reference to Henry VIII—six 6-line stanzas with burden.
1. BM Addit. 31922, f. 54b.
Chappell, *Archaeologia* XLI. 378-9; Flügel, *Anglia* XII. 242; Padelford, *Early XVI Cent. Lyrics*, p. 90; Stevens, *Music & Poetry*, pp. 405-6; Stevens, *Music at Court*, p. 40.

2271.4   My soverayn saveoure to þe I calle
'þe prayere of þe pilgryme þat he sayes afore his deth:' poem occurring in only this MS. of Eng. tr. of the *Pèlerinage de la vie*—twelve stanzas rime royal.
1. Melbourne: Victoria Pub. Lib., f. 94a.

2271.6   My swetharte & my lyllye floure
A commendation to his mistress—eight cross-rimed quatrains.
1. Bodl. 12653, f. 4a.
Padelford and Benham, *Anglia* XXXI. 316-7.

2272.5   My thought oppressed my mynd in trouble
A lament of a rejected love, without time for pleasure—four stanzas rime royal.
1. BM Addit. 31922, f. 116b.
Flügel, *Anglia* XII. 253-4; Stevens, *Music & Poetry*, p. 422; Stevens, *Music at Court*, pp. 86-9.

2273   [St. 5 occurs separately in Rolle's *Meditations on the Passion:* see 918.5].
Allen, *Eng. Writings of Rolle*, p. 133; *Oxford Book Christian Verse*, p. 1; Comper, *Life & Lyrics of Rolle*, pp. 275-7; Williams, *New Book Eng. Verse*, p. 27.

2277   Burney, *Hist. Music*, 1782, II. 544-5; Stevens, *Music & Poetry*, p. 353.

2277.3   My wofull hairt me stoundis throw þe vanis
Christ describes his crucifixion, by [?Jhon] Clerk—eleven 8-line stanzas with refrain: '*Benedicta sit sancta Trinitas.*'
1. Advocates 1. 1. 6, f. 31a.
Bannatyne MS., Hunt. Club, II. 82-4; Ritchie, *STS* n.s. XXII. 77-9.

2277.5　　　My wofull hert of all gladnesse baryeyne
　　　　　　A complaint against his obdurate mistress—two 8-line stanzas.
　　　　　　　1. BM Addit. 5665, f. 65b.
　　　　　　　　Fehr, *Archiv* CVI. 279; Stevens, *Music & Poetry*, p. 339.

2277.8　　　My whofull herte plonged yn heuynesse
　　　　　　A complaint against his mistress—two stanzas rime royal (following 3613).
　　　　　　　1. Camb. Un. Ff. 1. 6, f. 153a.
　　　　　　　　Robbins, *PMLA* LXIX. 638.

2279　　　　A love song of a mistress for her absent lover—seven 3-line stanzas.
　　　　　　　Robbins, *PMLA* LXIX. 633-4.

2281　　　　1. Bodl. Lat. misc. c. 66 [*olim* Capesthorne], f. 92b.
　　　　　　　Robbins, *PMLA* LXV. 260-2.

2281.5　　　My yeris be yong even as ye see
　　　　　　A girl's expression of love by Thomas Wyatt—six 5-line stanzas including refrain: 'Yf yt ware not,' and 2-line burden.
　　　　　　　1. BM Addit. 17492, f. 78b.
　　　　　　　　Foxwell, *Poems*, I. 325; *Early Eng. Carols*, pp. 314-5; Muir, *Wyatt*, p. 136.

2282　　　　York, *MLN* LXXII. 484-5; Bowers, *Shakespeare Qr.* III. 110-1.

2284　　　　Förster, *Archiv* CI. 48.

*2284.3　　*.. nature y-sette in sowr ymage
　　　　　　In praise of his mistress—fragment of one stanza rime royal.
　　　　　　　1. Trinity Dublin 662, p. 174 (page mutilated, leaving ends of lines only).

*2284.5　　*Nauueþ my saule bute fur and ys
　　　　　　May the Lord preserve us—last ten lines of a religious poem.
　　　　　　　1. Jesus Oxf. 29, Part II, f. 189a.
　　　　　　　　Morris, *EETS* 49. 100-1; Segar, *Med. Anthology*, p. 37.

Nay mary nay mary I Peter
Burden to 1540.5.

Nay nay Ive it may not be iwis
Burden to 1226.

2284.8 Ne bee þe day neuere so longe / euere comeþe euensong
A couplet in a Latin sermon. [Cf. 2662, I. 578; 4004, vv. 5479-80; Heywood's *Prouerbes*].
1. Merton Oxf. 248, f. 146b.

2285 [Utley 211].
2. Trinity Camb. 43, f. 24a.
1. *Rel. Ant.*, II. 15; Wright, *Piers Plowman*, 1856, p. 552;
2. Förster, *Archiv* CIV. 304.

2287 Robbins, *Hist. Poems*, p. 24.

2288 [Possibly scraps of three unrelated love songs].
[Delete: Floyer and Hamilton, *Cat.*, 1906, p. 30.] Wilson, *Lost Lit.*, p. 177; Robbins, *Sec. Lyrics*, p. xl; C. Sisam, *N&Q* CCX. 245.

Ne no thyng ys to man so dere
An extract from *Handlynge Synne* in praise of women [Utley 212]: see 778.

2288.5 Ne sey neruer such a man a Iordan was / and wente he to gogeshale panyles
Fragment of a song, considerably mutilated.
1. Bodl. 13679, Item I (d).
Heuser, *Anglia* XXX. 174; Dronke, *N&Q* n.s. VIII. 245.

*2288.8 *Ne thurst men neuer in londe / After fairer children
Floris and Blaunchefur — in couplets.
1. Camb. Un. Gg. 4. 27, Part II, p. 1 (vv. 824); 2. Cotton Vitellius D. iii. f. 6a (vv. 451); 3. Egerton 2862 [*olim* Trentham Hall], f. 98a (vv. 1083); 4. Advocates 19. 2. 1, f. 100a (vv. 861).

1, 2. Lumby, rev. McKnight, EETS 14. 51-74, 101-14; 3, 4. A. B. Taylor, Oxford 1927; 3. French and Hale, *ME Met. Rom.*, pp. 824; 4. Hartshorne, *Anc. Met. Tales*, pp. 81; Laing, *A Penni Worth of Witte*, Abbotsford Club

1857, pp. 15-44; crit. text. Hausknecht, *Samml. Eng. Denkmäler* V, Berlin 1885 (vv. 1296).

2289   Sauerstein, *Charles d'Orléans*, 1899, p. 65.

2289.3   Nede not y loue wher men loue me
         Three little songs: of love, of sorrow, of joy—three short cross-rimed quatrains in a Latin sermon.
         1. Arras: Bibl. de la Ville 184, f. 1b.
         Friend, *PMLA* LXIX. 984.

Ner hope harte wolde breste   See 1251.5.

2289.5   Neuere to ʒelden & euere to crauen / Maket man fewe frendis to hauen
         De beneficiis—one couplet.
         1. Advocates 18. 7. 21, f. 32b.

Newes newes
     Burden to 102.3.

2289.8   Nixt that a turnament wes tryid
         'The Justis betuix the tailyeour and sowtar,' by William Dunbar—nine 12-line tail-rime stanzas. [Cf. 515.5].
         1. Pepys 2553, pp. 162-5 (prefixed by vv. 1-12, 109-120 of 2623.3); 2. Advocates 1. 1. 6, f. 111a; 3. Asloan, f. 210a; 3a (xix cent. transcript). Edinburgh Univ. La. III. 450/1.
         1. Craigie, *STS* n.s. VII. 184-7; 2. Ramsay, *Evergreen*, I. 247-53; *Bannatyne MS.*, Hunt. Club, II. 316-9; Small, *STS* IV. 122-6; Ritchie, *STS* n.s. XXII. 295-8; MacKenzie, *Dunbar*, pp. 123-6; Kinsley, *Dunbar*, pp. 53-7; 3a. Laing, *Dunbar*, I. 54-8; Paterson, *Dunbar*, pp. 214-8; Schipper, *Dunbar*, pp. 134-8; and *DKAW* XL (IV). 43-8; Baildon, *Dunbar*, pp. 67-70.

2290   [Cf. 4166.5. Utley 213].
         Kaiser, *Anthologie*, p. 462; Bowers, *MLN* LXXIII. 328-9.

No catell no care *leticia*   See 3209.

2290.5   No [ew]yll wyll do and do no mys / Fle fro evyll felyschip
         Flee evil—one couplet.
         1. Jesus Camb. 59, f. 151b.
         James, *Cat.*, p. 94.

2291.5 No kinde of labore is a thing of shame
Not work, but idleness is blameworthy—one couplet.
1. Durham Univ. Cosin V. iii. 9, f. 61a (repeated at f. 69b).
Furnivall, *EETS* lxi. 192, 205.

Noo man is wrechched but him self yt were
La response du ffortune au pleintif   See 3661.

2292   1. Bodl. 21876, f. 35a.

2293 No more ne will i wiked be
Dickins and Wilson, *Early ME Texts*, pp. 130-1; Kaiser, *Anthologie*, p. 277; Kaiser, *Med. Eng.*, p. 294.

2293.5 No wondre thow I murnyng make
Sore I sigh—seven quatrains with refrain: 'alone I lyue alone' and 2-line burden. [Cf. burden alone 266.5. Cf. also 377.5 and 266.3].
1. Public Record Office, Excheq. Misc. 22 / 1 / 1, recto.
Saltmarsh, *Antiquaries Journal* XV. 12-16; Saltmarsh, *Two Med. Lyrics*, Cambridge 1933; Robbins, *Sec. Lyrics*, pp. 154-5.

Noble Markis youre humanyte   See O Noble Markis.

2293.6 Nobles report your matynis in this buke
Five riming lines at end of 'Porteus of Noblenes.'
Chepman and Myllar, 1508 (STC 20120); *facs.* Beattie, *Edinb. Bibl. Soc.* 1950, p. 5; *repr.* Stevenson, *STS* LXV. 68.

2293.8 Non sigheth so sore / as þe gloton that mai no more
A proverbial couplet.
1. Balliol 354, f. 191b.
Dyboski, *EETS* ci. 129.

2294   Taylor, *Roxburghe Club* XLIV. 161-2.

2296   Searle, *Chronicle of John Stone*, Cambridge Antiq. Soc. Pub., Octavo Series, XXXIV. 100.

2297   1. Durham Univ. Cosin V. ii. 13, ff. 112b-113a.

2300.3   Noghte to lyke þow me to lake / For this schrowyll byhynd my bake
           A colophon at the end of a nineteen foot prayer roll written by Percival, Premonstratensian Canon at Coverham Abbey, Yorkshire—ten couplets.
           1. Glazier G. 39.
              Legge, *Antiquary* X. 111; Bühler, *Speculum* XXXIX. 278.

           Nova nova Aue fit ex Eua
           Burden to 889.

2300.6   Now all men mowe sen be me / That wordys Joye is vanyte
           Six couplets on worms' meat.
           1. Worcester Cath. F. 10, f. 208a.
              Owst, *Lit. & Pulpit*, p. 530.

2300.8   Now Barbara the spouse of criste that moche art of myght
           Colophon to ME prose life of St. Barbara—four monoriming lines.
           1. Durham Univ. Cosin V. iv. 4, f. 76a.

2302   1. Ellis, *Specimens*, 1803, I. 265-8; Brandl and Zippel, *ME Sprach- u. Literatur.*, pp. 144-5.

2304   14. Winchester Coll. 33, f. 48a; 15. Public Record Office, C. 47 / 34 / 1, No. 5, f. 1a (opening couplet cut off at top).
           7. Zupitza, *Anglia* I. 393 (vv.1-16, 57-68); D'Evelyn and Mill, *EETS* 235.1

2305   Emerson, *ME Reader*, pp. 8-13 (extracts); Hall, *Early Middle English*, pp. 112-7 (extracts).

2306   1. Longleat 30, f. 19a.

2306.5   Now culit is Dame Venus brand
           'Of luve erdly and divine,' by William Dunbar—fifteen quatrains each with 2-line refrain. [Utley 215].
           1. Advocates 1. 1. 6, f. 284b.
              [Hailes,] *Anc. Scot. Poems*, pp. 100-3; Sibbald, *Chronicle*, II. 20-3; *Sel. Poems of Dunbar*, Perth 1788, pp. 83-6; Laing, *Dunbar*, I. 221-4; Paterson, *Dunbar*, pp. 303-6; *Bannatyne MS.*, Hunt. Club, IV. 826-9; Small, *STS* IV.

179-82; Schipper, *Dunbar*, pp. 351-3; and *DKAW* XLII (IV). 49-51; Baildon, *Dunbar*, pp. 182-5; Ritchie, *STS* n.s. XXVI. 91-4; MacKenzie, *Dunbar*, pp. 101-4; Kinsley, *Dunbar*, pp. 68-9 (extract).

2307.5 Now do I know you chaungyd thought
A rebuke to his 'newfangled' mistress—six quatrains. [Utley 217.].
1. BM Addit. 18752, f. 77b and f. 139b.
1a & b. Reed, *Anglia* XXXIII. 353, 368.

2308.3 Nowe everyman in hys begynnyng / Thanke his God
'The working of the phylozophers stone'—vv. 169.
1. Massachusetts Hist. Soc., Winthrop 20 c, ff. 157b-158b.

2308.5 Now fayre fayrest off euery fayre
To the Princess Margaret on her arrival at Holyrood, A.D. 1503, by William Dunbar—seventeen lines.
1. Royal App. 58, f. 17b.
Hawkins, *Hist. Music*, 1776, III. 32; repr. Strickland, *Queens of Scotland*, I. 58; Burney, *Hist. Music*, III. 32; Rimbault, *Songs & Ballads*, p. 27; Laing, *Dunbar*, I (Suppl.) 280; Small, *STS* IV. 279; Schipper, *Dunbar*, p. 92; and *DKAW* XL (IV). 1-2; Flügel, *Anglia* XII. 265-6; Flügel, *Neuengl. Lesebuch*, p. 160; Baildon, *Dunbar*, p. 38; MacKenzie, *Dunbar*, pp. 178-9.

2308.8 Now fayreste of stature formyd by nature
The lover's appeal to his mistress for mercy—four stanzas rime royal (following 751).
1. Cotton Vesp. D. ix, f. 188b.
Robbins, *Sec. Lyrics*, pp. 201-2.

2309 94 stanzas rime royal with inserted 'bill of complaynt' of seven 8-line stanzas.
Gentleman's Magazine, May 1842, pp. 468-70 (extracts).

2311 A heartless mistress—thirteen quatrains.
Robbins, *Sec. Lyrics*, pp. 139-41.

2312.5 Now glaidith euery liffis creature
'Of the Nativitie of Christ,' attributed to William Dunbar—five 8-line stanzas with refrain.
1. Advocates 1. 1. 6, f. 27a.

Laing, *Dunbar*, II. 55-6; *Bannatyne MS.*, Hunt. Club, II. 67-8; Small, *STS* IV. 324-5; Schipper, *Dunbar*, pp. 448-50; and *DKAW* XLIII (I). 60-2; Baildon, *Dunbar*, pp. 233-4; Ritchie, *STS* n.s. XXII. 63-6.

2315   Rickert, *Anc. Eng. Xmas Carols*, pp. 204-5; Stevens, *Med. Carols*, p. 7; Robbins, *Early Eng. Xmas Carols*, p. 22.

2317   Wright, *Polit. Poems*, II. 238-42.

2318   To his mistress—one stanza rime royal with introductory couplet: 'O penful harte that lyes in travvail / And in tene luk vp merely for somer hit schall.' [Actually an extract from Hawes' *Pastime of Pleasure* (4004), vv. 2542-8 occurring separately. For a longer extract which includes this same stanza, see 2532.5).

1. Hunterian Mus. 230, f. 246b.
Robbins, *Sec. Lyrics*, p. 152.

2319   1. D'Evelyn, *Peter Idley's Instructions*, p. 216.

2320   [The English quatrain does not occur in the following MSS.: A (French). Royal 20. B. xlv; B (Latin). Royal 5. C. iii; Royal 7. A. i; C (English). Harley 3490; Harley 4012; Harley 5441].

A. Old French Texts:
15. Pembroke Camb. 258, f. 129a; 16. *olim* George Smith [*olim* Harmsworth Sale, Oct. 1945, Lot 2018] (Sotheby Sale, Feb. 2, 1960, Lot 317), Art. 2.

1, 3. *Eng. Lyr. XIII C.*, pp. 1, 166; 1, 3, 6, 10, 11, 12. *Register*, I. 17, 45, 139, 310, 363, 446; 1. H. W. Robbins, *La Merure de Seinte Eglise*, p. 63; Onions, *Med. Aevum* XVII. 33; Mossé, *Handbook*, p. 202; 2. Wilson, *Early ME Lit.*, p. 266; Cutler, *Explicator* IV, No. 1, p. 7; Kaiser, *Anthologie*, p. 178; Kaiser, *Med. Eng.*, p. 214; 3. Whiting, *Speculum* IX. 221; Davies, *Med. Eng. Lyrics*, p. 54; 7. Mustanoja, *How the Good Wife*, p. 93.

B. Latin Texts:
16. Camb. Un. Mm. 6. 17, f. 28b.

1, 3, 5, 7, 8, 12, 13, 14, 15. *Register*, I. 11, 23, 93, 146, 181, 376, 394, 410, 452.

C. English Texts:
8. BM Addit. 22283; 9. NLW Peniarth 395, p. 344; 10. Longleat 32.

2, 4, 7. *Register*, I. 40, 118, 387.

2321 1. Bodl. 20552 (a transcript of four plays from MS. 2).

2322 Botzenmayer, *Heroic Deeds* & *Knightly Adventures*, Westermann Texte, Englische Reihe, No. 129.

2323.3 Now has Mary born a flour / all þis world to gret honour
A song to the B.V.—two fragmentary stanzas.
1. BM Addit., 5666, f. 3a.

Now haue y told ȝow þow y it ȝelpe
Unique lines in the Bühler MS. of 1408.

2323.5 Now haw y vryt alle / ȝyf me drynk of gode ale
English couplet translating common Latin colophon: '*Nunc scripsi totum pro christo da michi potum*' (preceding).
1. Wellcome Hist. Med. Lib. 405, f. 66b.
Moorat, *Cat.*, I. 273.

Now hertely ye bee welcome into this hal   See 3563.5.

2323.8 Now helpe fortune of thy godenesse
A plea to Fortune for success in love—four lines.
1. BM Addit. 5665, f. 71b.
Fehr, *Archiv* CVI. 280; Stevens, *Music* & *Poetry*, p. 341.

2325.5 Now holde him silf from loue let se þat may
A roundel, translated from the French of Charles d'Orleans (Champollion-Figeac, p. 26).
1. Harley 682, f. 61b.
Taylor, *Roxburghe Club* XLIV. 138; Steele, *EETS* 215. 106.

Now I haue declared þowe þis
Prologue (Trinity Camb. 600) to 970.

2329 5. Foster, *Essays* & *Studies in Honor of Carleton Brown*, p. 151.

Nv yh she blostme sprynge   See 3963.

2330 fifty-three couplets. [Singer 803. Cf. 1931.5].
Ashmole, *Theatrum Chemicum*, pp. 344-47.

2331 Now ich wille þet ye ywyte hou hit is y-went
[Cf. 3579].
1. Arundel 57, f. 94a.
Stevenson, *Roxburghe Club* LXXII. 211; Baugh, *Hist. Eng. Language,* 1935, p. 480; 1957, p. 476; Mossé, *Handbook,* p. 221; Brandl and Zippel, *ME Sprach- u. Literatur.,* p. 237; Kaiser, *Anthologie,* p. 166; Kaiser, *Med. Eng.,* p. 198.

2332 Kele, repr. Bramley and Stainer, *Xmas Carols,* no. xxxii; Wright, *Percy Soc.* IV. 58; Sandys, *Christmastide,* p. 232; Husk, *Songs of Nativity,* p. 54; Bullen, *Carols & Poems,* pp. 10-11; Rickert, *Anc. Eng. Xmas Carols,* p. 104; 1. Greene, *Sel. Eng. Carols,* p. 72.

Now in the name of our lord ihesus
Clopton Church extracts of Lydgate's *Testament:* see 2464.

Now yn this medow fayre and grene   See 2034.5.

2333 Husk, *Songs,* p. 179; Bullen, *Carols & Poems,* pp. 250-1; Rickert, *Anc. Eng. Xmas Ca ͻls,* pp. 110-2.

2334 Schulz, *Huntington Lib. Bull.* No. 6, pp. 165-7.

2335 1. Corp. Christi Oxf. 237, f. 243b (vv. 16).
2. Robbins, *Hist. Poems,* pp. 149-50.

2336 Davies, *Med. Eng. Lyrics,* pp. 73-4.

2338 fifteen couplets.
Bentley, *Excerpta Historica,* pp. 279-80; Robbins, *Hist. Poems,* pp. 186-7.

Now is the Rose of Rone growen to a gret honoure
Burden to 1380.

2339 1. Sylvester, *Garland of Xmas Carols,* p. 9; 2. James and Macaulay, *MLR* VIII. 77-9; 3. Rickert, *Anc. Eng. Xmas Carols,* pp. 112-5.

2341 Patterson, *JEGP* XX. 274-5.

2342 Rickert, *Anc. Eng. Xmas Carols,* pp. 172-3.

2343   [Dated Oct. 4, 1500].
Robbins, *Sec. Lyrics*, pp. 3-4; Greene, *Sel. Eng. Carols*, p. 57.

2345   3. Glazier G. 9, Art 2 [*olim* Berkeley].

2346   Rickert, *Anc. Eng. Xmas Carols*, p. 243; Greene, *Sel. Eng. Carols*, p. 66.

[Now know I t]hat reson in the fayleth
Cecil fragment of 3327.

Now knoweth ȝe alle that ben here
See 4184 (Rylands Lib. MS.).

2348   1. Harley 2942, f. 4a.
Robbins, *American N&Q* II. 148.

Now let vss talke of Mount of Flodden   See 1011.5.

2349.3   Now lythis off ane gentill knycht
Of Sir Thomas Norray, by William Dunbar—nine 6-line tail-rime stanzas.
1. Camb. Un. Ll. 5. 10, f. 8a; 2. Pepys 2553, pp. 3-5.
    2. Pinkerton, *Anc. Scot. Poems*, II. 359-61; Laing, *Dunbar*, I. 124; Paterson, *Dunbar*, p. 170; Small, *STS* IV. 192; Schipper, *Dunbar*, pp. 204-5; and *DKAW* XLI (IV). 4-7; Baildon, *Dunbar*, pp. 96-7; Craigie, *STS* n.s. VII. 2-4; MacKenzie, *Dunbar*, pp. 63-4; Kinsley, *Dunbar*, pp. 85-7.

Nowe Lorde Iesu I crye þee nowe mercy
Concluding couplet to a series of proverbs: see 299.5.

2349.5   Now lufferis cummis with larges lowd
'The Petition of the Gray Horse, Auld Dunbar,' by William Dunbar—eleven 6-line stanzas with 2-line refrain, and a concluding '*Responsio Regis*' in four couplets.
1. Camb. Un. Ll. 5. 10, ff. la, lb, 14a (vv. 55-66, 1-24, 67-74, 25-53); 2. Pepys 2553, p. 18 (vv. 23-54 only); 3. Harley 1703, f. 79b.
    1. Schipper, *Dunbar*, pp. 274-7; and *DKAW* XLI (IV). 76-9; Baildon, *Dunbar*, pp. 139-41; Craigie, *STS* n.s. XX.

40-1; 2. Pinkerton, *Anc. Scot. Poems*, I. 112; Sibbald, *Chronicle*, I. 339-40 (extracts); Craigie, *STS* n.s. VII. 19-20; 3. MacCracken, *MLN* XXIV. 110-11; *comp. text*. Laing, *Dunbar*, I. 149-51; *repr. Blackwood's Magazine*, Feb. 1835; Eyre-Todd, *Med. Scot. Poetry*, pp. 208-10. Paterson, *Dunbar*, pp. 282-5; Small, *STS* IV. 215-7; MacKenzie, *Dunbar*, pp. 46-8; Kinsley, *Dunbar*, pp. 94-6.

Now make we merthe al & sum
Burden to 2316.

2349.8   Now man behald þis warldis vaniteis
Moralizing verses on the inevitability of death—five quatrains.
1. Pepys 2553, p. 326.
Craigie, *STS* n.s. VII. 393.

Now may we myrthis make   See 2377.

Now marcy Jhesu I wyll amend
Burden to 2272.

Now of a prophete I will ȝow tellen þat was called ȝakarye See 574.

Nowe of this matter to you most cleere   See 2666.

2354.3   Now of wemen this I say for me
'In prais of wemen,' by William Dunbar—vv. 34 in couplets. [Utley 219].
1. Pepys 2553, pp. 294-5; 2. Advocates 1. 1. 6, f. 278b.
1. Craigie, *STS* n.s. VII. 345; 2. Laing, *Dunbar*, I. 95-6; Paterson, *Dunbar*, pp. 138-9; *Bannatyne MS.*, Hunt. Club, IV. 809-10; Small, *STS* IV. 170-1; Schipper, *Dunbar*, pp. 77-8; and *DKAW* XL (II). 76-8; Baildon, *Dunbar*, pp. 28-9; Ritchie, *STS* n.s. XXVI. 75-6; MacKenzie, *Dunbar*, pp. 83-4.

2354.5   Nowe or ever I begynne / I will tell right by and by
A short alchemical poem (not in Ashmole, *Theatrum Chemicum*)—ten long lines.
1. Bodl. 7625, p. 19.

2356 [Variant of 1791].
Robbins, *Hist. Poems*, p. xliii.

Now raygneth pride in price   See 1791.

2358.5 Now shall youe her a tale fore youre dysport
The Gossips' Meeting—in quatrains with refrain: 'Good gosyp.' [For a version in 6-line stanzas see 1362. Utley 107].
1a. Cotton Vitellius D. xi, f. 43b (st. 1-6); 1b. Cotton Titus A. xxvi, f. 161a (st. 7-26).
1a. Robbins, *British Mus. Qr.* XXVII. 12-13; 1b. *Ritson, Anc. Songs*, 1790, p. 77; 1829, I. 136-40; Wright, *Carols*, Percy Soc. XXIII. 104-7; Dyboski, *EETS* ci. 187-8; Arber, *Dunbar Anthology*, pp. 108-12; Flügel, *Anglia* XXVI. 213-5; J. E. Masters, *The Gossips*, Shaftesbury 1926; *Early Eng. Carols*, pp. 283-4.

2359 Segar, *Med. Anthology*, pp. 63-4 (5 st. only); Brook, *Harley Lyrics*, pp. 60-2; Kaiser, *Med. Eng.*, pp. 288-9 (5 st. only); Davies, *Med. Eng. Lyrics*, pp. 69-71.

Now synge we as we were wont / Uexilla regis prodeunt
Burden to 1119 (Kele text).

2360 An English version of a French proclamation from a mystery play—vv. 22 in short couplets.
Robbins, *MLN* LXV. 32.

Now seth that prynce is gone of excellence
Dedication to Henry VI in Hardyng's *Chronicle:* See 710.

2361 [Cf. 3254.5, 3255.5, 4187.5].
1. Sloane 1986, ff. 27a-56b.

2361.5 Now þe bok takeþ on honde / Wales to fore Engelonde
'Of the londe of Wales,' a verse description of Wales in Trevisa's translation of Higden's *Polychronicon* (Book I, Cap. 38)—vv. 460 in doggerel couplets. [Cf. 1637.6. Ringler 52].
1. St. John's Camb. 204, ff. 60b-63b; 2. Cotton Tiberius D. viii; 3. Harley 1900; 4. Stowe 65; 5. BM Addit. 24194; 6. Aberdeen Univ. 21, f. 37a; 7. Chetham Lib. 11379; 8. Hunterian Mus. 83; 9. Penrose 12; 10. Morgan Lib. M. 875.

Trevisa, *Discripcion of Britayne*, Caxton, 1480 (STC 13440a); *repr.* Dibdin, *Typo. Antiquities*, I. 146-8 (vv. 83-114, 125-50, 183-8); de Worde, 1498 (STC 13440b); Trevisa, *Prolicronycon*, Caxton, 1482 (STC 13438); *repr.* Wright, *Poems of Walter Mapes*, Camden Soc. XVI. 345-55; de Worde, 1495 (STC 13439); Treveris, 1527 (STC 13440); 1. Babington and Lumby, *Rolls Series* XLI, i. 395-431 (odd pages); Berdan, *Early Tudor Poetry*, pp. 169-70 (extracts).

2363 1. Trinity Dublin 652, ff. 338a-356.
Adams, *Chief Pre-Sh. Dramas*, pp. 243-62.

2364 6. Harley 78, f. 30a.
2. Robbins, *Sec. Lyrics*, p. 101; 5. Fehr, *Archiv* CVI. 54; Fehr, *Archiv* CIX. 71; Stevens, *Music & Poetry*, p. 356.

2370 Stevens, *Med. Carols*, p. 93.

2371 2. Yale Univ. 163 [*olim* Wagstaff 9, *olim* Petworth 8], f. 29a (last four lines only).
2. *Register*, I. 477.

2372 about 200 long irregular lines, sometimes falling into prose, interspersed with Latin.
1. St. John's Oxf. 94, ff. 149a-151a.

2374 [Cf. 2504].

2375 thirteen lines.
2. Camb. Un. Gg. 4. 27, I a, f. 490b; 3. Bodl. 1782, f. 51b (fragment: vv. 7).
2. Skeat, *Oxf. Ch.*, I. 359; *Early Eng. Lyrics*, p. 20; Robinson, *Chaucer*, 1933, p. 362; 1957, p. 318; Davies, *Med. Eng. Lyrics*, pp. 132-3.

2376 [Cf. st. 5 of 356].
[Delete: *Robbins*, MLN XLIII].

2377 1, 2. Stevens, *Med. Carols*, pp. 14, 94; 1. Robbins, *Early Eng. Xmas Carols*, p. 20; 2. Rickert, *Anc. Eng. Xmas Carols*, p. 177; 3. Greene, *Sel. Eng. Carols*, p. 60.

Nowe will ye be mery & can ye be merye
Burden to 3530.5.

Now will you be merye And can you be merye
Burden to 2668.8.

Now witeþ alle þat been here   See 4184.

2380   thirty irregular riming lines.
Calderhead, *MP* XIV. 7-8; Robbins, *Eng. Studies* XXX. 134-6.

2381   1. Copley, *Seven Eng. Songs*, 1940, No. 3; Robbins, *Sec. Lyrics*, pp. 159-60; Kaiser, *Anthologie*, p. 299; Kaiser, *Med. Eng.*, p. 468; Davies, *Med. Eng. Lyrics*, pp. 178-9; 2. Mason, *Humanism & Poetry*, pp. 169-70.

2382   Furnivall, *EETS* 15 orig. ed. 225; rev. ed. 254.

2383   Furnivall, *EETS* 15 orig. ed. 48-51; rev. ed. 76-9; Wülcker, *AE Lesebuch*, II. 124.

2384   Rickert, *Anc. Eng. Xmas Carols*, pp. 28-9.

Newell Newell newell newell / Thys ys þe songe of Angell Gabryell
Burden to 3736 (Hillwood MS.).

Nowell nowell nowell nowell / This sayd the aungell Gabryell
Burden to 1984.5.

Nowell nowell nowell nowell / Who ys there that syngith so
Burden to 681.

2384.3   O Albeon of all landes to behold
Metrical prophecy on England—in couplets.
1. Bodl. 13814, f. 119a.

2384.5   O altitude of alle science
Song at Allhallows: poem occurring in only this MS. of Eng. tr. of the *Pèlerinage de l'Ame*—five stanzas rime royal.
1. Melbourne: Victoria Pub. Lib., f. 194b.

2384.8   O beauteous braunche floure of formosyte
To his mistress—eight stanzas rime royal.
1. Trinity Camb. 599, f. 2a.
Wilson, *Anglia* LXXII. 402-4.

2386	Alternative Envoy to *La belle dame sans merci* (1086)—two stanzas rime royal (followed by 823). Robbins, *Sec. Lyrics*, p. 206; Seaton, *Sir Richard Roos*, pp. 113-4; Bennett, *RES* n.s. XIII. 175-6.
2388	Rickert, *Anc. Eng. Xmas Carols*, pp. 179-80; Stevens, *Med. Carols*, p. 83.
2388.5	O blessid Albone O martre moste benygne Hymn to St. Alban—five stanzas rime royal. [An extract from 3748 (vv. 1696-1716, 1724-30, 1717-23), separately preserved in a Book of Hours]. 1. Fitzwilliam Mus. 40-1950, f. 135a [*olim* Yates Thompson 83, 'Talbot Hours'].
2392.5	O blessyd Johan the Euangelyst A carol to St. John—five quatrains and 2-line burden. *Christmas Carolles*, Kele, ca. 1550 (STC 5205); *facs*. Reed, *Xmas Carols*, p. 53; *repr*. *Early Eng. Carols*, p. 68.
2393	A prayer to Henry VI—six 8-line stanzas. [Cf. 333-5]. 1. Ushaw: St. Cuthbert's Coll. 10, flyleaf. James, *Memoir of Henry VI by Blacman*, pp. 50-1.
2393.5	O blessed lord how may this be A loving mistress complains her heaviness—one 5-line stanza. 1. BM Addit. 5665, f. 69b. Fehr, *Archiv* CVI. 279; Stevens, *Music & Poetry*, p. 341.
2394.5	O blessed lord of heuyn celestiall A political carol honoring Prince Arthur—three 10-line stanzas with burden: 'From stormy wyndis…preserue the estrige fether.' 1. BM Addit. 5465, f. 104b. Stafford Smith, *Eng. Songs*, p. 11; Rimbault, *Songs & Ballads*, no. 21; Flügel, *Neuengl. Lesebuch*, p. 159; *Early Eng. Carols*, pp. 295-6; Stevens, *Music & Poetry*, pp. 280-1.
2395	Furnivall and Locock, *Roxburghe Club* CXLV. 454-5.
2397	Furnivall, *EETS* 15 orig. ed. 81-2; rev. ed. 112-3.
2400	Rickert, *Anc. Eng. Xmas Carols*, p. 15.

O blyssful lord on hye what shall I doo   See 540.

Oo blisful psalme and song celestiall   See 2200.

2400.5 O certeyn deth that now hast ouerthrow / Richard Quatremayns
    Epitaph on a brass, A.D. 1460, at Thame Church—ten irregular lines.
    Pettigrew, *Chronicle of Tombs*, p. 47.

2401.5 O cryst iesu pyte and mercy haue
    Epitaph, A.D. 1420, for Alice Thorndon at Frettenham, Norfolk—one stanza rime royal.
    Ravenshaw, *Antiente Epitaphes*, p. 7.

2403.3 O Christe thou hast restorede my soule
    Prefatory prayer to an alchemical tract—one quatrain.
    1. Copenhagen Old Coll. 3500, flyleaf.
    Retrospective Rev. II. 415.

2403.5 O crystys precyus hart / whose precyus blood oute start
    A prayer by the passion—fourteen lines. [Cf. 2548.5].
    1. Gorhambury, flyleaf [present location not known].
    Gibbs, *N&Q* 6 s. VIII. 443.

2407   three 8-line stanzas.

2409   Stevens, *Med. Carols*, p. 78.

2409.5 O dere God behold þis worlde so transytorye
    'The Lamentatyon of Edward, late Duke of Buckyngham,' A.D. 1521—nine stanzas rime royal. [Cf. 158.9].
    1. Bodl. 12653, f. 49b.
    Padelford and Benham, *Anglia* XXXI. 364-5.

2412   Wilson, *MLN* LXIX. 19; Person, *Camb. ME Lyrics*, p. 34.

2412.5 O desirerabull dyamvnt distinit with diversificacion
    An aureate invocation of his absent mistress—lines each ending in *-ion*.
    1. Harley 541, f. 208a.

2420   1. Advocates 1. 1. 6, p. 20 and f. 24a.
       1a, 1b. Ritchie, *STS* 3 s. V. 35-5; *STS* n.s. XXII. 58;
       1b. Laing, *Henryson*, 1865, p. 39; Wood, *Henryson*, pp. 163-5; Elliott, pp. 122-4.

2420.5 O eternall and persones three
        '*O lumen indeficiens o claritas se[e]mpiterna:*' a prayer to God—vv.40.
        1. Massachusetts Hist. Soc., Winthrop 20 c, f. 154a.

        O excellent pryncesse and Quene celestyall   See 3955.5.

2421   a 'symple letter.' [Cf. 752].
       Robbins, *Sec. Lyrics,* pp. 126-8.

       O fayre Dido most noble in constaunce
       An extract (II. 2171-2233) from *The Fall of Princes* in MS. Harley 2251 only [Utley 220]. See 1168.

2424.5 O fayre madame if so ye dare not loo
        Love me, madame, 'in spite of daunger and his affynyte' (associated with Charles d'Orléans)—three 8-line stanzas and 4-line Envoy.
        1. Harley 682, f. 135a.
        Taylor, *Roxburghe Club* 1827, XLIV. 265-6; Steele, *EETS* 215. 198-9.

2428   [Ringler 54].
       8. Camb. Un. Kk. 1. 6, ff. 73a-77b; 9. BM Addit. 34193, f. 63b; 10. Hatfield; 11. Melbourne: Victoria Pub. Lib., f. 161b.
       Pylgremage of the Sowle, Caxton, 1483 (STC 6473).

2432   Comper, *Spiritual Songs,* p. 178; Greene, *Sel. Eng. Carols,* p. 120.

2436   *Gentleman's Magazine,* May 1842, p. 462 (extracts).

2437	eight stanzas rime royal, with introductory and concluding couplets. [Utley 221]. Cords, *Archiv* CXXXV. 297-8; Robbins, *Sec. Lyrics*, pp. 220-2; Kaiser, *Med. Eng.*, p. 481 (7 st. only).
2437.5	O ffresshes flour Title (three words only) of a courtly love lyric mentioned in a bill of a music teacher *ca*, A.D. 1473-5. 1. Public Record Office C 47 / 37 / 11, f. 3a. Hanham, *RES* n.s. VIII. 271.
2439	*Gentleman's Magazine*, May 1842, p. 468.
2439.5	O gentyll & most gentyll Ihesu yow save A love letter to his disdainful mistress—two stanzas rime royal. 1. Bodl. 12653, f. 71a. Padelford and Benham, *Anglia* XXXI. 395.
2440	A lover's good fortune—one stanza rime royal. Wilson, *MLN* LXIX. 20.
	O glorious crosse that with holy blode See 914.
2440.5	O glorious feste among al other Song at Candlemas: poem occurring in only this MS. of Eng. tr. of the *Pèlerinage de l'Ame*—five stanzas rime royal. 1. Melbourne: Victoria Pub. Lib., f. 202a.
2442	2. Thompson (Portland, Oregon) [*olim* Amherst 20], f. 1b.
2443	[Cf. 3776].
2444	Kaiser, *Med. Eng.*, p. 509.
	O gloryous mayde for that heuynesse See 447.
2445	10. Chetham Lib. 6709, ff. 282b-284a (9 st.). *Suffolk Garland*, Ipswich 1818, pp. 351-5.
2446	Kaiser, *Med. Eng.*, p. 510.

2446.5   O glorious quene of all floures floure
            'A miracle of oure lady done to ser Amery knyght'—one
            stanza rime royal and ten quatrains. [Cf. 59, 1641].
            1. Trinity Dublin 432, f. 63b.
              Brotanek, *ME Dichtungen*, pp. 67-8.

            O God alone in heuen werynge crowne   See 3452.1.

2449   2. Camb. Un. Add. 2585 (1), f. 2b.
            2. Robbins, *MLN* LXVI. 505.

2451   A prayer to Christ and the Virgin—184 lines. [This is
            a composite text: st. 1 = st. 5 of 1752; st. 2 = st. 1 of MS.
            Egerton 3245 of 615; st. 3-16 = 775, complete; st. 17 = st. 1
            of 241; st. 18-27 = MS. Longleat 29 of 2121; then come vv.
            23, generally in couplets, using lines from MS. Bodl. 6922*
            of 2119].

2451.5   O god þat in tyme all thingis did begin
            Poem on Time by John Skelton—thirteen 8-line stanzas.
            1. Egerton 2642, f. 130a (st. 7, 9, 10, 11); 2. Advocates
            1. 1. 6, f. 82a; 3. Trinity Dublin 661, pp. 3-5 (st. 7, 9,
            10, 11 only).
              Certayne Bokes, Kynge and Marche, n.d. (STC 22599); *repr.*
              Dyce, *Skelton*, I. 137-8; Dyce and Child, *Skelton & Donne*,
              I. 160-1; Henderson, *Skelton*, 1931, p. 11; 1948, 1959,
              p. 21; Hughes, *Skelton*, pp. 35-6; Day, n.d.; Lant, n.d.;
              Workes, Marshe, 1568 (STC 22608); *repr.* [? J. Bowle,]
              1736; Chalmers, *English Poets*, II. 266; 2. Bannatyne MS.,
              Hunt. Club, II. 227; Ritchie, *STS* n.s. XXII. 208-11.

2453   *Early Eng. Carols*, p. 211; Stevens, *Med. Carols*, p. 108.

2454   Robbins, *Hist. Poems*, pp. 199-201.

            O gracious lyle of pore folk chef patron
            Prayer to St. Giles (four 8-line stanzas with Envoy) follow-
            ing his life: see 2606.

2457.5   O gracious Princes guid and fair
            'Of the same James [Dog, keeper of the Queen's Wardrobe]
            quhen he hed plesett him,' by William Dunbar—six qua-
            trains with refrain: 'He is na dog he is a lam.' [Cf. 3496.3].
            1. Camb. Un. Ll. 5. 10, f. 44b; 2. Pepys 2553, p. 339.
              2. Pinkerton, *Anc. Scot. Poems*, I. 92-3; Sibbald, *Chronicle*,

I. 279; Laing, *Dunbar*, I. 111; repr. *Blackwood's Magazine*, Feb. 1835; Paterson, *Dunbar*, p. 177; Small, *STS* IV. 197-8; Schipper, *Dunbar*, pp. 201-2; and *DKAW* XLI (IV). 3-4; Zupitza, *AE Uebungsbuch*, pp. 206-7; Baildon, *Dunbar*, p. 95; Craigie, *STS* n.s. VII. 414; MacKenzie, *Dunbar*, pp. 62-3; Kinsley, *Dunbar*, p. 88.

2459   1. Chetham Lib. 6709, ff. 284b-285b.

2461   'Ane Ballat of Our Lady,' attributed to William Dunbar (in Bodl. 3354 attributed to Chaucer).
2a. Edinburgh Univ. 521 (transcript).
2a. Laing, *Dunbar*, I (Suppl.). 305.

2462.5 O holy St. George o very champion
Divers heroes of the family of Willoughby in a poem by James Packe, 'out of an old roll of parchemin'—eight stanzas rime royal.
1. Harley 245, f. 107b.

2463   O hope in dede þou help me / Godes moder I pray þe
[trans. '*O spes in morte me salua maria precor te,*' by 'Wilfridus'].

2464   13. Leyden Univ. Vossius 9, ff. 117a-135b; 15. Victoria and Albert Mus. Dyce 33 (transcript of Pynson).
Clopton text painted on scroll (see also Parker, *Hist. of Long Melford*, 1873, p. 128; Conder, *Church of Holy Trinity*, 1887, p. 54; Waller, *Journal Brit. Archaeol. Assoc.* II. 187-8; pr. Trapp, *RES* n.s. VI. 7-11).
5. Bennett, *STS* 3 s. XXIII. 270-4.

2465   2. Pepys 2553, p. 173.
2. Craigie, *STS* n.s. VII. 197-9.

2466   O Iesse yerde florigerat / The fruyt of lyff &c.

2469   1. Bodl. 6667, f. 110a; 3. Longleat 30, f. 12b.

2469.5 O Jhesu ful of myght markyd in þi mageste
A prayer for the king—three lines.
1. Durham Univ. Cosin V. iii. 24, f. ii recto.

2471   eight lines, followed by prose petitions.

2473	twenty-two stanzas generally rime royal. 1. Longleat 30, f. 13b; 2. Huntington HM 142, f. 11b (9 st.; ends imperfectly).
2475	one mono-riming quatrain. Robbins, *Sec. Lyrics*, p. 149.
2476	Stevens, *Med. Carols*, p. 111 (burden only).
2478	four 8-line stanzas. 1. Bodl. 3354, ff. 231a, 230a. Robbins, *Sec. Lyrics*, pp. 197-8.
2478.5	O Lady myne to whom thys boke I sende An epistle to his mistress, including a Dialogue between the Lover and Dame Nature—thirty-two stanzas rime royal. [Followed by 928.5]. 1. Trinity Camb. 599, ff. 4a-6b. Wilson, *Anglia* LXXII. 407-15.
2478.8	O lady sterre of iacob glorie of israel / Of all blessid '*Oracio de sancta Maria in anglicis verbis*'—six stanzas rime royal. 1. Bodl. Lyell 30, f. 176a.
2479	following *The Cuckoo and the Nightingale* (3361). 1. Bodl. 3896, f. 147b. *Chaucer*, Thynne, 1532 (STC 5068); *Chaucer*, Stow, 1561 (STC 5075); *Chaucer*, Speght, 1598 (STC 5077); Urry, *Chaucer*, 1721, p. 545; Bell, *Poets of Great Britain*, XI. 171; [Anderson,] *Poets of Great Britain*, I. 501; Chalmers, *English Poets*, I. 366; *British Poets*, Chiswick 1822, V. 27; *Aldine Brit. Poets*, 1845, VI. 128; 1866, IV. 85; Bell, *Chaucer*, IV. 347; Ellis, *Floure and Leafe*, Hammersmith 1896; 1. Skeat, *Oxf. Ch.*, VII. 359; 2. Vollmer, *Bonner Beiträge zur germ. und rom. Phil.* XVII. 46-7.
2482.5	O Lobbe Lobe on thy sowle God haue mercye 'The Epytaphye of Lobe, the kynges foole' [to Henry VIII]—seven stanzas rime royal. [Cf. Schoeck, *MLN* LXVI. 506-9]. 1. Bodl. 12653, f. 27b. Halliwell, *Nugae Poeticae*, pp. 44-6; Padelford and Benham, *Anglia* XXXI. 346-7.

2483	[...prose version occurs in Harley 1706, ff. 17b and 84a]. 1. *Rel. Lyr. XV C.*, pp. 216-7.
2486	O Lord God O Crist Ihu / O sueit saluiour &c. [A verse rendering of a prose prayer on f. 146a, pr. Bennett, *STS* 3 s. XXIII. 240]. Bennett, *STS* 3 s. XXIII. 259-61.
2487	O lord god comforte of care On careful speech—one quatrain.
2490	The dilemma of an unfortunate lover—two cross-rimed quatrains.
2491	five 8-line stanzas. 1. Cotton Vesp. D. ix, f. 189a. Robbins, *Sec. Lyrics*, pp. 122-4.
2492	[The first line opens a prayer in Advocates 1. 1. 6, f. 41a, pr. *STS* n.s. XXII. 104-5].
2493	2. Fitzwilliam Mus. 56, ff. 123a-142b. O lord right dere / þi wordes I here *Responsio humana:* See 2504.
2494	Robbins, *Sec. Lyrics*, pp. 20-1.
2496	The Pains of Love, a love epistle.
2497	James, *Cat.*, III. 16-7. *O lumen indeficiens o claritas se[m]piterna* See 2420.5
2497.5	O lusty flour of ȝowth benyng and bricht To the Queen Dowager, by William Dunbar—five 8-line stanzas with refrain: 'Devoyd langour and leif in lustiness.' 1. Advocates 1. 1. 6, f. 238b. Brydges and Haslewood, *Brit. Bibl.*, IV. 191-2; Laing, *Dunbar*, II. 45-6; Paterson, *Dunbar*, pp. 297-8; *Bannatyne MS.*, Hunt. Club, III. 689-91; Small, *STS* IV. 326-7;

Schipper, *Dunbar*, pp. 343-5; and *DKAW* XLII (IV). 41-3; Baildon, *Dunbar*, pp. 177-8; Ritchie, *STS* n.s. XXIII. 323-4; MacKenzie, *Dunbar*, pp. 180-1.

2500.5   O man more than madde what ys þi mynde
A warning against deceitful women—eight stanzas rime royal. [Utley 223].
1. Bodl. 12653, f. 69b.
Padelford and Benham, *Anglia* XXXI. 393-5.

2501.5   O man Remembre the great kyndnes
'*Da tua dum tua sunt*'—four lines.
1. Bodl. 815, f. 20b.

O man the belle is solemplye rownge   See 4028.3.

2504   [Cf. also 2507].
1. Bodl. 819, f. 74b (*Querela diuina* only); 2. BM Addit. 37605, f. 192a (transcription &c.).
Pepwell, 1521 (STC 20972); 2 (inscription in church). *Journal Brit. Archaeol. Assoc.* XXX. 231.

2507   1-3. Ross, *Speculum* XXXII. 276; 2. Person, *Camb. ME Lyrics*, p. 11; 3. Comper, *Life & Lyrics of Rolle*, p. 318; Davies, *Med. Eng. Lyrics*, p. 168.

O marble herte and yet more harde perde
An extract (vv. 717-24) in MS. BM Addit. 17942 occurring separately: see 1086.

2509   [Delete entire entry].

O mercy quene and emperesse   See 2169.

2510   2 and 3. [Delete these MSS.].
Chaucer, Stow, 1561 (STC 5075); *Chaucer*, Speght, 1598 (STC 5077); Urry, *Chaucer*, 1721, p. 556; Bell, *Poets of Great Britain*, XIII. 127; [Anderson,], *Poets of Great Britain*, I. 585.

2511   [Followed by 1587].

2514	4. NLW Peniarth 196, p. 149. 2. Holthausen, *Archiv* CXL. 33; Holthausen, *Palaestra* CXLVIII: *Anglica* II, 70-2.
2515	A prophecy—seventy-six lines. [vv. 28, 31-35 occur separately in 3308.5].
2516	6. Bodl. 21722, ff. la-289b, 301a-306a; 16. Gloucester Cath. 5, f. la (vv. 26426); 18. Rylands Lib., English 1, f. 2a; 19. Morgan Lib. M. 876 [*olim* Helmingham Hall], f. la (vv. 23868); 20. *olim* Harmsworth [*olim* Phillipps 3113], f. la (Sotheby Sale, Oct. 1945, Lot 1963) (vv. 28090); 21. Harvard Coll. Eng. 752 [*olim* Ashburnham 131], f. la (vv. 28000); 22. Bodl. 13679, ff. 3, 2 (I. 460-537; 623-701); 23. *olim* Temple, Newton Park, Bristol (Sotheby Sale, June 16, 1941, Lot 153). 12. Bergen, *EETS* &c.
2517	Robbins, *Sec. Lyrics*, pp. 132-3; Davies, *Med. Eng. Lyrics*, p. 273.
2518	[Utley 225]. Robbins, *Sec. Lyrics*, pp. 138-9; Mason, *Humanism & Poetry*, pp. 176-7; Davies, *Med. Eng. Lyrics*, pp. 271-2.
2520	1. Advocates 1. 1. 6, p. 43 and f. 56a. 1a, 1b. Ritchie, *STS* 3 s. V. 71-3; *STS* n.s. XXII. 139; 1b. Laing, *Henryson*, 1865, p. 27; Wood, *Henryson*, pp. 211-2.
2521	1b. Robbins, *Studia Neophil.* XXVI. 61-4.

O mortal man cal to remembraunce / This text See 3563.5.

2522.5	O mortall man lyfte up thyn eye / And put all 'The crafte to lyue well'—three 8-line stanzas. de Worde, 1505; *repr.* Dibdin, *Typo. Antiquities*, II. 121.
2523	2. BM Addit. 21410, f. 168a (fragment: st. 1 only). 2. Bergen, *EETS* cxxiv. 65.
2523.5	O mortall man remembir nycht and day '*Memento homo quod cinis est*,' 'Quod Lichtoun'—six 8-line stanzas with this refrain.

              1. Advocates 1. 1. 6, f. 48a.
              Bannatyne MS., Hunt. Club, p. 129; Ritchie, *STS* n.s. XXII. 119-20.

2524   A scurrilous balade against his mistress—three stanzas rime royal. [Cf. 4230. Utley 226].
              1. Trinity Camb. 599, f. 205b (inserts 4230 after st. 1).
              Chaucer, Stow, 1561 (STC 5075); *Chaucer*, Speght, 1598 (STC 5077); Urry, *Chaucer*, 1721, p. 558; Bell, *Poets of Great Britain*, XIII. 133; [Anderson,] *Poets of Great Britain*, I. 568; Chalmers, *English Poets*, I. 564; Skeat, *Chaucer Canon*, p. 124; Person, *Camb. ME Lyrics*, p. 40.

2525   [Delete entire entry].

           O most blessid Fader omnipotent   See 914.

2526   1. [Delete this MS.].
            Dyce and Child, *Skelton & Donne*, II. 345-6.

2528   Bennett, *STS* 3 s. XXIII. 274-5.

2529   five stanzas rime royal with 4-line Envoy: 'Farewell swet harte,' [St. 2 is adapted from *Temple of Glas* (851), pr. Schick, *EETS* 60. 31; and also occurs separately in Advocates 1. 1. 6, pr. *Bannatyne MS.*, Hunt. Club, III. 29].

2530.5   O my desyre what eylyth the
           A lover's complaint—two 8-line stanzas with refrain: 'O my desyre what eylyth the.'
           1. BM Addit. 5465, f. 10a.
              Fehr, *Archiv* CVI. 53; Stevens, *Music & Poetry*, p. 354.

2531.5   O my hart and O my hart
           'My hart it is so sore,' attributed to Henry VIII—one quatrain.
           1. BM Addit. 31922, f. 22b.
              Chappell, *Archaeologia* XLI. 374; Flügel, *Anglia* XII. 232; Trefusis, *Songs Henry VIII*, Roxburghe Club CLXI.9; Stevens, *Music & Poetry*, p. 390; Stevens, *Music at Court*, p. 17.

O my hart is wo
Burden to 4023.

2532.3 O my lady dure / I am your prisoner
A love song—one couplet.
1. Royal App. 58, f. 16b.
Flügel, *Anglia* XII. 265.

2532.5 O my swete lady & exelente goddas
Praise of his mistress—twenty-five stanzas rime royal. [Actually an extract from Hawes' *Pastime of Pleasure* (4004); the last stanza also occurs separately as 2318].
1. Bodl. 12653, f. 18a.
Padelford and Benham, *Anglia* XXXI. 333-8.

O noble Markis yowre humanyte
Chaucer's Clerk's Tale in Naples MS. (begins st. 6); extracts printed *Rel. Ant.*, II. 68. See 4019.

2533 Stevens, *Med. Carols*, p. 77.

2533.5 O orient lyghte & kinge eterne
Song at the Ascension: poem occurring in only this MS. of Eng. tr. of the *Pelerinage de l'Ame*—five stanzas rime royal.
1. Melbourne: Victoria Pub. Lib., f. 208a.

2535.5 O painefull hart in peiyns syȝht
A disconsolate lover—two cross-rimed quatrains.
1. Bodl. 13679, f. 6a.
Frankis, *Anglia* LXXIII. 299.

2536 [Delete entire entry].

O penful harte that lyes in travvail
Introductory lines (indicating melody) to 2318.

2536.5 O pereles Prynce of Peace / And Lorde of Lordes all
The evil state of morality among clergy and laity—twelve short cross-rimed quatrains.
1. Morgan Lib. *Life of St. Winifred*, Caxton, 1485 (STC 25853), first blank folio, verso.
Bühler, *Anglia* LXXII. 420-1.

2536.8   O pytefull Creater concerning erthly sepulter
   Epitaph, A.D. 1496, for Catherine Burlton and Richard, her husband, at Dartford, Kent.
   Weever, *Anc. Funerall Monuments,* 1631, p. 334 (STC 25223).

2538   2. Canterbury Cath. Memorandum, on a blank leaf near the end (st. 14 et seq.).
   2. *Hist. MSS. Comm. Report* IX, App., p. 108 (2 st. only); R. A. L. Smith, *Cant. Cath. Priory,* 1943, pp. 198-9 (1 st. only).

2541   [Utley 227].
   3. Harley 2251, f. 244b.
   2. Hammond, *Eng. Verse Chaucer-Surrey,* pp. 115-8.

2541.5   *O quem mirabilia* good Lord thy werkys been
   Ballade about King John, Otto, and Philip—three stanzas rime royal.
   Fabyan, *New Chronicles,* 1516 (STC 10659); repr. Ellis, 1811, p. 322; Wilson, *Lost Lit.,* p. 194 (first st. only).

2542   A hymn to the B. V. by James Ryman—ten quatrains with refrain: '*Regina celi letare.*'

   O quene of heuen þat syttist in se   See 507.

2546   R. Lant, ca. 1542; *Certayne Bokes,* Kynge and Marche, n.d. (STC 22599); J. Day, n.d.; *Workes,* Marshe, 1568 (STC 22608); Dyce, *Skelton,* I. 139-40; Dyce and Child, *Skelton & Donne,* I. 162; Henderson, *Skelton,* 1931, pp. 14-16; 1948, 1959, pp. 13-15; Hughes, *Skelton,* pp. 37-8 (4 st. only).

2547   Robbins, *Sec. Lyrics,* pp. 218-9.

2547.3   *O Rex regum* in thy realme celestialle
   The House of Stanley: *Flodden Field*—twenty-six stanzas rime royal. [Cf. 366.8, 2549.5].
   1. Harley 293, f. 55a; 2. Harley 367, f. 120a; 3. Harley 2252, f. 45b; 4. BM Addit. 27879, p. 117.
   1, 2. Weber, 1808; 2. Evans, *Old Ballads,* 1810, III. 58; Dolman, *Gentleman's Magazine,* 1886, CCXXI.16; 4. Ritson, *Anc. Songs,* p. 210; Hales and Furnivall, *Percy Folio MS.,* I. 318.

2547.5 O rote of trouth o princess to my pay
His virtuous mistress—five lines.
1. BM Addit. 5465, f. 38b.
Fehr, *Archiv* CVI. 58; Stevens, *Music & Poetry*, p. 363.

2548.5 O rufully perchyd ryath hand of Cryste Iesu
On the five wounds—eleven couplets. [Cf. 2403.5].
1. Gorhambury, flyleaf [present location now known].
Gibbs, *N&Q* 6 s. VIII. 443.

2549.5 O Schotland thow was flowryng / in prosperus welthe
Lament on the misfortunes following Flodden—six stanzas rime royal. [Cf. 366.8, 2547.3: and Dickins, *LSE* VI. 74].
1. BM Addit. 45102 (u).
Wright, *British Mus. Qr.* XII. 13-17.

2550 Davies, *Med. Eng. Lyrics*, pp. 183-4.

2551 2. Laing, *Henryson*, 1865, p. 30; Wood, *Henryson*, pp. 205-7; Elliott, pp. 119-20.

2551.5 O synfull man þir ar þe xl dayis
'The maner of passyng to confessioun,' by William Dunbar— ten stanzas rime royal.
1. Arundel 285, f. 161a.
Laing, *Dunbar*, I. 225-7; Paterson, *Dunbar*, pp. 72-4; Small, *STS* IV. 280-2; Schipper, *Dunbar*, pp. 354-7; and *DKAW* XLII (IV). 51-5; Baildon, *Dunbar*, pp. 185-7; MacKenzie, *Dunbar*, pp. 167-9; Bennett, *STS* 3 s. XXIII. 257-9.

2551.8 O sisters too / how may we do
The Coventry Carol—three 6-line stanzas with Lullay burden, occurring in the Coventry Pageant of Shearmen and Tailors (3477).
No MS. extant.
Sharpe, *Diss. on the Pageants*, 1825, pp. 114, 116-17 (from a copy by Thomas Mawdycke, 1591, from a transcript by Robert Croo, 1534; both texts now destroyed); Craig, *EETS* lxxxvii. 32; Halliwell, *Ludus Coventriae*, Shakespeare Soc. 1841; Bramley and Stainer, *Christmas Carols*, no. lxi; Pollard, *XV Cent. Prose & Verse*, p. 272; Rickert, *Anc. Eng. Xmas Carols*, pp. 76-7; *Oxford Book*

Carols, p. 44; Early Eng. Carols, p. 71; Robbins, Early Eng. Xmas Carols, p. 74; Davies, Med. Eng. Lyrics, pp. 292-3; and many other editions.

2552.5   O soorowe of all sorowes my harte doeth dere
'The lamentatyon of the Ladye Gryffythe'—three stanzas rime royal. [For a companion poem see 3962.5].
1. Bodl. 12653, f. 30a.
Padelford and Benham, Anglia XXXI. 349-50.

O sop of sorrow sor kin into care
Cresseid's Complaint against Fortune in Henryson's Testament of Cresseid: see 285.

2557   four 6-line stanzas &c.
Edinburgh Univ. 205, f. iii verso.

O swete Angell that keepithe me / Bryng me to blysse I pray the
The 'versicull' concluding 2560.

2560.5   O swete harte dere & most best belouyd
A love letter—seventeen cross-rimed quatrains.
1. Bodl. 12653, f. 55a.
Padelford and Benham, Anglia XXXI. 372-4.

2562.5   O svete lady mayden mylde / pray for me
A simple prayer attached to a scroll—two couplets.
1. BM Addit. 37049, f. 29b.

2567   A Compleynt attributed to Charles d'Orleans or to the Duke of Suffolk.
1. Robbins, Sec. Lyrics, pp. 185-6.

2568   Robbins, PMLA LXIX. 639-42; Person, Camb. ME Lyrics, pp. 35-8.

O thou Phelippe founder of new falshede   See 3682.

2571   [A.D. 1414].

2571.5   O thou most noble pastour chosen by God
The Mayor of Waterford's metrical epistle to Walter, Arch-

bishop of Dublin, refusing to recognize Lambert Simnel as King of Ireland, A.D. 1487—44 doggerel stanzas rime royal.
1. Dublin State Paper Office (ca. A.D. 1600).
T. Crofton Croker, *Pop. Songs of Ireland*, 1839, pp. 318-331.

2574   The 'Magnificat' in 8-line stanzas (II. 981-1060). [Ringler 55]. 1. Bodl. 2253, f. 1a (begins I. 71); 6. Bodl. 14634, f. 1a; 7. Bodl. 27643, ff. 1a-94b (ends VI. 454). 10. Camb. Un. Kk. 1. 3, Part X, f. 2a (begins I. 75); 15. Arundel 168, f. 66a (begins I. 414; ends III. 1208); 19. Harley 2382, f. 1a (begins I. 427); 19a. Sloane 297, f. 88 (a fragment: one leaf from Harley 2382: III. 1671-1741); 24. Harley 5272, f. 1a (begins I. 419); 25. Sloane 1785, f. 14a (begins I. 434; ends I. 795); 26. BM Addit. 19252, f. 4a (begins I. 113); 27. BM Addit. 19452, f. 2a (begins I. 31; ends VI. 277); 30. Advocates 19. 3. 1, f. 176a (Books IV-VI); 31. Chetham Lib. 6709, f. 6a (a copy of Caxton); 32. Durham Univ. Cosin V. ii. 16, f. 5a; 33. Hunterian Mus. 232, f. 1a (ends VI. 308); 35. Soc. of Antiquaries 134, f. 1a (begins II. 222); 36. Longleat 15, ff. 2a-104b (ends VI. 128); 37. *olim* Harmsworth [*olim* Mostyn Hall 85], f. 2a (Sotheby Sale, Oct. 16, 1945, Lot 2019); 38. Univ. of Illinois 85 [*olim* Mostyn Hall 257], ff. 1-85 (begins at v. 118 of Chap. III); 39. Chicago Univ. 566 [*olim* Cockerell], f. 6a (begins I. 173); 41. Huntington HM 144 [*olim* Huth 7], f. 11a (II. 1-504 only); 42. Rome: English Coll. 1306, ff. 2a-66b (begins II. 365); 43. Yale Univ. 281, ff. 1-114.

The Lyf of Our Lady, Caxton, 1484 (STC 17023); Robert Redman, 1531 (STC 17025); 17. Tame, *Eng. Relig. Lit.*, 1879 (Bk. I - Bk. II. 1095); 30. Turnbull, *Visions of Tundale*, 1843, pp. 85-137 (Bks. IV-VI); 32. *crit. ed.* Lauritis, Klinefelter, and Gallagher, *Duquesne Studies, Philological Ser.* 2, 1961.

2577   [For an indulgence see 3305.8].
10. Blairs Coll. 13 (vv. 152); 12. Thompson (Portland, Oregon) [*olim* Amherst 20], f. 2a; 13. Longleat 30, f. 7a; 16. Osborn 22a [*olim* Fitzgerald] (roll: vv. 66); 17. Osborn 22b [*olim* Fitzgerald] (roll: vv. 88).

2577.3   O uery lyfe of swetnes and hope
A prayer to the B. V., paraphrasing the antiphon, '*Salve regina &c.*' (*Anal. Hymn.* L. 318-19)—five 3-line stanzas with 2-line burden: '*Salve regina mater misericordie &c.*' (Possibly ends imperfectly).

Christmas Carolles, Kele, ca. 1550 (STC 5205); *facs.* Reed, *Xmas Carols*, p. 62; *repr. Early Eng. Carols*, p. 155.

2577.5   O very lord o loue o god alas
A love complaint, erroneously attributed to Lord Thomas Howard—four stanzas rime royal, adapted from Chaucer's *Troilus and Criseyde* (3327), Book IV. 288-308, 323-29. [Preceded by introductory couplet (IV. 13-14): see Southall, *RES* n.s. XV. 143. Cf. also 1418.5].
   1. BM Addit. 17492, f. 29b.
      Muir, *Proc. Leeds Philos. & Lit. Soc., Lit. & Hist. Section*, VI. 265-6.

2578.5   [O wauering W]orlde all wrapped in wretchidnes
Elegy on the death of Henry VII, A.D. 1509, perhaps by Hawes (but not by Skelton)—seven 8-line stanzas.
   1. Durham Cath. Prior's Kitchen, Bp. Hatfield's Survey, Registrum Parvum II, f. 174a.
      de Worde, n.d. (Douce E. 20) (STC 13075); repr. Dyce, *Skelton*, II. 399-400; Dyce and Child, *Skelton & Donne*, II. 362-4; Scammell and Rogers, *RES.* n.s. VIII. 169-70.

2579   1a. Neilson and Webster, *Chief. British Poets*, pp. 227-9; Boyd, *ME Miracles*, pp. 56-61.

2579.3   O what a treasure ys love certeyne
'My ladye loveth me'—one quatrain.
   1. Bodl. 6659, f. 100a.
      Wagner, *MLN* L. 455.

2579.5   O when be dyvyne deliberatioun / Of persons thre
An Envoy to the B. V.—six stanzas rime royal. [Follows immediately 1507].
   1. Advocates 1. 1. 6, p. 6 and f. 39b.
      Chepman and Myllar, 1508 (STC 5099); *facs.* Beattie, *Edinb. Bibl. Soc.* 1950, p. 134; *repr.* Stevenson, *STS* LXV. 204-5; 1a, 1b, Ritchie, *STS* 3 s. V. 9; *STS* n.s. XXII. 102; 1b. *Bannatyne MS.*, Hunt. Club, p. 109.

2580   [Utley 229].
      Robbins, *Sec. Lyrics*, pp. 225-6.

2583   O wofull hert prisound in grete duresse

2585	3. Camb. Un. Ff. 5. 45, f. 13b. 1. MacCracken, *EETS* 192. 656-7; 2. Wager, *PQ* XV. 377-83 (extract).
2586	Rickert, *Anc. Eng. Xmas Carols*, pp. 184-5.
2587	Urry, *Chaucer*, 1721; Bell, *Poets of Great Britain*, 1782, IV.
2587.5	O wreche be war this warld will wend the fro 'Of the warldis vanitie,' by William Dunbar—three 8-line stanzas with refrain: '*Vanitas vanitatum et omnia vanitas.*' 1. Pepys 2553, p. 195. Laing, *Dunbar*, I. 201-2; Paterson, *Dunbar*, pp. 62-3; Small, *STS* IV. 244; Schipper, *Dunbar*, pp. 386-7; and *DKAW* XLII (IV). 84-5; Zupitza, *AE Uebungsbuch*, p. 207; Baildon, *Dunbar*, pp. 207-8; Craigie, *STS* n.s. VII. 221; MacKenzie, *Dunbar*, pp. 150-1.
2588.5	O ye all that ben or haue byn in dyssease A plea to lovers for sympathy—five stanzas rime royal. 1. Trinity Camb. 599, f. 3b. Wilson, *Anglia* LXXII. 404-5.
2590	6. Leyden Univ. Vossius 9, f. 29b. *Fall of Princes*, Appendix, Tottel, 1554; *repr.* Dugdale, *Hist. of St. Pauls*, 1658; Bergen, *EETS* cxxiii. 1025-44; 7. Bergen, *EETS* cxxvi. 45.
2590.5	O ye dere frendys whych sall here aftyr be Epitaph, A.D. 1463, of Richard Payne at St. Nicholas Acons Church, London—seven couplets. Weever, *Anc. Funerall Monuments*, 1631, p. 412 (STC 25223); Pettigrew, *Chronicles of Tombs*, p. 48.
	O ye folkes all which have devocion See 4246.
2591	7. Coventry Corp. Record Office, ff. 70a-74b; 8. Rome: English Coll. 1306, f. 111b (82 st., omits 7 & 52). *Horae Beate Marie Virginis*, Fakes, ca. 1521 (20 st. only) (STC 15932).
2592	4. Chetham Lib. 6709, ff. 193a-198b.

2594	Advice resented: a dialogue between an unhappy lover and the Advocate of Venus—fourteen stanzas rime royal. 1. Corp. Christi Oxf. 61, ff. 66b, 67a. Robbins, *Sec. Lyrics,* pp. 169-72; Bowers, *PQ* XXXI. 212-4.
2595	'The Parliament off Cupyde gode of love'—sixteen stanzas rime royal and 4-line Envoy.
2597	1. Bodl. Lat. misc. c. 66 [*olim* Capesthorne], f. 94a col. i. Robbins, *PMLA* LXV. 269-70.
2598	Brusendorff, *Chaucer Tradition,* pp. 457-60; Hammond, *Eng. Stn.* XLIII. 12 (extracts).
2599	O ye prynces þat prechyd hase my hert A love lyric on the unkindness of his mistress—one stanza rime royal. 1. Lambeth 432, f. 94b. Robbins, *MLN* LXIX. 553.
	O ye peple that louers yow prebende Envoy to 2595.
2602	[Utley 230]. 1. Bodl. 6919, end cover; 2. Naples: National Lib. XIII. B. 29, p. 146. 1. Lauritis, Klinefelter, and Gallagher, *Life of Our Lady,* p. 40; 2. Vallese, *La Novella del Chierico di Oxford,* Naples 1939, p. 77.
	O you that putt youre trust and convidence See 4263.3.
	O [indefinite pronoun] See One.
2602.2	*Oblesse oblesse que porar obler* / All hevy thought A roundel (associated with Charles d'Orleans)—vv. 14. 1. Harley 682, f. 102b. Taylor, *Roxburghe Club* 1827, XLIV. 189; Steele, *EETS* 215. 143.
*2602.3	*Of a chaunce ichil ȝou telle / at whilom in þis lond bifelle 'A Penni Worthe of Witte'—vv. 400 in couplets. [Cf. 1897].

           1. Advocates 19. 2. 1, ff. 257a-258b.
           Laing, *Abbotsford Club* 1857, pp. 1-14; Kölbing, *Eng. Stn.* VII. 113-17.

2602.4   Of a clene maide I was borne
           Contra luxuriam—four lines. [Followed by 1709.5].
           1. Sloane 2275, f. 245a.

2602.6   Of a day of wel & of a day of wo
           On doomsday—one couplet.
           1. Camb. Un. Ii. 3. 8, f. 145b.

           Of a gode begynnyng comyth a gode endying   See 37.5.

           Off a rose a louely rose
           Burden to 1914.

2604   Morris, *Specimens*, 1867, pp. 105-7; Brook, *Harley Lyrics*, pp. 42-3.

2605   1. Segar, *Med. Anthology*, pp. 27-31 (13 st. only).

2605.5   Off eftyr [?] Catyffe hoo may better ys
           Two very faded couplets, abusively ribald.
           1. Caius 513, f. 83b.

2606   4. Leyden Univ. Vossius 9, f. 1a.
           1. MacCracken, *EETS* cvii. 161-73; 2. Horstmann, *AE Leg. 1881*, pp. 371.

2607   3. Arras: Bibl. de la Ville 184, f. 1b (part of v. 1).
           3. Friend, *PMLA* LIX. 984.

           Of all creatures women be best
           Burden to 1485.

2607.5   Of all good thinges the worlde brought forth
           A faithful friend—one couplet.
           1. Durham Univ. Cosin V. iii. 9, f. 47a.
             Furnivall, *EETS* lxi. 171.

2608   1a (xix cent. transcript). Egerton 2257, ff. 101a-104b.
             Perry, *EETS* 26 orig. ed. 97-105; rev. ed. 88-95.

2609   Brotanek, *ME Dichtungen*, pp. 116-21; Robbins, *Hist. Poems*, pp. 210-5.

2609.5   Of all nacyons vnder the heuyn
             'Agaynst a comely coystrowne,' by John Skelton—ten stanzas rime royal.
             Pynson, n. d.; *repr.* Hawkins, *Hist. Music*, 1776, III. 40-2; Dyce, *Skelton*, I. 15-18; Dyce and Child, *Skelton & Donne*, I. 19-22; Henderson, *Skelton*, 1931, pp. 119-21; 1948, 1959, pp. 34-6; *Workes*, Marshe, 1568 (STC 22608); *repr.* [? J. Bowle,] 1736; Chalmers, *English Poets*, II. 300.

2610   1. NLW Deposit: Porkington 10, ff. 87b-89b.

2611   1. BM Addit. 16165, ff. 244b-245a (a blank space follows for a third st.).

2612   [Delete entire entry].

             Offe al the enmys þat I can fynd
             Burden to 4198.

2613   Bowers, *Univ. of Florida Monographs, Humanities* XII. 33-43.

2613.5   Of al þe merueile of merlyn how he makys his mone
             An animal prophecy attributed to Merlin—twelve quatrains.
             1. Harley 2382, f. 127b.

2614   An English translation of the '*Semita Recta*' of Albertus Magnus on the Elixir—thirty-two couplets. [Singer 177].

2614.5   Of Alle þe witti men and wise I warne Alle i þe wache
             The Papelard Priest—nine 10-line stanzas with 'O and I' refrain.
             1. BM Addit. 45896 (roll), Art. 1.
             Smith, *London Med. St.* II. 42-5.

2615   1. Child, *Ballads*, 1864, 1878, VIII. 101-16; Kaiser, *Med. Eng.*, pp. 441-3 (vv. 162 only).

2616   Allen, *Rolle*, p. 403.

    Of alle þyngis þat god made   See 4218.

2617.5 Of alle thinges that I can fynde
    On hope—one couplet, 'quod Carter.'
    1. Durham Univ. Cosin V. iii. 9, f. 36b.
    Furnivall, *EETS* lxi. 155.

2619   1. Davies, *Med. Eng. Lyrics*, pp. 210-11.

2619.2 Of all werkys in this worlde that ever were wrought
    Commemoration of Geoffrey Barber who built a bridge near Abingdon, A.D. 1457—23 quatrains and two couplets (with alliterative phrases).
        Leland, *Itinerary*, 1745, VII. 74; *repr.* Hearne, *Itinerary of John Leland*, 1769, VII. 79; L.T. Smith, *Leland's Itinerary*, 1910, V. 116-8.

    Of Anton story who lyste to lere   See 1197.8.

2619.5 Of bewtie yet she passith all
    'What wold she more'—eight quatrains with this refrain.
    1. BM Addit. 18752, f. 33a.
    Reed, *Anglia* XXXIII. 349-50.

2619.8 Off benefice schir at everie feist
    To the King, by William Dunbar—six 5-line stanzas with refrain. [Cf. 2621.5 and 3118.8].
    1. Camb. Un. Ll. 5. 10, f. 10a; 2. Pepys 2553, pp. 8 and 321. 2a, 2b. Craigie, *STS* n.s. VII. 8-9, 385-6; 2a. Small, *STS* IV. 208; Schipper, *Dunbar*, pp. 256-8; and *DKAW* XLI (IV). 58-60; Baildon, *Dunbar*, pp. 127-8; 2b. Pinkerton, *Anc. Scot. Poems*, I. 104-5; Sibbald, *Chronicle*, I. 315 (extracts); Laing, *Dunbar*, I. 159-60; Paterson, *Dunbar*, pp. 275-6; MacKenzie, *Dunbar*, p. 28.

    Of Columbyne I wyll sow tell
    See 3754 (Trinity Camb. 759).

2621   Clive, *Roxburghe Club* 1835, L. 90-102; Liljegren, *Eng. St.* LVII. 87-98.

2621.5 Off every asking followis nocht
'Of discretioun in asking,' by William Dunbar—nine 5-line stanzas with refrain: 'In asking sowld discretioun be.' [Cf. 121.5, 2619.8, 3118.8, and 3783.3].
1. Camb. Un. Ll. 5. 10, f. 21a; 2. Pepys 2553, p. 259 (vv. 16-20 wanting); 3. Advocates 1. 1. 6, p. 45 and f. 61a.
2. Craigie, STS n.s. VII. 289-90; 3a, 3b. Ritchie, STS n.s. XXII. 150-2; 3 s. V. 76-7; 3b. Ramsay, Evergreen, II. 82-4; repr. Ramsay and Earlier Scot. Poets, p. 274; [Hailes,] Anc. Scot. Poems, pp. 56-8; Sibbald, Chronicle, II. 7 (extracts); Laing, Dunbar, I. 165-6; Select Poems of Dunbar, Perth 1788, pp. 52-4; Paterson, Dunbar, pp. 238-40; Bannatyne MS., Hunt. Club, II. 165-7; Small, STS IV. 84-6; Eyre-Todd, Med. Scot. Poetry, pp. 206-7; Schipper, Dunbar, pp. 248-9; and DKAW XLI (IV). 49-51; Baildon, Dunbar, pp. 121-2; MacKenzie, Dunbar, pp. 31-4.

2622 Robbins, Sec. Lyrics, p. 12; Wilson, Lost Lit., p. 179; Speirs, Med. Eng. Poetry, p. 61.

2623.3 Off Februar the fiftene nycht
'The Dance of the Sevin Deidly Synnis,' by William Dunbar—vv. 120, generally in 12-line tail-rime stanzas.
1. Camb. Un. Ll. 5. 10, f. 11b; 2. Pepys 2553, pp. 12-16 and 161-2 (vv. 1-12, 109-120; and see 2289.8); 3. Advocates 1. 1. 6, f. 110a.
2. Craigie, STS n.s. VII. 12-16, 183-4; 3. [Hailes,] Anc. Scot. Poems, pp. 32-6; Ramsay, Evergreen, I. 240-6; repr. Ramsay and Earlier Scot. Poets, p. 255; Sibbald, Chronicle, I. 282-6; Select Poems of Dunbar, Perth 1788, pp. 33-7; Laing, Dunbar, I. 49-53; repr. Kaufman, Traité de la langue...Dunbar, 1873, pp. 23-46; Paterson, Dunbar, pp. 206-11; Bannatyne MS., Hunt. Club, II. 312-5; Small, STS IV. 117-20; Eyre-Todd, Med. Scot. Poetry, pp. 192-6; Schipper, Dunbar, pp. 127-33; and DKAW XL (IV). 37-43; Baildon, Dunbar, pp. 63-6; Arber, Dunbar Anthology, pp. 41-9; Ritchie, STS n.s. XXII. 291-4; MacKenzie, Dunbar, pp. 120-3; Kinsley, Dunbar, pp. 50-3.

Of farly fare who so wyll fynd   See 944.

Of ferlyis of this grete confusion   See 2139.

2623.8 Of festres ther ben maneres two
How to distinguish between hot and cold festers—one monoriming quatrain.
1. Sloane 2457, f. 23b.

2624 3. Robbins, *Sec. Lyrics,* pp. 72-3; 4. Person, *Camb. ME Lyrics,* pp. 50-2.

2625 [Utley 232].
3. Bodl. 11951, f. 88b (8 st.); 10. Leyden Univ. Vossius 9, f. 102b.
4. Furnivall, *EETS* 15 orig. ed. 45-7; rev. ed. 73-5; Neilson and Webster, *Chief British Poets,* pp. 222-3.

2626 Skeat, *Minor Poems,* p. 470.

2627 [Prose versions: Delete Sloane 140; for Ashmole 1397 read Ashmole 1379; add Bodl. 7707, p. 81; Pepys 878, f. 170a; Sloane 120, Sloane 122, Sloane 3215. For comparable verse texts cf. 417.8, *1496.3, and 3754].
[Revise listing of MSS. as follows:]
1. Bodl. 7719, Part III, f. 3a ('Betayne' only: vv. 12); 2. Bodl. 7760, ff. 117b-118b (Betony only: vv. 86); 3. Camb. Un. Dd. 10. 44, ff. 123b-128a (vv. 600); 4. Pepys 1661, pp. 288-309; 5. Trinity Camb. 921, ff. 35b-46a (vv. 600); 6. Trinity Camb. 1117, ff. 179a-181a ('Beton,' vv. 86; 'Centory,' vv. 18; 'Egremonye,' vv. 8); 7. Sloane 140, ff. 53a-56b (Betony, vv. 86; Centory, vv. 18); 8. Sloane 147, ff. 94a-112a (vv. 600); 9. Sloane 1571, ff. 14b-36b (vv. 666); 10. Sloane 2457, ff. 2a (vv. 300); 11. BM Addit. 17866, f. 5a (var.: vv. 753); 12. Uppingham School; 13. Society of Antiquaries 101, f. 90b; 14. Stockholm Royal Lib., X.90, pp. 49 (vv. 965); 15. Bühler 21 [*olim* Phillipps 7008], ff. 26b-45b (vv. 918).
2, 3, 8. Rohde, *OE Herbals,* pp. 43-4, 193-6 (extracts); 11. Garrett, *Anglia* XXXIV. 164-83; 14. Stephens, *Archaeologia* XXX. 364-95; *repr.* London 1844; Holthausen, *Anglia* XVIII. 307-30; 15. Bühler, *Studies in Med. Lit. to Baugh,* pp. 289-93 (extracts).

*Of hym I haue herde myche good / I graunte See 1915 (STC 13687).

2627.5 Of is lif of foly & of synn þorw lawe
Four irregular lines on the folly of the world.
1. Caius 221, f. 22a.

2631 [Also found in Spenser's *Shepherd's Calendar,* Eclogue III].

Of hony men gadyr out swetnesse   See 401.

2631.5 Of humylite and lowlinis comethe grace
Pride and Envy destroy Virtue—one couplet.
1. Trinity Dublin 69, f. 124b (added in xvi cent. hand).

2632.5 Off Lentren in the first mornyng
'All erdly joy returnis in pane,' by William Dunbar—ten quatrains with this refrain.
1. Pepys 2553, p. 319 (vv. 17-20 wanting); 2. Advocates 1. 1. 6, f. 48b.
1. Craigie, *STS* n.s. VII. 382-3; 2. [Hailes,] *Anc. Scot. Poems,* pp. 109-11; *Select Poems of Dunbar,* Perth 1788, pp. 91-3; Laing, *Dunbar,* I. 209-10; Paterson, *Dunbar,* pp. 60-2; *Bannatyne MS.,* Hunt. Club, II. 131-2; Small, *STS* IV. 76-7; Schipper, *Dunbar,* pp. 331-2; and *DKAW* XLII (IV). 29-30; Baildon, *Dunbar,* pp. 170-1; Ritchie, *STS* n.s. XXII. 121; MacKenzie, *Dunbar,* pp. 145-6.

2633 [Utley 233a].
Herrtage, *EETS* xxxiii. 510.

2634 [Delete: Compare 2161].
Robbins, *Sec. Lyrics,* pp. 130-2.

2635 Off love were lykynge of to lere
Ipomadon (Version A)—8890 lines in 12-line stanzas.

Of March take the first C   See 1502.

2635.5 Of mary a mayd withowt lesyng / this day was borne
A carol listing the events in the live of Christ—seven quatrains and Latin burden, '*Te deum laudamus* &c.'
1. Camb. Un. Add. 7350, f. ib.
Robbins, *PMLA* LXXXI.

2636 *Oxford Hist. Music,* 1932, p. 340; Stevens, *Med. Carols,* p. 75.

*2636.5 *Of mary de... / With all þis noo
Fragment of a carol, perhaps on the Annunciation, with a Farewell refrain.

        1. Camb. Un. Add. 2764 (1), C.

*2639.5   *Of my chambyr he is and born in pallacye
Fragment of a poem on *Sir Eger de Femyne*—nine lines only. [Cf. 1624].
1. Sloane 1212, f. 101a.

2640   [Utley 235].
Robbins, *Sec. Lyrics*, p. 223; Davies, *Med. Eng. Lyrics*, p. 165.

2641   James, *Cat.*, II. 279; Person, *Camb. ME Lyrics*, p. 71.

2642   [For a xvi cent. version by Henry Parker in Chatsworth MS., see Wright, *EETS* 214. Utley 236].
1. Schleich, *Die ME Umdichtung von Boccaccio's De Claris Mulieribus, Palaestra* CXLIV.

2645   five 9-line stanzas.
2. Wehrle, *Macaronic Hymn Tradition*, pp. 30-1; Dickins and Wilson, *Early ME Texts*, pp. 125-6; Segar, *Med. Anthology*, pp. 125-6; Kaiser, *Anthologie*, p. 241; Kaiser, *Med. Eng.*, p. 286; Davies, *Med. Eng. Lyrics*, pp. 53-4.

2646   Furnivall, *EETS* 15 orig. ed. 240; rev. ed. 268.

2646.5   Of oure lefdy marie bigynneþ now here þe pleynt
Verse introduction and conclusion to ME prose narration of Passion—two couplets.
1. Pepys 2498, pp. 449, 459.
James, *Cat.*, III. 109; Påhlsson, *Recluse*, p. v.

2647   8. Brown, *EETS* 169. 73.

2649   Böddeker, *AE Dicht.*, pp. 135-8; Robbins, *Hist. Poems*, pp. 27-9.

2650.5   Of Saynt George oure ladyes knyght / Of whome no torment coude haue myght
Introductory couplet to an English prose prayer.
1. Bodl. 21575, f. 77b; 2. Thompson (Portland, Oregon) [*olim* Amherst 20], f. 13b.

2651 Clive, *Roxburghe Club* 1835, L. 8-41; Serjeantson, &c.

2652.5 Of saynt Steuen goddes knyght / That preched the fayth
A carol to St. Stephen—nine quatrains and burden. [Cf. var. 1363.5].
Christmas Carolles, Kele, ca. 1550 (STC 5205), pp. 33 and 42 (var. 4 st.); *facs.* Reed, *Xmas Carols*, pp. 51, 60; *repr. Early Eng. Carols*, pp. 64, 63.

2654 Robbins, *Sec. Lyrics*, pp. 32-3.

2656 On preparing the Philosopher's Stone, ascribed in MS. 21 to Richard Carpenter (cf. Thorndike, IV. 351-3)—generally forty-eight couplets, but there are numerous variants (MSS. 4, 7, 18, 23) which are listed here for convenience. [See further 3721; and the related verses for Ripley's Emblematical Scroll, 1364.5. Singer 817].
1. Delete this MS.; 7. Bodl. 7624, p. 110 (vv. 10); 11. Bodl. 7653, f. 17b (vv. 10 additional), and f. 18b (vv. 8); 12. Bodl. 7010 (Ashmole 1490, previously misnumbered Bodl. 7655), f. 47a (vv. 47); 13. Delete this MS.; 14. Delete this MS.; 16. Corpus Christi Oxf. 226, f. 57a; 20. Delete this MS. [See 595]; 23. BM Addit. 32621 (vellum roll: text ascribed to James Standysh); 25. Sloane 1098, f. 10a and ff. 25b-26a (vv. 12); 26. Wellcome Hist. Med. Lib. 519, f. 62a (vv. 80), and f. 63b (var., vv. 40); 27. Princeton Univ. Gen. Coll. 93.
16. Robbins, *Sec. Lyrics*, pp. 82-4.

2657 English song against the Flemings, perhaps by Lydgate [see MacCracken, *Anglia* XXXIII. 283-6] &c.

2657.5 Off seche cvmplayn
Title (three words only) of a courtly love lyric mentioned in a bill of a music teacher ca. A.D. 1473-5.
1. Public Record Office C. 47 / 37 / 11, f. 3b.
Hanham, *RES* n.s. VIII. 271.

Off suche thyngis here be tawghte by delygence   See 1514.

2658 Hazlitt, *Remains*, III. 44-53.

2659.3 Of the blessed counsellour Saynt Roche
Introductory couplet to a Latin prayer to St. Roch.
1. Bodl. 21575, f. 82a; 2. Thompson (Portland, Oregon) [*olim* Amherst 20].

2659.6 Of the blessed martire saynt Sebastyane / Whos greuous paynes none tell can
  Introductory couplet to a ME prose prayer.
  1. Bodl. 21575, f. 80a; 2. Thomson (Portland, Oregon) [*olim* Amherst 20], f. 14a.

Of the ground there is a hell   See 1364.5.

2660.1 Of þe holy omelies now j wil blynne
  Concluding couplet to ME devotional prose tract.
  1. Pepys 2498, p. 212.
  Påhlsson, *Recluse*, p. iv.

2660.3 Of þe sautere on englische here is þe gynnynge
  Couplet introducing ME prose translation of Psalter.
  1. Pepys 2498, p. 263.
  James, *Cat.*, III. 107; Påhlsson, *Recluse*, p. iv.

Of the schynyng stone take klier lyȝthe   See 2656.

2660.6 Of þe vprist of Crist as Nichodemus gan telle
  Couplet introducing ME prose *Gospel of Nicodemus*.
  1. Pepys 2498, p. 463.
  James, *Cat.*, III. 110; Påhlsson, *Recluse*, p. v.

2661 [St. 1 = st. 16 of 919; st. 2 has a 'Blind eat fly' refrain, cf. 1944. Utley 239].
  Chaucer, Stowe, 1561 (STC 5075); *Chaucer*, Speght, 1598 (STC 5077); Urry, *Chaucer*, 1721, p. 553; Bell, *Poets of Great Britain*, XIII. 115; [Anderson,] *Poets of Great Britain*, I. 582; Chalmers, *English Poets*, I. 560.

2662 [Singer 808. Ringler 56].
  A Text: 17. Stow 950, f. 1a (begins I. 166; many leaves lost; ends III. 361); 24. Newberry Lib., Louis H. Silver 3 [*olim* Castle Howard], f. 1a &c.; 25. *olim* Hastings (Ashby-de-la-Zouche) (Quaritch Sale Cat.) (begins Pro. 342; a few leaves lost); 31. Plimpton 265, f. 4a (begins Pro. 504); 32. Rosenbach Foundation 1083/29 [*olim* Aberdeen]; 33. Madrid: Escorial G. II. 19.
  B Text: 5. Nottingham Univ. Mi LM 8 [*olim* Wollaton Hall], f. 1a; 7. Taylor, Princeton [*olim* Phillipps 8192, f. 1a; 8. Laurence Witten, New Haven, Sale Cat. 5, No. 24, f. 9a (begins I. 231; several leaves lost; ends perfectly).

C Text: 8. Bodl. Lyell 31 [*olim* Clumber], ff. 165.
Separate stories:
1. Bodl. 12900, f. 25a (VIII. 2377-2970, Conclusion); 8. Penrose 6 &c...f. 5a (V. 5551-6048 &c); 9. London: Univ. Coll. Fragment Ang. 1 [*olim* Phillipps 22914] (four leaves: V. 775-966, 1159-1542, 1735-1926); 10. R. C. Pearson, Cambridge, Sale Cat. 13, 1953, Item 219, ff. 8 (I. 1361-2602).

    Caxton, 1493 [=1483] (STC 12142); Berthelette, 1532 (STC 12143); 1554 (STC 12144).

2663   Brewer, *Mon. Franciscana*, Rolls Series IV, i. 606; Robbins, *Hist. Poems*, pp. 163-4; Davies, *Med. Eng. Lyrics*, pp. 141-2.

2663.5   Of these sayynges Cristyne was aucteuresse
Epilogue to Earl Rivers' translation of 'Dictes and Sayengs of the Philosophres' (cf. 3581)—two stanzas rime royal. [Ringler 57].
    Morale Prouerbes of Cristyne, Caxton, 1478 (STC 7273); Dibdin, *Typo. Antiquities*, I. 74-5; Blades, *Life & Typography of Caxton*, II. 148-9; Crotch, *EETS* 176. 32; Aurner, *Caxton*, pp. 236-7.

*Of þine swete wordes ich am swiþe glad   See 877 (f. 181a).

2664.5   Of this chapell se here the fundacyon
The Foundation of the Chapel of Walsingham—one quatrain and twenty stanzas rime royal. [Ringler 58].
    Pynson, ca. 1490-1500 (STC 25001); *repr.* Huth, *Fugitive Tracts*, 1 s. 1875, No. 2.

2665   Rickert, *Anc. Eng. Xmas Carols*, p. 122; Stevens, *Med. Carols*, p. 9.

2666   [Sometimes followed by 3257. Singer 862].
3. Bodl. 7624, pp. 82-3 (vv. 49); 4. Bodl. 7628, p. 30; 5. Bodl. 7654, ff. 72b-73b (vv. 68); 6. Sloane 1092, f. 5b; 7. Sloane 3580 B, ff. 182a-183a; 8. Sloane 3667, f. 119b; 9. Univ. of Pennsylvania, Smith 4, f. 51b.

Off þy sorow be nott to sad / Of þy ioy be not to glad
A proverbial couplet (pr. *Oxford Dict. Eng. Proverbs*, p. 605) from 3502.

Of titan magnesia take the clere lyght   See 2656.

2667   [Delete entire entry].

Of Troye throw hard fechynge   See 1181.

2668   [Singer 1009].
On removing spots made by wine, water, and milk.
1. Harley 2251, f. 76b; 4. Delete this MS.
3. Bühler, *RES* XII. 237; 5. Steele, *Academy* XLV. 395.

Offe witte & wisdome þe begynnynge   See 3502 (Longleat).

Off women now þis I say for me   See 2354.3.

2668.3   Of wonders that shull fall after our day
A prophecy—ninety-two irregular riming lines.
1. Bodl. 4062, f. 9b.

2668.5   Oft bryngeth on day / þat alle þe ȝere not may
A proverb—one couplet. [Cf. Heywood].
1. Bodl. 1654, f. 10a; 2. Bodl. 21626, f. 13b; 3. Rylands Lib. Latin 394, f. 6a.
1, 2. Förster, *Eng. Stn.* XXXI. 16; Förster, *Festschrift zum 12 Deutschen Neuphilologentage*, p. 44; 3. Pantin, *BJRL* XIV. 95.

2668.8   Ofte hathe this songe bene put in vre
A song by John Redford with varying refrains for use for Christmas and Easter—twenty-two 6-line stanzas aaaabb including a 'Merie' refrain and 7-line heading: 'Now will you be merye.' [Cf. 3530.5 with similar 'burden'].
1. BM Addit. 15233, f. 51b.

Oiez seynours vne demaunde   See 3828.

2671   Bowers, *Med. Studies* XVII. 230-2.

2672   5. Blackburn Pub. Lib. [*olim* Petworth 3], f. 167a.
5. Furnivall, *N&Q* 4 s. II. 577-8 (beg. and end only: vv. 23).

2673   [Ringler 23].
2. Ipswich County Hall Deposit: Hillwood [*olim* Brome], f. 39a (ends imperfectly).

Pynson, ca. 1493 (with intro. couplet) (STC 17325); Redman, ca. 1532; repr. Corser, *Collect. Anglo-Poet.* VIII, Chetham Soc., 1878, pp. 385-9 (extracts).

Old man wytles / ʒong chyld rekles   See 1820.

2674   Proverbial sayings on absence—three couplets.

Old men been scornyd / women arn wowed   See 906 (MS. Trinity Camb. 1157).

2674.5   *Omnes gentes plaudite / Car nostre saueyour est ne*
A macaronic carol of the Nativity in Latin, French, and English—five quatrains and burden.
1. Egerton 3307, f. 51b.
    Stevens, *Med. Carols*, p. 36; Greene, *Sel. Eng. Carols*, p. 68.

2675   Rickert, *Anc. Eng. Xmas Carols*, p. 244; Robbins, *Sec. Lyrics*, p. 5.

2678   Segar, *Med. Anthology*, pp. 33-4 (vv. 28 only).

2681   Rickert, *Anc. Eng. Xmas Carols*, pp. 186-7; Comper, *Spiritual Songs*, p. 95; Greene, *Sel. Eng. Carols*, p. 127.

2682   1. Bodl. Lat. misc. c. 66 [*olim* Capesthorne], f. 106b.
    Robbins, *MLN* LVIII. 362-3; Robbins, *PMLA* LXV. 276-9.

*2684.5   *...on earde / and alle þeo i-sceaftan þe to him to sculen
Fragments of an alliterative poem, the Address of the Soul to the Body, written as prose—vv. 349.
1. Worcester Cath. F. 174, ff. 63b-66b.
    Sir Thomas Phillipps, *Fragments of Aelfric's Grammar*, 1838; Singer, *Departing Soul's Address to the Body*, 1845; E. Haufe, *Die Fragmente der Rede der Seele an dem Leichnam in der Kath. zu Worcester*, Greifswald 1880; R. Buchholz, *Die Fragmente der Reden der Seele* &c., Erlanger Beiträge VI; Kaiser, *Med. Eng.*, p. 208 (extracts).

*2685.5   *On folie was myn silwyr leyd
The wickedness of the Times—in 8-line stanzas.
1. Camb. Un. Add. 4407, Art. 19 (g) (vv. 24).
    Skeat, *MLR* VII. 150 (one st. only).

2685.8   On fut suld be all Scottis werre
   Scotia sit guerra pedibus—seven couplets trans. seven Latin lines in Fordun's *Scotichronicon* (Book XII, Cap. x).
   1. Harley 712; 2. Edinburgh Univ. 186.
   Hearne, *Joannis de Fordun Scotichronicon*, Edinburgh 1759, II. 232; Pinkerton, *Anc. Scot. Poems*, I. lxxxvi.

2686   A. Peter Langtoft:
   3. Cotton Julius A. v, f. 147a; 8. Delete this MS.; 12. All Souls 39, f. 101b; 13. Harley 114, f. 135b.
   2-5, 10. Wright, *Camden Soc.* VI. 293, 393; 10. Wilson, *Lost Lit.*, p. 209.

   On the gronde ther is an hille   See 1364.5.

2689.5   On þis ne trist I me nout ... / þis have I now y-bouth
   A couplet in Nicolas Bozon's *Contes moralisés*.
   1. Gray's Inn 12, f. 37a.
   Smith, *SATF*, p. 110; Wilson, *LSE* VI. 45; Ross, *Neuphil. Mitteilungen* L. 208.

2691.3   Ones forsworne / evere forlorne
   A proverbial tag.
   1. Harley 741; 2. BM Addit. 25184; 3. Lincoln's Inn.
   1, 2. Riley, *Year Book 18 & 19 Edward III*, Rolls Series XXXI. 291; 1. Woodbine, *Speculum* XVIII. 431, fn. 5.

2691.5   O beggur is wo / þat anoþer in þe town goo
   A proverbial couplet.
   1. Bodl. 21626, f. 23a; 2. Rylands Lib. Latin 394, f. 12a.
   Förster, *Festschrift zum 12 Deutschen Neuphilologentage*, p. 49; 2. Pantin, *BJRL* XIV. 100.

2691.8   One cock sufyse xv hynnys / scase xv men suffise one woman
   '*Dictio hisopii*'—one couplet (with Latin version).
   1. Arundel 220, f. 1a.

   On dai bringd that al ier ne mai   See 2668.5.

2692   [For later versions in printed *Horae* see Bühler, *Studies in Renaissance* VI. 228-9].

   One god only thow shalt love   See 2695.5.

2695 Furnivall, *EETS* 15 orig. ed. 224-5; rev. ed. 253.

2695.5 One only god thou shalt loue and worship perfytely
  The Ten Commandments—ten riming lines. [Cf. 2692, 3689.5. For texts in *Horae* see Bühler, *St. in Renaissance* VI. 228-9].
  1. Morgan Lib. *Royal Book*, Caxton, 1486, sg. b. ii, verso (added in early xvi cent. hand).
  Ordynarye of Crysten Men, de Worde, 1502 (STC 5198); 1506 (STC 5199); *repr.* Dibdin, *Typo. Antiquities*, II. 103; *Kalender of Shepherdes*, Pynson, 1506 (STC 22408); *repr.* Furnivall, *Captain Cox*, Ballad Soc. VII. lxxx; 1. Bühler, *St. in Renaissance* VI. 228.

2696 Bowers, *Southern Folklore Qr.* XVI. 249-50.

2697 an extract from Wintoun's *Chronicle* (399) occurring separately—vv. 64 in couplets. [And in texts of the *Chronicle*, e.g., Cotton Nero D. xi, f. 207a; Royal 17. D. xx, f. 276b (vv. 74), pr. Laing, *Remains*, rev. Small, Edinb. 1885, pp. 196-7; rev. Hazlitt, 1895, I. 305-6].
  Craigie, *STS* n.s. VII. 125-7; Amours, *STS* LVII. 368.

2698 On ƺeer oþer to / wrong wylle on honde go
  An English proverb—two short couplets in *Le Dite de Hosebondrie* by Walter de Henley. [Cf. 4113].
  1. Bodl. 15516; 2. Bodl. 21672; 3. Merton Oxf. 321; 4. Camb. Un. Ee. 1. 1, f. 251a; 5. Camb. Un. Hh. 3. 11: 6. Corpus Camb. 301, f. 141b; 7. Trinity Camb. 1438, f. 99b; 8. BM Addit. 6159, f. 222b; 9. Canterbury Cath., Register J; 10. Canterbury Cath., Register P; 11. Guildhall, Liber Horn; 11a (xix cent. transcript). Camb. Un. Add. 4026; 12. NLW Peniarth 22; 13. ? Sir A. Acland Hood, St. Audries, Somerset [present location not known]; 14. ? Northumberland D. xi. 1 [present location not known]; 15. Paris: Bibl. nat. f. fr. 7011.
  de Worde, n.d. (STC 25007); 4. Lamond, *Walter of Henley's Husbandry*, 1890, p. 4; Mustanoja, *How the Good Wife*, p. 75 n.; Mustanoja, *Neuphil. Mitteilungen* IL. 130; 9. *Hist. MSS. Comm. Report* IX, App., p. 75.

2700 Bowers, *PMLA* LXX. 217-22.

2700.5 Orri be y-var be Alriche
  English couplet in a Latin *Fabula de duobus canibus*.
  1. Royal 7. E. iv, f. 163a.
  Wright, *Percy Soc.* VIII. 108.

2701   Chepman and Myllar, 1508 (18 leaves only) (STC 13148); repr. Craigie, *Facs.* Lekpreuik 1570, Appendix; 1. Eyre-Todd, *Early Scot. Poetry,* 1891, pp. 190-220 (extracts).

Oure beninge princesse and lady souereine   See 2200.

2702.5   Our fader celestyall almyghty
A version of the *Pater Noster.*
Flower of Commandments, de Worde, ca. 1510 (STC 23876).

2703   '*Pater Noster in anglico,*' the clauses of the *Pater Noster* as remedies against the sins.
2. Ellis, *EETS* vii. 443; Ellis, *E. E. Pronunciation,* Chaucer Soc. 2s, IV. 443; Camden, *Remains,* 1636, p. 24; 1870, p. 28; Weever, *Anc. Funerall Monuments,* 1631, p. 152 (STC 25223.)

2704   1. Person, *Camb. ME Lyrics,* p. 27; 2. Hussey, *Medium Aevum* XXVII. 10.

2708.5   Oure fader þat art in heuen / þin name be halowed with meke steuen
The *Pater Noster.*
1. Trinity Dublin 211, at end (a).

Oure fote folk / þut þam in pe polk   See 3252.

2711   2. Longleat 30, f. 24a.

2711.5   Our gracyous god moost in magnyfycence
'The remors of conscyence' — sixty-seven 8-line stanzas. [Ringler 59].
   de Worde, ca. 1500 (STC 20882).

2714   4. Pepys 1584, f. la; 7. Delete this MS.; 12. Harvard Coll. Eng. 530, f. la (vv. 1-138 wanting).
11. Furnivall, *EETS* 15 orig. ed. 168-203; rev. ed. 198-232; 3. Person, *Camb. ME Lyrics,* p. 3 (vv. 385-448 only).

Oure kyng at westminster he laye
   Passus I of Cotton MS. variant of 969.

2716   1. Chappell, *OE Pop. Music*, I. 25-9; Méril, *Poésies Populaires Latines*, 1843, p. 101; *Oxford Hist. Music*, 1932, II. 7-9; Robbins, *Hist. Poems*, pp. 91-2; Greene, *Sel. Eng. Carols*, p. 156; Davies, *Med. Eng. Lyrics*, pp. 168-9; 1a. Burney, *Hist. Music*, 1782, II. 384-7; Nicolas, *Agincourt*, 1833; Rimbault, *Musical Illustrations of Bp. Percy's Folio MS.*, 1850, pp. 18, 60; 2. Stevens, *Med. Carols*, p. 6.

2718   1. Morris, *EETS* 46, 131-49.

2719   three couplets (with couplet heading).

        Oure lord Iesu Crist in bethlem was borne   See 624.

2723.5   Ur lauerd þat alle michtes may / In even and erthe þi wille þou mai
        A prayer to Christ for mercy—two 8-line stanzas.
        1. Camb. Un. Add. 2585 (2), f. 2b.

2725   [Cf. 3028].
        1. Pepys 2125, f. 131a (vv. 1503); 2. Leeds Univ. Brotherton 501, ff. 92a-99b [*olim* Maggs Bros. Sale Cat. No. 580, Item 450].
        2. Lightbown, *MLR* XLVII. 323-9.

2727   1. Trinity Dublin 516, f. 32a.
        Robbins, *Hist. Poems*, pp. 191-3.

2729.5   Owte of darkness I will leade thee
        'By the Grace of God,' alchemical verses—vv. 21 followed by prose commentary.
        1. Univ. of Pennsylvania, Smith 4, f. 80b.

2730   Rickert, *Anc. Eng. Xmas Carols*, pp. 118-20.

2731   Stevens, *Med. Carols*, p. 98.

2732   Rickert, *Anc. Eng. Xmas Carols*, pp. 116-7.

2732.5   Out of the mouth o[f] a holy man / Shal come good lernynge and wysedom
        A proverbial couplet.
        Salamon and Marcolphus, Leeu, Antwerp ca. 1492 (STC 22905); *facs.* Duff, London 1892.

2733 2. Camb. Un. Ll. 1. 11, f. 32a (st. 1, 4, 2).
1, 2. Stevens, *Med. Carols*, pp. 18, 114; 1. Rickert, *Anc. Eng. Xmas Carols*, pp. 165-6; Greene, *Sel. Eng. Carols*, p. 64; Davies, *Med. Eng. Lyrics*, pp. 195-6; 2. Robbins, *Early Eng. Xmas Carols*, p. 18.

2735 [Utley 243].

2736.2 Pallas Euander his sone lieþ here
Epitaph of the giant Pallas—three monoriming lines in Trevisa's translation of Higden's *Polychronicon* (Book I, cap. 24).
1. St. John's Camb. 204; 2. Cotton Tiberius D. vii; 3. Harley 1900; 4. Stowe 65; 5. BM Addit. 24194; 6. Aberdeen Univ. 21; 7. Chetham Lib. 11379; 8. Hunterian Mus. 83; 9. Penrose 12; 10. Morgan Lib. M. 875.

Trevisa, *Discripcion of Britayne*, Caxton, 1480 (STC 13440a); de Worde, 1498 (STC 13440b); Trevisa, *Prolicronycon*, Caxton, 1482 (STC 13438); de Worde, 1495 (STC 13439); Treveris, 1527 (STC 13440); 1. Babington and Lumby, *Rolls Series* XLI, i. 225; Mätzner, *AE Sprachproben*, II. 363.

2736.4 Palmers all our faders were
Epitaph, A.D. 1407, on Thomas Palmer of Snodland, Kent.
Ravenshaw, *Antiente Epitaphes*, p. 5.

2736.6 *Parce mihi* o lord most excellent
Moralizing stanzas on the approach of death—two 8-line stanzas. [Cf. 561].
1. BM Addit. 18752, f. 77a.
Reed, *Anglia* XXXIII. 353.

2736.8 Pardon alas why saye I so
'Farewell my loue and my dere'—four quatrains.
1. BM Addit. 18752, f. 149a.
Reed, *Anglia* XXXIII. 368-9.

Parting parting / I may well synge
Refrain to 13.3.

2737.5 Passetyme with good cumpanye / I loue and shall unto I dye
'The Kynges Balade'—three 10-line stanzas. [For moralized version see Craigie, *STS* n.s. IX. 63].
1. BM Addit. 5665, f. 136b (one st.) and again at f. 141b; 2. BM Addit. 31922, f. 14b.

1, 2. Chappell, *OE Pop. Music*, I. 44, 42; 1a, 2. Stevens, *Music at Court*, pp. 10, 11; 1. Stafford Smith, *Musica Antiqua*, I. 44; Rimbault, *Songs & Ballads*, p. 37; Stevens, *Music & Poetry*, p. 344; 2. Chappell, *Archaeologia* XLI. 372-3; Briggs, *Madrigals*, PMMS 1893, no. 6; Flügel, *Anglia* XII. 230; Flügel, *Neuengl. Lesebuch*, p. 146; Furnivall, *Captain Cox*, Ballad Soc. VII. cxlix; Trefusis, *Songs Henry VIII*, Roxburghe Club CLXI. 1-2; *Oxford Book XVI Cent. Verses*, pp. 36-7; *Early Eng. Lyrics*, pp. 212-13.

Pastymes of yough sum tyme among   See 3706.5.

2741   1. Christchurch Cath. Dublin (vellum account roll, 1337-1346).

2741.5   Pes lordyngs I prai ȝow pes / And of ȝour noys
Prologue to a play—vv. 36 in six-line stanzas.
1. Durham Cath., Prior's Kitchen, Archid. Dunelm 60, dorso.
Cooling, *RES* n.s. X. 172-3.

2742   [Cf. Puttenham, *Arte of English Poesie*, ed. Willcock, 1936, p. 208; and Hughey, I. 87; II. 16; Arundel, Harington, f. 20a, pr. Hughey, I. 87].
7. Harley 629, f. 97a; 10. Soc. of Antiquaries 134, f. 30a; 14. Bodl. 14634, f. 109a; 15. Rylands Lib. Latin 201, f. 130a.
7, 13, 14. Lauritis, Klinefelter, and Gallagher, *Life of Our Lady*, pp. 31, 44, 27; 2, 7. *Rel. Ant.*, I. 315; 2, 11. Brotanek, *ME Dichtungen*, pp. 15-16; 4. Robbins, *Sec. Lyrics*, p. 81; Kaiser, *Med. Eng.*, p. 396; Davies, *Med. Eng. Lyrics*, p. 240; 7. Hughey, *Arundel Harington MS.*, II. 16; 9. *Bibliotheca Anglo-Poetica*, 1815, p. 187; 15. Fawtier, *BJRL* V. 389.

2743   1. *Register*, I. 371.

2743.5   Pecunia maket wrong rith
On the power of money—four lines.
1. Advocates 18. 7. 21, f. 14a.
Owst, *Lit. & Pulpit*, p. 317.

2744   Gordon, Oxford 1953; Hillman, Coll. St. Elizabeth Press, New Jersey, 1958; Cawley, 1963.

2746   Person, *Camb. ME Lyrics*, pp. 26-7.

2747   [For a Latin version see Wright, *Poems of Walter Mapes*, Camden Soc. XVI. 226].
                2. Balliol 8, f. 222b (var. burden & fragment st. 1).
                    1. Ritson, *Anc. Songs*, 1877, p. 116; Sibbald, *Chronicle*, III. 229; Wright, *Camden Soc.* XVI. 361; Robbins, *Sec. Lyrics*, pp. 50-1; Kaiser, *Anthologie*, p. 317; Kaiser, *Med. Eng.*, p. 550; 2. Mynors, *Cat.*, p. 7.

2749   Maister Benet [? Burgh].
                    Förster, *Archiv* CI. 53-5; Furnivall, *N&Q* 4 s. I. 455-6.

2749.5   Peters brother where lyest all night
                The White Benedictus, a spell—eighteen irregular lines.
                1. Bodl. Gough Horae, de Worde, 1502, margin.
                Suffolk Garland, Ipswich 1818, pp. 354-5.

2751   Wilson, *Osiris* VI. 427 (in part); Robbins, *Sec. Lyrics*, p. 76.

2751.5   Phebus out of gemini his course when he adualyd
                Peregrinatio humani generis, a versification of the prose of Prior Hendred of Leominster—180 stanzas rime royal.
                Pylgrymage of Man, Pynson, 1508 (STC 19623); Faques (STC 19918).

2753   [Compare 1907.5 and 2794].

2753.5   Persyd wyth payne wounded full nygh the hart
                A lover's plaint—one stanza rime royal.
                1. BM Addit. 18752, f. 90b.
                Reed, *Anglia* XXXIII. 363-4.

2754   [Cf. 3918.5].
                A. Peter Langtoft:
                    1. Bodl. 3904, f. 5a; 4. Cotton Julius A. v, f. 145b (vv. 12); 9. Delete this MS.; 13. Harley 114, f. 134a.
                B. Robert Mannyng of Brunne [See 1995] (vv. 18).
                    1, 3, 7, 11. Wright, *Camden Soc.* VI. 392-3, 286; 10. Legge, *Anglo-Norman Lit.*, p. 352; 11. Flügel, *Neuengl. Lesebuch*, p. 506; Wilson, *Lost Lit.*, p. 208.

2755   13. Winchester Coll. 33, f. 12a.
                    6. D'Evelyn and Mill, *EETS* 236. 697.

2755.5   Petyously / Constrayned am I
        Sorrow at parting, sometimes ascribed to John Skelton—three 8-line stanzas.
        1. Royal App. 58, f. 19a; 2. Rosenbach 678, Boethius, *De Disciplina Scholarum*, Deventer 1496 [*olim* Heber Incunabula, Sotheby Sale Cat. 1834, Part III, No. 810], f. iii (5 st) [Cf. 497].
        1. Flügel, *Anglia* XII. 266-7; 2. Birch, *Athenaeum*, 1873, p. 679; *repr.* Ashton, *Ballade of Scottyshe Kyng*, p. 19; Kölbing, *Zur Charakteristik Skeltons*, 1904; Henderson, *Skelton*, 1931, p. 19; Hughes, *Skelton*, p. 207.

2756   Chalmers, *English Poets*, I. 517-8; 2. Robinson, *Chaucer* 1933, pp. 620-1; 1957, pp. 526-7.

2756.5 Pla-ce-bo / Who is there who
        'Phyllyp Sparowe,' by John Skelton—vv. 844 in 'skeltonics.'
        Kele, n. d. (STC 22594); *repr.* Dyce, *Skelton*, I. 51-94; Dyce and Child, *Skelton & Donne*, I. 61-108; Flügel, *Neuengl. Lesebuch*, pp. 67-71 (extracts); Henderson, *Skelton*, 1931, pp. 59-98; 1948, 1959, pp. 60-100; Hughes, *Skelton*, pp. 10-34, 87-95 (vv. 1-616, 998-1214); Williams, *Selection*, pp. 57-100; Pinto, *Selection*, pp. 44-71 (extracts); *Oxford Book XVI C. Verse*, pp. 17-30 (extracts); *Poets of Eng. Lang.*, I. 371-413; J. Wyght, n.d.; Kitson, n. d.; *Workes*, Marshe, 1568 (STC 22608); *repr.* [? J. Bowle], 1736; Chalmers, *English Poets*, II. 290-300.

2757   Robbins, *Harvard Theol. Rev.* XLVII. 58; Robbins, *Sec. Lyrics*, p. 1.

2757.3 Please ytt your grace dere harte to gyffe audyence
        'Helpe me of my payne'—four stanzas rime royal.
        1. Bodl. 12653, f. 1a.
        Padelford and Benham, *Anglia* XXXI. 312.

2757.5 Pleasure yt ys / to here Iwys
        Praise God in nature, probably by William Cornish—vv. 13.
        XX Songes, de Worde, 1530 (STC 22924); Imelmann, *Shakespeare-Jahrbuch* XXXIX. 134; Flügel, *Anglia* XII. 595; Flügel, *Neuengl, Lesebuch*, p. 114; *Early Eng. Lyrics*, p. 160; *Oxford Book XVI C. Verse*, p. 38; Davies, *Med. Eng. Lyrics*, p. 292.

2759 (including 'Adiew' anaphora). [St. 8, 4, 14, 17-19 in Clopton Chapel, Church of Holy Trinity, Long Melford, Suffolk; pr. Parker, *History of Long Melford*, 1873, pp. 128; Condor, *Church of Holy Trinity*, 1887, pp. 54; Trapp, *RES* n.s. VI. 5-6].

2760 1. Bodl. Lat. misc. c. 66 [*olim* Capesthorne], f. 93b col. ii. Robbins, *PMLA* LXV. 267-8.

Preised be þou kyng & blessed be þou kyng   See 2017.5.

2766 Dedicatory prologue to Stephen Scrope's version of Christine de Pisan's *Epitre d'Othéa* (addressed to Humfrey Duke of Buckingham or to Sir John Fastolf)—in couplets (with succeeding verse introductions to each of the 100 chapters, one quatrain for cap. vi and following).
1. St. John's Camb. 208, f. 1a (missing one leaf); 2. Longleat 253, f. 4b (lacks prologue); 3. Morgan Lib. M. 775, f. 200b (prologue begins incomplete, vv. 34).
2. Warner, *Roxburghe Club* 1904, CXLI. 5-6 (and interspersed verse, *passim*); 3. Bühler, *Anglia* LXXVI. 266.

2766.2 Pray for bowlay þat owght this booke
A book motto.
1. Trinity Camb. 913, f. 109b.

2766.3 Praye for me all that ye maye
A prayer for the writer.
1. Balliol 329, f. 172b.
Mynors, *Cat.*, p. 340.

2766.4 Pray for the sowl al ye that liue in sight
Epitaph, A.D. 1477, for Sir Geoffrey Gate at High Esterne, Essex—five monoriming lines.
Weever, *Anc. Funerall Monuments*, 1631, p. 620 (STC 25223).

2766.5 Pray for the sowl of Mawd Dauy / Whos corps here vndyr do ly
Epitaph, A.D. 1491, at Northfleet, Kent—six lines.
Weever, *Anc. Funerall Monuments*, 1631, p. 332 (STC 25223).

2766.6 Pray for the sawlys of John Caxton and of Jone
Epitaph, A.D. 1485—vv. 12.
Somner, *Antiq. Canterbury,* 1640, p. 327 (STC 22918); 1703, App., p. 69; Pettigrew, *Chronicles of Tombs,* p. 49; Blades, *Life & Typography of Caxton,* I. 270.

Pray not to God wyth thy lyppes only
See 324 (MS. Sloane 1360).

Pray we now with all our might
Epilogue (6 couplets) to 2147.

2766.8 Pray we to God that all may gyde
For victory in France, A.D. 1513, a round—five lines.
1. BM Addit. 31922, f. 103a.
Chappell, *Archaeologia* XLI. 383; Flügel, *Anglia* XII. 250; Flügel, *Neuengl. Lesebuch,* p. 161; Stevens, *Music & Poetry,* p. 418; Stevens, *Music at Court,* p. 75.

Praye you all my freendys deere   See 1342.

2766.9 Prey ye for the sowl in wey of cheritie / Of Richard Bontfant
Epitaph, A.D. 1459, at Stone, Kent—vv. 10.
Weever, *Anc. Funerall Monuments,* 1631, p. 333 (STC 25223); Ravenshaw, *Antiente Epitaphes,* p. 12; Pettigrew, *Chronicles of Tombs,* p. 46.

2767 [Utley 247].
Chaucer, Stow, 1561 (STC 5075); *Chaucer,* Speght, 1598 (STC 5077); Urry, *Chaucer,* 1721, p. 555; Bell, *Poets of Great Britain,* XIII. 121; [Anderson,] *Poets of Great Britain,* I. 583; Chalmers, *English Poets,* I. 561-2.

Prenegard prenegard / þus bere I myn baselard
Burden to 1896.

2768 three 7-line stanzas and 4-line Envoy.

2769 1a. Person, *Camb. ME Lyrics,* p. 27; 1b. Bloomfield, *Seven Deadly Sins,* p. 169.

2770 2. Pepys 1584, f. 107b.

2771 1, 2. *Early Eng. Carols,* pp. 239-40.

2773   seven alliterative monoriming epithets.
            Bloomfield, *Seven Deadly Sins*, p. 168.

2776   Bloomfield, *Seven Deadly Sins*, p. 208.

2777   fifteen 12-line stanzas.
            Bennett, *England Chaucer-Caxton*, pp. 203-6 (10 st. only); Rickert, *Chaucer's World*, pp. 374-8; Kaiser, *Med. Eng.*, p. 322 (10 st. only); Robbins, *Hist. Poems*, pp. 157-62.

2778   1. MS. to be established, f. 35a.

2779   *Early Eng. Carols*, p. 353; Greene, *Sel. Eng. Carols*, p. 186.

2780   [See 3638.3].
            9. BM Addit. 34801, f. 2a (fragment, vv. 46).
            1. Ford, *Age of Chaucer*, pp. 289-301; 3. Halliwell, *Nugae Poeticae*, pp. 49-63; 9. Hornstein, *PMLA* LXXVIII. 455.

2781   (including Nine Worthies).
            1. Loomis, *MP* XV. 217-8 (extracts).

Pryncesse of wo and wepynge proserpyne   See 1168.

2782   one couplet. [Skelton's *Bowge of Courte* (1470.5) v. 253 may refer to this piece. The first five words are duplicated in v. 970 of 851 and v. 897 of 729.5, but there is no further resemblance].
            Trend, *Zeitschrift für Musikwissenschaft* VIII. 50; Wilson, *Lost Lit.*, p. 178; Robbins, *Sec. Lyrics*, p. 275.

2783   two 8-line tail-rime stanzas.
            Robertson and others, *Scottish Records*, 1804, p. 49: *repr.* Reeves, *MLN* IX. 206.

Preuy penawns discretly / devoute preyre clerly
    See 317 (Bodl. MS. 2224).

2784   [Ringler 61].
            6. Cotton Calig..A. ii, f. 17a; 6a (transcript by Bp. Percy). BM Addit. 39547, f. 90a; 8. Harley 2407, f. 76a (66 st.); 11. *olim* Brudenell, Lamport Hall [*olim* Cardigan], f. 304a (vv. 1-366 only) (Sotheby Sale, Feb. 1959); 12. Boston Pub.

Lib. 92 [*olim* Gurney], ff. 187a-189b (st. 1-16 wanting); 14. Leyden Univ. Vossius 9, f. 42a.

Chorle and the birde, Caxton, ca. 1477 (STC 17008); *facs.* Jenkinson, 1906; Caxton, ca. 1492 (STC 17009); *repr.* Sykes, *Roxburghe Club* 1818, XVI; Pynson, ca. 1493 (STC 17010); de Worde, ca. 1500 (STC 17011); Mychel, 1540 (Selden D. 45); 7. Neilson and Webster, *Chief British Poets*, pp. 208-13; 8. Bowers, *MLN* XLXI. 91-3 (8 st. only).

Proface welcome welcome   See 3587.

2784.5   *Psallemus cantantes / Domino noua cantica dantes*
A hymn to St. John Evangelist—eleven 8-line stanzas inc. refrain, 'Amice christi Iohannes' (cf. bur. 2443), the first stanza wholly in Latin. [A Latin hymn in Bodl. 29734, f. 40b, shares st. 1; pr. Wright, *Percy Soc.* XXIII. 60; *Early Bodl. Music*, II. 182].

Christmas Carolles, Kele, ca. 1550 (STC 5205); *facs.* Reed, *Xmas Carols*, pp. 28-32.

2785.5   Put not in this world to much trust
The vanity of the world—one couplet. [Cf. 397].
1. Harley 2321, f. 149a.
Rel. Ant., I. 208.

2787   [vv. 13-16 occur in Joannis de Fordun, *Scotichronicon*, pr. Edinburgh 1775, II. 474].
5. Royal 17. B. xvii, f. 99a (vv. 13-16 only, followed by 2319).

1-5. Aspin, *AN Pol. Songs*, pp. 161-4, 158, 159; 2. *Rel. Lyr. XIV C.*, p. 259; 4. Marsh, *Hist. Eng. Language*, pp. 247-8; Kaiser, *Med. Eng.*, p. 379.

2788   [Followed by 4053.5].
Wells, *Manual*, p. 533.

2789   2. Harley 665, f. 296a (2 st. with Latin interspersed).

2791   2. [Delete this MS].

2792   Perry, *EETS* 20. 47.

2792.3   *Qui creauit celum* lully lully lu
The processional song of the nuns of Chester, entirely in

Latin except for alternating English Lullay refrains: 'lully lully lu' and 'byby byby by.'
1. Huntington Lib. EL. 34. B. 7 [olim Ellesmere].
Legg, *Processional of Nuns of Chester*, Henry Bradshaw Soc. XVIII. 18; *New Oxford Hist. Music*, III. 117.

Quid petis O fily   See 3438.3.

2793   one couplet with Latin equivalent (followed by 3464.5).

2793.5   R shall rech & the p shall prech
Doggerel prognostics and prophecies—ten lines trailing off into prose.
1. Lansdowne 762, f. 97b (inserted into MS.), f. 96a (copied from f. 97a).

2794   1. Bodl. 15409, Item 5.

2794.2   Ravyshed was I that well was me
A song on the Princess Mary's dancing with her father Henry VIII—six quatrains.
1. Bodl. 6659, f. 100b; 2. Cotton Titus D. xi, f. 56b (title only: first three words).
1. *Rel. Ant.*, I. 258.

2794.4   Rasyd is my mynde
An unkind mistress—one cross-rimed quatrain.
1. Royal App. 58, f. 16b.
Flügel, *Anglia* XII. 265.

2794.6   Reche me mi rocke quet alfled
Three monoriming lines in a Latin sermon.
1. Tübingen Univ. Deposit: Berlin Preussische Staatsbibliothek, Lat. theol. fol. 249, f. 134a.

2794.8   Rede distinctly / pray deu[ou]tly
'A spesiall Glasse to loke in daily:' precepts in -ly—thirty-four irregular riming lines. [Cf. 317, 324, 799, 3087, 3102].
1. London Univ. 278 [olim Mostyn 259], f. 22b.
Whitford, *Imitation of Christ*, Wyer, ca. 1530 (STC 23961) (vv. 28); and later printings; *repr*. Raynal, New York 1872, pp. 402-4; 1908, p. 267; *repr*. with 1. Pafford, *Studies to Sir Hilary Jenkinson*, pp. 515-6, 313-4.

2795   1. Bodl. 21876, f. 32b.
        Whiting, *EETS* 184. x.

2796.5 Resun bade I schulde write / think micul and speke lit
        Inscription on a mazer belonging (in 1930) to Major Thorold
        [Cf. 938, 942].

2797   [Delete entire entry].

        Resoun me bad and redde as for the best   See 2538.

        Reson wondrith that witte no tel can   See 4181.

*2797.5 *...red rosse fayre and sote
        Fragment of refrain song probably for marriage of Princess
        Margaret to James IV, A.D. 1503. [Cf. Stevens, *Music &
        Poetry*, p. 427].
        1. New York Pub. Lib. Drexel Fragments 4180.

        Redresse of sorweful O Cytherea   See 851.

2803.5 Reioyse England / And vnderstande
        'How the Douty Duke of Albany &c.,' by John Skelton—vv.
        532 in 'skeltonics.'
        Workes, Marshe, 1568 (STC 22608); *repr.* [? J. Bowle,] 1736;
        Chalmers, *English Poets*, II. 254-8; Dyce, *Skelton*, II.
        68-84; Dyce and Child, *Skelton & Donne*, II. 321-39;
        Henderson, *Skelton*, 1931, pp. 322-37; 1948, 1959, pp. 398-
        412.

2805   Robbins, *Anglia* LXXII. 386-7; Robbins, *Hist. Poems*, pp.
        150-2.

        Remembre John this þat shineth bright   See 3563.5.

2806.5 Remember man the payne and smart / Wich Christ
        A remembrance on the Passion—two 10-line stanzas.
        1. Harley 4826, f. 146b.

        Remembre youre promys made yn baptym   See 1123.8.

2809   [Utley 249].

2811.5   Renownit ryall right reuerend and serene
'Welcum to Bernard Stewart, Lord of Aubigny,' by William Dunbar, May, A.D. 1508—twelve 8-line stanzas (including acrostic on Barnardus) with refrain: 'With glorie and honoure lawde and reuerence.' [Cf. 1444.5].
Chepman and Myllar, 1508 (ends incompletely); *facs*, Beattie, *Edinb. Bibl. Soc.* 1950, pp. 171-4; *repr.* Laing, *Dunbar*, I. 129; Laing, *Knightly Tale of Golagros*, 1827; Paterson, *Dunbar*, pp. 266; Small, *STS* IV. 59; Schipper, *Dunbar*, pp. 291-5; and *DKAW* XLI (IV). 93-7; Baildon, *Dunbar*, pp. 150-3; Stevenson, *STS* LXV. 241-4; MacKenzie, *Dunbar*, pp. 131-3; Kinsley, *Dunbar*, pp. 18-19.

2811.8   Rest after gret trauelyng
Two couplets in a Latin sermon.
1. Camb. Un. Ii. 3. 8, f. 144a.

2814   Adams, *Chief Pre-Sh. Dramas*, pp. 212-24.

Rex I sitt and loke about   See 1822.

Richard kyng henri sone to engeland com   See 727.

2818.2   Richard Nordell lyeth buryd here
Epitaph, A.D. 1500, for Richard Nordell and his wife at St. Edmund's Church, Lombard Street, London—vv. 16 in couplets (including vv. 4 on Abuses of Age; cf. 906 and 1206.8). Weever, *Anc. Funerall Monuments*, 1631, pp. 19, 412-3 (STC 25223); Ravenshaw, *Antiente Epitaphes*, p. 15.

*R[ichard went agayn] wel stille   See 1979 (MS. 7a).

2818.3   Riches are gotten with labor holden with feare
A moralizing couplet. [Cf. 397].
1. Harley 2321, f. 148a.
Rel. Ant., I. 208.

2818.6   Rydynge al alone with sorowe sore encombred
'Epitaffe of the moste noble & valyaunt Iasper late duke of Beddeforde,' A.D. 1495—introduction and twenty sections in many different verse forms. [Ringler 62].
Pynson, ca. 1496 (14477); *repr.* (from a transcript in a Pepys MS.) Dyce, *Skelton*, II. 347-98; Dyce and Child, *Skelton & Donne*, II. 347-61.

2818.8   Ryght as all stringis ar reullit in ane harp
'*De regimene principum bonum consilium*' from the *Liber Pluscardensis*—in rime royal stanzas.
1. Bodl. 3888, ff. 190a-191b (vv. 291); 1a (transcript). Marchmont A. C. 15; 1b (1675 transcript). Bodl. 8915, ff. 562b-567a; 2. Pepys 2553, p. 96 (vv. 308).
Chepman and Myllar, 1508 (vv. 224) (STC 3307); *facs.* Beattie, *Edinb. Bibl. Soc.* 1950, pp. 101-8; *repr.* Laing, *Knightly Tale of Golagros,* 1827; Stevenson, STS LXV. 171-8; 1, 1a. Craigie, STS n.s. XX. 74-91; 1a. Skene, *Liber Pluscardensis,* I. 391-400 (*Historians of Scotland,* VII, Edinb. 1811); 2. Craigie, STS n.s. VII. 115-25.

2820   [Cf. also 856.5].
2. Harley 2251, f. 152b; 4. BM Addit. 29729, f. 288b (vv. 7); 6. Yale Univ. 163 [*olim* Petworth 8], f. 29a; 7. Rylands Lib. Latin 201, f. 227a.
3. Brusendorff, *Chaucer Tradition,* p. 436; 7. Fawtier, *BJRL* V. 389.

Right as smale flodes encrece to watres feele   See 1874.

2820.3   Right as the rose excelleth all floures *inter ligna floriga*
On good wine—thirteen long macaronic couplets.
1. Durham Cath., Prior's Kitchen, Bp. Hatfield's Survey, p. 149.

2820.5   Ryght as the stern of day begouth to schyne
'The Golden Targe,' by William Dunbar—thirty-one 9-line stanzas.
1. Pepys 2553, pp. 64-6, 73-6, 81; 2. Advocates 1. 1. 6, f. 345a.
Chepman and Myllar, 1508; *facs.* Beattie, *Edinb. Bibl. Soc.* 1950, pp. 89-100; *repr.* Sibbald, *Chronicle,* I. 253-63; Laing, *Knightly Tale of Golagros,* 1827; Laing, *Dunbar,* I. 11-21; Kaufmann, *Traité de la langue...Dunbar,* 1873, pp. 23-46; *repr. Blackwood's Magazine,* Feb. 1835 (extracts); Paterson, *Dunbar,* pp. 29-40; Small, STS IV. 1-10; Eyre-Todd, *Med. Scot. Poetry,* pp. 159-69; Stevenson, STS LXV. 159-68; MacKenzie, *Dunbar,* pp. 112-19; Kinsley, *Dunbar,* pp. 25-33; 1. Craigie, STS n.s. VII. 89-97; Schipper, *Dunbar,* pp. 101-13; and *DKAW* XV (IV). 9-19; Baildon, *Dunbar,* pp. 45-52; 2. [Hailes,] *Anc. Scot. Poems,* pp. 9-19; Ramsay, *Evergreen,* I. 22-37; *repr. Ramsay and Earlier Scot. Poets,* pp. 263; *Select Poems of Dunbar,*

Perth 1788, pp. 1-11; *Bannatyne MS.*, Hunt. Club, IV. 995-1003; Arber, *Dunbar Anthology*, pp. 7-17; Ritchie, *STS* n.s. XXVI. 252-61.

2821 [Utley 252].

2821.3 Rycht airlie on Ask Weddinsday
'The twa cummeris,' by William Dunbar—six 5-line stanzas with refrain. [Utley 251].
1. Camb. Un. Ll. 5. 10, f. 19b; 2. Pepys 2553, pp. 57-8; 3. Aberdeen, Town Clerk's Office, Minute Book of Sasines, III; 4. Advocates 1. 1. 6, f. 137a.

3, 4. Laing, *Dunbar*, I (Suppl.). 312-3,I.81-2; 2. Pinkerton, *Anc. Scot. Poems*, I. 113-14; Craigie, *STS* n.s. VII. 64-5; Kinsley, *Dunbar*, pp. 77-8; 3. Small, *STS* XVI. 249-50; 4. Sibbald, *Chronicle*, I. 232-3; Paterson, *Dunbar*, pp. 93; *BannatyneMS.*, Hunt. Club, III.386-7; Small,*STS* IV. 160; Schipper, *Dunbar*, pp. 73-4; and *DKAW* XL (IV). 72-4; Baildon, *Dunbar*, pp. 25; Ritchie, *STS* n.s. XXIII. 14-15; MacKenzie, *Dunbar*, pp. 84; Kinsley, *Dunbar*, pp. 77-8.

2821.5 Rycht fane wald I my quentance mak / withe Sir penny
Sir Penny—seven 8-line stanzas. [Cf. 1480, 2747, 3209].
1. Camb. Un. Ll. 5. 10, f. 40a; 2. Pepys 2553, p. 330; 3. Advocates 1. 1. 6, f. 144a.

2. Craigie, *STS* n.s. VII. 399-400; 3. Sibbald, *Chronicle*, III. 227; [Hailes,] *Anc. Scot. Poems*, pp. 193-5; Ramsay, *Evergreen*, I. 27; *Caledonian Muse*, 1785, p. 164; *Bannatyne MS.*, Hunt. Club, p. 409; Ritchie, *STS* n.s. XXIII. 35-6; Wright, *Poems of Walter Mapes*, Camden Soc. XVI. 362.

Right fresshe flour whos I ben haue and shal
'*Litera Troili:*' See 3327.

2824 Robbins, *Sec. Lyrics*, p. xx.

Right is deed and þat is rewþe   See 2145.

2825 1. Pepys 2011, f. 78a.
Bühler, *MLN* LII. 2-4.

2826 4. Sloane 1787, f. 107a; 5. Sloane 3667, f. 92a; 6. Univ. of Pennsylvania, Smith 4, ff. 1a-10.

2827.5 Right wel beloved prentise / I commande me to your gentil-
nesse
A humorous letter 'send by R.W. to A.C.'—twenty-seven
couplets.
1. Bodl. 12653, f. 8a.
Padelford and Benham, *Anglia* XXXI. 321-2.

2829 Robbins, *Hist. Poems*, p. 327.

2830.5 Robyn Hod in scherewod stod
A fragment of a Robin Hood ballad—four lines only.
1. Lincoln Cath. 132, f. 100a.
Morris, *MLR* XLIII. 507-8; Wilson, *Lost Lit.*, p. 140.

Robynn lyth in grene wode bowndyn See 1317.

2831 1a (xix cent. transcript). BM Addit. 30371, f. 77a.
1. Eyre-Todd, *Med. Scot. Poetry*, pp. 91-5; Arber, *Dunbar Anthology*, pp. 146-50; *Oxford Book English Verse*, pp. 16-20; Neilson and Webster, *Chief British Poets*, pp. 383-4; *Poets of Eng. Lang.*, I. 296-301; Wood, *Henryson*, pp. 151-4; Elliott, pp. 125-8.

2831.2 Rolling in my rememberaunce / Off court
'The Variance of Court,' by Stewart—ten 5-line stanzas.
1. Camb. Un. Ll. 5. 10, f.35a; 2. Pepys 2553, p. 311; 3. Advocates 1. 1. 6, f. 94a.
2. Craigie, *STS* n.s. VII. 370-2; 3. [Hailes,] *Anc. Scot. Poems*, p. 204; *Bannatyne MS.*, Hunt. Club, pp. 269-70; Sibbald, *Chronicle*, II. 44; Ritchie, *STS* n.s. XXII. 249-51.

2831.4 Rome no þing is þere to þe
In praise of Rome—one quatrain in Trevisa's translation of Higden's *Polychronicon* (Book I, cap. 24).
1. St. John's Camb. 204; 2. Cotton Tiberius D. vii; 3. Harley 1900; 4. Stowe 65; 5. BM Addit. 24194; 6. Aberdeen Univ 21; 7. Chetham Lib. 11379; 8. Hunterian Mus. 83; 9. Penrose 12; 10. Morgan Lib. 875.
Trevisa, *Discripcion of Britayne*, Caxton, 1480 (STC 13440a); de Worde, 1498 (STC 13440b); Trevisa, *Prolicronycon*, Caxton, 1482 (STC 13438); de Worde, 1495 (STC 13439); Treveris, 1527 (STC 13440); 1. Babington and Lumby, *Rolls Series* XLI, i. 213; Mätzner, *AE Sprachproben*, II. 359.

2831.6   *Rorate celi desuper* / Hevins distill your balmy schouris
On the Nativity, by William Dunbar—seven aureate 8-line stanzas with refrain: '*Et nobis puer natus est.*'
1. Advocates 1. 1. 6, f. 27a.

[Hailes,] *Anc. Scot. Poems*, pp. 104-6; Laing, *Dunbar*, I. 236-8; Paterson, *Dunbar*, pp. 67-9; *Select Poems of Dunbar*, Perth 1788, pp. 87-9; *Bannatyne MS.*, Hunt. Club, II. 69-70; Small, *Dunbar*, STS IV. 72-3; Schipper, *Dunbar*, pp. 367-8; and *DKAW* XLII (IV). 65-6; Baildon, *Dunbar*, pp. 193-4; Ritchie, *STS* n.s. XXII. 65; MacKenzie, *Dunbar*, pp. 154-5; Kinsley, *Dunbar*, pp. 1-2.

2831.8   Ros Mary most of vertewe virginale
'Ane ballat of our lady,' by William Dunbar—six 8-line stanzas with refrain: '*O mater Jhesu salve Maria.*'
1. Harley 1703, f. 79b (8 st., with 10 addit st. by William Forrest, ca. 1558); 2. Edinburgh Univ. 205, f. 183b (vv. 1-40); 3. Asloan, f. 301a.

1. MacCracken, *MLN* XXIV. 110-11; 2. Stevenson, *STS* LXV. 24-5; 3. Laing, *Dunbar*, I (Suppl.). 283-4; Small, *STS* IV. 272-3; Schipper, *Dunbar*, pp. 372-4; and *DKAW* XLII (IV). 69-72; Baildon, *Dunbar*, pp. 197-8; Craigie, *STS* n.s. XVI. 271-2; *crit. text.* MacKenzie, *Dunbar*, pp. 175-7.

2832   8. Wilson, *Library* IV, ii. 264; 4. Foster, *Essays in Honor of Carleton Brown*, p. 156.

2832.2   Rutterkyn is com vnto oure towne
A satire on gallants, perhaps by John Skelton—four quatrains and burden: 'Hoyda, hoyda.' [Cf. Speech of Abusione in *Magnificence* (223.5), Stage 2, scene 12].
1. BM Addit. 5465, f. 101b.

Hawkins, *Hist. Music*, 1776, III. 9-16; Dyce, *Skelton*, II. 245-6; Dyce and Child, *Skelton & Donne*, III. 218-9; Rimbault, *Songs & Ballads*, p. 31; Briggs, *Songs & Madrigals*, PMMS 1881, pp. [M] 1-4; Flügel, *Neuengl. Lesebuch*, p. 147; *Early Eng. Lyrics*, p. 248; Henderson, *Skelton*, 1931, p. 37; 1948, 1959, p. 25; Stevens, *Music & Poetry*, p. 380.

2832.5   Rowe the bote Norman / rowe to thy lemman
Fragment of a popular song made by the watermen of Thames to John Norman, mentioned in early chronicles.

Fabyan, *New Chronicles*, 1516 (STC 10659); Ellis, 1814, p. 628; Kingsford, *Chronicles of London*, p. 164; Wilson, *Lost Lit.*, p. 204.

2834 three 8-line tail-rime stanzas.

2834.3 S mysed in myndes and merke þer a P
A political prophecy—thirty-six alliterative lines.
1. Cotton Rolls II. 23, Art. 9.

Sacrylege in Englyssh ys as I can
See 1540 (MS. Arundel, f. 57a).

2834.5 Sad and solitaire sittand myn allone
'Think on thy end and thow sall never syn'—five 8-line stanzas with this refrain.
1. Pepys 2553, p. 222.
Craigie, STS n.s. VII. 250-1.

2837 5. National Lib. of Wales 5043, ff. 3a-3b (fragment).

2838 2. Bodl. 3938, f. 33a (col. 2).

2839 17. Lambeth 223, f. 65b.
9. D'Evelyn and Mill, EETS 235. 54.

2842 7. D'Evelyn and Mill, EETS 235. 238-41.

2843 7. D'Evelyn and Mill, EETS 235. 211-4.

2844 18. Bodl. Eng. poet. e. 94, a single leaf (vv. 1-6, 11-38, 43-71).
8. D'Evelyn and Mill, EETS 235. 148-55.

2845 8. Gray's Inn 20, ff. 2a-2b (fragment).
4. D'Evelyn and Mill, EETS 236. 586-90.

2847 2. Horstmann, AE Leg. 1881, pp. 1-10; Emerson, Reader, pp. 135-43.

2848 13. D'Evelyn and Mill, EETS 236. 543-50.

2849 Clive, Roxburghe Club, 1835, L. 116-36; Serjeantson, EETS 206. 110-29.

2850 19. Winchester Coll. 33, f. 51b.
9. D'Evelyn and Mill, EETS 235. 19.

2854	1 (with vv. 1-34 from 4). Horstmann, *EETS* 87. 24-5; 10. D'Evelyn and Mill, *EETS* 235. 214-17.
2855	in Vernon Golden Legend—in short couplets.
2856	7. D'Evelyn and Mill, *EETS* 235. 217-20.
2858	7. D'Evelyn and Mill, *EETS* 236. 373-84.
2860	3. McCann,, *Downside Rev.* XLI. 48-53; 6. D'Evelyn and Mill, *EETS* 235. 122.
2861	1. McCann, *Downside Rev.* XLI. 53-5.
2863	in Vernon Golden Legend—in short couplets.
2864	Bowers, *MLN* LXIX. 160-3.
2866	10. D'Evelyn and Mill, *EETS* 235. 47-54.
2868	vv. 738 in couplets. 16. Ripon Minster, fragment 33; 17. Wisbech Mus. H. 6. 29, two binding strips (fragment). 1 (with vv. 68-247 from 13). Horstmann, *EETS* 87. 220-40. 8. D'Evelyn and Mill, *EETS* 235. 180-204; *comp. text* (4). M. Bälz, *Die ME Brendanlegende des Gloucesterlegendars*, Stuttgart 1909; 13. *Cambridge Book Prose & Verse*, pp. 345-7 (extracts).
2872	15. Nottingham Univ. Mi LM 7/1 [*olim* Wollaton Hall], f. 161 (vv. 5-25, 39-59); 16. Public Record Office C. 47 / 34 / 1, No. 5, f. 4a (vv. 1-82). 7. D'Evelyn and Mill, *EETS* 235.37; 15. *Hist. MSS. Comm. Report*, Middleton MSS., 1911, pp. 622-3.
2873	2, 3, 8. B. E. Lovewell, &c.
2874	7. D'Evelyn and Mill, *EETS* 235. 78-81.
2875	15. D'Evelyn and Mill, *EETS* 236. 515.
2876	7. D'Evelyn and Mill, *EETS* 235. 315-27.

2878   8. D'Evelyn and Mill, *EETS* 235. 340-81.

2879   1. Egerton 3309 [*olim* Castle Howard], pp. 1-203.

2880   20. Winchester Coll. 33, f. 24a; 21. G. Allan, of Darlington (MS. not further identified).
            10. D'Evelyn and Mill, *EETS* 235. 118-21; 21. C. Sharp, *History of Hartlepool*, App. pp. xxiii-xxv.

2881.5   Sayn denes þat es me dere / For hes lof / drenk and make gud cher
        Inscription on a drinking cup, property of Pembroke Coll., Cambridge.

2882   6. D'Evelyn and Mill, *EETS* 236. 434-9.

2883   6. Camb. Un. Add. 2585 (3) (vv. 124).

2884   22. Ripon Minster, fragment 33.
            1 (with vv. 107-160 from 4). Horstmann &c.; 10. D'Evelyn and Mill, *EETS* 235. 204-11; 18. Morris and Skeat, *Specimens*, 1889, p. 19 (vv. 1-92).

2886   13. D'Evelyn and Mill, *EETS* 236. 492-511.

2887   1. Lord Francis Hervey, *Corolla S. Eadmundi*, 1907, pp. 362-6; 11. D'Evelyn and Mill, *EETS* 236. 511-5.

2888   3. G. E. Moore, *ME Verse Life of Edward the Confessor*, Philadelphia 1942, pp. 1-40.

2889   8. D'Evelyn and Mill, *EETS* 235. 110-8.

2890   in two MSS.
        2. Winchester Coll. 33, f. 20b.

2891   4. Langton Brown, *Saint Egwine and his Abbey of Evesham*, 1904, pp. 167-75.

2892   1. York Minster XVI. G. 5, f. 98b.

2894   1 (with vv. 86-179 from 9). Horstmann, *EETS* 87. 393-402.

2895   —vv. 24 (Fabian) and vv. 90 (Sebastian, as in 2896).
          14. Delete this MS.; 15. Winchester Coll. 33, f. 49b.
            6. D'Evelyn and Mill, *EETS* 235. 15.

2896   Seint Fabian þretten зer pope was in rome
          —vv. 4 (Fabian) and vv. 90 (Sebastian, as in 2895).
          5. Lambeth 223, f. 53a.

2903   Blundevill, *Fower Chiefest Offices Belonging to Horsemanship*, 1571; repr. E.B., *N&Q* 6 s. I. 54; Kittredge, *Witchcraft in Old and New England*, 1929, p. 220; Greene, *Sel. Eng. Carols*, p. 228; 1. Robbins, *Sec. Lyrics*, p. 61.

2904   2. Parker, *MLN* XXXVIII. 97.

2905   10. D'Evelyn and Mill, *EETS* 235. 155-9.

2906   9. Cotton Jul. D. ix, f. 132b.
          6. D'Evelyn and Mill, *EETS* 236. 384-9.

2907   1. Horstmann, *Archiv* LVII. 307-8.

2910   19. Winchester Coll. 33, f. 30a.
          10. D'Evelyn and Mill, *EETS* 235. 81-4.

2910.5   Seynt gregor with oþir popes / & bysshoppes yn feer
          A xylographic indulgence accompanying an Image of Pity ca. A.D. 1423—four long lines.
          Collected Papers of Henry Bradshaw, 1889, p. 97; Axon, *Trans. Lancs. & Cheshire Antiq. Soc.* X. 105; Dodgson, *English Woodcuts, no. 2*; Schreiber, *Handbuch*, 869, D. 2.

2911   2, 3. Birch, *Memorials of St. Guthlac*, pp. xxix (vv. 1-24), xxx (vv. 105-24); Forstmann, *Bonner Beiträge* XII. 32 (vv. 1-24), 22.

2912   16. Public Record Office C. 47 / 34 / 1, No. 5, f.2a (vv. 1-89).
          7. D'Evelyn and Mill, *EETS* 235. 5-8.

2916   4. National Lib. Wales 5043, ff. 1, 2 (fragment, inc. *Narracio bona*).

2918   Seint Iemes þe holi Apostle guod is to habbe in mone
       8. D'Evelyn and Mill, *EETS* 235. 327-40.

2920   in 'expanded' North. Hom. Cycle. [Cf. 2920.5]
       3. Edinb. Coll. Phys.
          3. Small, *Met. Homilies*, pp. 25-7; Morris, *Specimens*, 1867, pp. 146-8.

2920.5 Sain Jerom telles that fiften / Ferli takeninges
       The Fifteen Signs before Doomsday, in one MS. of the North Hom. Cycle, with accompanying Latin text. [Cf. 2920].
       1. Edinb. Coll. Phys., f. 19b.
          Small, *Met. Hom.*, pp. 25-9; Morris, *Specimens*, 1867, pp. 146-8; Morris and Skeat, *Specimens*, II. 83-6.

2921   [Cf. 3973].

2922   15. Cotton Jul. D. ix, f. 137a.
       6. D'Evelyn and Mill, *EETS* 236. 428-34.

2928   1. Bodl. 3938, f. 194b.

2932   11. D'Evelyn and Mill, *EETS* 236. 594-610; 18. Furnivall, *E. E. Poems*, pp. 106-7 (extract).

2945   8. D'Evelyn and Mill, *EETS* 235. 241-6.

2949   9. D'Evelyn and Mill, *EETS* 235. 31-2.

2950   20. Cotton Titus A. xxvi, f. 204b; 21. Public Record Office C. 47 / 34 / 1, No. 5, f. 3a (vv. 1-44 wanting).
       10. D'Evelyn and Mill, *EETS* 235. 32-7.

2951   3. Schleich, *Archiv* CLI. 25-34; 8. D'Evelyn and Mill, *EETS* 235. 62-70.

2954   14. D'Evelyn and Mill, *EETS* 236. 533-43.

2956   6. D'Evelyn and Mill, *EETS* 235. 279-91.

2957   8. D'Evelyn and Mill, *EETS* 236. 358-64.

2959   11. D'Evelyn and Mill, *EETS* 236. 476-83.

2960	1. Peebles, *Legend of Longinus*, 1911, pp. 94-5; 5. D'Evelyn and Mill, *EETS* 235. 84-5.
2961	14. Furnivall, *E. E. Poems*, pp. 101-6; D'Evelyn and Mill, *EETS* 236. 566-71.
2963	forty-one lines in couplets. 1. BM Addit. 46919 [*olim* Phillipps 8336], f. 211a. Gneuss, *Anglia* LXXVIII. 185-6.
2973	5. D'Evelyn and Mill, *EETS* 236. 439.
2987	8. D'Evelyn and Mill, *EETS* 235. 291-302; 15. Mätzner, *AE Sprachproben*, pp. 200-7.
2988	3, 7. Hewlett, *Rolls Series* LXXXIV, i. 73; 3. Wilson, *Lost Lit.*, p. 172; 4. *Register*, I. 199; 11. Hall,*Early Middle English*, I. 5; Davies, *Med. Eng. Lyrics*, p. 51.
2989	9. D'Evelyn and Mill, *EETS* 235. 127-8.
2990	21. Winchester Coll. 33, f. 25a; 22. Bodl. Eng. poet. e. 94, single leaf (vv. 293-320, 325-46); 23. Bodl. 8⁰ G. 40. Med. (fragment: vv. 182-7, 213-9) 9. D'Evelyn and Mill, *EETS* 235. 136-48.
2991	14. BM Addit. 10301, f. 150b. 7. D'Evelyn and Mill, *EETS* 236. 364-73.
2994	7. D'Evelyn and Mill, *EETS* 235. 302-15.
2995	Rickert, *Anc. Eng. Xmas Carols*, pp. 3-5.
3004	9. D'Evelyn and Mill, *EETS* 235. 159-60.
3004.5	Saint Martin was a nobill man / For in his barnhede Life of St. Martin in 'expanded' North. Hom. Cycle. [Cf. 416, 3006]. 1. Cotton Tiberius E. vii, f. 268a; 2. Harley 4196, f. 188a. 2. Horstmann, *AE Leg. 1881*, pp. 152-5.
3005	14. D'Evelyn and Mill, *EETS* 236. 483-92.
3017	6. D'Evelyn and Mill, *EETS* 236. 397-402.

3018   Small, *Met. Hom.*, pp. 34-8.

3021   6. Morris, *Specimens*, 1867, pp. 151-4.

3026   18. Winchester Coll. 33, f. 39a.
            9. D'Evelyn and Mill, *EETS* 235. 70-1.

3027   4. BM Addit. 37787, f. 15b; 6. Quaritch Sale Cat., 1931 Illuminated MSS., Item 82, and Cat. 609, 1943, Item 500.
            4. N. S. Baugh, *Worcestershire Misc.*, pp. 103-4.

3028   [Cf. 554.3 and 2725].
            2. Cotton Tiberius E. vii. f. 90a (vv. 2154); 3. Penrose 6 [*olim* Delamere], f. 175b (fragment: vv. 37); 4. Delete this MS.

3029   Parts I-III. 15. Corp. Christi Camb. 145, f. 149b (transferred from Parts I-II only. MS. 5).
            5. D'Evelyn and Mill, *EETS* 236. 402-28; 10 (Part III only). Mätzner, *AE Sprachproben*, pp. 137-47.

3030   4. National Lib. Wales 5043, f. 3a (fragment).

3031   recorded by Geoffrey of Durham.
            Hall, *Early Middle English*, I. 5; Wilson, *Lost Lit.*, p. 173.

3033   1 (with vv. 361-448 from MS. 16). Horstmann, *EETS* 87. 240-55; 16. D'Evelyn and Mill, *EETS* 236. 550-66.

3035   19. Winchester Coll. 33, f. 17b.
            8. D'Evelyn and Mill, *EETS* 235. 71-8.

3036   12. Camb. Un. Add. 2585 (3) (last 34 vv.).
            7. D'Evelyn and Mill, *EETS* 236. 357-8.

3037   18. National Lib. Wales 5043, ff. 4a, 4b (fragment).
            9. D'Evelyn and Mill, *EETS* 235. 85-110.

3039   1. Horstmann, *EETS* 87. 199-220.

3041   17. Winchester Coll. 33, f. 38a (Conversion only).
            8. D'Evelyn and Mill, *EETS* 235. 264-74.

3042	7. D'Evelyn and Mill, *EETS* 235. 162-3.
3046	16. Winchester Coll. 33, f. 37a. 7. D'Evelyn and Mill, *EETS* 235. 246-64.
3048	20. Winchester Coll. 33, f. 31b. 10. D'Evelyn and Mill, *EETS* 235. 164-7.
3050	10. D'Evelyn and Mill, *EETS* 236. 456-60.
3051	17. Winchester Coll. 33, f. 44b. 7. D'Evelyn and Mill, *EETS* 235. 179-80.

Seynt Sebestian was a man of a gret honour   See 2895.

3051.5   Sanct salvatour send silver sorrow
To the King, by William Dunbar—seven 5-line stanzas with refrain: 'My panefull purs so priclis me.' [Cf. 3116.5].
1. Advocates 1. 1. 6, f. 113b.

[Hailes,] *Anc. Scot. Poems*, pp. 87-8; *Select Poems of Dunbar*, Perth 1788, pp. 73-4; Sibbald, *Chronicle*, I. 280-1; Laing, *Dunbar*, I. 157-8; Paterson, *Dunbar*, pp. 203-4; *Bannatyne MS.*, Hunt. Club, II. 322-4; Small, *STS* IV. 129-30; Schipper, *Dunbar*, pp. 232-3; and *DKAW* XLI (IV). 34-5; Baildon, *Dunbar*, pp. 112-13; Ritchie, *STS* n.s. XXII. 301-2; MacKenzie, *Dunbar*, pp. 1-2.

3052	8. D'Evelyn and Mill, *EETS* 235. 59-60.
3055	7 (with 13). D'Evelyn and Mill, *EETS* 236. 448-56.
3058	Ritson, *Anc. Songs*, 1790, p. 83; Child, *Ballads*, 1864, 1878, I. 316-18; Gummere, *OE Ballads*, pp. 295-6; Sylvester, *Garland of Xmas Carols*, pp. 2-4; Bullen, *Carols & Poems*, pp. 33-5; Sargent and Kittredge, *Ballads*, no. 22; Rickert, *Anc. Eng. Xmas Carols*, pp. 123-4; *Oxford Book Christian Verse*, pp. 42-3; Leach, *Ballad Book*, pp. 107-8.
3059	9. D'Evelyn and Mill, *EETS* 236. 590-4.
3060	1, 5. J. Earle, *Gloucester Fragments*, 1861, pp. 78-83; 6. D'Evelyn and Mill, *EETS* 235. 274-9.

3063   Seint Thomas þe guode Apostle I-martyred was in Inde
       8 (with vv. 1-308 from 15). D'Evelyn and Mill, *EETS* 236. 571-86.

3064   2. Bodl. 2567; 5. Pepys 2344, p. 528 (vv. 1-24); 9. Harley 2277, f. 226a; 11. Bodl. 1596; 12. Bodl 6924, f. 259a; 13. Camb. Un. Add. 3039; 14. Corpus Christi Camb. 145, f. 217b; 15. Cotton Jul. D. ix, f. 265b; 16. Lambeth 223.
       10. Mätzner, *AE Sprachproben*, p. 192; 14. D'Evelyn and Mill, *EETS* 236. 690.

3065   3 (with 5 st. from 2). MacCracken, *EETS* cvii. 304-10.

3066   8. D'Evelyn and Mill, *EETS* 235. 61-2.

3067   8. D'Evelyn and Mill, *EETS* 235. 25-31.

3068   19. Lambeth 223, f. 50b.
       10. D'Evelyn and Mill, *EETS* 235. 8-15.

3068.5 Salamon seyth ther is none accorde
       Proverbs—fifteen couplets (vv. 25-26 = vv. 1-2 of 4137).
       1. Trinity Camb. 1450, f. 70a.
       Person, *Camb. ME Lyrics*, pp. 52-3.

3070   2. Bodl. 29734, f. 20a (4 st.).
       2, 3. Rickert, *Anc. Eng. Xmas Carols*, pp. 179, 178; 3. Stevens, *Music & Poetry*, p. 51.

3072   Zupitza, *Archiv* LXXXIX. 318-9.

       Salue sancta parens   See 182.

3074   [Ringler 63].
       Lidgate, *Stans puer*, Caxton, ca. 1477 (STC 17030).

3074.3 Sanctus beda was iboren her on bretone mid us
       Alliterative lines complaining of William the Conqueror's foreign prelates—vv. 16.
       1. Worcester Cath. F. 174, f. 63a.
       Phillipps, *Fragment of Aelfric's Grammar*, 1838, p. 5; Wright, *Bibl. Brit. Lit.*, I. 59; Varnhagen, *Anglia* III. 424-5; Hall, *Early Middle English*, I. 1; Dickins and Wilson, *Early ME Texts*, p. 2.

3074.6 Sauns remedye endure must I
The sleepless lover—three long quatrains with internal rime.
1. Bodl. 6659, f. 99b.
Wagner, *MLN* L. 454.

3077.5 Salviour suppois my sensualitie
'Ane orisoun,' by William Dunbar—one 8-line stanza.
1. Camb. Un. Ll. 5. 10, f. 40a; 2. Pepys 2553, p. 326.
2. Laing, *Dunbar*, I. 235; Paterson, *Dunbar*, p. 87; Small, *STS* IV. 267-8; Schipper, *Dunbar*, pp. 366-7; and *DKAW* XLII (IV). 64-5; Baildon, *Dunbar*, p. 193; Craigie, *STS* n.s. VII. 393; MacKenzie, *Dunbar*, p. 154; Kinsley, *Dunbar*, p. 67.

3078 [Utley 254].
1. Dickins and Wilson, *Early ME Texts*, p. 119; Whiting, *Speculum* IX. 220; 2. Herbert, *Cat. Rom.*, III. 529 (couplet only); Coulton, *Life in the MA*, I. 149.

3078.5 Sey nou man quat þinket þu
A cross-rimed quatrain translating: '*Dic homo quid speres &c.*'
1. Advocates 18. 7. 21, f. 87b.

3079.2 Say the best and bere the softe / ontaust tunge greuith ofte
A couplet motto on a scroll in one MS. of Hoccleve's *De Regimine Principum* (2229).
1. Camb. Un. Hh. 4. 11, f. 44a and again at f. 72a.

Say þe best or be stylle See 3079.8.

3079.3 Sey þu vessel of wrechednesse
Two couplets translating: '*Dic homo vas scelerum &c.*'
1. Advocates 18. 7. 21, f. 87b.

3079.4 Say to our lady *aues* seuen
A rubric recommending prayer to the Heart of Christ.
1. Bodl. Lat. misc. c. 66 [*olim* Capesthorne], f. 129b.

3079.5 Say trouthe be not fals / Telle no talis
A couplet motto on a scroll in one MS. of Hoccleve's *De Regimine Principum* (2229).
1. Camb. Un. Hh. 4. 11, f. 36a.

3079.7   Saye well ys a worthy thyng
          Do well preferable to Say well—nine quatrains and burden.
          [Cf. Tilley D 402, S 123].
          1. Advocates 1. 1. 6, f. 83a (21 couplets); 2. Victoria and
          Albert Mus., Dyce 45, f. 41b.
          1. *Bannatyne MS.*, Hunt. Club, p. 230; Ritchie, *STS* n.s.
          XX. 212-3.

3079.8   Say well or be styll / Suffyr and haue all thy wyll
          Two couplets advocating caution (including 'had y wyst').
          [Cf. 3081].
          1. Harley 665, f. 302a; 2. Bühler 21, f. iii recto (vv. 3 with
          4 Latin lines).
          2. Bühler, *Studies in Med. Lit. to Baugh*, p. 287.

3080   The Battle of Bannockburn Avenged, by Laurence Minot.
          Warton, *History Eng. Lit.*, rev. Hazlitt, III. 122; Flügel,
          Neuengl. Lesebuch, p. 96; Mätzner, *AE Sprachproben*,
          I. 323; Wülcker, *AE Lesebuch*, I. 77; Zupitza, *AE Uebungs-
          buch*, 1928, p. 164; Kaiser, *Anthologie*, p. 369; Kaiser,
          Med. Eng., p. 381; Robbins, *Hist. Poems*, p. 30.

*3080.5   *Second day of þat seynte
          The Fifteen Signs before Doomsday—vv. 18. [Cf. 1823].
          1. BM Addit. 40166 (C. 3), f. 12a (starts at 2nd Day and
          ends at 6th Day).

3081   [=vv. 99-100 of 3502, MS. Bodl. 14526].
          and as comment of Third Cock in story in *Gesta Romanorum*
          (cf. 3322.3 and 2238.5); e.g.: 13. Harley 2270; 14. Harley
          5259, f. 60a; 15. Harley 7333, f. 224b; 16. BM Addit. 9066,
          f. 19b.
          12. *Register*, II. 6; 13, 15. Madden, *Roxburghe Club*,
          1838, LV. 147, 515; 14, 16. Herbert, *Cat. Rom.* III. 206,
          309; 15, 16. Herrtage, *EETS* xxxiii. 175.

3082   four stanzas rime royal.

          See / Me / Be / kinde
          An extract from Hawes' *Conuersion of Swerers* (3354.5).

3083   [Cf. Brown, *MLN* LIV. 131-3].
          5. Victoria and Albert Mus., Dyce 34 (Dyce's transcript
          of de Worde print).

3084   *The Remedy of Love*—nineteen stanzas rime royal as Prologue, and sixty-two stanzas as text. [For an extract occurring separately see 3648.8; cf. also 1409.3. Utley 255].
Chaucer, Thynne, 1532 (STC 5068); *facs.* Skeat, 1905, pp. 758; *Chaucer*, Stow, 1561 (STC 5075); *Chaucer*, Speght, 1598 (STC 5077); Urry, *Chaucer*, 1721, p. 526; Bell, *Poets of Great Britain*, XII. 157; [Anderson,] *Poets of Great Britain*, I. 550; Chalmers, *English Poets*, I. 538-42.

3084.3   Seeke to defend thyself from synne
On the Seven Deadly Sins—seven quatrains and concluding 6-line stanza.
1. BM Addit. 17013, f. 5a (added in xvi cent. hand).
Francis, *EETS* 217. 340.

3084.6   Selde erendeʒ wel þe loþe / And selde pledeʒ wel þe wroþe
A proverbial couplet.
1. BM Addit. 35116, f. 24b.
W.C. Bolland, *Year Books*, p. 77; Stanley, *Owl and Nightingale*, 1960, pp. 126-7.

3086   Metcalfe, *STS* XVIII. 361-72

3087   [See further 2794.8].
1. Revise MS. number: Bodl. 6704, f. 70a (vv. 11); 3. Revise MS. number: Bodl. 15444, f. 143a (vv. 7).
Bayte and Snare of Fortune, Wayland, n. d.; repr. Dibdin, *Typo. Antiquities*, III. 531; 3, 4. Meech, *MP* XXXVIII. 122, 131; 5. *Register*, I. 216.

3088   1. Harley 116, f. 170b (vv. 3).
1. *Rel. Ant.*, I. 316; 2. Robbins, *Archiv* CC. 342.

3091   9. Cotton Titus A. xxvi, f. 202b.
9. Huber, *Die Wanderlegende von den Siebenschläfern*, Leipzig, 1910, p. 165.

*3091.5   *Schall come trewly as y ow say
Concluding ten quatrains of a prophecy.
1. NLW Peniarth 50, pp. 263-4.

*Schall haue ʒowr dessyer þe same ʒer   See 3694.3.

Shall I go to her agayn onys to prove
The second quatrain of 2490.

Shall y leue of and let hur go
Three concluding stanzas of 3179.

Sale mak wus al at do   See 1844.5.

3097.3   Shall we all die / We shall die all / All die shall we /Die all we shall
A palindromic type of epitaph of four words in four lines. Pettigrew, *Chronicle of Tombs*, p. 63.

3097.6   She is gentyll & also wysse
The beauty of his mistress—six 3-line stanzas (including refrain) and burden: 'My lady is a prety on.'
1. Harley 7578, f. 85a.
Fehr, *Archiv* CVII. 57-8; *Early Eng. Lyrics*, p. 83; *Early Eng. Carols*, p. 303.

She may be callyd / a souerant lady   See 66.5.

3098   [Utley 257].

3098.3   She þat hathe a wantan eye / & can convey ytt wysselye
Wanton and nice—sixteen quatrains. [Utley 258].
1. Bodl. 12653, f. 31b.
Padelford and Benham, *Anglia* XXXI. 352-3.

3098.5   Sche þat I loue alle þermoost & loþist to begile
His mistress ever in his thoughts—one 6-line stanza including an 'Y and O' refrain. [Cf. 3418].
1. Huntington Lib. HM 503, f. 129b.
Greene, *Medium Aevum* XXX. 170.

*3098.6   *Sche was fairest of all / The kyng....
Two fragments from a romance of Apollonius of Tyre—about 140 lines in quatrains.
1. Bodl. 21790, ff. 2.
Halliwell, *New Boke about Shakespeare*, London 1850, pp. 1-13; A. H. Smyth, *Shakespeare's Pericles and Apollonius of Tyre*, Philadelphia 1898, pp. 249-55; J. Raith,

Die alt- und me Apollonius-Bruchstücke, Munich 1956, pp. 78-84.

Schelde us fra þe paynes of hell   See 1950.5.

3098.8   Short rede / good rede / slewe the bisshop
A tag in Leland, *De Rebus Brit.*, II. 417.

3099   *Gentleman's Magazine,* May 1842, pp. 463-4 (extracts).

3100   Person, *Camb. ME Lyrics,* p. 29.

3100.5   Siker to dele to alle maner men / To tellen of is time nouere no man kan
A couplet translating '*Mors cunctis certa nil est incertius hora.*'
1. Advocates 18. 7. 21, f. 87b.

3101   Six riming lines on Deliverance in an English prose homily. [Cf. 89.5, 91.5, 1628.5, 1848].
Grisdale, *Leeds Texts & Monographs* V. 48.

3102   3. BM Addit. 37790, f. 225a; 4. Bodl. Holkham misc. 41 [*olim* Holkam Hall 675], p. 98; 6. Bodl. 505, f. 219b; 7. Bodl. Lat. lit. e. 17, f. 53a (vv. 5); 8. Sloane 775, f. 55b.
1. Coxe, *Cat. Laud. MSS.,* p. 254; 2. Person, *Camb. ME Lyrics,* p. 75; 3. *Cat. Add. MSS.,* 1906-10, p. 155.

3104.5   Simenel hornes / ber non þornes / alleluya
A tag.
1. Trinity Camb. 1109, f. 419a.
James, *Cat.,* III. 91; Wilson, *Lost Lit.,* p. 182; Everett, *MA* XXII. 34.

Since   See Sith.

3106   Furnivall, *EETS* 15 orig. ed. 235-6; rev. ed. 264.

3109   2. *olim* Merton 25, f. 58a [Breslauer Cat. 90, Item 16].

3112   six 7-line stanzas with 4-line burden.
Christmas Carolles, Copland, ca. 1550 (Douce fragments f. 48); *facs.* Reed, *Xmas Carols,* pp. 12-14; *repr. Early Eng. Carols,* pp. 128-9.

3113   4. Trinity Dublin 516, ff. 108a-110a (vv. 140).

3114   1. Univ. Coll. Oxf. 154, f. ii recto.

Synge to oure lorde a new songe
One of the prayers in 1975 (st. 4).

Syng vp hart syng vp hart
Burden to 3118.5.

3115   2. Wolfenbüttel, Herzoglichen Bibliothek 2819, ff. 149b-150b.

3115.5   Synk and say / leet and tak / holde and have
Three irregular lines on sin in Latin homiletic notes.
1. Peterhouse 218, f. 15a.

3116.5   Schir at this feist of benefyce
'Quhone mony benefices vakit,' by William Dunbar—three 5-line stanzas. [Cf. 3051.5].
1. Camb. Un. Ll. 5. 10, f. 9b; 2. Pepys 2553, pp. 7 and 316. 2a, 2b. Craigie, STS n.s. VII. 6-7, 376-7; 2b. Pinkerton, Anc. Scot. Poems, I. 101; Small, STS IV. 205; Schipper, Dunbar, pp. 255-6; and DKAW XLI (IV). 57-8; Baildon, Dunbar, pp. 126-7; MacKenzie, Dunbar, pp. 27; comp. text. Laing, Dunbar, I. 156.

3117   Wülcker, AE Lesebuch, I. 78; Kaiser, Med. Eng., p. 383; Robbins, Hist. Poems, p. 31.

*3117.2   *Sire emperoure Dred ye no thynge
A fragment from a Caesar Augustus play—vv. 13 in 8-line tail-rime stanzas.
1. Bodl. 6621, f. 168a.
Robbins, Anglia LXXII. 32.

3117.3   Schir for ȝour grace bayth nicht and day
To the King, 'That he war Jhone Thomsonnis man,' by William Dunbar—eight quatrains with refrain: 'God gif ye war Johne Thomsonnis man.'
1. Pepys 2553, p. 194.
Pinkerton, Anc. Scot Poems, I. 120-1; Sibbald, Chronicle,

I. 322-3; Laing, *Dunbar*, I. 113-4; Paterson, *Dunbar*, pp. 281-2; Small, *STS* IV. 218; Schipper, *Dunbar*, pp. 235-6; and *DKAW* XLI (IV). 36-8; Baildon, *Dunbar*, pp. 113-14; Craigie, *STS* n.s. VII. 220-1; MacKenzie, *Dunbar*, pp. 38-9; Kinsley, *Dunbar*, pp. 91-2.

*3117.4 *...sire he seis and sonenday is nouwe
The Life of Joseph of Arimathea—in alliterative lines.
1. Bodl. 3938, f. 403a (vv. 709).
Skeat, *EETS* 44. 1-23.

3117.5 Schir I complane off injuris
'Complaint to the Kyng aganis Mure,' by William Dunbar—four 7-line stanzas.
1. Camb. Un..Ll. 5. 10, f. 11a; 2. Pepys 2553, p. 10.
2. Pinkerton, *Anc. Scot. Poems*, I. 107-8; Ramsay, *Evergreen*, II. 209-11; Laing, *Dunbar*, I. 117-18; Paterson, *Dunbar*, p. 173; Small, *STS* IV. 210-11; Schipper, *Dunbar*, pp. 227-8; and *DKAW* XLI (IV). 28-30. Baildon, *Dunbar*, pp. 109; Craigie, *STS* n.s. VII. 10; MacKenzie, *Dunbar*, p. 5.

3117.6 [Ser Iohn Mandev]elle and Sir Marc of Veneese
'Off the Grete Caan Emperour of Tartaria,' an extract from Mandeville's *Travels*—vv. 313 in 8-line stanzas. [Cf. 248.5]
1. Bodl. 3692, ff. 113b, 109a-112b, 115a.
Rel. Ant., II. 113-5 (vv. 185-282); Hazlitt, *Remains*, I. 155-8 (vv. 185-282); Seymour, *AUMLA* XXI. 42-50.

3117.7 Schir Jhon Sinclair begowth to dance
'Of a dance in the quenis chalmer' by William Dunbar—seven 7-line stanzas.
1. Camb. Un. Ll. 5. 10, f. 45a; 2. Pepys 2553, pp. 340-1.
2. Pinkerton, *Anc. Scot. Poems*, I. 94-6; Sibbald, *Chronicle*, I. 275-7; Laing, *Dunbar*, I. 119-20; Paterson, *Dunbar*, pp. 164-6; Small, *STS* IV. 199-200; Schipper, *Dunbar*, pp. 123-5; and *DKAW* XL (IV). 33-5; Baildon, *Dunbar*, pp. 60-2; Craigie, *STS* n.s. VII. 415-16; MacKenzie, *Dunbar*, pp. 60-1; Kinsley, *Dunbar*, pp. 83-5.

3117.8 Schir Johine the Rose ane thing thair is compiled
'The Flyting of Dunbar and Kennedie,' by William Dunbar—vv. 552 in 8-line stanzas.
1. Camb. Un. Ll. 5. 10, f. 58a; 2. Pepys 2553, pp. 53-4, 59-63, 69-72, 77-80; 3. Advocates 1. 1. 6, f. 147a.

Chepman and Myllar, 1508 (vv. 316-552 only); *facs.* Beattie, *Edinb. Bibl. Soc.* 1950, pp. 137; *repr.* Stevenson, *STS* LXV. 209-16; Laing, *Knightly Tale of Golagros* &c., 1827; Small, *STS* IV. 11-29; 2. Craigie, *STS* n.s. VII. 71-88; 3. Ramsay, *Evergreen*, II. 47-75; *repr. Ramsay and Earlier Scot. Poets*, pp. 267-73; Sibbald, *Chronicle*, I. 351-8 (extracts); ; Laing, *Dunbar*, II. 65-86; *Bannatyne MS.*, Hunt. Club, III. 420-37; Ritchie, *STS* n.s. XXIII. 44; 3 (vv. 1-315 and C&M print). MacKenzie, *Dunbar*, pp. 5-20; *comp. text.* Schipper, *Dunbar*, pp. 150-89; and *DKAW* XL (IV). 50-99; Paterson, *Dunbar*, pp. 313-14; Baildon, *Dunbar*, pp. 71-88.

3118   1. Bodl. 1129, f. 1a.

Schir lett it nevir in toun be tald   See 2349.5.

3118.2   Sir Rawland Vaux that sometime was the lord of Triermaine
            Epitaph—two couplets (perhaps spurious).
            Beauties of England, III. 125.

3118.4   Syr sheryffe for thy sake
            Robin Hood and the Sheriff of Nottingham: fragment of a drama—vv. 42 in couplets.
            1. Trinity Camb. [*olim* W. Aldis Wright, *olim* Le Neve (Norroy)]; 1a. transcript by Stukeley; 1b. transcript by Bradshaw.
            1. Greg, *Malone Soc. Collections*, I. 120-4 (with *facs.*); Adams, *Pre-Sh. Drama*, pp. 345-6; 1a. J.M.G., *N&Q* 1 s XII. 321-2; 1b. Child, *Ballads*, 1864, 1878, V. 429-30; and *Pop. Ballads*, III. 90; Manly, *Specimens*, I. 279-81.

3118.5   Sur songe in tyme past hath ben doune a doune
            A 'ballet' sung at the Conduit in Cheap in honor of Edward VI, ca. 1548—six long quatrains and burden.
            1. Coll. of Arms I. 7, f. 37b.
            Strype, *Eccles. Memorials*, 1822, II, ii. 329; Esdaile, *Age of Elizabeth*, 1915, p. 1; *Early Eng. Carols*, pp. 297-8.

3118.6   Schir ȝe have mony seruitours
            A Remonstrance to the King, by William Dunbar—vv. 88 in couplets.
            1. Pepys 2553, p. 196.

	Laing, *Dunbar*, I. 145-8; *repr. Blackwood's Magazine*, Feb. 1835; Paterson, *Dunbar*, pp. 228-32; Small, *STS* IV. 220-2; Schipper, *Dunbar*, pp. 270-3; and *DKAW* XLI (IV). 72-5; Baildon, *Dunbar*, pp. 136-8; Craigie, *STS* n.s. VII. 222-4; MacKenzie, *Dunbar*, pp. 36-8; Kinsley, *Dunbar*, pp. 88-91.
3118.8	Schir ȝit remember as of befoir To the King, by William Dunbar—seventeen 5-line stanzas with refrain: 'Exces of thocht dois me mischeif.' [Cf. 2619.8 and 2621.5]. 1. Camb. Un. Ll. 5. 10, f. 34a (last 2 st. only); 2. Pepys 2553, p. 295; 3. Advocates 1. 1. 6, f. 94b. 2. Craigie, *STS* n.s. VII. 346-8; MacKenzie, *Dunbar*, pp. 41-3; 3. [Hailes,] *Anc. Scot. Poems*, pp. 82-6; *Select Poems of Dunbar*, Perth 1788, pp. 69-73; Sibbald, *Chronicle*, I. 316-9; Laing, *Dunbar*, I. 161-4; Paterson, *Dunbar*, pp. 277-80; *Bannatyne MS.*, Hunt. Club, II. 271-4; Small, *STS* IV. 104-7; Schipper, *Dunbar*, pp. 259-62; and *DKAW* XLI (IV). 60-4; Baildon, *Dunbar*, pp. 128-31; Ritchie, *STS* n.s. XXII. 251-4; Kinsley, *Dunbar*, pp. 92-3 (extract).
*3119.5	*...sit amonges the knyghtes all / ... at te counsell Of Discreet Behaviour—six quatrains and burden. 1. Harley 4294, f. 81b (text badly defaced at left-hand margin). *Rel. Ant.*, I. 252; *Early Eng. Carols*, p. 234.
3120	[Entry transferred to 3173.5].
3121	8. Coventry Corp. Record Office, ff. 57a-69b.
3122	6. Harley 3362, f. 36a.
3125	Sith fortune hathe me set thus in this wyse Robbins, *PMLA* LXIX. 635.
3126	1a (xix cent. transcript). BM Addit. 20091, ff. 50b-57b; 2. Lansdowne 418, f. 88a.
3127	Robbins, *Hist. Poems*, pp. 221-2.
3130	Girvan, *STS* 3 s. XI. 176.
3131	Stevens, *Music & Poetry*, pp. 368-9.

3131.5   Sin it is lo / that I muste goo / & pass yow ffroo / my lady dere
   An English scribble to his lady dear—four short lines.
   1. Royal 19. B. iv, f. 98a.
    Robbins, *Anglia* LXXXII. 12.

3133   5. Robbins, *Hist. Poems*, pp. 145-6.

3135   seven 6-line stanzas, heading, and 3-line burden.
   1. BM Addit. 46919 [*olim* Phillips 8336], f. 208b, and trial draft (vv. 7) on f. 84b.
    1a. *Rel. Lyr. XIV C.*, p. 253.

3135.5   Since of a womans breestes I was fostered
   Enjoy what Nature gives—one cross-rimed quatrain.
   1. Durham Univ. Cosin V. iii. 9, f. 56a.
    Furnivall, *EETS* lxi. 184.

3137   Ford, *Age of Chaucer*, pp. 315-32.

3138   Sibbald, *Chronicle*, I. 55; Craigie, *STS* n.s. IX. 103-7.

3140   three 8-line stanzas and 5-line Envoy.

3140.5   Sen that I am a presoneir
   'Bewty and the Presoneir,' by William Dunbar—fourteen 8-line stanzas with refrain.
   1. Camb. Un Ll. 5. 10, f. 8a (vv. 1-16 only); 2. Advocates 1. 1. 6, f. 214a.
    1. Craigie, *STS* n.s. XX. 58; 2. Laing, *Dunbar*, I. 22-6; Paterson, *Dunbar*, pp. 100-4; Eyre-Todd, *Med. Scot. Poetry*, pp. 177-81; *Bannatyne MS.*, Hunt. Club, III. 607-10; Small, *STS* IV. 164-7; Schipper, *Dunbar*, pp. 113-16; and *DKAW* XL (IV). 23-6; Baildon, *Dunbar*, pp. 53-6; Arber, *Dunbar Anthology*, pp. 18-22; Ritchie, *STS* n.s. XXIII. 249-52; MacKenzie, *Dunbar*, pp. 104-7; Kinsley, *Dunbar*, pp. 21-4.

3142   2. Camb. Un. Add. 2585 (1), f. 2a.
   1. Arber, *Dunbar Anthology*, p. 124; 2. Robbins, *MLN* LXVI. 505; Davies, *Med. Eng. Lyrics*, p. 182.

3143	Death's Warning to the World—rime royal: partly from *The Fall of Princes* (1168), I. 764-70, 806-12, 918-24, 925-31, 960-6. 1. Wager, *PQ* XV. 377-83 (extracts).
3143.5	Sythen the furste þat were here or may be An appeal for unity against the French in 1452—vv. 120 in 8-line stanzas. 1. Trinity Dublin 516, f. 194a.
3144	Tolkien and Gordon, Oxford, 1925, 1949; Ford, *Age of Chaucer*, pp. 351-430; Cawley, 1963.
3144.5	Syne the tyme I knew yow fyrst 'Why soo vnkende'—six couplets with this burden. 1. Royal App. 58, f. 6a. Flügel, *Anglia* XII. 261; *Early Eng. Carols*, p. 305.
3145	[See also *4194.5. Ringler 64]. 2. Sloane 1044, ff. 248a-b (fragment: vv. 216). *Guy of Warwick*, Pynson, ca. 1490-1500 (STC 12540) (three leaves: vv. 4663-4722, 5023-5142 of Copland); de Worde, ca. 1500 (STC 12541) (one leaf: vv. 7293-7382 of Copland); Copland, 1561 (STC 12542); *repr*. Schleich, *Palaestra* CXXXIX.
3151	*Gude and Godlie Ballates*, 1578; *also repr*. Eyre-Todd, *Med. Scot. Poetry*, p. 75; FitzGibbon, *E. E. Poetry*, p. 87; Mitchell, *STS* XXXIX. 238-9; *repr. from* 1621. Neilson and Webster, *Chief British Poets*, p. 360; with 1. Lawson, *Kingis Quhair*, 1910, pp. 102, 103; 1. Girvan, *STS* 3 s. XI. 176.
	Syn till ane turnament fast þai hyit See 2289.8.
3153	[For miracles performed at Hailes Abbey see *311.5].
3154	[Delete: Book II of 'Ratis Raving.' For Book I see 2235.] Girvan, *STS* 3 s. XI. 52-65.
3154.5	Sithe ye haue me chalyngyd M[aster] Garnesche Against Garnesche, a flytyng by John Skelton—vv. 469 in rime royal stanzas, couplets, and 'skeltonics.' 1. Harley 367, ff. 101a-109b.

Dyce, *Skelton,* I. 116-31; Dyce and Child, *Skelton & Donne,* I. 132-53; Henderson, *Skelton,* 1931, pp. 122-37; 1948, 1959, pp. 150-64; Pinto, *Selection,* pp. 80-2 (extracts).

3155　　　Gutch, *Robin Hood,* I. 373-4; Dickins and Wilson, *Early ME Texts,* pp. 10-12; Williams, *New Book Eng. Verse,* pp. 24-5; Kaiser, *Anthologie,* p. 364; Kaiser, *Med. Eng.,* p. 349; Davies, *Med. Eng. Lyrics,* pp. 55-6.

3156　　　1, 2, 3. Furnivall, *EETS* 69. 20-79; 99-100 (vv. 1-42); 4. *Rel. Ant.,* II. 64-5 (vv. 12 only).

Syse is ever the best chaunce of the dyce　See 734.8.

3157　　　sixteen lines.
　　　　　Robbins, *Sec. Lyrics,* pp. 71-2.

3158　　　Slombrynge ryght chonceful ful of unkyndenes
　　　　　two 8-line and two 7-line stanzas.
　　　　　1. Trinity Camb. 921, f. 95a.

Smale pathis to the grenewode
Burden to 2007.5.

3161　　　Rickert, *Anc. Eng. Xmas Carols,* pp. 74-6.

So dye shall then all cristyn men
Burden to 1587.

3162　　　2. Robbins, *Sec. Lyrics,* p. 182.

3162.5　　So fer I trow from remedy
　　　　　A lover's complaint—one stanza rime royal.
　　　　　1. BM Addit. 5465, f. 6b.
　　　　　Fehr, *Archiv* CVI. 52; Stevens, *Music & Poetry,* p. 353.

3163　　　*Gentleman's Magazine,* May 1842, pp. 471-2.

3163.5　　So gret vnkyndnes wythoute diseruyng
　　　　　'A falce surmysing'—in irregular lines.
　　　　　XX Songes, de Worde, 1530 (STC 22924); Imelmann, *Shakespeare-Jahrbuch* XXXIX. 129; Flügel, *Anglia* XII. 591-2.

3164   1. BM Addit. 34360 [*olim* Phillipps 9053], f. 21b.
Brusendorff, *Chaucer Tradition*, pp. 277-8; Robinson, *Chaucer*, 1933, p. 628; 1957, p. 533.

3165   [vv. 5-8 = vv. 9-12 of 1349.5. Cf. Kenney, *JAMS* VIII. 199; Bukofzer, *Musical Qr.* XXVIII. 25; *New Oxford Hist. Music*, III. 131-2].
1. Yale Univ. 9, ff. 61b-63.
Menner, *MLQ* VI. 382; Kenney, *Journal American Musicological Soc.* VIII. 201-2.

So laughyng in lap layde   See 3438.3.

3167.3   So longe ic haue lauedi / yhoued at þi gate
The devoted but unrequited lover, one cross-rimed quatrain in a Latin sermon. [Cf. 3860.3].
1. Tübingen Univ. Deposit: Berlin Preussische Staatsbibliothek, Lat. theol. fol. 249, f. 131a.
Robbins, *Anglia* LXXXII. 13.

3167.6   So longe þou may on þe stone spete / þat at þe laste it woll be wete
A proverbial couplet.
1. Bodl. 21626, f. 29b; 2. Rylands Lib. Latin 394, f. 21b.
1. Förster, *Festschrift zum 12 Deutschen Neuphilologentage*, p. 56; 2. Pantin, *BJRL* XIV. 107.

So many pointed caps / Laced with double flaps   See 3168.2.

3168.2   So propre cappes / So lytle hattes
'The maner of the world now a dayes,' possibly by John Skelton—in quatrains with refrain.
1. Sloane 747, f. 88b.
Copland, n. d.; Collier, *Percy Soc.* I. 2-8; Henderson, *Skelton*, 1931, pp. 144-50; 1948, 1959, pp. 133-9; Gant, *Skelton*, pp. 45-8; with 1. Dyce, *Skelton*, I. 148-54; II. 200-3; Dyce and Child, *Skelton & Donne*, II. 428-33, 434-7.

3168.4   So put yn fere I dare not speke
A lover's lament on his wounded heart—three stanzas rime royal.
1. BM Addit. 5665, f. 137b.
Fehr, *Archiv* CVI. 283; Stevens, *Music & Poetry*, p. 345.

    *So þat at myn ending day See 3231 (Edinburgh Univ. MS.).

3168.6 Sa tretit thai that his sone wed
    On the marriage of Robert to Elizabeth Moor—two popular couplets in the chronicles of Fordun and Wintoun.
    1. Edinburgh Univ. 186.
    Hearne, *Joannis de Fordun Scotichronicon,* Edinburgh 1749, II. App. 15.

    So trusteth youre People with affiaunce See 2200.

3170 Salomon seyth ther is none accorde
    thirty lines in couplets (includes 1999, 4117, 4137).
    Person, *Camb. ME Lyrics,* pp. 52-3.

3171 [Utley 264; and 265, Lambeth MS.].
    2, 3. *Early Eng. Carols,* pp. 267-8; 2. [Masters,] *Rymes of Minstrels,* pp. 30-1.

3171.5 Some desarve or they desyer
    Unequal distribution—two short couplets 'quod Carter.'
    1. Durham Univ. Cosin V. iii. 9, f. 55b.
    Furnivall, *EETS* lxi. 183.

3172 [Utley 266].
    Rel. Ant., I. 258-9.

    Sum giffis for thank sum for threitt See 3768.3.

3172.5 Some hornes doe weare and blowe them not
    A proverbial couplet.
    1. Camb. Un. Dd. 6. 45, f. 105b (added in xvi cent. hand).

3173 MacCracken, *EETS* 192. 813-8.

3173.5 Summe maner mater worlde I fayne meve
    Truth and Conscience—fourteen 12-line stanzas.
    1. Wellcome Hist. Med. Lib. 673 [*olim* Phillipps 18134; Quaritch Sale Cat. 164], f. 8a.
    Kane, *London Med. St.* II. (Part I). 61-5.

3174 1. Caius Camb. 383, p. 190.
    Robbins, *Sec. Lyrics,* pp. 30-1.

3174.5   Sum men speke muche evyll be women
A punctuation poem against women by Richard Hatfield—one stanza rime royal. [For two similar poems of cf. 232 and 3909.6].
1. BM Addit. 17492, f. 18b.
Flügel, *Neuengl. Lesebuch*, p. 39; Padelford, *Early XVI Cent. Lyrics*, p. 95; Muir, *Proc. Leeds Philos. & Lit. Soc., Lit. & Hist. Section* VI. 261; Hughey, *Arundel Harington MS.*, II. 210.

Som men thynke that ye shall haue penalte   See 3903.5 (Lansdowne).

3175.5   Summe sende yleus / and summe sende nadderes
Six lines on Wade, inserted in a Latin sermon on humility.
1. Peterhouse 255, Part II, f. 49a.
James, *Academy*, Feb. 1896, p. 137; Wilson, *Lost Lit.*, p. 17.

3176   [Cf. 1585.5].
2. Rosenthal, *Vitae Patrum in Old & ME Lit.*, pp. 156-8.

3178   2. Rosenthal, *Vitae Patrum in Old & ME Lit.*, pp. 159-60.

3180   [Utley 270].
Ritson, *Anc. Songs*, 1877, p. 111.

Sum tyme I was with loue bounde   See 3194.

3181   Sauerstein, *Charles d'Orléans*, 1899, pp. 44-5.

3182   de Worde (STC 20034).

3183   2. Advocates 1. 1. 6, f. 45b (ascribed to 'Chawseir') and p. 29.
Chaucer, Thynne, 1532 (STC 5068); *repr*. Bell, *Poets of Great Britain*, I. ccxlv; Chaucer, Stow, 1561 (STC 5075); Chaucer, Speght, 1598 (STC 5077); Urry, *Chaucer*, 1721 (unpag. preface); Bell, *Works of Chaucer*, IV. 421; 2. *Bannatyne MS.*, Hunt. Club, II. 123; Ritchie, *STS* n.s. XXII. 113-15; *STS* 3 s. V. 48-50.

3183.5   Somtyme in Rome a pope ther was / that god loued
The Life of St. Gregory's Mother [=Trental]—in quatrains. [Cf. 3184].
Pynson, ca. 1500 (STC 24267); de Worde, 1515 (STC 12352); Mychell, ca. 1548 (12353).

3184   [Cf. 467.5; 3183.5].

3185   1. Bodl. 6927, ff. 42a-53b; 3. Cotton Titus A. xxiii, ff. 2a-53b.

3186   'De duobus veris amicis' (in Sithia and Climonen, part of 422).
Horstmann, AE Leg. 1878, p. 34.

3187   A Text: 5 (with vv. 1-134, 3180-4328, from C2). Weber, Met. Rom., III. 3-153; 5 (with vv. 1-119 and vv. 2771 ff. from 1& 4). Brunner, EETS 191.
D Text: 1. Asloan, f. 161a (imperfect, vv. 2780); 1a (xix cent. transcript). Edinburgh Univ. La. III. 481; 1b (xix cent. transcript). Edinburgh Univ. La. IV. 27/28 (incomplete).
1. Craigie, STS n.s. XVI. 1-88.

3188   [Delete: in one MS. of the South English Legendary.]

3189   Noyes, Sussex Arch. Soc. IX. 318-9; Robbins, PMLA LXV. 255.

3190   [See 2218 for stanzas incorporated into another poem]. 13. Ipswich County Hall Deposit: Hillwood [olim Brome], f. 80b; 14. Cotton Otho A. xviii (MS. destroyed, preserved in transcript, 1721, by William Thomas); 15. Coventry Corp. Record Office, f. 76b.
Urry, Chaucer, 1721, p. 547; Chalmers, Eng. Poets, I. 553-4; 12. Brotanek, ME Dichtungen, pp. 10-11; Stow, 1561, repr. [Anderson,] Poets of Great Britain, I. 577-8; 6. Pace, St. in Bibliography IV. 119-20; Robinson, Chaucer, 1933, p. 632; 1957, p. 537; 11. MacCracken, MLN XXIII. 214; 12. Pace, MLN LXIII. 460; 13. Smith, Commonplace Book, p. 19; 14. Pace, Speculum XXVI. 306-7; mod. ed. Clarke, Riches of Chaucer, II. 304.

    Somtym wee warr as yee now bee   See 3220.7.

3193.5   Somewhat musing / and more mourning
A virelai by Earl Rivers on the eve of his execution, A.D. 1483—five 8-line stanzas.
1. Fitzwilliam Mus., unnumbered fragment; 2. Cotton Vesp. A. xii, f. 170b; 3. BM Addit. 5465, f. 34a; 4. BM Addit. 31922, f. 120b; 5. Wells Cath. fragment; 6. New York Pub. Lib. Drexel Fragments 4183.
2. Hearne, *Rossi Warwicensis Historia Regum Angliae,* 1716, 1745, p. 214; Percy, *Reliques,* 1839, II. 46; 3. Arber, *Dunbar Anthology,* p. 180; Stafford Smith, *Eng. Songs,* no. 9; Turner, *Hist. England,* III. 465; *Chronicles of White Rose,* p. 209; Ritson, *Anc. Songs,* p. 149; 3, 4. Stevens, *Music & Poetry,* pp. 361-2, 423-4; 4. Flügel, *Anglia* XII. 254-5; Stevens, *Music at Court,* pp. 90-4.

3194   4. London Univ. [*olim* Sterling; *olim* Clopton], ff. 97b-114b. (vv. 2209).

Sum wemen wepen of peure feminite
See 854 (BM Addit. MS. 29729). [Utley 269].

Sone for þat in armys diffusenes is   See 3118.

3195   two 12-line and one 14-line stanzas.
1. Lambeth 853, p. 155 (lacks last four lines); 2. BM Addit. 25006, f. 11b; 3. ? Buckland House, at end of *Mirror of Sinners.*
1. Furnivall, *EETS* 32 orig. ed. 34-5.

3196   two 4-line stanzas (= st. 1 & 2 of 3784.6; and cf. 3784.5).
1. Bodl. 6936, f. 65b (st. 1 only).
1, 2. Brotanek, *ME Dichtungen,* p. 49; 1. Black, *Cat. Ashmole MSS.,* p. 91; 2. Mustanoja, *How the Good Wife,* pp. 72-3.

3197   2. Leyden Univ. Vossius 9, f. iii verso.
Chaucer, Stow, 1561 (STC 5075); *Chaucer,* Speght, 1598 (STC 5077); Urry, *Chaucer,* 1721, p. 557; Bell, *Poets of Great Britain,* XIII. 130; [Anderson,] *Poets of Great Britain,* I. 585; Chalmers, *English Poets,* I. 563; 2. van Dorsten, *Scriptorium* XIV. 325.

3199.3 Son crokith the tre / that crokid will be
A proverbial couplet.
1. Balliol 354, f. 191b.
Dyboski, *EETS* ci. 129.

3199.5 Sore I sye & sore I may
Three sorrowful things—three couplets. [Cf. 3969].
1. Bodl. 21626, f. 20b (vv. 3-4), and f. 24a (vv. 6); 2. Harley 3362, f. 4a (var. vv. 3-4); 3. Rylands Lib. Latin 394, f. 13b.
1, 3. Pantin, *BJRL* XIV. 101; 1. Förster, *Festchrift zum 12 Deutschen Neuphilologentage*, pp. 49, 51.

3199.8 Sore this dere strykyn ys
An enigmatic stricken deer carol—six cross-rimed quatrains with a 3-line burden: 'Blow þy horne hunter.' [Utley 271].
1. Royal App. 58, f. 7b (bur. only); 2. BM Addit. 31922, f. 39b.
1, 2. Chappell, *OE Pop. Music*, I. 39-40; Flügel, *Anglia* XII. 262, 238-9; Stevens, *Music at Court*, p. 29; 1. Stafford Smith, *Musica Antiqua*, I. 31; Flügel, *Neuengl. Lesebuch*, p. 152; 2. Stevens, *Music & Poetry*, pp. 400-1.

3200.5 Sorwe of his kare / ioye of his weilfare
A short prayer—six short lines.
1. Trinity Dublin 312, f. 123b.

3201 nine couplets.

3202 Delete: [in one MS. of the *South English Legendary*.]

3203 Zimmerman, Königsberg, 1901.

3205 1. Longleat 55, f. 55a.

3206 *Epitaphium eiusdam Ducis Glowcestrie*, A.D. 1447—thirteen 8-line stanzas.
1. Robbins, *Neuphil. Mitteilungen* LVI. 243-7; Robbins, *Hist. Poems*, pp. 180-3.

3206.5 Souerayn lorde in erth most excellent
A carol for the king (perhaps Henry VII)—two stanzas rime royal and burden: 'Enforce yourself as goddis knyght &c.'
1. BM Addit. 5465, f. 115b.

Stafford Smith, *Eng. Songs,* p. 11; Briggs, *Madrigals,* PMMS 1893, no. 3; Fehr, *Archiv* CVI. 68; *Early Eng. Carols,* pp. 296-7; Stevens, *Music & Poetry,* p. 383.

3206.8   Soveraygne lorde welcome to your citie
A roundel (vv. 14) sung by Fourteen Virgins, inserted in the pageant verses for the Entry of Henry VI into London, by Lydgate. [For version in MSS. see 3799].
Fabyan, *New Chronicles,* Pynson, 1516 (STC 10659); *repr.* Ellis, 1811, p. 604; Gattinger, *Wiener Beiträge* IV. 26.

3207.5   Speke frensche & constrwe arte / And þu shalt selde come to þy parte
A proverbial couplet.
1. Bodl. 21626, f. 19a; 2. Rylands Lib. Latin 394, f. 8b.
1. Förster, *Festschrift zum 12 Deutschen Neuphilologentage,* p. 48; 2. Pantin, *BJRL* XIV. 97.

Speke Parotte I pray yow for Maryes saake   See 2263.5.

3208   3. Small, *Met. Hom.,* p. xiv (first and last st. only).

3209   [Cf. Heywood. Tilley G 247, S 707].
2. Bodl. 21626, f. 15b (vv. 1-2 only); 3. Sloane 2232, f. 9b (var. vv. 4); 4. Rylands Lib. Latin 394, f. 7a.
1. Robbins, *Sec. Lyrics,* p. 57; Kaiser, *Med. Eng.,* p. 550; 2. Förster, *Festschrift zum 12 Deutschen Neuphilologentage,* p. 45; 4. Pantin, *BJRL* XIV. 96.

3209.5   Stanche blood stanche blood / So dyd Noes flood
A charm to stop bleeding—four short lines.
1. Harley 665, f. 302a.

3211   6. Trinity Dublin 301, f. 194a.
1. Kaiser, *Anthologie,* p. 218; Kaiser, *Med. Eng.,* p. 260; 3. Dickins and Wilson, *Early ME Texts,* pp. 129-30; Brook, *Harley Lyrics,* pp. 56-7; Davies, *Med. Eng. Lyrics,* pp. 86-8; 4. Brown, *Eng. Lyr. XIII C.,* p. 204.

3212   Brown, *Rel. Lyr. XIV C.,* p. 55; Davies, *Med. Eng. Lyrics,* p. 115.

3213   [Cf. Emmerig, *Bataile of Agyncourt im Lichte geschichtlicher Quellenwerke,* 1906].

1. Cotton Cleop. C. iv, f. 25b.
Nicolas, *History of Battle of Agincourt*, 1833, pp. 281-2; Robbins, *Hist. Poems*, pp. 74-7.

3214 [Utley 272].

Still on my wayis as I went   See 3889.5.

Stynte now moder and wepe no more
See 14 (Worcester Cath. MS.).

*3216.5 *...stod ho þere neh / þat leueli leor wid spald ischent
'*Compassio Marie*,' based on '*Stabat iuxta Christi crucem*' — seven 6-line stanzas (about 3 or 4 st. missing at the beginning). [Cf. 1697].
1. Bodl. 9995, p. 175.
Napier, *Archiv* LXXXVIII. 182-3; Napier, *EETS* 103. 77-9; *Eng. Lyr. XIII C.*, pp. 8-10; *Early Bodl. Music*, II. 8-9.

3217 3. Eyre-Todd, *Early Scot. Poetry*, 1891, pp. 73-127 (extracts).

3218.3 Straunge men þat needeþ / þat lond
Peaceful England—vv. 26 in couplets in Trevisa's translation of Higden's *Polychronicon* (Book II, cap. 41).
1. St. John's Camb. 204; 2. Cotton Tiberius D. vii; 3. Harley 1900; 4. Stowe 65; 5. BM Addit. 24194; 6. Aberdeen Univ. 21; 7. Chetham Lib. 11379; 8. Hunterian Mus. 83; 9. Penrose 12; 10. Morgan Lib. M. 875.
Trevisa, *Discripcion of Britayne*, Caxton, 1480 (STC 13440a); de Worde, 1498 (STC 13440b); Trevisa, *Prolicronycon*, Caxton, 1482 (STC 13438); de Worde, 1495 (STC 13439); Treveris, 1527 (STC 13440); 1. Babington and Lumby, *Rolls Series* XLI, ii. 19-21.

3218.5 Stroke oule and schape oule and evere is oule oule
A proverb in Nicholas Bozon's *Contes moralisés*.
1. BM Addit. 46919 [*olim* Phillipps 8336], f. 122b; 2. Gray's Inn 12, f. 20a.
1. Owst, *Lit. & Pulpit*, p. 44; Ross, *Neuphil. Mitteilungen* L. 203; 2. Smith, *SATF*, p. 23; Förster, *Festschrift zum 12 Deutschen Neuphilologentage*, p. 58; Herbert, *Cat. Rom.*, III. 104.

3219   Furnivall, *EETS* 15 orig. ed. 242; rev. ed. 268.

3220   thirteen lines, most of them illegible.
        1. Harley 2942, f. 122a.

3220.5 Such as I am such sall ye be
        Epitaph of Simon and Agnes Street, A.D. 1440, at St. Anthony's Church, London—vv. 11 in couplets. [Cf. 3220.7].
        Weever, *Anc. Funerall Monuments*, 1631, p. 404 (STC 25223); Pettigrew, *Chronicles of Tombs*, p. 44.

3220.7 Such as ye be some time ware wee / Suche as wee are suche schall ye be
        Epitaph for Sir Robert Drury, but lines common elsewhere, e.g., for William Chichele, A.D. 1425 (vv. 12); John Woode (vv. 6).
        Weever, *Anc. Funerall Monuments*, 1631, pp. 730, 803 (STC 25223); *Beauties of England: Suffolk*, p. 75; Pettigrew, *Chronicles of Tombs*, pp. 45, 64; *Records of Buckinghamshire*, IV. 22; Ravenshaw, *Antiente Epitaphes*, p. 8; Evans, *English Art 1307-1461*, p. 174; Gray, *N&Q* n.s. VIII. 135.

3220.9 *Summa totalis / Nescio que qualis*
        On the difficulties of logic—nine macaronic Latin and English lines.
        1. Corpus Christi Camb. 329, last page.
        James, *Cat.*, II. 153.

3221   Segar, *Some Minor Poems*, pp. 50-3; Segar, *Med. Anthology*, pp. 46-8 (extracts); Kaiser, *Med. Eng.*, p. 285.

3222   [Utley 273].
        Delete: [Stengel, *Cod. MSS. Digby 86*, pp. 64;] Add:
        1. Dickins and Wilson, *Early ME Texts*, pp. 71-6.

3223   Chappell, *OE Pop. Music*, *facs.* and p. 13; Burney, *Hist. Music*, 1782, III. 407-11; Stafford Smith, *Musica Antiqua*, I. 7; Rimbault, *Anc. Vocal Music*, no. 13; FitzGibbon, *E. E. Poetry*, p. 1; Segar, *Med. Anthology*, p. 93; *Oxford Book English Verse*, p. 1; Dickins and Wilson, *Early ME Texts*, p. 118; Funke, *ME Reader*, p. 47; Schofield, *Music Review* IX. 81; Kaiser, *Med. Eng.*, pp. 463, (*facs.*) 450; Manning, *Explicator* XVIII. 2; Davies, *Med. Eng. Lyrics*, p. 52; *facs.* Garnett, *Eng. Lit.*, I. 124; *facs.* James, *Abbeys*, frontispiece; *facs.* Mossé, *Handbook*, p. 201.

3223.5   Somer passed / and wynter well begon
          The xv Ioyes of Maryage, a translation, perhaps by Robert Copland, of *Les quinze joyes de mariage*—Prologue in eleven 7-line stanzas, Prohemye in thirty 7-line stanzas, text in couplets. [Utley 274].
              de Worde, ca. 1507 (15258) (Douce frag. e. 10); de Worde, 1509 (STC 15258); *repr.* Wilson, *Batchelars Banquet.*

3224.5   Songen alle wid one steuene
          English couplet describing the shepherds' songs in a French picture Bible.
          1. BM Addit. 47682 [*olim* Holkham Hall 666].
              Skeat, *British Museum Qr.* XVI. 26.

          Superne lucerne guberne this pestilens   See 2420.

3225.5   *Surrexit Dominus de sepulchro* / The Lord is rissin
          On the Resurrection, attributed to William Dunbar—five 8-line stanzas with refrain: '*Surrexit sicut dixit allalua.*' [Cf. 688.3].
          1. Advocates 1. 1. 6, f. 34b.
              Laing, *Dunbar*, II. 61-2; *Bannatyne MS.*, Hunt. Club, III. 93-4; Small, *STS* IV. 154-5; Schipper, *Dunbar*, pp. 454-5; and *DKAW* XLIII (I). 75-7; Baildon, *Dunbar*, pp. 237-8; Ritchie, *STS* n.s. XXII. 87-8.

3226   3. Harley 5036, f. 25a; 4. Trinity Dublin 160, f. 161a.

3227   1. Arundel 292, f. 71b.
          Haupt and Hoffman, *Altdeutsche Blätter*, II. 146-7; Lindberg, *Archiv* CI. 395; Coulton, *Life in the MA.* III. 99 (mod.); Robbins, *Sec. Lyrics*, p. 106; Kaiser, *Med. Eng.*, p. 475; Speirs, *Med. Eng. Poetry*, pp. 94-5; Davies, *Med. Eng. Lyrics*, p. 213.

3228   (with acrostic on Stanlei, Sir Thomas, Baron Stanley, A.D. 1459).
          Furnivall, *EETS* 15 rev. ed. 291-2; Sauerstein, *Charles d' Orléans*, 1899, p. 47.

3228.3   Swete harte be trwe / chavnge for [no] newe / Come home to me agene
A religious love parody—seven 6-line stanzas. [Cf. 2086, 3318.4].
1. Victoria and Albert Mus., Dyce 45, f. 22a.
Greene, *Sel. Eng. Carols*, p. 225 (2 st. only).

3228.5   Swet harte I loue yow more feruent than my fader
A letter from a lady to her fickle lover—two 8-line stanzas.
1. Bodl. 12653, f. 63a.
Padelford and Benham, *Anglia* XXXI. 384.

3231   6. Edinb. Univ. 114, f. i (last 8 lines only); 7. Lambeth 559, f. 14a (last 6 lines only).
5. N. S. Baugh, *Worcestershire Misc.*, pp. 101-3; 7. *Register*, I. 440-1.

3232   1. Bodl. Don. C. 13, f. 166a.
facs. B. D. Brown, *Bodl. Qr. Record* VII. 1.

3233   [For other MSS. see 3231 and 3483].
3. BM Addit. 47663 (M) [*olim* Burton] (fragment of 36 lines; ends imperfectly); 4. *olim* Fellowes, f. 166b (Sotheby Sale Cat., June 7, 1964, Lot 231) (vv. 50).

Swete iesu heuene king / Fayr and best of alle thyng
See 3236 (st. 14 of Harley MS. 2253).

3235   A nativity carol on the life of Christ.
Greene, *Sel. Eng. Carols*, p. 74; Davies, *Med. Eng. Lyrics*, p. 241.

3236   [Cf. 1747.5; 1779.5. The quatrain (= st. 14 of MS. 2) appears separately as '*Ora pro Anglia, Sancta Maria, quod Thomas Cantuaria*' in some early prints of Chaucer; cf. Purves, *Canterbury Tales*, 1870, p. 292; Gilman, *Chaucer*, 1879, III. 655].
4. Fitzwilliam Mus. 355 (a) (st. 14 of Ms. 2 only); 5. *olim* George Smith (Harmsworth Sale, Lot 2018, Oct. 1945; Sotheby Sale, Feb. 2, 1960, Lot 317), Art. 3 (14 st.); 6. Illuminated Missal, flyleaf, st. 14 of MS. 2 only [Present location not known].

2, 3. *Rel. Lyr. XIV C.*, pp. 7-9, 245; 1. *Eng. Lyr. XIII C.*, pp. 91-2; *Oxford Book Christian Verse*, pp. 4-5; 2. Brook, *Harley Lyrics*, p. 51; 6. Brydges and Haslewood, *British Bibliographer*, 1812, II. 200.

3237   Kaiser, *Anthologie*, p. 309; Kaiser, *Med. Eng.*, p. 475.

3238   [Cf. 1732.5, 3680.5].
2. Balliol 8, f. 222a (st. 4 only); 6. Trinity Dublin 155, pp. 109-119 (69 quatrains); 7. Longleat 29, ff. 55a-56b, 58b (100 quatrains with 8 'Mary' quatrains added in margins); 8. Huntington EL. 34. B. 7 [*olim* Ellesmere], f. 83b (31 quatrains).
5. N. S. Baugh, *Worcestershire Misc.*, pp. 129-42; 8. Legg, *Henry Bradshaw Soc.*, pp. 30-3.

3238.3   Swet Ihesu that on the Rode / Boutast us &c.
A prayer to Christ in a xiv cent. Sarum *Horae*—three stanzas.
1. *olim* Sowter, ff. 111a-115 [Sotheby Sale, May 20, 1947, Lot 371].

3238.5   Zuete iesu þin holy blod
A simple prayer by Christ's shedding his blood—one tailrime stanza.
1. Arundel 57, f. 2a.
Morris, *EETS* 23. 1.

3241   7. Quaritch Sale Cat. Illuminated MSS., 1931, Item 82; and Cat. 609, 1943, Item 500.
5. N. S. Baugh, *Worcestershire Misc.*, p. 102.

3242.5   Swete lamman dhin are
Refrain of love song forgetfully substituted by priest for '*Dominus vobiscum,*' as related by Giraldus Cambrensis.
Brewer, *Rolls Series* XXI, ii. 120; Brown, *Eng. Lyr. XIII C.*, p. xi; Wilson, *Lost Lit.*, p. 174; Davies, *Med. Eng. Lyrics*, p. 30.

3243   [Following 3777.5].
Bennett, *STS* 3 s. XXIII. 180-2.

3243.3   Sweit rois of vertew and of gentilness
'To a ladye,' by William Dunbar—three 5-line stanzas.
1. Pepys 2553, p. 320.

Pinkerton, *Anc. Scot. Poems*, I. 89; Sibbald, *Chronicle*, II. 23-4; Laing, *Dunbar*, I. 27; Paterson, *Dunbar*, pp. 42; Small, *STS* IV. 223; Eyre-Todd, *Med. Scot. Poetry*, p. 186; Schipper, *Dunbar*, p. 117; and *DKAW* XL (IV) 26-7; Baildon, *Dunbar*, pp. 56; Craigie, *STS* n.s. VII. 383-4; MacKenzie, *Dunbar*, pp. 99; Kinsley, *Dunbar*, p. 21; Davies, *Med. Eng. Lyrics*, pp. 246-7.

3246.5   Swynes halle / fendes falle
Riming headings in a sermon on the failings of women.
1. Merton Oxf. 248, f. 131a.
Pfander, *Pop. Sermon*, p. 50.

3248.5   Take a wobster þat is leill
Three impossibilities—three couplets.
1. Pepys 2553, p. 338.
Craigie, *STS* n.s. VII. 412.

3249   [All texts show extreme variations, some MSS. are followed by further couplets. Further variants exist in xvi and xvii cent. MSS. Singer 857].
[Delete entire listing of MSS. and substitute as follows:]
1. Bodl. 6954, ff. 127a-128a (vv. 72); 2. Bodl 7010, f. 142a (fragment); 3. Bodl. 7010, ff. 142a-142b; 4. Bodl. 7624, II, ff. 82b-83 (vv. 49); 5. Bodl. 7628, pp. 23-30 (vv. 174); 6. Bodl. 7630, V, ff. 19b-20b; 7. Bodl. 7630, VIII, D, ff. 26b-28a; 8. Bodl. 7630, VIII, I, ff. 45a-46b (vv. 70); 9. Bodl. 7630, VIII, I, ff. 49a-50 (vv. 56); 10. Bodl. 7652, ff. 47b-38a (vv. 56); 11. Bodl. 7653, f. 18b (vv. 4); 12. Bodl. 7657, VIII, pp. 127-30 (vv. 173); 13. Trinity Camb. 1119, f. 83b (vv. 56); 14. Sloane 288, f. 164a (vv. 52); 15. Sloane 317, f. 94a (vv. 124); 16. Sloane 1091, ff. 105a-108a (variant); 17. Sloane 1092, ff. 3b-5b; 18. Sloane 1092, f. 62a (imperfect); 19. Sloane 1098, ff. 19b-21a; 20. Sloane 1098, f. 22a; 21. Sloane 1098, f. 47a (vv. 20); 22. Sloane 1842, f. 11a; 23. Sloane 3580 B, ff. 181a-182a; 24. Sloane 3667, f. 118a; 25. Sloane 3688, ff. 74b-78; 26. Sloane 3747, ff. 106b-108a; 27. Clifton Coll. Lib. (vv. 72); 28. Trinity Dublin 389, f. 101a (vv. 196); 29. Wellcome Hist. Med. Lib. 519, f. 69b (vv. 110); 30. Petworth 99, ff. 13-16; 31. Copenhagen Old. Coll. 3500; 32. Massachusetts Hist. Soc., Winthrop 20, ff. 154a-155a (vv. 186); 33. Univ. of Pennsylvania, Smith 4, ff. 76-77.

31. *Retrospective Review*, II. 415 (beg. & concluding lines only).

Take heavy softe colde & dry   See 3721.

3249.6   Tayk hed at all tymes to god mayk the redy
         Be prepared for death—one long couplet.
         1. Royal 7. C. ix, f. 192a.

3252   [Delete entire entry].

         Take hede of castellys and of towres hye   See 3917.5 (Garrett MS.).

3252.5   Take hede vnto my fygure here abowne
         A warning accompanying a picture of Death as skeleton, introducing 1563—eight lines. [Cf. 4049.6].
         1. BM Addit. 37049, f. 32b.
         Brunner, *Archiv* CLXVII. 30.

3253   [Sometimes followed by four more lines. Singer 852].
         2. Bodl. 7630, VIII, F, f. 36a; 3. Harley 2407, f. 2b (var.).
         Ashmole, *Theatrum Chemicum*, p. 434; 1. Singer, *Alchemical MSS.*, II. 579.

3254   11. Gray's Inn 15, f. 72b (vv. 12).

3254.5   Take onyons and mense them wele
         'Sauce for a mawlerd rostid'—three couplets. [Cf. 2361, 3255.5].
         1. Pepys 1047, f. 15a.

3255.5   Take the croppe of rede brere
         'All maner herbys gode for potage'—vv. 13 in couplets. [Cf. 2361, 3254.5].
         1. Pepys 1047, f. 16a.

         Take the Father that Febys so brith   See 2656.

3256   [See 746].
         MacCracken, *EETS* 192. 424; Stevens, *Music & Poetry*, p. 161; Seaton, *Sir Richard Roos*, p. 221; Robbins, *Eng. Lang. Notes* I. 1.

         Take thou Phebus that is so bright   See 1364.5.

3256.1   Take thou this treatise thi time therin to vse
Make the most of time—one alliterative quatrain.
1. Huntington EL 26. C. 9, f. ii recto (added in xvi cent. hand).
Manly and Rickert, *Canterbury Tales*, I. 152.

3256.3   Take iij clateras
Riddle on women—ten irregular lines. [For a variant cf. 3552. Utley 275].
1. Ipswich County Hall Deposit: Hillwood [*olim* Brome], f. 1b (written as prose).
Smith, *Commonplace Book*, p. 12.

3256.6   Tak tyme in tyme and no tyme defer
Four moralizing couplets (concluding with first two lines of 512.8). [Cf. 4095].
1. Camb. Un. Ll. 5. 10, f. 58a; 2. Pepys 2553, p. 294; 3. Advocates 1. 1. 6, f. 122a and f. 147a.
2. Craigie, *STS* n.s. VII. 344; 3. *Bannatyne MS.*, Hunt. Club, p. 346; Ritchie, *STS* n.s. XXII. 324, n.s. XXIII. 44.

3257   Alchemical verses, '*ad mineralia alteranda in terram cristallinam,*' ascribed to Pearce the Black Monk—in couplets. [Sometimes following 2666. Singer 849, 849A].
1. Bodl. 7628, p. 31 (vv. 9 Eng.; vv. 4 Latin); 3. Bodl. 7654, f. 74b (vv. 37); 4. Trinity Camb. 1119, f. 83b (vv. 9); 5. Sloane 1092, f. 6b; 6. Sloane 1098, f. 21b; 7. Sloane 1842, f. 16a (vv. 9); 8. Sloane 3580 B, f. 183a; 9. Sloane 3667, f. 120b; 10. Sloane 3747, f. 15a.

3258   2. [Delete this MS.]
Certaine Worthye Manuscript Poems, Robert Dexter, London 1597 (STC 21499) (vv. 995); *repr.* Edinburgh 1812; repr. with 1. Wright, *EETS* 205. 38-99.

3259   eight lines.
Patterson, *Shakespearean Studies*, 1916, p. 447; Copley, *Seven Eng. Songs*, 1940, no. 7; *New Oxford Hist. Music*, III. 125-6; Robbins, *Sec. Lyrics*, p. 8.

3260 1. Bodl. 1797, f. 20b (vv. 52).
1, 2. Robbins, *Hist. Poems*, pp. 55-7, 275; 2. Wright, *Polit. Poems*, I. 224; Wright, *Pop. Superstitions*, II. 266; Kaiser, *Anthologie*, p. 373; Kaiser, *Med. Eng.*, p. 386.

3262 2. Pepys 1584, f. 106b.

Telle ichulle of þe holi man seint Sebestian   See 2896.

3263.5 Telle me nowe qwate is þi rede / Thorgh Moises lawe I am but dede
A couplet in a sermon.
1. Bodl. 29746, f. 124b.
Little, *Franciscan Papers*, 1943, p. 250.

3265 [For other texts, some with Prologues, see 73, *1538.5, 1905, and 4253. For pictorial prognostications see Woodborough roll, BM facs. 480 A, B].

3265.5 Tell you I chyll / If that ye wyll
'The Tunnyng of Elynour Rummyng,' by John Skelton—vv. 623 in 'skeltonics.' [Utley 277].
1. BM Addit. 22504 (transcript from early print).
Certayne Bokes, Lant, ca. 1545 (STC 22598); Kynge and Marche, ca. 1560 (STC 22599); *repr.* Dyce, *Skelton*, I. 95-115; Dyce and Child, *Skelton & Donne*, I. 109-31; Henderson, *Skelton*, 1931, pp. 99-118; 1948, 1959, pp. 112-30; Hughes, *Skelton*, pp. 39-61; Day, n.d. (STC 22600); *Workes*, Marshe, 1568 (STC 22608); *repr.* [? J. Bowle,] 1736; *repr.* Chalmers, *English Poets*, II. 267-71; Busbie and Loftis, 1609; S. Rand, 1642; *repr. Harleian Miscellany*, I. 415; Isaac Dalton, 1718.

3266 13. Leeds Univ. Brotherton 501 [Maggs Bros. Sale Cat. 1930, 1931; Sotheby Sale, Mar. 14, 1949, Lot 309], ff. 117a-122b.
5. D'Evelyn and Mill, *EETS* 235. 221.

þah—see under þeh. [And under Though - conjunction].

*That dred was sone after / Rayled full of redd roses   See 1011.5.

þat dwellyth but a lytil stonde   See 105.5.

*þat ful eneþe eny more me miȝt þer on bringe   See *3634.1.

3270.5 That goodly las / When she me bas
> Margaret meek—three 8-line stanzas with a 4-line refrain and introductory heading.
> 1. BM Addit. 5465, f. 89b.
>> Hawkins, *Hist. Music*, 1776, III. 22-3; Rimbault, *Songs & Ballads*; Briggs, *Songs & Madrigals*, PMMS 1891, pp. [M] 5-14; Flügel, *Neuengl. Lesebuch*, p. 142; Stevens, *Music & Poetry*, pp. 376-7.

3271 six quatrains and burden.

*That her maidens fairer was / And also brighter shene
> *Sir Lamwell* (Douce fragment): See *1367.1.

*3271.5 *That hym were better to be dede
> Fragment of a tale involving a man and an ass—in couplets.
> 1. Peterborough Cath. Fragments (parts illegible).
>> Dibdin, *Northern Tour*, I. 22 (vv. 21 only).

3272.5 þat ich et þat ich hadde
> Three gnomic lines on possessions. [Cf. 3274; for a variant incorporated into an epitaph cf. 374.5].
> 1. Pembroke Camb. 32, f. 153a.
>> Förster, *Anglia* XLII. 147; James, *Cat.*, p. 35.

3273 11. Balliol 239, f. 77b.

3274 [Cf. 3272.5].
> 3. NLW Peniarth 356, p. 298.

3276 1. BM Addit. 43406 [*olim* Mulchelney Abbey], end flyleaf xiv verso.

3278 Furnivall, *EETS* 15 orig. ed. 240; rev. ed. 268; *Register*, I. 352.

þat in þy sorewe forsake þe not See 3280.

*3281.5 *þat it apertly was apayed for profit þat he feld
> *William of Palerne*—5540 alliterative lines.
> 1. King's Camb. 13, f. 4a.
>> Madden, *William and the Werwulf*, Roxburghe Club 1832, XLVIII; Skeat, *EETS* i.

That it was a febill oke   See 1627.5.

3282   6. *Register*, I. 525.

3283   Stevens, *Med. Carols*, p. 29; Robbins, *Early Eng. Xmas Carols*, p. 34.

3285   'Certeyn rewles' to ascertain a trustworthy man.
1. Bodl. 6777, f. 213a.

*3287.5   *That monny hardie knycht of gret renoune ǀ / Into the feild
Gilbert Hay's *Buik of Alexander*—approximately vv. 20,000 in couplets. [For a Scottish prose version by Hay, see *STS* 1896, 1914].
1. BM Addit. 40732 [*olim* Taymouth Castle]; 2. BM Addit. 41063 (v) [*olim* Taymouth Castle], ff. 8.
2. Laing, 1834 (priv. pr.).

3289   5. Small, *Met. Homilies*, pp. 68-73.

3290   7 (with vv. 88-172 from 4). Small, *Met. Homilies*, pp. 164-7.

3290.5   That nobull blyn lade fortuen
On the Lady Fortune—four faded lines. [Cf. 3408].
1. ? Lambeth 223, f. 1a.

3291   a love epistle. [Cf. 869].
Furnivall, *EETS* 15 orig. ed. 43-4; rev. ed. 71-2; Robbins, *Sec. Lyrics*, pp. 190-1.

3291.5   That Pers said / Me think it is laid.
Two reflective stanzas added by Mannyng to his trans. of Langtoft's six AN stanzas on Merlin's prophecies fulfilled in King Edward.
1. Inner Temple, Petyt 511, Part VII; 2. Lambeth 131.
Hearne, *Chronicle*, p. 282; Wright, *Rolls Ser.* XLVII, ii. 268.

3292.3   That [th]at is swete in thy mumme / geue thy felawe summe
A proverbial couplet. [Cf. Heywood].
1. Bodl. 21626, f. 25a; 2. Harley 3362; 3. Rylands Lib. Latin 394, f. 15a.

1. Förster, *Festschrift zum 12 Deutschen Neuphilologentage*, p. 52; 3. Pantin, *BJRL* XIV. 102.

That the citesaynes mit gret deal   See 3098.6.

3292.5   That the hert þynkyt / the mowte spekyt
A proverbial tag.
1. Bodl. 15444, f. 140b.
Meech, *MP* XXXVIII. 119.

3297.3   That was my ioy is now my woo and payne
A lady's complaint and the lover's reassurance—two stanzas rime royal. [Cf. 3297.5].
1. BM Addit. 5465, f. 31b.
Stafford Smith, *Eng. Songs*, no. 17; Fehr, *Archiv* CVI. 57; Stevens, *Music & Poetry*, pp. 360-1.

3297.5   That was my woo is nowe my most gladness
Paradoxes of a servant of love—one stanza rime royal. [Cf. a companion piece 3297.3].
1. BM Addit. 5465, f. 12b.
Burney, *Hist. Music*, 1782, II. 546-7; Flügel, *Neuengl. Lesebuch*, p. 142; Stevens, *Music & Poetry*, p. 356.

*þat wele begynnes and fayles in nede   See 245 (Marlborough MS.).

3300   4. Dugdale, *Monasticon*, II. 129; Thorpe, *Diplom. Ang. Aevi Sax.*, 1865, p. 180; *Quattuor Coronatorium Antigrapha*, I, Part 3, p. 29.

3302.3   Thalmyghty god that made eche creature
Henry Medwall's *Nature*—in varying stanzas.
Rastell, ca. 1530 (STC 17779); *repr.* Brandl, *Quellen des Weltlichen Dramas in England*, 1898, pp. 75-158; Farmer, London 1907; Farmer, Amersham 1914; Harbage, p. 18; *facs. Tudor Facsimile Texts*, 1908.

3302.5   The auncient acquaintance madam betwen vs twayn
A reproof to an erring lady, by John Skelton—six stanzas rime royal. [Utley 279].

Dyuers Balettys, ? Pynson, n. d. (STC 22604); *repr*. Dyce, *Skelton*, I. 23-4; Dyce and Child, *Skelton & Donne*, I. 28-30; Henderson, *Skelton*, 1931, pp. 29-30; 1948, 1959, pp. 28-9; *Poets of Eng. Lang.*, I. 368-9.

The angell sayde to the that the fruyt of thi body sulde be blyssyde
Two irregular long riming lines introducing Worcester Cath. MS. of 427.5.

3305   a translation of *Angelus ad Virginem* (cf. 888).

3305.2   þe apocalips in Englissch here now makeþ ende
Couplet concluding ME prose version of Apocalypse. [For introductory couplet see 3305.4].
1. Pepys 2498, p. 263.
James, *Cat.*, III. 107; Påhlsson, *Recluse*, p. iv.

3305.4   Þ'apocalips on englisch makeþ here gynnyng
Couplet introducing ME prose version of Apocalypse. [For concluding couplet see 3305.2].
1. Pepys 2498, p. 226.
James, *Cat.*, III. 107; Påhlsson, *Recluse*, p. iv.

3305.6   þe articulus of þe fay / Tech þi parichones þus & sey
'*Articuli fidei.*'
1. Trinity Dublin 211, at end (c).

3305.8   The armes of crist both god and man / Seynt Pieter þe pope discryued
Indulgence for the *Arma Christi* devotions (1370, 2577, and 4200, in three MSS. only)—seventeen irregular couplets.
1. Royal 17. A. xxvii, f. 80a (vv. 32); 2. Blairs Coll. 13; 3. Longleat 30, f. 11b.

3306   3. Cox [*olim* Harmsworth].
1, 2. Robbins, *Hist. Poems*, pp. 273, 54; 1. Arnold, *Memorials of St. Edmund's*, Rolls Series XCVI, iii. 295; Dickins and Wilson, *Early ME Texts*, p. 10; Wilson, *Lost Lit.*, p. 192; 3. J. S. Cox, *Literary Repository*, 1957, IV. 1.

3306.3 The bakarse boy is vere craynke
'My good boy:' a nonsense poem, possibly erotic—eleven quatrains and concluding six lines.
1. Durham Univ. Cosin V. ii. 13, ff. 3a, 2b.

3306.5 The beme schall bynde that berys the assise
A political prophecy—seven quatrains.
1. NLW Peniarth 26, p. 62.

3306.8 The beistlie lust the furious appetyte
'Ballate aganis Evill Women,' attributed to William Dunbar —six stanzas rime royal. [Utley 282].
1. Camb. Un. Ll. 5. 10, f. 39b; 2. Pepys 2553, p. 325; 3. Advocates 1. 1. 6, f. 262a; 4. Lismore, p. 77 (present location not known; st. 2 & 3 ascribed to Chaucer).
    1. Small, *STS* IV. 266-7; 2. Schipper, *Dunbar*, pp. 439-42; and *DKAW* XLIII (I). 50-4; Craigie, *STS* n.s. VII. 391-2; Baildon, *Dunbar*, pp. 228-9; 3. *Bannatyne MS.*, Hunt. Club, V. 765-6; Ritchie, *STS* n.s. XXVI. 32-3; 4. Craigie, *STS* n.s. XX. 124.

The begynnyng es of three   See 3428 (extract F).

The bella the bella / we maydins beryth the bella   See 3863.5.

3307.5 The better that thi state be / The better wysdom behouys the
A proverbial couplet.
1. Bodl. 21626, f. 30a.
Förster, *Festschrift zum 12 Deutschen Neuphilologentage*, p. 56.

The Bird of Hermes is my name   See 1364.5.

3308   James, *Cat.*, II. 148 (st. 1 only); Robbins, *Hist. Poems*, p. 90.

3308.5 The blak schal blede & þe blewe schal fare & fed
A political prophecy—in long lines, generally couplets (immediately following 734.8), actually vv. 28, 31-35 of 2515 occurring separately.
1. Trinity Camb. 1157, f. 41a (vv. 7); 2. Cotton Cleo C. iv, f. 123b (vv. 12; precedes 734.8); 3. Harley 559, f. 39a; 4. Lansdowne 762, f. 96a (vv. 6).

3310   2. Dickins and Wilson, *Early ME Texts*, pp. 127-8 ('*Ubi sunt*' st. only); Kaiser, *Anthologie*, p. 194; Kaiser, *Med. Eng.*, p. 221 ('*Ubi sunt*' st. only); Speirs, *Med. Eng. Poetry*, p. 89 ('*Ubi sunt*' st. only); Davies, *Med. Eng. Lyrics*, pp. 56-9.

3311   Furnivall, *EETS* 15 orig.ed. 243; rev. ed. 268.

*3312   *þe borys hed haue we in broght
        The concluding quatrain of a Boar's Head carol.
        1. St. John's Camb. 259, f. 1a.
            James and Macaulay, *MLR* VIII. 68; *Early Eng. Carols*, p. 321; Green, *Sel. Eng. Carols*, p. 209.

3313   *Carolles*, de Worde, 1521 (STC 5204); repr. Hearne, *Guilielmi Neubrigensis Historia*, 1719, III. 745; Strutt, *Horda Angel-Cynnan*, 1775, III. 110; Brand, *Pop. Antiquities*, rev. Ellis, I. 448; Sandys, *Carols*, p. 19; Sylvester, *Garland of Xmas Carols*, p. 142; Rickert, *Anc. Eng. Xmas Carols*, p. 260; Davies, *Med. Eng. Lyrics*, p. 278; *facs.* Reed, *Xmas Carols*, p. 3; 1. Segar, *Some Minor Poems*, p. 14; Dyboski, *EETS* ci. 33; Furnivall, *EETS* 32. 388; Robbins, *Sec. Lyrics*, p. 48.

3314   Sylvester, *Garland of Xmas Carols*, p. 155; Rickert, *Anc. Eng. Xmas Carols*, p. 257; Robbins, *Sec. Lyrics*, pp. 49-50.

3315   Stafford Smith, *Musica Antiqua*, I. 22; Sylvester, *Garland of Xmas Carols*, p. 157; Rickert, *Anc. Eng. Xmas Carols*, p. 258; Stevens, *Med. Carols*, p. 66; Robbins, *Early Eng. Xmas Carols*, p. 13; Greene, *Sel. Eng. Carols*, p. 91.

3318   seven couplets.
        1. Balliol 354, f. 7a; 2. Harley 5086, f. 99a; 3. Bodl. 8606, f. 82a.
            1. Flügel, *Anglia* XXVI. 100; 2. F. Smith, *Early Hist. Veterinary Lit.*, 1919, I. 110.

3318.2 The bred is flesche in our credance
        On the host—one 6-line stanza. [Cf. 1561.5, 1640].
        1. Durham Univ. Cosin V. v. 19, f. 73a.

3318.3 The brwett of evill tonges what woman can eschew
On defamation—one couplet.
1. Durham Univ. Cosin V. iii. 9, f. 56a.
Furnivall, *EETS* lxi. 184.

3318.4 The burne ys this world blynde
Christ's appeal from the Cross—thirteen 6-line tail-rime stanzas with 3-line burden: 'Cum ouer the borne Bessey.' [All texts show some variations. Cf. 3228.3; for a secular version see 2263.5; for late xvi cent. political adaptations see Rollins, *SP* XXI. 56, 205, Nos. 587 and 2377].
1. Bodl. 6659, f. 100a (2 st.); 2. Emmanuel 263, f. i recto; 3. Trinity Camb. 1157, f. 55b (12 st.); 4. BM Addit. 5665, f. 143b (burden and st. 1 only).
2. Brie, *Eng. Stn.* XXXVII. 25 (extract only); 4. Furnivall, *Captain Cox,* Ballad Soc. VII. clxxxi; Briggs, *Madrigals,* PMMS 1893, no. 2; Stevens, *Music & Poetry,* p. 348.

3318.6 The catte seeth wele / Whoos berde she lycke shall
A proverbial couplet. [Cf. 3894.6].
Salamon and Marcolphus, Leeu, Antwerp, ca. 1492 (STC 22905); *facs.* Duff, London 1892.

3318.7 The catte the ratte and Louell our dogge / Rulyth all England vnder a hogge
England in 1485 under Richard III—one couplet by Wyllyam Colyngbourne posted on the doors of St. Paul's Cathedral, preserved in many early printed chronicles. [Cf. *Mirror for Magistrates,* p. cxxxviii a. Tilley C 143].
Fabyan, *New Chronicles,* Pynson, 1516 (STC 10659); *repr.* Ellis, 1811, p. 672 [cf. 3955.5]; Hall, *Chronicles,* 1809, p. 395; Holinshed, *Chronicles,* 1807, III. 422; *DNB* IX. 284; Flügel, *Neuengl. Lesebuch,* p. 269 (and cf. 507); Davies, *Camden Soc.* LXIV. 91; Sheppard, *Camden Soc.* n.s. XIX. 96; Wilson, *Lost Lit.,* p. 199; Roskell, *BJRL* XLII. 168; Robbins, *Hist. Poems,* p. xxxviii.

3318.8 The catte wolle fyssh ete / but she wol not her fote wete
A proverbial couplet. [Cf. Heywood; Meech, *MP* XXXVIII. 130; Tilley C 144].
1. Bodl. 15444, f. 142b; 2. Trinity Camb. 1149, f. 351a; 3. Harley 2321, f. 146b; 4. Harley 3362, f. 5a; 5. Rylands Lib. Latin 394, f. 2b.

1. Meech, *MP* XXXVIII. 121; 2, 3, 4. Förster, *Eng. Stn.* XXXI. 7; 3. *Rel. Ant.*, I. 207; 4. Förster, *Anglia* XLII. 202; 5. Pantin, *BJRL* XIV. 93.

3319 [Delete entire entry].

3321 twenty stanzas rime royal. [Utley 283].

3322 Sharp, *Antiquities of Coventry*, pp. 235-6; Robbins, *Hist. Poems*, pp. 63-4.

3322.1 The cyte of heuen is set on so hye a hylle
The City of Heaven—five couplets. [Followed by 3707.7].
1. BM Addit. 37049, f. 67a.

3322.3 The cok seithe in his songe / that thow dost thin husbonde wrong
Riming comment of the first cock in the Story of the Three Cocks in the *Gesta Romanorum*—one couplet. [Cf. 1391.8; 2238.5 and 3081].
1. Harley 5259, f. 60b; 2. Harley 7333, f. 224b; 3. BM Addit. 9066, f. 19b.
2, 3. Herrtage, *EETS* xxxiii. 175; 1. Herbert, *Cat. Rom.*, III. 206; 2. Madden, *Roxburghe Club* 1838, LV. 146.

þe comb yt ys of red coral   See 4185.5.

3322.5 þe comyng of þy gest / ȝif þou lowe feed hys best
A proverbial couplet.
1. Harley 3362, f. 3a.

3322.8 þe comaundementz expouned here enden I ȝou seie
Couplet concluding ME prose text on Commandments.
1. Pepys 2498, p. 226.
James, *Cat.*, III. 107; Påhlsson, *Recluse*, p. iv.

3323.5 þe craft of alle craftys it is þe craft of lowe
A couplet in a Latin sermon on confession.
1. Balliol 219, f. 234b.
Mynors, *Cat.*, p. 214.

3324 six quatrains, English alternating with Latin.
Robbins, *Sec. Lyrics*, p. 104.

3325 Furnivall, *EETS* 15 orig. ed. 225; rev. ed. 254.

3327 [A Latin trans. by Sir Francis Kinaston, A.D. 1639, with Eng. from Thynne, occurs in Bodl. 29640. Ringler 65].
5. Camb. Un. Gg. 4. 27, I a, ff. 13a-126b (begins I. 71); 7. St. John's Camb. 235, ff. 1a-119b; 14. Durham Univ. Cosin V. ii. 13, f. 4a.
Extracts:
G. Trinity Camb. 652, f. 171b (3 st.: III. 302-22; see 3535). H. Durham Univ. Cosin V. iii. 11, f. 100b (II. 1106-7 misquoted); I. Lord Salisbury Lib., Cecil fragment (I. 764-833); J. Huntington EL 26. A. 13, f. iii (scrap); K. BM Cat. 643. m. 4 (transcript by William Thomas in 1721 of burned Cotton Otho A. 18, pasted into copy of Urry's *Chaucer*, II. 548).
[For further extracts appearing as separate poems see 848.5, 1418.5, 1422.1, 1926.5, 2577.5].

Caxton, 1482 (STC 5094); H. Campbell, *PMLA* LXXIII. 306 (*with facs.*); Furnivall, *Chaucer Soc.* 1 s. LXIII, LXIV; J. Pace, *Speculum* XXVI. 307-8.

3327.5 þe ende of lagthre is woþ
The sorrow of the world—two couplets.
1. Magdalen Oxf. 27, f. 103a.
Coxe, *Cat.*, p. 18.

3328 Robbins, *Sec. Lyrics*, pp. 44-5.

The farther I go the more behynde   See 3437.

3328.5 The ffather of heuyn from aboue / Hathe sent his son
A carol to the Trinity—ten quatrains and Latin burden, '*Te deum laudamas* &c' [St. 1 = st. 1 of 2168].
1. Cambridge Univ. Add. 7350, f. ia.

3329 2. Rickert, *Anc. Eng. Xmas Carols*, pp. 65-6.

*3339.5 *The feynd þat is bath fel and bald / Principal tempir he
On Man's Three Foes, a fragment of about 140 lines of a didactic treatise.
1. Bodl. 16032, ff. 91a-92b.

*3339.8	*þe furste braunce is als I tolde right A double leaf of an instructional religious poem, the first page very faded and stained by damp—88 couplets. 1. Camb. Un. Add. 4407, Art. 27.
3343	1. Reed, *Xmas Carols*, pp. xxx-xxxi; Husk, *Songs*, p. 8; Rickert, *Anc. Eng. Xmas Carols*, pp. 223-4; Greene, *Sel. Eng. Carols*, p. 56; Davies, *Med. Eng. Lyrics*, pp. 167-8.
3344	Rickert, *Anc. Eng. Xmas Carols*, pp. 180-1.
3347	Sandys, *Carols*, p. 58; Rickert, *Anc. Eng. Xmas Carols*, pp. 205-6; Niles, *Carol Study Book*, 1948, p. 22.
3347.5	The first vj yeres of mannes byrth and aege Man's life compared to the months of the year (six years = one month), adapted from the French—twelve cross-rimed quatrains. [Cf. *Kalendar of Shepherdes*]. *Horae*, Paris, 1527; *Horae*, London, 1537 (STC 15999); &c.; Bühler, *St. in Renaissance* VI. 233-4.
3348	10. Coventry Corp. Record Office, f. 76b. *Chaucer*, Thynne, 1532 (STC 5068); [Anderson,] *Poets of Great Britain*, I. 579; Clarke, *Riches of Chaucer*, II. 306; 5. Robinson, *Chaucer*, 1933, p. 632; 1957, p. 536.
3349	[For variant cf. 2921; also cf. 3973].
3351	[Preceded by 4053.5].
3352	1. Bodl. 3904, f. 7b; 4. Cotton Julius A. v, f. 147b; 9. Delete this MS.; 13. Harley 114, f. 136b. 1, 3, 7, 11. Wright, *Camden Soc.* VI. 394-5, 295-6; 11. Wilson, *Lost Lit.*, p. 209.
3352.5	The formyst fadere þat formed ȝou alle Dialogue between Lucidus and Dubius. [Cf. 3430.5]. 1. Winchester Coll. 33, ff. 54b-64b.
3353	Furnivall, *EETS* 15 orig. ed. 237; rev. ed. 255-6.
3354.5	The frutefull sentence and the noble werkes *The Conuersion of Swerers* by Stephen Hawes—forty-six

stanzas rime royal (including 4216) and short-line emblem verses (See / Me / be kynde). [Cf. Church, *PMLA* LXI. 636-50; Berdan, *Early Tudor Poetry*, p. 90].

de Worde, 1509 (STC 12943); Butler, ca. 1530 (STC 12944); Copland, 1551; crit. ed. Laing, *Abbotsford Club* XXXII.

3355   2. Camb. Un. Ii. 3. 8, f. 68a and f. 68b.

The further I goo the more behynde   See 3437 (Huntington MS.).

3357   Furnivall, *EETS* 15 orig. ed. 230; rev. ed. 257.

3357.5   The gentyll poets under cloudy figures

The Comfort of Lovers, by Stephen Hawes, a debate between Amour and Pucelle—126 stanzas rime royal (including Prohemye).

de Worde, ca. 1515 (STC 12942.1).

3361   fifty-eight 5-line stanzas. [MSS. 3 & 4 add a Balade and Envoy, 2479. Utley 286].

5. Camb. Un. Ff. 1. 6, f. 22a (followed by 383); 6. Delete this MS.

Chaucer, Speght, 1598 (STC 5077); Urry, *Chaucer*, 1721; Bell, *Poets of Great Britain*; [Anderson,] *Poets of Great Britain*, I; *British Poets*, Chiswick 1822; [Pickering's] *Aldine British Poets*; R. Bell, *Works of Chaucer*, IV; Crowell, *Works of Chaucer*; 3. Vollmer, *Berliner Beiträge zur germ. und rom. Phil.* XVII. 28-44.

3361.1   The good & bad happ that som women have had

The choice of a husband—three couplets. [A companion piece to 3361.6].

1. Arundel, Harington, f. 16b and f. 17b.

Hughey, I. 80, 83.

3361.3   þe gode mon on is weie

A single line fragment of an English song.

1. Bodl. 13679, Item I (b).

Heuser, *Anglia* XXX. 174; Wilson, *Lost Lit.*, p. 179.

3361.6   The good or evell fortune of all a mans lyffe

The choice of friends and a wife—three couplets. [A companion piece to 3361.1].

    1. Durham Univ. Cosin V. iii. 9, f. 66a (vv. 1-2); 2. Arundel, Harington, f. 16b and again f. 17b.
    1. Furnivall, *EETS* lxi. 200; 2. Hughey, I. 80, 82.

3362 1, 2. Girvan, *STS* 3 s. XI. 80-100; Mustanoja, *How the Good Wife*, pp. 176-96.

3363 Mustanoja, *How the Good Wife*, pp. 173-5.

3364 six couplets.

3365 Mätzner, *AE Sprachproben*, I. 115.

3372 [Also in early printed books, e.g., *Liber Festivalis*, 1483].
    1. Cotton Claudius A. ii, ff. 123b and 128a.
    Peacock, *EETS* 31. 21, 24; Wordsworth and Littlehales, *Old Service Books*, p. 271 (preface only).

3372.1 The grete vertus of oure elders notable / Ofte to remembre
    The morale prouerbs of Cristyne, translated by Anthony Widvill, Earl of Rivers—vv. 202 in couplets. [Ringler 66].
    Caxton, 1478 (STC 7273); Dibdin, *Typo. Antiquities*, I. 72-3; (vv. 1-26, 195-202 only); Pynson, 1526.

3372.2 The greatest Comfort in al temptacyon
    'The remembraunce of Crystes passyon'—one couplet, a typographic text on woodcut.
    Hylton, *Scala Perfectionis*, de Worde, 1533 (STC 14045); Dibdin, *Typo. Antiquities*, II. 41; Schreiber, *Handbuch*, VIII. 53 (916a, D. 12).

3372.4 The halte and the blind / ever ben behynde
    A proverbial couplet.
    1. Rylands Lib. Latin 394, f. 2b.
    Pantin, *BJRL* XIV. 93.

3372.5 The hare wente þe markyth scharlyt forto syll
    A proverbial couplet translating '*Forum lepus petabat* &c.'
    1. Bodl. 15444, f. 143b.
    Meech, *MP* XXXVIII. 124.

3372.6 The hart lovyt þe wood the hare lovyt þe hyll
    Satirical proverbs on women—four monoriming lines. [Cf. a

variant in *Oxford Dict. Nursery Rhymes*, p. 200. Utley 287].
1. Ipswich County Hall Deposit: Hillwood [*olim* Brome], f. 1a.
    Smith, *Commonplace Book*, p. 11.

3372.8 The hed of þe crow þat token call we
A fragment of an alchemical poem, perhaps a summary of Ripley's *Twelve Gates*—three stanzas rime royal.
1. Harley 486, f. 16a.

3373 thirteen couplets in a Latin text.
3. Lansdowne 344, f. 70a.

3375 vv. 141 in irregular riming lines.
1. Lansdowne 762, f. 59a.
    Bowers, *Anglia* LXXIII. 293-8.

3376 Robbins, *Sec. Lyrics*, pp. 113-4.

3376.5 The hye desire that Y have for to se
Have mercy, mistress, on me—one 6-line tail-rime stanza.
1. BM Addit. 5665, f. 68b.
    Fehr, *Archiv* CVI. 279; Stevens, *Music & Poetry*, p. 341.

3377 A Proheme of 24 stanzas rime royal and an Epistle, consisting of 100 sets of stanzas (in Texte generally one st. only) with prose Glose and Moralite.
    J. D. Gordon, Philadelphia 1942.

3381 2. Yale Univ. 163 [*olim* Petworth 8], f. 29a (st. 6 only).

3382 [Cf. 1149.5].
    Stevens, *Med. Carols*, p. 72.

The holy doghter of Syon   See 3674.

3384 13. Bodl. 9837, f. 69b; 14. Winchester Coll. 33, f. 35b.
5. D'Evelyn and Mill, *EETS* 235. 134.

3385 [Followed by 1037.3].
1. Greene, *Sel. Eng. Carols*, p. 112; 2. *Rel. Lyr. XV C.*, pp. 110-1; Rickert, *Anc. Eng. Xmas Carols*, p. 12; Stevens, *Med. Carols*, p. 2; Robbins, *Early Eng. Xmas Carols*, p. 60.

3387   2. Winchester Coll. 33, f. 39b.
          1. Horstmann, *Archiv* XLIX. 401 (vv. 1-10 only).

3388   18. Winchester Coll. 33, f. 45a.
          7. D'Evelyn and Mill, *EETS* 236. 390.

3389   [Incorporated in the Laud 'Sancta Crux' and in Winchester 33, f. 41b. Cf. 3387].
          20. Leeds Univ. Brotherton 501 [Maggs Bros. Sale Cat. 1930; Sotheby Sale, Mar. 14, 1949, Lot 309], ff. 107a-b, 102a-106b, 101a-b.
          9. D'Evelyn and Mill, *EETS* 235. 167.

3389.5   The honorable merchant Jon Pickering / And Elisabyth lie
          Epitaph, (allegedly) A.D. 1448 (? A.D. 1465) at St. Laurence-in-Jewry Church, London—eight lines.
          Weever, *Anc. Funerall Monuments*, 1631, p. 399 (STC 25223); Pettigrew, *Chronicles of Tombs*, pp. 48-9.

3389.8   þo ilke þat in nei sibreden ben founden
          Four couplets in a collection of friar sermons.
          1. Basle Univ. B. VIII. 4, f. 105a.
          Meyer and Burckhardt, *MA HSS. der Univ. Basel Beschreibendes Verzeichnis*, Abt. B, p. 852.

3391   Davies, *Med. Eng. Lyrics*, pp. 199-200.

          The Iues me acusyd / and peter refusyd   See 3318.4.

3397   A single quatrain occurring in a sermon, 'Redde racionem villicacionis tue,' preached by Wimbledon. [For numerous printed eds. cf. Sunde, p. vii].
          1. Camb. Un. Ii. 3. 8, f. 43b and f. 51b (vv. 2; var.); 5. Bodl. Eng. theol. f. 39 [*olim* Helmingham Hall], f. 37a; 6. Bodl. 4063, f. 16b; 7. Caius 334; 8. Sidney Sussex 74; 9. Harley 2398, f. 153a; 10. Royal 18. A. xvii, f. 198a; 11. Royal 18. B. xxiii; 12. BM Addit. 35213; 13. Leeds Univ. Brotherton 501, f. 67b.
          A Sermon, London, 1582 (STC 25830); 6. Sunde, *Götesborgs Högskolas [Universitets] Arsskrift* XXXI, v. 35.

          *The kyng when þis consale was done   See *298.5

3404   [Delete entire entry].

The kinges baner on felde is [splayd]   See 1119.

3405   1. BM Addit. 46919 [olim Phillipps 8336], f. 205a.

*3405.3 *The kinges son swer by godes crose / That he shulde
A xv cent. fragment of a variant text of *Bevis of Hamptoun* (corresponds to pp. 129-144 of Kölbing—see 1993).
1. Trinity Camb. 1117, ff. 149-152.

3405.5 The knyght knokett at the castell gate
A love song, possibly for a May disguising—eight couplets with 4-line burden.
1. BM Addit. 31922, f. 45a.
  Chappell, *Archaeologia* XLI. 381-2; Flügel, Anglia XII. 239-40; Flügel, *Neuengl. Lesebuch*, p. 135; *Early Eng. Lyrics*, p. 56; *Oxford Book XVI Cent. Verse*, p. 37; *Early Eng. Carols*, p. 312; Stevens, *Music & Poetry*, p. 402; Stevens, *Music at Court*, p. 33.

3405.8 The knowlege of god passythe comparysone
A Treatise bytweene Enformacione and Musyke by William Cornish (A.D. 1504)—Prologue of four stanzas rime royal and text of twelve stanzas rime royal.
1. Harley 43, ff. 88a-91b (imperfect); 2. Royal 18. D. ii, f. 163a.
  2. Flügel, *Anglia* XIV. 467; Hollander, *Untuning of Sky*, pp. 433-6.

3406   and with a concluding '*Tractatus de Spe*' and Epilogue. [Ringler 67].
3. Plimpton 256 [olim Castle Howard], ff. 1-34 (lacks st. 1-8 of Prologue or Proheme; with 10 addit. st. in conclusion).
De Curia Sapiencie, Caxton, ca. 1480 (STC 17015); 1. Hammond, *Eng. Verse Chaucer-Surrey*, pp. 258-67 (extracts); 2. Brunner, *Anglia* LXII. 260-62 ('*Tractatus de Spe*' & Epilogue only); 3. Bühler, *MLN* LIX. 6-7 (2 st. Proheme only).

3407   1a (transcript). Bodl. 3871, pp. 2-20.

3408   12. *Register*, I. 199.

3409   Brand, *Pop. Antiquities*, rev. Ellis, II. 379; Robbins, *Sec. Lyrics*, pp. 19-20.

þe leuys sothyn in wit wyn   See 3754 (MS. Harley 1735).

The lechys for seke mannys sake   See 2627 (MS. Bühler 21).

3411 twelve short lines.
  Early Eng. Lyrics, p. 170.

3412 [For extract see 4187.8. Roundel fragment also in MS. 2; see 2375. Ringler 68].
  6. Bodl. 10173, ff. 120a-131a; 9a (xix cent. transcript). Camb. Un. Add. 2794; 13. Harley 7333, ff. 129b-132b; 14. Delete this MS.; 15. Longleat 258, ff. 85a-101a.
  Rastell, ca. 1525 (STC 5093) (single leaf fragment); 9. Robinson, Chaucer, 1933, pp. 362-72; 1957, pp. 309-18; D. S. Brewer, 1960.

3412.3 The lylie that faire floure / Is the kyng of ffrance
  '*Declaracio signorum*' in various prophecies—nine couplets.
  1. Lansdowne 762, f. 52a.

þe lion is wonderliche stronge / & ful of wiles   See 3353.

3412.5 The lyon sens thre days as ded had bestylt
  English lines on political conditions in England, *ca.* A.D. 1460-1470—vv. 66.
  1. *olim* Greg [*olim* Huth 153; Goldschmidt Sale Cat. No. 71, 1943, Item 1], f. 16b.

3413 vv. 802.
  Haupt and Hoffman, *Altdeutsche Blätter*, II. 99-120.

3413.3 The lytyll prety nyȝhtygale / among the leuys grene
  'I loue none but you alone'—five cross-rimed quatrains.
  1. Royal App. 58, f. 9b (and imperfect var. at f. 8b).
  Rimbault, *Songs & Ballads*, p. 57; Furnivall, *Captain Cox*, Ballad Soc. VII. cxxviii; Briggs, *Songs & Madrigals*, PMMS 1891, p. 8; Flügel, *Anglia* XII. 263 (var. 262); Flügel, *Neuengl. Lesebuch*, p. 139.

3413.6 The lyver maketh a man to love
  Parts of the body influencing man's faculties—twelve irregular non-riming lines.
  1. Pepys 1036, f. 91a.

3414   2. BM Addit. 34360 [*olim* Phillipps 9053], f. 51a.
        2. Robinson, *Chaucer*, 1933, pp. 621-3; 1957, pp. 528-9.

3416.5 The lover trwe / In colour blew
        The significance of colors—three 6-line tail-rime stanzas.
        1. Trinity Camb. 1450, f. 76b.

        þe man þat him beþouhte   See 4129.

3418   [Cf. 3098.5].
        Robbins, *Sec. Lyrics*, pp. 16-17; Kaiser, *Med. Eng.*, p. 470 (lacks st. 5).

3422   [All texts show some variation. Cf. also 1603, 1605, 3578, 4182].
        1. Bodl. 7719, Part II, f. 1a (as prologue); 2. Bodl. 7778, Part III, p. 184 (as epilogue); 8. Delete this MS.; 9. Sloane 1314, f. 5a (vv. 6 addit.); 10. Sloane 2584, f. 13a (vv. 10 addit.); 11. Wellcome Hist. Med. Lib. 542 [*olim* Payne], f. 1a (vv. 36); 12. Sloane 140, f. 65b; 13. Sloane 340, f. 115b; 14. Sloane 374, f. 14a; 15. Sloane 382, f. 211a; 16. Sloane 442, f. 43a; 17. Sloane 468, f. 7a; 18. Sloane 468, f. 80b (vv. 10); 19. Sloane 963, f. 79b; 20. Sloane 3153, f. 2a (vv. 30); 21. Dawson Sale Cat. 102, Item 11 (1960).
        10. Robbins, *Sec. Lyrics*, pp. 95-6.

3423   [Cf. a prose text in Cotton Titus A. xxv, f. 105a].
        1. Harley 3542, ff. 84b-85a.
        Hutton, *Sword and the Centuries*, 1901, p. 36.

        The maner lyvyng of þe londe / As wel dyverse from Englond
        See 2361.5.

        The mayster to his man maketh his roys   See 4064.

        The masters that vsen blode letynge   See 3848.

3426   *Gentleman's Magazine*, June 1842, p. 467.

3427   2. Huntington Lib. EL 26. A. 13, f. iii.

3428   9. Bodl. 5167*, f. 1a (lacks vv. 1-181 and ends at v. 8426); 60. Rylands Lib. Eng. 90 [olim Ashburnham 136, olim Corser], f.2a; 61. Rylands Lib. Eng. 51, f. 1a (vv. 1-422 wanting); 62. Rylands Lib. Eng. 50, f. 1a; 65. Trinity Dublin 156, f. 2a; 67. Trinity Dublin 158, f. 2a (ends imperfectly); 69. Soc. of Antiquaries 687 [olim Bright], pp. 5-358 (ends imperfectly); 71. Yale Univ. Deposit: Osborne 31 [olim Greg, olim Phillipps 8343], ff. 2a (vv. 1-37 wanting); 73. Bühler 13 [olim Harmsworth]; 74. Foyle, Beeliegh Abbey [olim Harmsworth, olim Amherst 29], ff. 1a-146; 75. Leeds Univ. Brotherton 500 [olim Harmsworth, olim Neale], ff. 1a-147; 76. Helmingham Hall LJ. II. 1; 77. olim Horton Hold Hall (? perhaps MS. 88); 78. Univ. of Pennsylvania, Eng. 1 [olim Ireland Blackburne], ff. 14a-118a; 80. NLW Deposit: Porkington 20, f. 1a; 81. Univ. of Pennsylvania, Eng. 8 [olim Stonor Park], ff. 147a-159b (Prologue, I, II, part of III); 82. Harvard Coll. Eng. 515, f. 1a (vv. 1-160 wanting; text much abridged); 85. Newberry Lib. C. 19169, ff. 98; 87. Univ. of Virginia, Hench, f. 1a (vv. 1-156 wanting); 89. Leeds Univ. Brotherton 501 [olim Horton Hold Hall], ff. 1a-58a; 92. Camb. Un. Add. 6693 [olim Ashburnham App. 236], ff. 1a-179a; 93. Bodl. 8⁰ P. 4. At. Seld. = Selden supra 102*, ff. 15, 16 (Ker Pastedowns No. 1744) (vv. 26); 94. Douai Abbey, Woolhampton, Berks.

3429   15. Trinity Dublin 69, ff. 83b-95b, 65a-72b, 96a-123; 16. Bodl. Lyell empt. 6 [olim Phillipps 2734], f. 1a.

3430   1a (transcript ca. 1675). Bodl. 8915, f. 555a; 3. Brussels, Bibl. royale 4628.

3430.5   The myȝty maker that made al thynge
Discussion between Occupation, Idleness, Doctrine, and Cleanness—in couplets. [Cf. 3352.5].
1. Winchester Coll. 33, ff. 65a-73b.

3431   [Delete entire entry].

The myghty William Duk of Normandy   See 444.

3433   2. Magdalen Oxf. 93, f. 136b.

3434   [Delete entire entry].

The merthe of alle þis londe / maketh þe gode husbonde
Burden to 1405.5.

[382]

3435   twenty-three alliterative lines in couplets, and concluding 6-line tail-rime stanza.
1. Advocates 19. 3. 1, f. 10b; 1a (xix cent. transcript). Egerton 2257, f. 169a.

3435.5   The mone is myrke the lyon is bon
An English prophecy—eight couplets.
1. Bodl. 4062, f. 42b (written twice).

3436   [For burden cf. 3823].

3437   [Cf. also 1629].
5. Briggs, *Songs & Madrigals*, PMMS 1891, pp. [M] 19-22; Stevens, *Music & Poetry*, p. 352; 7. Furnivall, *N&Q* 5 s. IX. 342; Bühler, *MLN* LV. 567.

3438   [Utley 291].
Rickert, *Anc. Eng. Xmas Carols*, p. 263; Robbins, *Sec. Lyrics*, pp. 46-7; Greene, *Sel. Eng. Carols*, p. 93; Davies, *Med. Eng. Lyrics*, p. 228.

3438.3   The moder full manerly & mekly as a mayd
A moralization on the B.V. playing with the Christ Child—three monoriming quatrains and 4-line Latin burden: '*Quid petis O fili* &c.'
1. Peterhouse 195 (Latin burden only); 2. BM Addit. 31922, f. 112b.
2. Chappell, *Archaeologia* XLI. 384; Flügel, *Anglia* XII. 252-3; Flügel, *Neuengl. Lesebuch*, p. 121; Rickert, *Anc. Eng. Xmas Carols*, pp. 63-4; Stevens, *Music & Poetry*, p. 421; Stevens, *Music at Court*, pp. 82-5.

3438.6   The mowse goth a brode / When þe cat is not lorde
A proverbial couplet. [Tilley C 175].
1. Balliol 354, f. 200b.
Flügel, *Anglia* XXVI. 203; Dyboski, *EETS* ci. 132.

3438.8   The name of Iohan wel prays I may
Carol to St. John the Baptist—five 8-line stanzas and 4-line burden.
Christmas Carolles, Kele, ca. 1550 (STC 5205); *facs*. Reed, *Xmas Carols*, pp. 23-5; *repr. Early Eng. Carols*, p. 69.

3439.5 þe nyxtyngale synges / þat all þe wod rynges
　　　　The message of the song of the nightingale—two short couplets.
　　　　1. NLW Peniarth 356, p. 196.
　　　　　Robbins, *Anglia* LXXXII. 12.

3440　　11. Chetham Lib. 6709, ff. 199a-282b; 12. Yates Thompson 47 [*olim* Mostyn Hall 84], p. 1.

3442　　Chepman and Myllar, ca. 1508 (vv. 461); *facs.* Beattie, *Edinb. Bibl. Soc.* 1950, pp. 151-65; *repr.* Stevenson, *STS* LXV. 221-36; 1. *Bannatyne MS.*, Hunt. Club, p. 922; Laing, *Henryson*, 1865, p. 49; Wood, *Henryson*, pp. 129-48; 2. Craigie, *STS* n.s. XVI. 155-74.

3443　　4. BM Addit. 37049, f. 24a (vv. 4); 5. Bodl. Lat. misc. c. 66 [*olim* Capesthorne], f. 129b; 6. Wellcome Med. Hist. Lib. 632 [*olim* Pullen] (roll).
　　　　4. *Early Eng. Carols*, p. 401 (vv. 3 only).

3443.5 The nunne walked on her prayer
　　　　'*Inducas inducas / In temptationibus*'—in macaronic quatrains with this burden.
　　　　1. Camb. Un. Add. 7350, f. iia (8 st.).
　　　　Christmas Carolles, Kele, ca. 1550 (STC 5205) (4 st.); *facs* Reed, *Xmas Carols*, p. 37; *repr. Early Eng. Carols*, p. 311; Robbins, *PMLA* LXXXI.

3444　　3. Bodl. 2291, ff. 19a-21a; 7. Harley 364, f. 22a (st. 6, 10, 12, 13, 14).
　　　　7. Bowers, *MLN* LXVII. 534-6.

3444.5 The owle to þe stone and þe stone to þe owle
　　　　A proverbial tag.
　　　　1. Bodl. 15444, f. 141b.
　　　　　Meech, *MP* XXXVIII. 120.

　　　　þe passione as oure lefdy seiþ　　See 2646.5.

3445.5 The Perse owt off Northombarlande and a vowe to God mayd he
　　　　The Hunting of the Cheviot—in two parts, 25 and 45 cross-rimed quatrains. [For its later variant see 960.1; for a poem of an earlier border raid from which several st. are borrowed see 1620].

1. Bodl. 6933, ff. 15b-18a.

Hearne, *Guilielmi Neubrigiensis Historia*, 1719, I. lxxxii; Percy, *Reliques*, 1765, I. 4; *Annual Register*, 1766, VIII. 261-71; Wright, *Songs & Ballads*, Roxburghe Club 1860, LXXVIII. 24-8; Skeat, *Specimens*, p. 67; Ritson, *Anc. Songs*, p. 92; Child, *Ballads*, 1864, 1878, VII. 29-42; and *Pop. Ballads*, no. 162, III. 307-10; Flügel, *Neuengl. Lesebuch*, p. 198; Bronson, *English Poems*, I. 216; Sidgwick, *Ballads*, p. 177; Gummere, *OE Ballads*, pp. 105-15; Sargent and Kittredge, *Pop. Ballads*, pp. 393-7; Arber, *Dunbar Anthology*, pp. 63-8; Leach, *Ballad Book*, 447-54.

3446 The parfite lyfe to put in remembraunce
  [Ringler 69].
  Pynson, ca. 1495 (STC 19812).

3448 *Chaucer*, Thynne, 1532 (STC 5068); Hyll, ca. 1548 (STC 5100); Wotton, 1606 (STC 5101); *Works*, Thynne, 1542 (STC 5069); *repr.* Skeat, *Oxf. Ch.*, VII. 147-90; *Chaucer*, Stow, 1561 (STC 5075); *repr.* Urry, *Chaucer*, 1721, p. 178; [Anderson,] *Poets of Great Britain*, I; Chalmers, *English Poets*, I. 623-34.

3448.5 þe [pope] haþ graunt a ful fayre pardon
  An introductory 6-line rubric to 701.
  1. BM Addit. 37787, f. 12b.
  N. S. Baugh, *Worcestershire Misc.*, p. 98.

*3448.8 *The prince of prests to hym gan say
  The Stoning of St. Stephen—vv. 87 in cross-rimed quatrains.
  1. Canterbury Cath. Add. 68 [*olim* Ingilby], ff. 99a-b, 97a-b.
  Woodruff, *XV C. Guide Book*, pp. 84-6.

3449 2. Harley 7371, f. 80b (vv. 42)

3451 1. Trinity Dublin, f. 24a.

3451.5 The prophecy professed and j-pight / Of maiden Sibille
  A political prophecy—vv. 300 in quatrains.
  1. Cotton Rolls II. 23, Art. 18.

3452 10. Advocates 19. 2. 1, f. 66a (vv. 1-309).
  1. Horstmann, *Leben Iesu*, Munster & Regensburg, 1873.

3452.1   The prudent problems & the noble werkes / Of the gentyll poets
   A *Joyfull Medytacyon,* by Stephen Hawes (on the coronation of Henry VIII)—thirty-two stanzas rime royal including Prologue and *Excusacio auctoris.*
   de Worde, n.d. (STC 12953); Laing, *Abbotsford Club* 1865, XXXII; Flügel, *Neuengl. Lesebuch,* p. 371 (Prologue only).

3452.3   The sawter of mercy here endyd is
   A colophon to a ME prose tract—four lines.
   1. Durham Univ. Cosin V. v. 12, ff. 9b-10a.

3452.5   The red man here to his white wyfe
   A couplet on a scroll attached to alchemical symbols. [Singer 448].
   1. Egerton 845, f. 16a.
   Singer, II. 351.

3452.6   The red rose and the wythe / Be knyght togeder with grett delyghte
   On the Union of the Lancastrians and Yorkists, A.D. 1486—one couplet.
   1. St. John's Oxf. 57, cover.
   Robbins, *Hist. Poems,* p. 300.

3452.8   þe rede stremes renning
   Two couplets as sermon heads with Latin side notes: '*Respiciamus: oculis, auribus, gustu, tactu.*'
   1. Advocates 18. 7. 21, f. 122a.

3453   8. Huntington HM 64 [*olim* Phillipps 6883], ff. 72b-79a;
   9. Advocates 23. 7. 11 (vv. 34=vv 691-724 of MS. 15, 3029).
   9. Holthausen, *Archiv* XCVIII. 401.

3454   two couplets.
   Robbins, *Neophilologus* XXXVIII. 39.

3455   *Privy Council Books* VI. xxiv; Collier, *Camden Soc.* LXVII. 68; Robbins, *Hist. Poems,* pp. 201-3.

3456.5   The rose both white and rede
   'A lawde...for our souereigne Lord the Kyng [Henry VIII],' possibly by John Skelton—eight stanzas rime royal.

              1. Public Record Office, Treas. Receipt of Exchequer, B. 2. 8, pp. 67-9.

              Dyce, *Skelton*, I. ix-xi; Dyce and Child, *Skelton* & *Donne*, II. 340-2; Stopes, *Athenaeum*, May, 1914, p. 625; Henderson, *Skelton*, 1931, pp. 25-6; 1948, 1959, pp. 131-2.

3457   Rickert, *Anc. Eng. Xmas Carols*, p. 142; Robbins, *Hist. Poems*, pp. 92-3; Greene, *Sel. Eng. Carols*, p. 157.

              Te Rosse wolle into frawnse spryng
              Burden to 306.5.

3457.5   The Salerne Schoole doth by these lines impair

              A dietary—six couplets at end of a collection of Latin and English prose medical rules.

              1. A. Dickson Wright.

              Talbot, *Journal of Hist. of Medicine* XVI. 231.

              The skaterande Scottes / holde we for sottes   See 3558.5.

              þe Scottes / I telle for sottes   See 3558.5.

*3458.5   *[þe sec]ond is compunccion / [þat] some men callis contricion

              A long didactic poem emanating from Bridlington, divided into between 90 and 100 chapters. It has been badly damaged by fire. On f. 65b is a list of the chapters in Latin. The first lines of Chap. I are wanting.

              1. Cotton Vitell. F. xiii, ff. 2a-65a.

3460   Rickert, *Anc. Eng. Xmas Carols*, pp. 99-102; *Oxford Book Christian Verse*, pp. 2-4; Williams, *New Book Eng. Verse*, pp. 109-12; Greene, *Sel. Eng. Carols*, p. 69.

3461   Halliwell, *Nugae Poeticae*, 1844, pp. 13-20.

*3461.3   *The ship full mayny tempeste past / Hath reacht the quiet

              On Friendship—fifteen couplets (vv. 1-4 illegible).

              1. Camb. Un. Dd. 6. 9, ff. 86b.

3461.5   The sigh...ysse

              Fragments, mostly illegible, of the tenor part of a love song.

              1. Camb. Un. Add. 2750, recto (a).

3461.8   The sight which ferst my hart dyd strayne
         A lover's devotion — one 7-line stanza.
         1. Corpus Oxf. 4, f. 1b.

3463   9. *Register*, II. 6.

3464.5   The smaller pesun the more to pott
         Fairness of a woman corresponds to her flightiness — a couplet with a Latin distich. [Utley 293. Tilley P 137].
         1. Bodl. 21626, f. 26b; 2. Sloane 1210, f. 134a (following 2793); 3. Rylands Lib. Latin 394, f. 16b.
         1. Förster, *Festschrift zum 12 Deutschen Neuphilologentage*, p. 53; 2. *Rel. Ant.*, II. 40; Tilley, p. 527; 3. Pantin, *BJRL* XIV. 103.

3465   Kirke, *Reliquary* IX. 75; Robbins, *Sec. Lyrics*, p. 183.

3466   [Perhaps acephalous].

3472   Rickert, *Anc. Eng. Xmas Carols*, p. 209; Williams, *New Book Eng. Verse*, pp. 65-6.

3473   Rickert, *Anc. Eng. Xmas Carols*, p. 185.

3473.5   The sone shall þe f[adre slo]
         An English prophecy — probably about 300 lines in 9-line stanzas.
         1. Cotton Vitell. F. xiii, ff. 76b-81a (pages damaged).

3475   eleven quatrains.
         1. Camb. Un. Mm. 4. 41, f. 147a.
         Person, *Camb. ME Lyrics*, pp. 18-19.

3477   Adams, *Chief Pre-Sh. Dramas*, pp. 158-66 (vv. 475-end); Song alone: *Early Eng. Carols*, p. 50; Cutts, *Renaissance News* X. 3-8.

3477.3   The sterne is rissin of our redemptioun
         On the Nativity, attributed to William Dunbar — five 8-line stanzas with refrain: 'The sterne is rissin of our redemptioun.'
         1. Advocates 1. 1. 6, f. 30b.
         Laing, *Dunbar*, II. 59-60; *Bannatyne MS.*, Hunt. Club, II. 80; Small, *STS* IV. 328-9; Schipper, *Dunbar*, pp. 452-3;

and *DKAW* XLIII (I). 63-5; Baildon, *Dunbar*, pp. 236-7; Ritchie, *STS* n.s. XXII. 76.

3477.6   The stern of heven modre Marye
A hymn to the Virgin.
1. Victoria and Albert Mus., Reid 7, end leaf.

The sterre shoon boþe nyʒt & day
Introductory refrain to 3810.3.

3478.5   þe sonne is brithere þane þe mone
In praise of the Virgin—four lines translating '*Sol luna lucider.*'
1. Balliol 230.
Mynors, *Cat.*, p. 241.

3479   twelve long quatrains.

3480   Mason, *Hoccleve's Poems*, 1769.

3481.5   The sonedayes here thou masse and the festes of commaundment
The Five Commandments of the Church—five lines describing a cut in *The Ordynarye of Crysten Men*.
de Worde, 1502 (STC 5198); 1506 (STC 5199); repr. Dibdin, *Typo. Antiquities*, II. 103-4.

*3483.5   *þe tent ioy had our lady at þe feste of Architriclyne
Fifteen Joys of the B.V.—in couplets.
1. BM Addit. 37049, f. 68a.

3486.5   The thowghts within my brest
A love song ascribed to Henry VIII—one cross-rimed quatrain.
1. BM Addit. 31922, f. 29b.
Flügel, *Anglia* XII. 233; Stevens, *Music & Poetry*, p. 392; Stevens, *Music at Court*, p. 22.

3487   2. Förster, *Archiv* CIV. 308 (st. 1-7).

3487.5   The tyme of youthe is to be spent
'Goode dysporttys,' by Henry VIII—six couplets.
1. BM Addit. 31922, f. 28b.

Briggs, *Madrigals*, PMMS 1893, no. 1; Trefusis, *Songs Henry VIII*, Roxburghe Club CLXI. 10-11; Flügel, *Anglia* XII. 233; Flügel, *Neuengl. Lesebuch*, p. 147; Stevens, *Music & Poetry*, p. 392; Stevens, *Music at Court*, p. 22.

3488　　A Compleynt by the Duke of Suffolk, the healing of the wounded lover.

3489　　1. Camb. Un. Gg. 2. 6, f. 291a.

þe tonge brekyth bon / And hath hym sylfe non　　See 3792.5.

3490.6　　þe Tree of þe cros is wol bryȝte
A worthy tree—two couplets in a Latin sermon by Friar Nicolas Philip.
1. Bodl. 29746, f. 168a.

3491　　[Revise listing of MSS. as follows:]
A Text:
1. Bodl. 815, ff. 1a-20b; 2. All Souls 103, ff. 1a-12b (ends imperfectly, vv. 731); 3. Pepys 1461, ff. 1a-23b; 4. Harley 78, ff. 54a-69a (begins imperfectly at v. 75); 5. Harley 4011, ff. 120a-137b (lacks vv. 626-79; ends imperfectly at v. 1091); 6. Soc. of Antiquaries 101, ff. 50a; 7. Belfast: Queen's Univ. (a single leaf).
B Text (1):
8. Bodl. 14526, ff. 173a-193b; 9. Cotton Vitell. E. x, ff. 192a-207b (damaged by fire); 10. BM Addit. 40673 [*olim* Wrest Park], ff. 1a-16b; 11. Huntington Lib. HM 140 [*olim* Phillipps 8299], ff. 125a-140b.
B Text (2):
12. Harley 78, ff. 35a-52b; 13. Harley 78, ff. 53a-b (a single leaf: vv. 968-1042); 14. Harley 271, ff. 1a-25b; 15. Rylands Lib. Eng. 955, ff. 1a-2b, 4a-5b, 8a-27a; 15a (missing portion of 15 added in xvi cent. hand). Rylands Lib. Eng. 955, ff. 3a-b; 15b (missing portion of 15 added in xvi cent. hand). Rylands Lib. Eng. 955, ff. 6a-7b; 16. Boston Pub. Lib. 92 [*olim* Gurney 146], ff. 167a-184b; 16a (transcript of xvii cent. inserted at end). Boston Pub. Lib. 92.

Hakluyt, *Principal Navigations*, 1598, I. 187 (STC 12626); *repr.* Glasgow 1903, II. 114; Rhys, London 1907, I.. 174; Benham, Seattle 1922; Selden, *Mare Clausum*, 1635, p. 261; 1. Wright, *Pol. Poems*, II. 157-205; Hertzberg and Pauli, Leipzig 1878; *crit. ed.* Warner, Oxford 1926.

3492.3   The xij degrees of pacyence thou mayst beholde her
               The xii degrees of pacyence—one 8-line stanza (probably the first of twelve). [Ringler 69a].
                  Ars Moriendi, Caxton, 1491 (STC 786); facs. Nicholson, 1891; repr. Blades, 1869.

3492.5   The unlatit woman the licht man will lait
               'Indisciplinata mulier'—five couplets translating several Latin distiches in Fordun's Scotichronicon (Book XIV, cap. xxxi).
                  Hearne, Joannis de Fordun Scottichronicon, 1759, II. 376.

3493   1. Trinity Camb. 599, f. 67a and again at f. 179a.
               Person, Camb. ME Lyrics, p. 50.

               The veronycle I honour in worship of the   See 2577 (Bodl. 21575).

3495   Adams, Chief Pre-Sh. Dramas, pp. 304-24.

3496.3   The wardraipper of Venus boure
               'Of James Doig, kepar of the quenis wardrop,' by William Dunbar—six quatrains with refrain. [Cf. 2457.5].
                  1. Camb. Un. Ll. 5. 10, f. 44a; 2. Pepys 2553, p. 339.
                  2. Pinkerton, Anc. Scot. Poems, I. 90-1; Sibbald, Chronicle, I. 278; Laing, Dunbar, I. 110; Blackwood's Magazine, Feb. 1835; Paterson, Dunbar, p. 175; Small, STS IV. 195; Schipper, Dunbar, pp. 200; and DKAW XLI (IV). 1-2; Zupitza, AE Uebungsbuch, pp. 205-6; Baildon, Dunbar, p. 94; Craigie, STS n.s. VII. 413; MacKenzie, Dunbar, pp. 61-2; Kinsley, Dunbar, p. 87.

3496.6   The wednesdayes / astynence and holy fast
               'A lytel treatyse to faste on þe wednesday'—seventy couplets. [Ringler 70].
                  de Worde, ca. 1500 (STC 24224); repr. Huth, Fugitive Tracts in Verse, 1 s. 1874, no. 4.

3498   four stanzas rime royal.

3498.5   The whele off fortune who can hold / or stablysh yt
               'Farewell the best that euer was borne'—three stanzas rime royal.
                  1. Royal App. 58, f. 50a.
                  Flügel, Anglia XII. 269-70.

3499   6. *The Primer*, London 1891, I. 29.

3501   [related to Nicolas Bozon].
              2. Förster, *Archiv* CIV. 205-7.

3502   [Some of the couplets appearing separately in other MSS. are listed individually, e.g., 1151, 4034.6].
              4. Delete this MS.; 5. Longleat 29, ff. 131a-146b, lower margins (var., vv. 64); 6. Leyden Univ. Vossius 9, f. 107b.
              1. Schleich, *Anglia* LI. 221-4.

3502.5   The woud hath erys þe fylde syȝt
              Watch what you say—one proverbial couplet. [Tilley F 209, and cf. W 19].
              1. Trinity Camb. 1149, f. 351a; 2. Harley 3362, f. 5a; 3. NLW Peniarth 356, f. 297.
              1. Förster, *Eng. Stn.* XXXI. 8; 2. Förster, *Anglia* XLII. 202.

3504   7. Huntington Lib. EL 26. A. 13, f. ii.

3506   Furnivall, *EETS* 15 orig. ed. 230; rev. ed. 257; Bloomfield, *Seven Deadly Sins*, p. 166.

3507   8. Liverpool Univ. [*olim* Harmsworth], f. 202b.

3508   Clive, *Roxburghe Club*, 1835, L. 144-82.

3509   Clive, *Roxburghe Club*, 1835, L. 271-304; Serjeantson, *EETS* 206. 257.

3510   An animal prophecy—134 irregular riming lines. [Cf. 3945].
              1. Lansdowne 762, ff. 63b-65a.

3510.5   þe þanne we beseken þi seruans do good
              A couplet translating '*Te ergo quaesumus famulis tuis.*'
              1. Advocates 18. 7. 21, f. 95a.

þeh - conjunction

              þei Y synge & murþus make / it is not y wolde   See 2185.

3511   Furnivall, *EETS* 15 orig. ed. 253; rev. ed. 262.

3513 þey þou þe vulf hore hod to preste
[Cf. 734.5].
1. Whiting, *Speculum* IX. 219, fn. 2; 2. Wilson, *Lost Lit.*, p. 135; Steiner, *American Journal Philology* LXV. 67.

3513.5 Then a ded mon shall aryse & agrement make
A political prophecy—three quatrains.
1. Lansdowne 762, f. 54b.

3514 A long collection of Latin prophecies with some English verses scattered throughout.
1. Sidney Sussex Camb. 39, ff. 1a-69b.

3515.5 þan creu cacces An þan was it dey rybaudye
An English scribble.
1. Corpus Camb. 150, flyleaf.
James, *Cat.*, p. 339; Wilson, *Lost Lit.*, p. 181.

3516.5 þanne is abstinence of worþinesse / Wan man fastet fro wikednesse
A couplet translating '*Tunc est preclara apud Deum abstinencia cum animus ieiunat a viciis.*'
1. Advocates 18. 7. 21, f. 12a.

3517 2. Jesus Oxf. 29, f. 183a (vv. 132; sixteen introductory lines).
4. Kaiser, *Med. Eng.*, pp. 231-3 (vv. 112 only).

*3518.5 *Thenne the knyʒt and the stuard fre
Sir Amadace—generally in 12-line stanzas.
1. Advocates 19. 3. 1, f. 68a (vv. 778); 2. Bibl. Bodmeriana, Coligny, Genève [*olim* Ireland Blackburn], ff. 16a-34b (vv. 852).
1. Weber, *Met. Rom.*, III. 243-75; 2. Robson, *Camden Soc.* XVIII. 27-56; Stephens, *Ghost-Thanks*, Copenhagen 1869.

þan þou þi candul kaste to grownde   See 3372.

3520 2. Hereford Cath. O. iv. 14, f. 3a.

3521 [Utley 387].

3521.5 Ther be iiij thynges full harde for to knaw
'*Cordiale quatuor novissimorum*'—one couplet introducing

prose. [Ringler 71. Bühler, *ELN* I. 83 suggests rime accidental].
1. Lansdowne 762, f. 16b (transcribed from print).
Boke of Huntyng, St. Albans 1486 (STC 3308); *facs.* Blades, 1881; de Worde, 1496 (STC 3309); Caxton, n.d. (IB 49437); *repr.* Bühler, *English Lang. Notes* I. 83; 1. *Rel. Ant.*, I. 233.

There been thre thinges full harde to be knowen
   See 3521.5 (Lansdowne MS.).

3522.5   There ben women there ben wordis / There ben gese there ben tordys
Proverbial couplet against women. [Tilley W 600].
1. Bodl. 21626, f. 23a; 2. Rylands Lib. Latin 394, f. 12a.
1. Förster, *Festschrift zum 12 Deutschen Neuphilologentage*, p. 50; 2. Pantin, *BJRL* XIV. 100.

3523   [Utley 387].

3525   [Possibly a carol, the first stanza forming the burden]. Greene, *Sel. Eng. Carols*, p. 105.

þer childe is kynge   See 906 (MSS. Bodl. 1654 and Rylands Lib.).

*þere him graunted his wille ywis   See 209 (Advocates MS.).

3526   Kaiser, *Med. Eng.*, p. 295 (9 st. only).

3527   1. Rickert, *Anc. Eng. Xmas Carols*, pp. 117-8; Greene, *Sel. Eng. Carols*, p. 86.

3528   3. Bodl. 7630, Part VIII, F, f. 36a; 4. Sloane 1098, f. 14b.

3528.5   There is a boke men calles merlyns Bulbrane
Metrical prophecies, English and Latin, on English history— ten couplets.
1. Bodl. 4062, f. 34b.

Ther ys a chylde borne of a may   See 20.

3530.5   Ther ys a saying bothe olde & trwe
         A moral poem on honest mirth—six 6-line stanzas and a 4-line pseudo-burden. [Cf. 2668.8].
         1. Victoria and Albert Mus., Dyce 45, f. 15b.

*3533.5 *þer ys no merth yn noþir / A man þat haþ yteyd hym vp
         Against women—two cross-rimed stanzas (the first line rubbed out). [Utley 298a].
         1. Bodl. 21831, f. 99b.
            Rel. Ant., II. 113 (second st. only); Robbins, *Sec. Lyrics*, p. 38.

3534   Robbins, *Sec. Lyrics*, pp. 136-8.

3535   'The Tongue,' a composite poem incorporating three stanzas from Lydgate's *Fall of Princes* (1168), I. 4621-41, and three stanzas from Chaucer's *Troilus and Criseyde* (3327), III. 302-22—seven stanzas.

3536   five 3-line stanzas and burden.
         Early Eng. Carols, p. 130; Rickert, *Anc. Eng. Xmas Carols*, p. 8; Segar, *Med. Anthology*, p. 65; Stevens, *Med. Carols*, p. 10; Robbins, *Early Eng. Xmas Carols*, p. 66; Greene, *Sel. Eng. Carols*, p. 107.

3537   Greene, *Sel. Eng. Carols*, p. 132.

         There may areste me no pleasaunce   See 3878.

3538.5   There may to slouthe no nother qw...
         Moral admonitions—five stanzas rime royal.
         1. Harley 2202, ff. 71a-b.

3539   Hall, *Poems of Minot*, 1914, pp. 101-3; 2. Hearne, *Robert of Gloucester*, 1810, I. lxxxiii.

3540   [Ringler 72].
         Caxton, ca. 1484 (STC 5057); *repr.* Dibdin, *Typo. Antiquities*, I. 334.

3542   nine 8-line stanzas (possibly three balades) and 10-line Envoy. [Ringler 73].

        3. Bodl. 6943, f. 43b (eight 6-line st.; occurs separately);
        4. Bodl. 10173, f. 69b.
          Notary, ca. 1500 (STC 5089); *Chaucer*, Stow, 1561 (STC 5075); *repr.* Chalmers, *English Poets*, I. 363; 2. Robinson, *Chaucer*, 1933, pp. 633-4; 1957, pp. 537-8.

þer spring a welle al at here foot   See 2730.

Ther was a frier of order gray/ *Inducas*   See 3443.5.

þer was a knyȝt in a cunttre / that ryche man was   See 1641.

3546   [Cf. 1163].
           Furnivall, *EETS* 15 orig. ed. 35; rev. ed. 63.

3547   Rosenthal, *Vitae Patrum in Old & ME Lit.*, p. 158.

3549.5   There was one Octauyan / Octauyan of Rome Emperour
           'A caroll of the Innocentes'—eight 10-line stanzas including refrain: 'In Israel' and introductory burdens: 'Marke this songe for it is trewe.'
           Christmas Carolles, Kele, ca. 1550 (STC 5205); *facs.* Reed, *Xmas Carols*, pp. 54-8; *repr.* Bliss, *Bibl. Miscellanies*, 1813, p. 58; Sandys, *Carols*, pp. 23-6; Husk, *Songs of Nativity*, p. 45; Daglish, *Carols*, p. 35.

3551   [Cf. Raby, *Hist. Secular Latin Poetry*, II. 215].

3552   [For a variant cf. 3256.3. Utley 275. Cf. D'Urfey, *Pills to Purge Melancholy*, 1707, II. 127.].
           [Masters,] *Rymes of Minstrels*, p. 20; Padelford, *CHEL* II. 385.

3553   2a (xix cent. transcript). Egerton 2257, ff. 133a-136b; 4. Morgan Lib. M. 818 [*olim* Ingilby], f. 1a.
           1-5. Amours, *STS* XXXVIII. 177-245; 1. Laing, *Early Pop. Poetry*, rev. Hazlitt, 1895, I. 45-6.

*3553.5   *Therfore be thyn own frend
           Know Thyself—vv. 44 in 8-line stanzas with refrain: 'And know thyself wysely I rede.'
           1. Balliol 354, f. 156b.
             Flügel, *Anglia* XXVI. 70-1; Dyboski, *EETS* ci. 82-3.

Therefore ye Welshe men here after nurture lerne
Tag in Fabyan's *Chronicle* (ed. Ellis, p. 127): see 3955.5.

þese armis of Crist boþ god and man
Concluding rimed rubric to 2577.

*3553.8 *These be the diue techynges expresse / The which giveth
A poem to his mistress likening her to a tree in various seasons—about twenty folios.
1. Longleat 253 (first leaf missing).

3556.5 Thir ladyis fair that makis repair
'Of the ladyis solistaris at court,' by William Dunbar—six 12-line tail-rime stanzas. [Utley 301].
1. Camb. Un. Ll. 5. 10, f. 38b; 2. Pepys 2553, p. 324; 3. Advocates 1. 1. 6, f. 261a.
2. Craigie, *STS* n.s. VII. 390-1; MacKenzie, *Dunbar*, pp. 97-8; 3. Ramsay, *Evergreen*, I. 206-8; *Ramsay and Earlier Scot. Poets*, pp. 253; Sibbald, *Chronicle*, I. 251-2; Laing, *Dunbar*, I. 92-4; Paterson, *Dunbar*, pp. 136-8; *Bannatyne MS.*, Hunt. Club, IV. 762-3; Small, *STS* IV. 168-9; Eyre-Todd, *Med. Scot. Poetry*, pp. 204-5; Schipper, *Dunbar*, pp. 74-6; and *DKAW* XL (II). 74-6; Baildon, *Dunbar*, pp. 26-8; Ritchie, *STS* n.s. XXVI. 30-1.

These lechys for seke mannys sake   See 2627.

3557 1. Egerton 3245 [*olim* Gurney], f. 191b.

3558 [Probably copied from *Ars Moriendi*, Caxton, 1491 (STC 786); *facs.* Nicholson, 1891; repr. Blades, 1869; or from T. Betson's *Right Profitable Treatise*, de Worde, ca. 1500. Ringler 73a].

3558.5 These scaterande scottes / hold I for sottes
A song of victory over the Scots inserted in the *Brut* Chronicles and early prose chronicles. [For the Langtoft version see 841].
A. Brut Chronicle (numerous MSS., e.g.):
1. Bodl. 11539, Cap. CLXIX, not foliated; 2. Cotton Galba E. viii, f. 83a.
2. Brie, *EETS* 131. 191.
B. Printed Chronicles, e.g.:
Chronicles of England, Caxton, 1480 (STC 9991); Fabyan,

New Chronicles, Caxton, 1516 (STC 10659); repr. Ellis, 1811, p. 398; Rastell, Pastime of Peoples or Chronicles, repr. Ellis, 1811, p. 197; Weever, Anc. Funerall Monuments, 1631, p. 458 (STC 25223); Wright, Pop. Superstitions, II. 261; Wilson, LSE V. 44; Early Eng. Carols, p. liii.

3559.5   These xij aposteles under figure / I shall declare in short manere
On the Apostles—in rime royal stanzas.
1. Bristol: All Saints Church 2, f. 47a.

3559.8   These women all / Both great and small
Satire on woman's inconstancy—five 6-line stanzas with disclaiming refrain: 'But I will nott say so.' [Utley 304].
1. Harley 7578, f. 100b; 2; Folger Lib. 1186.2, a single folio (7 st.).
1. Ritson, Anc. Songs, 1877, p. 178; Oxford Book XVI C. Verse, p. 39.

3560   [See also 1538].
1. Bodl. 6923, f. 251b (vv. 454).
1. Horstmann, AE Leg. 1881, pp. 77-81.

3560.5   þies woundes smert bere in þi hert
Verses on a scroll accompanying a drawing of Christ's wounded heart—six lines.
1. BM Addit. 37049, f. 20a.
Comper, Life & Lyrics of Rolle, p. 318.

*Thay rad a fful gret pas   See *4194.5.

*[Thei] thonkeþ god þat al haþ wrou3t   See 3145 (Sloane).

3561.5   þeues frend and louerdes porse / Comune chest & crystes corse
A couplet translating Latin ascribed to St. Jerome.
1. Bodl. 2695, f. 229a.
Utley, Speculum XX. 109.

Thyn own cot y-had sem noon / The purpose þat þey layd
See 2577 (MS. Osborn 22b).

Thingis in kynde desyris thingis lyke   See 223.

Thingys passid remembre and well devide
See 576 (stanza on Prudence).

3563.5   Thinke and thanke prelate of grete prise
Six 'sotelties' at the banquet for the elevation of John Morton to the Bishopric of Ely in A.D. 1479—seven stanzas rime royal.
Arnold, *Customs of London,* 1502; 1521; *repr.* London 1811, pp. 238-40; J. Bentham, *Hist. and Antiquities of Ely,* App., p. 35; Coulton, *Life in the MA,* III. 150 (st. 1 only).

3565   [Delete entire entry].

þenc man of mi harde stundes
Couplet heading to 2079.5.

3565.5   Thenke man thi life mai not ever endure
Warning against false executors—four monoriming lines, on a tile fixed in pillar near west end of nave in St. Anne's Chapel, Great Malvern Priory, pr. James, *Abbeys,* 1926, p. 78; also on a tile in Salisbury Museum, pr. *Heritage* II. 208.

3566   Greene, *Sel. Eng. Carols,* p. 135.

3567   2. Brunner, *Anglia* LIV. 290-1.

3567.3   Think neuer noy Ill
The Saviour's plea—four lines.
1. Trinity Dublin 661, p. 69.

3567.6   þenk of þi cote þat is brith an gay
A couplet.
1. Advocates 18. 7. 21, f. 144a.

3568   [Cf. 3570.5].
2. Delete this MS.; 3. Corp. Christi Camb. 402, f. 65a.
3. d'Ardenne, *S. Iuliene,* Liége, 1936, p. xlv; *reissued EETS* 248. xlv; Tolkien, *EETS* 249. 123; 6. Day, *EETS* 225. 107.

3568.5 Thynke on hym and haue gode mynde / That to the was soo kynde
  A couplet in the story of Emperator Fredericus in the *Gesta Romanorum*. [Cf. 4074.5].
  1. Harley 5369, f. 48b.
    Gesta Romanorum, ? de Worde, ca. 1517 (STC 21286.1); repr. Herbert, *Cat. Rom.*, III. 192; with 1. Madden, *Roxburghe Club*, 1838, LV. 506.

3570.5 þenchen hu swart þing & suti is þe sunne
  A moral warning, inserted into a life of St. Margaret. [Cf. 3568].
  1. Bodl. 1898, f. 29b; 2. Royal 17. A. xxvii, f. 49a.
    1, 2. Mack, *EETS* 193. 34, 35.

3571 [Cf. Terry, *N&Q* s. viii, IV. 77; *Oxford Dict. Nursery Rhymes*, p. 380].
  5. Huntington HU 1051 [*olim* Ashby-de-la-Zouche], f. 48a.
    1. Robbins, *Sec. Lyrics*, p. 62.

3572 Furnivall, *Percy Soc.* II. 266; Robbins, *Sec. Lyrics*, p. 71; Jones, *Inst. Hist. Medicine Bull.* V. 554.

3574 1. Segar, *Med. Anthology*, p. 43; 2. Rickert, *Anc. Eng. Xmas Carols*, pp. 169-70; 2. Stevens, *Med. Carols*, p. 4.

3575 Reed, *Xmas Carols*, pp. 84-5.

3576 Bramley, *Rolle's Psalter*, 1884, pp. 1-2; Allen, *Rolle*, p. 174 (extracts).

  This book hat Ypocras / Oon of þe beest surgeon   See 3422.

3578 A verse preface to Macer's prose Virtues of Herbs—four lines.
  1. Sloane 963, f. 85b; 2. Trinity Camb. 1037, f. 1a.

3578.5 þis boc is ycome to þe ende / Heuene blisse god ous zende
  One couplet in *Ayenbite of Inwyt*. [Cf. 2331].
  1. Arundel 57, f. 94a.
    Morris, *EETS* 23. 263; Stevenson, *Roxburghe Club*, 1855, LXXII. 211.

3579 nine couplets.
Mätzner, *AE Sprachproben*, II. 61; Stevenson, *Roxburghe Club*, 1855, LXXII. 1; Brandl and Zippel, *ME Sprach- u. Literatur.*, p. 237; Kaiser, *Anthologie*, p. 166; Kaiser, *Med. Eng.*, p. 198.

3580 2. Harley 1251, f. 1a; 5. Harley 2320, f. 72b; 6. BM Addit. 30506, f. 169a; 7. Victoria and Albert Mus., Reid.
3. Littlehales, *EETS* 109. 1; 1. Robbins, *Sec. Lyrics*, p. 85; 2. Bennett, *England Chaucer-Caxton*, p. 161; Coulton, *Life in the MA*, II. 118 (mod.); 5. Wordsworth and Littlehales, *Old Service Books*, p. 60; 7. Douglas, *Burlington Mag.* I. 392.

3581 six couplets. [Cf. 2663.5, 4273.8].
2. Bühler 11 (xvii cent.).
Morale Prouerbes of Cristyne, Caxton, 1478 (STC 7273); Park, *Walpole's Cat. of Royal Authors*, 1806, I. 216; Dibdin, *Typo. Antiquities*, I. 62-3; 1. Bühler, *MLN* LXXII. 4-5.

3581.5 This Booke shewith to clerkes misticall conninge
Prologue to *Certayne Principall Questions drawen oute of Raymundes Questyonary* [actually a translation of Norton's Latin Prologue to his *Ordinal:* cf. 3772]—twenty couplets.
1. Bodl. 7642, Part II, ff. 90a-b; 2. Bodl. 7643, ff. 299b-300a.

3582 6. Coventry Corp. Record Office, f. 64b.

Thys boke vnto clarkes declaryth scyence greate   See 3581.5.

3583 [St. 2 = 1640].
Greene, *Sel. Eng. Carols*, p. 126.

3584 1560 lines in 8-line stanzas. [Ringler 74].
3. Asloan, ff. 263a-290a (vv. 1552).
de Worde, 1499 (STC 5643); 1, 2. Bennett, *STS* 3 s. XXIII. 64-169.

This borne ys the world blynd   See 3318.4.

3584.5   Thys chapell floryschyd with formosyte spectabyll
           A 4-line inscription at Holloway Church, Somerset.
           Beauties of England: Somerset, p. 388.

3585.5   Thys cros that heyr peyntyd is / Syng of the cros of bromholm is
           Text attached to a picture of the Rood of Bromholm.
           1. Fitzwilliam Mus. 55, f. 57b; 2. Prayer-roll, Sotheby Sale, Dec. 9, 1963, Lot 120.
              1. James, *Cat.*, p. 139.

           This day day dawes
             Burden to 1450.

3587   [Delete entire entry].

           This day ys borne a chylde of grace
             Burden to 54.5.

3593   [Utley 305].
           [Masters,] *Rymes of Minstrels,* p. 27.

3594   Robbins, *Sec. Lyrics,* pp. 18-9.

3595   Wilson, *Lost Lit.,* p. 180; Stevens, *Med. Carols,* p. 110.

3595.3   This hindir nycht halff sleiping as I lay
           'The Dreme,' by William Dunbar, a plea for money to King James IV—twenty-three 5-line stanzas.
           1. Camb. Un. Ll. 5. 10, f. 3b.
              Laing, *Dunbar,* I. 31-5; Paterson, *Dunbar,* pp. 233-7; Small, *STS* IV. 257-60; Schipper, *Dunbar,* pp. 242-7; and *DKAW* XLI (IV). 43-9; Baildon, *Dunbar,* pp. 117-21; Craigie, *STS* n.s. XX. 46-50; MacKenzie, *Dunbar,* pp. 127-30.

3595.6   Thys yonders nyght / I herd a wyght
           'Alas I dye for payne:' Christ's complaint—one 6-line tail-rime stanza.
           1. Royal App. 58, f. 12b.
             Flügel, *Anglia* XII. 265.

3596   1. Rickert, *Anc. Eng. Xmas Carols*, pp. 69-70; 3 (burden only). Stevens, *Med. Carols*, p. 10; Robbins, *Early Eng. Xmas Carols*, p. 72.

    This enders nyght / I sawe a sight / A sterne as bryght
    Burden to 3627.

3597   2. Briggs, *Madrigals*, PMMS 1893, no. 5; Bullen, *Carols & Poems*, pp. 21-2; Rickert, *Anc. Eng. Xmas Carols*, pp. 62-3; Segar, *Med. Anthology*, pp. 72-4; Stevens, *Music & Poetry*, pp. 366-7.

3598   ten 7-line stanzas.
    1. Camb. Un. Ll. 5. 10, f. 58a (st. 1 & 2 only).
    3. Schipper, Vienna 1894, pp. 35-6; *Bannatyne MS.*, Hunt. Club, II. 330-3; Kaufmann, *Traité de la langue...Dunbar*, 1873, p. 23; Schipper, *DKAW* XL (II). 34-6; Baildon, *Dunbar*, pp. 2-4; MacKenzie, *Dunbar*, pp. 51-3.

3598.5   Thys enders nyte / When sterres shone bryte
    A dialogue between Christ and the Sinner, with *chanson d'adventure* opening—two 6-line tail-rime stanzas and nineteen couplets.
    1. Victoria and Albert Mus., Dyce 45, f. 15a.

3599   fifteen 8-line tail-rime stanzas.
    Pinkerton, *Poems from Scarce Editions*, III. 189; Sibbald, *Chronicle*, I. 178-82; Child, *Ballads*, 1864, 1878, VIII. 147-52; Laing, *Henryson*, 1865, p. 10; Arber, *Dunbar Anthology*, pp. 151-5; *Oxford Book Eng. Verse*, pp. 20-5; *Oxford Book Christian Verse*, pp. 19-23; Wood, *Henryson*, pp. 173-6; Elliott, pp. 115-8.

3603   1. Rickert, *Anc. Eng. Xmas Carols*, pp. 160-1; Segar, *Med. Anthology*, p. 44 (5 st. only); Speirs, *Med. Eng. Poetry*, pp. 72-3 (omits st. 3, 4).

3603.5   þis goode booke Recluse here now makeþ ende
    Couplet at end of a prose *Regula anachoritarum*.
    1. Pepys 2498, p. 449.
    James, *Cat.*, III. 109; Påhlsson, *Recluse*, pp. v, 201.

3604   (in A.D. 1428).
    1. Robbins, *Sec. Lyrics*, pp. 88-90.

3604.5   This heuenly boke more precyous than golde
　　　　　Colophon by de Worde at end of Hilton's *Scala Perfectionis*
　　　　　—one 8-line stanza.
　　　　　　　de Worde, 1494 (STC 14042); *repr.* Duff, *XV Cent. English Books*, p. 53.

3609.6   This is a rewle to knowe without labour / When the mone chaungeth and in what houre
　　　　　A couplet introducing a prose table on the changes of the moon.
　　　　　1. Harley 2252, f. 159b; 2. Royal 17. B. xlvii, f. 48a.

3610   Furnivall, *EETS* 15 orig. ed. 236; rev. ed. 265 (vv. 2).

3611   The Complaint of Christ to Man and Man's answer (st. 10). [St. 9 = st. 9 of 3612].

3612   5, 7. Stevenson, *STS* LXV. 46-50, 298-301; 6, 7. Furnivall, *EETS* 15 orig. ed. 160-9; rev. ed. 190-9; 5. Laing, *Early Pop. Poetry*, rev. Hazlitt, 1895, I. 309-12.

3612.5   Thys ys Iohn Hancock ys boke
　　　　　Book plate consigning Thomas Carter to hell—one couplet.
　　　　　1. Durham Univ. Cosin V. iii. 9, f. 37b.
　　　　　Furnivall, *EETS* lxi. 156.

3613   one stanza rime royal. [Followed by 2277.8].
　　　　　Robbins, *PMLA* LXIX. 638; Robbins, *Sec. Lyrics*, p. 156; Jacob, *XV Cent.*, p. 486.

3614   [Delete entire entry].

　　　　　This is Robert Curzon his booke   See 1417.5.

3615   1. BM Addit. 10336, f. 3b.
　　　　　Bennett, *England Chaucer-Caxton*, p. 161.

3616   [Cf. 407.6. Singer 796].
　　　　　1. BM Addit. 15549, ff. 153a-168a; 2. Delete this MS.

3618   [Singer 861].

3618.5 This is the propheci þat thai have in wales
The fall of London, a political prophecy—two stanzas rime royal.
1. Trinity Dublin 516, f. 16a.

3619 Rickert, *Anc. Eng. Xmas Carols*, p. 172; Stevens, *Med. Carols*, p. 23.

3621 [Cf. 312].

3622 Bullrich, *Über Charles d'Orleans*, 1893, p. 22 (2 st.).

3623.5 This lady clere / that I sheu here
Man's soul his true love—three 6-line tail-rime stanzas with a secular burden-refrain: 'Who shall have my fayr lady &c.' (taken from 4098.6).
XX *Songes*, de Worde, 1530 (STC 22924); *repr.* Imelmann, *Shakespeare-Jahrbuch* XXXIX. 129-30; Flügel, *Anglia* XII. 592; Flügel, *Neuengl. Lesebuch*, p. 127.

3625 2. Fitzwilliam Mus. McClean 182 [*olim* Ashburnham App. 134], f. 9b (4 st.); 4. Delete this MS.; 5. Delete this MS. Treveris, 1559; *repr.* Brydges, *Censuria Lit.* IX. 369.

3627 1. Sylvester, *Garland of Xmas Carols*, pp. 5-8; Husk, *Songs*, p. 13; Bullen, *Carols & Poems*, pp. 15-18; F. E. Budd, *Book of Lullabies*, 1930, p. 34; 2. Bramley and Stainer, *Xmas Carols*, no. xxv; *Oxford Book Christian Verse*, p. 5; Segar, *Some Minor Poems*, pp. 44-7; Segar, *Med. Anthology*, pp. 68-71 (6 st.); 4. Brandl and Zippel, *ME Sprach- u. Literatur.*, p. 114; *comp. text.* Rickert, *Anc. Eng. Xmas Carols*, pp. 59-62 (8 st.).

3627.5 This lusty maij the quhich all tendre flouris
'Quare of Ielusy'—607 lines mainly in couplets, but partly in stanzas of varying length.
1. Bodl. 3354, ff. 221b-228b.
Laing, *Bannatyne Miscellany* II. 161; Lawson, *Kingis Quair*, 1910, pp. 104-23; Brown, *STS* 3 s. IV. 195.

3628 four 8-line stanzas and a 4-line 'Lullay' introduction: 'Thys yonder nyȝth y sawe a syȝte &c.'

3629 [Singer 859].

3630   Rickert, *Anc. Eng. Xmas Carols*, pp. 44-5.

3631   Delete: Second roundel follows.
       1. Harley 682, f. 61a.

3632   [Some MSS. have further stanzas added, but not by Lydgate. For variant texts see 444, 882, and 4174.3].
       [Revise listing of MSS. as follows:]
       1. Bodl. 1797, f. 65a (var., 10 st.); 2. Bodl. 1885, f. 45a; 3. Bodl. 2527, f. 184b; 4. Bodl. 3896, f. 330b; 5. Bodl. 6943, f. 75a; 6 (xvii cent. transcript of de Worde, 1530). Bodl. 10210, f. 51a; 7. Bodl. 11914, f. 78b; 8. Bodl. 11951, f. 187a; 9. Bodl. 12172, f. 121a; 10. Bodl. 22005 (a roll) (vv. 151); 11. Bodl. 29284 (a roll); 12. Bodl. 30437, f. 23a; 13. Bodl. Firth d. 14, ff. 96a-99 (from a 1483 print); 14. Lincoln Coll. Oxford; 15. Camb. Un. Add. 6686 [*olim* Ashburnham 140], p. 272; 16. Caius Camb. 249, f. 127a (to Henry V); 17. Jesus Camb. 56, f. 46a; 18. Trinity Camb. 601, f. 242a and f. 319a (to Edward IV); 19. Cotton Galba E. viii, ff. 2a-b; 20. Cotton Titus D. xx, f. 94a; 21. Egerton 1995, f. 110a; 22. Harley 2251, f. 2b; 23. Harley 2261, f. 446b; 24. Harley 7333, f. 149a; 25. Lansdowne 210, ff. 27a-42b (interspersed throughout a prose chronicle); 26. Lansdowne 699, f. 79a; 27. Lansdowne 762, f. 10a (to Henry VII); 28. Royal 18. D. ii, f. 181a (vv. 160, including introductory st.; continues to Henry VIII); 29. Stowe 69, f. 196a (to Richard II; imperfect); 30. BM Addit. 31042, f. 96a (to Edward I); 31. BM Addit. 34360, f. 60b (to Edward IV); 32. College of Arms LVIII, f. 335a; 33. Hertford County Record Office; 34. Ipswich Great Doomsday; 35. Lambeth 306, f. 17b; 36. Nottingham Univ. Me LM 1 [*olim* Mellish], end leaves; 37. Trinity Dublin 516, f. 28b; 38. Leyden Univ. Vossius 9, f. 92b; 39. Bühler 17 [*olim* Lyell, Quaritch Sale Cat. 699, no. 52], second flyleaf, recto & verso.

   Pynson, ca. 1518 (Bodl. Wood 536); de Worde, 1530; Bodl. Ashmole 456 (Printed Book); 7. Robbins, *Hist. Poems*, pp. 3-6; 8. Hearne, *Robert of Gloucester*, II. 585-95; 21. Gairdner, *Camden Soc.*, n.s. XVII. 49-54; 34. *East Anglian* n.s. I. 38 (extracts); 35. Gairdner, *Camden Soc.* n.s. XXVIII. 28-31.

3632.3   This mynyon ys in London
       A fine mistress — four 7-line stanzas with burden: 'Mynyon go trym.'
           XX Songes, de Worde, 1530 (STC 22924); *repr.* Imelmann, *Shakespeare-Jahrbuch* XXXIX. 130-1; Flügel, *Anglia* XII. 592-3; Flügel, *Neuengl. Lesebuch*, p. 145.

3632.6   þys nome ys also on honikomb þat ȝyfþ ous sauour and swetnesse
On the name of Jesu—four long monoriming lines by Friar William Herebert.
1. BM Addit. 46919 [olim Phillips 8336], f. 161a.

*3634.1   *Þis nue fryt of which yspe ... and
The seed sown in man's heart by Christ the gardener—probably thirteen long lines irregularly riming.
1. Kilkenny Corporation, *Liber primus Kilkenniensis*, f. 1a.
Seymour, *Proc. Royal Irish Academy* XLI. 205; Richardson, *N&Q* n.s. IX. 47.

3634.3   This nycht befoir the dawing cleir
'How Dunbar wes desyred to be ane freir,' by William Dunbar—ten 5-line stanzas.
1. Camb. Un. Ll. 5. 10, f. 42a; 2. Pepys 2553, p. 333; 3. Advocates 1. 1. 6, f. 115a.
2. Craigie, *STS* n.s. VII. 404-5; 3. [Hailes,] *Anc. Scot. Poems*, pp. 29-31; Sibbald, *Chronicle*, I. 240-2; *Select Poems of Dunbar*, Perth 1788, pp. 31-3; *Bannatyne MS.*, Hunt. Club, II. 327-8; Laing, *Dunbar*, I. 28-30; Skeat, *Specimens*, 1871, pp. 408-10; Paterson, *Dunbar*, pp. 184; Small, *STS* IV. 131-3; Browne, *Early Scot. Poets*, 1896, pp. 121-3; Schipper, *Dunbar*, pp. 239-41; and *DKAW* XLI (IV). 39-43; Skeat, *Specimens*, 1887, pp. 116-7; Baildon, *Dunbar*, pp. 116-7; Arber, *Dunbar Anthology*, pp. 28-30; Ritchie, *STS* n.s. XXII. 306-7; MacKenzie, *Dunbar*, pp. 3-4; Kinsley, *Dunbar*, pp. 43-4.

3634.5   This nyght I will wende my wey tide what bytide
A charm against thieves by the Four Apostles—in couplets.
1. Sloane 2584, f. 75a.

3634.6   This nycht in my sleip I wes agast
'The Devillis Inquest,' by William Dunbar—in 5-line stanzas.
1. Camb. Un. Ll. 5. 10, f. 18b (13 st.); 2. Pepys 2553, pp. 55-7 (13 st.); 3. Advocates 1. 1. 6, f. 132b (17 st.).
2, 3. Laing, *Dunbar*, II. 248; I. 45-8; 2. Craigie, *STS* n.s. VII. 62-4; 3. [Hailes,] *Anc. Scot. Poems*, pp. 37-41; Ramsay, *Evergreen*, I. 171-5; *Ramsay and Earlier Scot. Poets*, p. 247; *Select Poems of Dunbar*, Perth 1788, pp. 38-41; Paterson, *Dunbar*, pp. 95-8; *Bannatyne MS.*, Hunt. Club, III. 372-5; Small, *STS* IV. 144-8; Zupitza, *AE Uebungsbuch*, pp. 203-5; Baildon, *Dunbar*, pp. 31-3; Ritchie, *STS* n.s.

XXIII. 1-4; *comp. texts.* Sibbald, *Chronicle,* I. 290-4 (18 st.); Schipper, *Dunbar,* pp. 81-4; and *DKAW* XL (II). 81-4 (18 st.); MacKenzie, *Dunbar,* pp. 76-9 (21 st.).

3635 Rickert, *Anc. Eng. Xmas Carols,* pp. 43-4.

This nyghtes rest this nyghtes rest / adewe farewell &c. Refrain of 1449.5.

3635.5 This other day / I hard a may / Ryght peteusly complayne
A disconsolate mistress comforted—nine 6-line tail-rime stanzas with a 5-line 'Hey nony' burden. [Preceded by 135.5].
1. BM Addit. 31922, f. 36a.
Flügel, *Anglia* XII. 236-7; Flügel, *Neuengl. Lesebuch,* p. 135; *Early Eng. Lyrics,* pp. 59-61; Padelford, *Early XVI Cent. Lyrics,* p. xxxix (3 st. only); Stevens, *Music & Poetry,* pp. 397-8; Stevens, *Music at Court,* p. 27.

3636 (vv. 20; ends imperfectly).
Brotanek, *ME Dichtungen,* p. 34.

3637 on a chained Psalter belonging to John Harpur, who established the parish of Rushall, Staffordshire.
1. Nottingham Univ. Me LM 1 [*olim* Mellish], flyleaf.
Beauties of England: Staffordshire, 1813, p. 1103; Robbins, *Sec. Lyrics,* pp. 86-7.

3637.5 This rime mad an hermyte
An explanatory note added to the text of the Returned Hermit (314)—eight lines. [Also occurs as penultimate st. of 1869, MS. 5].
1. Camb. Un. Dd. 1. 1, f. 82b.
Small, *Met. Hom.,* pp. iii-iv; Robbins, *JEGP* XXXIX. 231.

3638 Rickert, *Anc. Eng. Xmas Carols,* p. 11; Stevens, *Med. Carols,* p. 13; Robbins, *Early Eng. Xmas Carols,* p. 68.

3638.3 This riall king Robert of cesile lond
A story of Kyng Robert of Cesyle—one stanza rime royal and eighteen quatrains. [Cf. 2780].
1. Trinity Dublin 432, f. 60a (vv. 79; ends incomplete).
Brotanek, *ME Dichtungen,* pp. 36-8.

3638.6   þis rewle ys gode / for lettynge of blod
              A series of couplets used as headings in a prognosticatory calendar, much faded.
              1. Bodl. 8465 a (a piece of vellum).

3639.5   This silver plate and riche araye / Of purple hewe
              Worldly pomp unnecessary—one cross-rimed quatrain.
              1. Durham Univ. Cosin V. iii. 9, f. 61a.
              Furnivall, *EETS* lxi. 192.

3641   five couplets, three quatrains, and two tail-rime stanzas.

3642.5   Thys the parlament of byrdys / Of hygh and low
              'The Parliament of Birds'—280 lines in quatrains.
              1. Lansdowne 210, ff. 74a-78b.

3643   Rickert, *Anc. Eng. Xmas Carols*, pp. 48-9; Greene, *Sel. Eng. Carols*, p. 63.

3644   Furnivall, *EETS* 15 orig. ed. 227; rev. ed. 256.

3645   *Gentleman's Magazine*, May 1842, p. 468.

3645.3   This tretise devysed it is / Of two knaues som tyme of Dis
              Epitaph for Adam Udersall and John Clarke, by John Skelton—vv. 131 in Latin and English 'skeltonics.'
              Workes, Marshe, 1568 (STC 22608); *repr.* [? J. Bowle,] 1736; Chalmers, *English Poets*, II. 320-4; Dyce, *Skelton*, I. 168-73; Dyce and Child, *Skelton and Donne*, I. 187-93; Henderson, *Skelton*, 1931, pp. 454-8; 1948, 1959, pp. 55-9.

3645.5   This vnryghtwys man said in is sawe
              Debate between devils and angels over the body of a repentant robber—thirty-seven couplets in a short prose narrative, probably from Jacques de Vitry.
              1. Royal 18. B. xxiii, f. 69b.

              Thys vyrgyn clere wythowtyn pere   See 3627.

3645.8   This voyce both sharp & also [shryll]
              '*Uenite ad iudicium*'—eight quatrains and 2-line burden.
              Christmas Carolles, Kele, ca. 1550 (STC 5205); *facs.* Reed, *Xmas Carols*, pp. 66, 63-4; *repr. Early Eng. Carols*, p. 245.

*This was the tenour of her talkynge   See 375 (Kele text).

3646.3   This waverand warldis wretchitnes
  'Of the warldis instabilitie,' by William Dunbar—twenty-five quatrains with refrain: 'For to considder is ane pane.'
  1. Camb. Un. Ll. 5. 10, f. 27a; 2. Pepys 2553, p. 178.
  2. Pinkerton, *Anc. Scot. Poems*, I. 115-9; Sibbald, *Chronicle*, I. 333-6; Laing, *Dunbar*, I. 204-8; Paterson, *Dunbar*, pp. 261-5; Small, *STS* IV. 226-9; Schipper, *Dunbar*, pp. 263-6; and *DKAW* XLI (IV). 64-8; Baildon, *Dunbar*, pp. 131-4; Craigie, *STS* n.s. VII. 202-5; MacKenzie, *Dunbar*, pp. 28-31.

3646.6   This wikide man coude non euel he wrowht
  The evil man—five couplets in a Latin exemplum.
  1. Bodl. 29746, f. 42b.

Thys wynde be resun ys called tentacyon   See 3525.

3647.3   Thys woman hath leued her vessell of clay / and in to þe cyte ys wend her way
  A couplet translating the text (John iv. 28) of a Latin sermon.
  1. Royal 8. D. x, f. 204a.
  Warner and Gilson, *Cat.*, I. 248.

3647.5   þis wondir wel vndir þis trone
  Ware the Wheel of Fortune—six lines.
  1. Harley 7322, f. 163a.
  Furnivall, *EETS* 15 rev. ed. 265.

3648.5   This worke deuysed is / For such as do amys
  'Ware the Hauke,' by John Skelton—vv. 329 in 'skeltonics.'
  Certayne Bokes, Kynge and Marche, n. d. (STC 22599); repr. Dyce, *Skelton*, I. 155-67; Dyce and Child, *Skelton & Donne*, I. 173-86; Henderson, *Skelton*, 1931, pp. 151-63; 1948, 1959, pp. 101-11; Hughes, *Selection*, pp. 144-8 (vv. 29-144 only); Day, n. d.; Lant, n.d.; *Workes*, Marshe, 1568 (STC 22608); *repr.* [?. J. Bowle,] 1736; Chalmers, *English Poets*, II. 263-5.

3648.8   This work quha sa sall sie or reid
  'Fle þe mys-woman,' with an exemplum—twelve stanzas rime royal. [Actually st. 20-29 and 38, 35 of *The Remedy of Love* (3084) occurring separately. Utley 306].

	1. Advocates 1. 1. 6, f. 258b. *Chaucer*, Stow, 1561 (STC 5075); Urry, *Chaucer*, 1721, p. 527; *Bannatyne MS.*, Hunt. Club, p. 755; Ritchie, *STS* n.s. XXVI. 24, 23.
3651	[Stanzas 3-9 appear separately as 576, &c. Ringler 40]. *Mars and Venus*, Notary, ca. 1500 (STC 5089) (st. 8-36 only).
3652	Stevens, *Med. Carols*, p. 106.
3653	1. Royal 13. D. i, f. 246b (vv. 78); 3. *olim* Phillipps 3338 [Robinson Sale Cat. 1950, item 28], f. 202b.
3654	Greene, *Sel. Eng. Carols*, p. 136.
3655	3. Harley 2251, f. 39a; 4. Delete this MS.
3656	[Utley 307]. 2. Delete this MS.; 6. Delete this MS. *Chaucer*, Stow, 1561 (STC 5075); *repr.* [Anderson,] *Poets of Great Britain*, I. 580; Clarke, *Riches of Chaucer*, II. 307; 1. Davies, *Med. Eng. Lyrics*, pp. 189-91.
3656.5	þis worlde is of so grete a space *Interrogacio juvenis & Responsio sapientis* — one cross-rimed quatrain. 1. BM Addit. 10392, f. 185a. Doyle, *Medium Aevum* XXX. 98.
3659	Stevens, *Med. Carols*, p. 30.
3660	'*Leaulte vault Richesse.*' 4. Camb. Un. Ll. 5. 10, f. 56b.
3661	[Ringler 75]. 10. Leyden Univ. Vossius 9, f. 94b. *Temple of Bras*, Caxton, ca. 1478 (STC 5091); *Chaucer*, Thynne, 1532 (STC 5068); [Anderson,] *Poets of Great Britain*, I. 578; 5. Robinson, *Chaucer*, 1933, pp. 630-1; 1957, pp. 535-6.
3662	Robbins, *MLR* LIV. 221-2.

3662.5　　Thomas Albone is my name / With hande and pene I write
　　　　　A scribe's excuse for poor writing: 'if my pene had bine beter'—two couplets.
　　　　　1. Morgan Lib. *Royal Book*, Caxton (added in xvi cent. hand).

3663.5　　Thomas knolles lyeth vnder this stone
　　　　　Epitaph, A.D. 1448—nine couplets.
　　　　　Pettigrew, *Chronicles of Tombs*, p. 430.

　　　　　Thomas of wandrith & of wough　　See 3665.

3665　　　1. Taylor, *Polit. Prophecy*, p. 165 (v. 1-30 only).

3665.3　　Thomas Stonne es at ham / god gif þe husband schame
　　　　　Riming phrases in a Latin sermon.
　　　　　1. Cotton Faustina A. v, f. 9b.

　　　　　*Thomas takes the Iuell and Ihesus thankis　　See 3665 (Camb. MS).

3665.6　　Those that lerne ne wyll / The commaundementes & lawes
　　　　　The reward of hell to those who forego the Commandments—one cross-rimed quatrain.
　　　　　Floure of the Commandments, de Worde, ca. 1510 (STC 23876).

3666　　　*Love's Labour Lost*, Variorum Edition, 1904, p. 283.

　　　　　Thou barrant wit ouirset with fantasyis　　See 4002.5.

*3667.5　　*Thow be wys dred thi nowne consyens
　　　　　One stanza rime royal, perhaps a draft of a poem or quotation, with corrections.
　　　　　1. Bodl. 6943, f. 134b (the beginnings of the lines may be imperfect).

3669　　　Rickert, *Anc. Eng. Xmas Carols*, pp. 126-7.

3670   [Ringler 76].
2. Bodl. 2078, ff. 5a-11a; 7. BM Addit. 16165, ff. 241b-243b, 256a-258b; 9. BM Addit. 17492, f. 91a (vv. 308-316 only).
Compleynt of Anelida, Caxton, ca. 1477 (STC 509); 3. Robinson, *Chaucer*, 1933, pp. 355-60; 1957, pp. 303-8.

3672   Person, *Camb. ME Lyrics*, pp. 8-9.

3673   6. Chetham Lib. 6709, ff. 284b-285b (7 st.).

3674   in quatrains and burden.
1. Bodl. 3340, f. 25b (7 st.); 2. Egerton 3307, f. 53a (8 st.).
1. Rickert, *Anc. Eng. Xmas Carols*, p. 17; 2. Stevens, *Med. Carols*, p. 36; Greene, *Sel. Eng. Carols*, p. 110.

3675   Thow holy moder off God almyght
'*Speciosa facta es suavis:*' a simple prayer to the B.V.—three quatrains.
1. Canterbury Cath. Add. 68 [*olim* Ingilby], f. 98a.
Woodruff, *XV Cent. Guide Book*, p. 79.

3676   1. BM Addit. 46919 [*olim* Phillipps 8336], f. 208b.

Thow lord whos lyst descendeþ from fer   See 2574 (MS. 30).

3677   [Followed by three English metrical prayers, in couplets: 1038.5, 1048.8, 1078.5].
1. Egerton 3143 [*olim* Newcastle, *olim* Clumber], f. 39b.
Haslewood, *Roxburghe Club* 1824, pp. 1-48; Bazire, *EETS* 228. 42-72.

3677.5   Thow man envired with temptacion
'*Paratus sum semper mori pro te*'—six lines.
1. BM Addit. 5665, f. 70b.
Fehr, *Archiv* CVI. 280; Stevens, *Music & Poetry*, p. 341.

3680   Furnivall, *EETS* 15 orig. ed. 238; rev. ed. 266.

3680.5   Thou most swettest of any thynge / To loue you
'A Songe of Loue to oure Lord Iesu Criste'—69 monoriming quatrains. [Cf. 3238].
1. *olim* J. W. Dod [present location not established].
Gentleman's Magazine, June 1848, pp. 612-4.

3682   fourteen 8-line stanzas.
        1. Sloane 252, f. 169a (vv. 43); 2. Rome: English Coll. 1306, f. 83b.
          2. Robbins, *Neophilologus* XXXIX. 138-40; Robbins, *Hist. Poems*, pp. 86-9.

3685   9. Ushaw: St. Cuthbert's Coll. 28; 10. Bodl. Lat. lit. e. 17, ff. 53b-54a.

3686   1. Bodl. 4127, f. 212a.

3687   12. Rylands Lib. Latin 201, f. 130a; 18. Foyle [*olim* Harmsworth; Sotheby Sale, Oct. 16, 1945, Lot 2131]; 19. Univ. of Illinois 71 [*olim* Harmsworth; Sotheby Sale, Oct. 16, 1945, Lot 2132].
          12. Fawtier, *BJRL* V. 389.

3689.5 Thou shalt worshyp one god onely
          The Ten Commandments—ten couplets ending in-ly. [Cf. 2693.5].
          Floure of the Commandments, de Worde, ca. 1510 (STC 23876); *Matyns of Our Lady*, de Worde, 1513 (STC 15914).

3691   [St. 4 ≠ st. 4 of 611].
          Davies, *Med. Eng. Lyrics*, p. 111.

3693   1. Yale Univ. 163 [*olim* Wagstaff 9, *olim* Petworth 8], ff. 125a-134a.

3694.3 Thow þat has cast iij sixes her / Shalt haue þy desyr
          Divination by means of dice—in quatrains. [Cf. More, *Book of Fortune*, translation of *Le livre de passetemps de la Fortune des Dez*]. [Cf. Utley 201].
          1. Sloane 513, f. 98b (vv. 74 only); 2. Aberdeen Univ. 123, ff. 149b-152b (vv. 188; ends incomplete); 3. Ipswich County Hall Deposit: Hillwood [*olim* Brome], f. 2a (vv. 95); 4. Boston Pub. Lib. 100, ff. 125b-128; 5. H. P. Kraus Sale Cat. 22, no. 21.
          3. Smith, *Commonplace Book XV Cent.*, pp. 15-18.

3694.6 Thow þat in hewin for our saluatioun
          'Ane orisoun quhen the governour past into France,' by

William Dunbar—five 8-line stanzas with refrain: 'For but thy helpe this kynrick is forlorne.'
1. Camb. Un. Ll. 5. 10, f. 28b; 2. Pepys 2553, p. 186.
2. Pinkerton, *Anc. Scot Poems*, I. 128-9; Sibbald, *Chronicle*, II. 24; Laing, *Dunbar*, I. 250-1; Paterson, *Dunbar*, pp. 299-301; Small, *STS* IV. 235-6; Schipper, *Dunbar*, pp. 381-3; and *DKAW* XL (IV). 79-81; Baildon, *Dunbar*, pp. 204-5; Craigie, *STS* n.s. VII. 210-11; MacKenzie, *Dunbar*, pp. 139-40.

3695　　1. Bennett, *STS* 3 s. XXIII. 275-6; Davies, *Med. Eng. Lyrics*, pp. 269-70.

3695.5　　Thow that lokyst on myn lykenes / & haste no pytey
Verses accompanying an 'Image of Pity'—vv. 12. [Cf. 3777.3].
1. Bodl. Lat. lit. e. 17, f. 73a.

3697　　Utley, *Harvard Theological Rev.* XXXVIII. 144; Robbins, *Hist. Poems*, p. 166; Kaiser, *Med. Eng.*, p. 323; Person, *Camb. ME Lyrics*, pp. 41-2.

3698　　two quatrains with concluding couplet. [Utley 309].
Robbins, *Hist. Poems*, p. 139.

3700　　1. BM Addit. 46919 [*olim* Phillipps 8366], f. 206b.
Kaiser, *Anthologie*, p. 242; Kaiser, *Med. Eng.*, pp. 287 (vv. 42 only); Davies, *Med. Eng. Lyrics*, pp. 95-7.

*3700.5　　*þou wost wol lytil ho is þi foo
A *chanson d'aventure* song of moral advice spoken by a bird—in quatrains.
1. Sloane 2593, f. 2a (last 5 st. only).
Wright, *Carols*, Warton Club IV. 1-2; Fehr, *Archiv* CIX. 41; *Early Eng. Carols*, p. 322.

3701　　Kaiser, *Med. Eng.*, p. 294.

Though (conjunction). And see under þeh.

3701.5　　Thocht all þe wod vnder the hevin þat growis
The wickedness of women: a companion piece to 1409.3—one 8-line stanza. (Utley 310].
1. Advocates 1. 1. 6, f. 258b.
Bannatyne MS., Hunt. Club I. c v; Ritchie, *STS* n.s. XXVI. 23.

Thow achylles in batayl me slow   See 3666.

3703   3. Edinburgh Univ. 205, f. ii verso (Prologue and First Fable); 4a (xix cent. transcript by Chalmers). Edinburgh Univ. La. III. 450/1, ff. 236-240.
Early prints: Charteris, 1570; with 1-4. Smith, STS LV. 3-315; Bassandyne, 1571; repr. Wood, Henryson, pp. 3-102; Sibbald, Chronicle, I. 90-114; Elliott, pp. 1-89; 3. Ritchie, STS n.s. XXVI. 117-28, 158-82, 206-45.

3703.3   Thowghe I be bonde yette am I ffree
An enigma: the bond of love—six quatrains.
1. Harley 2252, f. 133*a.
Flügel, Neuengl. Lesebuch, p. 139.

3703.5   Thofe I doo syng my hert dothe wepe
A lament: 'Sorow hath piercyd my hart so depe'—two stanzas rime royal.
1. Royal App. 58, ff. 18b-19b.
Flügel, Anglia XII. 266.

*Thoffe y owe syche too   See 3518.5.

3703.8   Tho it be late ere thou merci craue
Verses by God, a priest, and Death, attached to a drawing of a deathbed scene—three couplets.
1. BM Addit. 37049, f. 38b.

3704.3   þo iosep hadde is wif iwedded as hit fel in the lawe
The Annunciation and Nativity (following 574 and preceding 2717 in the Egerton MS.).
1. Egerton 1993, f. 30b.
Horstmann, AE Leg. 1875, pp. 82-100.

3704.6   Though man for his offence & gret demerit
Speech of Prelacy at the pageant celebrating the marriage of Prince Arthur to Princess Catharine—four stanzas rime royal.
1. Cotton Vitellius A. xvi, ff. 194a-b.

3706.2   Thowgh peper be blake / hit hath a good smakke
A proverbial couplet.
1. Balliol 354, f. 191b and f. 200a; 2. BM Addit. 37075, f. 70b; 3. Rylands Lib. Latin 394, f. 18b.

        1. Flügel, *Anglia* XXVI. 202; Dyboski, *EETS* ci. 128, 130; 3. Pantin, *BJRL* XIV. 165.

3706.3   Though phily3ophers of god knolege did opteyn
'The speech of Raphaell' at the pageant celebrating the marriage of Prince Arthur to Princess Catharine—five stanzas rime royal.
1. Cotton Vitellius A. xvi, f. 188a.

3706.4   Though poetts fayn that fortune by her chaunce
'*Auxilium meum a Domino*'—two quatrains and burden on this theme.
XX Songes, de Worde, 1530 (STC 22924); *repr.* Flügel, *Anglia* XII. 589-90; Flügel, *Neuengl. Lesebuch*, p. 114; Imelmann, *Shakespeare-Jahrbuch* XXXIX. 125; *Early Eng. Lyrics*, p. 159.

3706.5   Though sum saith that yough rulyth me
On youth and age, ascribed to Henry VIII—four 5-line stanzas including refrain.
1. BM Addit. 31922, f. 71b.
Chappell, *Archaeologia* XLI. 376; Flügel, *Anglia* XII. 246-7; Flügel, *Neuengl. Lesebuch*, p. 137; Trefusis, *Songs Henry VIII*, Roxburghe Club CLXI. 28-31; *Early Eng. Carols*, p. 297; Stevens, *Music & Poetry*, pp. 411-2; Stevens, *Music at Court*, pp. xviii, 52.

3706.6   Thowgh something in thys boke
An owner's verses on a copy of *Stimulus Amoris* in English—two stanzas.
1. Bodl. 2020, f. 64b (written over 4138).

3706.7   Thow that men do call it dotage
Constancy in love, attributed to Henry VIII—ten couplets.
1. BM Addit. 31922, f. 55b.
Chappell, *Archaeologia* XLI. 377; Flügel, *Anglia* XII. 243; Flügel, *Neuengl. Lesebuch*, p. 136; Trefusis, *Songs Henry VIII*, Roxburghe Club CLXI. 21-2; Stevens, *Music & Poetry*, pp. 406-7; Stevens, *Music at Court*, p. 41.

3706.8   Though that she can not redresse
To his mistress—six quatrains. [For related poem cf. 3706.9].
1. Royal App. 58, f. 3b.
Briggs, *Songs & Madrigals*, PMMS 1891, pp. xviii, 9; Flügel, *Anglia* XII. 259.

3706.9   Tho that ye cannot Redresse / Nor helpe me of my smart
         A love song 'to pete a mornyng hertt'—possibly seven quatrains with this refrain. [St. 1 = st. 1 of 3706.8, but later st. differ; last two st. may be part of another poem, ending imperfectly].
         1. Public Record Office, Exchequer Misc. E. 163 / 22 / 2, f. 57 (a single sheet, defective).
         Saltmarsh, *Antiquaries Journal* XV. 18.

3707.3   Though ye my love were nere a ladye fayre
         Farewell to a false love—three quatrains with a 4-line burden: 'Lost ys my love farewell adewe &c.'
         1. Bodl. 6659, f. 99a.
         Wagner, *MLN* L. 453.

3707.5   Though ye suppose all jeperdys ar paste
         On fickle fortune, by John Skelton—one stanza rime royal.
         Dyuers Balettys, Pynson, n.d. (STC 22604); *repr.* Dyce, *Skelton*, I. 26-7; Dyce and Child, *Skelton & Donne*, I. 33; Henderson, *Skelton*, 1931, 1948, 1959, p. 33.

3707.7   Thoghts ar so sotell and so slee
         Moralizing verses following 3322.1—one 8-line stanza abababab.
         1. BM Addit. 37049, f. 67a.

3707.8   Thoythis fre þat lykis me
         A love lyric—twelve cross-rimed quatrains.
         1. Trinity Dublin 157, ff. 87b, 88a.
         Robbins, *MLN* LXIX. 155-7.

*3708.5 *Thre flourys in a nyȝt can spryng / From euery floure &c.
         Fragment of an allegory, probably religious—five lines only.
         1. *olim* Perrins 33.
         Warner, *Cat. Rom.*, I. 100.

         Thre freris and thre fox maken thre shrewys   See 3815.5.

3709   [Preceded by 1292].
         1a (xix cent. transcript). Egerton 2257, f. 98a.
         Hughes, *Women Healers*, p. 32.

Thre heddelysse men playd at ball   See 1354.

3711.5   þre þinges it ben þat I holde þris
On a thief—three lines.
1. Pembroke Camb. 258, f. 135b.

3713.5   Through a forest as I can ryde / to take my sporte
The maid and the magpie, a love adventure, a dialogue between a betrayed maiden and her lover—seventeen cross-rimed quatrains.
1. Bodl. 12653, f. 56b.
Halliwell, *Nugae Poeticae*, 1844, pp. 42-4; Padelford and Benham, *Anglia* XXXI. 374-6; Child, *Pop. Ballads*, no. 111, II. 478-9; Sargent and Kittredge, *Pop. Ballads*, pp. 238-9.

Thorow a fforest þat was so longe   See 3820.

3716   On sudden death, a tag in the *Fasciculus Morum* (Foster No. 30).

3718   2. Harley 2251, f. 253b.

*3719.5 *Throw hys hond wyth hammur knak þai mad a gresely wound
Latter portion of a poem on the Passion—vv. 69 in 6-line stanzas with 'O and I' refrain.
1. Bodl. 6921, Part II, f. 134a.
Hammerle, *Archiv* CLXVI. 196-7.

Thurwe my ryȝt hande a nayle was driuen   See 1565.

3719.8   Throughout a garden greene & gay
The House of Stanley: The Rose of England, in praise of Sir William Stanley (executed A.D. 1495)—thirty-two quatrains.
1. BM Addit. 27879, p. 423.
Hales and Furnivall, *Percy Folio MS.*, III. 189-94; Sidgwick, *Ballads Illustrating Eng. Hist.*, p. 53.

3720   2. Robbins, *Hist. Poems*, pp. 176-80.

3721 Alchemical verses ascribed to George Ripley—in couplets. [Sometimes incorporated in 2656; all texts show considerable variation. Singer 863].
[Revise listing of MSS. as follows:]
1. Bodl. 6954, f. 55a (vv. 34); 2. Bodl. 7611, f. 150b; 3. Bodl. 7627, f. 77a (vv. 7); 4. Bodl. 7630, VIII, I, ff. 45a-46b; 5. Bodl. 7643, ff. 217b-218a; 6. Bodl. 11645, f. 43b (var., vv. 96); 7. Trinity Camb. 1120, f. 72a; 8. Sloane 288, ff. 73a-74; 9. Sloane 1098, ff. 33a-34a; 10. Sloane 1842, ff. 20b-22; 11. Sloane 3688, f. 66b; 12 Wellcome Hist. Med. Lib. 519, f. 65b.

Ashmole, *Theatrum Chemicum*, pp. 393-6; 3. Singer, II. 583.

3721.3 Thus endeth the lyfe of Robert the deuyll
Colophon at end of de Worde's printing of *Robert the Devil*—one cross-rimed quatrain.
de Worde, ca. 1502 (STC 21070); repr. London 1827, p. 56; de Worde, ca. 1517 (STC 21071).

*3721.5 *...thus hath mayd my payne
Fragment of a love song.
1. New York Pub. Lib. Drexel Fragment 4181.
Stevens, *Music & Poetry*, p. 427.

3721.8 Thus he sought in euery side
On Conscience—twelve lines.
1. Wellcome Hist. Med. Lib. 673, f. 8b.

3722 Robbins, *Sec. Lyrics*, p. 149.

3723 His chosen mistress (associated with Charles d'Orleans)—vv. 18.

Thus irobid in russet I romyd abowtyn
Vita de dowele dobet et dobest—vv. 757: An extract from *Piers Plowman*, B Text, Passus VIII; A Text, Passus IX-XI, in Harmsworth MS. See 1459.

3724.5 Thus musyng in my mynd gretly mervelyng
A variable mistress—one 8-line stanza.
1. BM Addit. 5465, f. 24b; 2. Fitzwilliam Mus., unclassified fragment; 3. New York Pub. Lib., Drexel Fragment 4183.
1. Stafford Smith, *Eng. Songs*, no. 16; Briggs, *Madrigals*,

PMMS 1893, no. 4; Fehr, *Archiv* CVI. 56; Stevens, *Music & Poetry*, p. 359.

3726.5 Thus worldly worschypp and honor wyth Fauour and fortun passyth day by day
Epitaph on Sir Harry Wever and his wife Joan—two long and three short lines.
Weever, *Anc. Funerall Monuments*, 1631, p. 393 (STC 25223).

3727.5 þi broþer in heuen is maister & kyng
The nearness of Christ, 'þi felaw & þi grom'—two couplets in a Latin sermon by Friar Nicolas Philip.
1. Bodl. 29746, f. 173a.

3729.5 Thy gilte is grett and þat is rewthe
'Rekewerynge is none and þat is trowthe:' the councillor's reply to a friend in need—one couplet.
1. Royal 18. B. xxiii, f. 64b.
Ross, *EETS* 209. 44.

3730 [Followed immediately by 229].
3. Longleat 29, ff. 53a-b.
2. Comper, *Life & Lyrics of Rolle*, pp. 261-4.

3734 1. Furnivall, *EETS* 15 orig. ed. 228-9; rev. ed. 260-1.

3734.5 Thy wyffe my frend is allwayes nowght
Moralizing lines on women—one quatrain.
1. Bodl. 4130, f. 169b.

3735 Sylvester, *Garland of Xmas Carols*, p. 150; Rickert, *Anc. Eng. Xmas Carols*, p. 256; Robbins, *Sec. Lyrics*, pp. 47-8.

3736 four monoriming quatrains in long lines with 'Nowell' burden.
3. Ipswich County Hall Deposit: Hillwood [*olim* Brome], f. 79b.
1. Chappell, *OE Pop. Music*, I. 30; Stevens, *Med. Carols*, p. 110; Robbins, *Early Eng. Xmas Carols*, p. 62; Greene, *Sel. Eng. Carols*, p. 113; 2. Rickert, *Anc. Eng. Xmas Carols*, pp. 35-6; 3. Smith, *Commonplace Book XV Cent.*, p. 122.

3737   Stevens, *Med. Carols,* p. 91; Robbins, *Early Eng. Xmas Carols,* p. 39.

3742   a political carol in support of Henry VI.
Robbins, *Hist. Poems,* pp. 198-9.

3742.5   Till horsis fote thou never traist
Don't trust women—one couplet translating Latin aphorism in Fordun's *Scotichronicon* (Book XIV, Cap. xxxii).
Hearne, *Joannis de Fordun Scotichronicon,* 1759, II. 377.

Tyme ys a thyng that no man may resyste   See 2451.5.

3743   1. Longleat 29, f. 145b (with a prose comment following which concludes with riming lines, ff. 146a-b).

3743.3   To a man of ple and motyng / a boke of scripture and wrytyng
Three lines in a sermon.
1. Bodl. 29746, f. 123b.
Little, *Franciscan Papers* 1943, p. 248.

3743.6   To a fowle syngyng
Man's life is transitory—four mnemonic riming lines. [Cf. 105.5].
1. Hereford Cath. O. iii. 5, f. 49b.

3744   Examples against women, by Lydgate—fifteen stanzas rime royal. [An extract from 1168, st. 1-4 = I. 519-60, 631-7; st. 10-15 = I. 6336, 6614-19, 6641-8. Utley 317].

3745   [Follows the Short Charter 4184, and precedes 1740].
1. Camb. Un. Add. 6686 [*olim* Ashburnham App. 140], p. 270.

3746   Lydgate's 'Reson and Sensuallyte,' freely translated from *Les Echecs amoureux* (vv. 1-4873).

3747   [Utley 326. Ringler 78].
Temple of Bras, Caxton, ca. 1478 (STC 5091); *Chaucer,* Stow, 1561 (STC 5075); *repr.* Chalmers, *English Poets,* I. 554-5; 1. Robinson, *Chaucer,* 1933, p. 634; 1957, pp. 538-9.

3748 [Cf. 2388.5].
5. Delete this MS.
2. John Herford, St. Albans, 1534.

3750 four stanzas &c. [The burden occurs as a round in Ravenscroft's *Pammelia*, 1609].
Stevens, *Music* & *Poetry*, pp. 373-4.

3751.3 To complayne me alas why shulde I so
A lover's plea for his reward—one stanza rime royal. [Cf. 870].
1. BM Addit. 5465, f. 15b.
Stafford Smith, *Eng. Songs*, no. 14; Fehr, *Archiv* CVI. 55; Stevens, *Music* & *Poetry*, p. 357.

To dy to day what haue I / Offended   See 2511.

3751.5 To dwell in court my freind gife þat thow list
'Rewl of anis self,' by William Dunbar—six 8-line stanzas with refrain. [Cf. Maitland's 'Counsell to his son beand in the court'].
1. Advocates 1. 1. 6, f. 68a.
[Hailes,] *Anc. Scot. Poems*, pp. 121-3; Laing, *Dunbar*, I. 179-80; *Bannatyne MS.*, Hunt. Club, II. 184-6; Small, *Dunbar*, STS IV. 98-9; Browne, *Early Scot. Poets*, 1896, pp. 127-9; Schipper, *Dunbar*, pp. 326-8; and *DKAW* XLII (IV). 23-6; Baildon, *Dunbar*, pp. 166-8; Ritchie, *STS* n.s. XXII. 167-9; MacKenzie, *Dunbar*, pp. 75-6.

3751.8 To elect the master of the mercerie hither am I sent
An inscription on a cup belonging to the Mercer's Company, London—one couplet.

*To euery man that is vnkynde   See 1841.

3753 three macaronic lines.

3754 [Prose versions: Delete: Harley 1735, Sloane 3215. Add: Bühler 21].
[Revise listing of MSS. as follows:]
1. Bodl. 1696, ff. 83a-89b (vv. 308, preceded by a prose introduction); 2. Bodl. 7625, VI, pp. 1-5 (vv. 290); 3. Bodl. 7683, pp. 19-28 (vv. 152); 4. Trinity Camb. 759, ff. 96b-127b (scattered couplets written on margins of medicinal properties of

such herbs as Columbine, Mint, etc.); 5. Harley 1735, ff. 51a-52b (preceded by a prose introduction, var.); 6. Sloane 3215, ff. 17b-24b; 7. Wellcome Hist. Med. Lib. 406 [*olim* Loscombe, *olim* Ashburnham App. 122], ff. 14a-20b (vv. 272); 7a (xix cent. transcript). BM Addit. 20091, ff. 80a-b (vv. 68 only).

    7. *Rel. Ant.*, I. 194-7 (part only: vv. 121); 7a. Irwin, *Anglia* LVII. 399-400 (vv. 250-272).

3755   [Revise listing of MSS. as follows:]
1. Bodl. 668, f. 1a; 2. Bodl. 1619, f. 38a; 3. Bodl. 11272, f. 13a; 4. Bodl. 32690, ff. 9, 10, 11, 12; 5. Rylands Lib. Eng. 51, f. 113a (defective text); 6. St. George's Chapel, Windsor, E. I. I, f. 32b; 7. Univ. of Pennsylvania, Eng. 1 [*olim* Ireland Blackburne], ff. 1a-13b.

    3. Adler and Kaluza, *Eng. Stn.* X. 232.

3756   Robbins, *Hist. Poems*, pp. 222-6.

3757   2. Morgan Lib. M. 775, f. 121b.

To encrease our ioy and blysse
Burden to 2039.5.

3758.5   To leve alone comfort ys none
The devoted lover—five 6-line tail-rime stanzas.
1. Royal App. 58, f. 10a.
    Stafford Smith, *Musica Antiqua*, I. 30; Flügel, *Anglia* XII. 263-4; Briggs, *Songs & Madrigals*, PMMS 1891, pp. xvii, 4-5.

3759   [Cf. Tilley L 228].
    1, 2. Hammond, *Eng. Verse Chaucer-Surrey*, pp. 237, 476; 1. Benham, *Eng. Lit. Widsith-Chaucer*, p. 351; Robbins, *Hist. Poems*, pp. 130-4.

3760   thirty-two 8-line stanzas.
    Segar, *Med. Anthology*, pp. 14-15 (6 st. only).

3760.5   To love þe swete Ihesu / is most medeful
Four riming lines in Rolle's *Meditations on the Passion*, B Text. [Cf. 981].
1. Bodl. 3657, f. 3b; 2. Camb. Un. Add. 3042; 3. Uppsala Univ. C. 494.

1. Allen, *Eng. Writings of Rolle*, p. 30; 2. Horstmann, *York. Wr.*, I. 94; 3. Lindkvist, *Skrifterutgifna Af K. Humanistika Veternskaps*, Uppsala 1917, XIX.

3761   (st. 3, 7, 11, 15 = st. 3, 4, 5, 10 of 1838).
        1. Trinity Camb. 599, f. 154b (23 st.).
        Chaucer, Stow, 1561 (STC 5075); *Chaucer*, Speght, 1598 (STC 5077); Urry, *Chaucer*, 1721, p. 552; Bell, *Poets of Great Britain*, XIII. 110; [Anderson,] *Poets of Great Britain*, I. 581; Chalmers, *English Poets*, I. 558.

3761.5   To Moyses lawe apeel I make / þe lawe of kynde I wille forsake
        A couplet in a sermon.
        1. Bodl. 29734, f. 124a.
        Little, *Franciscan Papers*, 1943, p. 249.

3765   Lovewell, *Life of St. Cecilia*, Boston, 1898, pp. 92-102.

3765.5   To saie you are not fayre I shall belye you
        Parody of a courtly panegyric, with ironic reversal, attributed to Lydgate—one quatrain. [Utley 321].
        1. BM Addit. 10336, f. 4a.
        Halliwell, *Percy Soc.* II. 271.

3766   [A part of 483].
        Brown, *EETS* 169. 81-3.

3767   [A part of 483].
        Brown, *EETS* 169. 83-4.

3767.5   To seek the way all partes to pleas
        The impossibility of pleasing sinners—one quatrain.
        1. Royal 12. E. xvi, f. 42a.

3768.2   To sorow in the mornyng
        On living soberly—six doggerel couplets by George Cely, ca. A.D. 1475.
        1. Public Record Office, C. 47 / 37 / 12, f. 32b.
        Hanham, *RES* n.s. VIII. 274.

3768.3   To speik of giftis of almous deidis
        'Of discretioun in geving,' by William Dunbar—twelve

5-line stanzas with refrain: 'In geving sowld discretioun be.' [Cf. 121.5, 2621.5].
   1. Camb. Un. Ll. 5. 10, f. 21b; 2. Pepys 2553, p. 260 (vv. 30-35 wanting); 3. Advocates 1. 1. 6, p. 46 (vv. 1-33 only) and f. 61b.
     2. Craigie, STS n.s. VII. 290-2; 3b. Ramsay, *Evergreen*, II. 84-7; *Ramsay and Earlier Scot. Poets*, p. 275; [Hailes,] *Anc. Scot. Poems*, pp. 59-62; Sibbald, *Chronicle*, II. 7-8 (extracts); *Select Poems of Dunbar*, Perth 1788, pp. 54-7; Laing, *Dunbar*, I. 167-9; Paterson, *Dunbar*, pp. 240-2; Small, STS IV. 87-9; Schipper, *Dunbar*, pp. 250-2; and DKAW XLI (IV) 52-4; Baildon, *Dunbar*, pp. 123-4; *Bannatyne MS.*, Hunt. Club, II. 167-9; MacKenzie, *Dunbar*, pp. 33-4; 3a, 3b. Ritchie, STS 3 s. V. 77-9; STS n.s. XXII. 152-4.

3768.6   To speik of science craft or sapience
        'Learning vain without guid lyfe' or 'Dunbar at Oxenfurde,' by William Dunbar—three 8-line stanzas with refrain: 'A paralous lyfe is vain prosperitie.'
        1. Camb. Un. Ll. 5. 10, f. 10b; 2. Pepys 2553, pp. 9 and 317.
          2. Pinkerton, *Anc. Scot. Poems*, I. 106; Laing, *Dunbar*, I. 199; Paterson, *Dunbar*, p. 159; Small, STS IV. 224; Ellis, *Specimens*, I. 378; MacKenzie, *Dunbar*, pp. 104; Kinsley, *Dunbar*, pp. 69-70; 2a, 2b. Craigie, STS n.s. VII. 9, 379-80; 2b. Schipper, *Dunbar*, pp. 322-3; and DKAW XLII (IV). 19-21; Baildon, *Dunbar*, p. 165.

      *To Tarse y fledde þat deþ to fle   See 3098.6.

3769.5   To þe blak draw þy knyf / With þe brown led þy lyf
        A proverbial couplet. [Tilley M 395].
        1. Harley 3362, f. 17a.
        Oxford Dict. English Proverbs, 1948, p. 536.

3769.8   To þe blisful Trinite be don all reuerens
        Introductory couplet, in one MS., to the *Prikil of Consciens* (3428).
        1. Egerton 3245 [*olim* Gurney], f. 1b.
          Robbins, *PMLA* LIV. 371.

3770.5   To ȝe fend I owe fewte / Truage homage and gret lewte
A couplet in a Latin treatise.
1. Harley 2316, f. 25b.
Rel. Ant., II. 120.

3771   2. Royal 12. B. xxv, f. 253b (parts illegible); 3. Sloane 3160, f. 137b.
1. Robbins, Sec. Lyrics, p. 59.

3772   [Singer 814].
[Revise listing of MSS. as follows:]
1. Bodl. 3652, ff. 2a-40a; 2. Bodl. 6938, pp. 1-123; 3. Bodl. 7010, ff. 277a-289; 4. Bodl. 7624, p. 79 (last 12 lines only); 5. Bodl. 7630, Part II, ff. 2a-96a; 6. Bodl. 7635, ff. 1a-44b; 7. Bodl. 7643, ff. 245a-298b; 8. Bodl. 8343, ff. 2b, 9b, 10, 11 (extracts only); 9. Trinity Camb. 910, ff. 3a-75b; 10. Trinity Camb. 1119, ff. 1a-49b; 11. Trinity Camb. 1269, f. 1a; 12. Harley 853, f. 26b; 13. Royal 18. B. xxiv, ff. 80a-138b; 14. Sloane 1198, ff. 1a-39b; 15. Sloane 1873, ff. 4a-16; 16. Sloane 2174, ff. 89a-116b; 17. Sloane 2532, ff. 1a-49; 18. Sloane 3580 B, ff. 61a-115a; 19. BM Addit. 10302, ff. 1b-67 (chapters 1-5 only); 20. Clifton Coll. Lib.; 21. Lincoln's Inn, Hale LXXIV, f. 1a; 22. Trinity Dublin 684, ff. 2a-5b; 23. Wellcome Hist. Med. Lib. 580, p. 1; 24. Longleat; 25. olim Petworth 103, f. 6b (?); 26. Massachusetts Hist. Soc., Winthrop 20 c, ff. 29a-65b and extracts on f. 90b.

3772.5   To the honour of our blessed lady
'A replycacioun agaynst certaine yong scolars &c.' by John Skelton—vv. 408, including Envoy, chiefly in 'skeltonics.'
Pynson, n.d.; Dyce, Skelton, I. 210-24; Dyce and Child, Skelton & Donne, I. 230-50; Henderson, Skelton, 1931, pp. 376-94; 1948, 1959, pp. 413-29.

3773   [Delete entire entry].

To the makyng of this preciouse midecyn   See 3257.

3774   [For variant texts see 2410 and 2573].

*...to þe nale tryll   See 1163.5.

3775.5   To þe Ihesu my trought I pligth / And to þe Mary his moder brigt
   Inscription on a brooch.
   Beauties of England: Westmorland, p. 107.

3776   [Cf. 2442].
   3, 5. Stevens, *Med. Carols,* pp. 10, 95, 105; 1. Greene, *Sel. Eng. Carols,* p. 79; 2. Segar, *Med. Anthology,* p. 103; Rickert, *Anc. Eng. Xmas Carols,* p. 126; 3. Davies, *Med. Eng. Lyrics,* p. 157.

3776.5   To the O marcifull saluiour myn Iesus
   'The tabill of confessioun,' by William Dunbar—in 8-line stanzas with refrain: 'I cry the mercy and lasar to repent.'
   1. Pepys 2553, p. 199 (19 st.); 2. Arundel 285, f. 1a (21 st.); 3. Advocates 1. 1. 6, p. 9 and f. 17b (20 st.).
   1. Craigie, *STS* n.s. VII. 224-9; 2. Bennett, *STS* 3 s. XXIII. 1-6; 3a, 3b. Ritchie, *STS* 3 s. V. 13; *STS* n.s. XXII. 42; 3a. Laing, *Dunbar,* I. 228-34; Paterson, *Dunbar,* pp. 75-81; *Bannatyne MS.,* Hunt. Club, II. 43-8; Small, *STS* IV. 65-71; Schipper, *Dunbar,* pp. 358-67; and *DKAW* XLII (IV). 55-64; Baildon, *Dunbar,* pp. 187-92; MacKenzie, *Dunbar,* pp. 163-7.

3777.3   To þam þat before þis ymage of pyte
   An indulgence of 32,765 years of pardon for reciting five *Pater nosters* and *Aves*—four irregular lines on a woodcut. [Cf. 3695.5].
   1. Bodl. Arch. G. e. 35.
   Dodgson, *English Woodcuts,* no. 3; Dodgson, *English Woodcuts in Ashmolean Mus.,* p. 33; Schreiber, *Handbuch* 866b, D.3, 9, 10.

*3777.5   *To þame þat luffis þe in cleynnes
   The Fifteen Ooes—vv. 326 in couplets. [Followed immediately by 3243].
   1. Arundel 285, f. 85a.
   Bennett, *STS* 3 s. XXIII. 170-80.

3778.5   To þis kyngdom brynge he ȝou & me / þat for vs deyid on rode tre
   An ascription—one couplet.
   1. Salisbury Cath. 103, f. 54b.
   Brandeis, *EETS* 115. 167.

3780   1. Lansdowne 762, f. 92a.

*3780.5   *To þi neȝbour fore loue of me / To make debate ny dyscorde
          Latter portion of a poem on the Nine Virtues by John
          Audelay—vv. 102 in 13-line stanzas.
          1. Bodl. 21876, f. 8a.
          Halliwell, *Percy Soc.* XIV. 51-4; Whiting, *EETS* 184. 46-9.

3782   [Utley 322].
          Robbins, *Sec. Lyrics*, p. 31; Kaiser, *Anthologie*, p. 297;
          Kaiser, *Med. Eng.*, p. 470; Davies, *Med. Eng. Lyrics*,
          pp. 283-4.

3782.5   To veri god & to alle trewe in Crist
          Jack Upland—in very rough alliterative verse. [Cf. *Reply by Friar Daw Topias* (4098.3), suggested by Skeat to be in prose. Also cf. *Jack Upland's Rejoinder* (1653.5)].
          1. Camb. Un. Ff. 6. 2, ff. 71a-80a; 2. Harley 6641, ff. 1a-25b.
          Jacke vp Lande, Gough, ca. 1536 (STC 5098); repr. Skeat, *Oxf. Ch.*, VII. 191; *Chaucer*, Speght, 1602 (STC 5080); 1687; Urry, *Chaucer*, 1721, p. 590; Foxe, *Acts and Monuments*, 1843, II. 357; Sibbald, *Chronicle*, II. 31-3 (extracts); Wright, *Polit. Poems*, II. 16.

*3783.5   *to weri with my heued
          The Conflict of Wit and Will—seven fragments.
          1. Camb. Un. York Missal (Res. b. 162), in binding.
          Dickins, *Leeds School Eng. Lang., Texts & Monographs*, IV. 15-19.

3784.6   To you beholders cowde I say more þan þis
          'The vij scoles:' instructions to children—introductory couplet and eight quatrains. [St. 1, 5 = 3196).
          1. Trinity Dublin 432, f. 61b.
          Brotanek, *ME Dichtungen*, pp. 48-9.

3785   Robbins, *Sec. Lyrics*, pp. 198-200.

3785.5   To yow mastres whyche haue be longe / a feynd loue·
          A scornful letter to a faithless mistress—seven 8-line stanzas with refrain: 'Wher many dogges be att a bone.' [Utley 324].

        1. Bodl. 12653, f. 62a.
        Padelford and Benham, *Anglia* XXXI. 382-4.

3785.8   To you my aungellys this precept ye assure
        Pageant verses at the Conduit at Paul's Gate for the return of Henry VI to London, A.D. 1432—two stanzas rime royal. [Adapted from 3799].
        Fabyan, *New Chronicles*, Pynson, 1516 (STC 10659); *repr.* Ellis, 1811, pp. 607-8; Gattinger, *Wiener Beiträge* IV. 29.

        To you my Ioy and my worldly plesaunce   See 3878.

3787   [Utley 325. Ringler 77].
        5. Harley 2251, f. 271a (lacks Envoy); 10. Camb. Un. Gg. 4. 27, I b, f. 35a; 11. BM Cat. 643, m. 4 (transcript by William Thomas in 1721 of burned Cotton Otho A. 18, pasted into copy of Urry's *Chaucer*, II. 548); 12. Coventry Corp. Record Office, f. 76b.
        Anelida and Arcyte, Caxton, ca. 1477 (STC 5090); Chaucer, Stow, 1561 (STC 5075); *repr.* [Anderson,] *Poets of Great Britain*, I. 579; 1. Davies, *Med. Eng. Lyrics*, pp. 136-7; 3. MacCracken, *MLN* XXVII. 228-9 (2 st.); Pace, *MLN* LXIII. 461; Pace, *Papers Bibl. Soc. Univ. Virginia* I. 117-18; 9. Bühler, *MLN* LII. 6; *crit. ed.* Robinson, *Chaucer*, 1933, p. 635; 1957, pp. 539-40; 11. Pace, *Speculum* XXVI. 307.

3788   *Chaucer*, Thynne, 1532 (STC 5068).

3788.5   Today in the dawnyng I hyrde þe fowles syng
        The names of birds—five long-line couplets, with sporadic medial rime.
        1. Harley 1002, f. 72a.
        Wright, *RES* n.s. II. 116.

3790   6. Emerson, *Reader*, pp. 148-54.

3792.5   Tonge breketh bon / wher bon he hathe non
        A proverbial couplet. [Cf. 102.5; 2078 (st. 17 of Harley MS.); Heywood; *Oxford Dict. Eng. Proverbs*, 1935, p. 552; 1948, p. 663; Tilley T 403].
        1. Bodl. 21626, f. 18b; 2. Balliol 354, f. 200b; 3. Trinity Camb. 1149, f. 351a; 4. Harley 3362, ff. 2b and 21a; 5. Rylands Lib. Latin 394, f. 8b.

1, 3. 4. Förster, *Eng. Stn.* XXXI. 6; 1. Förster, *Festschrift zum 12 Deutschen Neuphilologentage*, p. 47; 2. Flügel, *Anglia* XXVI. 203; Dyboski, *EETS* ci. 132; 4. Förster, *Anglia* XLII. 200; 5. Pantin, *BJRL* XIV. 97.

3793   6. Bodl. Lat. misc. c. 66 [*olim* Capesthorne], f. 26b; 7. Trinity Dublin 509, p. 104 (vv. 22).
4. Furnivall, *EETS* 32 rev. ed. 258-9; 6. Robbins, *PMLA* LXV. 259-60.

3798   1. Bodl. 3356, f. 206b (27 st.).

3799   [Another prose paraphrase in Egerton 1995. For adaptations of various stanzas into separate items in Fabyan's *Chronicle* see 227.5, 578.5, 728.5, 1924.4, 1929.3, 3206.8, 3785.8, 3866.3].
2. Cotton Julius B. ii, f. 89a; 6. Rome: English Coll. 1306, f. 67a.
2. McCracken, *Archiv* CXXVI. 75-97; roundel only: 6. Robbins, *Neophilologus* XXXIX. 132-3.

3799.3   Tprut Scot riueling / wiþ mikel mistiming / crop þu ut of kage
English abuse of Scots—three lines in Langtoft's *Chronicle* (not quoted by Mannyng) in two MSS. only.
1. Bodl. 3904, f. 4a; 2. College of Arms, Arundel XIV.
1, 2. Wright, *Pol. Songs*, p. 391; 1. Wilson, *Lost Lit.*, p. 207.

3799.6   Trendel an appull never so ferre / hyt will be know fro wheyre he comyth
A proverb in Nicolas Bozon's *Contes moralisés*. [Cf. 1384, vv. 135-9].
1. Harley 1288, f. 95b; 2. BM Addit. 46919 [*olim* Phillipps 8336], f. 123a; 3. Gray's Inn 12, f. 20a.
1, 2. Ross, *Neuphil. Mitteilungen* L. 203; 1, 3. Smith, *SATF*, pp. 206, 23; Förster, *Festschrift zum 12 Deutschen Neuphilologentage*, p. 59; 1. Herbert, *Cat. Rom.*, III. 103; 3. Wilson, *LSE* V 45; Owst, *Lit & Pulpit*, p. 44.

Tres sunt qui psalmos &c.   See 1214.9.

3800   1. MacCracken, *EETS* 192. 801-2.

3800.5   Trolly lolly loly lo / Syng Troly loly lo
'My love is to the grenewode gone'—five lines.
1. BM Addit. 31922, f. 43b.

Flügel, *Anglia* XII. 239; Stevens, *Music & Poetry*, p. 401; Stevens, *Music at Court*, p. 32.

3801   Mätzner, *AE Sprachproben*, I. 321; Kaiser, *Anthologie*, p. 369; Kaiser, *Med. Eng.*, p. 380.

3805   1. Trinity Camb. 263, f. 117b.

3806   Copley, *Seven English Songs*, 1940.

3807   Robbins, *Sec. Lyrics*, pp. 110-113.

3808   [Translated from the French of Laurence Calot; cf. *Revue des études historiques*, July 1909].

3808.5 Trust in my luf hy schall be trw
        A lover's lament—two cross-rimed quatrains (added in a xv cent hand in *The Blickling Homilies*).
        1. Princeton: Scheide Lib. 66, f. x recto.
        Blickling Homilies, Titusville, Pa., p. 65; Robbins, *Anglia* LXXXII. 11.

3809   Robbins, *Sec. Lyrics*, p. 101; Kaiser, *Med. Eng.*, p. 472; Person, *Camb. ME Lyrics*, p. 43.

3810   1. Bodl. 4127, f. 211b.

3810.3 Truth it is ful sekyrly
        The Visit of the Magi—96 lines in cross-rimed quatrains with an introductory refrain: 'The sterre shoon boþe nyȝt & day.' [Cf. 2033.3].
        1. Canterbury Cath. Add. 68 [*olim* Ingilby], f. 100a.
        Woodruff, *XV Cent. Guide Book*, pp. 81-4.

3810.6 Trouth it is that nobles lady lateryn
        'The speche of Vertu' at the pageant celebrating the marriage of Prince Arthur to Princess Catharine—four stanzas rime royal.
        1. Cotton Vitellius A. xvi, ff. 187a-b.

3811   *Castell of Pleasure*, de Worde, ca. 1517 (STC 18475); Pepwell, 1518 (STC 18476); *repr.* Cornelius, *EETS* 179.

3812   [Cf. 707.5, 1214.9, 1655.5. Utley 329].
Davies, *Med. Eng. Lyrics*, p. 198.

Twas a man als ic herd say   See 1642.

3813   17. Public Record Office, C 47 / 34/1, No. 5, f. 1b; 18. Winchester Coll. 33, f. 49b.
8. D'Evelyn and Mill, *EETS* 235. 4.

3815.3   Twenty wynter glad and blyth
Four lines at the end of a Durandus.
1. *olim* Cook-Davies [sold at Sotheby, June 15, 1959, Lot 205].

3815.5   Two frereus and a fox maken þre shrewes
One long couplet.
1. Bodl. 21626, f. 31a; 2. Bodl. Holkham misc. 39, f. 439b; 3. Rylands Lib. Latin 394, f. 25a.
1. Förster, *Festschrift zum 12 Deutschen Neuphilologentage*, p. 57; 3. Pantin, *BJRL* XIV. 109.

3815.8   Twoe men came riding ouer Hackney Hay
A prophecy on the fall of Reeves Abbey—two couplets.
1. Cotton Titus D. xii, f. 93b.
Rel. Ant., I. 205.

3816.5   Two partes in on ye may asspy / That is my name I may not tary
A riddling couplet with music.
1. Harley 1512, f. 2b.
Robbins, *Journal American Musicological Soc.* XVI. 77.

3817   Clive, *Roxburghe Club*, 1835, L. 1-8.

Two wyfes and one howse   See 3818.

3818   [Utley 332. Ringler 79. Tilley C 184].
3. B.M. IB 49408: *Cordiale quatuor novissimorum*, Caxton, n.d., f. 1 recto.
Boke of Huntyng, St. Albans, 1486 (STC 3308); *facs.* Blades, 1881; *repr.* Dibdin, *Typo. Antiquities*, II. 59: de Worde, 1496 (STC 3309); 2, 3. Bühler, *English Lang. Notes* I. 83, 84.

3818.5   Hudo make an ende of thy playe
           Couplet at end of *Gesta Romanorum*, translating '*Fac finem ludo, iam lusisti satis, Udo.*' [Cf. 849.5].
           1. BM Addit. 9066, f. 65a.
              Herbert, *Cat. Rom.*, III. 258.

3819   [Cf. *851.6].
           1. Arundel 292, f. 70b.
              Haupt and Hoffman, *Altdeutsche Blätter*, II. 145-6; Utley, *Speculum* XXI. 196-7; Hollander, *Untuning of Sky*, p. 425.

3820   Greene, *Sel. Eng. Carols*, p. 140.

3820.5   Vnder a law as I me lay / I herd a may
           'For faute of loue I stand alone'—one cross-rimed quatrain, possibly a religious parody of a secular lyric.
           1. York Minster, *Acta Capitularia* 1410-1429, f. 13a.
              Cawley, *Speculum* XXVI. 142-3.

3822   Rickert, *Anc. Eng. Xmas Carols*, pp. 20-1; Greene, *Sel. Eng. Carols*, p. 116; Davies, *Med. Eng. Lyrics*, pp. 236-7.

3822.3   Vndyr this ston lyeth in the holy plas / Ambros Cressacre
           Epitaph, A.D. 1477, in the Mercer's Chapel, London.
              Weever, *Anc. Funerall Monuments*, 1631, p. 401 (STC 25223).

3822.5   Under this ston William Wever doth ly
           Epitaph, A.D. 1409, in St. Bride's Church, London—three couplets.
              Weever, *Anc. Funerall Monuments*, 1631, p. 436 (STC 25223); Pettigrew, *Chronicles of Tombs*, p. 45.

3823   '*Ballade per antiphrasim*,' by Lydgate—four 8-line stanzas. [The same refrain also serves for 3436. Utley 334].

           Underneath a tre I dyde me set   See 418.

3823.5   Understonde þis verse and have mynde þeron / All þinges schul passe save to love god aloone
           A moralizing couplet (repeated in Latin).
           1. Arundel 286, f. 19b.

3824   [= st. 21 of Maydestone's penitential Psalm, 1961].

3825   2. Lambeth 557, f. 185b (st. 2, 1, only).
       2. Woolf, *RES* n.s. XIII. 9.

3825.5 Ondo ʒoure ʒatys princys to me
       Dialogue between Christ and the Princes of Hell—seven lines in a Latin sermon.
       1. Bodl. 29746, f. 169a.

3826   3. BM Addit. 22283, f. 146b.
       2. Comper, *Life & Lyrics of Rolle*, pp. 282-3.

3827   [For a further variant cf. 3826].

       Vnto the excellent power and nobles / of god cupide and venus the goddes
       Introductory couplet heading to 510.

3830.5 Vnto the holy and vndeuyded trynyte / Thre persones
       A 'Ballade' translated from Latin by Caxton—one stanza rime royal. [Cf. 527.5 and 927.5. Ringler 80].
       1. Chetham Lib. 6709, f. 156a (copied from Caxton).
           Lydgate, *Lyf of Our Lady*, Caxton, 1484 (STC 17023); *facs.* Blades, *Life & Typography of Caxton*, II. 172; *repr.* Dibdin, *Typo. Antiquities*, I. 340; Aurner, *Caxton*, 1926, p. 294; Crotch, *EETS* 176. 85; Lauritis, Klinefelter, and Gallagher, *Life of Our Lady*, p. 52.

3831   2. Royal 17. D. xviii, f. 100a.
       Robbins, *Sec. Lyrics*, pp. 92-3.

3832   [Utley 335].
       Cords, *Archiv* CXXXV. 296; Robbins, *Sec. Lyrics*, pp. 219-20; Davies, *Med. Eng. Lyrics*, pp. 244-5.

3832.5 Vp I arose *in verno tempore*
       A betrayed maiden's lament—four macaronic quatrains.
       1. Bodl. 6659, f. 98b; 2. BM Addit. 5665, f. 145b.
           2. Fehr, *Archiv* CVI. 284; Stevens, *Music & Poetry*, p. 348.

3836.5   Apon a mornyng of may
         The beginning of a *chanson d'aventure* of a man in black—
         three 6-line tail-rime stanzas with an introduction (? burden)
         of five lines: 'Wep no more ffor me.'
         1. Harley 1317, f. 94b.
            Rel. Ant., II. 39; *Early Eng. Carols*, p. 312.

3837   Davies, *Med. Eng. Lyrics*, pp. 229-30.

3838   133 lines in 13-line stanzas alternating with 'versus' of
         eight short lines.
         Robbins, *Hist. Poems*, pp. 98-102.

3843   [Delete entire entry].

         Opon a tyme when Ser Iohn Mandeville   See 3117.6.

3844   *Gentleman's Magazine*, 1799, LXIX. 33; Brand, *Pop. Antiquities*, rev. Ellis, III. 131.

3844.5   Upon temse fro london myles iij / In my chambir
         Venus presents to a dreamer a picture of a beautiful lady—
         two stanzas rime royal.
         1. Leyden Univ. Vossius 9, f. 112a.
            van Dorsten, *Scriptorium* XIV. 318.

*3844.8 *Vpon the cros duryng his passioun
         Parts of six stanzas rime royal on the Seven Times Christ
         shed his blood.
         1. Caius 804, fragment (a slip of vellum).

3845   1. Bodl. 798, f. 14b (followed by 1967.5); 12. BM Addit.
         5465, f. 67b (with 10-line burden).
            6. Furnivall, *EETS* 15 orig. ed. 141; 12. Stevens, *Music &
            Poetry*, pp. 371-2.

*3845.3 *Vppon þe hilles topps waking
         Metrical history of Birth and Life of Christ—short couplets.
         1. BM Addit. 39196 [*olim* Phillipps 9803], ff. 1a-23b.

3845.5   Apon the Midsummer evin mirriest of nichtis
'The tretis of the tua mariit wemen and the wedo,' by William Dunbar—vv. 530 in non-riming alliterative long lines. [Utley 336].
1. Pepys 2553, pp. 81-96.
Early print, n.p., n.d. (STC 7350) (vv. 1-103 wanting); *facs.* Beattie, *Edinb. Bibl. Soc.* 1950, pp. 177-89; *repr.* Laing, *Knightly Tale of Golagros*, 1827; Stevenson, *STS* LXV. 247-59; *repr. with* 1. Sibbald, *Chronicle*, I. 210-29; Laing, *Dunbar*, I. 61-80; MacKenzie, *Dunbar*, pp. 85-97; 1. [Pinkerton,] *Anc. Scot. Poems*, I. 44-64; Schipper, *Dunbar*, pp. 46-9; and *DKAW* XL (II). 45-69; Baildon, *Dunbar*, pp. 10-23; Craigie, *STS* n.s. VII. 98-115; Small, *STS* IV. 30-47; Kinsley, *Dunbar*, pp. 33-40 (extracts).

Apon thy cors vengeance vengeance thay cry
See 3117.8 (Chepman and Myllar print, begins v. 316).

3847   Furnivall, *EETS* 32 rev. ed. 219-20.

3848   [Revise listing of MSS. as follows:]
1. Bodl. 3461, f. 25a; 2. Bodl. 3478, f. 16a; 3. Bodl. 6733, f. 4b; 4. Bodl. 6795, f. 9a (vv. 110); 5. Bodl. 7627, f. 199a (vv. 68); 6. Bodl. 7719, Part I, pp. 96-8; 7. Bodl. 7722, Part I, E, ff. 25b-26 (vv. 94); 8. Trinity Camb. 921, ff. 33a-b (var., ends imperfectly); 9. Trinity Camb. 1037, f. 20a (last 36 vv. only); 10. Trinity Camb. 1440, f. 142b (vv. 82); 11. Egerton 1995, f. 79a; 12. Egerton 2572, f. 69a (vv. 56); 13. Lansdowne 680, f. 22b; 14. Sloane 100, f. 34a (vv. 92); 15. Sloane 357, f. 46a (vv. 92); 16. Sloane 540, A, f. 23a (vv. 108); 17. Sloane 610, ff. 5b-8; 18. Sloane 963, f. 71a; 19. Sloane 2457, f. 1a; 20. Sloane 3160, f. 149a; 21. BM Addit. 18216, f. 9b; 22. BM Addit. 30338, f. 212a; 23. Durham Univ. Cosin V. iii. 10, f. 41b (vv. 90); 24. Hunterian Mus. 258, p. 190 (vv. 10, inc. 4-line preface); 25. Wellcome Hist. Med. Lib. 406 [*olim* Loscombe], f. 1b (vv. 90); 26. *olim* Ashburnham App. 121, p. 74 (vv. 90); 27. Nat. Lib. of Medicine 4, ff. 16a-17a.

1. Robbins, *Sec. Lyrics*, pp. 77-80; 12. Furnivall, *EETS* liii. 228-9; 17. Pettigrew, *Archaeologia* XXX. 420 (extract); 24. Young, *Cat.*, p. 210; 26. *Rel. Ant.*, I. 189-91; 27. Mayer, *Bull. History of Medicine* VII. 388-90.

Verbum caro factum est
Burden to 795.

3849   A balade protesting devotion and fidelity—three 6-line tail-rime stanzas.
          1. Robbins, *PMLA* LXIX. 639.

3851   Robbins, *Hist. Poems*, pp. 144-5.

3856.5   W Wisdome *monstrat et adventus*
          An acrostic on the virtues of the Earl of Warwick—six lines.
          1. Trinity Dublin 432, f. 70b.
          Madden, *Archaeologia* XXIX. 332; Brotanek, *ME Dichtungen*, p. 136; Robbins, *Hist. Poems*, p. 380.

3857.5   Wel and wa sal ys hornes blawe
          A lament after the death of Robert de Neville, A.D. 1280—one quatrain.
          1. Lansdowne 207, f. 434a.
          Cat., II. 76; Raine, *Hist. Dunelm. Scriptores Tres*, Surtees Soc. IX. 112; Dodds, *Archaeol. Aeliana*, 4 s, I. 133; Dibdin, *Northern Tour*, I. 283; Wilson, *LSE* V. 49; Wilson, *Lost Lit.*, p. 187; Dickins and Wilson, *Early ME Texts*, p. 118; *New Oxford Hist. Music*, III. 114; Cottle, *JEGP* LXII. 764.

3858   Furnivall, *EETS* 15 orig. ed. 239; rev. ed. 267.

3859.5   Wake wel annot / þi mayden boure
          A fragment of a popular song in a Latin sermon—four short lines.
          1. Cotton Faustina A. v, f. 9a.
          Robbins, *Sec. Lyrics*, p. xxxix.

3860.3   Was he neuer good knape / þat had is dame at þe sate
          A proverbial couplet. [Cf. 3167.3].
          1. Bodl. 21626, f. 29b; 2. Rylands Lib. Latin 394, f. 21b.
          1. Förster, *Festschrift zum 12 Deutschen Neuphilologentage*, p. 56; 2. Pantin, *BJRL* XIV. 107.

3860.6   Was hit nevere mi kind / Chese in welle to finde
A couplet in Nicolas Bozon's *Contes moralisés*.
1. Harley 1288, f. 121b; 2. BM Addit. 46919 [*olim* Phillipps 8336], f. 126a; 3. Gray's Inn 12, f. 43a.

1, 3. Smith, *SATF*, pp. 215, 151; Förster, *Festschrift zum 12 Deutschen Neuphilologentage*, p. 59; Wilson, *LSE* VI. 46; 2. Ross, *Neuphil. Mitteilungen* L. 210.

3860.8   Was nevir in scotland hard nor sene
'At chrystis kirk of the grene,' attributed to King James I— in 9-line stanzas including this refrain.
1. Pepys 2553, p. 129 (23 st.); 2. Advocates 1. 1. 6, f. 99a (21 st.).

1. Craigie, *STS* n.s. VII. 149-55; 2. Ramsay, *Evergreen*, I. 1; Sibbald, *Chronicle*, II. 356; *Bannatyne MS.*, Hunt. Club, pp. 282-8; Ritchie, *STS* n.s. XXII. 262-8.

Water ffrozen Caymes broþer   See 597.5 (MS. Balliol 354).

3862.5   Water shall wax and wod shall wane
A political prophecy in *Joannis Rossi Warwicensis Historia*— four lines.
1. Cotton Vesp. A. xii, f. 116a.

Hearne, *Rossi Warwicensis Historia Regum Angliae*, 1716, p. 130.

3863.5   We be maydyns fayr & gent
The song of the light ladies—one quatrain and burden: 'The bella.'
1. New York Pub. Lib. Drexel Fragments 4184, 4185.

XX Songes, de Worde, 1530 (STC 22924); *repr.* Imelmann, *Shakespeare-Jahrbuch* XXXIX. 128-9; Flügel, *Anglia* XII. 591.

3864   Robbins, *Sec. Lyrics*, p. 6.

3866   twelve couplets.
Person, *Camb. ME Lyrics*, pp. 23-4.

3866.3   We ladyes thre all by one consent
Pageant verses by Nature, Grace, and Fourteen Virgins, at the return of Henry VI to London, A.D. 1432—three stanzas rime royal. [Adapted from 3799].

Fabyan, *New Chronicles,* Pynson, 1516 (STC 10659); *repr.* Ellis, 1811, pp. 603-4; Gattinger, *Wiener Beiträge* IV. 25-6.

3866.5   We lordis hes chosin a chiftane mervellus
'The lordis of Scotland to the Governour in France,' attributed to William Dunbar—five 8-line stanzas with refrain: 'In lak of justice this realme is schent allace.'
1. Advocates 1. 1. 6, f. 78b.
Laing, *Dunbar,* II. 47-8; *Bannatyne MS.,* Hunt. Club, II. 215-6; Small, *STS* IV. 237-8; Schipper, *Dunbar,* pp. 443-5; and *DKAW* XLIII (I). 54-7; Ritchie, *STS* n.s. XXII. 197; MacKenzie, *Dunbar,* pp. 181-2.

3867   Furnivall, *EETS* 15 orig. ed. 241; rev. ed. 269.

3868   1-3. Bliss, Oxford 1954; 3. Laing, *Remains,* rev. Hazlitt, 1895, I. 64-80; Ford, *Age of Chaucer,* pp. 271-87.

*3868.5   *We rede ye ffede / & ȝe shellen ffynde
Apparently a fragment of a lullaby—four lines (very faded).
1. Royal 20. A. i, f. 121b.
Early Eng. Carols, p. 329.

3870   1. Camb. Un. Ll. 5. 10, f. 55b; 2. Pepys 2553, p. 290; 4. Delete this MS.
2. Craigie, *STS* n.s. VII. 337-41; 3. *Blackwood's Magazine,* Feb. 1835; Sibbald, *Chronicle,* I. 234-9; *Ramsay and Earlier Scot. Poets,* p. 266; *Bannatyne MS.,* Hunt. Club, II. 292-6; Schipper, *Dunbar,* pp. 41-3; and *DKAW* XL (II). 40-3; Baildon, *Dunbar,* pp. 6-9; Neilson and Webster, *Chief Brit. Poets,* pp. 396-7; MacKenzie, *Dunbar,* pp. 56-9; Kinsley, *Dunbar,* pp. 98-100 (extracts).

*3870.5   *We Tib / Telle on
The Shrewsbury Fragments: single parts in non-cycle mystery plays—*Officium Pastorum* (vv. 50), *Officium Resurrectionis* (vv. 44), *Officium Peregrinorum* (vv. 81).
1. Shrewsbury School VI, ff. 37b-43a; 1a *(facs.).* Bodl. facs. d. 24.
Skeat, *Academy* 1890, I. 27; Manly, *Spec. Pre-Sh. Drama,* I. xxviii-xxxvii; Waterhouse, *EETS* civ. 1-7; Adams, *Chief Pre-Sh. Dramas,* pp. 73-8; Young, *Drama Med. Church,* II. 514-23.

3872   [Cf. Robbins, *Anglia* LXXV. 195-6].
    1. BM Addit. 46919 [*olim* Phillipps 8336], f. 205b.
    Davies, *Med. Eng. Lyrics*, p. 98.

    Wep no more ffor me swet hart   See 3836.5.

3874   [Utley 340].
    Brook, *Harley Lyrics*, pp. 35-6.

3876   A song of the Trinity.
    Christmas Carolles, Kele, ca. 1550 (STC 5205); *facs.* Reed, *Xmas Carols*, pp. 46-7.

3877   1. Greene, *Sel. Eng. Carols*, p. 55; 2. Bullen, *Carols & Poems*, p. 2; Sylvester, *Garland of Xmas Carols*, p. 79; Rickert, *Anc. Eng. Xmas Carols*, pp. 121-2; *Oxford Book Carols*, p. 213.

3878   Robbins, *PMLA* LXIX. 634-5.

3879   [Utley 341].
    Robbins, *Sec. Lyrics*, pp. 163-4.

3880   Furnivall, *EETS* 15 orig. ed. 5; Halliwell, *Camden Soc.* X. 32.

3880.3   Welcome faire lady fayrer than hesperus
    Speech of welcome to Princess Catharine at the pageant celebrating her marriage to Prince Arthur—three stanzas rime royal.
    1. Cotton Vitell. A. xvi, f. 192a.

3880.6   Welcum ffortune wellcum agayne
    Joy in his mistress' devotion—five quatrains. [Cf. *Gude & Godlie Ballatis*, *repr.* Laing, 1868, pp. 150-1; Mitchell, *STS* XXXIX. 222].
    1. BM Addit. 18752, f. 88a; 2. *olim* Ely Cath. fragment (present location not known).
    1. Reed, *Anglia* XXXIII. 360.

3881   Robbins, *Sec. Lyrics*, pp. 115-7.

3882	1. Egerton 3245 [*olim* Gurney], f. 185a; 2. Camb. Un. Gg. 5. 31, f. 4a (added in margin). 2. Robbins, *MP* XL. 139.
3883	6. Brussells: Bibl. royale, ff. 139-140; 7. Glazier G. 9 [*olim* Berkeley], Art. 3. 4. N. S. Baugh, *Worcestershire Misc.*, pp. 149-50.
3884	Person, *Camb. ME Lyrics*, p. 28.
3884.5	Welcome moost excellent high & Victorious Pageant verses spoken by Iusticia to Henry VII in A.D. 1486 at Bristol—four stanzas rime royal. 1. Cotton Julius B. xii, ff. 20a-b.
3885.5	Welcome nevew welcome my cousyn dere Pageant verses to Henry VII in A.D. 1486 at Worcester—twenty-three stanzas rime royal. 1. Cotton Julius B. xii, ff. 13b-17a.
3886	[Delete entire entry]. Welcombe you bretheren godely in this hall See 1386.5.
3887	[Delete entire entry]. Wyl be þow ster of se See 1034.5.
3887.5	Well chered / fayr hered Six properties of a woman—tag lines (following prose text on 18 Properties of a Horse). [Cf. Bühler, *Traditio* IV. 434 n]. 1. Huntington Lib. HU 1051, f. 62b.
3889.5	Well on my way as I forth wente / ouer a londe 'The Prophisies of Rymour, Reed, and Marlyng:' a later version of 365—vv. 628 in 8-line stanzas. [Cf. a shortened version, vv. 248, in *The Whole Prophesie of Scotland*, Waldegrave, Edinb. 1663; repr. Murray, *EETS* 61. 48-51. Cf. also 'Prophesie of Sir Thomas of Astledowne' in *Sundry Strange Prophecies*, 1652; repr. Albrecht, Univ. of New

Mexico Press, 1954; and see further, Albrecht, *Med. Aevum* XXIII. 88-95.
1. Bodl. 12653, f. 72b (cf. 3903.5); 2. Lansdowne 762, ff. 75a-88a ('Erceldoune,' to A.D. 1531).
2. Murray, *EETS* 61. 52-61; *comp. ed.* Sibbald, *Chronicle*, III. 129-35.

3891 [Delete entire entry].

Welle was hire mete   See 2037.5.

3892 two 6-line stanzas.

3892.5 Well were hym þat wyste / to wam he myst tryst
A proverbial couplet (appearing as vv. 1-2 of 3892 and 3893). [Also found on a xiv cent. ring, belonging to Sir Arthur Evans, exhibited at Exhibition of Eng. Med. Art, London 1930, Item 862].
1. Bodl. 15444, f. 144a; 2. Bodl. 21626, f. 17a.
1. Meech, *MP* XXXVIII. 125; 2. Förster, *Festschrift zum 12 Deutschen Neuphilologentage*, p. 46.

3893 Wel were hym þat wyst / to wham he might trist
A warning against false friends—one 6-line tail-rime stanza. [Cf. 3892].
1. Bodl. 7707, p. 82; 2. Royal 17. B. xlvii, f. 3b (lacks vv. 3, 6, to form two couplets).
1. *Cat. MSS. Ashmole*, 1845, p. 1186; Förster, *Festschrift zum 12 Deutschen Neuphilologentage*, p. 46; 2. *Register*, I. 366.

3894 [Delete entire entry].

Wel qwa wal thir hornes blau   See 3857.5.

3894.3 Wel worth the suffrance þat abatis strif
'And wo worthe the hastinesce þat reues man his lif'—a couplet in Nicolas Bozon's *Contes moralisés*.
1. Harley 1288, f. 94b; 2. BM Addit. 46919 [*olim* Phillipps 8336], f. 122a; 3. Gray's Inn 12, f. 19a.
1, 3. Smith, *SATF*, pp. 203, 20; Förster, *Festschrift zum 12 Deutschen Neuphilologentage*, p. 58; Ross, *Neuph*'. *Mitteilungen* L. 203; 1. Herbert, *Cat. Rom.*, III. 105; 3. Wilson, *LSE* VI. 45.

3894.6   Wel wot hure cat / whas berd he lickat
A proverbial couplet. [Cf. 3318.6. Tilley C 140].
1. Bodl. 21626, f. 23b; 2. Trinity Camb. 1149, f. 351a; 3. Harley 3362, f. 6a; 4. Sloane 747, f. 66a.
1. Förster, *Eng. Stn.* XXXI. 5; Förster, *Festschrift zum 12 Deutschen Neuphilologentage*, p. 50; 2. *Retrospective Rev.*, 1854, II. 309; 4. Förster, *Anglia* XLII. 203.

Wende kyng edward with his longe shankes   See 3918.5.

3895   Robbins, *Sec. Lyrics*, p. 105.

3896   1. Royal 4. A. xiv, f. 106b.
Birch, *Trans. Royal Soc. Lit.* 2 s. XI. 485; Kaiser, *Med. Eng.*, p. 144.

Were I in my castle of Bungey   See 1417.3.

Were not hope stedfaste / herte ofte sithe sholde brest
See 1251.5.

3897.5   Were þat þat is ido iet for to donne
An act beyond recall—one couplet.
1. Tübingen Univ. Deposit: Berlin Preussische Staatsbibliothek Lat. theol. fol. 249, f. 131b.

3898   Robbins, *Sec. Lyrics*, pp. 7-8; Wilson, *Lost Lit.*, p. 179.

3899   Robbins, *Hist. Poems*, p. 37.

3899.3   Westron wynde when wylle thou blow
Yearning for his mistress—one quatrain.
1. Royal App. 58, f. 5a.
Chappell, *OE Pop. Music*, I. 37; Stafford Smith, *Eng. Songs*, I. 31; Ritson, *Anc. Songs*, 1790, p. lv; 1829, I. lxxvi; Flügel, *Anglia* XII. 260; Flügel, *Neuengl. Lesebuch*, p. 138; *Early Eng. Lyrics*, p. 69; *Oxford Book XVI C. Verse*, p. 40; Robbins, *Sec. Lyrics*, p. xxxviii; *Poets of Eng. Lang.*, I. 426; Stevens, *Music & Poetry*, p. 130; Davies, *Med. Eng. Lyrics*, p. 291.

3899.6   Waylowy so dere boht þat it sal þus ben
          A xiii cent. scrap of English added on a margin.
          1. Caius 221, f. 18b.
          Robbins, Anglia LXXXII. 13.

3900.5   Weilawei þat ich ne span / þo ich into wude ran
          A couplet in a Latin sermon.
          1. Tübingen Univ. Deposit: Berlin Preussische Staatsbibliothek Lat. theol. fol. 249, f. 132b.
          Robbins, Anglia LXXXII. 13.

3901   [Cf. 1218.5].

3902   2. Aberdeen Univ. 154, f. 155b (vv. 4).

3902.5   Vaylaway whi ded y so / now ich am in alle wa
          The lament of the fallen virgin—one couplet.
          1. Balliol 220, f. 220b.
          Mynors, Cat., p. 216; Robbins, Anglia LXXXII. 13.

3903.3   What art þou & art so synge
          Dialogue between St. Christopher and the Christ Child—two couplets, on two scrolls on a mural on the north wall of Horley Church, Oxfordshire.
          Bennett, N&Q CLXXVI. 387.

3903.5   What can it auayle / To dryue forth a snayle
          'Colyn Cloute,' by John Skelton—vv. 1270 in 'skeltonics.'
          1. Bodl. 12653 (fragment; cf. 3889.5); 2. Harley 2252, ff. 147a-153b; 3. Lansdowne 762, f. 71a ('The Profecy of Skelton' = vv. 462-80 of Dyce text).
          Godfray, n.d.; Kele, n.d. (STC 22601); repr. with 3. Dyce, Skelton, I. 311-60, 329; Dyce and Child, Skelton & Donne, II. 125-69, 141-2; repr. Henderson, Skelton, 1931, pp. 282-321; 1948, 1959, pp. 250-87; Hughes, Poems, pp. 96-139; William, Selections, pp. 101-40; Pinto, Selections, pp. 88-97 (extracts); J. Wyght, n.d.; Kytson, n.d.; Workes, Marshe, 1568 (STC 22608); repr. [? J. Bowle,] 1736; Chalmers, English Poets, II. 280-90.

3903.8   What causyth me wofull thoughtis to thynk
          No thought can release me of my sore—one stanza rime royal.
          1. BM Addit. 5465, f. 4b.
          Fehr, Archiv CVI. 52; Stevens, Music & Poetry, pp. 352-3.

3904	Bennett, *STS* 3 s. XXIII. 234-6.
3905	All is vanity save good deeds—one stanza rime royal. Person, *Camb. ME Lyrics*, p. 49.
3905.5	What ich þole man by hand Five couplets in a Latin note on the Passion. 1. Brussels; Bibl. royal 2054, f. 48a.
3906	1. BM Addit. 46919 [*olim* Phillipps 8336], f. 210a. Davies, *Med. Eng. Lyrics*, pp. 94-5.
3907	Furnivall, *EETS* 15 orig. ed. 231; rev. ed. 259.
3908.5	Quhat is this lyfe bot ane straucht way to deid 'Of lyfe,' by William Dunbar—one stanza rime royal. 1. Pepys 2553, p. 310; 2. Advocates 1. 1. 6, f. 59b. 1. Laing, *Dunbar*, I. 235; Paterson, *Dunbar*, p. 87; Small, *STS* IV. 250; Schipper, *Dunbar*, p. 336; and *DKAW* XLII (IV). 83-4; Baildon, *Dunbar*, p. 207; Craigie, *STS* n.s. VII. 350; MacKenzie, *Dunbar*, p. 151; Kinsley, *Dunbar*, p. 67; 2. *Bannatyne MS.*, Hunt. Club, II. 204; Ritchie, *STS* n.s. XXII. 186.
3909.2	What joy ys yn hayn what sorow ys yn hell Four monoriming lines. 1. Worcester Cath. F. 12, pastedown.
3909.4	What lyf is þer here / þe lyf her is deyȝe The vanity of the world, by William Herebert—questions and answers in eight alternatively riming lines. 1. BM Addit. 46919 [*olim* Phillipps 8336], f. 179b. Gneuss, *Anglia* LXXVIII. 192.
3909.6	What man can perceyve that women be evyll A punctuation poem against women, by Richard Hatfield—one stanza rime royal. [For two similar poems see 232 and 3174.5]. 1. BM Addit. 17492, f. 18b. Flügel, *Neuengl. Lesebuch*, p. 39; Padelford, *Early XVI Cent. Lyrics*, p. 95; Muir, *Proc. Leeds Philos. & Lit. Soc., Lit. & Hist. Sect.* VI. 261; Hughey, *Arundel Harington MS.*, II. 209.

3910 eighteen stanzas rime royal with tr. into Latin hexameters.
1. College of Arms, Box 21, no. 16 [see Heralds' *Commem. Cat.* 1934, p. 37, and plate 42].
Dugdale, *Monasticon Angl.*, London 1846, VIII. 1600; repr. Horstmann, *O. Bokenams Leg. 1883*; Weever, *Anc. Funerall Monuments*, 1631, pp. 472-7 (STC 25223).

3910.5 What man that wille of huntyng leere
Envoy to Twici's prose *Treatise on Hunting* — one stanza rime royal. [Cf. 202].
1. Rome: English Coll. 1306, f. 160a.
Robbins, *Neophilologus* XXXIX. 134.

3911 Robbins, *Sec. Lyrics*, pp. 60-1.

3911.5 Quhat meneth this Quhat is this windir vre
Against the inconstancy of women, an extract from *The Complaint of the Black Knight* (1507), vv. 302-434, 456-469 — twenty-one stanzas rime royal. [Utley 345].
1. Advocates 1. 1. 6, f. 281a.
Chaucer, Stow, 1561 (STC 5075); Urry, *Chaucer*, 1721, p. 453; *Bannatyne MS.*, Hunt. Club, p. 817; Ritchie, *STS* n.s. XXVI. 82

3911.8 What nedys a pilgryme do þat wyll sped hym smert
Three monoriming lines in a Latin sermon.
1. Balliol 149, f. 73b.

What remedy what remedy   See 98.5.

3912.5 What shall happen alse weene
A prophecy for 1560 — two 5-line stanzas.
1. Cotton Galba E. ix, f. 66b.
Hulme, *EETS* c. xxiv.

3914 [Anderson,] *Poets of Great Britain*, I. 579; 1. Robinson, *Chaucer*, 1933, p. 639; 1957, p. 543.

3914.5 What shuld I say sithe faith is ded
'Trouth is exiled in whomanhede' — one couplet. [Var. of st. 1 of poem by Wyatt, ed. Muir, No. 143].
1. Bodl. 6919, end cover.
Seaton, *Sir Richard Roos*, p. 486; Lauritis, Klinefelter, and Gallagher, *Life of Our Lady*, p. 40.

3916   Arber, *Dunbar Anthology*, p. 123.

3917   Robbins, *PMLA* XLIX. 632-3; Davies, *Med. Eng. Lyrics*, pp. 237-8.

3917.3   What thynge maye sowne to gretter excellence
          Wynkyn de Worde's introduction to his edition of *Polychronicon*—five stanzas rime royal. [Ringler 81].
          1. Garrett 151, f. 1a (vv. 22-35 only).
          Trevisa, *Prolicronycon*, de Worde, 1495 (STC 13439); *repr.* Dibdin, *Typo. Antiquities*, II. 50; Treveris, 1527 (STC 13440).

3917.5   What thing restethe not now & then amonge
          The need for rest—a couplet.
          1. Durham Univ. Cosin V. iii. 9, f. 58a.
          Furnivall, *EETS* lxi. 187.

3917.8   Whatt tyme as Paris son of kyng Priame / lay sleping in a garden
          A description of the qualities of Venus, a dialogue—thirty-nine stanzas rime royal.
          1. Bodl. 12653, f. 64a.
          Padelford and Benham, *Anglia* XXXI. 385-93.

          What wee gaue we haue   See 1924.3.

3918.5   What wenes kynge Edwarde with his longe shankes
          Scots' abuse of Edward I at Berwick—five lines, found in most early chronicles and in most MSS. of prose *Brut*. [Cf. 2754. Ringler 80a].
          Chronicles of Englond, Caxton, 1480 (STC 9991), and later eds.; Fabyan, *New Chronicles*, Pynson, 1516 (STC 10659); *repr.* Ellis, 1811, p. 398; Rastell, *Pastime of People or Chronicles*, *repr.* 1811, p. 196; *Annales Angliae et Scotiae*, Rolls Series XXVIII, ii. 373; Wright, *Pop. Superstitions*, II. 261; Brie, *EETS* 131. 189; Wilson, *LSE* V. 43; Wilson, *Lost Lit.*, p. 208; Legge, *Anglo-Norman Lit.*, p. 353.

3919   [Utley 179].
           Robbins, *Sec. Lyrics*, p. 37.

3919.5   Whatt women be in dede why shold nott all men know
Women: fickle to their friends, spiteful to their foes—a long couplet signed 'Robert Iernegan.'
1. Trinity Camb. 1037, f. 205b (added on flyleaf in xvi cent. hand).

3920   *Early Eng. Carols*, p. 220.

When ase beareth vp syse   See 734.8.

3921   1a (xix cent. transcript). Egerton 2257, f. 99a.
1. Davies, *Med. Eng. Lyrics*, pp. 143-6.

3922   [Cf. 1596, vv. 98-9; 3921, vv. 1-4; and in many early chronicles. For further refs. cf. Meech, *MP* XXXVIII. 130. Tilley A 30].
MSS. include: Bodl. 15444, f. 142b; Harley 3352, f. 5a; &c.
Printings include: *Annales*, Stow, 1615, p. 293; Riley, *Thomae Walsingham Historia Anglicana*, Rolls Series XXVIII, ii. 32; Thompson, *Chronicon Angliae*, Rolls Series LXIV. 321; Dyboski, *EETS* ci. 131; Owst, *Lit. & Pulpit*, p. 291; *Oxford Dict. Eng. Proverbs*, p. 571; Meech, *MP* XXXVIII. 121; Eberhard, *Der Bauernaufstand vom Jahr 1381*, AF LI. 24; Robbins, *Anglia* LXXVIII. 202.

3923   [Cf. *22].

3923.5   Quhen Alexander our kynge wes dede
A popular lament (or '*Cantus*') on the times following the death of Alexander III of Scotland, A.D. 1286, occurring in Wintoun's *Chronicle* (399) at end of Book VII (vv. 3621-8), considered as the earliest extant Scottish political prophecy— two quatrains.
For MSS. see 399.
Macpherson, London, 1795; Laing, Edinburgh, 1872; Ellis, *Specimens*, I. 233; Eyre-Todd, *Med. Scot. Poetry*, p. 162; Eyre-Todd, *Scot. Ballad Poetry*, p. 17; Brandl and Zippel, *ME Sprach- u. Literatur.*, p. 649; *CHEL* II. 116; Murray, *Dialects Southern Counties Scotland*, p. 28; Amours, *STS* LVI. 145; Wilson, *LSE* V. 44; Wilson, *Early ME Lit.*, p. 271.

3924   1. Bodl. 1703, f. 111b.

3926.5   When al was husht and al was in sylens
One stanza rime royal in aureate language, apparently the beginning of an amateurish religious-moral poem, followed by related pen trials.
1. Trinity Dublin 423, f. 102b.

3927   [Possibly acephalous].
Rickert, *Anc. Eng. Xmas Carols*, pp. 54-5; *facs.* Reed, *Xmas Carols*, p. 15.

3927.3   When bale is hiest / þen boot is neste
A proverbial couplet. [Cf. 693; 3502, v. 14. Tilley B 59].
1. Bodl. 21626, f. 25b; 2. Rylands Lib. Latin 394, f. 15b.
1. Förster, *Festschrift zum 12 Deutschen Neuphilologentage*, p. 52; Pantin, *BJRL* XIV. 102.

3927.6   Whanne bloweþ þe brom / þanne wogeþ þe grom
Four short gnomic lines.
1. Trinity Camb. 1149, f. 351a.
Förster, *Eng. Stn.* XXXI. 5.

3928   [All MSS. are more or less imperfect, except 1 and 11. Ringler 82].
12. Cotton App. XXVII, ff. 3a-51b (vv. 1-3408); 16. BM Addit. 18632, ff. 6a-33b; 18. Durham Univ. Cosin V. ii. 14; 20. Delete this MS.; 21. *olim* Brudenell [*olim* Cardigan], f. 246a (Sotheby Sale, Feb. 1959); 22. Camb. Un. Add. 6864 [*olim* Gurney 150], f. 1a; 26. Delete this MS.; 28. St. John's Oxf. 256; 29. Coventry Corp. Record Office, f. 98a; 30. *olim* Campbell (Robinson Sale Cat. 74, 1944, No. 268); 31. Boston Pub. Lib. 94.
The Storye of Thebes, de Worde, ca. 1495 (STC 17031).

3928.3   Qwan browm beryth apelys and homulok hony browin
Impossibilities—one couplet translating a Latin distich. [Cf. 3999].
1. Bodl. Holkham misc. 39, f. 439b.

3928.5   When busy at my booke I was uppon a certain night
The Vision of Sir George Ripley, Canon of Bridlington.
1. Bodl. 7644, Part I, art. 3; 2. Bodl. 7652, f. 46b.
Ashmole, *Theatrum Chemicum*, p. 374.

Qwhen þe dyvyne deliberatioun   See 2579.5.

3929   1. Cotton Nero A. vi, ff. 196b.
        2. Robbins, *Hist. Poems*, pp. 194-6.

3932   four quatrains and burden.
        Sandys, *Christmas Carols*, pp. 2-3; Bramley and Stainer, *Christmas Carols*, no. 19; Sylvester, *Garland of Xmas Carols*, p. 76; Bullen, *Carols & Poems*, p. 6; Rickert, *Anc. Eng. Xmas Carols*, pp. 46-7.

3936   Clive, *Roxburghe Club*, 1835, L. 137-44.

3938   [Based on St. Anselm's *Deploratio male amissae virginitatis*.]
        1. Univ. of Pennsylvania, Eng. 1 [*olim* Ireland Blackburne], ff. 118b-120b.
        Dickins, *LSE* III. 33-6 (extracts).

3939   2. Brook, *Harley Lyrics*, p. 29; Kaiser, *Anthologie*, p. 241; Kaiser, *Med. Eng.*, p. 286.

3940   4. Bodl. Holkham misc. 39, f. 438a.

3941.5 Whan euery woo hathe easse / And euery wyshe his wyll
        The changes of fortune: on the impossibility of relief in love—one stanza rime royal.
        1. Durham Univ. Cosin V. ii. 13, f. 2a (written twice, first in 6 vv.) and f. 115a (var.).

3942   2. Advocates 1. 1. 6, p. 42 and f. 55a.
        2a, 2b. Ritchie, *STS* 3 s. V. 68-71; *STS* n.s. XXII. 137; 2b. *Bannatyne MS.*, Hunt. Club, p. 149; Laing, *Henryson*, 1865, p. 23; Wood, *Henryson*, pp. 179-81.

3943   [Ringler 83].
        [Revise listing of MSS. as follows:]
        1. Bodl. 6943, f. 78a (vv. 8, '*Profecia Merlini*'); 2. Bodl. 8113, p. 162; 3. Bodl. 9914, p. 253; 4. Bodl. 14526, f. 1b; 5. Bodl. Lat. misc. c. 66 [*olim* Capesthorne], f. 104a; 6. Camb. Un. Gg. 4. 27, I b, f. 4b; 7. Camb. Un. Ii. 3. 26, f. 161b (xvii cent. scrap); 8. Camb. Un. Ii. 6. 11, end flyleaf; 9. Pepys 1236, f. 91a; 10. Trinity Camb. 595, f. 3a; 11. Harley 1337, f. 105b; 12. Royal 17. A. xvi, f. 27b; 13. BM Addit. 24663, f. 1a ('wrytten by Iefferae Chauser'); 14. Fitzwilliam Mus. 355 (a); 15. Rylands Lib. Latin 201, f. 227a; 16. Trinity Dublin 516, f. 118a; 17. Illuminated Missal, flyleaf (vv. 9, tail-rime) [present location not known].

Anelida and False Arcyte, Caxton, ca. 1477 (STC 5090); *facs. Story of Queen Anelida,* Camb. 1905; *repr.* Dibdin, *Typo. Antiquities,* I. 311; Blades, *Life & Typography of Caxton,* II. 65; Skeat, *Oxf. Ch.,* I. 46; D'Evelyn, *Peter Idley's Instructions,* p. 230; Fawtier, *BJRL* V. 390; *Chaucer,* Thynne, 1532 (STC 5068); *Chaucer,* Stow, 1561 (STC 5075); *Chaucer,* Speght, 1598 (STC 5077); Bell, *Poets of Great Britain,* I. ccxlvii; Puttenham, *Art of English Poesie,* ed. Arber, p. 232; *British Poets,* Chiswick 1822, V. 179; [Pickering,] *Aldine British Poets,* 1845, VI. 287; 1866, VI. 307; Bell, *Chaucer,* III. 427; Gilman, *Chaucer,* III. 654; Skeat, *Chaucer Canon,* p. 115; 1. Skeat, *Atheneum,* 1896, CVIII. 874; Skeat, *Oxf. Ch.,* VII. lxxxi; 2. Urry, *Chaucer,* 1721, preface (unpaginated); Dibdin, *Typo. Antiquities,* II. 514; 5. Robbins, *PMLA* LXV. 275; 9. James, *Cat.,* III. 5; Robbins, *Sec. Lyrics,* p. 241; 10. Todd, *Gower & Chaucer,* p. 119; 15. Fawtier, *BJRL* V. 389; 16. Furnivall, *EETS* 9 xlvi; Furnivall, *Chaucer Soc.* 2 s. XIII. xlvi; Robbins, *Hist. Poems,* p. 121; 17. Brydges and Haslewood, *Brit. Bibliographer,* II. 200.

3945   in couplets.
1. Harley 2338, f. 28b (vv. 18; ends imperfectly); 2. Lansdowne 762, f. 52a (vv. 52).

3946   [Cf. 3999].
Person, *Camb. ME Lyrics,* p. 41.

3946.5   When Flora had oerfret the firth / In May
A balade—three 8-line stanzas with refrain: 'Whom I loue I dare nocht assay.'
1. Advocates 1. 1. 6, f. 218a.
[Hailes,] *Anc. Scot. Poems,* p. 239; Ramsay, *Evergreen,* I. 256; *Bannatyne MS.,* Hunt. Club, p. 621; Ritchie, *STS* n.s. XXIII. 262; Hinley, *Eng. Lyrics,* p. 25; Cohen, *Ballade,* pp. 297-8.

3947   2206 short lines with concluding stanza and Envoy (923), and final couplet.
1. BM Addit. 10303, ff. 1b-9a; 2. Longleat 256, ff. 2a-24b.
Chaucer, Speght, 1598 (STC 5077); Urry, *Chaucer,* 1721, p. 572; Bell, *Poets of Great Britain,* XI. 5; [Anderson,] *Poets of Great Britain,* I. 462; Chalmers, *English Poets,* I. 378; *British Poets,* Chiswick 1822, V. 73; Moxon, *Chaucer, p. 389;* [Pickering,] *Aldine British Poets,* 1845, VI. 177; 1866, V. 86; Bell, *Chaucer,* III. 439; *crit. ed.* Sherzer, Berlin 1903.

*3947.3   *When folk are festid and fed fayn wald þai here
The Romance of *The Wars of Alexander the Great*—about 5800 lines in irregular alliterative lines. [Cf. 4262, and a prose version in Lincoln Cath. 91, ff. 1a-49a].
1. Bodl. 6925, f. 1a (vv. 23-803 parallel 4262 (A); vv. 4019-4714 parallel 4262 B); 2. Trinity Dublin 213, ff. 27a-66b (vv. 678-3296, 3356-3426 of MS. 1, with an extra vv. 122); 3. James Fairhurst (fragment).
1, 2. Skeat, *EETS* xlvii; Stevenson, *Roxburghe Club* 1849.

3947.6   When fortune had me avaunsyd
Welcome, pain—two stanzas rime royal.
1. Royal App. 58, f. 21b.
Flügel, *Anglia* XII. 267.

3948   Ritson, *Anc. Songs*, 1877, p. 111; 1829, I. 129; Robbins, *PMLA* LXIX. 639.

3949   *Gentleman's Magazine*, May 1842, p. 465.

Whan Gabryell our lady grette   See 1920 (de Worde).

3950   two macaronic 5-line stanzas and Latin burden.
Rickert, *Anc. Eng. Xmas Carols*, pp. 128-9; Stevens, *Med. Carols*, p. 81.

When game is best / Hit is tyme to rest   See 4034.6.

3951.5   When gonewey shall on curtays calle
A prophecy following 3943 in one MS.—one 8-line stanza.
1. Pepys 1236, f. 91a.
Robbins, *Hist. Poems*, pp. 316-7.

Whan Harflete was gette that ryall toune
See 969 (Passus II of Cotton MS. var.).

3954.5 Quhen halie kirk first flurest in southheid
On conscience, by Gawin Douglas—four stanzas rime royal.
[Cf. Advocates 1. 1. 6, f. 89b].
1. Pepys 2553, p. 192.
Pinkerton, *Anc. Scot. Poems*, 1786; Small, *Works*, I. 121; Craigie, *STS* n.s. VII. 217-8.

3954.8 When I aduert in my remembraunce / The famous draughtes of poetes eloquent
The Example of Virtue, by Stephen Hawes—300 stanzas rime royal, inc. Prologue of four stanzas, in fourteen chapters.
de Worde, ca. 1510 (STC 12945); de Worde, ca. 1520 (STC 12946); de Worde, ca. 1530 (STC 12947); *repr.* Arber, *Dunbar Anthology*, pp. 219-95 (mod.).

Whan I aduerte to my remembrance   See 3955.

3955 six stanzas rime royal and one 8-line Envoy.[Ringler 84].
9. Harley 271, f. 26a (6 st.); 18. NLW Peniarth 481, f. 1a; 22. Rome: English Coll. 1306, f. 89a.
Caxton, ca. 1477 (STC 4850); ca. 1478 (STC 4851); ca. 1480 (STC 4852).

3955.5 When I aduertyse in my remembraunce / The manyfolde storyes
The Prologue to Fabyan's *Chronicle*—twenty-eight stanzas rime royal. [Cf. 4174.5].
Fabyan, *New Chronicles*, Pynson, 1516 (STC 10659); *repr.* Ellis, 1811, pp. 2-7.
[In the prose text are inserted numerous passages in verse, including some translations of hymns to the B.V. These are not given separate entries in this Supplement except where noted. Verses are found at the following pages of Ellis: 9, 19, 33, 40, 54, 74, 93, 126, 127, 146, 178, 185, 199, 200, 227-8, 238, 239-40 (Prologue to Part VII), 256, 259, 260 (1820.8), 264, 272, 275, 277, 281, 290 (Lenvoy), 293-5, 310, 314, 322-3 (2541.4), 335, 369, 388, 394, 405, 406-7, 420 (2039.3), 430, 431-2, 440 (1934), 488, 489, 569, 574-5, 590-1, 600-1 (1929), 603 (227.5), 603-4 (3866.3), 604 (3206.8), 604-5 (1929.3), 605 (1924.4), 605-6 (728.5), 606 (578.5), 606-7 (3785.8); 620, 672 (3318.7), 674-5, 682, 682-3.]

3956   A balade with refrain &c.

3957   Brusendorff, *Studies* &c., pp. 323-34.

3958   Whane I compleyne ther is no Resone
           A Lover's Plaint—fifty-five long lines with internal rime.
           1. Trinity Camb. 61, f. 100a.
              Person, *Camb. ME Lyrics*, pp. 55-6.

3958.5   When I hade nowght I did geve
           A promise to repay in time—six irregular lines.
           1. Sloane 3160, f. 173b.

3959   [Cf. 33.5 and 1484].
              Greene, *Sel. Eng. Carols*, p. 141.

           When I haue þat I wylle   See 3971.5.

3960.5   Quhen I len I am a freynd / And quhen I craif I am vnkynd
           Two couplets on the incommodities of lending. [Cf. 1297, 1400, 1640.5. Tilley F 723].
           1. Camb. Un. Ll. 5. 10, f. 57a; 2. Pepys 2553, p. 294; 3. Advocates 1. 1. 6, f. 122a and f. 147a.
              2. Craigie, *STS* n.s. VII. 344; 3a, 3b. Ritchie, *STS* n.s. XXII. 324; *STS* n.s. XXIII. 43; Ramsay, *Evergreen*, I. 107.

3961   Warton, *Hist. Eng. Poetry*, rev. Hazlitt, II. 38.

3962.5   When I reuolue yn my remembrance / Thys lyfe fugytyue
           The Epytaphye of Sir Gryffyth ap Ryse—nine stanzas rime royal. [See companion piece 2552.5; and cf. 3962].
           1. Bodl. 12653, f. 28b.
              Padelford and Benham, *Anglia* XXXI. 347-9.

3963   1. Brook, *Harley Lyrics*, pp. 54-5; Kaiser, *Anthologie*, p. 243; Kaiser, *Med. Eng.*, p. 286.

3964   twelve short lines.
              Davies, *Med. Eng. Lyrics*, p. 99.

3965   ten short lines.

3967   1. Bodl. 1687, f. 197b (adds 2 st. between 10 and 11).

Wan y thenke on þe hie tre
A song of sorrow: see 2289.3.

3969   [Cf. also 3199.5].
1. Balliol 354, f. 213b (followed by 2072.6).
1. Haupt and Hauffman, *Altdeutsche Blätter*, II. 142;
4. Kaiser, *Anthologie*, p. 204; Kaiser, *Med. Eng.*, p. 294.

3971   [Cf. 266.3].
Greene, *Sel. Eng. Carols*, p. 146.

When I wowe / golde in my glove   See 4020.6.

3973   5. Trinity Camb. 605, f. 1a (vv. 20), ff. 1b-6a (vv. 508),
f. 188a (vv. 78, inc. Fifteen Signs of Doomsday, from 3349);
10. Winchester Coll. 33, ff. 1a-11b.

3973.5 Qwen it is song it has no myht
Man compared to a summer flower—three lines.
1. Hereford Cath. O. iii. 5, f. 48b.

3975   2. Stevens, *Med. Carols*, p. 97.

Whan Ianus bifrons in cold Ienuarie
Extract (The Circumcision) from Lydgate's *Life of Our Lady* (Book IV): see 2574 (MS. 30).

3976.5 When Jesus Christ was twelve yeare olde
Twelve lines (ending incomplete).
1. Morgan Lib. *Royal Book*, Caxton.

3983   [Preceded by *Prohemium*, 4231. Utley 350].

Wanne king is radles   See 1820.

3985   11. Rylands Lib. Latin 201, f. 227a (vv. 2 only); 13. Wellcome Hist. Med. Lib. 673, f. 9a.
1, 2, 4-6, 10. Murray, *EETS* 141; 10. Fawtier, *BJRL* V. 389; Kaiser, *Med. Eng.*, p. 286; 13. Kane, *London Med. St.* II. 66-7.

When lordes wille is londes law　　See 3943.

3986　　　[Delete entire entry].

Whan lordes wol leese þeire olde lawes　　See 3943.

3987　　　Whan lordschype fayleth / gode felawschipe awayleth
　　　　　Signs of degeneracy—a couplet heading to 2262.3.
　　　　　　1. Trinity Dublin 516, f. 22b.
　　　　　　　Robbins, *PMLA* LXXI. 266; Robbins, *Hist. Poems*, p. 189.

3988　　　Stevens, *Med. Carols*, p. 87.

3989　　　Scott, *Minstrelsy of Scot. Border*, 1833; rev. Henderson, IV. 99; Robbins, *Hist. Poems*, p. 29.

3990.5　　Quhen Merche wes with variand windis past
　　　　　'The Thrissil and the Rois,' by William Dunbar—twenty-seven stanzas rime royal.
　　　　　　1. Advocates 1. 1. 6, f. 342b.
　　　　　　　Ramsay, *Evergreen*, I. 15-26; [Hailes,] *Anc. Scot. Poems*, pp. 1-8; *Ramsay and Earlier Scot. Poets*, pp. 220-2; *Select Poems of Dunbar*, Perth 1788, pp. 13-22; Sibbald, *Chronicle*, I. 264-72; *The Union*, Edinburgh 1753, London 1759, pp. 1-9; Brydges, *Restituta*, 1815, II. 508-15; Ritson, *Caledonian Muse*, 1821, p. 12; Laing, *Dunbar*, I. 3-10; *Blackwood's Magazine*, Feb. 1835; Kaufmann, *Traité de la langue...Dunbar*, pp. 23-46; Paterson, *Dunbar*, pp. 118-25; *Bannatyne MS.*, Hunt. Club, IV. 988-94; Skeat, *Specimens*, 1871, pp. 109-17; Small, *STS* IV. 183-9; Browne, *Early Scot. Poets*, pp. 114-21; Eyre-Todd, *Med. Scot. Poetry*, pp. 170-76; Schipper, *Dunbar*, pp. 93-100; and *DKAW* XL (IV). 2-10; Baildon, *Dunbar*, pp. 39-45; Arber, *Dunbar Anthology*, pp. 36-40; Smith, *Spec. Middle Scots*, pp. 27-34; Ritchie, *STS* n.s. XXVI. 246-52; MacKenzie, *Dunbar*, pp. 107-12; Kinsley, *Dunbar*, pp. 10-15.

3992　　　de Worde, 1509 (STC 19305).

3993　　　[Delete entire entry].

When mametri is beate downe　　See 3912.5.

3996   1. Davies, *Med. Eng. Lyrics*, pp. 117-19.

3997   6. Turnbull, *Legendae Catholicae*, p. 126.

3997.5   When me[n] profereth þe pigge open þe pogh
Beware a pig in a poke—one long couplet. [Cf. Heywood].
1. Bodl. 21626, f. 27b.
Förster, *Festschrift zum 12 Deutschen Neuphilologentage*, p. 54.

3998   Davies, *Med. Eng. Lyrics*, pp. 74-5.

3999   [Cf. Advocates 1. 1. 6, f. 155b, pr. *STS* n.s. XXIII. 66; f. 266a, pr. *STS* n.s. XXVI. 42; f. 266b, pr. *STS* n.s. XXVI. 44. Cf. 3928.3. For a later satirical religious adaptation see 4056.5. Cf. *JEFDSS* IV. 130. Utley 351].
3. B.M. IB 55252: Trevisa, *Bartholomeus Anglicus*, f. 477b.
1. FitzGibbon, *E. E. Poetry*, p. 200; C. Wells, *Nonsense Anthology*, p. 186; 2. [Masters,] *Rymes of Minstrels*, pp. 18-9; Robbins, *Sec. Lyrics*, p. 103; Davies, *Med. Eng. Lyrics*, pp. 223-4; 3. Utley, *PMLA* LX 346-7.

4000   six 7-line stanzas.
Early Eng. Carols, p. 229.

4001   1. NLW Deposit: Porkington 10, f. 200a.

4002   2. Heuser, *Anglia* XXVII. 293-7.

4002.5   Qvhen paill Aurora with face lamentabill
The Palice of Honour by Gawin Douglas—in 9-line stanzas (including Prologue and Text and Epilogue to James IV).
Copland, 1553 (STC 7073); Edinburgh 1579; *Select Works*, Perth 1787, pp. 1-88; Pinkerton, *Scotish Poems*, 1792; *Bannatyne Club* XVII; Small, *Works*, I. 1-81; Sibbald, *Chronicle*, I. 386-423 (selections); Davidson, Edinburgh 1540 (fragments); repr. Beattie, *Edinb. Bibl. Soc. Trans.* III. 31-46.

4004   [For extracts occurring separately see 2318, 2532.5].
de Worde, ca. 1509 (STC 12948); 1517 (STC 12949); *repr.* Mead, *EETS* 173; Hammond, *Eng. Verse Chaucer-Surrey*, pp. 268-86, 487-95 (extracts); Wayland, ca. 1554 (STC 12950); repr. Southey, *Sel. Works Brit. Poets*, 1831; Tottel, 1555

(STC 12951); Waley, 1555 (STC 12952); *repr.* Wright, *Percy Soc.* XVIII.

4005 [Ringler 85].
de Worde, ca. 1498 (STC 17005); de Worde, n.d. (STC 17006); *repr.* Jenkinson, 1906; de Worde, ca. 1500 (STC 17007).

4005.3 Quhen phebus fair wt bemis bricht
A song of impossibilities with lying refrain: 'Than will my reuerend lady on me rew'—six stanzas rime royal. [Cf. 3999. Utley 353].
1. Advocates 1. 1. 6, f. 249b.
Bannatyne MS., Hunt. Club, p. 728; Ritchie, *STS* n.s. XXIII. 356.

4005.5 Quhone pryd is in pryce / And wit is in covatyce
A political prophecy for Scotland's prosperity in A.D. 1581, incorporating a version of the Abuses of the Age (cf. 4006)—vv. 14 in couplets.
1. Camb. Un. Ll. 5. 10, f. 57a; 2. Pepys 2553, p. 293.
2. Craigie, *STS* n.s. VII. 342.

4006 3. Sloane 2578, f. 44b (variant, in -les).

Qwan prestis faylin in her sawes   See 3943 (MS. 17).

4007 [Delete entire entry].

4008 Qwhen Rome is removyde into Inglande
The Second Scottish Prophecy—in couplets. [All MSS. show considerable variations, but derive from an original short prophecy, Scottish in sympathy, developing some of the symbols used by Geoffrey of Monmouth. This entry incorporates 4007, 4009, 4010, 4011, all now deleted. Some MSS. include verses on the Abuses of the Age (4006)].
A Text:
1. Bodl. Lyell 35, ff. 24a-25b; 2. Camb. Un. Kk. 1. 5, IV, ff. 33a-34 (vv. 71); 3. NLW Peniarth 26, pp. 129-31; 4. NLW Peniarth 50, pp. 4-7 (vv. 90); 5. NLW Peniarth 94, pp. 174, 262, 167 (first vv. 35; then another 33 vv.; and last vv. 13); 6. National Lib. of Wales Addit. 441C, pp. 49-51 (vv. 86); 7. Llanstephen 119 (vv. 95); 8. Public Record Office, State Papers Henry VIII; 9. Westminster Abbey 27, f. 31b; 10. Mostyn 133, pp. 331-41 (vv. 96).

Fragments: a. Harley 559, f. 10a (vv. 7); b. Sloane 2578, ff. 44b-45a (a medley of single lines written as prose); c. Sloane 2578, f. 67a (vv. 1-40); d. NLW Peniarth 26, p. 127 (vv. 7).
B Text (begins at v. 16 of A Text):
11. Cotton Vesp. E. viii, ff. 21a-22b (vv. 87); 12. Sloane 1802, ff. 10b-14b (vv. 90).
C Text:
13. Cotton Cleo. C. iv, f. 86b (vv. 14); 14. Royal 7. A. ix, ff. 4a-4b (vv. 14); 15. NLW Peniarth 26, p. 122; 16. NLW Peniarth 94, p. 257; 17. Llanstephen 119, p. 177.

Whole Prophesie of Scotland, Waldegrave, 1603 (Prophecie of St. Beid, B Text, vv. 90); *repr.* Laing, *Anc. Scot. Prophecies*, Bannatyne Club, 1833, XLIV. 9; 2, 14. Robbins, *Hist. Poems*, pp. 118, 313; 2. Stevenson, *Maitland Club* XLVIII. 157; Lumby, *EETS* 42. 32; 8. Furnivall, *Ballads from MSS.*, Ballad Soc. 1868, I. 317; 13. Wright, *Polit. Poems*, II. 249; crit. ed. Haferkorn, *Beiträge zur englischen Philologie* XIX. 92, 104, 112, 114.

4009   [Delete entire entry].

4010   [Delete entire entry].

4011   [Delete entire entry].

4012   Rickert, *Anc. Eng. Xmas Carols*, pp. 124-5.

4014.5   When shall yor cruell stormes be past
A lover's plea and his lady's response—two 6-line stanzas.
1. Trinity Camb. 1450, f. 85b (added in a xvi cent. hand).

4014.8   Quhen sharpe & fairfeld are maried in fere
A prophecy—two couplets.
1. Rylands Lib. Latin 228, f. 49b.

When 6 is the best cast of the dyse   See 734.8.

4015   James, *Cat.*, I. 44 (st. 1 only).

4016   [Cf. 4167].

4017   [All texts show variations. Singer 812].
[Revise listing of MSS. as follows:]

1. Bodl. 6954, ff. 106b-113b (vv. 448); 2. Bodl. 7577, p. 254 (vv. 65; ends imperfectly); 3. Sloane 1098, ff. 47b-48a (var., about vv. 100); 4. Sloane 1098, ff. 5a-7a (short version); 5. Sloane 1423, ff. 37b-39b; 6. Sloane 1787, ff. 111a-117b; 7. Sloane 2036, ff. 22a-25a; 8. Sloane 3747, ff. 110a-115b; 9. Lichfield Cath.; 10. Massachusetts Hist. Soc., Winthrop 20 c, ff. 21a-24b.

Ashmole, *Theatrum Chemicum*, pp. 380-8 (short version).

4018   A political prophecy according to the throw of the dice, with an introduction of four lines—in couplets. [For texts without the introduction see 734.8].
[Revise listing of MSS. as follows:]
1. Camb. Un. Ii. 6, 11, flyleaf (vv. 14); 2. Cotton Rolls II. 23, Art. 19 (vv. 20); 3. Harley 559, f. 34a (vv. 23).
[Delete 5. Furnivall, &c.] 1. Furnivall, *Ballads from MSS.*, Ballad Soc. I. 477.

4018.5 Chwen sonday goth by E d and C/ And prime by on and too
A political prophecy—one quatrain (the first line similar to that of 4018).
1. Peniarth 26, p. 59.

When sparrowys bild church & stepulles hie   See 3999.

4019   [Ringler 86. Singer 807. Cf. Utley 38, 81, 261, 303, 339].
I. Perfect texts:
11. Rylands Lib. Eng. 113 [olim Hodson 39], ff. 6-194.
II. Imperfect texts:
19. Bodl. 6420 (Barlow 20), f. 1a [A. 574]; 46. *olim* Brudenell, Lamport: [*olim* Cardigan] (Sotheby's Sale, Feb. 1959), f. 1a [A.153]; 47. Princeton Univ. Lib. [olim Helmingham Hall], f. 1a [A. 1975]; 50. Penrose 6 [olim Delamere], f. 20a [A. 177], 54. Bibl. Bodmeriana, Coligny, Genève [*olim* Rosenbach 156, *olim* Phillipps 8136], f. 1a; 55. Rosenbach Foundation 1084/1 [*olim* Phillipps 8137], f. 1a [A. 2718].
III. Fragmentary texts:
62. (b) Rosenbach Foundation 1084/2 [*olim* W. A. White], ff. 11 [A. 4246]; 64. Newberry Lib., Louis H. Silver 2, (a) ff. 12; (b) ff. 12.
IV. Separate Tales:
Group B. 70. Delete this MS.; 74. Chetham Lib. 6709, ff. 173a-178b. [And cf. 4231].
Group F. 81. Delete this MS.: 82 (transcript by John Lane, 1615). Bodl. 21744, ff. v. verso -35a; 82a (transcript by John Lane, 1630). Bodl. 6937, f. 1a.

Group G. 83. Delete this MS.; 85. Chetham Lib. 6709, ff. 160a-173a.
V. Spurious Links:
ClT to FranklT. MSS. 6, 9, 15, 19, 37, 42, 49, 53.
MerchT to WBT. MSS. 9, 15, 19.
SqT to WBT. MS. 8.
PardT to ShipT. a. MSS. 1, 2, 4, 6, 9, 13, 15, 19, 21, 28, 29, 33, 37, 41, 42, 53. b. MS. 8.
FranklT to PhysT. Tyrwhitt.
NPT to SecNT. MSS. 5, 10, 11, 46.
CYT to PhysT. a. MSS. 1, 2, 4, 9, 15, 17, 18, 19, 21, 28, 33, 36, 38, 42, 44, 53. b. MS. 8
Concl. to ClT. MS. 17.
Concl. to SqT. MS. 18.

    Caxton, 1478 (STC 5082); Caxton, ca. 1484 (STC 5083); Pynson, ca. 1492 (STC 5084); de Worde, 1498 (STC 5085); *Chaucer*, Thynne, 1532 (STC 5068); Thynne, 1542 (STC 5069); Stow, 1561 (STC 5075); Speght, 1598 (STC 5077); Speght, 1602 (STC 5080).

4020   Halliwell, *Nugae Poeticae*, 1844, pp. 1-12.

4020.3   When that byrdes be brought to rest / Wythe joy & myrth
Your bird shall hop in my cage: a dialogue between a lover and a lass—eight cross-rimed quatrains.
1. Bodl. 12653, f. 60a.
Zupitza, *Archiv* LXXXVII. 433; Padelford and Benham, *Anglia* XXXI. 380-1.

4020.6   When þat I wowe / goold is in my glove inowe
Two proverbial couplets, tr. '*Cum procor, est aurum cirothecis* &c.'
1. Bodl. 21626, f. 28a; 2. Rylands Lib. Latin 394, f. 18a.
1. Förster, *Festschrift zum 12 Deutschen Neuphilologentage*, p. 55; 2. Pantin, *BJRL* XIV. 105.

4021   1. Fitzwilliam Mus. McClean 182, f. 139a.

4023   *Christmas Carolles*, Kele, ca. 1550 (STC 5205); *facs.* Reed, *Xmas Carols*, pp. 32-4.

4026   *Chaucer*, Speght, 1598 (STC 5077); *repr.* Urry, *Chaucer*, 1721, p. 473; Bell, *Poets of Great Britain*, XII. 83; [Anderson,] *Poets of Great Britain*, I. 532; Todd, *Gower & Chaucer*, p. 203; Chalmers, *English Poets*, I. 394; *British*

Poets, Chiswick 1822, V. 139; Moxon, *Chaucer*, p. 405; [Pickering,] *Aldine British Poets*, 1845, VI. 244; 1866, IV. 86; Bell, *Chaucer*, IV. 350; Ellis, *Floure and Leafe*, Hammersmith 1896; Skeat, *Oxf. Ch.*, VII. 361; Ashbee, London 1902; Pearsall, London 1962.

4028   Lives of four Julians &c.

*Whan the aungell Aue began   See 3385 (Kele text).

4028.3   Qwan the belle ys solemplye rownge
       Epitaph, A.D. 1481, for Sir Thomas Bettys—two couplets.
       Beauties of England, II. 209; Pettigrew, *Chronicles of Tombs*, p. 49.

Quan þe cherye was a flour þan hadde it non ston   See 1303.

4028.6   When the clot klyngueth and the cucko syngith
       In the spring a young man's fancy: a schoolboy's exercise—five riming lines with a Latin translation. [Cf. 430.8].
       1. Harley 1002, f. 72b.
       Wright, *RES* n.s. II. 119.

4029   The First Scottish Prophecy—in alliterative cross-rimed quatrains. [For a later adaptation see BM Addit. 28789, f. 239b; pr. Hales and Furnivall, *Percy Folio MS.*, III. 372-3].
       [Revise listing of MSS. as follows:]
       1. Bodl. Lyell 35, ff. 26a-27a; 2. Camb. Un. Kk. 1. 5, IV, ff. 25a-26a (vv. 139); 3. Caius 249, ff. 227b-228b (vv. 40); 4. Cotton Rolls ii. 23, Art 8 (vv. 75); 5. Harley 559, f. 43b (vv. 76); 6. Harley 1717, f. 249b (vv. 72); 7. Lansdowne 762, f. 62a (vv. 81, part of 365); 8. Sloane 1802, f. 7a; 9. Sloane 2578, ff. 15b-17a, and ff. 100b-102a (part of 365); 10. Sloane 4031, f. 189b (vv. 80); 11. BM Addit. 24663, ff. 13b-17b; 12. NLW Peniarth 26, pp. 39-41; 13. NLW Peniarth 50, pp. 1-3; 14. NLW Peniarth 58, p. 18; 15. Trinity Dublin 516, f. 114a (vv. 78; preceded by 4030.5); 16. Westminster Abbey 27, f. 82a; 17. NLW Deposit: Porkington 10, ff. 192a-193b.
       Whole Prophesie of Scotland, Waldegrave, Edinburgh 1603; *repr.* Laing, *Bannatyne Club*, 1833, XLIV. 6; 2. Lumby, *EETS* 42. 18; 4. Robbins, *Hist. Poems*, p. 115; 6. Hermentrude, *N&Q* 3 s. VIII. 326; *comp. text.* Brandl,

> Sitzungsberichte der königliche Preussischen Akademie der Wissenschaften, Berlin 1909, p. 1166; Haferkorn, Beiträge zur englischen Philologie XIX. 109.

4030.5 When þe dede arysen & comen hom
A political prophecy: wonders in England — two lines preceding 4029 in one MS.
1. Trinity Dublin 516, f. 114a.

4031 Horstmann, *York. Wr.*, I. 156.

4033 Furnivall, *EETS* 15 orig. ed. 220-21; rev. ed. 249-50.

When þe fote warmes   See 4079.3.

4034 [Delete entire entry].

When þe Flemmyng wer fressh florisshid   See 4056.8.

4034.3 Wen þe fox prechys / kep wyll þe ges
An English proverbial tag in a Latin and English collection.
1. NLW Peniarth 356, p. 195.

4034.6 When þe game ys best / yt ys tyme to rest
A proverbial couplet. [Occurs also in 3502].
1. Bodl. 1851, f. 99b; 2. Bodl. 14526, f. 54b; 3. Bodl. 15444, f. 141b; 4. Bodl. 21626, f. 21a; 5. Rylands Lib. Latin 394, f. 10b.
1. Schleich, *Anglia* LI. 222; 2. Zupitza, *Archiv* XC. 245; 3. Meech, *MP* XXXVIII. 120; 4. Förster, *Festschrift zum 12 Deutschen Neuphilologentage*, p. 49; 5. Pantin, *BJRL* XIV. 99.

4035 15. Egerton 833, f. 10b (var.); 16. Longleat 29, f. 3a.
9-12. Person, *Camb. ME Lyrics*, pp. 19-20; 3. *Eng. Lyr. XIII C.*, p. 222.

4036.5 Wen þe nese blakes and þe lyppe quakes
Signs of death — nine lines. [Cf. 4031, 4033, 4047].
1. Trinity Dublin 312, f. 152a.

4037   Strutt, *Horda Angel-Cynnan*, III. 151-2; Williams, *New Book Eng. Verse*, pp. 23-4; Dickins and Wilson, *Early ME Texts*, p. 123; Mossé, *Handbook*, pp. 207-8; Brook, *Harley Lyrics*, p. 63; Kaiser, *Anthologie*, p. 292; Kaiser, *Med. Eng.*, p. 464; Davies, *Med. Eng. Lyrics*, pp. 62-3.

4038   2. Aberdeen Univ. 154, f. 155b.

4038.5   When the pellican begynnyth to fle
         A political prophecy—eleven quatrains (ends imperfectly).
         1. NLW Peniarth 50, pp. 269-70.

4039   Hollander, *Untuning of Sky*, pp. 427-32.

4040   seven couplets.

4040.3   Wen þe rede is god / I þe litele þolemod
         Four short lines paraphrasing Latin: '*Non humilis paruus.*'
         1. Trinity Camb. 323, f. 28b.

4040.6   When þe rofe of þyn hous lithe on þi nese / Alle þe worldis blisse ys noth worthe a pese
         A proverbial couplet.
         1. Camb. Un. Ii. 3. 8, f. 172a.
           Owst, *Lit & Pulpit*, p. 43.

4041   [Delete this entry].

4042   [Preceded by a Balade introduction of five stanzas, 102.5].

4042.5   When þe snail renneþ and þe see brenneþ
         One gnomic couplet on cast of dice (?).
         1. Egerton 2788, f. 53b.

4043   467 lines in rough doggerel couplets.
         Hammond, *MP* XXI. 384-95.

4044   Dickins and Wilson, *Early ME Texts*, p. 127; Peter, *Complaint and Satire*, p. 73.

4044.3   Whan the whelpe gameth / the old dogge grenneth
A proverbial couplet.
1. Balliol 354, f. 200b.
Flügel, *Anglia* XXVI. 203; Dyboski, *EETS* ci. 132.

4044.6   When the wyntar wynddys ar vanished away
In praise of women—in 12-line stanzas.
1. Bodl. 6933, ff. 88a-90b.
Wright, *Songs & Ballads*, Roxburghe Club, 1860, LXXVIII. 145-9.

*When they to Calas come / all this comely meany   See 1011.5.

4046   preceded by Latin equivalent: '*Oculi cum occultentur* &c.'
Person, *Camb. ME Lyrics*, p. 21.

4049.2   When tho herd hat Rome
Conform to your surroundings—two couplets translating '*Cum fueris Rome* &c.' [Tilley R 165].
1. Bodl. 15444, f. 142b; 2. Balliol 354, f. 188a.
1. Meech, *MP* XXXVIII. 122; 2. Flügel, *Anglia* XXVI. 202; Dyboski, *EETS* ci. 130; Tilley, p. 575.

4049.3   Whanne þou begynnyst a thynge / thynk on the endynge
A proverb, also used as a motto on a scroll in one MS. of Hoccleve's *De Regimine Principum* (3831)—one couplet. [Cf. 37.5].
1. Bodl. 21626, f. 29a; 2. Camb. Un. Hh. 4. 11, f. 36a and f. 58a.
1. Förster, *Festschrift zum 12 Deutschen Neuphilologentage*, p. 55.

Whene þou commys before a lord   See 4153.

4049.5   When thou hast gathered all þat thou may
The inevitability of death—one couplet. [Cf. 397].
1. Harley 2321, f. 148b.
Rel. Ant., I. 208.

4049.6 Wen tho lest wenis *veniet mors te superare*
　　　　The inevitability of death—two macaronic couplets.
　　　　1. BM Addit. 37049, f. 33a (preceding 1563; cf. 3252.5); 2. York Minster XVI. G. 5, f. 26b.
　　　　　1. Brunner, *Archiv* CLXVII. 30.

4049.7 When þou lyes vnder þe ston
　　　　The sorrow and woe of Death—three couplets.
　　　　1. Hereford Cath. O. iii. 5, f. 48b.

4049.8 When þou myght no lengur spek
　　　　The death of Man—two couplets.
　　　　1. Hereford Cath. O. iii. 5, f. 49b.

4050　　(ca. A.D. 1191).
　　　　Stubbs, *Chronicle of Benedict of Peterborough*, Rolls Series XLIX, ii. 139; Riley, *Roger of Hoveden*, ii. 170; Saintsbury, *Prosody*, I. 28; Taylor, *Pol. Prophecy*, p. 22.

4051　　1. Jesus Oxf. 29, Part II, f. 184b.

4052.5 When thou shalte se towe knytte in one
　　　　A colophon at the end of Ripley's alchemical receipts—one cross-rimed quatrain.
　　　　1. Bodl. 11645, f. 71a.

4053　　[Cf. Bühler, *MLN* LVI. 351-5].
　　　　2. Durham Cath. B. iii. 34, dorso (15 quatrains).
　　　　　1. Förster, *Archiv* CXXVIII. 285-7.

　　　　Whan thy hed quakes *memento*　　　See 4035.

4053.5 Wan tyati can ournest me
　　　　On the mercy of Jesus—five macaronic lines. [Follows 2788 in the MS. and precedes 3351].
　　　　1. Ghent Univ. 317.
　　　　　Logeman, *Archiv* LXXXVII. 432.

4054　　Brown, *MLN* XLIX. 394.

4056   The second song in Rolle's *Form of Living* (cap. viii).
[These lines in varying form occur in the '*Cantus amoris*' —see 2270. For the First Song see 2017.5].
[Revise listing of MSS. as follows:]
1. Bodl. 1292, f. 13b; 2. Bodl. 1619, f. 85b; 3. Bodl. 1963, f. 148a; 4. Bodl. 3938, f. 336b col ii; 5. Bodl. 11272, f. 91b; 6. Bodl. 12143, f. 51b; 7. Univ. Coll. Oxf. 97, f. 146b; 8. Camb. Un. Dd. 5. 64, Part III, f. 15a; 9. Camb. Un. Ff. 5. 45; 10. Camb. Un. Hh. 1. 12; 11. Camb. Un. Ii. 4. 9; 12. Camb. Un. Ii. 6. 55; 13. Caius 669, f. 189a; 14. Trinity Camb. 322, f. 141a; 15. Trinity Camb. 1053, f. 111b; 16. Harley 1022, f. 57a; 17. Lansdowne 455, f. 38a col ii; 18. BM Addit. 22283, f. 149a; 19. BM Addit. 37790, f. 131a; 20. Chetham Lib. 6690; 21. Hereford Cath. P. i. 9; 22. Trinity Dublin 155, pp. 26-7; 23. Westminster School; 24. *olim* Gurney; 25. *olim* Harmsworth [*olim* Amherst]; 26. Longleat 29, f. 39a; 27. Huntington HM 127 [*olim* Powis]; 28. Paris: Bibl. Mazarine 514; 29. Paris: Bibl. St. Geneviève 339, f. 81a; 30. Morgan Lib. M. 818, f. 12a.

6, 8. Horstmann, *York. Wr.*, I. 34; 8. Allen, *Eng. Writings of Rolle*, p. 107; 18. Comper, *Life & Lyrics of Rolle*, pp. 224-5.

4056.3   Wanne hol man is turned into half man
Death comes fast—three lines in a Latin sermon.
1. Camb. Un. Ii. 3. 8, f. 84b.

4056.5   When wreneys weare wodknyves Cranes for to kyll
A lying-song satirizing priests' wives—seven quatrains. [Based on 3999. Utley 361].
1. Public Rec. Office, State Papers Henry VIII.
Furnivall, *Ballads from MSS.*, Ballad Soc. I. 313-5.

4056.8   When ye fflemmyng wer fressh florisshid in youre flouris
Mocking song against the Flemings (A.D. 1436)—thirty-three couplets inserted in a prose *Brut*.
1. Lambeth 6, f. 256a.
Williams, *Archaeologia* XXXIII. 130-2; Brie, *EETS* 136. 582-4; James and Jenkins, *Cat.*, p. 16; Robbins, *Hist. Poems*, pp. 83-5.

4057   1. Bodl. Lat. misc. c. 66 [*olim* Capesthorne], f. 93a.
Robbins, *PMLA* LXV. 263-4.

*Where ben men biforn ous were   See 3310 (Advocates MS.).

4058   vv. 560 in couplets.

4058.3   Wher be ye / My love my love
'No comfortyng but yow'—five 6-line tail-rime stanzas. [Possibly a modified carol in four stanzas and introductory burden].
1. BM Addit. 31922, f. 110b.
Flügel, *Anglia* XII. 251-2; Flügel, *Neuengl. Lesebuch*, p. 137; Stevens, *Music & Poetry*, pp. 420-1; Stevens, *Music at Court*, pp. 80-1.

4058.5   Were erys are there are causes / Where women be there are wordys
A proverbial couplet.
Salamon and Marcolphus, Leeu, Antwerp ca. 1492 (STC 22905); *facs.* Duff, London 1892.

4058.8   Where ffrom euer thys boke be com
Book plate of William Barbor—one couplet. [Cf. 4126].
1. Camb. Un. Ii. 6. 4, f. 1b.
Rel. Ant., II. 64; Bennett, *England Chaucer-Caxton*, p. 161; Robbins, *Sec. Lyrics*, p. 257.

4059   two stanzas rime royal. [Possibly 4241.5 serves as an Envoy].
1. Camb. Un. Ff. 1. 6, f. 20b.
Robbins, *PMLA* LXIX. 632; Person, *Camb. ME Lyrics*, p. 34.

4060   1. Trinity Camb. 263, f. 118a.
James, *Cat.*, I. 375 (vv. 1-2 only); Person, *MLQ* I. 243; Wilson, *MLN* LXIX. 22.

4062   1. Rylands Lib. Eng. 113, f. iii.
Furnivall, *EETS* 15 rev. ed. xlvi-xlviii; Robbins, *Hist. Poems*, pp. 111-13.

4063   Where so euer y be come ouer all / I belonge to the chappell of gonvylle hall
Wordsworth and Littlehales, *Old Service Books*, p. 62.

4064   vv. 597 in couplets. [Ringler 87, who suggests vv. 305-484 may have belonged originally to another work].
1. Bodl. 14637, ff. 1a-11a; 2. Lambeth 491 B, ff. 287a-294b.
Boke of Huntyng, St. Albans, 1486 (STC 3308); *facs.* Blades, 1881; de Worde, 1496 (STC 3309); *repr.* Flügel, *Neuengl. Lesebuch*, pp. 12-13 (extracts).

4064.5   Wher sorow dothe sorow slake
           Two gnomic couplets.
           1. Rylands Lib. Latin 228, f. 65b.

           Where þat dede flesche be in a mannys bowk   See 2627.

4065   1. Delete this MS.
           2. *Rel. Lyr. XV C.*, pp. 119-20; Rickert, *Anc. Eng. Xmas Carols*, pp. 168-9.

4066   Robbins, *Hist. Poems*, pp. 106-8.

4067   1. Egerton 3309 [*olim* Castle Howard], p. 204.

4068.3   Wherfor pray we to hym to make vs studfast yn our fay
           Two couplets in Mirk's *Festial*.
           1. Bodl. 4124; 2. Bodl. 17680; 3. Camb. Un. Dd. 10. 50; 4. Caius 168; 5. Cotton Claud. A. ii; 6. Harley 2403; 7. Harley 2417; 8. Southwell Cath. VII.
           2. Erbe, *EETS* xcvi. 20-1.

4068.6   Wherfore shuld I hang up my bow
           A 'jolly forester:' the lover still active—four quatrains and refrain, with 4-line introduction: 'I am a joly foster.' [For a companion piece see 1303.5].
           1. BM Addit. 31922, f. 69b.
              Flügel, *Anglia* XII. 245-6; Flügel, *Neuengl. Lesebuch*, p. 151; *Early Eng. Lyrics*, p. 246; *Early Eng. Carols*, p. 314; Stevens, *Music & Poetry*, pp. 410-11; Stevens, *Music at Court*, pp. 50-1.

4070.5   Whereto shuld I expresse / My inwarde heuynesse
           Until we meet again—six cross-rimed quatrains.
           1. BM Addit. 31922, f. 51b.
              Chappell, *OE Pop. Music*, I. 45-6; Flügel, *Anglia* XII. 241; Flügel, *Neuengl. Lesebuch*, p. 135; Trefusis, *Songs Henry VIII*, Roxburghe Club CLXI. 20; *Early Eng. Lyrics*, p. 55; *Oxford Book XVI C. Verse*, p. 35; Stevens, *Music & Poetry*, p. 404; Stevens, *Music at Court*, p. 37.

4071   Which had that affiaunce and inspiracion / The monasterie of workssoppe first to bee founde
             twenty-six stanzas rime royal.
           1 (1587 transcription). Lansdowne 205, ff. 167b-168b.

4073   Clive, *Roxburghe Club*, 1835, L. 61-90; Horstmann, *O. Bokenams Leg.*, pp. 54-80.

4073.3   While fortune the favorethe frendes thow hast plentye
            Friends fickle as Fortune—one 6-line stanza.
            1. Durham Univ. Cosin V. iii. 9, f. 64b.
            Furnivall, *EETS* lxi. 197.

4073.5   Quyles I am song whom schold I dred
            Warning to young notorious livers: a dialogue—three quatrains.
            1. Bodl. 1292, f. 186a.

4074.5   While I haue in mynde / The blode of hyme that was so kynde
            Three couplets in the *Gesta Romanorum*. [Cf. 3568.5].
            1. BM Addit. 9066, f. 53b.
            Madden, *Roxburghe Club*, 1838, LV. 406.

4076   Short preface of three couplets (tr. *Incendium Amoris*, XV. 189) and 44 short lines.

4076.5   Whiles I synge in selkouthe soune
            An irregular couplet in Rolle's English Psalter (Ps. 56). [For further MSS. see Allen, *Rolle*, pp. 170-7].
            1. Bodl. 4127, f. 85b; 2. Univ. Coll. Oxf. 64.
            1. Allen, *Eng. Writings of Rolle*, p. 16; 2. Bramley, Oxford 1884.

4077   Stevens, *Med. Carols*, p. 103.

            Quhylome in grece that nobill regioun   See 3183.

            Whilles lyue or breth is in my brest   See 2271.2.

4079   Owst, *Lit. & Pulpit*, p. 429.

4079.3   While the fote warmith / the shoe harmith
            A proverbial couplet. [Cf. Heywood].
            1. Bodl. 15444, f. 142b; 2. Balliol 354, f. 191b; 3. Harley 3362, f. 2b; 4. Rylands Lib. Latin 394, f. 4a.
            1. Meech, *MP* XXXVIII. 122; 2. Dyboski, *EETS* ci. 128; 4. Pantin, *BJRL* XIV. 94.

4079.6 While the gresse growith / the hors stervith
A proverbial couplet. [Cf. Heywood].
1. Bodl. 15444, f. 141b; 2. Bodl. 21626, f. 15b; 3. Balliol 354, f. 191b and f. 200b; 4. Harley 2321, f. 149a; 5. Rylands Lib. Latin 394, f. 7b.
2, 3, 4. Förster, *Festschrift zum 12 Deutschen Neuphilologentage*, p. 45; 1. Meech, *MP* XXXVIII. 120; 3. Flügel, *Anglia* XXVI. 203; Dyboski, *EETS* ci. 128, 132; 4. *Rel. Ant.*, I. 208; 5. Pantin, *BJRL* XIV. 97.

4079.8 Wil þe hund gnageþ bon / ifere neede he non
A proverbial couplet.
1. Trinity Camb. 1149, f. 351a; 2. Harley 3362, f. 7a.
1. Förster, *Eng. Stn.* XXXI. 8.

Wylum the wordule was stedefaste and stable
See 3190 (MS. Trinity Camb. 921).

4081 in 12-line stanzas. [Cf. 4132].
1. Penrose 6 [*olim* Delamere], f. 164a (fragment, vv. 308).

4082 1. Bodl. 11951, ff. 142b-155a (vv. 610 &c.).

4083 1. Univ. Coll. Oxf. 33, f. 70a (with 'V and I' refrain).

4085 Kaiser, *Anthologie*, p. 272; Kaiser, *Med. Eng.*, p. 321.

4086 Clive, *Roxburghe Club*, 1835, L. 103-16; Serjeantson, *EETS* 206. 98-110.

Whilom yeris passed in the old dawes   See 3926.

4088 1. Allen, *Eng. Writings of Rolle*, p. 149; Comper, *Life & Lyrics of Rolle*, p. 227; 3. Wilson, *Lost Lit.*, p. 182; 5. Hearne, *Johannes de Fordun Scotichronicon*, 1722, V. 1398.

4090 The fickleness of women—thirteen 8-line stanzas with refrain: 'Pulle of her bellys & let her go flye.' [Utley 365].

4091 [= st. 11 of 2251 occurring separately. Utley 366].

4091.6   Wo hath non herynde feethe synde
         Two couplets in a Latin sermon.
         1. Camb. Un. Ii. 3. 8, f. 101a.

4092   one 8-line stanza.
         Robbins, *Sec. Lyrics*, p. 101.

4093   [Utley 369].
         Robbins, *Hist. Poems*, p. 324.

         Quha in welth takis no heid / he sall hafe falt in tyme of neid   See 4095.

*4094   *Hwo is ate kinge bord / and wıle anon for a word
         English verses in pencil, almost illegible—vv. 46 in all (beginning probably lost).
         1. Royal 11. C. iii. f. 248b.

         Quho is at my windo quho quho   See 4284.3.

4094.3   Who is my loue / but god aboue
         Reflections on the Passion, including prayers—five stanzas with 4-line refrain-heading: 'My lufe murnis for me.' [A religious adaptation of 2261.4; cf. *Gude* & *Godlie Ballatis*, p. 140].
         XX *Songes*, de Worde, 1530 (STC 22924); repr. Sibbald, *Chronicle*, III. 274; Flügel, *Anglia* XII. 595; Flügel, *Neuengl. Lesebuch*, pp. 127-8; Imelmann, *Shakespeare-Jahrbuch* XXXIX. 133-4; Rickert, *Anc. Eng. Xmas Carols*, pp. 140-2.

4094.5   Who is so wounded or ille bate
         'How a sicke man schal dyate him'—in couplets.
         1. BM Addit. 17866, f. 4a.

4094.8   Ho may þe lynn fle þat by þe wode went
         Three lines in a Latin sermon.
         1. Camb. Un. Ii. 3. 8, f. 72a.

4095   Who of plente wyll take no hede / Shal fynde defawte yn tyme of nede
         A moralizing couplet (included in longer series of proverbs against lending money; cf. 1640.5, 3256.6).

  1. Bodl. 14526, f. 55a; 2. Camb. Un. Ll. 5. 10, f. 57a; 3. Pepys 2553, p. 294; 4. Advocates 1. 1. 6, f. 122a.
  1. Zupitza, *Archiv* XC. 247; *Oxford Dict. Proverbs*, 1948, p. 507; 3. Craigie, *STS* n.s. VII. 344; 4. *Bannatyne MS.*, Hunt. Club, p. 346; Ritchie, *STS* n.s. XXII. 324; n.s. XXIII. 43.

4095.5 Who openeth these gates what opened they also
  The speech of Policy at the pageant celebrating the marriage of Prince Arthur and Princess Catharine—three stanzas rime royal.
  1. Cotton Vitellius A. xvi, ff. 188a-b.

4096 Robbins, *Sec. Lyrics*, pp. 93-4.

4096.5 Who runneth over see ffrom place to place
  '*Caelum non animum mutat, qui trans mare currit*'—one couplet.
  1. Durham Univ. Cosin V. iii. 9, f. 63a.
  Furnivall, *EETS* lxi. 194.

4097 [Delete entire entry].

  Who seith the best shal neuer repent See 102.5.

4098 Morris, *EETS* 29. 267; Brandl and Zippel, *ME Sprach- u. Literatur.*, p. 235; Hall, *Early Middle English*, I. 128.

4098.1 Who seketh the renoune to haue / And eke the prayse
  Who would be famed for virtue, let him earn it by virtuous deeds—one cross-rimed quatrain.
  1. Durham Univ. Cosin V. iii. 9, f. 82b.
  Furnivall, *EETS* lxi. 223.

4098.3 Who shal graunten to myn eye a strong streme of teres
  The *Reply of Friar Daw Topias* to *Jack Upland* (3782.5)—in rough alliterative verse. [Cf. 1653.5].
  1. Bodl. 1642, ff. 2a-16b.
  Wright, *Polit. Poems*, II. 39.

4098.6   Who shall haue my fayre lady
A love song—two 3-line stanzas. [The first stanza is used as a burden for a religious adaptation in 3623.5].
1. BM Addit. 5465, f. 99b.
Rimbault, *Anc. Vocal Music*, part 10; Stafford Smith, *Eng. Songs*, no. 12; Flügel, *Neuengl. Lesebuch*, p. 144; Manly, *Eng. Prose & Poetry*, p. 92; *Early Eng. Lyrics*, p. 75; *Poets of Eng. Lang.*, I. 427; Stevens, *Music & Poetry*, p. 379.

*4098.8   *Whoe shall haue the egge saye ye
Six lines of a humorous song. [In same hand as 3999, MS. 3].
1. B.M. IB 55242: Trevisa, *Bartholomeus Anglicus*, in margins.

4099   [For fragments of this poem, st. 8, 14, 17, 18, 19, written on the walls of Clopton Chapel, Church of the Holy Trinity, Long Melford, Suffolk, cf. Trapp, *RES* n.s. VI. 1, 5].

4100   Girvan, *STS* 3 s. XI. 66-79.

4101   [=Wife of Bath's Prologue, vv. 654-7. Ringler 88].
2. B.M. IB 49437: *Cordiale quatuor novissimorum*, Caxton, n.d., f. 1a.
Boke of Huntyng, St. Albans, 1486 (STC 3308); *facs.* Blades, 1881; de Worde, 1496 (STC 3309); *repr.* Dibdin, *Typo. Antiquities*, II. 59; 2. Bühler, *English Lang. Notes* I. 83.

4102   [Cf. 4135.5].
2. Bodl. 2712, f. 268a.
2. Robbins, *Archiv* CC. 342.

4103   five mono-riming lines.
1. Lansdowne 762, f. 91b.

Who þat euer þe fader be   See 475.8.

Ho þat hym biþoȝte   See 1422.

4104   Robbins, *Sec. Lyrics*, p. 86.

4105.5   Who that lufes or likes to here / of gude mens lifes
   Life of St. John Thweng of Bridlington—vv. 239 in couplets.
   1. Quaritch Sale Cat. 824, ff. 84b-87 (ends imperfectly).

4106   [Ringler 89].
   1. Trinity Camb. 1450, f. 46a (vv. 6); 3. B.M. IB 49408: Alliaco, *Meditationes,* Caxton, n.d., f. 34b.
   Boke of Huntyng, St. Albans, 1486 (STC 3308); *facs.* Blades. 1881; de Worde, 1496 (STC 3309); *repr.* Dibdin, *Typo. Antiquities,* II. 59; 2. Bühler, *English Language Notes* I. 83.

4106.5   Who that mannyth hym with his kynne / And closith his croofte
   Proverbial lines—one quatrain. [Ringler 90].
   1. B.M. IB 49437: *Cordiale quatuor novissimorum,* Caxton, n.d., f. 1a.
   Boke of Huntyng, St. Albans, 1486 (STC 3308); *facs.* Blades, 1881; de Worde, 1496 (STC 3309); *repr.* Dibdin, *Typo. Antiquities,* II. 59; 1. Bühler, *English Lang. Notes* I. 84.

4106.8   Who that passyth by this way
   Epitaph, A.D. 1477, for William Read: a general request for prayers for the faithful departed, an inscription at St. Nicholas Olave Church—six lines.
   Weever, *Anc. Funerall Monuments,* 1631, p. 701 (STC 25223); Ravenshaw, *Antiente Epitaphes,* p. 11.

   Who þat strechet forþerre þan his wytel wyle reche   See 4113.

4108   A prayer tag added to a copy of the *Mirror of Simple Souls*—five lines.
   1. BM Addit. 37790, f. 225a.

4109.5   Who that wol lodge hymself herynne
   'The ballade that was wryton vpon the gate of the prouostis place of Tourmaday,' by William Caxton—nine 9-line stanzas.
   Blanchardyn and Eglantine, Caxton, 1489 (STC 3124); *repr.* Kellner, *EETS* lviii. 46.

4110.3   Wo þe þer be seþ Iesu my suete lif
A couplet translating 'Quis te lesit ita Iesu dulcissima vita &c.'
1. Advocates 18. 7. 21, f. 119a.

4110.5   Ho þan þat wile beyȝen him blis
Against pride—one cross-rimed quatrain in Lavynham's *Tretys*.
1. Bodl. 655; 2. Bodl. 12146; 3. Bodl. 21634; 4. Camb. Un. Ff. 6. 31; 5. Trinity Camb. 305; 6. Harley 211, f. 37a; 7. Harley 1197; 8. Harley 1288; 9. Harley 2382; 10. Royal 8. C. 1; 11. Leeds Univ. Brotherton 501; 12. London: Dr. Williams' Lib. Anc. 3; 13. Norwich: St. Peter's Hungate Mus. 48. 158. 926; 14. Soc. of Antiquaries 687 [*olim* Bright].
6. Zutphen, *A Litel Tretys by Lavynham*, pp. xiii, 5.

4110.8   Quho thinkis that he has sufficence
Of Content, by William Dunbar—seven 5-line stanzas.
1. Camb. Un. Ll. 5. 10, f. 5a; 2. Pepys 2553, p. 307.
1. Schipper, *Dunbar*, pp. 333-5; and *DKAW* XLII (IV). 31-3; Baildon, *Dunbar*, pp. 171-2; Craigie, *STS* n.s. XX. 50-1; 2. [Pinkerton,] *Anc. Scot. Poems*, I. 122-3; Laing, *Dunbar*, I. 189-90; Paterson, *Dunbar*, pp. 50-1; Small, *STS* IV. 230-1; MacKenzie, *Dunbar*, pp. 144-5; Craigie, *STS* n.s. VII. 366-7.

4112   4. Lansdowne 699, f. 85b (8 addit st.); 7. Leyden Univ. Vossius 9, f. 98b (8 addit. st.); 9. Nat. Lib. of Medicine 4, ff. 66b-67a.

4112.5   Quha will behald of luve the chance
Inconstancy of Love, by William Dunbar—three 8-line stanzas with the same rimes throughout. [Utley 372].
1. Advocates 1. 1. 6, f. 281a.
Brydges and Haslewood, *British Bibliographer*, 1814, IV. 192; Laing, *Dunbar*, I. 172; Paterson, *Dunbar*, p. 90; Bannatyne MS., Hunt. Club, IV. 816; Small, *STS* IV. 172; Schipper, *Dunbar*, p. 120; and *DKAW* XL (IV). 30; Baildon, *Dunbar*, pp. 58-9; Ritchie, *STS* n.s. XXVI. 81-2; MacKenzie, *Dunbar*, pp. 100-1.

4113   '*Hom dit a reprouver en Engleys:*' an English proverb—one long irregular couplet in *Le dite de hosebondrie* by Walter de Henley. [Cf. 2698. For a variant occurring separately cf. 1170.5].

1. Bodl. 15516, f. 16b; 2. Bodl. 21672, f. 188a; 3. Merton Oxf. 321, f. 153b; 4. Camb. Un. Dd. 7. 6, f. 52b; 5. Camb. Un. Dd. 7. 14, f. 228b; 6. Camb. Un. Dd. 9. 38, f. 252b; 7. Camb. Un. Ee. 1. 1, f. 251a; 8. Camb. Un. Hh. 3. 11, f. 78a; 9. Corpus Camb. 301, f. 141b; 10. Trinity Camb. 1438, f. 99b; 11. Lansdowne 1176, f. 132a; 12. BM Addit. 6159, f. 222b; 13. Canterbury Cath., Register J; 14. Canterbury Cath., Register P; 15. College of Heralds, Arundel XIV; 16. Guildhall, Liber Horn; 16a (xix cent. transcript). Camb. Un. Add. 4026; 17. NLW Peniarth 92; 18. ? Sir A. Acland Hood, St. Audries, Somerset [present location not known]; 19. ? Northumberland D. x 1 [present location not known]; 20. Paris: Bibl. nat. f. fr. 7011, f. 57b.

de Worde, n.d.; 7. Lamond, *Walter of Henley's Husbandry*, 1890, p. 4; Mustanoja, *How the Good Wife*, p. 75; Mustanoja, *Neuphil. Mitteilungen* IL. 132; 13. *Hist. MSS. Comm. Ninth Report*, App., p. 75.

4116.5   Quhom to sall I compleine my wo
'For in this warld may non assure,' by William Dunbar—seventeen 5-line stanzas with this refrain.
1. Camb. Un. Ll. 5. 10, f. 40b; 2. Pepys 2553, p. 331; 3. Advocates 1. 1. 6, f. 84a.

2. Craigie, *STS* n.s. VII. 401-3; MacKenzie, *Dunbar*, pp. 44-6; 3. [Hailes,] *Anc. Scot. Poems*, pp. 89-93; *Select Poems of Dunbar*, Perth 1788, pp. 75-8; Sibbald, *Chronicle*, II. 14; Laing, *Dunbar*, I. 195-8; Paterson, *Dunbar*, pp. 56-60; *Bannatyne MS.*, Hunt. Club, II. 234-6; Small, *STS* IV. 100-7; Schipper, *Dunbar*, pp. 280-2; and *DKAW* XLI (IV). 81-4; Baildon, *Dunbar*, pp. 142-5; Ritchie, *STS* n.s. XXII. 215-7.

4117   [Cf. 3170].
5. Univ. Coll. Oxf. 154, f. 121b.
1. *Register*, I. 41.

4118   [Delete entire entry].

Whose thought is cumbered and is not clene   See 4117.

4119   English and Latin verses on the beasts produced by various parts of the dead body: '*Ex cerebro bufo, de spina scorpio* &c.'—ten lines.

*4119.5 *Whoso beres palm þe tokne is þis
The Assumption of the Virgin—in 6-line stanzas.
1. Advocates 19. 2. 1, f. 73a (begins imperfectly).
Schwarz, *Eng. Stn.* VIII. 448-57.

4120.3 Wo so boleth myn kyn / ewere is the calf myn
Proverbial couplet used in a suit on bastardy (18 Edward III).
1. BM Addit. 35116.
Bolland, *Year Books*, p. 76; Woodbine, *Speculum* XVIII. 431, n. 5; Vinogradoff, *Essays in Med. History to Tout*, p. 191.

4120.6 Who so can rede may telle be mowthe
A story of an unhappy boy—one introductory stanza and vv. 18 in quatrains. [Cf. 36].
1. Trinity Dublin 432, f. 64b (ends imperfectly).
Brotanek, *ME Dichtungen*, p. 93.

4121 six 12-line stanzas with refrain: 'Thenke on this word, suffren I mot.'
1. NLW Peniarth 395, f. 345a.

4122 3. Gollancz, *EETS* lxxiii. 15-16; Boyd, *ME Miracles*, pp. 50-5.

4123 Boyd, *ME Miracles*, pp. 61-7 (1 & 4 only).

4123.5 Who soo euyr on thys boke do rede
To the reader—one stanza rime royal following the colophon.
1. Rylands Lib. *Chaucer*, Pynson.

Who-so euer on me doth loke   See 4138 (Bodl. 2020).

4126 [Cf. 4058.8].
Coulton, *Life in the MA*, II. 118; Bennett, *England Chaucer-Caxton*, p. 162; Robbins, *Sec. Lyrics*, p. 86.

4126.5 Who so euer thou hearest be it good or badde
Moral admonitions—thirteen couplets.
1. Harley 2389, f. 57b.

4127 Furnivall, *EETS* 32 rev. ed. 266-74.

4128.2   Who so goth to chirch aȝenst his will / he comyth home a-cursyd [still]
A proverbial couplet. [Cf. Bodl. 1562, f. 508a; pr. Smalley, *Med. & Ren. St.* III. 214].
1. Bodl. 21626, f. 15b; 2. Rylands Lib. Latin 394, f. 7b.
1. Förster, *Festschrift zum 12 Deutschen Neuphilologentage*, p. 47; 2. Pantin, *BJRL* XIV. 99.

4128.4   Ho so hade a clepart at hys bedyng
Five impossibilities (Evils of the Age) to restore the dead to life—four couplets, with a Latin version.
1. NLW Peniarth 356, p. 297.

4128.5   Woys hat a wyf & loȝt fort to suync
'*Qui provam habet conjugem qui odit laborare* &c.'—four monoriming lines.
1. Leicester City Lib., Old Town 4, p. 37.
Retrospective Rev. I. 419.

4128.6   Who so hath an euyll tonge / euer he spekyth that is wrong
A proverbial couplet.
1. Bodl. 21626, f. 21a; 2. Rylands Lib. Latin 394, f. 11a.
Förster, *Festschrift zum 12 Deutschen Neuphilologentage*, p. 49; 2. Pantin, *BJRL* XIV. 99.

4128.8   Qwoso have any quarrel or ple
On justice in Norwich in 1433—seven irregular lines.
1. Norwich City Book of Pleas, f. 72a.
W. Hudson, *Records of City of Norwich*, 1906, I. 334; Liebermann, *Archiv* CXVI. 185.

Whoso haue sore pappys or bolnyng / Make þis playstre   See 1408.

Whoso heweth to hy / þere falle chippis in his ye   See 1149.5.

4129   [Colwell's epitaph also pr. Weever, *Anc. Funerall Monuments*, 1631, p. 276; another version at Saffron Walden, *ib.*, p. 625. Stratford-on-Avon pr. Gray, *N&Q* n.s. VIII. 135, with refs.].

5. Aberdeen Univ. 154, f. 155b; 6. Hereford Cath. O. iv. 14, II, f. 223a; 8. Harley 5312, f. 1b; 9. St. Florian, Stiftsbibl. XI. 57.

6. *Register*, I. 446; 9. Kaiser, *Anthologie*, p. 277; Kaiser, *Med. Eng.*, p. 294; comp. text. Dibdin, *Typo. Antiquities*, II. 331.

4131   1. Leyden Univ. Vossius 9, f. 107a.

4132   4. BM Addit. 35288 [*olim* Ashburnham App. 247], f. 2a (vv. 12195; a leaf missing after f. 19); 5. Bodl. Lat. misc. b. 17 [*olim* Robartes = Clifden] (damaged fragment: vv. 6142-6344).

4134   5. Robbins, *PQ* XXXV. 91.

4135.5   Whoso loueth wel to fare
Proverbial verses originally on the walls of Launceston Priory, Cornwall—a series of four stanzas, twenty lines in all, with four Latin lines. [St. 1 = 1156; st. 2 = 4102; st. 4 = 1619].
1. Bodl. 2712, f. 268a.
Rose-Troup, *Devon & Cornwall N&Q* XIX. 154-6; Robbins, *Archiv*. CC. 342.

4136   French, *Chaucer Handbook*, pp. 238-42; Boyd, pp. 33-7.

Hoo so makyst at crystysmas a dogge lardyner   See 4106.

4137   one couplet, followed by five related couplets.
[vv. 1-2 also occur in 3068.5 (vv. 25-6); vv. 5-6 listed also under 1587.8; vv. 7-8 listed also under 860.3; vv. 9-10 also occur separately as 513; vv. 11-12 listed also under 1829.2. Ringler 92].
2. Bodl. 11951, f. 59a (vv. 1-2 only).
Lidgate, *Stans puer*, Caxton, ca. 1477 (STC 17030); *repr.* Dibdin, *Typo. Antiquities*, II. 225.

4138   Ho-so on me doth loke / I am my w... ladys boke
1. Bodl. 2020, f. 64b (much faded; partly covered by 3706.6).

4139   Six couplets of Moral Warning by Buntyng &c.
1. Camb. Un. Dd. 4. 54, f. 75a.

4140   Bowers, *Univ. of Fla. Monographs*, Humanities XII, 13-14.

4143 10. Worcester Cath. F. 19, f. 164a col ii.
      10. *Register*, I. 451.

4143.3 Whoso that wyll all feattes optayne
        The values of loving, ascribed to King Henry VIII—seven couplets.
        1. BM Addit. 31922, f. 38b.
           Flügel, *Anglia* XII. 236; Flügel, *Neuengl. Lesebuch*, p. 137; Trefusis, *Songs Henry VIII*, Roxburghe Club CLXI. 15; Stevens, *Music & Poetry*, p. 399; Stevens, *Music at Court*, pp. 28-9.

4143.5 Whoso that wyll for grace sew
        The need for constancy in love, ascribed to Henry VIII—two 6-line stanzas.
        1. BM Addit. 31922, f. 84b.
           Flügel, *Anglia* XII. 248; Trefusis, *Songs Henry VIII*, Roxburghe Club CLXI. 32-3; Stevens, *Music & Poetry*, p. 414; Stevens, *Music at Court*, p. 60.

4143.8 Whoso that wyll hymselfe applye
        An invitation to a tournament—four monoriming lines.
        1. BM Addit. 31922, f. 27b.
           Flügel, *Anglia* XII. 233; Stevens, *Music & Poetry*, p. 392; Stevens, *Music at Court*, p. 21.

4144   [Delete: Heuser, *Kildare-Gedichte*, p. 131].

4145   Horstmann, *EETS* 98. 407-42.

4145.5 Who-so wolle abyde / he shall wel be tyde
        A proverbial couplet.
        1. Bodl. 21626, f. 15b; 2. Rylands Lib. Latin 394, f. 7b.
           1. Förster, *Festschrift zum 12 Deutschen Neuphilologentage*, p. 45; 2. Pantin, *BJRL* XIV. 97.

4146   vv. 196 in couplets.
        1a (xix cent. transcript). BM Addit. 20091, ff. 75a-78a.
        1. Amherst, *Archaeologia* LIV. 157-72.

        Who-so wylle be hys soules leche   See 4182.

4148　　2. Bodl. 11598, f. 1a (vv. 24); 6. Trinity Camb. 1157, f. 24a (vv. 20); 8. Lansdowne 762, f. 2b (vv. 24); 9. Royal 17. B. xlvii, f. 59a (vv. 24); 10. BM Addit. 25001, f. 2b (vv. 20); 11. Lambeth 306, f. 203a (vv. 20); 13. Bodl. Lat. misc. c. 66 [*olim* Capesthorne], f. 101b (vv. 20); 15. BM Addit. 6702, f. 109a.

3, 5. Robbins, *Sec. Lyrics*, pp. 70-1, 249-50; 11. Furnivall, *EETS* 15 orig. ed. 24; rev. ed. 44; Gairdner, *Camden Soc.* n.s. XXVIII. xxvi; 13. Robbins, *PMLA* LXV. 275.

4149　　1a (transcript). BM Addit. 23198.

H. J. Whymper, *Const. Artis Geometria,* 1889; W. G. Speth, *Quattuor Coronatorium Antigrapha*, Margate 1889, I, parts i, viii (*inc. facs.*); D. Knoop, G. P. Jones, and D. Hamer, *Med. Mason*, Manchester 1933, pp. 261-9; H. Poole, *Gould's History of Freemasonry*, 1951.

4149.5　　Who so will do my commaundements

'The x commandementes of the deuill' — one cross-rimed quatrain and thirteen couplets.

Pynson, *Kalendar of shepherdes*, 1506 (STC 22408); *repr.* Furnivall, *Captain Cox*, Ballad Soc. VII. lxxx-xi.

4150　　[Ringler 93].

21. Lansdowne 344, f. 20a; 25. Ushaw: St. Cuthbert's Coll. 28; 27. Trinity Dublin 159, f. 160b; 28. Delete this MS.; 29. Laurence Witten, New Haven, Cat. 5, Item 51 [*olim* Helmingham Hall LJ. V. 14], f. 73b; 31. Camb. Un. Dd. 4. 51, f. 14a (fragmentary); 32. Camb. Un. Add. 6150, f. 11a; 33. Foyle [*olim* Harmsworth; Sotheby Sale, Dec. 16, 1945, Lot 2131]; 34. Univ. of Illinois 71 [*olim* Harmsworth; Sotheby Sale, Dec. 16, 1945, Lot 2132].

Speculum Christiani, de Machlinia, ca. 1486 (STC 26012).

4150.3　　Wo-so wile in soule hanne blisse

Four lines translating '*Absit ditari qui se wlt* &c.'

1. Advocates 19. 2. 1, f. 32b.

4150.6　　ho-so wyl not afore ȝe ȝee thyng on thys mangere

Nonsense verses — two couplets, preceded by three Latin and followed by two Latin lines.

1. Trinity Dublin 516, f. 115b.

4151　　[Occurs separately: see 1173. Delete: Cf. 1151].

4152   Furnivall, *EETS* 32 orig. ed. 299-327; rev. ed. 177-205.

4153   1a (xix cent. transcript). Egerton 2257, ff. 136a-137b; 2. Advocates 19. 3. 1, f. 28a (vv. 92; omits vv. 1-2).
            1. *facs.* W. G. Speth, *Quattuor Coronatorium Antigrapha*, Margate 1889, I, part i.

4154   8. Harvard Univ. Deposit: Richardson 22, f. 82b (ends imperfectly); 9. New York: Corning Mus. of Glass 6 [*olim* Currer], ff. 123b-130b.

4154.3   Who-so wyll the cronycles grathely loke
            Bede's prophecy—vv. 58.
            1. Bodl. 4062, ff. 41b-42a.

4154.5   Who-so wyll the even fast of Barabara water & brede
            Three couplets.
            1. Trinity Dublin 83, f. 1b.

4154.8   Wo-so wol this oureson saie / Be nyȝth other be daie
            A charm against thieves—ten couplets. [Cf. 939, 993, 1952.5, 3771].
            1. Sloane 2457, f. 7b.
            Bühler, *Speculum* XXXIII. 371.

4155   1. Bodl. 21959, f. 3a (a single leaf detached from MS. 4; last 11 lines only).
            5. Furnivall, *EETS* 32 orig. ed. 11-12; rev. ed. 260-1.

4155.3   Whoso with god wyll make his acorde
            Verses on the Works of Mercy.
            Flower of the Commandments, de Worde, ca. 1510 (STC 23876).

4155.5   Who-so with me playth fast / His play schall not longe last
            Three couplets in a *Narracio de gestis romanorum*.
            1. Camb. Un. Gg. 6. 26, f. 34b.

4159   Davies, *Med. Eng. Lyrics*, p. 119.

4160   4. Bodl. 8180, Part VI, f. 11a (vv. 1-29 only); 10. Cotton Titus C. xix, f. 141b; 11. *olim* Tenison, ff. 135b-137b.
            6b. Horstmann, *York. Wr.*, II. 374-5; 5. Davies, *Med. Eng. Lyrics*, pp. 173-5.

        Why shall not I
        Refrain to 2250.5.

4162.5   Whye shulde man dowtefully questyons make
        On faith and reason—twenty-nine quatrains.
        1. Victoria and Albert Mus., Dyce 45, f. 25b.

4163   1. Rylands Lib. Latin 395, f. 119b.

        Why soo vnkende Alas
        Burden to 3144.5.

4165   in 6-line stanzas inc. wheel and bob. [For a later redaction see 1992].
        1. Peterhouse Camb. 104, ff. 210a-212a (expanded version: vv. 468; ends imperfectly at v. 392 of MS. 2); 2. Advocates 19. 2. 1, ff. 328a-334b (vv. 476).
        1, 2. Brandl and Zippel, *ME Sprach- u. Literatur.*, pp. 184-201; 2. Kaiser, *Med. Eng.*, pp. 359-62 (vv. 174 only).

4165.5   Quhy will ʒe merchantis of renoun
        'To the merchantis of Edinburgh,' by William Dunbar.
        1. Camb. Un. Ll. 5. 10, f. 1b.
        Laing, *Dunbar*, I. 97-100; *Blackwood's Magazine*, Feb. 1835; Paterson, *Dunbar*, pp. 127-31; Small, *STS* IV. 261-3; Schipper, *Dunbar*, pp. 85-7; and *DKAW* XL (II). 85-7; Baildon, *Dunbar*, pp. 34-6; Craigie, *STS* n.s. XX. 41-4; MacKenzie, *Dunbar*, pp. 81-3; Kinsley, *Dunbar*, pp. 74-7.

4166   Stevens, *Music & Poetry*, p. 50 (4 st. only).

4166.5   Wylde bestys a man may make meke
        Women cannot be tamed—two couplets (occurring as vv. 9-11 in 2290).
        1. Bodl. 1502, f. ii verso.

4167   [Apparently derived from 4016, applied to marriage].

4168   1. Ritson, *Anc. Pop. Poetry*, 1833, pp. 61-7.

4169   Child, *Pop. Ballads*, no. 1, V. 283-4; Sargent and Kittredge, *Pop. Ballads*, pp. 1-2; Leach, *Ballad Book*, pp. 47-8.

4170   1b. *Eng. Lyr. XIII C.*, pp. 185-6.

4171   4. Stowe 949, f. 110b.
                1. Thiemke, *Palaestra* CXXXI. 1 (vv. 1-210).

4172   Kaiser, *Med. Eng.*, pp. 229-31 (extracts: vv. 118 only).

4172.5   Will ȝe offe þir poyntis lere
            Couplet introduction to a brief prose treatise on the points most pleasing to God.
            1. Bodl. 12143, f. 62a.
            Horstmann, *York. Wr.*, I. 110.

4174   2. Balliol 228, f. 319a.
                1. Coulton, *Life in the MA*, III. 22; 2. Mynors, *Cat.*, p. 235.

4174.3   Wyllyam conqueror Duke of Normandie / Conquered ynglond
            The Kings of England, an expanded and widely variant version of 3632, continuing to 1505—in quatrains.
            1. Bodl. 12299, f. ii verso, 1a, and lower margins of ff. 184b, 185a-b.

4174.5   Wilyam Rufus otherwyes William the Rede
            A rimed chronicle, drawing on Fabyan (3955.5) and Harding (710), continuing to Henry VIII—in couplets, with occasional stanzaic passages inserted.
            1. Pepys 2163, ff. 1a-643.

4174.8   William Victor and his wyf Grace / Under this stone
            Epitaph, A.D. 1486, at St. Alban's Abbey—eight lines.
            Weever, *Anc. Funerall Monuments*, 1631, p. 580 (dates 1408) (STC 25223); *Beauties of England*, VII. 101.

4175   one 8-line stanza. [v. 2 = v. 1969 of 935. Cf. 2668].
                1. Harley 2252, f. 2a; 2. BM Addit. 10106, f. 79a (vv. 7, rearranged).
                1-3. MacCracken, *EETS* 192. 724.

4176   W. Fleetwood, *Life & Miracles of St. Wenefrede*, 1713, pp. 125-7.

4176.5   Wynter etythe / what somer getithe
            A short proverbial couplet.
            1. Bodl. 15444, f. 140b; 2. Balliol 354, f. 191b and f. 200b;
            3. Rylands Lib. Latin 394, f. 2a.
            1. Meech, *MP* XXXVIII. 118; 2. Flügel, *Anglia* XXVI. 203;
            Dyboski, *EETS* ci. 128, 133; 3. Pantin, *BJRL* XIV. 92.

4177   Marsh, *Hist. Eng. Lang.*, p. 255; Ritson, *Anc. Songs*, 1790, p. 34; 1829, I. 65; 1877, p. 56; Ellis, *Specimens*, 1811, p. 65; *Oxford Book Eng. Verse*, p. 7; *Cambridge Book Prose & Verse*, p. 381; *Oxford Book Christian Verse*, pp. 7-8; Reed, *MLN* XLIII. 81; Funke, *ME Reader*, p. 49; Brook, *Harley Lyrics*, p. 53; Speirs, *Med. Eng. Poetry*, pp. 58-9.

4178   2. Trinity Camb. 599, f. 12a (6 Fables only) and f. 235a.

            Wisdome *monstrat et adventus*   See 3856.5.

4180   1. Merton Oxf. 248, f. 120a col. i.
            Register, I. 147.

4180.3   Wyse men alway / Affyrme and say
            'A mery jest how a sergeant would learne to play the frere,' by Thomas More, ca. 1503—in 12-line tail-rime stanzas. R. Jhones, n.d.; Notary, ca. 1515; Workes, *Rastell*, 1557; *facs.* & *repr.* Campbell, *Eng. Works*, pp. 327-32.

4180.6   Wyst euery man how bretell were his shen bon
            A proverb—one long couplet.
            1. Bodl. 21626, f. 30a; 2. Rylands Lib. Latin 394, f. 22a.
            1. Förster, *Festschrift zum 12 Deutschen Neuphilologentage*, p. 56; 2. Pantin, *BJRL* XIV. 107.

4181   [Ringler 95].
            [Cf. Inscription over door of a house in Gilesgate, Hexham; pr. A.B. Wright, *Hist. of Hexham*, 1823; A.B. Hinds, *Hist. of Northumberland*, III. 308; *repr.* Gray, *Arch. Aeliana* 4 s. XL. 185].
            10. Bodl. Lyell 34 [*olim* John Speed Davies], f. 194a; 12. Bodl. Eng. poet, b. 5, p. 5 (xvii cent.); 13. Lincoln Coll. Oxf., p. 598; 14. Egerton 2788, f. 53b; 15. BM Addit. 37505,

f. 200a (xix cent. transcript of text in a MS. Calendar, ca. 1400, owned by Edward Peacock); 16. Trinity Dublin 516, f. 205a; 17. Wellcome Hist. Med. Lib. 41, f. 16a.

Lidgate, *Stans puer*, Caxton, ca. 1477 (STC 17030); *repr.* Blades, *Life & Typography of Caxton*, II. 50; Duff, *XV Cent. English Books*, p. 76; 6, 9, 12. Gray, *Arch. Aeliana* 4 s. XL. 186; 3. Segar, *Med. Anthology*, p. 82; 13. *Pecock's Repressor*, Rolls Series XIX, ii. 623; 17. Moorat, *Cat.*, p. 27.

4182   in couplets. [Cf. 1603. Delete: Compare 3422].

[Revise listing of MSS. as follows:]

1. Bodl. 8613, f. iii (vv. 12); 2. Bodl. 21658, f. 1a (vv. 10); 3. Sloane 3285, f. 73a (vv. 10).

2. Robbins, *Sec. Lyrics*, p. 95.

4182.5   Wetes all that be here / Of that shall be lief and deer

Christ's Will and Testament — in couplets. [Cf. 4184].

1. Bodl. 5088, f. 79b (xvii cent.).

Astle, *Antiquarian Repertory*, I. 21.

4183   1-3. Fowler, *Surtees Soc.* LXXIV. 90-3; 3. Kemble, *Cod. Dipl. Aevi Sax.*, 1839-47, III. 188, 189; Thorpe, *Dip. Ang. Aevi Sax.*, 1865, pp. 182-3; W. G. Speth, *Quattuor Coronatorium Antigrapha*, Margate 1889, I, part iii, p. 27.

4184   [Cf. 4182.5].

1. Bodl. 6777, f. 109a; 8. Harley 6848, ff. 239b-240a; 11. BM Addit. 5465, f. 118b (as carol); 16. Camb. Un. Add. 6686 [*olim* Ashburnham App. 140], p. 270; 17. Harvard Univ. Deposit: Richardson 22, f. 71b; 18. Pepys 1036, ff. 7b-8 (var.); 19. Harley 3775, f. 138a; 20. Stowe 620, f. 11b; 21. Stowe 1055, f. 40a; 22. *olim* J. W. Dod (vv. 34).

11. Fehr, *Archiv* CVI. 69-70; Stevens, *Music & Poetry*, pp. 383-4; 15. James, *Cat.*, I. 300; 19. Riley, *Annales Mon. S. Albani, Amundesham*, Rolls Series XXVIII, Part V, i. 457-8; 22. *Gentleman's Magazine*, June 1848, p. 612.

With a betull be he smeton   See 4202.

4185   [Cf. also 1565].

1. Person, *Camb. ME Lyrics*, pp. 10-11; Davies, *Med. Eng. Lyrics*, pp. 207-8.

4185.5   Wyt a ... so wondyrleche grete / þe comb yt ys of red coral
On a cock—three lines.
    1. Caius 465, f. 89a.
       James, *Cat.*, II. 540 (part only); Wilson, *Lost Lit.*, p. 181.

4186   a series of love lyrics in varying forms for *Introibo, Confiteor, Misereatur, Officium, Kyrie, Gloria* and *Oryson*, vv. 145 in all.

4186.5   With boidekynnes was Cesar Iulius / Murdered at Rome
Four riming lines at end of *Serpent of Division*, quoting 'my maister Chaucer.' [Cf. Monk's Tale, vii. 2707].
    1. BM Addit. 48031 [*olim* Calthorpe, Yelverton 35], f. 156a;
    2. Harvard Coll. Eng. 530, f. 57b.
       2. Robinson, *Harvard St. & Notes in Philol.* V. 184.

4187   An admonition against excess.
       Robbins, *PQ* XXXV. 92.

4187.3   With constant cure eschewynge Ignoraunce
Life of St. Ursula—seventy-nine 8-line stanzas.
       de Worde, ca. 1520 (STC 24540.5); *repr. Roxburghe Club*, 1818.

4187.5   With egges and flowre a batour thou make
A recipe 'for fryturs'—seven lines in couplets. [Cf. 2361].
    1. Pepys 1047, f. 16a.

4187.8   Wyth empty honde men may no hawkes lure
One stanza rime royal. [vv. 1-2 = vv. 414-5 of Chaucer's Wife of Bath's Prologue. Ringler 94].
       Temple of Bras, Caxton, ca. 1478 (STC 5091); Furnivall, *Trial Forewords*, Chaucer Soc. 2 s., No. 8, 1871, p. 117.

4189   1. Trinity Camb. 1450, f. 62b; 2. Rylands Lib. Latin 395, f. 120a.
       1. Segar, *Med. Anthology*, pp. 61-2.

4189.5   Wiþ foure hors all snowe white / þou schalt sire Emperour wende
A couplet attributed to Ovid in Trevisa's translation of Higden's *Polychronicon* (Book I, cap. 24).

1. St. John's Camb. 204; 2. Cotton Tiberius D. vii; 3. Harley 1900; 4. Stowe 65; 5. BM Addit. 24194; 6. Aberdeen Univ. 21; 7. Hunterian Mus. 83; 8. Penrose 12; 9. Morgan Lib. M. 875.

Trevisa, *Discripcion of Britayne*, Caxton, 1480 (STC 13440a); de Worde, 1498 (STC 13440b); Trevisa, *Prolicronycon*, Caxton, 1482 (STC 13438); de Worde, 1495 (STC 13439); Treveris, 1527 (STC 13440); 1. Babington and Lumby, *Rolls Series* XLI, i. 239; Mätzner, *AE Sprachproben*, II. 368.

4191 Sauerstein, *Charles d'Orléans*, 1899, p. 29 (st. 1 only).

4192 six stanzas rime royal.

4194 Marsh, *Hist. Eng. Lang.*, p. 253; Brook, *Harley Lyrics*, p. 34; Kaiser, *Anthologie*, p. 296; Kaiser, *Med. Eng.*, p. 471.

With margerain ientyll   See 729.5.

*4194.5 *Wiht my lemman gan I wend / I went awai ay good paas
A fragment of *Guy of Warwick* — about 500 lines in couplets. [Cf. 3145].
1. BM Addit. 14408, ff. 74a-77b.
Phillipps, Middle Hill Press 1838; *repr.* Turnbull, *Abbotsford Club*, 1840, pp. xxviii-xlii.

4196 1. Leyden Univ. Vossius 9, f. 110a.
Brunner, *Archiv* CLXI. 41-2.

4197 [Cf. 905.5].
Little, *Arch. Cant.* LIV. 2; Greene, *Sel. Eng. Carols*, p. 53; Davies, *Med. Eng. Lyrics*, p. 231.

4198 [Cf. 4198.5].
Stevens, *Med. Carols*, p. 111 (burden only).

4198.5 With pyte moued to my payne I dyde me dres
'The example of euyll tongues' — seven stanzas rime royal. [Cf. 4198].
de Worde, ca. 1525 (STC 10608).

4198.8	With reste and pees / A man schal best encrees A proverbial couplet inserted in a chronicle. 1. Cotton Julius B. i; 2. Harley 565. [Nicolas,] *Chronicle of London*, 1827, p. 122.
4199	Robbins, *Sec. Lyrics*, p. 146. With sapyence tempre thi corage See 576 (stanza on *Sapiencia* or *Temperancia*).
4200	[For the indulgence see 3305.8]. 7. Longleat 30, f. 11a; 9. Camb. Un. Ee. 5. 13, f. 15b (7 st.). 4. Person, *Camb. ME Lyrics*, pp. 68-9.
4201.3	With sorowfull syghs and grevos payne / Thus ever to endure The lovers' next meeting—one quatrain. [Cf. 4201.6]. 1. BM Addit. 31922, f. 33b. Flügel, *Anglia* XII. 235; Stevens, *Music & Poetry*, p. 395; Stevens, *Music at Court*, p. 25.
4201.6	Wyth sorowful syghes and wondes smert / my hert ys persed A love lament—in quatrains. [Cf. 4201.3]. 1. BM Addit. 17942, f. 26a. Muir, *Proc. Leeds Philos. & Lit. Soc., Lit & Hist. Sect.* VI. 262.
4202	1. [Delete this MS]. 1. Delete: [Förster, *Festschrift* &c.]; 5. D'Evelyn, *Peter Idley's Instructions*, p. 226.
4205	1. Trinity Camb. 599, ff. 217a-234a. *Chaucer*, Stow, 1561 (STC 5075); *Chaucer*, Speght, 1598 (STC 5077); Urry, *Chaucer*, 1721, p. 560; Bell, *Poets of Great Britain*, XII. 105; [Anderson,] *Poets of Great Britain*, I.538; Chalmers, *English Poets*, I. 367; *British Poets*, Chiswick 1822, V. 28; Moxon, *Chaucer*, p. 333; [Pickering,] *Aldine British Poets*, 1845, VI. 130; 1866, IV. 1; Bell, *Chaucer*, IV. 280; Skeat, *Oxf. Ch.*, VII. 409.
4206	Robbins, *Sec. Lyrics*, p. 146; Wilson, *Lost Lit.*, pp. 184-5.
4208	Furnivall, *EETS* 15 orig. ed. 223; rev. ed. 252.

4209   vv. 78 in 6-line tail-rime stanzas (interlocking in st. 1-3). Kirke, *Reliquary* IX. 75-6; Robbins, *Sec. Lyrics*, pp. 120-2.

4211   James, *Cat.*, I. 439; Kaiser, *Med. Eng.*, p. 256.

4212.5   Withdrawith bodely lust & lykyng
What grace does—five lines in a Latin sermon.
1. Bodl. 29746, ff. 48a, 49a.

Wythin a garth vnder a rede rosere   See 1598.

4213.5   Withowt dyscord / And bothe accorde
True love, attributed to King Henry VIII—two 12-line tail-rime stanzas.
1. BM Addit. 31922, f. 68b.
     Flügel, *Anglia* XII. 237; Flügel, *Neuengl. Lesebuch*, pp. 136-7; Trefusis, *Songs Henry VIII*, Roxburghe Club CLXI. 26-7; Padelford, *Early XVI Cent. Lyrics*, p. 76; Stevens, *Music & Poetry*, p. 410; Stevens, *Music at Court*, p. 50.

4214.5   Wo ys hym þat hys wo and get wit wo ybounde
One couplet.
1. Trinity Camb. 1209, final flyleaf.

4215   2. Univ. Coll. Oxf. 154, f. 121b; 4. Public Record Office, Chancery Misc. 34 / 1 / 4.

4216   [From *Conuersion of Swerers* (3354.5), occurring separately; and cf. 3955.3, cap. 5].
Furnivall, *N&Q* 4 s. III. 9.

4217   1. Royal 8. F. iii, f. 2*b (illegible).

4217.3   Womanhod wanton ye want
An attack on 'Mastres Anne,' by John Skelton—four stanzas rime royal and concluding couplet. [Utley 383].
     A Comely Coystrowne, Pynson, n.d. (STC 22611); *repr.* Dyce, *Skelton*, I. 20-1; Dyce and Child, *Skelton & Donne*, I. 25-6; Henderson, *Skelton*, 1931, p. 35; 1948, 1959, p. 26; Gant, *Skelton*, 1949, pp. 17-8; *Workes*, Marshe, 1568 (STC 22608); *repr.* [? J. Bowle,] 1736; Chalmers, *English Poets*, II. 301.

4217.6   Womans herte vnto no creweltye
In praise of women—vv. 344-50 of Hoccleve's *Lespistre de Cupide* (666) occurring separately.
1. BM Addit. 17492, f. 89b.

4218   [Utley 385].
1. Camb. Un. Add. 5943, end wrapper, recto (text imperfect).

4219   [Utley 384].
1. Segar, *Med. Anthology*, p. 108; Greene, *Sel. Eng. Carols*, p. 142.

Women women loue of women   See 3171.

*...[w]orlde all wrapped in wretchydnes   See 2578.5.

4220   [A similar couplet occurs in Bromyard, under *Desperatio*; cf. *Gesta Romanorum*, Roxburghe Club, 1838, p. 529].

4223   Trend, *Music & Letters* IX. 112.

4224   Furnivall, *EETS* 15 orig. ed. 234; rev. ed. 263.

4225.5   Werdys lowe lestyth but a qwyȝle
Only Christ's love remains—two couplets in a Latin sermon by Friar Nicolas Philip.
1. Bodl. 29746, f. 174b.

4227   James, *Cat.*, p. 25.

4227.5   Wordly love is in herte bysy þouȝt
On worldly and spiritual love—two monoriming quatrains.
1. Bodl. Lat. lit. e. 17, f. 53a.

4229   Stevens, *Med. Carols*, p. 17.

4229.5   Worschip of vertu ys þe mede
Carol to St. George—three quatrains and burden.
1. Egerton 3307, f. 63b
Schofield, *Musical Qr.* XXXII. 513; Stevens, *Med. Carols*, p. 49; Copley, *N&Q* CCIII. 239; Greene, *Sel. Eng. Carols*, p. 124; Davies, *Med. Eng. Lyrics*, p. 185.

4230   [This poem does not occur in BM Addit. 16165 or in BM Addit. 34360, *pace* MacCracken, *EETS* 192. xvii. Utley 387].
3. Trinity Camb. 599, f. 205b (= st. 2 of 2524); 8. Copenhagen Royal Lib. 29264, f. 163a; 10. Rome: English Coll. 1306, f. 75a.
5. Brusendorff, *Chaucer Tradition*, p. 465; 9. Bühler, *EETS* 211. 368.

4231   = 5 st. of Chaucer's Monk's Tale Prologue, prefixed to 3983.

4232   Worshepfulle brother and euer yn mynde
six quatrains, followed by 5 lines.

4235   Meyer, *Romania* XV. 338; Robbins, *Anglia* LXXVIII. 193.

4235.5   Watt thou I be putt fer ought of conceyte and syght
'I have you all in remembrance both day and nyght' — one long couplet by Henry Berry, A.D. 1464. [Letter 483].
1. BM Addit.
Fenn, I. 278; Gairdner, *Paston Letters*, IV. 90.

4235.8   Worthy Iohn Leuckin stockfishmoner of London here is leyd
Epitaph, A.D. 1368 (probably later), at St. Michael's Church, Crooked Lane, London — four couplets.
Weever, *Anc. Funerall Monuments*, 1631, p. 410 (STC 25223).

4236   Robbins, *Hist. Poems*, pp. 148-9.

4237   [Utley 388].
Ramsay, *Evergreen*, I. 234; Ellis, *Specimens*, I. 366-8; Laing, *Henryson*, 1865, p. 8; FitzGibbon, *E. E. Poetry*, p. 90; Eyre-Todd, *Med. Scot. Poetry*, pp. 96-7; Wood, *Henryson*, pp. 169-70; Neilson and Webster, *Chief Brit. Poets*, pp. 384-5; Elliott, pp. 110-11.

4238.5   Wrappid in a schete as a ful rewli wretche
Epitaph, A.D. 1463, for John Baret at St. Mary's Church, Bury St. Edmunds — five couplets (preceded by introductory couplet).
Pettigrew, *Chronicles of Tombs*, p. 48; Ravenshaw, *Antiente Epitaphes*, pp. 12-13.

4239   2. *Rel. Lyr. XIV C.*, p. 237.

4241	1. St. John's Camb. 259, f. 1a (complete text).
	ȝare hit was isuteled See 4273.5.
4241.5	Ye ar to blame to sette yowre hert so sore A love lyric—one quatrain (perhaps as Envoy to 4059). 1. Camb. Un. Ff. 1. 6, f. 20b. Robbins, *PMLA* LXIX. 632.
4242	Arber, *Dunbar Anthology*, p. 125.
4242.5	ȝe ben my fader my creacion Song of the B.V. to the Christ Child—five quatrains inc. refrain: 'My owyn dyre sone lullay.' 1. Stanbrook Abbey 3, f. 241a. Ker, *Medium Aevum*.
4244	[Cf. 333 for text with introductory prologue].
4244.5	Ye crosbow men in trouthe ye haue gret nede The Order of Shooting with the crossbow—sixteen stanzas rime royal. 1. Arundel 359, ff. 26b-29b. *Retrospective Rev.* I. 206-8.
4246	3. Balliol 354, f. 148a.
4247	[Cf. 1181, 1181.5]. 2. [Delete this MS].
4249	3 (with Envoy from 2). MacCracken, *EETS* cvii. 84-6.
4250	1. Horstmann, *Archiv* LVII. 280 (vv. 112 only).
4251	1 (transcript from Thynne). Trinity Camb. 595, ff. 2a-3a.

Ye maydens of Englande nowe may ye morne   See 2039.3.

ȝe maistres þat vse blode lating
   Three introductory couplets prefaced to some texts of 3848.

4252   Ye men that will of Aunters mene / That lately in this Land hath bene
'The Felon Sew' or 'Felon Sowe and the Freeres of Richmonde,' a mock-heroic poem, possibly parodying *The Awnturs of Arthur* (1566)—forty-one 6-line tail-rime stanzas.
1. Ralph Rokeby (A.D. 1565, now lost); 1a (1654 transcript by Sir Thomas Rokeby); 1b (1712 transcript made for Richard Boylston); 1c (1815 transcript made by Langham Rokeby) [1a, 1b, 1c. present location not established]; 1d (xviii cent. transcript). Leeds Pub. Lib., Hopkinson; 1e (xix cent. transcript of 1d by Hunter). BM Addit. 24470, ff. 294-333.
1a. T. D. Whitaker, *Hist. of Richmondshire*, 1823; 1b. T. D. Whitaker, *Hist. of Craven*, 1805; repr. R. H. Evans, *Old Ballads*, 1810, III. 270; 1b (coll. 1c, 1d). A. W. C. Hallen, *Economia Rokebeiorum*, Edinburgh 1807; 1c (? or 1). Sir Walter Scott, *Rokeby*, 1813, note iii; rev. ed. 1830, note lii; R. Bell, *Early Ballads Illustrative of History*, 1877, p. 349; Robertson, *Scott's Poetical Works*, 1921, p. 402; crit. ed. Cowling, *Essays & St. by Members English Assoc*. VIII. 79-89.

4253   Robbins, *PQ* XVIII. 324 (Prologue only).

4254.5   Ye pop holy pristes full of presumcion
The galants' answer to the priests' accusations on dress (4255)—four quatrains.
1. Univ. Coll. Oxf. 154, f. ii recto; 2. Trinity Camb. 1157, f. 27a; 3. Harley 372, f. 113a.
3. Strutt, *Horda Angel-Cynnan*, 1775, III. 78; Wright, *Polit. Poems*, II. 251; Fairholt, *Percy Soc.* XXVII. 56.

4255   Against excess in men's apparel—two monoriming quatrains (followed by 4254.5). [Cf. 1874].
2. Univ. Coll. Oxf. 154, f. ii recto; 3. Trinity Camb. 1157, f. 27a.
1. Strutt, *Horda Angel-Cynnan*, 1775, III. 78.

4256   [Utley 396].
1. Grenoble Bibl. 873.

*4256.3 *...ye xall ete
A fragmentary carol of seven 3-line stanzas and burden.
1. St. John's Camb. 259, f. 13b.
James and Macaulay, *MLR* VIII. 85; *Early Eng. Carols*, p. 321.

4256.5   ȝe suln / rediliche / withouten abiding
Five mnemonic irregular-riming lines on 'ȝe suln turnen to god.'
1. Advocates 18. 7. 21, f. 123b

4256.8   Ye Sir [þat is] idronken / dronken dronken ydronken
The Drunkard's Song—two stanzas and linking line.
1. Bodl. 13679, Item I (1).
Heuser, *Anglia* XXX. 177; Robbins, *Sec. Lyrics*, p. 106; Wilson, *Lost Lit.*, p. 180; Kaiser, *Med. Eng.*, p. 480; Dronke, *N&Q* n.s. VIII. 246.

4257   Bergen, *EETS* cxxiv. 59-60 (extracts); Bowers, *Southern Folklore Qr.* XVI. 223-6; Robbins, *Hist. Poems*, pp. 233-5.

4258   seven long quatrains.
1. Bodl. 15409, item 2.

4258.3   Ye that be nobly groundid all in grace
Envoy to *Prohemium* (731.5) of Trevisa's translation of *De Proprietatibus Rerum*—one stanza rime royal. [For Prologue see 33].
de Worde, 1495 (STC 1536); repr. Dibdin, *Typo. Antiquities*, II. 318; Duff, *XV Cent. English Books*, p. 11.

Ye that ben sette most highest in dignyte   See 2590 (Fakes print).

4258.6   Ye that behold and see this dedely grave
Epitaph, A.D. 1473, for Peter Idley on a memorial brass (now destroyed) in the Abbey Church at Dorchester, Oxford—one stanza rime royal.
1 (xvii cent. transcript by Anthony à Wood). Bodl. 8505, f. 296a (vv. 7); 2 (xvii cent. transcript by Anthony à Wood). Bodl. 8586, f. 34b (vv. 4); 3 (xvii cent. transcript by Richard Symonds). Harley 165, f. 18b (vv. 4).
1-3, D'Evelyn, *Peter Idley's Instructions*, pp. 28, 29, 27; 3. Addington, *Abbey Church at Dorchester*, 1845, p. 137; Davis, *Parochial Collections*, Oxford Rec. Soc., 1922, Part II. 120.

4259   Furnivall, *EETS* 15 orig. ed. 232; rev. ed. 261.

4260   Bennett, *Chaucer & XV Cent.*, OHEL, p. 118; Robbins, *Sec. Lyrics*, p. xxv.

        Ȝe þat goȝt bi þe weye / abideȝt a litul stounde   See 4263.

4261   Robbins, *Hist. Poems*, pp. 203-5.

4263   Davies, *Med. Eng. Lyrics*, p. 125.

4263.3   Ye þat put your trust & confydence
- 'The lamentacioun off quene Elyȝabeth,' A.D. 1503, ascribed to Thomas More—twelve stanzas rime royal, with Latin lines. [Followed by 1206.9].
  - 1. Balliol 354, f. 175a; 2. Sloane 1825, f. 88b.
    - *Workes in the Englyssh Tonge*, Rastell, 1557; *facs. & repr.* Campbell, *Eng. Works*, pp. 335-7; *Oxford Bk. XVI C. Verse*, p. 15; 1. Flügel, *Anglia* XXVI. 184-8; Dyboski, *EETS* ci. 97-9.

4263.6   Ȝe þat sing hym bewar of gyle / Doth now penaunce a lytyll qwyll
- A couplet paraphrase of St. Matthew III. 2.
  - 1. Hereford Cath. O. iii. 5, f. 48a.

        Ye that this balad red shall
- Concluding couplet to *Isle of Ladies* (3947).

4264.5   Ȝe wymmen owyt herkeneþ alle
- Four lines in Latin instructions for parish priests.
  - 1. Camb. Un. Mm. 4. 41, f. 56b.

4265   vv. 24832 in couplets.
- 2. Cotton Vitell. C. xiii, f. 2a (does not include Chaucer's ABC hymn, but leaves a space for it; vv. 21600, lacking about vv. 2200); 4. Worcester Cath. C. i. 8 (fragment: Ker Pastedowns, No. 1984).

4265.5   Ye wryng my hand so sore / I pray yow do no more
- An amorous encounter—six stanzas and refrain.
  - *XX Songes*, de Worde, 1530 (STC 22924); *repr.* Hawkins, *Hist. Music*, 1776, III. 19-20; Imelmann, *Shakespeare-Jahrbuch* XXXIX. 126-7; Flügel, *Anglia* XII. 590-1.

        Yerly be þe morowe   See 700.

4266	18. Public Record Office, C. 47 / 34 / 1, No. 5, f. 1b; 19. Winchester Coll. 33, f. 49a. 9. D'Evelyn and Mill, *EETS* 235.3.
	Yas sen that the eyne that workis my weilfair See 3138.
*4267.5	*ȝutte y se but fewe canne sece The Wheel of Fortune—eight cross-rimed quatrains. 1. Bodl. 21652, ff. 1a-b (begins imperfectly). Bowers, *English Studies* XLI. 197-8.
4268	3. NLW Peniarth 395, pp. 346-7. 1. Robbins, *Hist. Poems,* pp. 57-60.
4269.5	ȝet shull Danos þes wanes / Her shull Danes fett banes Threat and counterthreats in A.D. 1367 in the Brut Chronicle. 1. Corpus Camb. 174, f. 190a. [And other MSS.]. Brie, *EETS* 136. 317.
4272.5	Yit wulde I not the causer faryd amysse A love lament—three stanzas rime royal (following 734). 1. Camb. Un. Ff. 1. 6, f. 153b. Robbins, *PMLA* LXIX. 638-9; Davies, *Med. Eng. Lyrics,* p. 220.
	Ynguar and Vbbe See 1267.5.
4273	Furnivall, *EETS* 15 orig. ed. 222; rev. ed. 251.
4273.3	ȝare hit was isuteled þurh wise and erndrake A 'text' in a Worcestershire sermon on the Incarnation—two couplets. 1. Worcester Cath. Q. 29, f. 130b. Stanley, *Eng. & Germanic St.* VII. 61.
4273.5	Yore was a londe / Wrathe & hate an honde One long couplet in a collection of Latin sermons. 1. Aberdeen Univ. 154, f. 155b. James, *Cat.,* p. 51.
	Yow and I and Amyas See 3405.5.

4273.8   Youe that haue redd the contentes of thy booke
Conclusion to Earl Rivers' translation of *Dictes of Philosophers* — three quatrains and couplets. [Cf. 3581].
1. Lambeth 265, at end (in early xvi cent. hand).
Bühler, *MLN* LXII. 5-6.

4274   On the faithlessness of women — two stanzas rime royal.

4278   [Utley 400].
[Masters,] *Rymes of Minstrels*, p. 23.

4279   [Utley 401].
Robbins, *Sec. Lyrics*, p. 38; Kaiser, *Anthologie*, p. 309; Kaiser, *Med. Eng.*, p. 475; Greene, *Sel. Eng. Carols*, p. 144.

4280   one 9-line stanza.
Wilson, *Lost Lit.*, p. 205.

Youer company / makes me so mery   See 4058.3.

4281.5   Yowre counturfetyng / with doubyll delyng
A deceiving mistress — two 8-line stanzas.
1. BM Addit. 5465, f. 22b.
Burney, *Hist. Music*, 1782, II. 541-3; Fehr, *Archiv* CVI. 56; Stevens, *Music & Poetry*, p. 358.

4282   [Utley 403].
1. FitzGibbon, *E. E. Poetry*, pp. 50-1; Robinson, *Chaucer*, 1933, p. 638; 1957, p. 542; Davies, *Med. Eng. Lyrics*, pp. 138-9.

4283.5   Your light grevans shall not me constrayne
A song to his uncertain mistress — four stanzas of three long riming lines and burden.
1. BM Addit. 5665, f. 38b.
Fehr, *Archiv* CVI. 273; Stevens, *Med. Carols*, p. 115; Stevens, *Music & Poetry*, p. 350.

4284   Arber, *Dunbar Anthology*, p. 125.

*4284.3 *...ʒoure seruand madame
A dialogue of the night visit—ten irregular stanzas with burden: 'Go fro my vindow go &c.' [Cf. Baskerville, *PMLA* XXXVI. 580-87; cf. a religious parody with similar burden: 'Quho is at my windo quho quho / Goe from my windo goe goe,' in *Gude & Godlie Ballatis*, ca. 1578; *repr.* Mitchell, STS XXXIX. 132; and cf. Sibbald, *Chronicle*, III. 227; and cf. Flügel, *Neuengl. Lesebuch*, p. 132].
1. Bodl. 3354, f. 230a (text often illegible).
Frankis, *Anglia* LXXIII. 301-2.

4284.5 Youre vgly token / My mynd hath broken
'Vppon a deedmans hede,' by John Skelton—vv. 59 in 'skeltonics.'
A Comely Coystrowne, ? Pynson, n.d. (STC 22611); *repr.* Dyce, *Skelton*, I. 18-24; Dyce and Child, *Skelton & Donne*, I. 23-5; Henderson, *Skelton*, 1933, p. 17; 1948, 1959, pp. 19-20; Hughes, *Skelton*, pp. 62-4; Gant, *Skelton*, pp. 15-17; Pinto, *Selection*, pp. 18-20; *Workes*, Marshe, 1568 (STC 22608); *repr.* [? J. Bowle,] 1736; Chalmers, *English Poets*, II. 301.

4284.8 Yry yry standard
A scrap on the Battle of the Standard, ca. A.D. 1138, in *Historia Anglorum* by Matthew of Paris.
Madden, *Rolls Series* XLIV, i. 260; Royster, *MLR* IV. 509.

APPENDIX A

Conversion Table of Acephalous Poems in the Brown-Robbins *Index*

All acephalous entries now appear in alphabetical order in the main section and are indicated by asterisks. Acephalous poems in the *Index* have the following new numbers in this *Supplement*.

*1	2478	*27	*819.5	*53	*3634.1		
*2	*78.5	*28	*823.3	*54	*3281.5		
*3	*196.5	*29	*842.5	*55	*3287.5		
*4	*282.5	*30	*851.6	*56	*3312		
*5	*295.5	*31	*854.3	*57	*3339.5		
*6	*296.3	*32	2358.5	*58	*3405.3		
*7	*296.6	*33	*944.5	*59	*3458.5		
*8	*298.5	*34	*1037.5	*60	*3461.3		
*9	*308.5	*35	*1132.5	*61	*3483.5		
*10	*301.3	*36	*1219.5	*62	*3518.5		
*11	*303.6	*37	*1367.1	*63	*3533.5		
*12	*304.5	*38	*1426.8	*64	*3553.5		
*13	*306.5	*39	*1492.5	*65	*3553.8		
*14	*309.5	*40	*1496.3	*66	3665		
*15	3452	*41	*1500.5	*67	*3700.5		
*16	*310.5	*42	*1538.5	*68	*3708.5		
*17	*316.3	*43	*1873.5	*69	*3719.5		
*18	*465.3	*44	*2284.5	*70	*3777.5		
*19	*295.8	*45	*2288.8	*71	*3780.5		
*20	*552.8	*46	*2602.3	*72	*3845.3		
*21	*557.3	*47	*2684.5	*73	*3870.5		
*22	586.5	*48	*3080.5	*74	*3947.3		
*23	*593.8	*49	*3117.4	*75	*4119.5		
*24	4256.8	*50	*3119.5	*76	*4194.5		
*25	*3844.8	*51	*3098.6	*77	*4256.3		
*26	*717.5	*52	*3216.5	*78	*4267.5		

APPENDIX B
Further Bodleian Summary Catalogue Numbers Used in the *Supplement*

Index — Corrigenda

Delete these references in *Index*, Appendix II

1119	Malone 941	7081	Ashmole 25
1994	Bodley 131	7629	Ashmole 1451
2305	Bodley 416	7655	Ashmole 1490
2538	Bodley 833	7662	Ashmole 1535
2907	Rawl. D. 328	7772	Ashmole 1481 I
3883	Fairfax 8	8447	Ashmole 1772
3888	Fairfax 14	11645	Rawl. B. 366
5167	Junius 56	12908	Rawl. D. 82
6733	Ashmole 391 v	14099	Rawl. D. 1370
6841	Ashmole 349	17686	Gouch Eccl. Top. 4
6953	Ashmole 754	18340	Gouch Liturg. 7

Supplement — Addenda

1049	Laud misc. 524	3554	e Mus. 54
1292	Laud misc. 210	3839	James 2
1562	Laud misc. 165	3843	James 6
1595	Laud misc. 647	3871	James 34
1619	Digby 18	3880	James 43
1642	Digby 41	3883	Fairfax 3
1654	Digby 53	3888	Fairfax 8
1873	Bodley 88 (printed book)	3894	Fairfax 14
1883	Bodley 34	3938	Eng. poet. a. 1 [Vernon]
1947	Bodley 100	4061	Hatton 26
1999	Bodley 131	4063	Hatton 57
2059	Bodley 608	4138	Hatton Donati 1
2090	Bodley 187	4192	Dodsworth 50
2224	Bodley 393	5088	Dodsworth 147
2285	Bodley 546	5136	Hatton 116
2305	Bodley 410	5167*	Junius 56
2538	Bodley 832		[Many Ashmole MSS, bound in one
2639	Bodley 791		volume, nevertheless have several S.C.
2649	Bodley 797		numbers.]
2670	Bodley 758	6616	Ashmole 970
2695	Bodley 828	6659	Ashmole 176
2712	Bodley 315	6704	Ashmole 349, I
3411	Selden supra 23	6733	Ashmole 391, II, 5
3478	Selden supra 90	6873	Ashmole 391, II
3493	e Mus. 23	6933	Ashmole 48

6937	Ashmole 53	11224	Rawl. A. 338
6953	Ashmole 745	11539	Rawl. B. 171
7007	Ashmole 1485, III, 3	11566	Rawl. B. 214
7010	Ashmole 1490	11645	Rawl. B. 306
7081	Ashmole Rolls 21	11946	Rawl. C. 81
7391	Ashmole 1113	11948	Rawl. C. 83
7628	Ashmole 1450, VII	12417	Rawl. C. 572
7654	Ashmole 1487, II	12506	Rawl. C. 662
7662	Ashmole Rolls 52	15161	Hearne's Diaries 38
7665	Ashmole 1489	15165	Hearne's Diaries 42
7722	Ashmole 1481	15516	Rawl. B. 471
7753	Ashmole 1386	15802	Rawl. liturg. f. 36
7772	Ashmole 1432	17680	Gough Eccl. Top. 4
8343	Ashmole 1451	18340	Gough Liturg. 7
8447	Ashmole Rolls 40	21672	Douce 98
8465[a]	Ashmole 8	21810	Douce 236
8505	Wood E. 1	28556	Corn. e. 2
8586	Wood B. 15	28557	Corn. e. 3
8606	Wood empt. 18	30161	Add. A. 60
8613	Wood empt. 25	32690	Eng. poet. e. 17
8714	Bodley 841	[S.C. numbers cease at 42088]	
8915	Jones 8		

APPENDIX C

Manuscripts in Private Possession: Present Locations

Present locations of MSS containing Middle English verse now or formerly in private possession, with a few major MSS in public collections often designated by name rather than by catalogue number. Where a MS has passed through several hands, the successive locations are given.

NAME	CONTENTS	LOCATION
Aberdeen	*Confessio Amantis*	Rosenbach Foundation 1083/29
Allan	*Index* 3880	Not established [G. Allan (Darlington)]
Aldenham	*Destruction of Jerusalem*	Goldschmidt Sale Cat. 50 (1938), Lot 59
Aldenham	*Horae*	Not established [1884 Cat., p. 84]
Aldenham 310	*Pricke of Conscience*	Univ. of Virginia: Hench 10
Aldenham	Life of St. Catherine	Harvard Coll. Richardson 44
Amherst 20	*Arma Christi*	Thompson
Amherst 23	Latin & ME prayers	BM Addit. 37787
Amherst 24	Sermons	Camb. Univ. Add. 5338
Amherst 26	*De Regimine Principum*	Merton 28
Amherst 28	Rolle, Juliana	BM Addit. 37790
Amherst 29	*Pricke of Conscience*	Harmsworth
Amherst 42	Magic	Wellcome Hist. Med. Lib. 510
Amherst 46	*Promptorum Parvulorum*	Sotheby Sale, Dec. 12, 1911, Lot 760
Amherst 135	*Form of Living*	Harmsworth
Anglesey	*Index* 2526	Not established
Appleby Castle	Ripley	Lord Hotham (Appleby Castle)
Armes	*Life of Our Lady*	Not established [not Univ. of California]
Arundel, Harington	Tudor poems (ed. Hughey)	Duke of Norfolk (Arundel Castle) [transcript: BM Addit. 28635]
Ashburnham 49	*Horae* (*Index* 914)	Not established
Ashburnham 52	*Primer*	BM Addit. 36683
Ashburnham 115	Lives of saints	Fitzwilliam Mus. McClean 128
Ashburnham 120	Tracts (*Index* 994)	Bibl. nat. n. a. 1. 693
Ashburnham 121	Medicine (*Index* 3848)	Not established
Ashburnham 122	Medicine	Wellcome Hist. Med. Lib. 406
Ashburnham 124	*Canterbury Tales*	Morgan Lib. M. 249
Ashburnham 125	*Canterbury Tales*	BM Addit. 35286
Ashburnham 126	*Canterbury Tales*	McCormick

[505]

Ashburnham 127	*Canterbury Tales*	Fitzwilliam Mus. 181
Ashburnham 128	Urry's transcriptions	BM Addit. 38181
Ashburnham 129	*Piers Plowman*	BM Addit. 35287
Ashburnham 130	*Piers Plowman* & *Pricke of Conscience*	Huntington Lib. HM 128
Ashburnham 131	*Troy Book*	Harvard Coll. Eng. 752
Ashburnham 132	Lydgate	Fitzwilliam Mus. 183
Ashburnham 133	Hoccleve	Gollancz
Ashburnham 134	Lydgate & Hoccleve	Fitzwilliam Mus. 182
Ashburnham 135	*Pricke of Conscience*	Fitzwilliam Mus. 131
Ashburnham 136	*Pricke of Conscience*	Rylands Lib. Eng. 90
Ashburnham 137	York pageant	BM Addit. 35290
Ashburnham 140	Charters of Christ	Camb. Univ. Add. 6686
Ashburnham 230	*Horae (Index* 1270)	Yates Thompson 57
Ashburnham 236	*Pricke of Conscience*	Camb. Univ. Add. 6693
Ashburnham 243	*Pricke of Conscience*	Not established
Ashburnham 244	*De Regimine Principum*	Garrett 137
Ashburnham 247	*Partenope de Blois*	BM Addit. 35288
Ashburnham 249	Astrology	Bodl. Lyell 37
Ashburnham 669	Prose lives of saints	BM Addit. 35298
Ashburnham	Plowman's Tale (inserted in a 1532 Chaucer)	Univ. of Texas 8
Ashby-de-la-Zouche	Alchemy & Medicine	Huntington Lib. HU 1051
Ashby-de-la-Zouche	*Confessio Amantis*	Quaritch Sale Cat.
Asloan	Scottish poems	Mrs. John McCombe [partial transcripts in Edinburgh Univ.: La. III. 450/1; La. III. 481; La. IV. 27-28]
Astley	Didactic poems	Morgan Lib. M. 775
Auchinleck	Scottish poems	Advocates 19. 2. 1
Bannatyne	Scottish poems	Advocates 1. 1. 6
Bateman	*Index* 981.3	Not established
Beauchamp	Beauchamp Hours	Fitzwilliam Mus. 41/1950
Bedford	*Cursor Mundi*	BM Addit. 36983
Belvoir Castle	*Fall of Princes*	Duke of Rutland (Belvoir Castle)
Bement	Religious poems	Huntington Lib. HM 142
Berkeley	*Horae*	Glazier G. 9
Billyng	Prayers by wounds	Not established
Blackburn: see Ireland Blackburn		
Blage	Tudor poems	Trinity Dublin 160
Blandford	Religious poems	Rylands Lib. Lat. 395
Bodmer	*Canterbury Tales*	Michael Bodmer (Coligny, Switzerland)
Bodmer	Metrical romances	Michael Bodmer (Coligny, Switzerland)
Borneman	*Index* 2119	Parke-Bernet Sale, Nov. 1955, Lot 796

Bowes Midland	*Handlynge Synne*	Osborn 5
Bramshill House	Life of Christ	BM Addit. 38666
Brechin Castle	Fordun's *Chronicle*	Earl of Dalhousie (Brechin Castle)
Brechin Castle	Wintoun's *Chronicle*	Earl of Dalhousie (Brechin Castle)
Bridgewater House: *see* Ellesmere		
Bright	*Pricke of Conscience*	Soc. of Antiquaries 687
Brome	Commonplace book	Hamilton
Brough Hall	*Horae* (printed book)	Sir John Lawson (Brough Hall)
Brough Hall	Psalter	Sir John Lawson (Brough Hall)
Brough Hall	*Rituale*	Sir John Lawson (Brough Hall)
Brudenell	Chaucer and *Siege of Thebes*	Sotheby Sale, Feb. 1959
Brudenell	Fragment: *Sydrac & Boctus*	George L. Brudenell (Lamport Hall, Northants.)
Buccleugh	*Siege of Rouen*	Quaritch Sale Cat. 304
Buckland House	Manual	? Sir. N. W. Throckmorton (Buckland House)
Buckland House	*Mirror of Sinners*	? Sir N. W. Throckmorton (Buckland House)
Bühler 5	Hardyng's *Chronicle*	Curt F. Bühler (New York)
Bühler 11	*Dictes* & *Sayings*	Curt F. Bühler (New York)
Bühler 13	*Pricke of Conscience*	Curt F. Bühler (New York)
Bühler 17	*Index* 3632	Curt F. Bühler (New York)
Bühler 21	Medicine	Curt F. Bühler (New York)
Burton	Fragments	BM Addit. 47663 (M)
Bute	*Confessio Amantis*	Marquis of Bute (London)
Bute	Northern Homilies	Marquis of Bute (London) [missing]
Calthorpe	*Serpent of Division*	BM Addit. 48031
Camoys	*Pricke of Conscience*	Univ. of Pennsylvania Eng. 8
Campbell	*Siege of Thebes*	Robinson Sale Cat. 74, 1944, No. 268
Campsall Hall	*Troilus* & *Criseyde*	Morgan Lib. M. 817
Canby	*Canterbury Tales*	Phillipps 8136
Capesthorne	Humphrey Newton's poems	Bodl. Lat. misc. c. 66
Cardigan	Chaucer & *Siege of Thebes*	Brudenell
Carlisle	*Confessio Amantis*	Silver 3
Carlisle	*Court of Sapience*	Plimpton 256
Carlisle	St. Cuthbert	Egerton 3309
Carlisle	Fragment (*Index* 3406)	Not established
Castle Howard: *see* Carlisle		

Chaderton	*Piers Plowman*	Horton Hold Hall
Challoner	*Horae*	York Minster: Chapter House
Charlemont	*Siege of Rouen*	Not established [Sotheby Sale, 1865]
Chirk Castle	Medicine	? Col. Myddleton-Biddulph (Chirk Castle, Denbigh)
Cholmondeley	*Stations of Rome*	Newberry Lib. Gen. Lib. Add. 12
Claverley	*Confessio Amantis*	Plimpton 265
Clifden	Fragments: *Parthenope* &c.	Bodl. Lat. misc. b. 17
Clopton	de Brunne	Folger Sh. Lib. 420312
Clopton	*Piers Plowman*	Sterling
Clumber	Brut *Chronicle*	Gordan Lib. 63
Clumber	*Confessio Amantis*	Bodl. Lyell 31
Clumber	Higden's *Polychronicon*	Gordan Lib. 64
Clumber	Robert of Knaresborough	Egerton 3143
Clumber	Voyage to Jerusalem	Sotheby Sale, 1937, Lot 1129
Cockerell	*Life of Our Lady*	Univ. of Chicago 566
Colchester Castle	Palladius	Bodl. 29620
Cole	*Index* 1941.8	Not established
Colville	Wintoun's *Chronicle*	Not established
Compton Hall	*Canterbury Tales* (Ashburnham 124)	Morgan Lib. M. 249
Compton Hall	*Canterbury Tales* (Ingilby)	Egerton 2864
Compton Hall	*Canterbury Tales* (Norton)	Egerton 2863
Compton Hall	*Canterbury Tales*	Rylands Lib. Eng. 113
Condover Hall	*Stations of Rome*	Newberry Lib. Gen. Add. 12
Cooke 21	Astrology (*Index* 3571)	? Davies Cooke (Owston, Yorks.)
Cooke 30	Commonplace book (*Index* 4148)	? Davies Cooke (Owston, Yorks.)
Cooke	Durandus	Sotheby Sale, July 15, 1959, Lot 205
Cox	*Catalogus Regum Angliae* (*Index* 906)	J. Stevens Cox (Dorset)
Cope	Life of Christ	BM Addit. 38666
Corser	*Pricke of Conscience*	Rylands Lib. Eng. 90
Coughton Court	Court roll	Throckmorton (Coughton Court, Warwickshire)
Currer	Mandeville's *Travels*	Corning Museum of Glass 6
Curzon	*Fall of Princes*	BM Addit. 39659
Davies	Chronicle	Bodl. Lyell 34
Deene Park: *see* Brudenell		
Delamere	*Canterbury Tales*	Penrose 6

Deritend House	*Index* 3529	Not established [? perhaps lost; not at Birmingham Pub. Lib.]
Devonshire	*Canterbury Tales*	Duke of Devonshire (Chatsworth House)
Devonshire	Fragments: Chaucer	Duke of Devonshire (Chatsworth House)
Devonshire	Chester plays	Huntington Lib. HM 2
Devonshire	Tudor poetry	BM Addit. 17492
Dewick	*Index* 704	Harmsworth
Dillon	Prayer book	Viscount Dillon
Dod	*Index* 4184	Not established [J. W. Dod (Cloverly)]
Drexel	Fragments: songs	New York Pub. Lib.
Dunrobin	Calendar (*Index* 4115)	Duke of Sutherland (Dunrobin, Scotland)
Eaton Hall: *see* Westminster		
Ecton Hall	*Fall of Princes*	Huntington Lib. HM 268
Ellesmere 26/A 13	Lydgate & Hoccleve	Huntington Lib. EL. 26. A. 13
Ellesmere 26/A 17	*Confessio Amantis*	Huntington Lib. EL. 26. A. 17
Ellesmere 26/C 9	*Canterbury Tales*	Huntington Lib. EL. 26. C. 9
Ellesmere 34/B 7	Processional	Huntington Lib. EL. 34. B. 7
Essex	Robert of Gloucester's *Chronicle*	Huntington Lib. HM 126
Fairfax	Songs & carols	BM Addit. 5465
Fairhurst	Fragment: *Wars of Alexander*	Not established [James Fairhurst]
Fellowes	Psalter	Not established [Sotheby Sale Cat. June 7, 1964, Lot 231]
Felton	de Guileville	Melbourne Pub. Lib.
Fillingham	Poems & romances	BM Addit. 37492
Findern	Chaucer apocrypha	Camb. Univ. Ff. 1. 6
Fitch	Songs & carols	Bodl. 29734
FitzGerald	*Arma Christi* rolls	Osborn 22
FitzWilliam	Palladius	Not established [photostats: Bodl. 31502]
Foyle	*Pricke of Conscience*	Christina Foyle (Beeleigh Abbey)
Foyle	*Miroure of Mans Saluacioune*	Christina Foyle (Beeleigh Abbey)
Foyle	*Speculum Christiani*	Christina Foyle (Beeleigh Abbey)
Frampton Court	*Peter Idley*	Bodl. Eng. poet. d. 45

Garrett 119	*Index* 687.3.	Princeton Univ. Deposit
Garrett 136	*Confessio Amantis*	Princeton Univ. Deposit
Garrett 137	*De Regimine Principum*	Princeton Univ. Deposit
Garrett 138	*Pricke of Conscience*	Princeton Univ. Deposit
Garrett 139	*Fall of Princes*	Princeton Univ. Deposit
Garrett 140	*Sowdon of Babylone*	Princeton Univ. Deposit
Garrett 141	*Amoryus* & *Cleopes*	Princeton Univ. Deposit
Garrett 142	Brut *Chronicle*	Princeton Univ. Deposit
Garrett 143	Religious poems	Princeton Univ. Deposit
Garrett 151	Trevisa	Princeton Univ. Deposit
Gatacre	*Confessio Amantis*	Plimpton 265
Glazier G. 9	*Horae*	W. S. Glazier (New York)
Glazier G. 39	Prayer roll (*Index* 2300.3)	W. S. Glazier (New York)
Gollancz	Hoccleve	Huntington Lib. HM 744
Gorhambury	*Index* 2403.5	Not established
Gower	*Speculum Vite*	Liverpool Univ.
Graham	XIV Cent. poems	? Sir Richard Graham (Cumberland)
Gray	*Confessio Amantis*	Maggs Sale Cat. 456, no. 184
Gray	Scottish poems	Advocates 34. 7. 3
Greg	*Abbey of Holy Ghost* (*Index* 3412.5)	Goldschmidt Sale Cat. 71 (1943), no. 1
Greg	*Pricke of Conscience*	Osborn 31
Gribbel	*Fall of Princes*	Not established [John Gribbel (Philadelphia)]
Grove	*Pricke of Conscience*	Huntington Lib. HM 125
Gurney 38	*Index* 2167	Not established
Gurney 75	Astrology	Camb. Univ. Add. 6860
Gurney 121	*Confessio Amantis*	Sotheby Sale, 1936, Lot 121
Gurney 146	*Libel of English Policy*	Boston Pub. Lib. 92
Gurney 150	*Siege of Thebes*	Camb. Univ. Add. 6864
Gurney 170	Morality plays	Folger Sh. Lib. 5031
Gurney	*Pricke of Conscience* & Lyrics (ed. *PMLA* LIV)	Egerton 3245
Hailes	Romance of Clariodus	Advocates 19. 2.5
Haistwell	*Canterbury Tales*	Egerton 2726
Halliwell	*Pricke of Conscience*	Not established [Sotheby Sale, 1920, Lot 515]
Hamilton	Commonplace book	Hillwood
Hamper: *see* Deritend House		
Harmsworth	*Catalogus Regum Angliae* (*Index* 906)	Cox
Harmsworth	*Fall of Princes*	Not established
Harmsworth	*Life of Our Lady*	Univ. of Illinois 85
Harmsworth	*Lumière des Laics*	Smith
Harmsworth	*Miroure of Mans Saluacioune*	Foyle

Harmsworth	*Piers Plowman*	Morgan Lib. M. 818
Harmsworth	*Pricke of Conscience* (Amherst 29)	Foyle
Harmsworth	*Pricke of Conscience* (Leighton)	Bühler 13
Harmsworth	*Pricke of Conscience* (Neale)	Leeds Univ. Brotherton 500
Harmsworth	Robert of Gloucester's *Chronicle*	London Univ. 278
Harmsworth	*Siege of Rouen*	Sotheby Sale, Oct. 15, 1945, Lot 1951
Harmsworth	*Speculum Christiani*	Foyle
Harmsworth	*Speculum Christiani*	Univ. of Illinois 71
Harmsworth	*Troy Book*	Sotheby Sale, Oct. 15, 1945, Lot 1963
Harmsworth	*Index* 704	Univ. of Pennsylvania Lat. 33
Harington I	Tudor poems	Egerton 2711 [transcript: BM Addit. 28636]
Harington II: see Arundel, Harington		
Harington-Hill	Tudor poems	BM Addit. 36529
Hastings: see Ashby-de-la-Zouche		
Hatfield	*Pilgrimage of the Soul*	Marquis of Salisbury
Hawkins	Religious poems	Huntington Lib. HM 183
Helmingham Hall LJ. I. 7	*Speculum Christiani*	Lord Tollemache (Helmingham Hall)
Helmingham Hall LJ. I. 10	Hardyng's *Chronicle*	Lord Tollemache (Helmingham Hall)
Helmingham Hall LJ. I. 11	Brut *Chronicle*	Lord Tollemache (Helmingham Hall)
Helmingham Hall LJ. I. 12	Chronicle	Lord Tollemache (Helmingham Hall)
Helmingham Hall LJ. II. 1	*Pricke of Conscience*	Lord Tollemache (Helmingham Hall)
Helmingham Hall LJ. II. 2	Homilies	Lord Tollemache (Helmingham Hall)
Helmingham Hall LJ. II. 9	Homilies (*Index* 2397)	Bodl. Eng. th. f. 39
Helmingham Hall LJ. III	*Canterbury Tales*	Princeton Univ. Lib.
Helmingham Hall LJ. IV. 3	Clement of Llanthony	Lord Tollemache (Helmingham Hall)
Helmingham Hall LJ. V. 14	*Speculum Christiani*	Laurence Witten, Sale Cat. 5 (1962), no. 51
Helmingham Hall LJ. VI. 22	Miscellanea	Lord Tollemache (Helmingham Hall)
Helmingham Hall	Trevisa	Morgan Lib. M. 875
Helmingham Hall	Lydgate & *Sir Generides*	Morgan Lib. M. 876
Hench 10	*Pricke of Conscience*	Univ. of Virginia: Hench

Henry VIII	Tudor poems	BM Addit. 31922
Henslow	Medical receipts	Not established
Hillwood	Commonplace book	Dennis Hillwood (Sherborne St. John): Ipswich County Hall Deposit
Hodson: see Compton Hall		
Hoe	*Life of Our Lady*	Huntington Lib. HM. 115
Holkham Hall 666	French Picture Bible	BM Addit. 47682 [All Holkham Hall MSS on microfilm in Bodl. Lib. MSS Film 478-493; & in Lib. of Congress]
Holkham Hall 667	*Canterbury Tales*	Earl of Leicester (Holkham Hall)
Holkham Hall 668	*Pricke of Conscience*	Earl of Leicester (Holkham Hall)
Holkham Hall 670	*Siege of Rouen*	Earl of Leicester (Holkham Hall)
Holkham Hall 671	Fabyan's *Chronicle*	Earl of Leicester (Holkham Hall)
Holkham Hall 675	Prose Passion with prayers	Bodl. Holkham Misc. 41
Holkham Hall	Miscellanea (Index 3815.5)	Bodl. Holkham Misc. 39
Hood	Walter de Henley	Not established [Sir A. Acland Hood (St. Audries, Somerset)]
Hopton Hall	Devotional prose tracts	? Henry Chandos-Pole-Gell (Derby)
Horton Hold Hall	*Piers Plowman*	Liverpool Univ. F. 4. 8
Horton Hold Hall	*Pricke of Conscience*	Maggs Sale Cat. 580, no. 449
Horton Hold Hall	*Pricke of Conscience*	Leeds Univ. Brotherton 501
Houghton 9	*Fall of Princes*	Arthur J. Houghton, Jr. (Maryland)
Howard de Walden	Poems & songs	Camb. Univ. Add. 5943
Huth 7	Burgh's *Cato*	Huntington Lib. HM 144
Huth 153	*Abbey of Holy Ghost* (*Index* 3412.5)	Greg
Huth	*Miroure of Mans Saluacioune*	Foyle
Huth	Prayer roll (*Index* 1011.8)	Not established
Huth	*Speculum Christiani*	Harmsworth
Ilchester	*Piers Plowman*	London Univ. V. 88 [transcript: Trinity Camb. 536]
Ingilby	*Canterbury Tales*	Compton Hall
Ingilby	*Piers Plowman*	Harmsworth
Ingilby	Rolle & English Psalter	Huntington Lib. HM 148

Ingilby	*Stations of Rome*	Canterbury Cath. Add. 68
Ireland Blackburn	Metrical romances	Bodmer
Ireland Blackburn	*Pricke of Conscience*	Univ. of Pennsylvania Eng. 1
Islip	*Horae* (*Index* 1727)	Lady Richmond (Islip, Oxford)

Jersey: see Osterly Park

Kilkenny Castle	English songs	Duke of Ormond (Kilkenny Castle)
Kimberley	*Fall of Princes*	Sotheby Sale, July 14, 1947, Lot 181
Knowsley Hall	*Titus and Vespasian*	Osborn 32

L'Estrange: see Devonshire (*Canterbury Tales*)
Leconfield: see Petworth

Lee	*Fall of Princes*	Morgan Lib. M. 124

Leicester: see Holkham Hall

Leighton	*Fall of Princes*	Harmsworth
Leighton	*Pricke of Conscience*	Harmsworth
Le Neve	*Horae*	Boston Pub. Lib. 1546
Littledale	*Index* 333.5	Miss O. Littledale (Oxford)
Longleat 15	*Life of Our Lady*	Marquis of Bath (Longleat, Somerset)
Longleat 29	Devotional prose & verse	Marquis of Bath (Longleat, Somerset)
Longleat 30	Devotional prose & verse	Marquis of Bath (Longleat, Somerset)
Longleat 31	*Pricke of Conscience*	Marquis of Bath (Longleat, Somerset)
Longleat 32	*Speculum Christiani*	Marquis of Bath (Longleat, Somerset)
Longleat 55	Red Book of Bath	Marquis of Bath (Longleat, Somerset)
Longleat 253	*Epître d'Othèa*	Marquis of Bath (Longleat, Somerset)
Longleat 254	*Fall of Princes*	Marquis of Bath (Longleat, Somerset)
Longleat 256	*Isle of Ladies*	Marquis of Bath (Longleat, Somerset)
Longleat 257	Lydgate & Chaucer	Marquis of Bath (Longleat, Somerset)
Longleat 258	Chaucer apocrypha	Marquis of Bath (Longleat, Somerset)
Longleat 298	*Scale of Perfection*	Marquis of Bath (Longleat, Somerset)
Longleat	Chronicles	Marquis of Bath (Longleat, Somerset)
Longleat	Medicine (*Index* 1910)	Marquis of Bath (Longleat, Somerset)

Longleat	Norton's *Ordinal of Alchemy*	Marquis of Bath (Longleat, Somerset)
Longleat	Prognostications (*Index* 970)	Marquis of Bath (Longleat, Somerset)
Loscombe	Medicine	Ashburnham 122
Loudoun	*Confessio Amantis*	Morgan Lib. M. 125
Lyme Hall	*Scottish Feilde*	? Richard Hegh (Lyme Park, Disley) [photostats: Bodl. Dep. c 130]
Lyell	*Fall of Princes*	Quaritch Sale Cat. 699, 1952, Lot 28
Lyell	Tudor poems	Univ. of Pennsylvania, Lat. 35
Lyte	*Horae*	Univ. of Illinois 76
Macro 5	Morality plays	Gurney 170
Macro 18	Astrology	Gurney 75
Macro 68	*Libel of English Policy*	Gurney 146
Macro 102	*Siege of Thebes*	Gurney 150
Macro 103	*Confessio Amantis*	Gurney 121
Maddocks	*Fall of Princes*	Sotheby Sale, Mar. 1, 1949, Lot 499
Maitland Folio	Scottish poems	Pepys 2553
Makculloch	Scottish poems	Edinburgh Univ. 205
McCormick	*Canterbury Tales*	Univ. of Chicago 564
Mellish	*Index* 3637	Nottingham Univ. Me LM 1
Mellon	Chansonnier	Yale Univ. 91
Merthyr	Fragment: Chaucer	L. C. Simons (Bridgend): Nat. Lib. Wales Deposit
Merton 25	*Index* 3109	Breslauer Sale Cat. 90, no. 16
Merton 28	*De Regimine Principum*	Breslauer Sale Cat. 90, no. 24
Merton	Mirk's *Festial*	Leeds Univ. Brotherton
Meyerstein:	*Sydrac and Boctus*	Quaritch Sale Cat. 713
Middleton: *see* Wollaton Hall		
Midland: *see* Bowes Midland		
Montagu	Calendar	Lord Montagu of Beaulieu
Mostyn 84	Lydgate	Yates Thompson 47
Mostyn 85	*Life of Our Lady*	Abbot Sale Cat.
Mostyn 186	*Horae*	Not established [Chester Beatty Sale, 1933]
Mostyn 257	*Life of Our Lady*	Harmsworth
Mostyn 258	*Siege of Thebes*	Abbot Sale Cat.
Mostyn 259	Robert of Gloucester's *Chronicle*	London Univ. 278
Mostyn 2722	*Fall of Princes*	Houghton
Mulliner	Mulliner Book music & songs	BM Addit. 30513
Myddleton-Biddulph: *see* Chirk Castle		

Narford	*Confessio Amantis*	Morgan Lib. M. 126
Naworth: *see* Carlisle		
Neale	*Pricke of Conscience*	Harmsworth
Newcastle	Robert of Knaresborough	Clumber
Norfolk	*Guiscardo* & *Ghismonda*	? MS lost [printed Robert Dexter, 1597]
North	*Pricke of Conscience*	Wellesley College 8
Northumberland 455	*Canterbury Tales*	Duke of Northumberland
Northumberland D. x. 1	Walter de Henley	Not established
Norton	*Canterbury Tales*	Compton Hall
Old Buckenham Hall	*Siege of Thebes*	? Prince Duleep Singh
Ormond	*Pricke of Conscience*	Leeds Univ. Brotherton 500
Osborn 5	*Handlynge Synne*	James M. Osborn: Yale Univ. Deposit
Osborn 22	*Arma Christi* rolls	James M. Osborn: Yale Univ. Deposit
Osborn 31	*Pricke of Conscience*	James M. Osborn: Yale Univ. Deposit
Osborn 32	*Titus and Vespasian*	James M. Osborn: Yale Univ. Deposit
Osterley Park	*Fall of Princes*	Rylands Lib. Eng. 2
Osterley Park	*Troy Book*	Rylands Lib. Eng. 1
Oxford	Fragments: Chaucer	(a) Rylands Lib. Eng. 63 (b) Rosenbach Foundation 1084/2
Payne	Medical tracts	Wellcome Hist. Med. Lib. 542
Peniarth 481	Burgh's *Cato*	Nat. Lib. Wales 481
Penrose 6	*Canterbury Tales*	Boies Penrose (Devon, Pennsylvania)
Penrose 11	Trevisa	Sotheby Sale, May 20, 1947, Lot 288
Percy Folio	Ballads & romances	BM Addit. 27879
Perrins 33	*Index* *3708.5	Not established
Perrins	Ripley scroll (*Index* 1364.5)	Not established
Perrins	Ripley scroll (*Index* 1364.5)	Kraus Sale Cat. 100, no. 32
Petre	*Speculum Vite*	Taylor
Petworth 2	de Guileville	New York Pub. Lib. Spencer 19
Petworth 3	Life of St. Margaret	Blackburn Pub. Lib.
Petworth 7	*Canterbury Tales*	Lord Leconfield (Petworth House)
Petworth 8	Religious prose & verse	Wagstaff 9
Petworth 97	Alchemy (Ripley)	Not established
Petworth 99	Alchemy (Norton)	Not established
Petworth 100	Alchemy	Not established

Petworth 102	Alchemy	Not established
Petworth 103	Norton's *Ordinal of Alchemy*	Not established
Phillipps 58	*Index* 707.5	Not established
Phillipps 1054	*Meditations Vitae Christi*	Michigan State Univ. 1
Phillipps 1099	Hoccleve & Walton	Rosenbach Foundation 1083/30
Phillipps 1805	English verses (ff. 3)	Preussische Staatsbibliothek Lat. 194
Phillipps 2298	*Confessio Amantis*	Garrett 136
Phillipps 2734	*Pricke of Conscience*	Strong
Phillipps 3113	*Troy Book*	Harmsworth
Phillipps 3126	*Pricke of Conscience*	Huntington Lib. HM 130
Phillipps 3311	Medical receipts	Wellcome Hist. Med. Lib. 404
Phillipps 3338	*Index* 3653	Robinson Sale Cat. 1950, lot 28
Phillipps 3784	Brut *Chronicle*	Folger Sh. Lib. 725-2
Phillipps 4204	Use of sword & spear	Not established
Phillipps 4254	*Fall of Princes*	Rosenbach Foundation 439/16
Phillipps 4255	*Fall of Princes*	Univ. of Chicago 565
Phillipps 6570	Fragments: Chaucer	(a) BM Addit. 9832 (b) Newberry Lib. Silver
Phillipps 6883	*South English Legendary*	Huntington Lib. HM 64
Phillipps 7008	Herbal	Bühler 21
Phillipps 8117	*Fall of Princes*	Garrett 139
Phillipps 8118	*Fall of Princes*	Gribbel
Phillipps 8122	Northern Homily Cycle	Univ. of Minnesota Z 822 N 81
Phillipps 8136	*Canterbury Tales*	Michael Bodmer (Coligny, Switzerland)
Phillipps 8137	*Canterbury Tales*	Rosenbach Foundation 1084/1
Phillipps 8151	Hoccleve	Huntington Lib. HM 111
Phillipps 8192	*Confessio Amantis*	R. H. Taylor, Princeton, New Jersey
Phillipps 8231	*Piers Plowman*	Huntington Lib. HM 137
Phillipps 8244	Alchemy	Not established
Phillipps 8250 [=8252]	*Piers Plowman* & *Troilus*	Huntington Lib. HM 114
Phillipps 8253	*South English Legendary*	Egerton 2810
Phillipps 8254	Northern Homily Cycle	BM Addit. 38010
Phillipps 8267	Fragment: Hoccleve	Not established
Phillipps 8299	Lydgate & Chaucer	Huntington Lib. HM 140
Phillipps 8306	*Promptorum Parvulorum*	Amherst 46
Phillipps 8310	*Robert the Deuyll*	Egerton 3132
Phillipps 8336	Herebert	BM Addit. 46919
Phillipps 8343	*Pricke of Conscience*	Osborn 31
Phillipps 8357	*Sowdowne of Babylone*	Garrett 140
Phillipps 8459	*Speculum Christiani*	Bodl. 32216

Phillipps 8820	Religious poems	Not established
Phillipps 8857	Brut *Chronicle*	Huntington Lib. HM 113
Phillipps 8923	Religious poems	Huntington Lib. HM 183
Phillipps 8942	*Confessio Amantis*	Folger Sh. Lib. SM 1
Phillipps 8980	Hoccleve	Huntington Lib. HM 135
Phillipps 9053	Lydgate	BM Addit. 34360
Phillipps 9056	*Piers Plowman*	BM Addit. 34779
Phillipps 9412	*Pricke of Conscience*	Huntington Lib. HM 139
Phillipps 9418	Medical tracts	New York Academy of Medicine 13
Phillipps 9472	Walton's *Boethius*	Camb. Univ. Add. 3573
Phillipps 9613	Chronicles	Folger Sh. Lib. 1232-3
Phillipps 9803	Life of Christ	BM Addit. 39996
Phillipps 9970	Fragment: Chaucer	Plimpton 253
Phillipps 11071	Sermons	Amherst 24
Phillipps 11077	Herbal	Huntington Lib. HM 58
Phillipps 11409	*Index* 809	Not established
Phillipps 11929	Prose tracts	Huntington Lib. HM 502
Phillipps 11955	Chaucer's *Astrolabe*	London Institute of Electrical Engineers
Phillipps 18134	*Index* 3120	Wellcome Hist. Med. Lib. 673
Phillipps 20420	Northern Homily Cycle	Huntington Lib. HM 129
Phillipps 22914	Fragment: *Confessio Amantis*	London Univ. Coll. frag. Ang. 1
Phillipps 23554	Fragment: *Fall of Princes*	Maggs Sale Cat. 849, No. 30 A
Phillipps 24309	Capgrave	Huntington Lib. HM 55
Plimpton 39	*Preces piae*	Columbia Univ. Deposit
Plimpton 80	*Index* 1727	Columbia Univ. Deposit
Plimpton 253	Fragment: Chaucer	Columbia Univ. Deposit
Plimpton 255	*Fall of Princes*	Columbia Univ. Deposit
Plimpton 256	*Court of Sapience*	Columbia Univ. Deposit
Plimpton 259	*Dictes & Sayings*	Columbia Univ. Deposit
Plimpton 263	Trevisa	Columbia Univ. Deposit
Plimpton 265	*Confessio Amantis*	Columbia Univ. Deposit
Plimpton Add. 2	Juliana Berners	Columbia Univ. Depsoti
Plimpton Add. 3	Religious poems	Columbia Univ. Deposit
Plimpton Add. 4	Fifteen Ooes	Columbia Univ. Deposit
Porkington 10	Poems & Romances	Nat. Lib. Wales Deposit
Porkington 20	*Pricke of Conscience*	Nat. Lib. Wales Deposit
Portland *see* Welbeck Abbey		
Powell *see* Horton Hold Hall		
Powis	Religious poems	Huntington Lib. HM 127
Pratt	Religious poems	Plimpton Add. 3
Pudsey	*Index* 333.5	Littledale
Pullen	Birth roll	Wellcome Hist. Med. Lib. 632
Raines	Burgh's *Cato*	? widow of Canon Raines, York

Ravensworth	*Confessio Amantis*	Morgan Lib. M. 690
Redgrave Hall	Dramatic fragment	BM Addit. Roll 63481 (B)
Reidpath	Scottish poems	Camb. Un. Ll. 5. 10
Richardson 22	*Index* 4184	William King Richardson: Harvard Univ. Deposit
Richardson 44	Life of St. Catherine	William King Richardson: Harvard Univ. Deposit
Ritson	Songs & carols	BM Addit. 5665
Robartes	Fragments: *Parthenope* & Northern Homily Cycle	Bodl. Lat. misc. b. 17
Robartes	Fragment: *Ancren Riwle*	Bodl. Eng. th. c. 70
Rutland *see* Belvoir Castle		
Schwerdt	Lydgate's Dietary (*Index* 824)	Sotheby Sale, Mar. 12, 1942
Scott	Ripley's *Twelve Gates*	Not established [John Scott (London)]
Sharp	Coventry plays	MS. burned in 1879
Silver 1	Fragment: Chaucer	Newberry Lib. Louis H. Silver
Silver 3	*Confessio Amantis*	Newberry Lib. Louis H. Silver
Silver 4	*Fall of Princes*	Newberry Lib. Louis H. Silver
Simeon	Religious poems	BM Addit. 22283
Smith	*Lumière des Laics*	Sotheby Sale, Feb. 2, 1960 [George Smith]
Sowter	*Horae*	Boston Pub. Lib. 1546
Stafford	*Confessio Amantis*	Huntington Lib. EL 26. A. 17
Stephens	Fragment: *Troilus*	? George Stephens (Edinburgh)
Sterling	*Piers Plowman*	London Univ.
Stockdale Hardy	Leicester Psalter	Not established
Stonehill	*Speculum Christiani*	Univ. of Illinois 71
Stonor Park	*Pricke of Conscience*	Univ. of Pennsylvania Eng. 8
Strong	*Pricke of Conscience*	Bodl. Lyell empt. 6
Sykes	Single York pageant	Yorkshire Philological Soc.
Talbot	Talbot Hours	Fitzwilliam Mus. 40/1950
Taylor	*Confessio Amantis*	Robert H. Taylor (Princeton, New Jersey)
Taylor	*Speculum Vite*	Robert H. Taylor (Princeton, New Jersey)
Taymouth Castle	Gilbert Hay's *Alexander*	BM Addit. 40732
Taymouth Castle	Gilbert Hay's *Alexander*	BM Addit. 41063 (V)
Temple	*Siege of Thebes*	Sotheby Sale, June 16, 1941, Lot 153

Tenison	*Poor Men's Mirror*	? Archbishop Tenison Lib. London
Thomas	*Horae* (Index 1165)	A. G. Thomas (Bournemouth)
Thompson *see* Yates Thompson		
Thompson	*Arma Christi*	Mrs. Eberly Thompson (Portland, Oregon)
Thornton	Religious poems	Lincoln Cath. 91 [sister MS. BM Addit. 31042]
Tollemache *see* Helmingham Hall		
Towneley Hall	Towneley Mystery Plays	Huntington Lib. HM 1
Trentham Hall	*Floris* & *Blancheflour*	Egerton 2862
Trentham Hall	Gower	? Duke of Sutherland (Trentham Hall)
Vernon	Religious poems	Bodl. 3938 (Eng. poet. a 1)
Wagstaff 9	Religious prose & verse	Yale Univ. 163
Welbeck Abbey 29/331	Brut *Chronicle*	Duke of Portland: BM Deposit
Welbeck Abbey 29/333	Song fragments	Duke of Portland: BM Deposit
Wemyss	Wintoun's *Chronicle*	Not established [transcript Harley 6909]
Westminster	*Piers Plowman*	Duke of Westminster's estate
Wheatley	Religious poems	BM Addit. 39574
Windsor	Carols	Egerton 3307
Wollaton Hall	*Confessio Amantis*	Nottingham Univ. Mi LM 8
Wollaton Hall	*Fall of Princes*	Quaritch Sale Cat. Illuminated MSS. 1931, No. 100
Wollaton Hall 163	Register of Burton Abbey	Nottingham Univ. Mi Dc 7
Wollaton Hall	Fragments: *South English Legendary*	Nottingham Univ. Mi LM 7/1
Wollaton Hall	*Speculum Vite*	Nottingham Univ. Mi LM 9
Wollaton Hall 7	Trevisa & *Abbey of Holy Ghost*	Plimpton 263
Worsley	*Pricke of Conscience*	Rylands Lib. Eng. 50
Wrest Park	Chronicles	Harvard Univ. Eng. 750
Wrest Park	*Libel of English Policy*	BM Addit. 40673
Wrest Park 5	*Sydrac and Boctus*	Meyerstein
Wright	Medicine (*Index* 3457.5)	A. Dickson Wright
Wright	*Index* 3118.4	Not established [W. Aldis Wright]
Wurzburg	*Fasciculus Morum*	Morgan Lib. M 298
Yates Thompson 47	Lydgate	Not established
Yates Thompson 57	*Horae* (*Index* 1270)	Not established

Yates Thompson 61	Primer	BM Addit. 36683
Yates Thompson 83	Talbot Hours	Fitzwilliam Mus. 40/1950
Yates Thompson	Beauchamp Hours	Fitzwilliam Mus. 41/1950
Yates Thompson	*Pricke of Conscience*	Garrett 138
Yelverton 35	*Serpent of Division*	BM Addit. 48031

APPENDIX D
Preservation of Texts

Corrected according to revised entries in this *Supplement*. *Index* or *Supplement* numbers in parentheses; changes in MSS in brackets.

117 MSS	*The Pricke of Conscience* (1193, 3428, 3429) [+3]
64 MSS	*The Canterbury Tales* (4019) [no change]
55 MSS	Lydgate's Dietary (824, 1418) [+9]
54 MSS	*Piers Plowman* (1458, 1459) [+4]
	Prayer to B. V. in *Speculum Christiani* (2119) [+6]
	South English Legendary [+20]
51 MSS	*Confessio Amantis* (2662) [+2]
46 MSS	Sentences of Philosophers in *Speculum Christiani* (2167) [+5]
45 MSS	Hoccleve's *De Regimine Principum* (2229) [+1]
44 MSS	Ten Commandments in *Speculum Christiani* (1491, 3687) [+4]
43 MSS	Lydgate's *Life of Our Lady* (2574) [+2]
42 MSS	English quatrain in *Speculum Ecclesie* (2320) [+6]
	Seven Deadly Sins in *Speculum Christiani* (1286, 4150) [+3]
41 MSS	'Erthe upon erthe' (703, 704, 705, 3939, 3940, 3985) [+5]
	Lydgate's Kings of England (882, 3632) [+4]
39 MSS	Nassyngton's *Speculum Vite* (245) [+4]
	Riming exhortation in *Speculum Christiani* (1342) [+4]
36 MSS	Precepts in -ly (317, 324, 799, 2794.8, 3087, 3102) [+6]
34 MSS	Lydgate's *Fall of Princes* (1168) [+4]
33 MSS	Burgh's *Cato major* (854) [+2]
	Verses on the Elixir (3429) [+19]
31 MSS	First song in Rolle's *Form of Living* (2017.5) [new entry]
30 MSS	Second song in Rolle's *Form of Living* (4056) [+22]
	Lydgate's *Siege of Thebes* (3928) [+4]
27 MSS	Cook's *Tale of Gamelyn* (1913) [new entry]
	Fasciculus Morum tags [-4]
	Phlebotomy (3848) [+10]
26 MSS	Norton's *Ordinal of Alchemy* (3772) [+7]
24 MSS	de Caistre's Hymn (1727, 1752) [+4]
	Lydgate's *'Stans puer ad mensam'* (1694, 2233) [+1]
	Ripley's *Twelve Gates* (595) [no change]
23 MSS	Chaucer's 'Truth' (809) [+3]
	Lydgate's *Troy Book* (2516) [+2]
	Preparing the Philosopher's Stone (2656) [-1]
	Walton's version of *Boethius* (1597) [no change]
22 MSS	Burgh's *Parvus Cato* (3955) [+1]
	Short Charter of Christ (4184) [+5]
20 MSS	Abuses of the Age (906) [+5]
	Introduction to a medical tract (3422) [+10]
	Lydgate and Burgh's *Secrees of Old Philosoffres* (935) [+1]
	Maydestone's version of the Psalms (1961, 3755) [-2]
	Proverb in Walter de Henley's *Hosebondrie* (4113) [new entry]

18 MSS   Long Charter of Christ (1174, 1718, 4154) [+1]
         Love-song to Jesus (1781) [+2]
         Prayer by the Holy Name (1703) [+6]
17 MSS   *Arma Christi* (2577) [+2]
         Assumption of the B.V. (1092, 2165, 2638, 3976) [no change]
         Chaucer-Merlin Prophecy (3943) [+5]
         Chaucer's *Troilus and Criseyde* (3327) [no change]
         First Scottish Prophecy (4029) [+6]
         Northern Homily Cycle [no change]
         Second Scottish Prophecy (4008) [new entry]
         'Sensus miratur' (4181) [+6]
16 MSS   Chaucer's 'ABC Hymn to the B.V.' (239) [+3]
         English translation of de Guileville [new entry]
         Libel of English Policy (3491) [+1]
15 MSS   Advice to Purchasers of Land (4148) [+1]
         Chaucer's 'Lak of Stedfastnesse' (3190) [+3]
         Hardyng's *Chronicle* (710) [+3]
         How to Find Easter (1502) [+7]
         Lydgate's 'Chorle and Bird' (2784) [no change]
         Lydgate's 'Dance of Macabre' (2590, 2591) [+2]
         Lydgate's 'Testament' (2464) [+1]
         On Herbs, especially Betony (2627) [+2]
         'Pees maketh plente' (2742) [+2]
         Proverb in Walter de Henley's *Hosebondrie* (2698) [new entry]
         Seege of Rouen (979) [+7]
14 MSS   Abuses of the Age (-les) (1820) [+4]
         Charm to staunch blood (624, 627.5) [new entry]
         Chaucer's *Parlement of Foules* (3412) [no change]
         Ipotis (220) [no change]
         Lavynham's *Tretis* tags [new entry]
         Lydgate's 'Why artow froward' (3845) [no change]
         Northern Passion (170, 1907) [no change]
         Robert of Gloucester's *Chronicle* (727) [-2]
13 MSS   Lay Folk's Catechism (406) [no change]
         Sapientia Patris (1276) [+4]
         Titus and Vespasian (1881) [+3]
         Wimbledon's sermon: quatrain (3397) [new entry]
12 MSS   *ABC of Aristotle* (471, 3793, 4155) [no change]
         Alchemical verses (3721) [new entry]
         Chaucer's 'Complaint to his Empty Purse' (3787) [+3]
         Chaucer's *Legend of Good Women* (100) [no change]
         Chester Plays (716) [no change]
         St. Godric's Hymn to the B.V. (2988) [no change]
         Langtoft's *Chronicle:* inserted songs [new entry]
         Lychefelde's 'Complaint to God' (2714) [-1]
         Lydgate's 'Hors Goose and Shepe' (658) [no change]
         Lydgate's *Life of St. Edmund* (3440) [no change]
         Lydgate's 'Rammeshorne' (199) [+1]
         Proverbial tag on youth and age (1151) [+4]

	Single stanza from *Fall of Princes* (674) [+1]

        Single stanza from *Fall of Princes* (674) [+1]
        Storia Lune (970, 1991, 3341) [+1]
11 MSS *'Cur mundus militat'* (4160) [+2]
        Hoccleve's *'Lespistre de Cupide'* (666) [+1]
        Hours of the Cross in the English *Primer* (3499) [no change]
        Kings of England (444) [new entry]
        Litany to the Cross (914) [no change]
        Meditation on the Passion (1761) [no change]
        Prayer of confession (3231, 3233) [+1]
        Thomas of Erceldoune's Prophecy (365) [new entry]
10 MSS Alchemical verses (3257) [new entry]
        Chaucer's 'Balade of Fortune' (3661) [no change]
        Chaucer's 'Gentilesse' (3348) [+1]
        Cursor Mundi (2153) [no change]
        Four things making man a fool (4230) [+1]
        Lydgate's *Interpretacio Misse* (4246) [no change]
        Lydgate's Kissing at the *Verbum caro* (2413, 4245) [no change]
        Lydgate's Women's Horns (2625) [no change]
        Ripley's *Mystery of Alchemists* (4017) [new entry]
        Sir Isumbras (1184) [no change]
        Speculum Gy de Warewyke (1101) [no change]
        Ten Commandments (3685) [+1]
        Trental of St. Gregory (83, 1653, 3184) [no change]
        Trevisa's translation of *Polychronicon:* inserted poems [new entry]
9 MSS   Against lending money, a tag (1297) [new entry]
        Alchemical verses (2666) [new entry]
        Chaucer's 'Complaint to Pite' (2756) [no change]
        Lay Folk's Mass Book (1323, 3507) [no change]
        Lydgate's 'Doctrine for the pestilence' (4112) [+1]
        Lydgate's Five Joys of the B.V. (2791) [-1]
        Lydgate's Kalendar (1721) [+1]
        Lydgate's *Temple of Glas* (851) [no change]
        St. Michael, Part III (3453) [+1]
        'Quia amore langueo' (1460) [no change]
        Remembrance of Mortality (4129) [new entry]
        Robert of Sicily (2780) [+1]
        Seven Joys of B.V. in Mirk's *Festial* (462) [no change]
        Seven Sages of Rome (3187) [no change]
        Wintoun's *Chronicle* (399) [no change]
        Wounds of Christ (4200) [+1]
8 MSS   Adulterous Falmouth Squire (2052) [no change]
        Chaucer's *Anelida and Arcite* (3670) [no change]
        Love-song to Jesus (3238) [no change]
        Lydgate's 'Black Knight' (1507) [no change]
        Lydgate's *'Consulo quisque eris'* (1294) [no change]
        Lydgate's *Life of St. Margaret* (439) [no change]
        Lydgate's 'Midsummer Rose' (1865) [no change]
        Lydgate's 'Song of Virtue' (401) [no change]
        Myrrour of Mankynd (1259) [no change]

Petition in Mirk's *Festial* (4068.3) [new entry]
Peter Idley (1540) [new entry]
Richard Coeur de Lion (1979) [new entry]
Ripley's scroll (1364.5) [new entry]
Seven Wise Counsels (576) [new entry]
Short metrical chronicle (1105) [no change]
Tag against English in Brut *Chronicle* (1934) [new entry]

APPENDIX E
Corrigenda for Subject and Title Index in the Brown-Robbins *Index*

Appeal of Christ to man (including *Quid ultra debuit*) *read* debui
Arimathea, Joseph of, *48 *read* *49
Authors: Bokenham, Oswald *read* Osbern

Barbara, S., life of, 3944 *read* 3994
Blessed Virgin Mary. Dialogues of: with Christ on Cross *delete* 2124; with Death, 834 *read* 1834
Bokenham, Oswald *read* Osbern

Charms, 1198 *read* 1199
Chaucer's dream (*Isle of ladies*), 3847 *read* 3947
Clerk: interlude with girl, 608 *read* 668

De regimine principium *read* principum
Dialogues. Clerk and maiden, 608 *read* 668
Dice: political prophecy by *delete* 3792

Fables, beast, by Henryson, 4144 *read* 3703
Fall of princes, extract of single stanza (?), 147 *read* 145 [*and delete*]

Gossips' meeting, 1853 *read* 1852
Gregory, S.: life of, 2916 *read* 2910
Griffith, David ap: verses by *read* to

Hyginus, Pope, life of, by Hoccleve *delete* by Hoccleve

James the less, S., life of, 2553 *read* 2353
Iankyn and Ionet, 178 *read* 179
Julian Apostate, S. *delete* S.
Julian, lives of the three *read* four

Katirin, acrostic on, 585 *read* 588
Kings of England, rimed charters of, by Lydgate, 1425 *read* 1513
Kingdom, a well ordered, 1821 *delete* entry

Latin hymns. *Ave maris stella*, 1801 *read* 1081
Lydgate, Epistle to Sibille, 3231 *read* 3321
— Lamentacioun of our lady Maria, 4049 *read* 4099
— Lauandres, tretise for, 4154 *read* 4254
— *Stans puer*, 2333 *read* 2233

Macer: *Virtues of herbs*, preface to, 3978 *read* 3578
Mannyng de Brunne, extracts, 625 *read* 516
Medical receipts: verses attached to (prose) collections of, 4183 *read* 4182

Newton, Humphrey [ed. pending, Robbins, *RES*] *read* *PMLA* LXV. 249-81

Paul, S.: life of *delete* 1790
Peace: prayer for 1722 *read* 1772
Prayers. On special occasions. For peace, 1722 *read* 1772
Psalm CXXIX, 2528 *read* 2522
Psalms by Myadestone *read* Maydestone
Pympe, John *read* Paston, John, I: letter to Margaret, 1360; letter from Pympe to John Paston, II, 866

Qui amore langueo *read* *Quia amore*

Religion *delete* rules of conduct for those in, 4019

Sir Tristrem, 1328 *read* 1382
Sixtus, S., life of, 1384 *read* 1584
Soldiers songs *delete* 1358
Speculum Christiani, exhortation, 1343 *read* 1342
Stans puer ad mensam, 2332 *read* 2233
Susannah, story of, 3353 *read* 3553

Wives' tales, 1853 *read* 1852
Women: praise of, *22 *read* *20
Wycliffite expansion of *Mass Book* *read* *Catechism*

SUBJECT AND TITLE INDEX

ABC poems: against pride of clergy, 455.8; on flowers, 1378.5; on morals and manners, 312.5; on ribald characterizations, 0.1.
Aberdeen, praise of, 541.5.
Abingdon bridge, commemoration of, 2619.2.
Absence: pangs of, 159.8; proverbial sayings on, 2674.
Absit ditari qui se wlt, 4150.3.
Abuses of the age (*see also* Evils of the times): 86.8, 1320, 2146, 2536.5, 2812.8, 3168.2, 3866.5, 4005.5.
Acrostics, poems containing, 735, 735.5, 1187, 1570.5, 1594, 1596.8, 1813, 2030.8, 2136, 2223, 2793.5, 2834.3, 3228, 3856.5; *and see* 1024, 1026, 1063.
Adam: reply of Mercy to, 1390.3; reply of Righteousness to, 1509.5.
Adam and Eve, life of, *1873.5.
Adam and Melchisedech, verse insert in prose text of, 1083.5.
Adare, Richard, epitaph for, 1206.8.
Admonition (*see also* Warnings): to man, 3560.5; to women, 4264.5.
— moral (*see also* Precepts, moral), 3538.5, 3570.5, *3667.5, *3770.5, 3823.5, 4126.5, 4187, 4256.5.
Advent, farewell to, 905.5.
Adversity, be cheerful in, 1470.8.
Advice, good: *see* Counsel, good *and* Precepts, moral.
'Advyce to luvaris,' by Dunbar, 1440.5.
'Advice to spend anis awin gude,' by Dunbar, 2072.8.
Aeneas, Dido's letter to, 811.5.
Aeneid, Douglas' translation of, 1842.5.
'Agaynst a comely coystrowne,' by Skelton, 2609.5.
— Dundas,' by Skelton, 1021.5.
— the prowde Scottes,' by Skelton, 1931.3.
— treason,' by Dunbar, 1587.3.
— venemous tongues,' by Skelton, 193.5.
Agincourt, battle of, 969.
Agnes, St., life of, *301.3.
'Alas I dye for payne,' 3595.6.
Alban, St., hymn to, 2388.5.
Albany, Duke of: orison on return to France of, 3694.6; plea to return to England addressed to, 3866.5; satirical attack on, 2803.5.
Alchemical poems, 407.6, 703.5, 1150.3, 1211.5, 1241.5, 1364.5, 1555.5, 1931.5, 2308.3, 2354.5, 2614, 2729.5, 3372.8, 3452.5, 3581.5, 3928.5, 4052.5.
Aldred, curse ascribed to, 1119.8.
Alewives poems (*see also* Gossips' meeting), 870.8, 1362, 2358.5, 3265.5 (Skelton).
Alexander the Great, Romance of wars of, 3947.3.
All Hallows: *see* All Saints.
'All maner herbys gode for potage,' 3255.5.
All Saints, song at, 2384.5.
'All erdly joy returnis in pane,' 2632.5.
Ambition, excessive, 1170.5.
'Amendis to þe telyouris and sowtaris,' by Dunbar, 515.5.
'Amerous balade by Lydegate,' 837.5.
Amys, Thomas, epitaphs for, 1187.5, 1285.5.
Anaphora: 'Adiew,' 2759; 'Considyr,' 2521; 'Farewell,' 765.3, 3720; 'I come,' 1289; 'I sayh,' 1353; 'Lorde,' 1975; 'Time,' 2451.5, 3256.6; 'Woe worth,' 160, 765.3.
Ancren Riwle, proverbial fragment in, 734.5.
'Anigmata,' 1396.
Animal noises, schoolboy's trans. of, 430.8.
— prophecy, 3510.
Anne, St., progeny of, 2153.5.
Annunciation: fragmentary poems on, *269.8, *2636.5; songs on, 1037.3; 1041.3, 1048.5.
— and Nativity, narrative of, 3704.3.
Anselm, St.: trans. of *Deploratio,* 3938.
Antichrist, birth of, by Dunbar, 2018.5.
Antidotarium Nicholai, riming opening to, 258.
Apocalypse: conclusion to, 3305.2; introduction to, 3305.4.
Apollonius of Tyre, romance of *3098.6.
Apostles, on the, 3559.8.
— Creed: *see* Creed.
Appeal of Christ to God the Father, 782.5.
— of Christ to man, 193.8, 490.5,

[526]

631.5, 813.5, *851.3, 1018.5, 1431.5, 2079.5, 2714, 3228.3, 3318.4, 3567.3, 3677.5, 3905.5.
— to the King to right wrongs, 3206.5.
Archery: on shooting with crossbow, 4244.5.
Argument of Morien and Merlin, 407.6.
Aristotle, advice attributed to, 1172.5.
Arthur, King: fragment of poem on, *295.8; as one of Nine Worthies, 1929.5.
— Prince: carol honoring, 2394.5; pageant verses for marriage of, 671.5, 1270.4, 1273.8, 1322.8, 1637.4, 2028.3, 2030.2, 2030.4, 3704.6, 3706.3, 3810.6, 3880.3, 4095.5; song on birth of, 1866.8.
'Articuli fidei,' teach parishioners, 3305.6.
Ascension, song at, 2533.5.
Ashwell, Thomas: music for anthem, 960.5.
Asperges, psalm arranged as trans. of, 1123.8.
Ass, story of man and, *3271.5.
Assumption of the B.V.: poem on, *4119.5; song of, 1249.5.
Astrological prognostications, 1201.5.
Astronomical lore, 1907.5.
Athelston, King: couplet attrib. to, 337.5.
Aubigny, Lord, welcome to, by Dunbar, 2811.5.
Audelay, John: Deadly sins and their remedies, *1492.5; Nine virtues, *3780.5.
Audi filia et vide, 2231.8.
Augustine, St., verses on, 1197.8.
Aula gaudescit, 1634.5.
Authors of Middle English and early Tudor verse: Berry, Henry; Bigot, Hugh; Bodmine; Bourscher, Richard; Buntyng; Carter; Caxton, William; Cely, George; Clerk; Clerke, John; Copland, Robert; Cornish, William; Crophill, John; de Worde, Wynkyn; Douglas, Gawin; Drake, Raff; Garnesche; Greenacres; Hay, Gilbert; Prior Hendred; Henry VIII; Hilton, Walter; Holland, Richard; Howard, Lord Thomas; James I; Jernegan, Robert; Kaye, Richard; Larrons, Patrick; Lavynham; Lichtoun; Lynne; Medwall, Henry; Mereley, John; Mersar [? John]; More, Thomas; Newton, Richard; Packe, James; Page, John; Paston, John; Peeris, William; Redford, John; Richardoune; Rivers, Lord (Anthony Wydville); Thorpe, William; Trevisa, John; Usk, Thomas; Walton, John; Wyatt, Thomas; Wikes, Nycholas; Womyndham, William; Wyllughby.
Auxilium meum a Domino, 3706.4
Ave cuius concepcio, 1070.3.
Ave Maria: paraphrase of, 1024; power to save, *465.3.
Ave maris stella, 1034.5.
Ave Rex anglorum, 1070.5.
Ayenbite of Inwyt: couplet in, 3578.5; invocation to, 1961.3; prefatory verses to, 539.5.

Baker, amulet for, against fever, 459.
Baker, John, benediction for, 1790.5.
'Balade [of Unstedfastness],' attrib. to Dunbar, 1466.5.
— of the Scottysshe Kynge,' by Skelton, 1822.5.
— *per antiphrasim*,' by Lydgate, 3823.
— vpon the gate of the prouostis place of Tourmaday,' by Caxton, 4109.5.
Ball, John: letters to rebels, 1790.8, 1791.
Ballade, triple, 828.
'Ballat of Our Lady,' 1082.5 (Dunbar), 2461 (Chaucer or Dunbar), 2831.8 (Dunbar).
— aganis evill women,' attrib. to Dunbar, 3306.8.
Banestre, Sir William, vision of, 1967.8.
Banknot, William, epitaph for, 1207.5.
Bannockburn: avenging of English defeat at, 3080; tag by Scots at, 2039.3.
Barbara, St., colophon to life of, 2300.8.
— Eve of, fasting on, 4154.5.
Barber, Geoffrey, commemoration of, 2619.2.
Barbor, William, bookplate of, 4058.8.
Baret, John, epitaph for, 4238.5.
Barlaam and Josaphat, 1585.5.
Barnet, Battle of, 899.
Barton, John, epitaph for, 1793.5.
Basle University fragments, 63.5, 442, 591.5, 3381.8.
Bastardy, verses used in suit on, 4120.3.
Batman, Stephan, bookplate of, 1411.5.
Beasts produced by parts of dead body, 4119.
Beatus venter qui te portauit, 1048.5.
Bede's prophecy, 4154.3.

[527]

Bedford, Jaspar Duke of: epitaph for, 2818.6.
Behaviour: advice on good, 552.5, 1636.8, 2000.5, 2289.5, 3307.5; foolish, 1149.8; rules for, 636.5, 1524.5, 2072.6, *3119.5.
Bek, Thomas Castleford of: Chronicle, 1559.
'Bele Aeliz' poem, 1470.
Benedict, St., Rule of: colophon for, 1197.6.
Berlin Staatsbibliothek fragments: 1631.3., 2794.6, 3167.3, 3897.5, 3900.5.
Berners, Juliana: *Book of Hawking*, colophon for, 1197.2.
Berry, Henry: verses in a Paston Letter, 4235.5.
'Best to be blyth,' by Dunbar, 886.5.
Bettys, Sir Thomas, epitaph for, 4028.3.
Betrayed maiden, 1330, 1589.5, 3409, 3832.5, 3902.5.
Bevis of Hamptoun, fragment of, *3405.3.
'Bewty and the presoneir,' by Dunbar, 3140.5.
Beauty, feminine: dangers of, 37.3, 817.5.
Bible, Wycliffite: colophon to, 1197.3.
Biblia pauperum, English version of, 576.5.
Bigot, Hugh: defiance of Henry III, 1417.3.
Bird, moral advice of, *3700.5.
— of paradise, 2231.3.
Birds, the names of, 3788.5.
— *Parliament of*, 3642.5.
'Birth of Antichrist,' by Dunbar, 2018.5.
Blessed Virgin Mary.
  Attributes of, 496.
  Ballades to, by Dunbar, 1082.5, 2831.8.
  Christ-child sings to, 3438.3, 4242.5.
  Christmas carol of, 1984.5.
  Envoy to, 2579.5.
  Fifteen joys of, *3483.5.
  Five joys of, *1037.5.
  Grace before meat to, 508.
  Hymns to, *1037.5, 1041.5, *3216.5, 3477.6.
  Joys of, 454.5, 1087.
  Laments of, 158.4, 377.5. 1448.5.
  Lullaby songs of 1448.5, 4242.5; *and see* 1575.5.
  Macaronic prayer to 2033.5.
  Miracles of, *282.5, *465.3, *1967.8.
  Moralization of play with Christ-child, 3438.3.
  Poems in praise of, 66.5, 1030.5, 1034.5, 1048.5, 1467, 2124.5, 2169, 2323.3, 3478.5.
  Prayers to, *196.5, 454.5, *995.2, 1034.5, 1036, 1037.3, 1070.3, 1807, 1833.5, 2033.5, 2121.5, 2124.5, 2169, 2478.8, 2562.5, 2577.3, 3675
  Sorrows of, 454.5.
  Tribulations of, 427.5.
  Truest of all, 1467.
Blessings, 210.5, 908.4, 1790.5.
Blickling Homilies, love lyric in, 3808.5.
Blindman's buff, tag for, 28.5.
Bliss, heaven's: prayer for, 879.5, 1871.8.
Blood, charms to staunch, 624, 627.5, 1946.5, 3209.5.
— Virtues of Christ's, 627.8.
— of Hayles: legend of, 3153; miracles of *311.5.
Boar's head carol, *3312.
Bodley Burial, 95.
Bodmine, Dominus Iohannes arcuarius canonicus: prayer to Christ, *711.5.
Body: address of Soul to, *2684.5; parts influencing faculties, 3413.6.
Boecius, speech of: at pageant, 2028.3.
Boethius, Walton's translation of: extracts occurring separately, 856.5, 1254, 2820.
Bonfant, Richard, epitaph for, 2766.9.
Book of fortune, by More, preface to, 2183.5.
— *of vices and vertues*, quatrain inserted in, 1436.5.
Bookplates, 1411.5, 1417.5, 1442.5, 1866.7, 2000.3, 2766.2, 3612.5, 4058.8, 4123.5.
Border warfare, 3445.5.
Borrowing, on, 1147.4; repayment of, 3958.5.
Bosworth Field, 981.3, 986.5.
Bourscher, Richard Daniel: verses by, 2245.4.
'Bowge of courte,' by Skelton, 1470.5; *and see* 2782.
Bozon, Nicolas: *Contes moralisés*, tags in, 635.5, 853.4, 1147.8, 1186.5, 1426.4, 1850, 2689.5, 3218.5, 3799.6, 3818.5, 3860.6, 3894.3.
Boy: loved *'carnaliter,'* 728.8; unhappy, 4120.6; with ulcerated hand, 1294.5.
Brews, Elizabeth: verses to John Paston, 1627.5.

Bridal feast, sotelties for, 461.5, 1270.8, 1331.5, 1386.5.
Bridlington, fragmentary verses from, *3458.5.
Brinton, tags in sermon, 807.5, 853.8.
Bristol, inscription on sword given to, 1796.5.
— pageant verses at, 2200.5, 2212.5, 3884.5.
Bromholm, Rood of: text attached to picture of, 3585.5.
Brooch, inscription on, 3775.5.
Brunne, de: tag in chronicle, 718.5.
Buckingham, Edward Stafford, Third Duke of: lament of, 158.9, 2409.5.
Buik of Alexander, by Hay, *3287.5.
Buntyng: moral admonition by, 4139.
Burgh, Benedict: extract from *Cato major*, 726.
Burlesques: of courtly love lyric, 2247.5; of female correspondence, 2261.8; of love epistle, 2827.5; of tournament, 2289.8 (Dunbar).
Burlton, Richard, epitaph for, 2536.8.

Caelum non animum mutat, 4096.5.
Caesar Augustus dramatic fragment, *3117.2.
Calliope, Skelton's service to, 585.5.
Calot, Laurence: trans. of, 3808.
Cambridge, Mayor of: student verses on, 1941.8.
Campshall Church, wall verses at, 1863.5.
Candlemas, song at, 2440.5.
Cantelowe, Margaret, epitaph for, 588.5.
Capgrave, John: *Solace of pilgrims*, tag in, 1083.5.
'Card lye down,' 1163.5.
Carlisle Cathedral, verses on stalls of, 1197.8.
Carmentis, 1924.5.
'Caroll of the Innocentes,' 3549.5.
Carter: couplet signed by, 484.5; condemned in book plate, 3612.5; verses by, 2617.5, 3171.5.
Catharine, Princess: *see under* Arthur, Prince.
— St.: *see under* Katherine, St.
Cato major, by Burgh: extract from, 726.
Cato, pagan yet Christian, 661.5.
Caution, need for, 68, 1824.6, 1829.2, 1829.5, 1941.5, 3079.8.
Caxton, John, epitaph for, 2766.6.

Caxton, William: 'Balade,' 527.5; 'Ballade' to Trinity, 3830.5; 'Ballade ... vpon the gate of the prouostis place of Tourmaday,' 4109.5; epilogue to *Lyf of Our Lady*, 927.5; epitaph for 2222.5.
Cely, George: on living soberly, 3768.2.
'Certeyn rewles' for ascertaining trustworthiness, 3285.
Chansonniers, European: English songs in, 135.3, 138, 2183, 2782, 3165.
Chamberleyn, John, epitaph for, 1770.5.
Chapel of Walsingham, foundation of, 2664.5.
Charity: absence of, 593.4; duty of, 1218.8.
Charlemagne, as one of Nine worthies, 1929.5.
Charms, 412.5, 605.5, 624, 627.3, 627.5, 860.5, 873.8, 1293.5, 1946.5, 1952.5, 2749.5, 3209.5, 3634.5, 4154.8.
Chattering in church, on (*see also* Tutivillus), 707.5.
Chaucer, Geoffrey: *Hous of Fame*, spurious conclusion to, 316.6; 'Lak of Stedfastnesse,' extracts from, 2218; *Troilus and Criseyde*, extracts from, 848.5, 1418.5, 1422.1, 1926.5, 2577.5, 3535.
— spurious ascriptions to: alchemical verses, 1931.5; chronicle, 1016; verses on swiving, 1635.
Chester, processional song of nuns of, 2792.3.
— Castle, verses on, 1637.6.
Chevy Chase, 960.1 (*and see Hunting of the Cheviot*).
Chichele, William, epitaph for, 3220.7.
Children: instructions for, 552.5, 3784.6; rimes used in games, 0.3, 28.5; tag for learning by rote, 430.5.
Christ (*see also* Jesus).
Appeal of, to God: *see under* Appeal
Appeal of, to Man: *see under* Appeal.
As book of love, 631.5.
As boy of twelve, 3976.5.
As gardener, *3634.1.
As groom, 3727.5.
Attributes of, 496.
'Balade' to, by Caxton, 527.4.
Birth of: *see under* Nativity.
Blood of, against sin, 627.8.
Complaint of: *see under* Complaint.
Description of, *1426.8.
Early life of, 3976.5.
Last will and testament, 4182.5.

Life of: carol describing, 2635.5; metrical history, *3845.3.
Love of man by: see under Love [religious].
Mourned by the Marys, 158.3.
On the Cross: description of, *296.6; devotions for, 1011.8; prepared to die for man, 3595.6, 3677.5; words of, *296.6.
Passion of: see under Passion.
Praise of, 1048.5, 1954.
Prayers to (and see Passion; Prayer tags), 11.5, *711.5, 1683.3, 1700.5, 1704.5, 1719.5, 1732.5, 1758.5, *1779.5, 1950.5, 1967.5, 2217.5, 2723.5, 3077.5, 3238.3, 3776.5.
Resurrection of, 688.3 (Dunbar), 1145.5.
Second coming, 1289.
Song of love to, 1732.5, 3680.5.
Sufferings of (see also Passion), 541.8, 2277.3, 3595.6.
Wounds of: see under Wounds.
Christ-child: carol on, 1575.5; plays with B.V., 3438.3; song of B.V. to, 4242.5; speaks with St. Christopher, 3903.3.
Christe qui lux es et dies, 620.5.
'Chrystis kirk of the grene,' by James I, 3860.8.
Christ's dialogue with sinner, 3598.5.
Christmas carols (see also Boar's head, Circumcision, Epiphany, Nativity), 54.5, 1984.5, 2217.5.
— song of schoolboy, 320.5.
— and Easter: song for use at, 2668.8.
Chronicles.
 based on Fabyan and Harding (to Henry VIII), 4174.5.
 Brut: inserted passages, 3213.
 later continuation of Harding, 4174.5.
 History of world (to A.D. 1518), 119.
 Kings of England, 3632, 4174.3 (to A.D. 1505).
Church, don't speak in (see also Chattering; Tutivillus), 813.8, 1214.9.
— Five commandments of the, 3481.5.
Circumcision of Christ, carol on, 2039.5.
Clariodus, romance of, *548.5.
Clarke, John, epitaph for, 3645.3.
Clergy: against pride of, 455.8; attack on, 2614.5; evil state of, 2536.5; place of: in three estates, 1494.5; satire on married, 4056.5.
Clerk, blinded by glory of B.V., *282.5.
Clerk, [? Jhon]: verses by, 2277.3.

Clerke, John, of Torryton: verses by, 1793.6.
Clopton Church wall verses, 2464.
Cock: description of, 4185.5; verses on, in *Gesta Romanorum*, 2238.5, 3081, 3322.3.
Cologne, three kings of, *854.3.
Colophons (see also Envoys; Epilogues), 189.5, 1179.5, 1197.1, 1197.2, 1197.3, 1197.4, 1197.5, 1197.6, 1218.5, 1241.5, 1596.5, 1965.5, 2300.3, 2323.5, 2660.1, 3305.2, 3452.3, 3578, 3603.5, 3604.5, 3637.5, 3721.3, 3815.3, 4052.5.
Colors: significance of, 3416.5; of urines, 1109.5.
'Colyn Cloute,' by Skelton, 3903.5.
Colyngbourne, William: satirical verses on Richard III, 3318.7.
Comfort of lovers, by Hawes, 3357.5.
Commandments of the church, five, 3481.5.
Commandments of the devil, ten, 4149.5.
Company, good, 2737.5.
Compassio Marie, *3216.5.
Complaint: against William the Conqueror's foreign prelates, 3074.3; of Christ, 490.5, 3595.6; of an exile, 158.8 (and see 120.5); of lover, 158.8, 270, 557.5, 648.5, 649.5, 675.8, 688.8, 835.5, 1418.5, 2245.1, 2277.5, 2530.5, 2577.5, 3144.5, 3162.5, 3808.5, 3958, 4201.6, 4272.5; of mistreated mistress, 2393.5; to the king, 649.8 (Dunbar); to her lover, 3297.3.
— *of the black knight*, by Lydgate: extract from, 3911.5.
— to the Kyng aganis Mure,' by Dunbar, 3117.5.
Compleint damours, 1388.
Compostella, itinerary to: tag in, 475.5.
— pilgrimage to, 1557.5.
Conception, on the, 1070.3.
Confession: forms of, 2551.5 (Dunbar); treatise on, *557.3, 694.
Conform, advice to, 4049.2.
Conscience, on, *3667.5, 3721.8, 3954.5 (Douglas).
— Remors of,' 2711.5.
— truth and, 3173.5.
Contentment, on, 4110.8 (Dunbar).
Contra luxuriam, 2602.4.
— *obstinatos*, 1136.3.
Conuersion of Swerers, by Hawes, 3354.5.
Cookery recipes: herbs for potage, 3255.5; recipe for 'fryturs,' 4187.5;

recipe for woodcock, 854.8; sauce for mallards, 3254.5.
Cornish, William: complaint, 120.5; praise God in nature, 2757.5; *Treatise bytweene enformacione and musyke*, 3405.8.
Cornish mystery play, English song in, 158.3.
Corpus Christi, song at, 1490.5.
'Counsale in luve,' by Dunbar, 753.3.
Counsel: against young men's, 1824.4; good (*see also* Precepts, moral), 194.5, 299.5, 552.5, 636.5, 836, 1172.5, 1218.8, 1409.5, 1427.5, 1468.5, 1570.8, 1587.8, 1596.8, 1829.5, 1941.5, 2522.5, 2818.8, 3079.7, 3079.8, *3553.5, 3751.5, 4068.3, 4135.5, 4187; on holding one's, 1817.5; on honest mirth, 3530.5; worldly wise, 465.5, 1427.5, 1923.5, 4049.2.
Courtly panegyric, parody of, 3765.5.
Coventry carol, 2551.8.
— made toll free, 1330.3.
Coverham Abbey, verses written at, 2300.3.
Covetousness, on, 865.8 (Dunbar), 1468.5.
Cowling Castle, inscription on, 1829.3.
Craft of lovers: portions incorporated, 1838.
Craft of philonomye, 935.
Crafte to lyue well, 2522.5.
Creed: clauses given to apostles, 662.5; how *Iudicare* came in, *851.6; paraphrase of, *1285, 1326.5.
Crophill, John: *Dayes of the Mone*, 1171; 'Loving cups,' 870.8; prayer tag, 981.5.
'Crosse rowe' poem, 0.1.
Cross of Bromholm, 3585.5.
Crossbow, order of shooting with, 4244.5.
Curses, 733.8, 1119.8, 1120.3, 1442.5.
Crucifixion: *see under* Christ; Passion.
Cuckold, on the, 543, 1137.5, 3172.5.
Cum procor est aurum, 4020.6.
Cupid, letter to, 4024.
— *Parliament of*, 2595.
Cupidity, 33.6.

Da tua dum tua sunt, 2501.5.
Dalusse, Robert, epitaph for, 334.5.
'Dame Pitiless,' 648.5, 2244.6.
'Dance of the sevin deidly synnis,' by Dunbar, 2623.3.

'Danger of wryting,' by Dunbar, 753.5.
Davy, Maud, epitaph for, 2766.5.
Days of the week, riddle on, 1396.
De beneficiis, 2289.5.
De dilectione cadus, 1415.5.
De duobus veris amicis, 3186.
de Guileville: see *Pèlerinage de l'âme*.
De modo vivendi, by Rolle: verses in, 995.3.
de Neville, Robert, lament on death of, 3857.5.
De proprietatibus rerum, trans. by Trevisa: envoy to, 4258.3; *Prohemium* to, 731.5.
De regimine principum, by Hoccleve: extract from, 1398; mottoes in one MS. of, 1587.8, 1704.5, 3079.2, 3079.5, 4049.3.
— *bonum consilium*, 2818.8.
de Worde, Wynckyn: colophon of *Robert the devil*, 3721.3; of *Scala perfectionis*, 3604.5; verses introducing *Polychronicon*, 3917.3.
Dead body, beasts produced by parts of, 4119.
Deadly sins and remedies, *1492.5.
Death: be prepared for, 484.5, 3249.6, 3252.5; 4049.3; dread of (*see also* Three sorrowful things), 673.5, 1370.5 (Dunbar); inevitability of, 672.4, 672.5, 2349.8, 3100.5, 4049.5, 4049.6; of man, 4049.8; on the approach of, 2736.6; patience in, 3492.3; prayer for grace at, 621.5; remembrance of, 550.5, 738.5, 1281.5, 2072.4, 2523.5, 2834.5, 3703.8, 4049.6; signs of, 853.8, 4036.5, 4040.6, 4049.8 (*and see* 4284.5); sorrow and woe of, 4049.7; swiftness of, 4056.3; thoughts of, prevent sin, 2834.5; warning by, 3143.
Deathbed scene, verses on a, 3703.8.
Debate: *see* Dialogues.
Deceit, on, 145.
Declaracio signorum in various prophecies, 3412.3.
Deer, carol of a stricken, 3199.8.
Defamation of women, on the, 3318.3.
Degeneracy of the age: *see* Abuses of the age, Evils of the time.
Delicta iuuentutis mee, 874.
Delight, pageant verses on, 1927.
Deliverance from sin, 3101.
Denis, St., drink for the love of, 2881.5.
Desert of religion, verses inserted in, 91.8, 1367.3.
Despair: charm for banishing, 860.5; prayer against, 1719.5.

Devil, ten commandments of the, 4149.5.
Devils debate with angels, 3645.5.
'Devillis inquest,' by Dunbar, 3634.6.
Dialogues.
  Amour and Pucelle, by Hawes, 3357.5.
  Betrayed maiden and lover, 3713.5.
  Christ and princes of hell, 3825.5.
  — and the sinner, 3598.5, 3611.
  Christopher, St., and Christ-child, 3903.3.
  Clerk and nightingale, *295.5.
  Courtier and maiden, 642.5.
  Devils and angels over body of robber, 3645.5.
  Dunbar and friend, 3634.3.
  Enformacione and musyke, by Cornish, 3405.8.
  Flyting of Dunbar and Kennedie, 3117.8.
  Jack Upland and friar, 1653.5, 3782.5, 4098.3.
  Juvenis et sapiens, 3656.5.
  Lover and advocate of Venus, 2594.
  — and Dame Nature, 2478.5.
  — and lass, 4020.3, *4284.3.
  Lucidus and Dubius, 3352.5.
  Maid and magpie, 3713.5.
  Mavis and lover, 1214.5.
  'Merle and the nichtingale,' 1503.5.
  Morien and Merlin, 407.6.
  Occupation, Idleness, Doctrine and Cleanness, 3430.5.
  Riotous young livers, 4073.5.
  Skelton and Garnesche, 3154.5.
  'Tua mariit wemen and the wedo,' by Dunbar, 3845.5.
  Venus and poet, 3917.8.
  Wooer and lady, 474.5.
Dice: casting by signs of Zodiac, 752.5; divination by, 3694.3; gnomic couplet on, 4042.5; on chance of, 2183.5; political prophecy by, 33.3, 734.8; preface to *Book of fortune*, 2183.5.
Dic homo quid speres, 3078.5.
Dic homo vas scelerum, 3079.3.
Dictio hisopii, 2691.8.
Dictes of philosophers, conclusion of Earl Rivers trans. of, 4273.8.
Dido's letter to Aeneas, 811.5.
Diet: moderation in, 1923.5; a sick man's, 4094.5.
Dietary, 3457.5.
Discretion: in asking, 2621.5; in behaviour, *3119.5; in giving, 3768.3; in taking, 121.5 (Dunbar); value of, 130.5.

Disputacio de sanguine Christi, English tag added to, 627.8.
Disputacio inter clericum et philomenam, *295.5.
'Do for thy self quhill thov art heir,' by Dunbar, 688.5.
'Do well' preferable to 'Say well,' 3079.7.
Doctrine, poem on religious, *3339.8.
Dog: and bone, 853.6; help my, 1730.5; in Latin *fabula*, 2700.5; love me, love my, 3322.5.
Dog, James, poems by Dunbar on, 2457.5, 3496.3.
Doomsday: Christ at, 3825.5, 3645.8; fifteen signs of, 2920.5, *3080.5; on, 2602.6.
Double˙ intendement, against, 1637.8.
Douglas, Gawin: *King Hart*, 1820.5; on conscience, 3954.5; *Palice of honour*, 4002.5; *XIII Bukes of Eneados*, 1842.5.
Drake, Raff: against the friars, 870.5.
'Dreme, The,' by Dunbar, 3595.3.
Dream visions, erotic, 1450.5, 1841.5, 3844.5.
Dress, against extreme fashions in, *1585.8, 2805.
Drinking: song of, 554.5; toast, 1940.5.
Drunkard's song, 4256.8.
Drury, Sir Robert, epitaph for, 3220.7.
Dubius, Dialogue with Lucidus, 3352.5.
Dunbar, William: 'Advice to spend anis awin gude,' 2072.8; 'All erdly joy returnis in pane,' 2632.5; 'Amendis to the telyouris and sowtaris &c.,' 515.5; 'Ane brash of wowing,' 1527; 'Ane his awin ennemy,' 1148.5; 'Ane orisoun,' 3077.5; 'Ane orisoun quhen the governour past into France,' 3694.8; 'Ballat of our Lady,' 1082.5 (*and see* 2461; 2831.8); 'Best to be blyth,' 886.5; 'Bewty and the prisoneir,' 3140.5; Birth of Antichrist, 2018.5; 'Cristes passioun,' 2497; 'Complaint to the King,' 649.8; 'Complaint to the Kyng aganis Mure,' 3117.5; Compliment to Queen Margaret, 912.5; 'Dance of the sevin deidly synnis,' 2623.3; 'Devillis inquest,' 3634.6; 'Dregy maid to the kyng,' 3870; 'Dreme, The,' 3592.3; Elegy on Bernard Stewart, 1444.5; 'Epitaph for Donald Owre,' 1587.3; 'Fenȝeit freir of Tungland,' 417.5; 'Flyting of Dunbar and Kennedie,'

3117.8; 'For in this warld may non assure,' 4116.5; 'Freiris of Berwick,' 384; 'General satyre,' 679.8; 'Gude counsale,' 479.5; 'Golden targe,' 2820.5; 'How Dunbar wes desyred to be ane freir,' 3634.3; 'How sall I governe me,' 1264.5; 'In prais of wemen,' 2354.3; Inconstancy of love, 4112.5; 'Justis betuix the tailyeour and sowter,' 2289.9; 'Kynd Kittok,' 2244; 'Learning vain without guid lyfe,' ('Dunbar at Oxenfurde'), 3768.6; 'Lament for the makars,' 1370.5; 'Maner of passing to confessioun,' 2551.5; 'Maner of the crying of ane playe,' 1119.3; 'Meditatioun in wynter,' 1599.5; 'Merle and the nichtingale,' 1503.5; New Year's gift to the King, 2267; 'Of a dance in the quenis chalmer,' 3117.7; 'Of content,' 4110.8; 'Of covetyce,' 865.8; 'Of deming,' 2226.5; 'Of discretioun in asking,' 2621.5; 'Of discretioun in geving,' 3768.3; 'Of discretioun in taking,' 121.5; 'Of folkis evill to pleis,' 861.5; 'Of James Doig, kepar of the quenis wardrop,' 3496.3; 'Of luve erdly and divine,' 2306.5; 'Of lyfe,' 3908.5; 'Of manis mortalitie,' 2143.5; Of Sir Thomas Norray, 2349.3; 'Of the changes of life,' 1356.5; 'Of the ladyis solistaris at court,'3556.5; 'Of the passioun of Christ,' 276.5, 2161.5; 'Of the warldis instabilitie,' 3646.3; 'Of the warldis vanitie,' 2587.5; 'On ane blakmoir,' 1934.5; 'On his heidake,' 2244.3; On the Nativity, 1657.5, 2312.5, 2831.6; On the Resurrection, 688.3; 'On the same James [Dog],' 2457.5; 'Petition of the gray horse, auld Dunbar,' 2349.5; 'Queinis reception at Aberdein,' 541.5; Remonstrance to the King, 3118.6; 'Rewl of anis self,' 3751.5; 'Solistaris in court,' 566; 'Tabill of confessioun,' 3776.5; 'Testament of Mr. Andro Kennedy,' 1330.5; 'Thrissil and the rose,' 3990.5; 'Tydingis fra the sessioun,' 293.5; 'To a ladye,' 3243.3; 'To a lady quhone he list to feyne,' 2247.5; To London, 1933.5; To the King, 2619.8, 3051.5, 3118.8; To the King 'that he war Jhone Thomsonnis man,' 3117.3; 'To the Lordis of the Kingis chalker,' 2258.5; 'To the merchants of Edinburgh,' 4165.5; To the Princess Margaret, 2308.5; 'To the Quene,' against catching the pox, 2032.5; To the Queen Dowager, 2497.5; 'Twa cummeris,' 2821.3; 'Tua mariit wemen and the wedo,' 3845.5; 'Welcum to Bernard Stewart,' 2811.5; Welcome to the Lord Treasurer, 1373.5; 'Quhone mony benefices vakit,' 3116.5; 'Without glaidnes awailis no tressour,' 470.5.

—Poems attributed to: 'Advyce to luvaris,' 1440.5; 'Ane ballat of our Lady,' 2461, 2831.8; 'Balade [of Unstedfastness],' 1466.5; 'Ballate aganis Evill Women,' 3306.8; 'Counsale in luve,' 753.3; 'Danger of wrytyng,' 753.5; 'Do for thy self quhill thov art heir,' 688.5; 'Freiris of Berwick,' 442.5; 'Lordis of Scotland to the Governour in France,' 3866.5; 'Of the Nativite of Christ,' 2312.5; On the Nativity, 1657.5, 3477.3; On the Resurrection, 3225.5.

Duplicity, attack on, 1626.
Durandus, conclusion of, 3815.3.
Durham, description of, 1608.5.
Durham Field: see Neville's Cross.

Earth upon earth, 702.5.
Ease, on living in, 1151.5.
Easter, how to find, 1502.
Edinburgh, rebuke to merchants of, by Dunbar, 4165.5.
Edward, Duke of Buckingham: lament of, 2409.5.
Edward I, Scots' abuse of, 3918.5.
Edward II, evil times of, 1992, 4144.
Edward III, motto of, 1214.2.
Edward VI, ballet honoring, 3118.5.
Eger de Femyne, Sir, fragment of poem on, *2639.5.
Ego Dormio, by Rolle: English verses in, 197.8, 1367.5.
Ego sum illy quy non youlte, 1273.5.
Elizabeth, queen to Henry VII: acrostic on, 735.5; anthem for marriage of, 960.5; epitaph for, 1206.9; lamentation of, 4263.3.
Ellendune, battle of, 718.5.
Ely, song of monks of, 2164.
Emblems in political prophecy, 552.3.
Emblematic scroll, by Ripley, 1364.5.
'En Parlament à Paris,' by Skelton, 1810.5.
Enemies, charm against, 412.5.
Enemy, oneself one's own, 1148.5.
England: appeal for unity of, against French, 3143.5; description of, in

Polycronicon, 3218.3; for victory of, 2766.8; kings of (to A.D. 1505), 4174.3; political condition in mid xv cent., 3412.5; prayer for nation of, 1717.3, 1955.5, 3206.5, 3236 (*and see* 2469.5); satire on state of (in A.D. 1485), 3318.7; unity at end xv cent., 3452.6.

Envoys ending texts (*see also* Colophons, Epilogues, Rubrics): alchemical tract, 1241.5; Apocalypse in prose, 3305.2; Commandments in prose, 3322.8; *De proprietatibus rerum*, trans. by Trevisa, 4258.3 (*Prohemium*); *Fall of princes*, one MS. only, 524; *Gesta romanorum*, 3818.5; *La belle dame sans merci*, alternative ending, 2386; medical collection, 3457.5; *Porteus of noblenes*, 2293.6; Pynson's *Chaucer*, to the reader, 4123.5; *Regula anachoritarum*, 3603.5; *Returned hermit*, added explanatory note, 3637.5; *Scala perfectionis*, by Hilton, 1596.5; *Treatise on hunting*, by Twici, 3910.5; veterinary directions, 1197.5.

Envy destroys virtue, 2631.5.

Epilogues (*see also* Envoys): *Dictes and sayengs*, 2663.5; *Lyf of Our Lady*, 927.5.

Epiphany: carols, 1070.5, 1220.5; fragment, *2033.3; poem, 3810.3.

Epistle from Mayor of Waterford, 2571.5.

Epistles, humorous, 2261.8, 2827.5.

— love, 564, 729, 733.1, 763.5, 765.3, 811.5, 1180, 1238, 1349.5, 1926.5 (adapted from Chaucer), 2267.5, 2421, 2439.5, 2478.5, 2510, 2560.5, 3228.5, 3785.5.

'Epitaph for Donald Owre,' by Dunbar, 1587.3.

'Epitaffe of . . . Iasper late duke of Beddeforde,' 2818.6.

Epitaphs, 143.8, 199.5, 334.5, 337.5, 374.5, 588.5, 679.5, 702.5, 703.3, 704, 765, 843.5, 1119.5, 1187.5, 1204.5, 1205.5, 1206.1, 1206.2, 1206.4, 1206.6, 1206.7, 1206.8, 1206.9, 1207.5, 1211.7, 1211.8, 1211.9, 1285.5, 1341.5, 1381.5, 1569.5, 1640.5, 1683.5, 1770.5, 1793.5, 1793.7, 1924.3, 2050.5, 2066.5, 2068.5, 2192, 2222.5, 2400.5, 2401.5, 2482.5, 2502.5, 2536.8, 2541.5, 2590.5, 2736.2, 2736.4, 2766.4, 2766.5, 2766.6, 2766.9, 2818.2, 2818.6, 3097.3, 3118.2, 3220.5, 3220.7, 3389.5, 3645.3, 3663.5, 3726.5, 3822.3, 3822.5, 3962.5, 4028.3, 4106.8, 4129, 4174.8, 4235.8, 4238.5, 4258.6.

'Epytaphye of Lobe, the Kynges toole,' 2482.5.

'Epytaphye of Sir Gryffyth ap Ryse,' 3962.5.

Erra Pater, Saying of: to husbandmen, 1426.1.

Erotic songs, 1344.5, 1641.5, 1824.8, 1863.3, 3306.3, 3443.5.

Erumpe et clama, 548.3.

Est homo res fragilis, 2066.8.

Everyman, 1341.8.

Evesham Abbey, seal of, 729.3.

Evil fellowship, avoid, 2290.5.

— man, 3646.6.

Evils of the time (*see also* Abuses of the age), 1088.5, 1602.5, 1810.5 (Skelton), 2536.5, *2685.5, 3168.2, 4116.5 (Dunbar), 4128.4.

'Example of euyll tongues,' 4198.5.

Example of virtue, by Hawes, 3954.8.

Extravagance, against, 1172.5, 3639.5, 4095.

— in dress: contrasted with Christ on the Cross, 1585.5; extract from *De regimine principum*, 1398; priests' attack on, 4255; reply of galaunts to priests, 4254.5.

Execution, poem by Lord Rivers on eve of his, 3193.5.

Executors, false, 3565.5.

Exile, complaint of an, 120.5.

Eye, a mortal foe to the heart, 158.2.

Fabyan's *Chronicle*: Prologue to, 3955.5; verse inserts listed separately, 227.5, 578.5, 728.5, 1820.8, 1924.4, 1929, 1929.3, 1934, 2039.3, 2541.5, 3206.8, 3318.7, 3785.8, 3799, 3866.3.

Fabula de duobus canibus, English verses in, 2700.5.

Fac finem ludo, 3818.5.

Faith and reason, on, 4162.5.

'Falce surmysing, A,' 3163.5.

Fall of princes, by Lydgate, extracts from, 711, 1592, 3143, 3535, 3744.

Falseness, on, 33.8, 3893.

'Farewell my loue and my dere,' 2736.8.

Farewell to world, by Edward Stafford, 158.9, 2409.5.

Fasting, on, 4154.5.

— on Wednesday, 3496.6.

— those excused from, 1570.5.

— when worthy, 3516.5.

'Fenʒeit freir of Tungland,' by Dunbar, 417.5.

[534]

Felix quem faciunt aliena pericula cautum, 859.5.
Felon sow, 4252.
Festers, two kinds of, 2623.8.
Festial, by Mirk, Prologue to, 956.5.
Fever, amulet for baker against, 459.
Fidelity in love, 2007.5.
Fifteen joys: *see under* Blessed Virgin Mary.
— Ioyes of maryage,' 3223.5.
— O's of Christ, *3777.5.
— Signs before Doomsday, *3080.5.
Findern Anthology, unique secular lyrics in, 12, 139, 159, 380, 383, 657, 734, 853, 1331, 2269, 2277.8, 2279, 2383, 2568, 3125, 3179, 3180, 3613, 3849, 3878, 3917, 3948, 4059, 4241.5, 4272.5.
Fingers, names of the, 1441.5.
Firumbras: see Sir Firumbras.
Fishing, art of, 1502.5.
Five commandments of the Church, 3481.5.
— dogs of London, 2262.3.
— wounds, prayer by, 1739.5.
'Fle þe mys-woman,' 3648.8.
Flemings, song against, 2657, 4056.8; *and see* 1497, 3682.
Flodden, lament on, 366.8, 2547.3, 2549.5; *and see* 1011.5.
Floris and Blauncheflur, *2288.8.
Flowers: ABC poem on, 1378.5; imagery of gathering, 642.5.
'Flyting of Dunbar and Kennedie,' 3117.8.
— an amorous, 456.5, 474.5.
Folly, censure of an upstart's, by Dunbar, 2609.5.
— the world's, 2627.5.
'For faute of loue I stand alone,' 3820.5.
'For in this warld may non assure,' by Dunbar, 4116.5.
Fordun's *Chronicle,* verses in, 299.8, 1824.4, 2685.8, 2787, 3168.6, 3492.5, 3742.5.
Foresight, need of, 2072.2.
Forester: *see* 'Jolly forester.'
Form of living, by Rolle, songs in, 2017.5, 4056.
Fornication with own wife, 326.5.
Fortune: beware of, 3707.5 (Skelton); *Book of,* 2183.5; determined by friends and wife, 3361.6; fickle, 3707.5, 4073.3, 4137; lover's good, 2440; lover's thanks to, 2440; moralizing poem on, 1580.5; on the Lady, 3290.5; plea for success in love to, 2323.8; rejected for God, 3706.4; reversals of, 3941.5, 3947.6; wheel of, 860.3, 3498.5, 3647.3, 4075, *4267.5.
Fortunes according to cards, 108.7, 2251.
Forum lepus petabat, 3372.5.
Four hard things, 3251.5.
— sorrowful things (*see also* Three sorrowful things), 861.8.
Fragments of songs and lyrics, 135.3, 135.5, 158.3, 179, 194, 231.5, 263.3, 266.3, 274, 455.5, 521.5, 684, 687.3, 734.5, *851.3, 865.5, 891, 900, 1120.5, 1123, 1142, 1163.5, 1176.5, 1214.4, 1252, 1260, 1265, 1273.3, 1276.8, 1301.5, 1335, *1339.5, 1389.5, 1393.5, 1445.6, 1470, 1492, *1500.5, 1631.3, 1798, 1799, 1871.5, *1944.5, 1999.5, *2012.3, 2037.5, 2043, 2182.3, 2236.5, 2261.2, *2284.3, 2284.5, 2288.5, 2323.3, 2437.5, 2622, 2630, 2636.5, 2657.5, 2782, *2797.5, 2832.5, 3125, 3131.5, 3167.3, 3242.5, 3264, 3361.3, 3461.5, 3515.5, *3721.5, 3778, 3836.5, 3859.5, *3868.5, 3899.6, 3900.5, 3902.5, *4098.8, 4185.5, 4212, *4256.3.
France: expedition of Henry V into, 969; for unity against, 3143.5; for invasion of (A.D. 1513), 134.5; for victory in, 306.8 (A.D. 1492), 2766.8; prophecy of rise of, 864.5.
Frederick the Emperor, 3567.5.
Freedom, gift of, 337.5.
French, appeal for unity against, 3143.5.
Friar Daw Topias, 3782.5.
Friars: against over-wandering, 870.5; how Dunbar was desired to be a, 3634.3; satirical couplet on, 3815.5.
'Freiris of Berwick,' attrib. to Dunbar, 442.5.
Friends: choice of, 3361.6; value of faithful, 2607.5; warning against false, 3893, 4073.3.
Friendship, on, 1439.8, *3461.3.
Frise, Isaace, acrostic on, 1596.8.
Fulgens et Lucrece, by Medwall, 5.5.

Gallants: against, 299.8, *1585.8; answer to priests' attack on, 4254.5; priests' attack on, 4255; satire on, 1874, 2832.3; spendthrift way of, 892.5; warning to, 143.8.
Galaunt: *see* Gallants.

Garlande of laurell, by Skelton, 729.5; and see 2782.
Garnesche, Skelton's flyting with, 3154.5.
Gate, Sir Geoffrey, epitaph for, 2766.4.
Gawain and Green Knight, couplet illustrating, 2262.5.
Gawain: see *Jeaste*.
General satyre, A,' by Dunbar, 679.8.
George, St.: carol to, 4229.5; invocation to, 2650.5.
Gesta Romanorum, verse tags in, 1251.5, 1391.8, 2238.5, 3322.3, 3081, 3568.5, 3818.5, 4074.5.
Jeaste of Syr Gawayne, The, *306.5.
Gast of Gy fragment, *554.3.
Giles, St., prayer to: see 2606.
Giving: gnomic lines on, 374.5, 908.2, 908.8, 1924.3; necessity of, 1218.8.
Gladness, wealth meaningless without, 470.5.
Gloucester, Duke of: in praise of, 711.
'Glotunis,' prayer for deliverance from, 1963.5.
Gnomic verses, 374.5, 403.5, 1162.6, 1640.3, 1829.5, 1924.3, 3171.5, 3272.5, 3927.6, 4042.5, 4064.5, 4214.5.
God: amends all, 1367.9; goodness of, 995.6; save King Harry, 960.3; slow to punish, 1001.5; Speed the plough, 964.5, 1405.5.
God's chosen, how to be one of, 995.3.
— generosity to man praised, 2757.5.
Golden mean, 512.5, 512.8, 1295.5, 1824.2, 3768.2.
'Golden targe,' by Dunbar, 2820.5.
'Gude counsale,' by Dunbar, 479.5.
— dysporttys,' by Henry VIII, 3487.5.
— medesyn yff a mayd have lost her madened &c,' 1409.1.
Gossips' meeting (*and see* Alewives poems), 603.5 (de Worde), 2358.5, 2831.3 (Dunbar).
Grace before meat, 508.
— good effects of, 4212.5.
'Gramercy myn own purse,' 33.5, 1484, 3959.
'Greenacres a lenvoye upon John Bochas,' 524.
Gregory, St., life of mother of, 3183.5.
Gregory's *Chronicle*, tags in, 1147.9, 1240.5.
Greyhound, properties of, 42.5.
Gryffythe, Lady, lament of, 2552.5.
— Lord, epitaph for, 3962.5.
Guest, on receiving a, 1938.5, 3322.5.

Guisborough, Walter of: tag, 1844.5.
Had I wist, 1223.5, 3079,8.
Hailes, miracles of the blood of, *311.5, 3153.
Hancock, John, bookplate of, 3612.5.
Hare, hunting of, 368.
Harfleur, siege of, 969.
Harley MS. 2253: facs. *EETS* 255.
Harrowing of hell, 1850.5, 3825.5.
Hatfield, Richard: punctuation poems by, 232, 3174.5, 3909.6.
Hawes, Stephen: *Comfort of lovers*, 3357.5; *Conuersion of swerers*, 3354.5; Elegy on HenryVII,2578.5; *Example of virtue*, 3954.8; *Joyfull medytacyon*, 3452.1; *Passetyme of pleasure*, 4004; extracts from, 2318, 2532.5.
Hawking: attack on a curate's, 3648.5 (Skelton); riming conclusion to prose notes on, 1197.2.
Hawks, women satirized in guise of, 4090.
Hawles, Harry, epitaph for, 1204.5.
Hay, Gilbert: *Buik of Alexander*, *3287.5.
Hayles: *see under* Hailes.
Headache, on his, by Dunbar, 2244.3.
Health (*and see* Diet; Medical use of herbs): advice to stay in good, 2032.5 (Dunbar), 4094.5; on festers, 2623.8.
Heart of Christ, rubric recommending prayer to, 3079.4.
Heaven: bliss of, 1871.8; City of, 3322.1; how to win, 2000.5.
— and Hell, 1939.5, 3909.2.
Hell, Harrowing of, 1850.5, 3825.5.
— reward of sinners, 3665.6.
'Helpe me of my payne,' 2757.3.
Hendyng, Proverbs of: extracts from, 549, 1427, 1429, 2817, 4143.
Hendred, Prior of Leominster: *Peregrinatio humani generis*, translation of, 2751.5.
Henley, Walter de: tags in *Husbondrie*, 2698, 4113.
Henry, Prince (son of Henry VIII), songs at birth of, 112.5, 120.4.
Henry II, a tale of, 987.5.
Henry III: defiance of, 1417.3; lament on death of, 1820.8.
Henry V: expedition into France, 969; God save the king, 910.
Henry VI: pageant verses for, 227.5, 578.5, 728.5, 1924.4, 1929.3, 3785.8, 3866.3; political carol in support of,

3742; prayer to, 333.5, 2393; verses spuriously attributed to, 1824.2.
Henry VII: anthem for marriage of, 960.5; elegy on, 2578.5; pageant verses for, 2199.5, 2200.5, 2212.5, 3884.5, 3885.5; political carol in support of, 3206.5.
Henry VIII: blessing on, 960.3; dances with daughter, 2794.2; 'Good dysporttys,' 3487.5; 'Holly and ivy' song, 409.5; love songs, 159.5; 676.5, 1420.5, 1866.5, 2531.5, 2737.5, 3486.5, 3487.5, 4143.3, 4143.5, 4213.5; song on constancy, 3706.7; songs on youth and age, 2025.5; 3706.5; songs complimenting, 558.3, 2794.2, 3456.5; songs referring to, 2271.2.
— fool of: epitaph for, 2482.5.
Herbal, couplet introduction to, 305.5.
Herbs: 'gode for potage,' 3255.5; preface for treatise on, 3578; virtues of, 417.8, 2026.5.
Herebert, Friar William: Christ's resurrection, 1145.5; couplet by, 2140.5; vanity of the world, 3909.4; verses on 'Jesu,' 3632.6.
Hereford, pageant verses at, 2199.5.
Hermit: life of a, 91.8; returned, 3736.5.
Hertford, mumming at, by Lydgate, 2213.
Hic bene se ditat qui semper inania vitat, 1140.5.
Hic habito clausis in tumulo, 1210.5.
Higden's *Polychronicon:* see Polychronicon.
Hilton, Walter: see *Scala perfectionis.*
'His awin ennemy,' by Dunbar, 1148.5.
Hoccleve, Thomas: *De regimine principum,* mottoes in scrolls in one MS. of, 1587.5, 1704.5, 3079.2, 3079.5, 4049.3; extracts from *Lespistre de Cupide,* 1609.5, 4217.6.
'Holly and Ivy' song attributed to Henry VIII, 409.5.
Holloway Church, Somerset: inscription at, 3584.5.
Holy Grail, by Lovelich, *842.5.
Holy Innocents, carol on, 2551.8, 3549.5.
Holyrood, Princess Margaret's arrival at, by Dunbar, 2308.5.
Homilies: see Sermons.
Honesty: how to ascertain, 3285; in dealing, 2072.6; in mirth, 3530.5.
Hope, on, 2617.5.
— for grace, 1009.5.

Horns and thorns, 3104.5.
Horologium sapientiae, versified supplement to, 1035.
Horse: first aid for sick, 1426.2; judged by hooves, 1439.5; properties of and medicines for, 1192.5; *and see* 1197.5; speaks to his master, 326.8. ·
Host, on the, 542, 3318.2.
Hosts, good, 908.4.
Hotspur: *see* Percy, Henry.
Hous of Fame, conclusion added to, 316.6.
'How a sergeant would learne to play the frere,' 4180.3.
— Dunbar was desyred to be ane freir,' by Dunbar, 3634.3.
— Ihesu crist herowede helle,' 1850.5.
— *iudicare* come in creed,' *851.6.
— sall I governe me.' by Dunbar, 1264.5.
— the douty Duke of Albany,' by Skelton, 2803.5.
— þe gosyps made a royal feest,' 603.5.
— þe louer is sette to serve þe floure,' 2178.
Howard, John, Duke of Norfolk: warning to, 1654.5.
Howard, Lord Thomas: verses attributed to, 2577.5.
Humfrey, acrostic on, 1187.
Humorous song, *4098.8.
Hundred meditations (verse supplement to *Horologium sapientiae*), 1035.
Hunger kills happiness, 33.9.
Hunting of the Cheviot, 3445.5 (*and see Chevy Chase*).
Husband, choice of, 3361.1.
Husbandman, song of, 1320.5.
— prognostics for, 1426.1.

I and O refrains: *see* O and I refrains.
'I loue none but you alone,' 3413.3.
Idleness is blameworthy, 2291.5.
Idley, Peter, epitaph for, 4258.6.
Illuminare Jerusalem, 1657.5.
Image of Pity, verses accompanying an, 2910.5, 3695.5, 3777.3.
Impossibilities, 1355.5, 3248.5, 3928.3, 4005.3, 4056.5, 4128.4.
'In baill be blyth for it is best,' 1470.8.
— besenysse,' 994.5.
— prais of wemen,' by Dunbar, 2354.3.
'*Indisciplinata mulier,*' 3492.5.
Indulgences promised for saying devotions, 720, 2910.5, 3305.8, 3448.5, 3695.5, 3777.3; *and see* 3079.4.

Inequality of distribution, 3171.5.
Innocents, Holy, carols on, 2551.8, 3549.5.
Inscriptions (see also Epitaphs; Graffiti; Wall verses): in churches, 337.5, 3584.5; on bronze jug, 675.5, 1172.8; on brooch, 3775.5; on choir stalls, 1197, 1197.8; on drinking cups, 2881.5, 3751.8; on mazer, 2796.5, 3751.8; on sword, 1796.5; on tiles, 1426.2, 3565.5; over entrance to Cowling Castle, 1829.3.
Interrogacio juvenis & Responsio sapientis, 3656.5.
Invocation to *Ayenbite of Inwyt*, 1961.3.
Ivy, carol of, 1651.5.

Jack Upland, 3782.5.
Jack Upland's rejoinder, 1653.5.
Jacques de Vitry, *exemplum* in, 3645.5.
James I: 'At chrystis kirk of the grene,' 3860.8; *Kingis quair*, 1215; verses by Shirley on death of, 42.3.
— IV, marriage of, *2797.5.
Janglers in church, against (and see Tutivillus), 813.8.
Jeaste of Syr Gawayne, *306.5.
Jelusy, Quare of, 3627.5.
Jernegan, Robert: verses, 3919.5.
Jerome, St., couplet ascribed to, 3561.5.
Jerusalem, itineraries to, 883, 986, 1557.5.
Jhesu Christe Domine qui supra nos sedes, 1963.5.
Jesus (see also Christ): love of sweet, 3760.5; on the mercy of, 4053.5; on the name of, 3632.6; riddle on name of, 717, 1528.5; troth plighted to, 3775.5.
Jesus conditor alme, 120.2.
Johan of Guldeuorde, greeting of, 2128.5.
John of Gaunt, grant of, 1321.5.
— King, verses on, 2541.5.
— the Baptist, St., carol to, 3438.8.
— the Evangelist, St.: carol to 2392.5; hymn to, 2784.5.
— Thomsonnis man: verses to the king on, by Dunbar, 3117.3.
— Thweng, St., life of, 4105.5.
Joannis Rossi Warwicensis Historia, prophecy in, 3862.5.
'Jolly forester' songs, 1303.3, 1303.5, 4068.6; *and see* 3199.8.
Joseph of Arimathea, life of, *3117.4.

'Justis betuix the tailyeour and sowtar,' by Dunbar, 2289.8.
Joys of B.V.: *see under* Blessed Virgin Mary.
— of love, recollections of, 14.5.
Judgement: avoid hasty, 675.5; no escape from, 2226.5; summons to, 3645.8.
Juggler and the Baron's daughter, 1194.5.
Julius Caesar, on, 1322.5.
Justice in Norwich, 4128.8.
Justicia, pageant verses by, 3884.5.

Kateryn, acrostic on, 1829.8.
Katharine, Princess: *see under* Arthur, Prince.
Katherine, St.: acrostic on, 588; charm against despair, 860.5; grace before meat to, 508; life of, *309.5.
Kaye, Richard: poems in hand of, 312.5, 1270.1.
Kennedy, Walter: 'Flyting of Dunbar and Kennedie,' 3117.8.
King Arthur: *see under* Arthur.
— *Hart*, by Douglas, 1820.5.
— *Palaan*, 1585.5.
— Robert of Cesyle, 3638.3.
'Kynges balade,' 2737.5.
Kings of England, 4174.3 (to A.D. 1505).
Knight-errant, glamour of, 1827.
Know thyself, *3553.5.

La belle dame sans merci, alternative envoy to, 2386; *and see* 823.
Lady Bessy, The most pleasant song of, 981.3.
— Fortune, on, 3290.5.
— Godiva's ride, couplet on, 1330.3.
— Gryffythe, Lamentatyon of, 2552.5; *and see* 3962.5.
'Lament for the makars,' by Dunbar, 1370.5.
'Lamentatyon of Edward, late Duke of Buckyngham,' 2409.5.
— of our lady for sweryng,' 158.4.
— off quene Elysabeth,' 4263.3.
— of the Kyng of Scottes,' 366.8.
— of the Ladye Gryffythe,' 2552.5.
Laments: for King Alexander, 3923.5; of a betrayed maiden, 3832.5, 3902.5; on death of Robert de Neville, 3857.5.
Lancastrians and Yorkists, 3452.6.
Langtoft's *Chronicle*, English verses in, 718.5, 3799.3; *and see* 3291.5.
Larrons, Patrick: a lover's plea, 1338.5.
Latin hymns (including antiphons).

Ave domyna sancta Maryia, 451.5.
Ave maris stella, 1034.5.
Ave regina celorum, 454.5.
Christe qui lux es et dies, 620.5.
Jesus conditor alme, 120.2.
Salve regina, 2577.3.
Vexilla regis prodeunt, 1119.
Latin mottoes and aphorisms, 33.6, 108, 173.5, 222.5, 230.5, 496, 568, 629, 644.5, 733.3, 825.8, 827.8, 859.5, 874, 995.8, 1001.5, 1013.5, 1137.3, 1140.5, 1162.7, 1175, 1210.5, 1262, 1273.5, 1415.5, 1445.5, 1545, 1634.5, 1636, 1636.3, 1793.9, 1863, 1863.8, 1864, 2005, 2083, 2095, 2137, 2145, 2146, 2231.8, 2323.5, 2463, 2501.5, 2685.8, 2691.5, 2757, 2793, 3078.5, 3079.3, 3100.5, 3167.3, 3273, 3464.5, 3478.5, 3485, 3510.5, 3516.5, 3521, 3523, 3561.5, 3742.5, 3928.3, 4040.3, 4049.2, 4091.3, 4096.5, 4103, 4110.3, 4150.3.
Launceston Priory verses, 4135.5.
Lavynham's *Litil tretis*, tags in, 621.5, 879.5, 4110.5.
Lawde . . . for our souereigne Lord the Kyng [Henry VIII],' 3456.5.
'Lay of Sorrow,' 482.
'Le roi qui ne ment,' *586.5.
Learning, true, disregarded, 1602.5.
— vain without guid lyfe,' by Dunbar, 3768.6.
'Leaulte vault richesse,' 3660.
Lechery, warning against, 551.
Lending: incommodities of, 1640.5, 1924.3, 3960.5; verses on, 374.5, 3272.5, 3274.
Lento pede procedet divinitas, 1001.5.
Lespistre de Cupide, by Hoccleve: extracts from, 1609.5, 4217.6.
Les quinze joyes de mariage, 3223.5.
Letter of Dydo, 811.5.
Leuckin, John, epitaph for, 4235.8.
Liber Pluscardensis, verses in, 2818.8.
Lichtoun: 'Memento homo,' 2523.5.
Life: compared to summer flower, 3973.5; on the religious, 1356.3; preparation for death, 3908.5.
Lyf of Our Lady, epilogue to, by Caxton, 927.5.
Light ladies, song of (and see Wanton's song), 3863.5.
Lion, on the, 3412.5.
'Lytel treatyce to faste on þe wednesday,' 3496.6.
Lobe, epitaph for, 2482.5.
Logic, difficulties of, 3220.9.

London: address to Lord Mayor, 1547.5; approach of Earl of March to, 1147.9; complimentary verses on, 1933.5 (Dunbar); Five dogs of, 2262.3; pageant verses in, 1240.5, 1547.5; pageant verses for return of Henry VI, 227.5, 578.5, 728.5, 1924.4, 1929.5, 3206.8, 3866.3; prophecied fall of, 3618.5.
Looking glass verses, 1999.
Lord Treasurer, welcome to, 1373.5.
'Lordis of Scotland to the Governour in France,' attrib. to Dunbar, 3866.5.
Lothbrog, three sons of, 1267.5.
Love [religious]: Christ's, 265.5; Christ's alone abides, 4225.5; Christ's for man, 823.5; man's soul is true, 3623.5; true, 103.5; parodies of secular love songs, 3228.3, 3623.5, 3820.5.
Love [secular]: affected by envy, 1422.5; be not dissuaded from, 1866.5; bond of, 3703.3; constancy in, 3706.7, 4143.5; contrasts of, 1328.3; counsel in, 753.5 (Dunbar); disconsolate, 932.5 (Skelton); earthly and divine, 1503.5, 2306.5 (Dunbar), 4227.5; ephemeral nature of a clerk's, 173.5; girl's expression of, 2281.5 (Wyatt); girl's progress in, 302.5, 2034.5; in youth, *317.5; inconstancy of, 4112.5 (Dunbar); May song of, 558.5, 1504.5; mutual, 2182.6, 2245.3; nature of, 1864.5; no relief from, 98.5, 3941.5; pain of, 14.5, 3947.6; pangs of, 13.3, 266.5, 1414.5; paradoxes of, 1328.3, 3297.5, 3703.3; plea to Fortune for success in, 2323.8; present pain and past pleasure of, 14.5; prisoner of, 2532.3; renunciation of, 120.6; secret, 158.6; scorn of, 1485.5; success and failure in, 1328.3; three essentials for, 1170; three leaves of, 1328.7; treasure of, 2579.3; true, 1017.5, 1176.5, 1176.8, 1489.5, 2245.3, 2245.4, 4213.5; unrequited, 13.5, 1329.5; values of, 4143.3; wounds of, 763.5, 925, 3168.4, 4201.6.
— adventures, 340.5, 642.5, 1449.5, 2034.5, 3405.5, 3635.5, 3713.5, 3836.5, 3844.5, 4265.5.
— letters: *see under* Epistles.
— songs: *see under* Mistress.
Love-days, admonition to officers of justice at, 312.
Love-longing for Christ, 1367.3, *1779.5, 3680.5.

—for his mistress, 3899.3.
Lover: absent, 2279; baffled, 2619.5, 4283.5; banished, 120.5; blissful, 3880.6; deluded, 1636.5, 2231.5 (Skelton); departing, 765.5; despairing, 557.5, 1356.8, 2224.5; devoted, 729, 2245.6, 3758.5; disconsolate, 1214.5, 2535.5; dismissed, *4284.3; distressed, 13.3, 120.7, 135.5, 146.5, 155.5, 159.5, 506.5, 1449.5, 2245.1, 2535.5, 2753.5, 2794.4, 3270.5, 3486.5, 4281.5; exiled, 120.5, 688.8; faithful, 143.5, 1176.5, 1176.8, 1273.3, 1328.5, 1328.8, 1414.8, 2007.5, 2028.8, 3098.5, 3413.3, 3758.5, 3849, 4070.5; false, 158.7; fickle, 3228.5; forsaken, 263.3, 263.5, 2244.6, 2250.3; happy, 2579.3; hopeful, 3751.3; jealous, 1422.5; made prisoner, 340.5, 2532.3, 3140.5; misunderstood, 3163.5; old but active: see Jolly forester; praised, 2271.2; rebellious, 1270.2; rejected, 155.5, 2272.5, 2277.5, 2277.8, 2311; schizophrenic, 1328.3; scornful, 2524, 3785.5, 4005.3; sleepless, 1449.5, 3074.6; unloved, 1329.5; unrequited, 3167.3; woebegone, 1531.5, 2293.5; would-be, 1999.5; wounded, 3168.4, 3488, 3703.5; yearning, 1295.8.
Lover's: anguish at separation, 1620.5, 2755.5, 4070.5; blame of self, 4241.5; devotion, 143.5, 3098.5, 3461.5; dialogue with a mavis, 1214.5; dialogue with Dame Nature, 2478.5; dialogue with lass, 4020.3; dialogue with mistress, 4014.5; dilemma, 2490; dismissal of false love, 3703.3; faith in prayer, 4213.5; farewells, 120.5, 765.5, 2736.8, 3131.5; lady unkind, 2277.8, 3243.3; laments, 146.5, 155.5, 158.8, 263.5, 266.5, 270, 557.5, 564, 676.5, 2262.5, 2268, 2272.5, 2293.5, 2599, 3168.4, 3808.5, 4201.6, 4272.5; mistress his only comfort, 4058.3; New Year's gift, 837.5; offer of service, 753.8; pains, 1414.5; plaint, 648.5, 649.5, 835.5, 1418.5, 2757.3; plea, 113.5, 190.5, 681.5, 870, 1176.5, 1176.8, 1328.2, 1338.5, 2195.5, 2308.8, 2311, 2439.5, 2753.5, 2757.3, 3376.5, 3706.9, 3751.3, 4014.5; pledge, 2245.6; prayer, 3724.5; testament, 1826; thanks to Fortune, 2440; torments, 1414.5, 3947.6.
Lovers: advice to, 479.5, 1440.5; appeal for sympathy to, 2588.5; defend all true, 2261.4; warning to, 263.8.

Lovers' next meeting, 4201.3.
Lovelich, Henry: *The Holy Grail,* *842.5.
'Lufaris complaynt,' 564.
Loving cups, by John Crophill, 870.8.
Lucidus, dialogue with Dubius, 3352.5.
Ludgate, epitaph in chapel at, 679.5.
Lullay songs: religious, 1448.5, 2024, 2551.8, 2792.3, 4242.5; *and see* 1575.5; secular, 2231.5, *3868.5.
Lusigen, romance of, *819.5.
Luxury (*and see* Extravagance): against, 2602.4; on a life of, 1151.4.
Lydgate, John: Sts. Alban and Amphibal, extract from, 2388.5; 'Ballade per antiphrasim,' 3823; *Fall of Princes,* extracts from, 1592, 3535, 3744; Hymn to B.V. ascribed to, 1046; Lover's New Year gift, 837.5; *Three kings of Cologne,* *854.3; verses in school of, *1037.5.
Lynne: praise of women, *552.8.
Lyric fragments: *see* Fragments.

Macaronic poems, 120.4, 320.5, 451.5, 694.5, 707.5, 870.5, 892.5, 1021.5, 1214.9, *1285, 1330.5 (Dunbar), 1464.5, 1498.5, 1605.5, 1655.5, 1844.5, 2033.5, 2143.5, 2674.5, 2784.5, 3443.5, 3832.5, 3950, 4049.6, 4053.5.
Macer: Virtues of herbs, 2026.5; preface to, 3578.
Magi, visit of the, *2033.3, 3810.3.
Magnyfycence, by Skelton, 223.5.
Maid and the magpie, 3713.5.
—bereft, 3820.5.
Maiden, lament of betrayed, 1330, 1589.5, 3409, 3832.5, 3902.5.
Maidenhead, restoration of, 1409.1.
Maledictions: *see* Curses.
Man: death of, 4098.8; ephemeral nature of, 67.5, 105.5, 1134.5. 2066.8, 2300.6, 3743.6, 3973.5; nature of, 1429.5.
Mandeville's *Travels,* 248.5, 3117.6.
'Maner of passyng to confessioun,' by Dunbar, 2551.5.
—of the crying of ane playe,' by Dunbar, 1119.3.
—of the world now a dayes,' attrib. to Skelton, 3168.2.
'Manerly Margery mylk and ale,' attrib. to Skelton, 456.5.
Maners, John, epitaph for, 843.5.
Man's: heart the garden of Christ, *3634.1; life compared to months of

year, 3347.5, to summer flower, 3973.5; proneness to evil, 3703.3; three foes, *3339.5.
Manners, ABC poem on, 312.5.
Mansfield, anchoress of: poem ascribed to, 1046.
Mansfield, Richard, epitaph for, 1206.7.
March, Earl of: couplet on his approach to London, 1147.9.
Margaret, Princess: complimentary verses on, 2308.5 (Dunbar); marriage to James IV, *2797.5.
— Queen, complimentary verses on, 912.5 (Dunbar).
— Queen (wife of Henry VI), wicked counsel of, 372.
— meek, song to, 3270.5.
— St., grace before meat to, 508.
Marriage: caution in, 1392; pageant verses for Prince Arthur and Princess Catharine's: see under Arthur; shun, *3533.5; sotelties for marriage feast, 461.5, 1270.8, 1331.5, 1386.5.
— XV Ioyes of, 3223.5.
Martin, St., life of, 3004.5.
Mary, St.: see Blessed Virgin Mary.
Mary Magdalene, St.: life of, *304.5; prayer to, 2993.
Mary, Princess, dances with father (Henry VIII), 2794.2.
Mavis, lover's dialogue with a, 1214.5.
May: morning adventure in, 3836.5; song for disguising in, 3405.5; songs of, 558.5, 1504.5.
Mazer, inscription on a, 2796.5, 3751.8; and see 675.5, 1172.8.
Medical receipts: book of, *1496.3; introduction to collections of, 1603, 1605, 2191.5, 4182.
— use of herbs, 417.8, 2026.5, 2627.
'Meditatioun in wynter,' by Dunbar, 1599.5.
Medwall, Henry: Fulgens et Lucrece, 5.5; Nature, 3302.3.
Melbourne MS.: see Pèlerinage de l'âme.
Melusine, tale of, *819.5.
Memento homo quod cinis est, 2143.5, 2523.5.
— mori, 2072.4.
— nostri Domine, 1967.3.
Mercer's Company, inscription on cup of, 3751.8.
Merchants of Edinburgh, rebuke to, 4165.5.
Mercy: couplets advocating, 832; in-

dispensability of, 77; of Jesus, 4053.5; works of, 825.3, 4155.3.
Mereley, John: behaviour of an 'ydell parson,' 853.2.
'Merle and the Nichtingaill,' by Dunbar, 1503.5.
Merlin: argument with Morien, 407.6; birth of, 611.5; prophecies of, 611.5, 1253.5, 2613.5, 3528.5, 3889.5.
Mersar, [? John]: warning to women, 158.7.
Michael, St., invocation to, 1227.
Miracle plays: see Mystery plays.
— of our ladye done to ser Amery knyght,' 2446.5.
Miracles at Hailes Abbey, *311.5, 3153.
— of the Blessed Virgin: clerk blinded by glory of, *282.5; monk sees vision of, *465.3.
Mirk's Festial: prologue to, 956.5; verses in, 4068.3.
Miroure of mans saluacioune, 1511.5.
Mirror of St. Edmund, verse introduction to, 1188.5.
Mirror of simple souls, prayer tag in, 4108.
Mirth, on honest, 3530.5.
Miserere: trans. of Asperges, 1123.8.
— nobis, 2217.5.
Mistress: absent, 13.3, 113.5, 146.5, 1334, 2412.5, 2245.1; chosen, 3723; coy, 2255.3; deceiving, 4281.5; devoted, 2200.3, 2250.5, 3880.6; disconsolate, 2393.5, 3635.3; disdainful, 263.8, 649.5, 2439.5; erring, 3302.5 (Skelton); faithless, 120.6; false, 79.5; 3707.3; hardhearted, 13.5, 2599; newfangled, 2307.5; obdurate, 2277.5, 2277.8, 2308.8, 3144.5, 3706.9; Parisian, 694.5; pitiless, 648.5, 675.8, 1598.3, 2161, 2244.6, 2311; uncertain, 4283.5; variable, 3724.5.
— envoys to his, 923, 928.5, 2030.6.
— like a tree, *3553.8.
— longing for his, 3899.3.
— love songs to his, 724, 765.5, 865.5, 871.5, 1295.8, 1422.3, 1598.3, *2012.3, 2015, 2028.5, 2182.6, 2195.5, 2200.3, 2271.5, *2284.3, 2318, 2384.8, 2412.5, 2424.5 (Orleans), 2532.3, 2547.5, 2579.3, 2736.8, 3097.6, 3131.5, 3387.5, 3413.3, 3632.3, 3706.8, 3706.9, 3707.8, 3800.5, 3946.5, 4058.3, 4098.6, 4241.5.
— praise of, 1414.8, 1829.8, 2250.5, 2532.5, 2619.5, 3097.6.
Mnemonic verses, 633.5.

[541]

Mocking song of his mistress, 1300, 1934.5, 2524, 3785.5.
Moderation: golden mean, 512.5, 512.8, 1295.5; in diet, 1923.5.
Moleyns, Dame Katherine, benediction for, 1790.5.
Monastery, prayer for, 1038.5, 1078.5.
Money (see also Borrowing, Lending): appeals for, by Dunbar, 2349.5, 3051.5, 3116.5, 3118.8, 3595.3; danger of, 228.8, 2078.5, 2818.3; greed and, 2619.8 (Dunbar); mine own purse, 33.5, 1484, 3959; power of, 465.5, 2743.5; promise to repay, 3959.5; Sir Penny, 2821.5.
Monk's Tale, by Chaucer: one stanza as Prohemium to Fall of Princes, extract, 4231.
Months: man's life compared to, 3347.5; verses on illustrations of, 1275.
Moon: prognostics by, 1436.3; table of changes by, 3609.6; to find Easter by, 1502; to the new, 985.5.
Moor, Robert and Elizabeth, on marriage of, 3168.6.
Morale prouerbs of Cristyne, trans. by Earl Rivers, 3372.1.
Morality plays, 223.5, 3352.5, 3430.5.
More, Thomas: 'How a sergeant would learne to play the frere,' 4180.3; 'Lamentacioun off quene Elyȝabeth,' 4263.3; preface to the *Book of fortune*, 2183.5; tapestry verses, 1270.6; trans. into Latin of English lyric, 506.5; verses ascribed to, 1156.
Morien and Merlin: alchemical verses, 407.6.
Mortality: recollection of, 550.5; reminders of 672.4, 672.5, 2143.5.
Morte d'Arthur fragment, *295.8.
Morton, John, Bishop of Ely: banquet sotelties for, 3563.5.
Motet, fragment of, 687.3.
Mum and the Sothsegger, *296.3.
Mummings (including Pageants), 227.5, *338.5, 578.5, 671.5, 728.5, 1240.5, 1270.4, 1273.8, 1322.8, 1547.5, 1637.4, 1924.4, 1927, 1929.3, 2028.3, 2030.2, 2030.4, 2199.5, 2200.5, 2212.5, 2213, 2214, 2215, 2216, 2360, 3117.2, 3704.6, 3706.3, 3785.8, 3810.6, 3866.5, 3880.3, 3884.5, 3885.5, 4095.5.
Mure, complaint against, by Dunbar, 3117.5.
Music, founder of, 1924.5, 1931.8.
— God be praised for, 651.5.

Mutability (see also Transitoriness, World), 1356.5, 1824.2.
'My hart it is so sore,' attrib. to Henry VIII, 2531.5.
— hart she hath and euer shall,' 1414.8.
Mystery plays, 95, 2360 (Proclamation only), *3117.2, *3870.5.
— ladye loveth me,' 2579.3.
— ladyes water mill,' 1641.5.
— love is to the grenewode gone,' 3800.5.
— true harte hathe slayne me,' 763.5.

Narracio de gestis romanorum, verses in a, 4155.5.
Nativity, ballades and songs of the, 34.5, 54.5, 1657.5 (Dunbar), 2312.5 (Dunbar), 2674.5, 2831.6 (Dunbar), 3477.3.
— narratives of, 3704.3, *3845.3.
Nature, by Medwall, 3302.3.
Nature: dialogue between lover and Dame, 2478.5; enjoy the gifts of, 3135.5; pageant verses by, 3866.3; praise God in, 2757.5.
Neville's Cross, battle of: 1992.5, 3117; popular song fragment on, 1445.6.
Neville, Robert de, lament over, 3857.5.
'New caroll of our lady,' 1984.5.
New Year, carol of the, 1540.5.
New Year's gift, a lover's, 837.5 (Lydgate).
Newton, Richard, verses by, 3189.
Nichodemus, gospel of: introduction to, 2660.3.
Nightingale: 'Merle and the,' 1503.5 (Dunbar); message of, 3439.5.
Nine nobles (see also Nine worthies), 1181.5.
— virtues: see under Virtues.
— worthies (see also Nine nobles), 1270.1, 1322.5, 1929.5, 2781.
Noblesse, speech of: at pageant, 2030.4.
Nolo mortem peccatoris, 782.5.
Non humilis paruus, 4040.3.
Nonsense verses, 35.5, 102.3, 488.5, 1354, 1409.1, 1605.5, 2250.8, *2285.5, 3248.5, 3928.3, 4056.5, 4150.6.
Nordell, Richard, epitaph for, 2818.2.
Norray, Sir Thomas, satire on, by Dunbar, 2349.3.
Norton's *Ordinal*: trans. of Latin prologue to, 3581.5.
Norwich, on justice in, 4128.8.
Number puzzles, 805, 1528.5.
Nun, tempted, 3443.5.

[542]

—Why I can't be a,' *316.3.
Nunc scripsi totum, 2323.5.
Nupcie moriar quia nubere dulce est, 827.5.
Nursery rimes, 0.3, 28.5; *and see* 3372.6, 3521.
Nurture and nature, 995.4.
Nutbrown maid, 467.

'O and I' refrains, 2003.5, 2614.5, 3098.5, *3719.5.
O lumen indeficiens o claritas sempiterna, 2420.5.
O mater Jhesu salve Maria, 2831.8.
O spes in morte, 2463.
Oaths, against using, 158.4.
Obstinacy, against, 1136.3.
Occupations of months, 1275.
Oculi cum occultentur, 4046.
'Of a dance in the quenis chalmer,' by Dunbar, 3117.7.
—covetyce,' by Dunbar, 865.8.
—deming,' by Dunbar, 226.5.
—discretioun in asking,' by Dunbar, 2621.5.
—discretioun in geving,' by Dunbar, 3768.3.
—discretioun in taking,' by Dunbar, 121.5.
—folkis evill to pleis,' by Dunbar, 861.5.
—James Doig, kepar of the quenis wardrop,' by Dunbar, 3496.3.
—lyfe,' by Dunbar, 3908.5.
—luve erdly and divine,' by Dunbar, 2306.5.
—manis mortalitye,' by Dunbar, 2143.5.
—the changes of life,' by Dunbar, 1356.5.
—the ladyis solistaris at court,' by Dunbar, 3556.5.
—the Nativitie of Christ,' by Dunbar, 2312.5.
—the Passioun of Christ,' by Dunbar, 276.5, 2161.5.
—the same James [Dog] quhen he hed plesett him,' by Dunbar, 2457.5.
—the warldis instabilitie,' by Dunbar, 3646.3.
—the warldis vanitie,' by Dunbar, 2587.5.
Omne seminarium voluptatis venenum puta, 222.5.
Omnis amor clerici amor clerici, 173.5.
'On ane blakmoir,' by Dunbar, 1934.5.

—his heid-ake,' by Dunbar, 2244.3.
—the changes of life,' by Dunbar, 1356.5.
Oracio ad beatum Robertum, 1048.8.
—*de sancta Maria*, 2478.8.
—*Presidentis* (invoking St. Robert), 1078.5.
Order of shooting with the crossbow, 4244.5.
Ordynarye of Crysten men: verses describing a cut in, 3481.5.
'Orisoun,' by Dunbar, 3077.5.
—quhen the governour past into France,' by Dunbar, 3694.6.
Orleans, Charles Duc d': poems commonly linked to, 2424.5, 2602.2, 3723; translation into English of French poem of, 2325.5.
Ossory: *see* Red book of Ossory.
Our Lady: *see* Blessed Virgin Mary.
Over-ambition, on, 1170.5.
Ovid, verses attrib. to, in Trevisa's trans. of *Polychronicon*, 4189.5.
Owayne Miles, *303.6.
Owl and nightingale: couplets by Master John, 2128.5.
Owre, Donald, epitaph for, by Dunbar, 1587.3.

Packe, James: poem on Willoughby family, 2462.5.
Page, John: *Siege of Rouen*, 979.
Pageants: *see* Mummings.
Palice of honour, by Douglas, 4002.5.
Palindromic epitaph, 3097.3.
Pallas, epitaph of, 2736.2.
Palmer, Thomas, epitaph for, 2736.4.
Papelard priest, 2614.5.
Paratus sum semper mori pro te, 3677.5.
—off Cupyde gode of love,' 2595.
—of foules, by Chaucer, one stanza from, 4187.8.
Partenay, romance of, *819.5.
Passion: described by Christ, 2277.3; meditations on, 11.5, 1011.8, 1747.5, 4094.3; pains of, 541.8, 664.3, 2277.3, *3719.5, 3905.5; prayers by, 1709.5, 2403.5, 3238.5, *3844.8; remembrance of, 2806.5; song of, 1320, 2161.5 (Dunbar); verses on, 2646.5; vision of, 276.5; worship of, *310.5.
Passetyme of pleasure, by Hawes, 4004; extracts from, 2318, 2532.5.
Pastimes free of vice, 3487.5.
Paston, John: verses in letter from,

1360; in letter to, 1627.5; *and see* 2267.5, 4235.5.
Pater noster, 2702.5, 2703, 2708.5.
— tract on, *827.8.
Patience: twelve degrees of, 3492.3; virtue of, 95.8.
Patriotism, songs of, 134.5, 306.8, 910.
Patris sapientiae, an alchemical poem, 1150.3.
Paul, St., day of: prognostics for coming year by, 1426.1.
Paula, St., life of, *717.5.
Payne, Richard, epitaph for, 2590.5.
Pearce the Black Monk: verses attrib. to, 3257.
Peeris, William: metrical chronicle, 631.8.
Pèlerinage de l'âme: songs in Melbourne MS. of English trans. of, 34.5, 528.5, 1041.3, 1249.5, 1490.5, 2271.4, 2384.5, 2440.5, 2533.5.
Penitence, song of, 0.2.
'Penni worthe of witte,' *2602.3.
Percy, Henry (Hotspur), verses on, 1185.
— House of: chronicle by William Peeris, 631.8.
Peregrinatio humani generis, 2751.5.
Pestilence, prose tract on: couplet ending, 189.5.
'Petition of the gray horse, auld Dunbar,' by Dunbar, 2349.5.
Philip, Friar Nicholas: tags in sermons, 636.5, 908.6, 1938.5, 3490.6, 3727.5, 4225.5.
'Phyllyp Sparowe,' by Skelton, 2756.5.
Philosopher's stone, 1558, 2308.3.
Pickering, Jon, epitaph for, 3389.5.
Piers, John, epitaph for, 1211.9.
Pilgrim, prayer of, 2271.4.
Pylgrymage of man, 2751.5.
Pilgrimage, itineraries for, 883, 986.
— to Compostella: tag in, 475.5.
— to Jerusalem: way stations of, 1557.5.
Pity, types of, 86.3.
— image of: verses on, 2910.5, 3695.5, 3777.3; *and see* 1863.5.
Planctus Marie carol, 377.5.
Planets, courses of, 1907.5.
Plough, God speed the, 964.5, 1405.5.
Plus pi, acrostic on, 1570.5.
Political prophecies: *see under* Prophecies.
Polycana, wife of Marcolphus, 286.5.
Polychronicon: verses in Trevisa's trans. of, 399.5, 746.5, 1426.5, 1637.6,
2361.5, 2736.2, 2831.4, 3218.3, 4189.5.
Porteus of noblenes, riming conclusion to, 2293.6.
Possessions, on, 3272.5.
Pox, warning against catching, by Dunbar, 2032.5.
'Prayer aseen dispeyre or mysbeleue,' 1719.5.
— of þe pilgryme þat he sayes afore his deth,' 2271.4.
— value of, 826.
Prayer-roll, colophons to, 2300.3, 2562.5, 3585.5.
Prayer-tags, 1009.5, 1496.5, 1683.3, 1683.5, 1700.5, 1704.5, 1709.5, 1728, 1758.5, 1955.5, 1965.5, 2121.5, 2562.5, 3200.5, 3228.5, 3775.5, 3778.5, 4108.
Prayers.
To Blessed Virgin: *see under* Blessed Virgin Mary.
By Christ and his Passion, 11.5, *296.6, 1838.5, 2403.5, 3238.5, 4094.3.
For use in church: for the dead, *2284.5.
Household: morning, 1950.5; night, 1513.5; to staunch blood, 1946.5; *and see* 624, 627.5.
Of sinners: composite prayer to Christ and B.V., 2451; for care in speech, 2487; for deliverance from 'glotunis,' 1963.5; for heaven's bliss, 879.5; to God, 553.5, 1967, 1967.5, 2420.5, 3200.5; to the Trinity, 790.5.
On special occasions: for England, 1717.3, 1955.5, 3236; for the king, 2469.5; for the realm, 3694.6 (Dunbar); for victory in France, 306.8, 2766.8.
Precepts, moral (*see also* Counsel, good), 113.8, 194.5, 228.5, 461.8, 502.5, 636.5, 675.5, 706, 1218.8, 1941.5, *3700.5, 4126.5.
— ending in -ly, 596, 2794.8.
Pricke of conscience, colophon to, 1197.1; introductory couplet to, 3769.8.
Pride, against, 4110.5.
— of clergy, against, 455.8.
Priests' attack on gallants' dress, 4254.5; *and see* 4255.
Prince Henry: *see* Henry, Prince.
Proclamations to mystery plays, 2360, 3741.5.
'Proface,' a Christmas carol, 54.5.
Prognostics: by dice, 3694.3; by letters,

2793.5; calendar of, 3638.6; for travelling, 1201.5, 1436.3; from New Year's Day, *1538.5; from St. Paul's Day, 1426.1; of wonders to befall, 2668.3.

Prologues and prefaces to: *Antidotarium Nicholai*, 258; *Ayenbite of inwyt*, 1227, 1961.3; *Book of fortune*, 2183.5; *Book of medicines*, 1603, 1605; *Cordiale quatuor novissimorum*, 3521.5; 'Disputacion betwyx þe body and wormes,' 3252.5; Fabyan's *Chronicle*, 3955.5; Hours of the Cross, 3448.5; Mirk's *Festial*, 956.5; *Mirror of St. Edmund*, 1188.5; Norton's *Ordinal*, 3581.5; *Polychronicon*, 3917.3 (de Worde); prose *Apocalypse*, 3305.4; prose devotional tract, 1435; prose *Gospel of Nicodemus*, 2660.6; prose herbal, 305.5; prose narration of Passion, 2646.5; couplets introducing prose prayers, 2650.5, 2659.3, 2659.6; prose table on changes of moon, 3609.6; prose trans. of Psalter, 2660.3; Scrope's version of *Epitre d'Othèa*, 2766; *Speculum medicorum*, 2191.5.

'Propreties of a goode grehunde,' 42.5; and see 1176.

Prophecies, animal, 2613.5, 3510.

— by cast of dice, 33.3, 734.8, 3694.3, 4018.

— political (by Bridlington, Merlin, Rymour, &c.), 23.5, 33.3, 285.5, *308.5, 366.5, 552.3, 607.3, 611.5, 734.8, 864.5, 1153.5, 1253.5, 1507.5, 1564, 2384.3, 2515, 2613.5, 2668.3, 2793.5, 2834.3, 3091.5, 3306.5, 3308.5, 3412.3, 3435.5, 3437.5, 3451.5, 3513.5, 3514, 3528.5, 3618.5, 3862.5, 3889.5, 3912.5, 3923.5, 3951.5, 4005.5, 4008, 4014.8, 4018.5, 4030.5, 4038.5, 4154.3.

Prophecy: allegory of, *3708.5; for A.D. 1560, 3912.5; letter, 2834.3; interpretation of symbols in, 3412.3; of fall of Reeves Abbey, 3815.8; on English history, 3528.5; on 'sharpe and fairfeld,' 4014.8.

— earliest Scottish, 3923.5.
— First Scottish, 4029.
— Second Scottish, 4008.

Proverbial couplets (single and in brief sequences), 33.9, 34.8, 37.3, 37.5, 39.5, 40.5, 63.8, 69.5, 77, 81.5, 95.5, 106.5, 108.5, 190.3, 228.5, 231.5, 299.5, 326.5, 397, 404.5, 407.5, 407.8, 411.5, 465.5, 474, 475.8, 512.5, 512.8, 513, 548.8, 644.5, 672.3, 675.5, 687.5, 733.3, 735.3, 769.5, 790.8, 793.5, 802.5, 817.5, 853.6, 853.8, 860.3, 908.2, 908.8, 946.5, 1009.3, 1136.5, 1137, 1137.5, 1142.5, 1147.2, 1147.6, 1149.5, 1150.5, 1152.5, 1162.5, 1162.8, 1162.9, 1174.5, 1174.8, 1223.5, 1251.5, 1354.5, 1445.5, 1587.8, 1627.5, 1628.8, 1634.5, 1635.5, 1636.3, 1636.8, 1640.3, 1793.9, 1814.5, 1829.2, 1829.5, 1867.5, 1941.5, 2289.5, 2293.8, 2631.5, 2668.5, 2691.3, 2691.5, 2691.8, 2698, 2732.5, 3068.5, 3079.2, 3079.8, 3081, 3084.6, 3167.6, 3170, 3172.5, 3199.3, 3207.5, 3218.5, 3292.3, 3292.5, 3307.5, 3318.6, 3318.8, 3322.5, 3372.4, 3372.5, 3372.6, 3438.6, 3444.5, 3464.5, 3502, 3502.5, 3522.5, 3706.2, 3729.5, 3769.5, 3792.5, 3799.6, 3815.5, 3818, 3860.3, 3892.5, 3894.6, 3927.3, 3997.5, 4020.6, 4034.3, 4034.6, 4040.6, 4044.3, 4049.2, 4058.5, 4079.3, 4079.6, 4079.8, 4095, 4106, 4106.5, 4113, 4120.3, 4128.2, 4128.6, 4145.5, 4176.5, 4180.6, 4198.8.

Proverbs: *of Cristyne*, trans. by Earl Rivers, 3372.1; of Hendyng: *see* Hendyng; of Solomon, 3068.5, 3170.

Provisions, good use of, 342.5.

Prudence, counsels of, 836.

Psalter: prologue to a prose, 2660.3; verses in Rolle's, 301.5, 1397.5, 1664.5, 4076.5.

Punctuation poems, 3174.5, 3909.6.

Pupilla oculi, verses on efficacy of prayer in, 826.

Purchas: *Pilgrimes*, 1557.5.

Purse: *see under* Money.

Quanto longiorem pacienciam, 733.3.

Queen Dowager, advice to, by Dunbar, 2497.5.

'Queinis reception at Aberdein,' by Dunbar, 541.5.

Qui me deridet non inde risus abibit, 1162.7.

Qui provam habet conjugem, 4128.5.

Quinze joyes de mariage, 3223.5.

'Quare of ielusy,' 3627.5.

Quis te lesit ita Iesu dulcissima vita, 4110.3.

Quo warranto, attack on statute of, 1844.5.

'R.W. to A.C.,' humorous letter from, 2827.5.

Raphaell, speech of: at mumming, 3706.3.

Raymundes Questyonary, 3581.5.

Read, William, epitaph for, 4106.8.

Reason: and faith, 4162.5; and treason, 404.5; and will, 1294.3.
Rebellion of A.D. 1381, 1498.5, 1790.8.
— of A.D. 1469, 1409.8.
Receipts, cookery, 854.8, 3254.5, 4187.5.
— medical, *1496.3.
Red Book of Ossory, tags in, 684, 891, 1120.5, 1123, 1214.4, 1265, 3891.
Redde racionem villicacionis tue, 3397.
Redford, John: song for Christmas and Easter, 2668.8.
Reeves Abbey, prophecy on, 3815.8.
Regula anachoritarum, couplet ending prose, 3603.5.
Religious instruction, *3339.8.
— life, 1356.3.
— parodies of secular love songs, 3228.3, 3623.5, 3820.5; *and see* 2737.5.
'Relucent mirror,' by Skelton, 194.5.
Remedy of love, 3084; extracts from, 1409.3, 3648.8.
'Remembraunce of Crystes passyon,' 3372.2.
Remonstrance to the king, by Dunbar, 3118.5.
'Remors of conscyence,' 2711.5.
Repentance: inducements to, 995.8; sin and, 1863.8.
Reply of Friar Daw Topias, 4098.3.
'Replycacioun agaynst certaine yong scolars,' by Skelton, 3772.5.
Rest, universal need of, 407.5, 3917.5.
Resurrection, on the, 688.3, 1145.5, 3225.5 (Dunbar).
'Rewl of anis self,' by Dunbar, 3751.5.
Ribald poems, 0.1, 769.5.
Richard the redeles: see *Mum and the Sothsegger*.
Richard III, satirical couplet on, 3318.7.
Richardoune: on precious stones, 904.
Riches (*see also* Money), bring sorrow, 2818.3.
Riddles, 597.5, 717, 754.5, 805, 1396, 1528.5, 2030.8 (letters), 3256.3, 3552, 3816.5.
Ring, inscription on, 3892.5.
Ripley, George: alchemical verses attrib. to, 3721; colophon for alchemical receipts, 4052.5; Emblematic scroll, 1364.5; summary of *Twelve gates*, 3372.8; Vision of, 3928.5.
Rivers, Earl: *Dictes of Philosophers*, conclusion to, 4273.8; dedication to, 3581; epilogue for 2663.5; *Morale prouerbs of Cristyne*, 3372.1; Virelai, 3193.5.

Robbers: *see* Thieves.
Robert of Knaresborough, prayers to, 1038.5, 1048.8, 1078.5.
Robert of Sicily: legend of, 1898.5; story of, 3638.3.
Roberte the Deuyll, 1898.5; colophon at end of, 3721.3.
Robin Hood, *834.5, 2830.5, 3118.4.
Roch, St., invocation to, 2659.3.
Roland and Vernagu, *823.3.
Roland, song of, *1132.5.
Rolle of Hampole, Richard: *De modo vivendi*, verses in, 995.3; *Ego dormio*, verses in, 197.8, 1367.5; *Form of living*, songs in, 2017.5, 4056; *Incendium amoris*, poem in, 1715; *Meditations on the Passion* (Text A), 11.5, 918.5; (Text B), 3760.5; *Pricke of conscience*, colophon ascribing to, 1197.1; Psalter, verses in, 301.5, 1397.5, 1664.5, 4076.5; prayer attrib. to, 1954; preface to tract in style of, 1435; verses in scroll, 1367.8.
— verses accompanying a picture of, 91.8.
Romans of Partenay, *819.5.
Rome: pilgrimage to, 1557.5; praise of, 2831.4 (Trevisa); when at, 4049.2.
Rood of Bromholm, text attached to picture of, 3585.5.
Roos, T.: couplet by, 2030.6.
Rose of England, 3719.8.
Roses, Wars of: unity concluding, 3452.6.
Rossi, Joannis: prophecy in, 3862.5.
Roundels, 1749, 2039.5, 2325.5, 2602.2, 3891.
Rounds, 266.5, 676.5, 688.8, 1214.6, 1214.7, 1637.2, 2766.8.
Rubrics: ending Wycliffite Bible, 1197.3; ending *Speculum vite*, 1197.4.
Ruffyn, St., legend of, *1219.5.
Rutterkin, 2832.3.
Ryman, James: song in praise of St. Francis, 1542.

Sacrament, on the, 1561.5.
Sacred Heart, 3560.5.
'Seynt Thomas Lottis,' 805.
Saints: *see under name in question for gospels, life, legends, and prayers.*
Saints days, mnemonic verses on, 633.5.
Saturnus, 1924.5.
'Sauce for a mawlerd rostid,' 3254.5.
Salve regina, 2577.3.
Say well or say nought, 3079.8.

Scala perfectionis, by Hilton: verses in de Worde's edition of, 1596.5, 3372.2, 3604.5.
Scholars of Cambridge, threatening verses by, 1941.8.
Schoolboy (*and see under* Children): Christmas song of, 320.5; exercises, 378.5, 430.8, 1631.5, 4028.6; first tag for learning by, 430.5.
Scotia sit guerra pedibus, 2685.8.
Scotland: Bannockburn, verses about, 2039.3, 3080; Flodden, lament on, 366.8, 2547.3, 2549.5; prophecy favorable to, 4005.5; in absence of Duke of Albany, 3866.5.
Scots: abuse of English by, 3918.5; English abuse of, 3799.3; English song of victory over, 3558.5; *and see* 841; poems by Skelton against, 1021.5, 1822.5, 1931.3, 2803.5.
Scots' abuse of Edward I (*and see* Bannockburn), 3918.5.
Scottish Feilde, 1011.5.
— *Legendary*, *301.3, *309.5.
— Prophecy: First, 4029; Second, 4008.
— Troy fragments, *298.5.
Scribe's: concluding formula, 467.5, 2323.5; excuse, 3662.5; prayer, 2766.3.
Scriveners play, 1273.
Scrolls, tags in, 1367.8, 1431.5; in MS. of *De regimine principum*, 1587.8, 1704.5, 3079.5, 4049.3.
Scurrilous verses, 0.1, 1300, 2605.5, 2524, 3306.3, 3522.5, 3785.5.
Sebastian, St., invocation to, 2659.6.
Second coming of Christ, 1289.
Seed in man's heart, *3634.1.
Self-discipline, on, 1264.5 (Dunbar).
Semita recta, trans. of, 2614.
Sergeant would play friar, 4180.3.
Sermons, short verses in: *see* Tags.
Serpent of division, concluding lines of, 4186.5.
Seven deadly sins: *see under* Sins.
— Scoles,' 3784.6.
— times Christ shed his blood, *3844.8.
— principal virtues, *272.5.
Shepherds' songs described, 3224.5.
Shirley, John: verses on death of James I, 42.3.
Shooting with crossbow, 4244.5.
Shrewsbury play fragments, *3870.5.
Shrift: *see under* Confession.
Sic in te diligo, 1414.5.
Signs of death, 4036.5.

Simnel, Lambert, denied recognition as king, 2571.5.
Simony, against, 4085.
Sinner, lament of, 141.5, 142, 161.5, 945.5.
Sinners, impossibility of pleasing, 3767.5.
Sinning with one's own wife, 326.5.
Sins: clauses of *Pater noster* as remedies against, 2703; dance of, 2623.3 (Dunbar); seven deadly, *1492.5 (Audelay), 3084.3.
Sir Amadace, *3518.5.
— *Eger de Femyne*, *2639.5.
— *Firumbras* (*see also* Firumbras), *593.8, *944.5.
— *Lamwell*, *1367.1.
— Penny, 2821.5.
— *Tristrem*, 1382.
Skelton, John: 'Agaynst a comely coystrowne,' 2609.5; 'Against Dundas,' 1021.5; Against Garnesche, 3154.5; 'agaynst the prowde Scottes,' 1931.3; 'Against venemous tongues,' 193.5; Attack on 'Mastres Anne,' 4217.3; 'Ballade of the scottysche kynge,' 1822.5; 'Bowge of courte,' 1470.5; 'Colyn Cloute,' 3903.5; Disconsolate love, 932.5; Elegy on Henry VII, 2578.5; 'En Parlament à Paris,' 1810.5; Epitaph for Adam Udersall and John Clarke, 3645.3; *Garlande of laurell*, 729.5; 'How the douty Duke of Albany,' 2803.5; Lamentation of soul of Edward IV, 2192; 'Lawde ... for our souereigne Lord the Kyng,' 3456.5; Lover deceived, 2231.5; *Magnyfycence*, 223.5; 'Maner of the world nowadayes,' 3168.2; 'Manerly Margery mylk and ale,' 456.5; On death of Earl of Northumberland, 1378; On fickle fortune, 3707.5; On time, 2451.5; 'Phylyp Sparowe,' 2756.5; Praise of his beloved, 1829.8; Prayer to the Trinity, 2546; 'Relucent mirror,' 194.5; 'Replycacioun agaynst certaine yong scolars,' 3772.5; Reproof of erring lady, 3302.5; Satire on gallants, 2832.3; Service to Calliope, 585.5; Sorrow at parting, 2755.5; 'Speke, Parrot,' 2263.5; 'Tunnyng of Elynour Rummyng,' 3265.5; 'Vppon a deedman's hede,' 4284.5; Verses presented to Henry VII, 2526; 'Ware the hauke,' 3648.5; *Why come ye nat to courte*, 813.3.

Skipworth, Richard, epitaph for, 1569.5.
Slander, against, 193.5.
Sloth, on, 1998.5.
Sober living, on, 3768.2.
Sol luna lucider, 3478.5.
Solomon, proverbs of, 3170; *and see* 3068.5.
Salomon and Marcolphus, verses on Marcolphus' wife in, 286.5.
Song fragments: *see* Fragments.
— of love to Criste,' 1732.5; *and see* 3680.5.
— *of Roland,* *1132.5.
Sorrow at parting, attrib. to Skelton, 2755.5.
— hath pierced my hart so depe,' 3703.5.
— of the world, 3327.5.
Sorrowful things: *see under* Three.
Sotelties, 461.5, 1270.8, 1331.5, 1386.5, 3563.5.
Soul, man's true love, 3623.5.
Soul's address to body, *2684.5.
South English Legendary: 184, 728, 2994, 3042, 3060; extract, 1441.5; fragment, *306.3.
'Speke, Parrot,' by Skelton, 2263.5.
'Spesiall glasse to loke in daily,' 2794.8.
Speciosa facta es suavis, 3675.
Speculum Christiani, introduction to *Quinta tabula* in, 2233.5.
— *Ecclesie,* verses in, 1940.5.
— *Humane salvacionis,* trans. of, 1511.5.
— *Medicorum,* prologue to, 2191.5.
— *Sacerdotale,* couplet in, 210.5.
— *Vite,* riming conclusion to, 1197.4.
— *Vite Christi,* tag concluding, 1965.5.
Speech: careful, 802.5, 2487, 3503.5; dangers of hasty, 102.5, 106.5, 1409.5, 1817.5, 1941.5; honest, 271.5.
Spells: *see* Charms.
Spending (*see also* Lending), 1924.3.
Spenser, Jone, epitaph for, 1211.8.
Spies everywhere, 3502.5.
Sports, dangers of excessive, 1014.5.
Springtime and love (*and see under* May), 4028.6.
Spurious links in *Canterbury Tales,* 4019.
Spyeer, John, epitaph for, 1341.5.
Stabat iuxta Christi crucem, a *Compassio Marie* based on, *3216.5.
Standard, battle of: tag for, 4284.8.
Stanlei (Sir Thomas, Baron Stanley), acrostic on, 3228.

Stanley, House of: poems commemorating, 981.3, 986.5, 1011.5, 2547.3, 3719.8.
— Sir William, praise of, 3719.8.
Stanza linking, 2179.
Stars and planets, 1907.5.
Stephen, St., carols to, 1363.5, 2652.5.
— stoning of, *3448.8.
Stewart: 'Variance of court,' 2831.2.
— Bernard, Lord of Aubigny: complimentary verses on, 2811.5 (Dunbar); elegy on, 1444.5 (Dunbar).
Stimulus amoris, verses with, 3706.6.
Stirps beate Anne, 2153.5.
Stokes, R., epitaph for, 2068.5.
Stone, John: verses in chronicle, 2296.
Stoning of St. Stephen, *3448.8.
Street, Simon, epitaph for, 3220.5.
Study, against excessive, 407.5.
— how to succeed in, 39.5.
Sufferance, on, 1999, 3170, 4121.
Suffolk, Earl of: Compleynt by, 1826; verses against, 556.5.
Surrexit Dominus de sepulchro, attrib. to Dunbar, 3225.5.
Suso: *see Horologium sapientiae.*
Swearing, against, 158.4.
Swiving, ballade by Chaucer on, 1635.
Sword, inscription on, 1796.5.
Sydrac and Boctus, 772, 2147.
Symbols: used for colors, 3416.5; used in alchemy, 3452.5; used in prophecies, 3412.3.

'Tabill of confessioun,' by Dunbar, 3776.5.
Tags in homilies, sermons, and similar didactic works, 33.8, 49, 51, 63.5, 65.5, 86.3, 89.5, 91.5, 103.5, 105.5, 141.5, 156, 197.5, 210.5, 222.5, 230.5, 301.5, 400, 457, 475.5, 517.5, 548.3, 591.5, 593.5, 602, 607.5, 607.8, 627.8, 628, 633, 635.5, 636.5, 661, 664.5, 672.5, 733.5, 782.8, 807.5, 823.5, 825.5, 825.8, 827.5, 834, 849, 853.3, 853.4, 853.6, 853.8, 858.5, 873.5, 879.5, 908.6, 995.6, 1013.5, 1123.5, 1145, 1147.8, 1186.5, 1210.5, 1218.5, 1228, 1260, 1265.5, 1270, 1271, 1276.5, 1281.5, 1289, 1294.5, 1332, 1390.3, 1392.5, 1426.4, 1428, 1490, 1493.5, 1498.8, 1509.5, 1524.5, 1551, 1606.8, 1611, 1628.5, 1631.3, 1664.5, 1700.5, 1777,

1833.8, 1843.8, 1848, 1850, 1871.8, 1902, 1936.5, 1938.5, 1975, 2039.8, 2066.8, 2077.5, 2089, 2099, 2140.5, 2231.8, 2256, 2284.8, 2289.3, 2289.5, 2291.5, 2300.6, 2328, 2617.5, 2646.5, 2650.5, 2689.5, 2693, 2700.5, 2736, 2794.6, 2811.8, 3101, 3115.5, 3175.5, 3218.5, 3246.5, 3263.5, 3279.8, 3294, 3323.5, 3389.8, 3397, 3452.8, 3490.6, 3496, 3510.5, 3516.5, 3518, 3567.6, 3646, 3646.6, 3647.3, 3665.3, 3727.5, 3729, 3729.5, 3743.3, 3760.5, 3761.5, 3770.5, 3799.6, 3825.5, 3859.5, 3860.6, 3891, 3892.5, 3894.3, 3897.5, 3900.5, 3902.5, 3905.5, 3911.8, 3937, 4056.5, 4080, 4084, 4091.6, 4093, 4094.8, 4096.5, 4202, 4212.5, 4264.5, 4273.3, 4273.5.

Tailors, satires on, by Dunbar, 515.5, 2289.8.

Talbot, John, prayer for, 1786.5.

Talis of the fyve bestes, *393.3.

Tapestry verses, 1270.6.

Te ergo quaesumus famulis tuis, 3510.5.

Temple of glas, verses adapted from, 2161.

Ten Commandments, 1856.5, 2692, 2695.5, 3689.5.

— couplet introducing tract on, 3322.8.

— hell reward of those foregoing the, 3665.6.

— of devil, 4149.5.

Testament of love, concluding couplet for, 945.8.

— of Mr. Andro Kennedy,' by Dunbar, 1330.5.

Thief, on a, 3711.5.

Thieves: charm against, 873.8, 1293.5, 1952.5, 4154.8; verses against, 242.5, 1952.5; prayer against, 939.

'Think on thy end and thow sall never syn,' 2834.5.

Thomas Aquinas, St., prayer attrib. to, 1967.

— of Canterbury, St., carol on, 187.5.

Thorndon, Alice, epitaph for, 2401.5.

Thorpe, William: against pride of clergy, 455.8.

Threat and counter threat, 4269.5.

Three cocks, riming comments of (in *Gesta Romanorum*), 2238.5, 3081, 3322.3.

— estates: clergy's place in, 1494.5.

— foes of man, *3339.5.

— impossibilities, 3248.5.

— *Kings of Cologne*, *854.3 (Lydgate).

— Marys, song of, 158.3.

— points of mischief, 3522.

— sorrowful things (*see also* Four sorrowful things), 738.5, 3199.5.

'Thrissil and the Rois,' by Dunbar, 3990.5.

'Thi lady hath forgoten to be kynd,' 506.5.

'Tydingis fra the sessioun,' by Dunbar, 293.5.

Tiles, verses on, 1426.2, 3565.5.

Times: all aspects of, 2451.5 (Skelton); irremedial loss of, 1998; make the most of, 3256.1, 3256.6.

Timor mortis conturbat me, 1370.5, 2066.5.

Titles appropriate for rulers, 86.5.

'To a ladye,' by Dunbar, 3243.3.

— a ladye quhone he list to feyne,' by Dunbar, 2247.5.

— the lordis of the kingis chalker,' by Dunbar, 2258.5.

— the merchantis of Edinburgh,' attrib. to Dunbar, 4165.5.

Tombstone inscriptions: *see* Epitaphs.

Tongue: composite poem on, 3535; destructive power of, 102.5, 3079.2, 3318.3, 3792.5, 4128.6; example of evil, 4198.5; hasty, 106.5, 802.5, 1409.5; rules against sins of, 1436.5; venemous, 193.5 (Skelton); wicked, 1256.5.

Tournament: invitation to, 4143.8; love song at, 2271.2.

Tractatus de spe, 3406.

Transitoriness (*see also* Mutability; Vanity; *and see under* Man): of life, 105.5, 269.5, 3743.6, 3973.5; of world, 197.8.

Travellers, prognostications for, 1201.5, 1436.3.

'Tretis of the tua mariit wemen and the wedo,' by Dunbar, 3845.5.

Tree in various seasons, mistress like a, *3553.8.

— of Jesse, pageant of, 578.5.

Trent Codex fragment, 135.3.

Trevisa: verses in *De proprietatibus rerum*, 731.5, 4258.3; in *Polychronicon*, 399.5, 746.5, 1426.6, 1637.6, 2361.5, 2736.2, 2831.4, 3218.3, 4189.5; added by Caxton, 3917.3.

Trinity: ballade to, 3830.5; carols to, 772.5, 3328.5; prayer to, 790.5; songs to, 528.5, 3876.

Troilus and Criseyde: *see under* Chaucer.

Troy: Scottish Troy fragments, *298.5.

True love: banished, 2261.6; man's soul his, 3623.5; on, 103.5, 1489.5, 2007.5, 2245.3.
Trustworthiness, rules for ascertaining, 3285.
Truth, on speaking the, 271.5.
— and conscience, 3173.5.
Tunc est preclara, 3516.5.
'Tunnyng of Elynour Rummyng,' by Skelton, 3265.5.
Tubal Cain, 1924.5, 1931.8.
Tutivillus, 707.5, 1214.9, 1655.5, 3812.
Twelve degrees of patience, 3492.3.
Twici's *Treatise on Hunting*, envoy to, 3910.5.
'Twa cummeris,' by Dunbar, 2821.3.
Tyranny, four victims of, 861.

Udersall, Adam, epitaph for, 3645.3.
Ugolino of Pisa, 28.8.
Unity against the French, 3143.5.
'Vppon a deedman's hede,' by Skelton, 4284.5.
Urines, verses introducing a tract on, 1109.5, 1201.3.
Urse, Aldred's curse on, 1119.8.
Ursula, St., life of, 4187.3.
— speech of, at pageant, 2030.2.
Usk, Thomas: *Testament of Love*, concluding couplet for, 945.8.

Vanity (*see also* Mutability; Transitoriness): against worldly, 2300.6; of life, 3905; of this world, 853.8, 2349.8, 2587.5, 2785.5, 3909.4.
'Variance of court,' by Stewart, 2831.2.
Vaux, Sir Roland, epitaph for, 3118.2.
Uenite ad iudicium, 3645.8.
Ventus cum pluuia, 644.5.
Venus: lover and advocate of, 2594; presents gift to dreamer, 3844.5; qualities of, 3917.8.
Verbum Domini, verses on, 1871.3.
— *Domini comparatur*, 1498.8.
Vernagu: *see* Roland.
Veterinary directions, 1192.5, 1197.5, 1426.2.
Vexilla regis prodeunt: see 1119.
'Vice through violence putteth vertue vnto flyte,' 1455.4.
Victor, William epitaph for, 4174.8.
Victory in France, song for, 306.8.
Virelai, 353, 3193.5.
Virgil, trans. of lines from, 399.5.
Virgin Mary: *see* Blessed Virgin Mary.
Virginity: lament for lost, 3902.5; mock medicine for lost, 1409.1.

Virtue: effect of pride and envy on, 2631.5; overcome by vice, 1455.5; speech of, at mumming, 3810.6; to be earned, 4098.1.
Virtues of herbs, 417.8.
— Seven principal, *272.5; mumming with, *338.5.
— Nine, *3780.5.
Vision, erotic, 1450.5, 1841.5.
— of sire William Banestre, knyght,' 1967.5.
Vite Ade et Eve, *1873.5.
Viuimus hic sorte, 230.5.
Voeux du paon, extract from, *586.5.

Wade, verses on, 3175.5.
Wales, description of, 2361.5 (Trevisa).
Wall verses (*see also* Epitaphs; Inscriptions), 1863.5, 1924.5, 1937, 2192, 2464, 3584.5, 3903.3, 4109.5, 4135.5, 4181.
Walsingham Chapel, foundation of, 2664.5.
Walton: *see* Boethius.
Wanton behaviour reproved, 4217.3.
Wanton's song (*and see* Light ladies), 1286.5, 1269.5, 3025.
Wantons win quick favor, 3556.5; *and see* 2255.6, 3097.6, 3098.3.
'Ware the hauke,' by Skelton, 3648.5.
Warnings: against women, 2500.5; excess in sports, 1014.5; false executors, 3565.5; false friends, 3893; false men, 158.7; lechery, 551; marrying in haste, 1392.
— to all, 411.5; Duke of Norfolk, 1654.5; improvident, 1162.6; lovers, 263.8, Mayor of Cambridge, 1941.8; officers of justice, 312; scholars, 407.5; Walter, Archbishop of Dublin, 2571.5; women, 158.7; young rakes, 4073.5.
Wars of Alexander the Great, 3947.3.
Warwick, Earl of: acrostic on, 3856.5.
Water of life, 1606.8.
Waterford, epistle of Mayor of, 2571.5.
Watermen's song, 2832.5.
Wealth: causes trouble, 228.8; unequal distribution of, 3171.5.
'Welcum to Bernard Stewart, Lord of Aubigny,' by Dunbar, 2811.5.
Wells, John, gives sword to Bristol, 1796.5.
Wench, spend money on a, 87.5.
Wentworth, William, epitaph for, 1211.7.

'Westron wynde,' 3899.3.
Wever, Sir Harry, epitaph for, 3726.5.
— William, epitaph for, 3822.5.
Wey: Latin Itinerary to Compostella, tag in, 475.5; *Itineraries to Jerusalem*, 883.
'What wold she more,' 2619.5.
'Quhone mony benefices vakit,' by Dunbar, 3116.5.
White Benedictus, 2749.5.
'Why art thow thus my mortall foe,' 158.2.
— *come ye nat to courte*, by Skelton, 813.3.
— I can't be a nun,' *316.3.
— soo unkende,' 3144.5.
Widvill, Anthony: see Rivers, Lord.
Wife (*see also* Women): erring, 81.5, 817.5; how to choose, 3361.1; virtuous, 40.5; worsts husband, 3648.8.
Wikes, Nycholas: verses by, 2195.3.
Will, defeated by reason, 1294.3.
William the Conqueror, complaint against foreign prelates of, 3074.3.
— *of Palerne*, *3281.5.
— Rufus, chronicle beginning with, 4174.5.
Wyllughby: series of proverbs signed by, 1628.8.
Willoughby family, 2462.5.
Wilson, John, acrostic on, 1594.
Wimbledon: tag in sermon by, 3397.
Winchester dramatic texts, 3352.5, 3430.5.
Window verses, 1330.3.
Wine, water, and milk: removing spots made by, 2668.
— good, 2820.3.
Winifred, St., hymn to, 854.5, 1808.5.
Wintoun's *Chronicle*, extracts in, 1377, 2697, 3168.6, 3923.5.
Wise use of provisions, 342.5.
Wit and will, conflict of, *3783.5.
'Without glaidnes awailis no tressour,' by Dunbar, 470.5.
Woe: on, 4214.5; turned to bliss, 197.5.
Woeful thoughts, no release from, 3908.8.
Womanhood, truth exiled in, 3914.5.
Women: abuse of, 3492.5, 3522.5, 3845.5; advice to, 158.7; cannot be tamed, 4166.5; contrariness of, 108.5; easily defamed, 3318.3; erring, 37.3, 81.5, 817.5; examples against, 3744; failings of, 37.3, 81.5, 3246.5, *3533.5, 4166.5; falseness of, 79.5, 1355.5, 2500.5, 3914.5; fickleness of, 2195.3, 3559.8, 3911.5, 3919.5, 4090; flightiness of, 108.5, 3464.5; garrulity of, 106.5, 3322.5, 4058.5; kind and unkind, 13.8; lecherousness of, 2691.8, 3464.5; moralizing lines on, 3734.5; praise of, 40.5, *552.8, 1409.3, 2354.3 (Dunbar), 4044.6, 4217.6; riddle on, 3256.3, 3522; satires on, 108.7, 994.5, 1362, 2358.5, 3098, 3174.5, 3256.3, 3372.6, 3492.5, 3909.6; six properties of, 3887.5; truth about, 3919.5; ugliness of, 1300; untrustworthiness of, 3742.5; vitriolic, 106.5; wickedness of, 3306.8, 3701.5; wiles of, 1166.5.
Womyndham, William: book motto of, 1442.5; curse on those miscalling him, 733.8.
Woodcock, receipt for preparing, 854.8.
Worcester, pageant verses at, 3885.5.
Wordes of a good horse to his mayster,' 326.8.
— of þe first sphere,' 1211.5.
World: history of, 119; sorrow of, 3327.5; unstableness of, 1356.5, 2632.5 (Dunbar), 3646.3 (Dunbar); untrustworthiness of, 4116.5; upside down, 506.5; vanity of, 2587.5 (Dunbar), 2785.5, 3909.4.
Worldly joy, transitoriness of, 2300.6, 2632.5 (Dunbar).
— love and spiritual, 4227.5.
Worms, man the meat of, 2300.6.
Wounds of Christ: charm against evil, 627.3; on the five, 2548.5; prayers by, 250.5, 1739.5, 1961.5; remedies for sins, 269; tag on, 607.8, 813.5.
Wrechedness: flee, 1140.5; how to avoid, 1436.2; happiness in, 1470.8.
Wulfhade and Ruffyn, Sts., legend of, *1219.5.
Wyatt, Thomas: poems ascribed to, 813.6, 1270.2, 2281.5; *and see* 1485.5, 3914.5.

Xylographic texts, *338.5, 2910.5; *and see* 3372.5, 3695.5, 3777.3.

'Y and O' refrain: *see* 'O and I.'
'ʒe suln turnen to god,' 4256.5.
Youth and age, song on, 3706.5.
— against counsel of, 1824.4.

Zodiac, casting dice by signs of, 752.5.

www.ingramcontent.com/pod-product-compliance
Lightning Source LLC
Chambersburg PA
CBHW020630230426
43665CB00008B/107